Catholic higher education
in America

Catholic
higher education
in America

A history

Edward J. Power
Boston College

APPLETON-CENTURY-CROFTS
EDUCATIONAL DIVISION
MEREDITH   CORPORATION   New York

Preface

In 1958 I wrote *A History of Catholic Higher Education in the United States,* a book that dealt mainly with the nineteenth century origins of American Catholic colleges. In this book, which represents another decade of study and research, I want to re-examine the history of nineteenth-century Catholic higher education from a broader perspective, adding to it interesting and significant interpretations of twentieth-century developments in Catholic college and universities.

It seems important to say directly that Catholic higher learning did not appear suddenly in full-grown institutional form in the United States. Several difficult years of educational growth were endured before schools called colleges succeeded in fulfilling the expectations their titles implied. In this history, then, because the first years were foundational years, although not in a strict sense years when authentic higher learning was cultivated, I believe it historically appropriate, and probably essential, to show how Catholic schools matured, and while they were maturing, how they struggled to become institutional representatives of a genuine higher learning.

A book of this kind is clearly heavily indebted to the work of others; and I gladly acknowledge this debt to the scholars whose books, monographs, and articles I have read and quoted and to Boston College for a grant enabling me to carry out this work. A special acknowledgement is due the always accommodating reference librarians at the Boston College Library: Mrs. Muriel B. Bliss and Mrs. Katherine W. Jaffe; and a note of particular gratitude is due Mr. Joseph M. McCarthy for help graciously given in a careful and perceptive reading of proofs.

E.J.P.

v

Contents

I
The formative years
1786-1870

I

The Church and higher learning

The Catholic Church in Colonial America

From the first colonizations in the New World to the 1870s the Catholic Church in North America was administered along missionary lines.[1] While this arrangement had a direct impact on ecclesiastical business—appointments of bishops, discipline of clergy, church support, and local applications of canon law—for the real management of the Church came from Europe, its effects on educational attitude and practice were apparent also. The Church, determining to gain a doctrinal foothold in the New World, and especially in English America with its inherent hostility to Catholicism, preferred to subordinate education to religious goals. Thus, from the outset, all schools from primary through college grades were preoccupied with preserving tenets of faith and with teaching policies ensuring the allegiance of Catholic people to their Church. A good end could shape its own means.

Twentieth-century criticism of this subordination of intellectual to denominational values is all too popular, but, at the time, the Church was faced with the fundamental problem of survival in a society having neither sympathy nor love for its dogmas or ministers. Perhaps society's fears were farfetched and inconsistent with the fundamental bases of Catholicism, but this did not diminish the force of such catchwords as

---

[1] From the first Catholic settlements in English America to 1908, the Church was accorded missionary status and was administered from Rome through the Congregation of the Propagation of the Faith. See John Gilmary Shea, *History of the Catholic Church in the United States* (New York, John G. Shea, 1888), I, 52, 59; and Theodore Roemer, *The Catholic Church of the United States* (St. Louis, B. Herder and Co., 1950), pp. 85–91. This practice made it easy for critics of Roman Catholicism to capitalize on the argument that the Church represented foreign, anti-American influences. See Edwin H. Burton, *The Life and Times of Bishop Challoner, 1691–1781* (New York, Longmans, Green and Co., 1909), II, 125–127.

no-popery, anti-Romanism, foreign prelates, and clerical domination. Protestant Americans of the colonial period were terrified by the prospect of the Roman Catholic Church gaining control over colonial politics and religion; officially and unofficially they bent every effort to prevent such a catastrophe. Laws discriminating against Catholics often made the offering of Mass illegal, and were used to intimidate and persecute Catholic clergymen whenever they were found;[2] in addition, the schools adopted anti-Catholic policies and warned pupils openly against the dangerous, insidious influence of the Roman creed.[3] If we agree that these fears had some historical foundation, and that Catholics had too often persecuted their fellow Christians in the name of true religion, we can understand the popular antiCatholic attitudes of colonial Protestants. Still, the fears were exaggerated, as history has shown, and the terrible apparition of a vengeance-seeking Catholic Church had no real basis in fact.

To protect itself against this hostility, based primarily on fear, and to safeguard orthodoxy among its communicants, the Church naturally enough exploited all the tools at its command, sometimes even trying to devise new ones to counteract the powerful forces pitted against her.

An ancient theory of Christian education, which had its origin in the writings of the Church Fathers, was, to all intents and purposes, jettisoned at this point. We may remember that it had dispensed the Church from literary teaching—from the ordinary work of schools—and commissioned the home, supplemented by the good offices of the Church's ministers, to instil theological and moral virtue and protect children from moral contagion and vice.[4] In actual practice, the Church had organized

---

[2] See W. W. Hening (ed.), *The Statutes at Large; Being a Collection of all the Laws of Virginia* (Richmond, Samuel Pleasants, Jr., 1809), I, 268–269; N. B. Shurtleff (ed.), *Records of the Governor and Company of the Massachusetts Bay in New England* (Boston, William White, 1854), III, 112; W. H. Browne (ed.), *Archives of Maryland. Proceedings and Acts of the General Assembly of Maryland, January 1637/38–September 1664* (Baltimore, Maryland Historical Society, 1883), I, 340–341; and *The Acts and Resolves, Public and Private, of the Province of Massachusetts Bay* (Boston, Wright & Potter, 1869), I, 423–424.

[3] See Burton Confrey, *Secularism in American Education: Its History,* Educational Research Monographs, vol. 6, no. 1 (Washington, The Catholic University of America, 1931), pp. 27–29; Henry Brann, *The Life of John Hughes* (New York, Benziger Bros., 1892), pp. 2–10; John Gilmary Shea, *op. cit.,* p. 83; *United States Catholic Historical Magazine,* vol. III, 532; Sister Mary Augustina Ray, *American Opinion of Roman Catholicism in the Eighteenth Century* (New York, Columbia University Press, 1936), pp. 157–164; and Philip R. McDevitt, "How Bigotry was Kept Alive by Old-Time Textbooks," *American Catholic Historical Society Records,* 24 (1908), 257–261.

[4] St. John Chrysostom, *On Vainglory: and how Parents should bring up their Children,* 19 in M. L. W. Laistner, *Christianity and Pagan Culture in the Later Roman Empire* (Ithaca, Cornell University Press, 1951); and H. I. Marrou, *A History of Education in Antiquity* (New York, Sheed and Ward, 1956), pp. 314–316.

classes for basic doctrinal instruction, from time-to-time established parish schools mainly for the elementary education of boys who might train for the priesthood, and founded theological schools for the education of priests when it became apparent that the older apprenticeship system—the bishop training assistants in his own household—would no longer do.[5] This left the entire field of grammar teaching—what we today call secondary education—and the specialized areas of study (save for theology) to schools outside ecclesiastical jurisdiction. These schools were frequented regularly and openly by Christian (Catholic) teachers and students. Possibly the Church was only making the best of a bad situation in allowing the intellectual side of educa-tion under her auspices to go uncultivated; and this policy of intellectual noninvolvement was challenged occasionally by less temperate Christians, who viewed with alarm and suspicion anything having a pagan—and classical—flavor.[6] As long as schools were available early Christians attended them, even amid debates that their faith was thus endangered.

The first official departure from this policy is found in the pronounce-ments of Pope Gregory the Great (540–604), who, speaking from the linguistic security of a social milieu wherein Latin, or a language akin to Latin, was the vernacular, denounced classical studies as unnecessary and contaminating for Christians.[7] But where a policy of indifference or antagonism to classical study was ecclesiastically feasible in Italy, it was not so in European lands without the same social affinities for and contacts with the Latin-Greek heritage. Gregory's policy was a luxury the Church, in the long run, could ill afford : Latin, the Fathers said, was a divine language, and every priest must know it.[8]

Gregory's policy could be tolerated while the schools of the Roman Empire remained in operation, but when they disappeared in the wake of political collapse, the Church was inevitably drawn into the business of education on a broad, and heretofore unpredictable, scale.

From roughly the time of Cassiodorus (480–575) until the mid-twentieth century the Church perpetuated a policy of superintending all education and

[5] *Ibid.*, pp. 334–336; P. R. Cole, *Later Roman Education in Ausonius, Capella, and the Theodosian Code* (New York, Teachers College Press, 1902); T. Haarhoff, *Schools of Gaul, a Study of Pagan and Christian Education in the Last Century of the Western Empire* (New York, Oxford University Press, 1920).

[6] See, for example, Tertullian, *On Idolatry;* and St. Basil's well-known essay *On the Reading of the Profane Authors;* also, G. L. Ellspermann, *The Attitude of the Early Christian Fathers Towards Pagan Literature and Learning* (Washington, The Catholic University of America,1949).

[7] See R. R. Bolgar, *The Classical Heritage and Its Beneficiaries* (Cambridge, Camb-ridge University Press, 1954), pp. 96–98; and E. K. Rand, *Founders of the Middle Ages* (Cambridge, Mass., Harvard University Press, 1928), pp. 25–28.

[8] Edward J. Power, *Evolution of Educational Doctrine* (New York, Appleton-Century-Crofts, 1969), pp. 147–150.

of conducting its own schools where such action seemed necessary.[9] In Catholic countries—whether the schools were Church-controlled or Church-supervised—formal education was largely absolved from engaging in religious polemic, apologetics, and defensive teaching, because threats to orthodoxy were eliminated by political policy, but in countries where law was inimical to the Catholic religion—and here we may list English colonial America and the early United States—the Church's posture was different : it sought to defend the faith from all assaults and insulate Catholics from heresy. Guarding religious faith thus became the principal function of the American Catholic school. Where we are now able to make a valid distinction between the Church teaching and the Church learning (the former a doctrinal presentation, the latter a search for truth with the university as a principal instrument,)[10] we must recognize that seventeenth-, eighteenth-, and nineteenth-century Catholics could not. Our world and theirs wear different faces.

The Church must be established before it can teach : and this leads us to an elaboration of the Church's colonial foundations. When Spanish adventurers and French settlers came to North America, they were always accompanied by Catholic clergymen, a natural enough circumstance because these people embraced the Catholic faith and, moreover, had the official sanction of public policy for doing so.[11] While the pioneer priests attended to the spiritual needs of their co-religionists, they also did their best to convert the native Indians to Catholicism. As long as French and Spanish colonization lasted, and wherever it was located, the Catholic Church was secure, but time, energy, and the fortunes of history made English, not Spanish or French, America the principal political force in the New World, so we must turn our attention to English America if we are to discover the roots of ecclesiastical foundations that later matured enough to generate developments in higher education and at the same time preconditioned the Church to attach unique objectives to higher learning in this strange, often hostile, New World.

Making haste slowly in matters of higher learning, Catholics lived in America for a long time before they endeavored to establish a college. Yet their seeming procrastination is easily explained : in the first place, especially before the Revolutionary War, their numbers were too few to allow them

[9] See Cassiodorus Senator, *An Introduction to Divine and Human Readings,* translated by Leslie Webber Jones (New York, Columbia University Press, 1946).

[10] John E. Walsh, "The University and the Church," in Edward Manier and John W. Houck (eds.), *Academic Freedom and the Catholic University* (Notre Dame, Ind., Fides Publishers, Inc., 1967), pp. 103–118.

[11] F. W. Blackmar, *Spanish Colonization in the Southwest* (Baltimore, Johns Hopkins University, 1890), pp. 15–18; and Thomas O'Gorman, *A History of the Roman Catholic Church in the United States* (New York, American Church History Series, 1895), pp. 121–132.

to initiate such an imposing venture; in the second place, they evidenced no clear understanding or appreciation of the values of higher learning.[12] As persons, Catholics in colonial America may have had profound respect for learning and the worth of formal schooling and as individuals may have sought out educational opportunities in Europe, but their Church entertained no such policy toward colleges as can be found by studying the annals of religious effort to establish Harvard, Yale, Princeton, William and Mary, Brown, Columbia, Rutgers, Washington, Washington and Lee, Hampden-Sidney, Transylvania, Dickinson, and St. John's.[13] These schools arose from a commitment each denomination made to the preservation of learning; and while we continue to debate the nature and depth of this commitment—whether it was merely to the training of clergymen or decently educated gentlemen—its reality cannot be gainsaid. Donald Tewksbury's pioneer studies tell us of 182 permanent colleges established before the Civil War, of which 175 were subject to direct denominational control;[14] and among them were twenty-eight Catholic colleges, although Tewksbury does not credit Catholics with such a large number either because his criteria for college founding are different from ours or because he was misled by institutional histories or reports which are notoriously undependable for precise historical information. In any case, some commitment to higher learning was secure and apparently irrevocable among Congregationalists, Episcopalians, Presbyterians, Baptists, and Dutch Reformers almost a century before the idea for a Catholic college ever entered John Carroll's mind.[15]

Debates over the nature of collegiate commitment and the clarity of college purpose, which tend to represent these early nonCatholic colleges as

12 See Thomas T. McAvoy, "The American Catholic Minority in the Later Nineteenth Century," *The Review of Politics,* 15 (July, 1953), 275–302; W. Ong, *American Catholic Crossroads* (New York, Macmillan Company, 1959), pp. 93–101; and T. A. Becker, "Shall We Have a University?" *The American Catholic Quarterly Review,* I (April, 1876), 23–53.

13 George P. Schmidt, "Intellectual Crosscurrents in American Colleges," *American Historical Review,* 42 (October, 1936), 46–67; C. C. Crawford and L. V. Koos, "College Aims Past and Present," *School and Society,* 14 (December, 1921), 505–506; and Samuel Eliot Morison, *Harvard College in the Seventeenth Century* (Cambridge, Mass., Harvard University Press, 1936), I, 141–147.

14 Donald Tewksbury, *The Founding of American Colleges and Universities Before the Civil War* (New York, Teachers College Press, 1932), p. 90.

15 Willard Sperry, *Religion in America* (Cambridge, Cambridge University Press, 1946); K. S. Latourette, *The Great Century, 1800–1914* (London, Eyre and Spottiswoode, 1941); W. W. Sweet, *The American Churches* (New York, Abingdon-Cokesbury Press, 1947); W. W. Sweet, *Religion in the Development of American Culture* (New York, Charles Scribner's Sons, 1952); and E. B. Greene, "The Puritan Counter-Reformation," *Proceedings of the American Antiquarian Society,* 42 (New Series, 1932), 39–41.

simple seminaries and later Catholic colleges as true representatives of higher learning, illustrate wishful thinking at its worst and must not be taken seriously.[16] Undeniably most early colleges, regardless of the religious creed under whose auspices they were conducted, tried to be true to a variety of educational and religious objectives. Their spirit was missionary, for they wanted to spread their faith throughout the land; they sought to prepare ministers for their sects; and, on occasion, they admitted boys frankly interested in secular learning to their classrooms. Very likely they were seldom, if ever, liberally oriented; yet the classics formed some part of every college curriculum. Few, we think, were divinity schools exclusively; yet some openly and honestly conducted courses or programs leading students to the profession of theology.

Catholic parents anxious to give their sons opportunities for higher studies were decidedly atypical in colonial days, but those who were would have been extremely uneasy about enrolling them in colonial colleges, for in both teaching and religious discipline such colleges, beginning with Harvard and ending with Charlestown College, including places like the Universities of Georgia and Pennsylvania (and excepting only Brown, which was more flexible) were totally and uncompromisingly Protestant.[17]

In 1634, when the predominantly Catholic expedition landed in Maryland, and for decades thereafter, no one spoke of an urgent need for higher learning under Catholic direction. True, the requirements of religious teaching were affirmed in precept and practice; some elementary instruction was obviously necessary for the good of the settlement and was provided in lower schools conducted by the Jesuits. There are equivocal references to a college in the Maryland colonial community and some correspondence mentions encouragement given the local Jesuits to maintain their college at Newtown.[18] But the term college then, whatever it signifies today, was probably used to designate, not a school of higher studies but, in the classic sense, a grammar school. Serious discussion concerning the establishment of an institution of higher learning would surely have been premature, for as late as 1770 there were hardly more than 22,000 Catholics in all the colonies along the Atlantic Ocean. Their numbers increased slowly until 1820, when

---

[16] Critical persons were aware of this attitude. See Augustus J. Thébaud, *Forty Years in the United States of America* (New York, United States Catholic Historical Society, 1904), II, 351–353.

[17] Perry Miller, *The New England Mind: The Seventeenth Century* (New York, Macmillan Company, 1939), pp. 75–79; Thomas J. Wertenbaker, *Princeton, 1746–1896* (Princeton, N. J., Princeton University Press, 1946), pp. 11–21; and Beverly McAnear, "College Founding in the American Colonies, 1745–1775," *Mississippi Valley Historical Review*, XLII (June, 1955), 24–36.

[18] Thomas Hughes, *History of the Society of Jesus in North America* (New York, Longmans, Green and Co., 1907–1917), I, 346, 460.

estimates run as high as 195,000; and then, following the 1830s and the era of Irish immigration, to 663,000 in 1840, and 1,980,000 in 1852.[19]

With sharp increases in the Catholic population, the shortage of priests quickly reached a crisis stage. Depending mainly on missionaries dispatched to the colonies by religious orders and the wandering clerical fraternity, which for its own reasons had fled the jurisdiction of European bishops to enjoy the greater ecclesiastical latitude of a colonial climate, the Church in America had been content to ignore provisions for the preparation of a native clergy. In the long run this was probably unwise, for the Church, administered from abroad and staffed at home by foreign-born priests, could not escape an unAmerican image. But on this question of clerical supply, Catholics had few options to exercise and they continued to welcome the immigrant priest, despite the growing awareness that a foreign clergy was an unsatisfactory, temporary solution to the problem of clerical manpower. Necessity, again the mother of invention, translated this obvious, critical need for a native clergy into motives for founding the first Catholic colleges.

An extended treatment of Catholic colonial history falls outside the ambit of this book's purpose; our interest is directed at higher learning's motives and institutions growing out of the Catholic colonial experience. It was a history, as McCluskey has wisely said, "of survival and adaptation."[20] Restrictive laws kept Catholics outside the main currents of political and cultural life; official denominational exercises were frequently proscribed and in many colonies Catholic schools were prohibited from functioning. Maryland's law of 1704, "An Act to Prevent the Growth of Popery," illustrates, in its provisions to deport any Catholic who kept a school, boarded students, or instructed children, repressive legislation typical of most colonies. Thus, to suppose that Catholics in the colonies could have followed in the footsteps of their nonCatholic countrymen to establish schools and affirm a strong official policy toward education under Catholic control would be to expect the impossible.[21]

The national period, however, allowed for some erosion in ancient animosities toward Catholicism; most of the old penalties relative to

[19] Gerald Shaughnessy, *Has the Immigrant Kept the Faith?* (New York, Macmillan Company, 1925), pp. 27, 73, 117, 125, 134; and Shea, *op. cit.*, I, 449.

[20] Neil G. McCluskey, *Catholic Education in America* (New York, Teachers College Press, 1964), p. 2.

[21] M. A. C., "Education in Louisiana in French Colonial Days," *American Catholic Quarterly Review*, XI (July, 1886), 395–418; M. A. C., "Education in New Orleans in Spanish Colonial Days," *American Catholic Quarterly Review*, XII (April, 1887), 253–277; R. H. Lord, *et al. A History of the Archdiocese of Boston* (New York, Sheed and Ward, 1944) I, 3–33; A. J. Riley, *Catholicism in New England to 1788* (Washington, The Catholic University of America, 1936); and Peter Guilday, *The Life and Times of John Carroll* (New York, Encyclopedia Press, 1922), pp. 790–795.

religious worship and keeping schools were lifted, although only four of the original thirteen states gave Catholics at their constitutional conventions the right to vote or hold office.[22]

So prior to the national period there is a long bleak time when Catholics engaged in educational work clandestinely, when their schools were *ad hoc* scholastic ventures intent on fulfilling a pragmatic purpose, but were unable to afford the luxury of thinking about generating influences for the schools they surely hoped would follow. Although the records about them are incomplete and highly fragmented, schools were conducted in Maryland, Pennsylvania, and New York, of the English colonies; in Detroit, St. Louis, and elsewhere in the French colonies; and mission schools were established in Florida, New Mexico, and California where Spanish settlements prevailed.[23] The first opportunities for education within the present boundaries of the United States were provided by Franciscan friars in Florida and New Mexico. In French America missionaries were active too : most prominent were the Jesuits, but the Sulpicians, Recollect Fathers, and Capuchins engaging in missionary work found time after dispensing the sacraments to give some religious and literary instruction.[24]

The first Catholic literary—that is, non-doctrinal—teaching in the English colonies was informally conducted by the Jesuits in Maryland. Beginning, we might suppose, almost with debarkation, this informal, or at least unorganized, instruction was terminated when a school could be opened. The records we have date the school in St. Mary's City around 1640, and classify it as elementary in character. Yet broader academic scope may have been planned for it : in September, 1640, the Jesuit General, Mutius Vitelleschi, wrote to the Director of the Maryland mission, probably

---

[22] Theodore Roemer, *op. cit.,* pp. 95–96.

[23] For details here, see J. A. Burns and Bernard J. Kohlbrenner, *A History of Catholic Education in the United States* (New York, Benziger Bros., 1937), pp. 18–96; William J. McGucken, *The Jesuits and Education* (Milwaukee, Bruce Publishing Co., 1932), pp. 45–59; H. S. Spalding, *Catholic Colonial Maryland* (Milwaukee, Bruce Publishing Co., 1931), pp. 129–141; H. I. Priestley (ed.), *The Luna Papers* (Deland, Florida State Historical Society, 1928), II, 257–261; G. S. de Meras, *Pedro Menéndez de Avilés* . . . J. T. Connor (Deland, Florida State Historical Society 1923), pp. 259–270; F. W. Hodge, George Hammond, and A.Rey (eds.), *Fray Alonso de Benavides' Revised Memorial of 1634* (Albuquerque, University of New Mexico Press, 1945), pp.100–103; and Antonine Tibesar (ed.), *The Writings of Junipero Serra* (Washington, Academy of American Franciscan History, 1955), I, 3–9.

[24] John Gilmary Shea (ed.), *Discovery and Exploration in the Mississippi Valley* (New York, J. S. Redfield, 1852), pp. 152–153; Edward J. Fortier, "The Establishment of the Tamarois Mission," *Transactions* of the Illinois State Historical Society, no. 13 (1909), 236–237; Claude L. Vogel, *The Capuchins in French Louisiana, 1772–1776* (Washington, Catholic University of America Press, 1928), pp. 25–26; and C. G. Herbermann, *The Sulpicians in the United States* (New York, Encyclopedia Press, 1916), pp. 140–193.

in response to some information he had been given, to say : "The hope held out of a college I am happy to entertain; and when it shall have matured, I will not be backward in extending my approval."[25] The Jesuit General probably used the term, college—then especially broad in its academic implications—in about the same way that contemporary educators speak of a high school, although one distinguished historian of this period is willing to concede that the General may only have been writing about the community house—the place where Jesuits resided—for the Maryland mission.[26] In any case, whatever the sense of the General's reference, the evidence suggests that the Jesuits were successful in opening and conducting a secondary school in Newtown, Maryland, as early as 1673, one capable of preparing boys for St. Omer, a Jesuit school of higher studies in France. It is barely possible that additional subjects were added to the Newtown school's curriculum by 1677, making it a pioneer institution of higher learning.[27] Yet no evidence now extant allows us to conclude that the Newtown school, if it ever operated as a post-secondary institution, formulated any long-range plans to perpetuate higher studies.

In addition to Newtown, other Catholic schools under Jesuit direction were probably established in Maryland in 1745, 1752, and 1757. The most prominent was Bohemia Manor School (1745), remotely located near the Pennsylvania border. A Catholic school was opened in New York City around 1685, and fifteen were established in Pennsylvania in the late seventeenth and early eighteenth centuries : at Philadelphia (St. Mary's Parish), Conewago, Sportsman's Hall, Carlisle, Milton, York, Taneytown, Frederick, Littlestown, Brandt's Chapel, Hanover, Haycock, Reading, Goshenhoppen, and Lancaster. Time, however, has eroded and obscured the histories of these early schools.[28]

Catholic attitudes toward higher learning

When we review the evolution of Catholic higher education in the United States, two historically significant factors become apparent : first, before 1783 no evidence points to any serious Catholic consideration of

[25] Hughes, *op. cit.*, I, 346.

[26] John M. Daley, *Georgetown University: Origin and Early Years* (Washington, Georgetown University Press, 1957), p. 2.

[27] See Burns and Kohlbrenner, *op. cit.*, pp.44–48; McGucken, *op. cit.*, pp. 45–59; and Spalding, *op. cit.*, pp. 129–141.

[28] Goshenhoppen appears to have been the most flourishing of these Catholic settlements. Its baptismal records are reproduced in the *Records of the American Catholic Historical Society*, II, 316–322; III, 303–398; VII, 345–393; XI, 45–60, 196–207, 303–307; and LXI, 56–63, 112–123, 185–192, 248–262.

higher learning, except as it related to the pressing need for native clergy, and then the topic being considered and discussed was clerical, not collegiate, education; second, the posture Catholics assumed on the question of higher learning was prescribed by clerical opinion. Except for Orestes Brownson's articles on education, Catholic education, and higher education in his *Review*, launched in Boston in the 1830s and continued later in New York City, and Elizabeth, New Jersey, no Catholic layman in the first seven decades of the nineteenth century made public statements either on the need for, or the quality of, Catholic schools or colleges.[29] This strange and striking lay silence on a question vital to them is one of the greatest paradoxes in American education. It is impossible to believe that laymen were totally barren of educational reactions; yet the discipline of the Church kept them silent, and only a man like Brownson, who revolted against garden-variety Catholicism, and deplored lay submission to clerical edicts on subjects outside ecclesiastical spheres, had enough courage to criticize and recommend.

Brownson had earlier participated in debates over the common school —for example, he had on various occasions challenged the educational philosophy of Horace Mann—and to some extent was successful in stimulating Catholic interest in it. College education, he averred, should also be scrutinized, and the Catholic colleges then in the process of evolution should be made to define their proper place in the American democratic community.[30] In the first place, he argued, Catholic colleges should become schools suited to the educational taste and temper of the United States by discarding their affinities for European models;[31] in the second place, they should abandon their ecclesiastical exclusiveness : they should be schools for laymen wherein knowledge is stressed, not seminaries for prospective clerics wherein piety is accorded pride of place. They should, moreover, once having clearly marked out their goal, avoid premature expansion :

The principle of established classes and terms of admission, of regarding every pupil as a candidate for a degree, of uniform statutory regulations, of matriculation and of residence, does not enter into the system. Though empowered to confer

---

[29] For Brownson's attitudes on Catholic colleges during this period, see Orestes A. Brownson, "Our Colleges," *Brownson's Quarterly Review*, 15 (April, 1858), 209–244; and for an interpretation of Brownson's position relative to Catholic education, see my articles, "Brownson's Theory of Education," *Records of the American Catholic Historical Society*, LXII (September, 1951), 142–171; "Brownson's Views on Responsibility for Education," *Records . . .* , LXII (December, 1951), 221–252; and "Brownson's Attitude Towards Catholic Education," *Records . . .* , LXIII (June, 1952), 110–128.

[30] Orestes A. Brownson, "Our Colleges," *Brownson's Quarterly Review*, 15 (1858), 210–212.

[31] *Ibid.*, p. 231.

degrees they are rarely conferred or applied for. The relations formed by students with the college are not essentially different from those between a well-grown child and the school-mistress of a neighbouring village. The institution continues to be an educational omnibus wherein the votaries of science enter unceremoniously, and continue up the ascent as far as suits either their curiosity or convenience, and no farther.[32]

Brownson complained of the tendency of Catholic colleges to mix candidates for the bachelor of arts degree with students who were only engaged in elementary-school studies : the same rules, the same supervision, and sometimes the same instruction were applied to all without regard for motivation, age, or ability. In such a chaotic atmosphere there could be no real attention to scholarship nor could the student as a person be accorded the educational dignity due to him. In a word, Brownson indicted Catholic colleges for disregarding the personalities of their students. And he indicted them further for their inability to perceive that the collegiate plan they were following had only a provisional origin and "thus a system that in its best aspect could only have been provisional has become the model."[33] He criticized the lack of imagination in the curriculum of Catholic colleges and complained of the length and disorder of the seven-year program.[34] He doubted the capacity of most Catholic college presidents to be good educational leaders, since so few of them had direct college experiences, and he dismissed the whole corps of prefects as obstacles to a decent education.[35] More importantly, Brownson interpreted the goals of Catholic colleges to be moral and religious rather than intellectual (a judgment in which we should concur); they were, he argued, inappropriate primary goals for an educational institution. Even so, the colleges failed in achieving their stated purposes : "We only know this much, that in most cases that have fallen under our observation, the graduates of our colleges appear to us very deficient in both mental and moral culture, and even in literary attainments and general culture."[36]

It should be observed that over a period of nearly a quarter century Brownson had not changed his mind : the Catholic colleges, he thought, were weak, misguided, and inefficient. They neither were nor wanted to be real colleges :

What can a boy only sixteen or seventeen learn of philosophy and natural sciences in simply one year's study? We have been studying philosophy for over fifty years,

[32] *Ibid.*, p. 213.
[33] *Ibid.*, pp. 215–216.
[34] *Ibid.*
[35] *Ibid.*
[36] Orestes A. Brownson, "Our Colleges," *Brownson's Quarterly Review,* 24 (1875), 251.

and even now hardly know its A B C. It is ridiculous to suppose that even a clever lad of eighteen can have learned enough philosophy, mental or moral, to be of any practical use to him. The college, as it now is, or was a few years ago, is only a respectable grammar-school.[37]

In order to eliminate the weaknesses of the Catholic college, Brownson proposed that definite levels of instruction be organized. Without seeking the suppression of any college then in existence (1875), he recommended that four levels of Catholic education be established : the parochial schools, preparatory schools (conducted by Jesuits, Lazarists, Christian Brothers, and others), colleges under the management of religious communities, and a university. The university, the capstone of the system, would be managed by the most competent persons without regard for their lay or clerical status and its teachers would come from the ranks of the academically qualified. In addition to being the ornament of Catholic education, such a university could set intellectual and educational standards for the Catholic community to follow; for the colleges it could be both a source of inspiration and a means for marking out decent goals in higher learning.[38]

Brownson's example, however, not only went unemulated by the very persons who were to support the schools and colleges and trust their children to them, but he himself was attacked with charges of disloyalty and heterodoxy both by laymen and clerics who thus muffled his thunder and short-circuited the influence of his arguments.[39] The fact of clerical domination over all Catholic education, too clear to require special documentation, is especially apparent in the attitudes Catholics inherited or formed about higher education.

So when we talk about Catholic attitudes to higher learning, we mean the attitudes of the clergy, for lay opinion was either non-existent or obscure. Either from teaching or habit Catholics must have come to believe that education was a subject reserved for persons with theological training and holy orders, for lay initiative in Catholic education, either in establishing schools, ascertaining their objectives, or molding their curricula, is unrecorded in archival documents or library chronicles, except in three cases where short-lived colleges were founded and conducted by laymen.[40] Exceptions here prove no rule. Because priests and bishops held canonically

37 *Ibid.,* pp. 254–255.

38 *Ibid.*

39 Bishop Francis P. Kenrick to Orestes A. Brownson, February 12, 1855, University of Notre Dame Archives; Archbishop John Hughes to Orestes A. Brownson, October 3, 1863, UNDA; and Henry F. Brownson, *Orestes A. Brownson: Latter Life* (Detroit, Henry F. Brownson, 1898), p. 287, and Thomas T. McAvoy, "Orestes A. Brownson and Archbishop John Hughes in 1860," *Review of Politics,* XXIV (January, 1962), 19–47.

40 See Bernard C. Steiner, *History of Education in Maryland,* U. S. Bureau of Education Bulletin No. 19, 1894, pp. 173, 267; *Report of the United States*

accredited leadership roles and positions of authority, lay contributions to the success of Catholic schools are easily obscured. Laymen supported the schools, although the academic history of Catholic institutions follows the usual, and approved, Catholic technique of heaping praise on clerics and crediting them with full responsibility for the success of any undertaking. Catholic clergymen have fed for centuries on the myth of their superiority over laymen, and laymen have enjoyed keeping the myth alive, especially in the histories of colleges. With these attitudes of self-abnegation, there was not the slightest resentment generated in the face of clerical domination over education, even when priests preached sermons and bishops wrote pastorals affirming parental rights in education.[41] Catholics were disinclined to interpret their spiritual fathers literally. When Brownson, or a lesser-known local figure whose name is obliterated by time, tried to speak to the educational issue or give answers to an entirely open question, he was ignored, reprimanded, or criticized for dangerous heterodoxy by a conservative laity and a clergy who regularly misinterpreted the good of the Church in terms of vested self-interest.[42]

We must not, however, begin by assuming that education—especially higher education—was a burning question of the day. Bishops made predictable pronouncements on the subject and priests followed suit, but their preoccupations were elsewhere.[43] Catholics were unquestionably dedicated to the proposition that teaching should be offered in schools free from prejudice and hostility, but all this could be taken for granted, and once the principle was stated it required only repetition, not further elaboration or illumination. Implementation of the principle was infinitely more difficult than its articulation, but even here no effort was made to solicit, sample, or reflect lay opinion. Policies and practices pertaining to Catholic education at all levels were determined by the bishops, or translated by them from Roman directives; since the colonial period knew no resident bishop, the policies of European dioceses, missionary orders, or Roman congregations

---

Commissioner of Education, 1870, pp. 508–509; and John Lamott, *History of the Archdiocese of Cincinnati* (New York, Frederick Pustet Co., 1921), pp. 284–285.

41 Bernard McQuaid, *The Public School Question* (Boston, Duffy and Co., 1876), p. 9; P. Bayma, "The Liberalistic View of the Public School Question," *The American Catholic Quarterly Review,* II (1877), 17; Daniel F. Reilly, *The School Controversy, 1891–1893* (Washington, The Catholic University of America Press, 1943), pp. 107–115; and Neil G. McCluskey, *Catholic Viewpoint on Education* (Garden City, N. Y., Doubleday-Image, 1962), pp. 53–61.

42 See Thomas I. Cook and A. B. Leavelle, "Orestes A. Brownson's *The American Republic,*" *Review of Politics,* IV (January, 1942), 70–87; and "Instruction of the Congregation of Propaganda de Fide Concerning Catholic Children Attending American Public Schools," *The Pastor,* IV (June, 1886), 232–237.

43 John Gilmary Shea, *The Hierarchy of the Catholic Church in the United States* (New York, The Office of Catholic Publications, 1886).

were adopted and made to fit colonial circumstances. This rigid system was altered somewhat, and for the better, we should think, when John Carroll was appointed apostolic prefect in 1784. From this time forward it is possible to speak of a Catholic attitude toward colonial- and national-period education without having to append a note that the attitude was transplanted. John Carroll may be the greatest man we meet in the history of American Catholic education, for if anyone can be given credit for inaugurating an entire system of education in the United States, it must be he. Born in Maryland, educated first in the Maryland Catholic schools and then in Jesuit schools in Europe, entering the Society of Jesus, becoming a priest, and finally returning to America, he soon became the recognized leader and spokesman among his brother priests. His stature is reflected further in his appointment as apostolic prefect in 1784 and his elevation to the episcopacy as the first Bishop of Baltimore in 1790.[44]

Carroll's identification with the Society of Jesus, although he disengaged himself from the Society when it was suppressed in 1773, gave him excellent credentials for dealing with education. While he was acting only in the role of a colonial priest, his correspondence shows a keen awareness of the need for schools and colleges. Undoubtedly the urgency of his concern is explained mainly by the critical shortage of colonial priests : missionaries who long before had come to America were getting old, and while Europe could always be counted on to supply some clergy, Carroll was fully aware of the contribution a native clergy could make to the Church. Thus, Carroll's first pronouncements on education, after he was endowed with episcopal authority, were directed to the lower schools with admonitions that they prepare boys for a colonial seminary which he hoped might eventually be created.[45]

Before and during Carroll's first years as prefect, he hoped to satisfy any Catholic need for secular higher studies by cooperating in the establishment of non- or inter-denominational colleges. We know the part he played in the early stages of the founding of an undenominational college in Baltimore, and he spoke enthusiastically of "a college in Philadelphia, and it is proposed to establish two in Maryland, in which Catholics can be admitted, as well as others, as presidents, professors, and pupils. We think accordingly of establishing a seminary, in which they can be trained to the life and learning suited to that state."[46] Although Carroll later found it impossible to approve these schools because their 'neutral' religious climate was fundamentally altered, at this time he certainly supported a Catholic utilization of them, and on various occasions tried to persuade friends in Europe to

---

[44] Guilday, *op. cit.,* p. 373.

[45] Shea, *History of the Catholic Church in the United States,* II, 260; and Daley, *op. cit.,* p. 42.

[46] Shea, *History of the Catholic Church in the United States,* II, 260.

recommend promising young men to serve as professors in the new colleges.[47]

The University of Pennsylvania, started as the College, Academy, and Charitable School of Philadelphia by Benjamin Franklin in 1749, was the Philadelphia college referred to in Carroll's correspondence; neither of the two colleges in Maryland may have materialized; one must have been the projected college which listed Carroll as a cooperating founder.[48] Its plans, we know, were unrealized. But we do not have to identify these colleges in order to feel the full weight of Carroll's thought on higher education: the initial form of Catholic higher learning was to be theological; and seminaries for the preparation of priests occupied the minds of Catholic clerical leaders throughout most of the formative period. Carroll, moreover, while not insensitive to prejudice and hostility directed toward Catholics, preferred not to dwell on such things probably because the atmosphere in Maryland was more moderate than in some other parts of the country; so he entertained visions of Catholic students and teachers participating in already existing colleges.[49] Whether this was an ideal solution to a vexing problem or only an acceptable expedient is hard to determine; it did have precedential support however, for Catholics had often allowed lower schools, not specifically Catholic in teaching or perspective, and sometimes clearly and openly classical, to handle the first years of a future theology student's education.[50] By Carroll's time, we must admit, the seminary was the prescribed institution for educating a priest; and while not counseling innovation, Carroll was, nevertheless, fully aware of the role medieval and modern universities had played in theological training.[51]

This attitude of optimism about the acceptability of nonCatholic lower schools and colleges was reversed abruptly within the space of a few short years, however, and we are left to wonder why Carroll at first thought them promising. We may, at the outset, absolve him from the charge of insufficient knowledge of the contemporary colonial schools and of an exaggerated liberalism, both of which could have generated this false optimism, for neither fits the man's character. What remains is this: the colonial schools, heretofore immune to the threat of Catholic enrollment, altered their learning atmosphere when faced with the prospect of Catholic students and allowed dormant antiCatholic dispositions to awaken and

[47] Daley, op. cit., p. 49.

[48] Burns and Kohlbrenner, op. cit., p. 63; The Maryland Journal and Baltimore Advertiser, XIII, May 31, 1786; and J. T. Scharf, Chronicles of Baltimore (Baltimore, Turnbull Brothers, 1874), p. 243.

[49] John Gilmary Shea, A History of Georgetown College (New York, P. F. Collier, 1891), p. 8.

[50] See Lloyd McDonald, The Seminary Movement in the United States, 1784–1833 (Washington, The Catholic University of America, 1927), pp. 62–71.

[51] Edward Devitt, "Georgetown in the Early Days," Records of the Columbia Historical Society, XII (1909), 21–25; and D. A. Casserly, "Georgetown College," Scribner's Monthly, XX (May, 1880), 35–39.

infuse their books, teaching, and scholastic environment. So Carroll's hope
that Catholics could utilize existing educational facilities was abortive and
he was compelled to seek other alternatives. By December, 1785, he was
writing not about the imminent establishment of a seminary, but about the
founding of a preparatory academy : "The object nearest my heart now,
and the only one that can give consistency to our religious views in this
country, is the establishment of a school, and afterwards a seminary for
young clergymen."[52]

The die was cast and for nearly the next full century every post-
elementary school under Catholic auspices accepted as an irrevocable
commission the principle that secondary schools should eventually add
college studies to their curricula and thus prepare young men for divinity
studies in a seminary. Nearly every Catholic secondary school and college
of the formative period made the seminary, the capstone to the system, a
part of its long-range academic plan.[53]

If Carroll's December, 1785 pronouncement was not the theoretical
foundation for Catholic education in the United States, it was at least a
prophetic anticipation, for the object nearest Carroll's heart became, in fact,
the practical educational goal for Catholics. When, six years later, Georgetown Academy opened its doors to students, the first step was taken toward
the implementation of Carroll's new plan.

After 1785, Carroll, the acknowledged leader among the Catholic clergy
in Maryland, moved quickly, though not in an ill-considered or precipitous
manner, to realize what now stands as a tradition-studded educational goal,
for, as we know, he had pondered what seemed to be an educational conundrum almost ever since his return to America in 1774. As early as 1783 the
Catholic clergy in Maryland had agreed on local ecclesiastical organization
and had formed a general chapter. This chapter was empowered by common
consent to handle issues falling within the Church's jurisdiction. So, using the
machinery of the chapter, Carroll proposed at its November, 1785 meeting
to find solutions to two vexing educational problems : the training of youth
and the education of priests.[54] Georgetown College may be seen as the
first-fruits of Carroll's policy, although it must be admitted that the college's
historians themselves usually prefer other evidences of founding.[55] It may,
moreover, be regarded as the initiation of a system of Catholic education in

[52] Carroll to Plowden, December 15, 1785, quoted in Shea, *A History of Georgetown College*, p. 9.

[53] Agatho Zimmer, *Changing Concepts of Higher Education in America Since 1700*
(Washington, Catholic University of America Press, 1938), pp. 94–99; and Sebastian
A. Erbacher, *Catholic Higher Education for Men in the United States, 1850–1866*
(Washington, The Catholic University of America, 1931), pp.60–70.

[54] Hughes, *op. cit.,* I, Part II, 665–666.

[55] See Daley, *op. cit.,* p. vii; J. Fairfax McLaughlin, *College Days at Georgetown
and Other Papers* (New York, J. B. Lippincott, 1899), pp. 13—15; J. Fairfax

the United States.[56] At this November meeting, Carroll recommended the opening of an academy for the purpose of giving boys a foundational education for the seminary.

While we suffer from some uncertainty about the details of opposition, not all the clergymen attending the November, 1785 meeting in Whitemarsh, Maryland, were enthusiastic about the proposed institution, and some were guardedly opposed to it. In the first place, some of Carroll's confreres believed an academy, with stated intentions of becoming a college and a seminary, was premature; they were unable to see either sources of support for the school, students who might be prepared to attend it, or teachers qualified to staff it. Besides, some may have resented Carroll's having already, as early as August of 1786, contacted Cardinal Antonelli, Secretary of the Congregation de Propaganda Fide, explaining plans for a school and seminary and asking for a ratio studiorum—a plan of studies—for the two branches.[57] The members of the loyal opposition had no illusions about the quality of existing schools and their suitability for Catholic children, especially for boys with a religious vocation, but they were reluctant to endorse an educational venture whose prospects of success appeared so dim. The generators of opposition along these lines were few, and whatever their misgivings—whether they adverted to the fact that the Catholic school for colonial America should not be a warmed-over version of European church schools goes unrecorded—we doubt whether they pressed or expressed them with fervor; the main opposition to the proposed school was based on other, non-academic considerations. Money had to be raised to establish the school, and additional reserve funds ought to be available to ensure its stability through the first lean years, for even Carroll's most optimistic estimates relative to the school's success did not envision it as a self-supporting institution for several years. Various means were available for raising funds, but they were slow and none included guarantees of success : a general subscription was one, but with few Catholics in the country, and even fewer wealthy ones, this way had little promise; solicitors could be appointed to seek money in the West India Islands and in Europe, but this, too, was slow and uncertain. Carroll recommended a better way : many ex-Jesuits held in their own names property once belonging to the Society of Jesus. This property, obtained by Jesuits who accompanied various groups of colonial settlers, and originally deeded to the Society, was later assigned to individual Jesuits when the Society was suppressed. Carroll's proposition was to dispose of this land and use the proceeds to finance the building of a school. He was asking ex-Jesuit priests who came to Whitemarsh to release to him

McLaughlin, "The Beginnings of Georgetown College," *The Catholic World*, XLVI (February, 1888), 610–619; and Shea, *A History of Georgetown College*, pp. 10–11.

[56] Guilday, *op. cit.*, pp. 790–791.

[57] Daley, *op. cit.*, pp. 32–33.

property they held in their names. Many ex-Jesuits in the United States, fiercely loyal to the Society, were confident of the Society's imminent restoration; they were thus unwilling to appropriate to other use resources that might later be needed by the Society. To fragment or dispose of such property was, they thought, tantamount to foresaking the Society at a time when its clandestinely-held resources should be kept secure and intact. Being an ex-Jesuit himself Carroll could understand and sympathize with this argument—although he was considerably less sanguine about the Society's restoration than other ex-Jesuits—so in order to achieve the support of the ex-Jesuits for his academic adventure and the funds he needed to sustain it, he was ready to compromise : a satisfactory agreement was reached when Carroll promised that in the event of the Society's restoration the college would be "surrendered into her hands."[58]

With the practical matter of financial support partially settled, the clerical assembly could proceed to approve Carroll's plan and state in the "resolves" that "a school be erected for the education of youth, and the perpetuity of the body of clergy in this country."[59] In this statement of purpose for the new school, we detect no departure from college objectives stated first in the founding of Harvard College, viz., that the school should ensure a regular and uninterrupted supply of clergymen.[60] History does not tell us that one hundred and fifty years made much difference to college foundations, or that Georgetown's founders affirmed any objectives, or entertained any attitudes about higher learning, distinguishing them from the divines responsible for the origin of Harvard. What was deemed a good and worthy objective a century and a half earlier, was still meritorious. Yet, it should not be thought that the total picture of young Georgetown, or the general Catholic attitude toward higher education, can be stated in the simple pronouncement that the school directed its efforts at the education of clergymen. There was something more.

With the college's location determined and the first building under construction, Georgetown faced its first crisis : the sale of ex-Jesuit property had not realized enough money to finance the project, so an appeal for funds was cleverly inserted in a broadside entitled "Proposals to Establish an Academy at George Town, Patowmack River, Maryland." This document served a dual purpose : it was, as we have said, an appeal for funds, but it was also a supplementary statement of the school's purpose and a prospectus. The new academy, the Proposals stated, was to "unite the means of com-

---

58 Guilday, *op. cit.,* p. 456.

59 The complete "Resolves" are quoted in Hughes, *op. cit.,* I, Part II, 665–666; Shea, *A History of Georgetown College,* pp. 10–11; Guilday, *op. cit.,* p. 451; and James S. Easby-Smith, *Georgetown University in the District of Columbia* (Chicago, Lewis Publishing Co., 1907), I, 22–23.

60 See Samuel E. Morison, *Harvard College in the Seventeenth Century,* I, 141–147.

municating Science with an effectual Provision for guarding and preserving the Morals of Youth."[61] NonCatholic students were welcome, but were required, the circular stated, "to conform to a general and uniform discipline."[62] This generous invitation to nonCatholic students is perplexing in view of the school's expressed intention to prepare boys for the Catholic priesthood. Perhaps Carroll and his counselors wanted to create an image of tolerance and openness for their school; even with Protestant students its focus would not be less Catholic and this liberal policy on admission suggested a Catholic willingness to cooperate and share educational opportunities with their nonCatholic fellow citizens. There was, moreover, a dearth of higher schools in the vicinity of Washington, so it was understandable that Carroll might have wanted to upgrade learning for the sake of the common good. Fearing a rekindling of old antiCatholic animosities if Georgetown wore an exclusive and uncompromising Catholic face, Carroll may have adopted an apparently liberal code of admission for the same reasons that led most colonial priests to oppose for about two decades the erection of a colonial ecclesiastical see and the appointment of a bishop in the English colonies.[63] Additionally, the history of Protestant benefactions to Catholic institutions could not be overlooked, nor could tuition payments from a full complement of students—whether Protestant or Catholic—be ignored in a school fighting for its financial life. Apparently some Protestants, putting the general welfare of religion above their own denominational views, were willing, not only to contribute to the school, but to send their sons there as well. So the statement permitting enrollment of nonCatholic students may have reflected only enough tolerance to keep the channels open for Protestant financial help. On another level, however, the open-door admissions policy was checkmated by the rule that nonCatholic students were required to conform to the general discipline of the school; or to put the regulation plainly : all students were obliged to attend and participate in Catholic devotions and rituals, although they were "at liberty to frequent places of Worship and [religious] Instruction appointed by their parents."[64]

The Proposals neither limited the geographic area the school should serve nor restricted admission to students clearly ready for a secondary school course. The policy was stated this way : the academy was ready to enroll students "as soon as they have learned the first Elements of Letters, and will conduct them through the several Branches of Classical Learning to that State of Education from which they may proceed with Advantage to the Study of higher Sciences in the University of this or those neighboring

[61] An original of the "Proposals" is preserved in the Georgetown University Archives. It is quoted in Easby-Smith, *op. cit.,* p. 25; and Daley, *op. cit.,* pp. 34–35.

[62] *Ibid.,* p. 35.

[63] *American Catholic Historical Researches,* XII (January, 1895), 44–45.

[64] Daley, *op. cit.,* p. 35.

States."[65] But it would also offer studies in "Reading, Writing, Arithmetic, the easier Branches of the Mathematics, and the Grammar of our native Tongue."[66] The Proposals, we must remember, were intended to cultivate prospective benefactors, so to take at face value all their promises may be misleading. Yet, they define the school in broad terms, making it elementary and secondary in character and standards, with some talk about preparing youth for the universities. What they really meant was college, not university, preparation, because in 1788, the year the Proposals were published, no American university capable of involving students in professional or graduate studies of university caliber was in evidence.[67] It was scarcely possible for Georgetown Academy to have been raised to the level of, say, the German classical gymnasium, and qualified to prepare students for genuine university curricula. A secondary school course was entirely satisfactory as a foundation for seminary study, however, and historians of seminaries in the United States acknowledge that throughout the formative period for colleges, perhaps as far forward as the founding of the Catholic University of America in 1884, the seminaries were definitely collegiate, not university, in scholastic standards.[68]

The Proposals are interesting, too, for what they neglect to say. For example, no allusion is made to a college course of study, although some ambiguity attaches to the meaning of the academy as a preparatory school; nor do they mention predivinity curricula. If we look only at the Proposals our understanding of Georgetown's objectives and their reflection of Catholic attitudes toward higher learning during these early years will be incomplete.[69] They bespeak, however, a broad approach to educational opportunity, encompassing the elementary branches of education and giving some attention to English grammar. This last point is singular and worth our notice, for the regular grammar schools of the day were indifferent to English grammar study despite the fact that their prospectuses promised to prepare young men for life in an English-speaking society.[70] Persistent in their neglect of this provision, they continued their undiminished determination to teach the Latin classics and to praise them as the finest

[65] *Ibid.*

[66] *Ibid.*

[67] See George Paul Schmidt, "Colleges in Ferment," *American Historical Review,* XIX (October, 1953), 19–42.

[68] See John Talbot Smith, *Our Seminaries: An Essay on Clerical Training* (New York, Longmans, Green and Co., 1896), pp. 51–59; and John Lancaster Spalding, *Means and Ends of Education* (Chicago, McClurg and Co., 1897), pp. 212–216.

[69] If one is to criticize Daley's fine book, it must be on this point, for he pays scant heed to the "Resolves" (see p. 34), and does not distinguish them from the "Proposals," although they were discrete documents separated in their publication by a period of two years.

[70] Robert Middlekauff, *Ancients and Axioms* (New Haven, Yale University Press, 1963), pp. 171–183.

ornaments of a decent education, because these curricula were justified by the best traditions of secondary education. So the willingness of the Georgetown Academy to make English grammar a part of its course of study ruptures tradition in a modest way and allows it to take a place alongside Franklin's Academy as a school unafraid of prudent innovation.[71] Lavish and undeserved praise must be avoided : the English curriculum at Georgetown was put up with but unloved (the English teacher's qualifications were regularly downgraded) and was the product of concession to circumstances not educational principle, for Catholic educators were unable to admit that knowledge of a vernacular had inherent worth. They, too, were caught in the inflexible grip of the Latin tradition and accorded Latin studies pride of place, but for them—although not so much for their nonCatholic counterparts—Latin clearly had utility.

But these are side issues and we should return to the mainstream. By not mentioning the academy as a preparatory seminary, the Proposals allowed the real purposes of the institution to go unstated. With the Proposals alone for guide, any complete resolution of a debate over Georgetown's original objectives is foreclosed. As it is, the Resolves may be taken into account as better evidence of institutional intent, because the Proposals, never intended as an educational manifesto, were published as a supplementary document enabling the projected school to put its best public foot forward. Looking again at the Resolves, we find a fundamental attitude toward higher learning. John Carroll, unquestionably the principal figure in the founding of Georgetown and determining its objectives, is unequivocal and explicit in reaffirming what the Resolves had clearly stated : "on this Academy is built all my hope of permanency and success of our H. Religion in the United States."[72] And in 1790, after Carroll had concluded an agreement with the Sulpicians to open a seminary in Baltimore, he could further elaborate his hope and define Georgetown as a school of classical education for boys who would enter clerical life.[73] So far nothing had been said about liberal learning nor was any reference made to training in the secular professions; the evolution of Catholic attitudes on higher learning was curtailed by the demands of clerical necessity and, up to this point, centered on the education of priests.

Later letters, sermons, pastorals, and ecclesiastical documents reflect undiminished confidence in an attitude equating higher learning with the establishment and support of seminaries; apparently the idea that Catholic laymen might benefit from higher studies under the direction and guidance of the Church never entered the minds of Carroll and his associates.

[71] Leonard W. Labaree, et al. (eds.), *The Papers of Benjamin Franklin* (New Haven, Yale University Press, 1959), III, 397–421.

[72] Carroll to Plowden, March 1, 1788, quoted in Daley, *op. cit.*, p. 47.

[73] See Guilday, *op. cit.*, p. 467.

Appointed Bishop of Baltimore in 1790, John Carroll, in the same year, encouraged the Sulpician Fathers to come to the United States to lay the foundation for a seminary which might open when students from Georgetown were ready. Although Georgetown had yet to enroll its first student, Carroll was beginning to reshape his plans for the school; its potential as a seminary was de-emphasized in favor of its character as a preparatory school. This attitude is evident in his 1792 pastoral letter, which further bespeaks both his unalterable commitment to clerical education and an almost total indifference to higher learning aimed in any other direction.[74]

With Georgetown the first stanchions for Catholic higher learning were in place and with Carroll's pastoral of 1792 the hierarchical structure of the American Church began to take shape. Thus the stage was set for a development of educational doctrine, and we should be interested in knowing the bishops' part in nurturing this doctrine and applying it to higher education. It would be a pleasant exercise to report that the bishops' official pronouncements confirmed an unwavering commitment to Catholic colleges and, moreover, exemplified their appreciation of higher learning as both broad and liberal. Historical accuracy forbids such license; instead we must make our way through ponderous, pedantic, ecclesiastical prose—sometimes finding encouraging statements about higher education, but often meeting with what amounts to a conspiracy of silence—to discover haphazard policies and equivocal attitudes towards secular studies in Catholic colleges.

Reading, writing, and religious instruction were never in jeopardy, and, in general, education had the bishops' wholehearted endorsement; but they spoke in an educational language woefully unresponsive and often irrelevant to the education of the people of a country as yet unable to draw on an indigenous intellectual tradition. Reflecting his appraisal of education's vital significance, Carroll begins the pastoral letter in 1792, after an appropriate ecclesiastical introduction, with a commentary on education. He speaks first of the parents' duties in educating their children, but never goes beyond purely moral and religious teaching, and while we should hesitate to gainsay the role of such teaching in the lives of men, it should be recorded that as a broad policy statement it left too much unsaid. Carroll proceeds to explain and, we should think, advertise Georgetown, a school "under the superintendence and government of some of my reverend brethren" expected to educate youth in "useful learning, and those of our own religion, in its principles and duties."[75] While he was probably only describing the administrative plan for Georgetown in his reference to the superintendence and

74 See Peter Guilday, *The National Pastorals of the American Hierarchy* (Washington, National Catholic Welfare Conference, 1923), pp. 1–15. Neil G. McCluskey has reprinted several of these pastoral letters in his *Catholic Education in America* (New York, Teachers College Press, 1964).

75 Guilday, *The National Pastorals*, p. 4.

government of the academy being in the hands of clerics, this description eventually achieved the status of a dogmatic assumption stipulating that any authentic Catholic school must be managed and controlled by ecclesiastics. Had this phrase been omitted from Carroll's pastoral—it was by no means essential to a meaning he wanted to convey—Catholic schools of the nineteenth century might not perhaps have worn a different administrative face; but as it was, the clerical monopoly over education was given official recognition, and apparent approval, and all Catholics seemed anxious to make what was in the beginning merely an accident of rhetoric an article of academic faith. Neither time nor experience with schools has shaken the implicit confidence of Catholic people in the ability of their clergymen to interpret education's ends and means perfectly or to manage schools faultlessly. On the point of "useful learning" Carroll appears to be more liberal than, in fact, he was, for by useful learning he meant classical foundations in grammar and rhetoric, counting them pre-eminently useful to the seminary student and priest.

The Bishop invites Catholic parents to send their sons to Georgetown whenever their finances allow, and he ends his appeal for the school by urging his readers to consider the good effects the academy might have even on persons unable to occupy its classrooms. Informally or incidentally, Georgetown could prepare teachers. Young men who after attending Georgetown did not enter an ecclesiastical seminary could return to their homes prepared to open schools, or assist pastors in teaching, and thus by continuing the educational practices learned in the college—"uniting much attention to religion with a solicitude for other improvements"—generate an increase in piety by carefully instructing children in the principles of Christian faith and morality.[76] But this was not all, for Carroll has not yet stated Georgetown's fundamental attraction : "The school, dear brethren, if aided by your benevolence, and favoured with your confidence, will be the foundation of an additional advantage to true religion in this our country. . . . may we not reasonably hope, that one of the effects of a virtuous course of education will be the preparing of the minds of some, whom providence may select, to receive and cherish a call from God to an ecclesiastical state?"[77] The question is plainly rhetorical, and Carroll allows it to go unanswered.

His final remarks on the subject of education treat of the Sulpicians' seminary at St. Mary's College in Baltimore; and he solicits from Catholics both patronage and endowment for the new institution, coming perilously close to implying that when schools for clerical education are able to fulfill the Church's requirements, Catholics can forget any questions they may have entertained about the future of higher learning. Seeing the society of

76 *Ibid.*
77 *Ibid.*, pp. 4–5.

the United States—from which Catholic laymen were fundamentally inseparable—from amongst the insulations of clerical life, Carroll's educational philosophy was too narrow to generate a policy of encouragement and active support for colleges with objectives geared to the inarticulate secular aspirations of lay Catholics.

Policies once stated with authority, clarity, and force, particularly in religious societies paying allegiance to tradition and precedent, are normally dispensed from the ardors of reexamination and reformulation. They become part of a conventional wisdom and depend on repetition for their validation. Thus in pastoral letters and hierarchical pronouncements for a half-century following Carroll's episcopacy, we look in vain for a reversal or liberalization of this narrow attitude toward higher education in general and, in particular, the college education of Catholic laymen. Carroll's attitudes on higher education, sustained by the machinery of religious precedent, achieved venerable standing, and were reflected in ecclesiastical policy statements issuing from important Church councils right down to 1884, when the Third Plenary Council broke new ground for Catholic higher education. During this ninety-year interlude the Catholic-college movement was not stagnant—noteworthy progress was made along a variety of academic avenues—but the official policy of the Church was still encumbered by the limitations and prescriptions of former attitudes, and the colleges, to all intents and purposes, were estranged from the one institution that could have given them counsel, love, understanding, and support.

From 1792 to 1829 Church leaders eschewed a national conciliar assembly, so high-level amendments or supplements to Carroll's educational policies were impossible. In 1829 a pastoral letter to the laity issued from the First Provincial Council of Baltimore.[78] Its contents picture the Church in the United States, graduating from a simple missionary venture, confronted by a variety of complex problems pertaining to ecclesiastical jurisdiction and religious discipline. Yet, education was made to stand still: in the pastoral letter, written probably by Bishop John England,[79] Catholic education is discussed in two separate sections; one is concerned with the education of priests and restates John Carroll's policy relative to the establishment and support of seminaries;[80] the other, considerably longer, commends to Catholic parents the Church schools then in operation. By 1829 it was possible to speak of Catholic schools and recommend their attendance with the force of episcopal authority, something the earlier pastoral was

[78] An ecclesiastical province is composed of several dioceses. While each bishop has independent jurisdiction over his own diocese, a provincial council is sometimes convened to discuss common issues and enact common church regulations.

[79] For John England's productive ecclesiastical career, see Peter Guilday, *The Life and Times of John England* (New York, The America Press, 1927).

[80] Guilday, *The National Pastorals*, p. 23.

unable to do. So the author of the letter says : "How well would it be, if your means and opportunities permitted, were you at this period to commit your children to those whom we have, for their special fitness, placed over our seminaries and our female religious institutions? It would be at once the best mode of discharging your obligations to your children, and of aiding us in promoting the great object which we have already endeavoured to impress upon your minds."[81] The "great object" was, of course, spiritual welfare and allegiance to Catholic doctrine; thus the schools are clearly defined by the bishops as religious institutions primarily and secondly as literary agencies. But it is important to notice that the letter demurs from making an unalterable or timeless commitment to religiously superintended, separate schools. To interpret this statement—"were you at this period to commit your children to the care of those whom we have . . . placed over our seminaries and our female religious institutions?"—as a qualification rather than a rhetorical flourish means that the bishops conceived their educational edicts to have temporary application; they were expedients constructed to mute the antiCatholic voice of ordinary American schools which otherwise Catholic children would almost unavoidably attend.

On the evidence of this pastoral the enthusiasm of Catholic clerical leaders for higher education is open to doubt, as is the attention they were willing to pay it, for nothing in the pastoral, save the pronouncement adjuring support for the seminaries, makes us think about Catholic colleges. An especially generous interpretation of the pastoral letter to the clergy from the same council, particularly the paragraph dealing with the instruction of youth, could convert it to a broad endorsement of clerical activity in Catholic education on all levels, but a literal reading of the text, contextually more appropriate, finds the bishops exhorting Catholic clergymen to "devote themselves to the instruction of children in the way of the God of truth."[82] To challenge the merit of such advice to priests is unthinkable, yet we should regard it as a commission to teach catechism and whenever possible the fundamentals of a literary syllabus and not an apostolic decree to excavate the treasuries of higher learning.

The Second Provincial Council of Baltimore convened in 1833 to review the condition of the Church in the United States and prescribe remedies for a variety of doctrinal and disciplinary maladies. While the council was preoccupied with subjects other than education (and this fact is reflected in its decrees), it did, nevertheless, enact legislation with tangential relationships to education : decrees or recommendations were made concerning the erection of diocesan seminaries, the establishment of a better system of parochial schools, and the appointment of a committee of prelates to censor

81 *Ibid.,* p. 26.
82 *Ibid.,* p. 58.

textbooks used in American schools containing erroneous information on matters of Catholic faith and discipline.[83]

This ambitious countermeasure—a board of censors for schoolbooks— never had any chance of success and the committee's work, if ever started, was certainly unproductive; yet, the rationale subserving its appointment was by no means trivial. Hoary indictments, malicious charges, and tired old wives' tales about Catholic beliefs and practices had too often invaded schoolbooks and the country's children were being fed on a regular diet of antiCatholic diatribe. An equitable hearing for Catholicism was impossible while this continued, so the committee's commission was highly significant. But it was powerless to correct or interdict these school practices and they continued for some decades to come without noticeable abatement. Uprooting the antiCatholic bias in "public" schools had to await the dawning of a new, more liberal era in American life, and it required some relaxation of rigid, inflexible antiProtestant prejudices entertained by a majority of Catholics as well.

A pastoral letter summarizes the action of the Second Council of Baltimore (1833) and publishes current Church policy. Education is treated in a succinct statement, freer from embellishments and obscurities of ecclesiastical rhetoric than former statements on the subject, and is acknowledged as a social and religious enterprise of the highest importance. For the first time higher education is approached as something more than predivinity or divinity training and a meaningful declaration is made about schools and colleges.

We have accordingly, at all times, used our best efforts to provide, as far as our means would permit, not only ecclesiastical seminaries to insure a succession in our priesthood and its extensions; but we have moreover sought to create colleges and schools in which your children, whether male or female, might have the best opportunities of literature and science, united to a strict protection of their morals and the best safeguards of their faith.[84]

Now we have, not a new policy, but an old one restated with broader educational dimensions : education's moral and religious purposes are reaffirmed, safeguards to faith are preserved, colleges and schools—whether for boys or girls—stripped of their dour monastic image, are allowed some independence as secularly-oriented academic refuges. Earlier pastorals, we recall, had paid uncommitted literary education scant heed, or none at all, and had put all Catholic schools in the business of supplying ministers for the Church. The Council of 1833, then, is a landmark and a good omen of better things to come in Catholic higher education : for the first time

[83] *Ibid.,* p. 61.
[84] *Ibid.,* p. 74.

in official language and policy, colleges form one branch of higher education, seminaries form another.

This generous policy was destined for dormancy, however, for the sting of antiCatholic books, attitudes, and actions made the prelates attending the Third Provincial Council of Baltimore (1837) assume a defensive posture unmatched by any previous council of the Church in the United States. A number of overt actions had brought the hostility of some Americans to Catholicism out into the open,[85] so the bishops devoted a long pastoral letter of guidance and admonition to Catholics in which they deplored the unhealthy religious climate of the United States. With well-founded chagrin they expressed their convictions clearly and candidly, but we must resist a temptation to recount both the conditions triggering their reactions and the reactions themselves. These preoccupations kept them from implementing the broader policy on higher education stated four years before; in the end they could only entreat Catholics to maintain "those institutions which we have created for the education of your children. It is our most earnest wish to make them as perfect as possible, in their fitness for the communication and improvement of science, as well as for the cultivation of pure solid and enlightened piety."[86] The bishops mildly regret the slow rate of progress toward high quality Catholic schools, and they blame the unfavorable American religious climate for this, but then make a self-serving comparison :

Yet, these notwithstanding [the unfavorable conditions], we are persuaded, that amongst those under our superintendence, are to be found, some of the most scientific and literary houses of education which our nation possesses; some establishments for the instruction of youth, male and female, in which there are successfully taught those speculative and practical lessons which inform the understanding, regulate the imagination, cultivate the taste, ameliorate the heart, improve the disposition, impress the importance and obligation of fulfilling every social, civic, domestic and religious duty, and teach the best mode of their performance.[87]

They hope, they say, that the schools conducted under their supervision will "furnish an abundant supply of useful citizens and christians, fitted for conferring blessings upon that country which protects them and that religion which they profess."[88]

The statement tends to equate civic and religious outcomes from a

---

[85] See Sister Mary Augustina Ray, *American Opinion of Roman Catholicism in the Eighteenth Century;* Ray A. Billington, *The Protestant Crusade, 1800–1860* (New York. Macmillan Co., 1938); and Gustavus Myers, *A History of Bigotry in the United States* (New York Random House, 1943).

[86] Guilday, *The National Pastorals,* p. 115.

[87] *Ibid.,* pp. 115–116.

[88] *Ibid.,* p. 116.

properly Church-sponsored system of schools, and whether this was the intended meaning or simply an accident of rhetoric, it put the Church on record as admitting the place of civic as well as religious virtue in formal education. This superficial evaluation of Catholic schools intrigues us, for the quality and superiority averred for them as scientific and literary institutions must have been bred out of hope or good intentions. After all, it is hard to understand how the bishops arrived at this conclusion, for we see no evidence of data collected, nor had they made any study of nonCatholic schools and colleges on which valid comparisons could be based. While they may have been correct in believing that the best Catholic schools were superior to some nonCatholic schools, the generality of the statement—to say nothing about their obvious lack of familiarity with nonCatholic institutions—may have had the effect of lulling Catholic school and college teachers and administrators into a state of academic euphoria. At the same time, in a paragraph dealing with the need for books inoffensive to Catholics, and reflecting action taken by the council in creating a committee of Catholic college presidents to supervise the preparation of textbooks for Catholic schools, they emphasized the dangers to Catholics of using books either in schools, colleges, or public libraries which, they said, were filled with errors and misrepresentations about the Catholic Church.[89] This adamant stand had the effect of putting Catholics on guard against all nonCatholic schools, and it reinforced what was rapidly becoming a ghetto mentality in a nascent Catholic academic community.

Where the pastoral letter of the Council of 1837 reads like a debater's rejoinder, the three-year interlude separating it from the Fourth Provincial Council of Baltimore was marked by social metamorphoses more hospitable to Catholicism, and the prelates at the Fourth Council, looking forward to better days, seem willing to forget the violence and scandalmongering of the past.[90] Still, in the longest pastoral statement yet on Catholic education, they are uncompromising in their determination to make Catholic children attend Catholic schools and they accompany their edict with the clear implication that the Church alone has the responsibility to make the schools safe places for Catholic children. The principle is old, but now its dogmatic tone is sharp and no allowance is made for an education standing outside the Church's jurisdiction or competence. And the bishops do not forget the dangerous, insidious residue from nonCatholic books used, they say, in the general schools of the country. If we may assume that nonCatholic schools were acceptable to Catholics—a doubtful and almost meaningless assumption in the light of acerbic commentaries on them—then books and other instruments of instruction used in the schools were hastily and summarily condemned. Whenever Catholic parents took these episcopal prom-

89 *Ibid.,* p. 114.
90 Billington, *op. cit.*

ulgations seriously, they were deprived of any options to exercise in the education of their children.

The pastoral devotes one brief paragraph to higher education. Beginning with an admission that for men's colleges "much remains to be done by their multiplication," the bishops shift to more general educational considerations : "We exhort you for the sake of your children, your country and your religion, to come to our aid for the purpose of making the effort thus to provide for the literary, moral and religious education of one sex as well as of the other."[91] The paragraph terminates with this statement : "We have exposed to you the danger of their [the colleges'] position, we confide in your charity and in your zeal." The exposition of danger to which the bishops allude is nowhere clear, however, and we are left to assume that they were talking about fiscal jeopardy, since neither political, religious, nor scholastic implications can be extracted from the letter's context.

Perfunctory heed having been paid to the colleges—now assumed to be principally lay schools—the bishops could turn their attention to the education of priests, a topic handled by ecclesiastical writers with zeal and devotion. Often prosaic and frequently redundant when recommending higher education for laymen, they became eloquent and convincing in solicitations for seminary support. A vocabulary of priority and urgency may be expected from a profession sincerely dedicated to self-perpetuation, but the obvious absence of reasonable balance in official pronouncements on seminaries vis-à-vis colleges, and in consequence, the selling of college education at discount, was something less than Catholics had a right to expect from clerical leaders commissioned to guard their general welfare. Still, the examination of episcopal myopia is unilluminating and alone it fails to explain why the bishops were unable to see the values of lay higher learning more clearly. In the last analysis, their indifference to higher learning was a product of their own academic experiences and the environment of the episcopal office.[92] Thus, a precise statement of an academic policy maintaining a proper respect for lay and clerical education, nurtured by an intimate understanding of and appreciation for liberal and professional learning in lay colleges, was impossible for American bishops of this genre. And we must be forbearing in our indictments of men whose reactions to higher education were conditioned by their experiences, or lack of them, in connection with it.

The Fifth (1843), Sixth (1846), and Seventh (1849) Provincial Councils of Baltimore (for sufficient or insufficent reasons) ignored the topic of higher education entirely, and save for one paragraph in the pastoral letter follow-

91 *Ibid.,* p. 135.

92 See John D. Donovan, "The American Hierarchy: A Social Profile," *The American Catholic Sociological Review,* XIX (June, 1958), 98–112.

ing the Fifth Council on instructing young Catholics in the inheritances of their religion,[93] the general subject of education does not intrude upon their deliberations. These were the years when Catholic colleges began to shape their personalities as literary and scientific rather than merely ecclesiastical schools; this was the time, when they began to multiply sharply; so a historian might assume that Church leaders, sensitive to these developments, would have been ready with new policies or, if they seemed likely to apply, with fresh interpretations of old ones. But this was not so, and the schools, managed by clerics accustomed to taking their cues from the bishops, were allowed to proceed as if the world was unchanged since the time of John Carroll, when a general policy for Catholic higher education was first elaborated. In this critical period, Catholic colleges, leaderless and undirected by bishops preoccupied with definitions of Church doctrine, were left to wander along academic pathways unaccompanied by the traditional wisdom of the Church.

After the Seventh Provincial Council of Baltimore, which in some respects had plenary standing,[94] the Church's national administrative structure was expanded to include additional provinces; it was no longer possible to convene the bishops of the country under the aegis of the Baltimore province. Thus, in 1852, the bishops of the United States met in plenary council.[95] The deliberations of the Council led to more comprehensive decrees and somewhat longer pastoral letters, because the maturing Church had a variety of new, and old, problems to face. On the subject of education, the Council said it was guided by a papal encyclical of 1851 directing bishops of the world to provide for the religious education of Catholic youth.[96] In what amounts to a policy statement, the Council's pastoral letter calls Catholic parents' attention to the danger of secular education in the ordinary schools of the country and adds : "To avert this evil give your children a Christian education, that is an education based on religious principles, accompanied by religious practices and always subordinate to religious influence."[97] And in ominous language the pastoral moves the Church into an educational monopoly by warning parents of what may happen to their souls if their "children should perish through [their] criminal neglect, or [their] obstinate refusal to be guided in the discharge of . . . parental duties, by the authority of God's Church."[98] Guidance is a nice word, but the prelates were, in fact, demanding obedience to their promulga-

---

[93] Guilday, *The National Pastorals,* pp. 152–153.

[94] Plenary, or acting for the entire United States, because it included bishops not attached to the province of Baltimore (see *ibid.,* p. xi).

[95] *Ibid.,* pp. 181–182.

[96] *Ibid.,* p. 191.

[97] *Ibid.,* p. 190.

[98] *Ibid.*

tions on education, and when God was their authority what Catholic parent could demur?

Despite the solicitude the bishops claimed to have for Catholic education—and on this point we take them at their word—the best they could say about higher education was again put in the context of clerical education. Yet, even on this subject, their policy does not extend beyond the support of seminaries, and the need for parental cooperation in cultivating vocations to holy orders, to the higher ground of academic plans for a seminary system with affiliated colleges wherein some training for the secular professions might be offered. The pastoral of 1852 reads as if Catholic colleges which nominally, at least, had been visible for seven decades were as yet unknown to the United States.

The period during which Catholic colleges were founded nears termination with the Second Plenary Council of 1866. The pastoral letter issued by the Council touches on two subjects of interest to us here : church–state relations and the education of youth. The prelates are at pains to clarify the Church's position vis-à-vis civil authority, and they make an immensely pragmatic statement about the Church's rights to hold and transfer property at the advent of a period when the Church was launching an extensive and expensive system of Church schools. While the letter's assertions relative to church-state accommodations may satisfy canonists,[99] it would seem to have dubious standing among constitutional lawyers, save as an interesting historical document. Yet, understandably, the bishops could hardly have stated their case in any other way, and in the long run, even without the consent of civil authority to the principles fundamental to the Catholic argument, the Church was successful in protecting its huge financial investment.

The section on education, seemingly regressive rather than progressive, is a disappointment; and if it is a face-value reflection of the best episcopal thinking on the subject, we should not be surprised by the haphazard record of Catholic colleges throughout the entire formative period. Writing in clichés, the bishops remind Catholics of the importance of an education thoroughly infused with religious principles, and they warn Catholic parents that any system of education—they mean the public system—not allowing for religious teaching is certain to foment disaster both to those who patronize it and society at large. Children, they say, are not to be listened to when questions about the goals of teaching are asked. And then with a single rhetorical blow they strip education of worthwhile ambitions : "Education to be good," the bishops opine, "need not necessarily be either high or ornamental, in the studies or accomplishments it embraces."[100] While it may not be evil for a young man to aspire to the best advanced education, parents should prepare their children "for the duties of the state

99 *Ibid.*, pp. 205–207.
100 *Ibid.*, p. 215.

or condition of life they are likely to be engaged in : do not exhaust your means in bestowing on them an education that may unfit them for these duties."[101] Assuming the possibility of predicting stations in life, or accepting as a fact the future insignificance of Catholics in American society, the hierarchy goes on record as pronouncing too much education to "be a sure source of disappointment and dissatisfaction, both for yourselves and for them."[102] If this is not a retraction of earlier timid support for colleges, it is, at least, a recitation of doubt that higher education for laymen is worth the trouble. Instead of having educational ambitions for children, the prelates say :

Accustom them from their earliest years to habits of obedience, industry, and thrift: and deeply impress on their minds the great principle, that happiness and success in life, as well as acceptance with God, do not so much depend on the station we fill, as on the fidelity with which we discharge its duties. Teach them, that the groundwork of true happiness must be placed in habitual and cheerful submission of our wills to the dispensations of Providence, who has wisely consulted for the happiness of all, without, however, bestowing on all an equal share of the goods of fortune.[103]

Strangely, and with a slight intrusion of doctrinal inconsistency, the bishops now see personal advancement as a holy game-of-chance, and rather than encourage their coreligionists to use all education's resources to upgrade themselves as individuals and as members of society, they timidly counsel them not to reach too high.

Catholic parents reading this epistle of anxious compromise should surely have been dissuaded from seeking higher education for their sons and daughters; Catholic college administrators, caught in tangled traditions and ambiguous episcopal policies, and thereby dispensed from an unqualified commitment to academic standards and quality, must have read this pastoral as a vote of confidence for collegiate mediocrity and academic conservatism. At the end of a long period of valiant expenditures of material resources and human talent, the bishops, in effect, told the colleges they had so far done enough and should avoid the hazards of dreaming about greater accomplishments for the future.

Yet their solicitude for education remains unblunted : the bishops encourage the establishment of Catholic protectories and industrial schools, where "under the influence of religious teachers, the waywardness of youth may be corrected, and good seed planted in the soil in which, while men slept, the enemy had sowed tares."[104] In paying heed to protectories and

101 *Ibid.*
102 *Ibid.*
103 *Ibid.*, pp. 215–216.
104 *Ibid.*, p. 217.

industrial schools they seem to downgrade colleges, but their best words are reserved for preparatory and theological seminaries. They report that diocesan seminaries, though flourishing, still require financial support, and they lament the dearth of enrollments in these schools. The fault, they say, "cannot be attributed to any deficiency of ours in such efforts as circumstances have enabled us to make;"[105] and thus absolving themselves by rhetorical circumlocution, they assign the fault to "many parents" who have not sufficiently encouraged their sons to enter the seminaries, and have sometimes discouraged them by "painting in too glowing colors the advantages of a secular life."[106] Ecclesiastical statements perpetuated the myth that secular professions were of secondary value, if not actually unworthy of a Catholic man, and they regularly sold college education for the layman at discount.

These Catholic attitudes of doubt and recrimination during a period when Catholic colleges were seeking stability and clarity of purpose, though not entirely unnatural in such a frantic era in the religious history of the United States, inevitably clamped a brake on progress Catholic colleges might have made had episcopal support been unrelenting and unequivocal.

105 *Ibid.*
106 *Ibid.*

2

Catholic college founding

Evidences of founding

Historians of academic institutions employ a variety of historical evidence to record and justify a college founding date. Thus, the question, "When is a college founded?" is by no means restricted to the Catholic field, although both for Catholic and nonCatholic colleges it must always stand in the shadow of larger historical issues. In the earliest days of the first authentic universities in medieval Europe the tug of war began, with every university claiming and trying to prove an origin more ancient than any of its counterparts.

Anxieties over priority of establishment led to a conventional assumption that academic institutions, like wine, improve with age, and conveniently ignored what everyone knew about the inappropriateness of the analogy : age alone controls neither the quality of colleges nor of wine. With remarkably few exceptions, however, American colleges followed the custom of using the earliest possible date to mark their founding; and when these dates were taken too seriously they blurred a more important history and provided ammunition for decades of smoldering but inconsequential debate. In the United States neither public, private, independent, nor church-related colleges can be rendered guiltless of honoring the assumption that old age guarantees academic quality.

Harvard College, for example, has historical roots in a 1636 money appropriation made by the General Court of Massachusetts Bay Colony, and Harvard dates its origin from that moment. Yet not until 1638 was a dwelling converted to instructional use; continuous teaching commenced four years later; and a charter made the school a legal entity in 1650.[1]

---

[1] Samuel Eliot Morison, *Harvard College in the Seventeenth Century* (Cambridge, Mass., Harvard University Press, 1936), I, 5–8. The 1850 charter is reprinted in

When, we are entitled to ask, was Harvard founded? The charter for the College of William and Mary was issued in 1693; but land for educational purposes was granted in 1619 by the Virginia Company, a college plan was written in 1622, and an act granting additional land to the college was passed by the Provincial Assembly in 1660.[2] The University of Pennsylvania has six dates—1740, 1743, 1749, 1751, 1753, 1755—each of which is evidentially justified as a founding date, depending on criteria historians acknowledge as proof of a college founding.[3] Princeton, Yale, Columbia, and the Universities of North Carolina, Charlestown, and Louisville are other good examples of institutions whose dates of origin may be interpreted with considerable latitude.[4]

Owing partly to an atmosphere of suspicion toward Catholic institutions in the late colonial and early national periods, the colleges were often born in stealth, and their records, if any were kept, were allowed to perish. In addition, Catholic educational pioneers, seldom imbued with the keen historical sense so characteristic of nonCatholic-college founders, kept registers and records for themselves, not future generations. Thus, Catholic college origins are shrouded in obscurity; and even the best chronicles lack an enviable historical precision. In any case, the historian of Catholic colleges faces, on this issue of evidences of founding, a problem common to American college historians, although his task is compounded, as we have said, by a paucity of dependable records: what academic event or institutional development should be accepted as conclusive evidence that a place of higher learning was established? In the long run, the whole matter of definitive founding dates may be trivial, or in the absence of complete historical data, inconsequential. Nevertheless, striving for accuracy and precision befits history, and we should think it worth the trouble to look for criteria of founding in order to set consistent rules for assigning historical priority to the schools whose origins we study.

Georgetown's chroniclers usually, and somewhat uncritically, use 1789 as the college's founding date; in that year the land which subsequently

---

Richard Hofstadter and Wilson Smith, *American Higher Education: A Documentary History* (Chicago, University of Chicago Press, 1961), I, 10–12.

[2] See Herbert B. Adams, *College of William and Mary*, U. S. Bureau of Information, Circular of Information No. 1, 1887; and Hamilton W. Mabie, "The University of Virginia," *Outlook*, 65 (August, 1900), 789.

[3] Edward P. Cheyney, *A History of the University of Pennsylvania, 1740–1940* (Philadelphia, University of Pennsylvania Press, 1940), pp. 45–52.

[4] See Thomas Jefferson Wertenbaker, *Princeton, 1746–1896* (Princeton, N. J., Princeton University Press, 1946); E. M. Coulter, *College Life in the Old South* (Athens, University of Georgia Press, 1951); John Howard Amringe, *Historical Sketches of Columbia University, 1754–1876* (New York, Columbia College, 1876); Norman Foerster, *The American State University* (Chapel Hill, N. C., University of North Carolina Press, 1937); and Albea Godbold, *The Church College of the Old South* (Durham, N. C., Duke University Press, 1944).

became the college site was deeded to John Carroll and his associates for seventy-five pounds sterling. But other dates—some with historical justification—have been used to mark the inauguration of Catholic higher education in the United States. J. Fairfax McLaughlin, in his *College Days at Georgetown,* is at pains to make Georgetown's cradle the Jesuit school established at St. Mary's City in colonial Maryland in 1634.[5] To take McLaughlin seriously, or to accept theories of origin identifying Georgetown with the Jesuit school in Newtown, Maryland, opened around 1673, or the Bohemia Manor School, founded about 1745, substitutes imagination for historicity. Better alternatives are available which merit at least equal consideration as evidences of founding with the transfer of a property deed. Three years prior to 1789, John Carroll and his clerical confreres developed a plan for the creation of an academy and college, and this plan, we should think, might command our historical attention in the same way that the General Court's appropriation to Harvard College has influenced historical judgments on Harvard's founding. In 1790, four years after Carroll's college plan—the "Resolves"—was submitted and approved, a college building was about ready, according to Carroll's correspondence : "I think we shall get enough of it [the building] completed this summer to make a beginning of teaching."[6] Georgetown admitted its first students in 1791,[7] and the college was chartered by the United States Congress in 1815.[8]

Uncertainty about the founding date is not particular for Georgetown alone among Catholic colleges : Mt. St. Mary's, St. Louis, Spring Hill, Xavier (Ohio), Holy Cross, Loras, St. Francis, Notre Dame, Villanova, St. Vincent, and Boston College, to name only the most obvious, have a variety of dated events which could be construed as foundation and from these a historian must choose.[9] His craft demands criteria for finding a path through such historical mazes.

[5] J. Fairfax McLaughlin, *College Days at Georgetown and Other Papers* (New York, J. B. Lippincott, 1899), pp. 17–21; and J. Fairfax McLaughlin, "The Beginnings of Georgetown College," *The Catholic World,* XLVI (February, 1888), 610–619.

[6] Quoted in John Gilmary Shea, *A History of Georgetown College* (New York, P. F. Collier, 1891), p. 13.

[7] See Daley, *op. cit.,* pp. 62–63; J. Fairfax McLaughlin, "William Gaston, The First Student of Georgetown College," *Records of the American Catholic Historical Society,* VI (1895), pp. 77–83; and J. H. Schauinger, *William Gaston, Carolinian* (Milwaukee, Bruce Publishing Co., 1949), p. 9.

[8] *Annals of the Congress of the United States.* Thirteenth Congress, Third Session, September 19, 1814–March 3, 1815 (Washington, Gates and Seaton, 1854), vol. 3, col. 1106.

[9] See Francis P. Cassidy, *Catholic College Foundations and Development in the United States, 1677–1850* (Washington, Catholic University of America, 1924), pp. 13–72; Walter J. Meagher and William J. Grattan, *The Spires of Fenwick: The History of the College of the Holy Cross, 1843–1963* (New York, Vantage Press, 1966), pp. 33–56; Thomas T. Taaffe, *A History of St. John's College* (New York, Catholic

A close reading of college history in the United States compels us to believe that consistency is lacking in ascertaining college founding dates: one institution honors a school plan, a legislative enactment or appropriation; another prefers procurement of land; still others recognize the erection of buildings; a few measure their origins from the onset of teaching or the conferral of academic degrees; finally, some demand as a criterion legal recognition in a college charter. An abundance of criteria leads inevitably to confusion, and if we take the colleges at their word we are left with a smudged historical picture.

Without dogmatically prescribing for all academic histories, what should be taken for the purposes of this history as the best evidence of founding? In the first place, some justification attaches to a college plan, such as the "Resolves," in Georgetown's case, or action by the General Court, in Harvard's, as evidence of college founding. Every school begins with a plan, an idea, or a legislative proposal and, although plans may be modified by external forces or crippled by the unrealistic visions of their formulators, the initial expectations for it naturally become part of its integral and dominating structure. Denied a cohesive plan, a school, or college drifts aimlessly along academic pathways; its best promise is an undistinguished future; its worst, an inchoate agency incapable of passing muster in the company of decent schools. But with a plan, which must antedate construction, students, and teaching itself, an essential condition for what is presumably an intellectual agency has been met. If implementation of the college plan leads to teaching and learning, this criterion of founding is confirmed in the institution's day-to-day life. But if a college plan is entirely abortive, the historian who accepts this criterion is uncomfortably plagued by a college whose only reality is on the pages of his book. Archives are well-stocked with plans for projected colleges, such plans representing at once the first and last genuine effort to create a college. The best single example of this may be found in various and elaborate proposals for the establishment of a national university.[10]

Publication Society, 1891), pp. 49–59; Thomas C. Middleton, *Historical Sketch of St. Thomas of Villanova* (Villanova, Pa., Villanova College, 1893), pp. 19–22; Oswald Moosmuller, *Bonifaz Wimmer* (New York, Benziger Bros., 1891), pp. 128–130, 140–144; Arthur J. Hope, *Notre Dame, One Hundred Years* (Notre Dame, Ind., University of Notre Dame Press, 1943), pp. 24–33; Michael J. Kenny, *Catholic Culture in Alabama* (New York, American Press, 1931), pp. 48–56; Mathias M. Hoffmann, *Story of Loras College, 1839–1939* (Dubuque, Ia., Loras College Press, 1939); G. J. Garraghan, "The Origin of Boston College," *Thought,* 17 (December, 1942), 617–656; and G. J. Garraghan, "Some Early Chapters in the History of St. Louis University," *St. Louis Catholic Historical Review,* 5 (April, 1923), 99–128.

[10] See A. O. Hansen, *Liberalism and American Education in the Eighteenth Century* (New York, Macmillan Company, 1926), pp. 129–139; John W. Hoyt, *Memorial in Regard to a National University* (Washington, Government Printing Office, 1892);

Land procurement is another frequently employed criterion for determining a college founding date, for with land—either rented, purchased, or received as a gift—collegiate promoters possessed physical, and in the deed, tangible evidence of their intentions. Yet, several college plans matured thus far before being summarily abandoned. Again, hopes for a college went on occasion beyond land acquisition to the construction, rental or renovation of buildings for instructional use. But dilemmas arise here, too: Buildings designed for education were sometimes converted to house factories or distilleries. Of what consequence was a plan, a plot of land, or a building if teaching and learning were never actually initiated? The appointment of a president, the selection of a faculty, or the admission of students, may each merit some consideration as evidences of founding, yet collegiate character was absent, one may argue, until a school offered the community its first academic product, a graduate.

Considering only nonpublic college founding allows for several alternatives, and generates a surplus of confusion, but to introduce the public college clouds the historical picture even more. Acceding to common practice, public colleges and universities dated their origins from legislative authorizations, although in many cases, and measured against other criteria of founding, these authorization dates were merely anticipatory of academic functions that began years, or decades, later. Legislative action as a plan for the establishment of a school or college is not fundamentally different from plans formed by interested citizens, founding committees or chapters, or informal boards of trustees. So much is readily admitted. Thus, if single, rather than dual, standards are preferred for arriving at realistic dates of origin for colleges in the United States, the "plan" may be embraced as an attractive, consistent, and useful criterion, although even its most judicious employment will sometimes bewilder us.

Finally, the criterion with obvious legal clarity, the college charter, must be mentioned. Early American colleges, however, paid the business of acquiring a charter scant heed, conducted their programs freely, and openly granted degrees without petitioning either the colony or the state for legal authority to do so. But this vexed no one because the colleges were unafraid of government intrusions and felt no urgency to protect their rights vis-à-vis the state by contract; and states, anxious to have flourishing educational institutions within their borders but temporarily content with educational *laissez-faire,* were happy to be relieved of a responsibility for colleges. Had these pleasant attitudes continued undisturbed by state encroachments on collegiate policies, American higher education would wear today a face of independence freer from marks of government inter-

and Charles Van Hise, "A National University a National Asset," in National Education Association *Proceedings,* 1912, pp. 210–220.

vention and initiative. But beginning with the state's determination to guide Dartmouth College toward educational policies assumed to be more responsive to public need,[11] these attitudes of permissiveness changed, and after the Dartmouth College decision of 1819[12]—which proscribed state infringement of valid college charters—states jealously guarded their chartering authority and, in addition, enacted legislation forbidding uncharted colleges from conferring academic degrees.[13] The old order—when a college applied for a charter whenever convenience or pride dictated—therefore changed abruptly after the 1820s; with later nineteenth-century colleges the chartering date is a reasonably reliable indication of a college's inception. But before this, chartering dates and colleges' founding had had no dependable correlation. Most colleges of the earlier era were deeply immersed in the business of higher education and granted degrees without bothering about legal blessings. The earliest Catholic colleges followed this practice, witnessed, for example, by Georgetown's 1815 chartering date, and after the decade critical for state policies on college charters (1819–1829) added unique means for circumventing the chartering requirement. For reasons they must have considered sufficient, state legislators sometimes refused charters to Catholic colleges—the College of the Holy Cross is probably the best example—[14] so the colleges without charters continued their instructional programs and arranged to have academic degrees for their students awarded by other Catholic colleges. For slightly more than a decade Holy Cross graduates were awarded Georgetown degrees.[15]

Despite the legal sanction bestowed on a college by a charter, complete confidence in it as a way of determining founding and assigning dates of origin must be withheld. The record contains legal and historical freaks : chartered colleges which never became functioning schools;[16] and schools

[11] William G. North, "The Political Background of the Dartmouth College Case," *New England Quarterly,* XVIII (June, 1945), 181–203.

[12] "The Trustees of Dartmouth College v. Woodward," *Reports of Cases Argued and Decided in the Supreme Court of the United States,* IV (Newark, N. J., 1882), pp. 555–600.

[13] G. W. Knight, "The State and the Private College," *Educational Review,* 10 (June, 1895), 57–70; and John S. Brubacher and Willis Rudy, *Higher Education in Transition* (New York, Harper and Row, Publishers, 1958), pp. 339–340.

[14] Orestes A. Brownson, "The College of the Holy Cross," *Brownson's Quarterly Review,* 6 (April, 1849), 372–395; and Meagher, *op. cit.,* pp. 50–56. Villanova, too, may have had trouble getting a charter. See Edward J. Power, "Formative Years of Catholic Colleges Founded Before 1850," *Records of the American Catholic Historical Society,* LXV (March, 1954), 24–39; and Edward J. Power, "Brownson's Attitude Towards Catholic Education," *Records of the American Catholic Historical Society,* LXIII (June, 1952), 125.

[15] Meagher, *op. cit.,* p. 56.

[16] Erbacher, *op. cit.,* pp. 9–30.

with valid charters which for their own reasons chose to remain institutions of elementary and secondary education.[17]

For all its legal appeal, chartering, which normally implies the existence of an institution qualified by the state to grant academic degrees, is hardly a completely trustworthy criterion for deciding questions of origin.

To assert the incontestable superiority of one criterion for judging the validity of college founding dates betrays more temerity than prudence; yet we should be uneasy without a consistent norm for appraising the testimony of college records. It is easy to be swamped by the details of origin of several hundred Catholic colleges, but this peril should not deter us from at least trying to find historical precedence by employing a consistent rubric. In this history a single criterion is needed, and despite its shortcomings, we accept as the criterion a clearly stated plan for the establishment of a college.

Founders of Catholic colleges

The history of Catholic education in the United States, it has been said, must be written in conjunction with that of the development of religious communities.[18] While they contain some elements of truth, such pronouncements must not be applied uncritically or unreservedly to the colleges. Seventy-three contemporary Catholic colleges for men are controlled by religious communities and eleven are under the direct superintendence of the bishop in whose diocese they are located; but these colleges were not always bred and nurtured by the authorities, congregations, or orders now conducting them. Forty-two Catholic colleges were founded from 1786 to 1849 : eighteen owed their origin to the bishop of a diocese, eighteen to religious communities or persons representing religious congregations, and five to secular priests who conducted them as private-venture institutions. One school—Jefferson College, located at Convent, Louisiana—had a brief and perished history; reconstruction of the most basic details of its founding is impossible.[19]

Before 1850, eight of eighteen colleges founded by bishops as diocesan institutions were transferred to religious communities; the five private-venture colleges exchanged their private status for either diocesan or religious-community control.[20] The pressure on private-venture schools to

[17] See Edward J. Power, *A History of Catholic Higher Education in the United States* (Milwaukee, Bruce Publishing Co., 1958), pp. 255–275.

[18] McCluskey, *op. cit.,* p. 28.

[19] Power, *A History of Catholic Higher Education in the United States,* p. 263.

[20] *Ibid.,* p. 32.

surrender their independence bespoke an official unwillingness to concede that Catholic higher learning could be handled safely in a personally-owned school largely immune to episcopal command; besides, it documented a thesis that such schools, with obviously limited resources, were incapable of employing and maintaining properly qualified faculties. We have, moreover, sampled the attitudes of nineteenth-century bishops toward lay-oriented Catholic colleges[21] and sense in them a determination to relieve themselves of responsibility for institutions they no longer genuinely loved. The colleges they founded were commissioned to educate future priests : as long as the colleges satisfied the bishops by fulfilling this goal they retained episcopal favor, but when programs for laymen began to distort and disturb the ideals of clerical education—and when the colleges either welcomed or were indifferent to this shift in institutional objectives—the hierarchy's fervor for collegiate higher education began to cool.

From 1850 to 1900, one hundred and fifty-two Catholic colleges for men were established : ninety-eight by religious communities, thirty-five by bishops, twelve by priests and two by laymen as private-venture schools. Too little is known of five colleges founded during these years to allow classification.[22] From 1901 to 1955, fifty-three Catholic colleges for men were founded by religious communities, and nineteen by bishops; a single college, even during this period, had a history sufficiently cloaked in obscurity to make us uncertain about the auspices of its origin.[23] Since 1955, although the distinction between colleges for men, coeducational schools, and colleges for women has been somewhat eroded, religious communities were responsible for establishing three colleges, while a bishop was the principal figure in founding one.

Despite the bishops' historical penchant for paying little more than lip service to higher education for laymen, it is apodictically clear that both permission and fundamental encouragement to establish colleges derived from them—especially after 1850—for the canonical structure of the Church admitted of no such initiative without the bishop's approval. While an individual bishop may not have been enthusiastic about higher learning for laymen or impressed with such inherent values as he himself perceived in it, he was, nevertheless, determined to strengthen and sustain Catholicism in his ecclesiastical jurisdiction by using all means available. He could lend support to a school wherein religious objectives were paramount, and thus hope to serve the Catholic people of his diocese; in other words, few

---

[21] Guilday, *The National Pastorals,* pp. 17–150.

[22] See Erbacher, *op. cit.,* pp. 32–63; Edward J. Power, "Formative Years of Catholic Colleges Founded Before 1850," *Records of the American Catholic Historical Society,* LXV (March, 1955), 19–34; and Power, *A History of Catholic Higher Education in the United States,* p. 32.

[23] *Ibid.*

bishops aimed at creating citadels of learning capable of attracting students the country over. Their commitment to higher education was too narrow for such academic idealism; they wanted, instead, a community college which would function as an educational arm of the Church. This educational policy was nailed to their episcopal masts.

Yet, while acknowledging the central role often taken by bishops in creating institutions of higher learning, the instances where their support was grudgingly given or actually withheld must not be glossed over. With an imperfect understanding of higher learning and a tendency to magnify its potential dangers to articles of faith, as evidenced in the pastoral letters and decrees emanating from the country's early Church councils,[24] the bishops wanted a clear demonstration of a college's ability to strengthen religion before conferring their blessing upon it. If nineteenth-century bishops merit commendation rather than lavish praise for their active sponsorship of colleges, we cannot resist picturing them, too, in the ambivalent position of being riders on the bandwagon of higher education without ever being its drivers. On the other hand, any portrayal of the bishops as strident enemies of higher education is exaggerated and unhistorical; lacking an instinctive appreciation for higher learning, and depending perhaps too heavily on their affinities for inflexibly interpreted ecclesiastical doctrines, they could be friendly toward higher learning without devotion and critically negative without hostility. This uncertainty had good reasons to excuse it. If at times the bishops seemed as humanistic and liberal as John Carroll himself, they often turned quite another way and, victims of some urgent anxiety, took refuge in the emotional extreme of absolute rejection. Thus, we find them every so often driven from the citadels of their common sense into a more or less whole-hearted acceptance of a policy of flight, from which, when the contretemps subsides, they again withdraw, to put forward with the usual hesitations the balanced views of compromise. During these calmer periods the bishops encouraged religious communities to open schools—almost half the colleges founded by religious orders owe their origin to a bishop's invitation to open a college in his diocese—and contributed significant moral and physical resources to keep them going. No doubt many a bishop may at first have considered establishing his own college, but sensing the multiple problems of management and staffing, decided instead to seek assistance from religious communities more conversant with the business of higher learning.

[24] See Alfred Baudrillart, "Catholic Universities II," *The Catholic Mind*, VII (1909), 41–49; Austin O'Malley, "Catholic Collegiate Education in the United States," *The Catholic World*, LXVII (June, 1898), 289–304; John T. Murphy, "Catholic Secondary Education in the United States," *The American Catholic Quarterly Review*, XXII (July, 1897), 449–464; and Ralph Adams Cram, *The Nemesis of Democracy* (Boston, Marshall Jones Co., 1918).

However much a bishop may have wanted religious orders and their colleges in his diocese, he was nevertheless uneasy because he could not exercise direct juridical control over them. It was within his power, of course, to expel a religious community, but this was not the point : he wanted his voice heeded on educational policy and his best tools were those of diplomacy. He had plenty of reasons for losing confidence in the colleges. The private-venture college with a priest-owner created a greater problem for a bishop's tender conscience, for it was even less susceptible of indirect control than religious-community colleges. Various forms of persuasion, and sometimes the rubric of religious obedience, were employed to make the bishop's authority felt; but in the long run this was untidy and ineffective, so as a matter of policy the bishops vigorously discouraged and, in clerical circles, refused to countenance the private-venture school. Its career, deprived of episcopal sanction, was therefore ephemeral, and if its halls were to remain open to students it had to be transferred to the bishop himself or to a religious order of his choosing. Private-venture in Catholic higher education was made to seem unconventional, or worse, unorthodox; and when laymen engaged in private-venture colleges (three such schools were opened during the decade 1850–1860)[25] the foundations of Church doctrine and Catholic education were assumed to be in peril. Bishops, religious and secular clerics, and Catholic laymen conspired to render these schools sterile : bishops withheld their approval or support and by their negative attitudes informally interdicted them; clerics spoke of them with unconcealed hostility; and more importantly, Catholics, following their leaders' cues and imagining educational evils where none existed, simply refused to enroll their sons in colleges not controlled and staffed by priests, seminarians, or brothers.[26] Lacking both intellectual and religious sophistication, Catholics identified a fundamentally Catholic education with instruction by persons in some grade of holy orders; and this durable myth infected Catholic thought for years to reinforce a clerical monopoly over all levels of Catholic education.[27]

[25] Erbacher, *op. cit.,* pp. 34, 45, 49.

[26] Orestes A. Brownson, "Roman Catholic Higher Education in the United States," *Brownson's Quarterly Review,* XVIII (June, 1861), 32–47.

[27] See Augustus J. Thèbaud, "Superior Instruction in Our Colleges," *The American Catholic Quarterly Review,* VII (October, 1882), 81–109; James F. Loughlin, "The Higher and Lower Education of the American Priesthood," *The American Catholic Quarterly Review,* XV (January, 1890), 101–122; S. J. Browne, "Catholic Colleges in America Today," *Irish Ecclesiastical Record,* 69 (January, 1927), 20–28; George J. Johnson, "Recent Developments in the Catholic College," *Catholic School Journal,* 30 (March, 1930), 96–98; A. J. Burrowes, "The Catholic College," *National Catholic Education Association Bulletin* 16 (November, 1919), 159–174; and G. Bull, "Function of the Catholic College," *Truth,* 37 (August, 1933), 20–22.

Motives for founding

Catholic colleges were products of the national rather than the colonial period; before 1786 Catholics were either unable or unwilling to enter the field of higher learning and provide foundations to compete with such colleges as Harvard, Yale, and Columbia for places in the history of colonial higher education.[28] The inability of Catholics to establish colleges was rooted, in part, in the unfavorable atmosphere prevailing in the colonies, for, as we have said, they were often disfranchised, subjected to inequitable economic competition, socially untolerated, and legally proscribed from taking the kind of action, or even leading the kinds of lives, motivating them to seek college training for their sons.[29] Yet while we admit these broad social frustrations, it would probably be wrong to overstress them or to use them as excuses for almost total inactivity in Catholic higher learning. We have a sufficient sample of early Catholic attitudes to know that they reflected neither an official collective nor an unofficial individual affinity for advanced education.[30] With remarkably few exceptions parents of colonial Catholic children were themselves poorly educated, and as the colonies expanded, with Catholics becoming more numerous, the general level of their educational accomplishments appears to have stood still.[31] Little in the thin academic experience of adult Catholics made them think higher education a prize worth having; when this disadvantage was coupled with the attitudes of the Catholic clergy, themselves unfamiliar with and often suspicious of "too much learning,"[32] the possibilities of establishing higher schools became remote indeed. Clerical pronouncements warned Catholics of dangers to their faith in the lower and higher schools of the country; speaking of the need to educate people in relation to their expected stations in life, they conveyed a tone of indifference to all higher learning not aimed at preparing young men for a seminary. The face of higher learning was

[28] See J. A. Burns, *Catholic Education: A Study of Conditions* (New York, Longmans, Green & Co., 1917), pp. 8–18.

[29] J. A. Burns, "Early Jesuit Schools in Maryland," *Catholic University of America Bulletin*, 13 (July, 1907), 73–85.

[30] See "The Catholic Element in the History of the United States," *The Metropolitan*, V (October, 1857), and Editorial.

[31] Joseph H. Fichter, *Religion as an Occupation* (Notre Dame, Ind., University of Notre Dame Press, 1961), p. 66; and John D. Donovan, *The Academic Man in the Catholic College* (New York, Sheed and Ward, 1964), pp. 47–65.

[32] See John D. Donovan, "The American Catholic Hierarchy: A Social Profile," *The American Catholic Sociological Review*, XIX (June, 1958), pp. 98–112; and John Talbot Smith, *The Training of a Priest: An Essay on Clerical Education with A Reply to Critics* (New York, Longmans, Green & Co., 1908).

distorted, unintentionally perhaps; nevertheless, such learning was made to appear as something unnecessary, at best, or, at worst, dangerous.[33]

Despite these obvious and inescapable impediments to the establishment of Catholic higher education in the United States, we should not spend too much time with them, for they neither illuminate college development nor show how Catholics overcame their academic caution and, with the establishment of Georgetown College, entered the field of higher learning. Nor should we ignore the fact, as the early builders of Catholic colleges seemed to, that colonial higher education was already about a century and a half old by the time the first Catholic college was founded. Catholic colleges may have had some special problems of adjustment but they also faced others which older colleges had been meeting for a hundred and fifty years, and nothing on the record shows them trying to learn from the experiences of colleges preceding them. Every early American college led a hazardous life; all were faced with ever-present obstacles to survival, and Catholic colleges shared this common vulnerability : of forty-two Catholic colleges started between 1786 and 1850 only ten were permanent.[34] This record of survival compares favorably with nonCatholic colleges founded before 1850 —a 25 percent survival rate for Catholic colleges as compared with a 20 percent survival rate for nonCatholic colleges—[35] although it must be said that nonCatholic colleges had a history covering nearly two centuries, while the Catholic colleges' survival rate applies to only one-quarter of that time. Once we understand why Catholic colleges were founded, we shall be in a better position to sense the reasons for their failures.

One motive always present in the establishment of Catholic higher schools, although seldom emphasized—and sometimes not even consciously apprehended—was intellectual development. The latent attachment Catholics had to learning was deeply imbedded in their intellectual tradition;[36] their religion had a creed demanding, at least for its clerics, considerable literary facility, so it was impossible for laymen, priests or bishops to gainsay either the validity or the relevance of this tradition. Still, in the early years of the nineteenth century the tradition was largely antiseptic, figuring generally, not specifically, in the motivations generating pre-1850 Catholic college foundings. Available evidence supports the assumption that before 1850 no Catholic college was established with the purpose of intellectual develop-

---

[33] Orestes A. Brownson, "The School Question," in the *Works of Orestes A. Brownson*, XIII, 243; "Catholic Schools and Education," *Brownson's Quarterly Review*, III (June, 1862), 496; and "Present Catholic Dangers," *Brownson's Quarterly Review*, II (July, 1857), 118.

[34] Power, *A History of Catholic Higher Education in the United States*, pp. 33–34.

[35] Tewksbury, *op. cit.*, p. 28.

[36] See L. Willcart, "A Catholic College in the Seventeenth Century," *The American Catholic Quarterly Review*, 30 (October, 1905), 745–758.

ment, a commitment to the intellectual life or liberal learning, uppermost in the minds of its founders.[37]

During the sixty-four years preceding 1850, three principal college-founding motives predominated : to offer a preparatory or preliminary education for boys aspiring to the seminary; to create a center for missionary activities from which the good offices of religion might diffuse the message of the Church to unconverted people or to supply the benefits of religion to Catholics in sparsely-settled and far-flung dioceses of a wilderness America; and to conduct a Catholic house of study and discipline where boys and young men might live in a controlled environment and thus cultivate moral and religious virtue. To some degree, we should think, every Catholic college of the formative period reflected all these motives in its founding, although, depending on special circumstances, one or other motive was perhaps emphasized.

Catholic college historians have noticed the seminal item of motivation, but for the most part they have interpreted Catholic motives in concert with those recognized as authentic among earlier nonCatholic colleges. Thus, Erbacher perpetuated Zimmer's[38] and Cassidy's[39] attitudes when he wrote about the specific aims of Catholic colleges and counted them the same, "except for their predominantly religious purpose, . . . as those of the ordinary liberal arts colleges of America at the time."[40] While the history of early colleges seldom allows us to speak with much confidence about ordinary liberal arts curricula, because of multiple variations from one to another college in teaching levels and subjects taught, or to discount striking religious purposes among all colleges, Erbacher, nevertheless, added this broad commission for Catholic colleges : "[they] endeavored by means of a religious training, mental discipline, and liberal culture, to produce the complete christian character."[41] Taking literally the published hopes along with the statements in colleges' prospectuses—which too often went unnoticed in day-to-day teaching—these historians are able to share Morison's optimistic belief that liberal culture, not training for the religious ministry, was the goal early American colleges hoped to achieve.[42]

---

[37] See Augustus J. Thébaud, *Forty Years in the United States of America* (New York, United States Catholic Historical Society, 1904), pp. 351–353.

[38] Agatho Zimmer, *Changing Concepts of Higher Education in America Since 1700* (Washington, Catholic University of America Press, 1938), p. 96.

[39] Cassidy, *op. cit.*, pp. 86–95.

[40] Erbacher, *op. cit.*, p. 65.

[41] *Ibid.*

[42] Samuel Eliot Morison, *The Founding of Harvard College* (Cambridge, Mass., Harvard University Press, 1935), p. 247, says: "In other words, the advancement and perpetuation of learning were the broad and ultimate objects of the foundation; the education of ministers was the immediate purpose; the fear of an illiterate clergy was the dynamic motive. Theological learning was to be included, but not to the

Although historical debate relative to colonial-college purpose subsides slowly, due, no doubt, to the fact that there are several plausible historical interpretations, which makes dogmatism untenable, we should want to know more about this purpose, if it is true that Catholic colleges were prone to accept it, adding, as Erbacher confidently asserts, "a predominantly religious purpose." One hundred and fifty years separate the first college in the English colonies—Harvard—from the first Catholic college in what is now the United States—Georgetown. And while no Catholic college historian, surely not Erbacher,[43] Zimmer,[44] or Cassidy,[45] claimed that Catholic colleges were simply denominational colonial colleges all over again, it would be hard to believe in their total immunity to social and academic forces generated by earlier institutions of higher learning. Thus, we can admit that Georgetown was influenced by the translations of academic purpose made, for example, among the venerable nine,[46] without at the same time agreeing that these influences were consciously solicited or that Georgetown was a mere prototype of American colleges preceding her.[47]

The permanent colleges preceding Georgetown on the American scene offer an interesting and varied academic portrait : beginning with Harvard (1636) and ending with the College of Charlestown (1785), they include William and Mary (1693), Yale (1701), Princeton (1746), Columbia (1754), the University of Pennsylvania (1755), Brown (1765), Rutgers (1766), Dart-

exclusion of other branches of learning. This distinction between ultimate and immediate objects, between "the tree of knowledge" and its most noble branch, was clear to everyone in the puritan century; nobody then thought of calling Harvard a "theological seminary" or "divinity school." Harvard was, in fact, less ecclesiastical than Oxford or Cambridge, and a smaller proportion of her graduates than of theirs became clergymen."

While this interpretation has a great deal to recommend it, it probably does not reflect precisely either the conditions of founding or the motives of the founders. The Puritan century may not have called the Harvard of the seventeenth century a divinity school, but the thirteenth would have and the twentieth does. Morison may not be giving due credit to the doctrine of formal or mental discipline, which had a secure place in Harvard, or the Congregational approach to theology, when he argues that many Harvard graduates did not become ministers. Yet, fifty-two percent of Harvard's seventeenth-century graduates did become ministers (see Richard Hofstadter and C. DeWitt Hardy, *The Development and Scope of Higher Education in the United States* (New York, Columbia University Press, 1952), p. 7).

43 Erbacher, *op. cit.,* pp. 64–68.

44 Zimmer, *op. cit.,* pp. 97—99.

45 Cassidy, *op. cit.,* pp. 82–95.

46 Harvard, William and Mary, Yale, Princeton, Columbia, Pennsylvania, Brown, Rutgers, and Dartmouth are the "venerable nine."

47 What appears to be the best supporting evidence is a statement in Georgetown's prospectus wherein it is said that the school has "the promising prospect of being a complete nursery of learning equal to those in the United States whose institution was earlier, and have taught this [school] to emulate the same" (*Prospectus of 1798*).

mouth (1769), Washington (1782), Washington and Lee (1782), Hampden-Sidney (1783), Transylvania (1783), Dickinson (1783), St. John's (1784), and the University of Georgia (1785). With the exception of the Universities of Pennsylvania and Georgia, they were established by religious denominations and, in the beginning, at least, were commissioned to fulfill certain religious objectives in connection with teaching. Even the two nondenominational colleges could not avoid religious entanglements, for the University of Pennsylvania submitted successively to Episcopal and Presbyterian influences before accepting government from the state,[48] and the University of Georgia, according to Coulter's perceptive observation, "was stamped with Christian principles, [but] no minister presided at its birth."[49] Remaining aloof to religious rivalries during its first quarter-century, the University of Georgia thereafter discarded the Jeffersonian code[50] and ignored the advice of its first president, Josiah Meigs, to surrender to denominational pressures.

A preponderance of evidence confirms the first colleges in the English colonies as religious institutions, their habitual use of academic nomenclature notwithstanding, and no one has tried to dispute or denigrate their religious character, a character they guarded zealously for decades. Of 182 permanent pre-Civil War colleges, identified by Tewksbury, 175 were controlled by religious denominations.[51] The seventeen earliest colleges which still survive represented five denominations : three Congregational, five Episcopal, five Presbyterian, one Baptist, one Dutch Reformed; Pennsylvania and Georgia varied between Episcopal, Presbyterian, and in Georgia's case, Baptist control.

Despite Morison's scholarly demurrals, the image of the colonial college as a school with religious content and purpose, a place where sects might prepare suitable candidates for the religious ministry, remains unblemished. The description of Harvard by nineteenth-century historians as a divinity school, Morison maintained, is misleading; he ascribed the clerical black to medieval traditions nurturing Harvard,[52] and asserted that students

[48] See Cheyney, *op. cit.*, pp. 122, 132, 172, 179.

[49] Coulter, *op. cit.*, p. 151.

[50] The Jeffersonian code may be expressed as follows : Bring the rival denominations together to mix their views, soften their asperities, liberalize and neutralize their prejudices. The outcome was to have been a general religion of peace, reason, and morality. See J. S. Patton, *Jefferson, Cabell and the University of Virginia* (New York, Neale Publishing Co., 1906), pp. 155–161.

[51] Tewksbury, *op. cit.*, p. 90.

[52] See Samuel K. Wilson, "The Genesis of American College Government," *Thought,* I (December, 1926), 416. The medieval traditions at Harvard were hardly pure, for they had been modified by a more modern Cambridge University. "Harvard . . . was founded according to the Cambridge model; [but] the Cambridge of that day was a university in which abnormal conditions had produced a temporary

aspiring to the ministry waited for their bachelor's degrees before pursuing specialized training in theology.[53] Admitting the passionately sincere religious motives of the Puritans and their unwillingness to "leave an illiterate Ministry to the Churches," Morison nevertheless argued that this was merely the immediate motive; the broader purpose, or the ultimate objective of the institution, was the advancement of learning and general culture.[54] If Morison was right, and one does not doubt the Puritans' commitment to hard and honest learning—for their entire tradition reflects an interest in mental refinement—then one must turn the question somewhat and ask : when was the immediate motive de-emphasized to allow for a prosecution of general cultural objectives? It would be reasonable to suppose that this transformation took some time. In any case, Thwing,[55] Boone,[56] Beard,[57] and Tewksbury[58] refuse to countenance Morison's interpretation of Harvard's purpose, and by extension the purpose of all colonial higher education. Missionary zeal, they averred, was not the motive for founding Harvard or any of the venerable nine, but a desire to dominate the social and political life of the New World as well as serve the objectives of institutionalized religion. McAnear, while taking into account a certain religious inspiration in colonial college founding, deduced a spirit of rationalism in the colonial mentality and maintained that rationalism, more than anything else, motivated the various sects to nail to their doctrinal and dogmatic mast the flag of higher learning.[59] Admittedly, any measurement of the effects of rationalism in colonial life is difficult, yet it was evident in literary societies, library associations, and perhaps in some colleges—like the University of Pennsylvania—where, as a matter of policy, theological studies were at first excluded. Still, nondenominational colleges were notoriously unsuccessful in securing allegiance from people wanting to attend or willing to support higher schools; and we might take this to mean that the majority wanted their colleges to abet the objectives of organized religion.

---

departure from traditional standards; this temporary condition, having been reproduced at Harvard, passed from the first to other institutions of colonial growth, and thereafter was accepted as the American plan for governing a college" (*ibid.*).

[53] Morison, *The Founding of Harvard College,* p. 8.

[54] *Ibid.,* p. 247.

[55] Charles F. Thwing, *American Colleges in American Life* (New York, Putnam, 1897), pp. 2–3.

[56] Richard Boone, *Education in the United States* (New York, D. Appleton, 1894), p. 29.

[57] Charles A. and Mary Beard, *The Rise of American Civilization* (New York, Macmillan Company, 1927), I, 52.

[58] Tewksbury, *op. cit.,* p. 81.

[59] See Beverly McAnear, "College Founding in the American Colonies, 1745–1775," *The Mississippi Valley Historical Review,* XLII (June, 1955), 24–25.

In 1754 President Clap re-stated Yale's purpose : "The original end and design of colleges was to instruct and train up persons for the work of the ministry. . . . The great design of founding this school was to educate ministers in our own way."[60] This forthright acknowledgement may have gone too far, for neither Yale nor any other colonial college restricted itself solely to training ministers; all extended the perimeters of their curricular boundaries and welcomed students with secular objectives. Nevertheless, the colonial college was a denominational school intended, first, to serve the religious sect responsible for its creation, and second, to tend to the cultural and academic needs of its students. Created by a religious sect, the college could hardly ignore legitimate sectarian requirements; and with clergymen and religiously-minded laymen at the college's helm to set the tangents of the college course, it never occurred to any responsible college officer to demand a new setting on the academic compass. Yet in this clear denominational context strident sectarian exclusivism was avoided by permitting, so reliable public pronouncements said, the admission of students without imposing any religious test. Harvard's records explain that religious tests were forbidden; Yale's officials stated publicly that persons of all denominations were admitted without any inquiry at the time of admission or later into their religious beliefs. The charters of Columbia, Princeton, and the University of Pennsylvania legally proscribed religious tests, although such prohibitions were probably unnecessary because nonconforming students were not likely to matriculate in schools unable to satisfy their fastidious religious appetites. When a student took these liberally-stated edicts at face value, he could usually testify to the zeal of the president and professors who inevitably tried to convert him to a truer brand of Christianity.[61]

Assessing college-founding motives of dogmatic sects is an easy exercise, but evangelical religions founded colleges too, and we are sometimes puzzled by the worth they attached to higher learning when, as a matter of simple orthodoxy, they inveighed against a learned ministry. If we are unwilling to assume that their colleges arose because of mere whim or sectarian pride, and if we admit that both training in theological doctrine and ritualistic devotion were unnecessary for the proper performance of church services, we are left to find their motives elsewhere. A plausible, and probably correct, interpretation discovers their motives in feelings of cultural inferiority :

[60] See Richard Hofstadter and Walter P. Metzger, *The Development of Academic Freedom in the United States* (New York, Columbia University Press, 1955), pp. 163–177.

[61] See Clifford K. Shipton, *Biographical Sketches of Those Who Attended Harvard College in the Classes of 1722–1725* (Boston, Massachusetts Historical Society, 1945), p. 36; Hofstadter and Hardy, *op. cit.*, pp. 5–6 ; and Walter C. Bronson, *The History of Brown University, 1764–1914* (Providence, Brown University Press, 1914), p. 6.

evangelical ministers were often rude, ignorant men, and this made prominent members of their congregations uneasy. They wanted an "educated ministry," which bespeaks a general cultural education, not a "learned ministry," which implies a prescribed dogmatic and ritualistic training. In order to offer a decent education to young men who were to be their ministers they established colleges. To have allowed prospective ministers to attend existing denominationally-dogmatic colleges would surely have created vexing problems : boys would be uncomfortable in a strange, hostile, religious climate, and during their impressionable years home-inculcated religious beliefs would be jeopardized. The Baptists, for example, founded Brown University in 1765, and twenty-one additional colleges before the Civil War, in order to educate ministers in their own way, while at the same time allowing for enough instructional flexibility to make Jews and Quakers feel welcome.[62]

Undoubtedly compelling circumstances in the American way of life contributed to the chief general, and religious, motive for college founding, but to maintain that the only goal of denominational colleges before the Civil War was instruction of a learned or educated clergy is simplistic; still, if we acknowledge clerical training as a principal function for pre-Revolutionary colleges, it must also be recognised that in postRevolutionary colleges, without this function being weakened in any way, other important purposes were attached to the college course. Thus, if Catholic colleges of the early nineteenth century had followed the example of colleges of earlier foundation on the important point of college purpose, they would not have been narrow clerical schools. The issue, then, is to what extent they subscribed to the doctrine of imitation and incorporated into their institutions the evolving purposes of the more mature denominational college.

In the first place, except for the one instance when John Carroll was sympathetically involved in the founding of a nondenominational college,[63] Catholics followed a policy of non-cooperation, or even hostility, toward the colleges of other denominations.[64] And while we should think some influences from the earlier denominational to the later Catholic college unavoidable, instances of voluntary or conscious imitation go unrecorded. The model Catholics were determined to follow is indicated in Carroll's correspondence, where he appealed to Rome for a *ratio studiorum*,[65] and the advice forthcoming was followed in shaping Georgetown's academic

---

[62] *Ibid.*, pp. 1–33.

[63] J. A. Burns and Bernard J. Kohlbrenner, *A History of Catholic Education in the United States* (New York, Beniger Bros., 1937), p. 63.

[64] An editorial, "What is the Outlook for Our Colleges?" *The American Catholic Quarterly Review,* VII (July, 1882), 63–65.

[65] Daley, *op. cit.,* pp. 32–33.

policies. In turn, because Georgetown was a model for all Catholic colleges of the formative period, Roman recommendations affected them too.[66] Next, a Catholic college, unless it were a misnamed seminary, could not have shared the pre-eminent purpose of earlier denominational colleges in clerical preparation, for, since the Council of Trent, professional clerical education was reserved to the seminary.[67] Finally, the early nineteenth-century Catholic college was unenthusiastic about the cultural values promised by higher education; despite statements of praise for general culture found in early prospectuses, the colleges' curricula contain no evidence that these statements implied anything more than reasonable facility in Latin. We are left, then, with the definite impression that Catholic colleges during most of the formative period mirrored neither in objectives nor day-to-day teaching the colleges preceding them on the American scene; their purpose must be phrased another way: Having both institutional and instructional goals, Catholic colleges aspired to seminary status while offering a course of studies aimed at preparing young men for professional theological study. If we are correct, it is impossible to endorse a common generalization that Catholic colleges of the formative period had a zealous affinity for liberal values in higher learning.[68]

Although never neglecting the possibility of institutional upgrading to seminary status, Catholic colleges of the nineteenth century were regularly preoccupied with other purposes and inspired by other motives. Some Catholic colleges radiated missionary activity, but before they became colleges they had been mother houses for mission priests and were redesigned to play an educational role, not perhaps in teaching the unconverted but in providing a steady source of income to maintain the mission band.[69] In the life of such colleges, remotely located from commercial and cultural centers, liberal learning was an impractical, pedantic pursuit for which the school had decided antipathies. In competition with the spiritual requirements of frontier Catholics, liberal learning always suffered in these mission-oriented colleges. In addition, American Indians were assumed to need denominational cultivation, and Catholic missionaries had an indelible and praiseworthy record of service to them, both in preaching the doctrines of

---

[66] Power, *A History of Catholic Higher Education in the United States,* p. 80.

[67] McDonald, *op. cit.,* pp. 9–11.

[68] See Cassidy, *op. cit.,* pp. 86–90; Zimmer, *op. cit.,* pp. 97––98; and Erbacher, *op. cit.,* pp. 88–91.

[69] Colman J. Barry, "Boniface Wimmer, Pioneer of the American Benedictines," *The Catholic Historical Review,* XII (October, 1955), 272–296; James R. Bayley, *Memoirs of the Rt. Rev. Simon William Bruté, D. D.* (New York, The Catholic Publishing Co., 1876); and Brother Beniedus, *Seventy-Five Years of Service, 1859–1934: An Historical Sketch of St. Michael's College* (Santa Fe, New Mex., St. Michael's College, 1934).

Christianity and teaching useful information and skills.[70] This work, obviously too important to ignore, could not be asked to mark time while the hares of polite learning were chased through classical texts. The college was pressed into service, Erbacher writes, because bishops and priests "considered the Catholic college one of the best means of accomplishing the task of keeping the faith alive in the hearts of the people . . . , and of spreading the gospel among those not yet of the fold. It was their firm conviction that young men who were trained to live up to the Catholic ideal of life would become loyal citizens of their country and useful members of society. For this reason they made every endeavor to place higher education within the reach of all without distinction."[71] Although Erbacher's appraisal may not be entirely innocent of wishful thinking in regard to the zeal of Catholic bishops in placing higher education within the reach of all, his interpretation of the colleges' missionary motive has the ring of authenticity.

A third principal motive for Catholic college founding during the formative period, especially before 1850, was the clergy's desire to cultivate devotional practices among Catholic youth and under the controlled environment of the Catholic college to mold a character capable of resisting threats to faith. After reviewing the contagion Catholics were prone to feel in nineteenth-century American society, Zimmer justifies this motive by saying : "Something had to be done to keep the students in the Catholic colleges where their faith would be protected against the irreligious currents of the day, especially agnosticism, which was being encouraged and propagated by the philosophy of Comte, Mill, and Spencer and their like; by writers like H. T. Buckle, and by anti-Catholic movements such as that identified with the American Protective Association."[72] Zimmer is undoubtedly correct in affirming the Catholic college as a safe haven where Catholic students were immunized from dangers to faith and morals, although such immunizations were sometimes ineffective; every episcopal pronouncement on education from John Carroll's first pastoral letter to the documents of the Third Plenary Council warned Catholics about the evils of education outside their own schools, and while these warnings were only infrequently directed at higher schools, the bishops never meant to exclude Catholic colleges from their counsels of caution.

Various college spokesmen ratified these episcopal admonitions : Edward Sorin, for example, the founder and first president of the University of

---

[70] M. P. Dowling, *Reminiscences of the First Twenty-Five Years at Creighton* (Omaha, Burkley Printing Co., 1903); G. J. Garraghan, "The Beginnings of St. Louis University," *St. Louis Catholic Historical Review*, I (January, 1919), 85–102; and M. J. Spalding, *Sketches of the Early Catholic Missions from their Commencement in 1787 to the Jubilee of 1826–27* (Louisville, 1844).

[71] Erbacher, *op. cit.*, p. 64.

[72] Zimmer, *op. cit.*, p. 97.

Notre Dame, described his school as a "seat of learning, religion, and of good morals."[73] Some bishops, leaning heavily on the colleges' ability to produce students of impeccable moral and religious character, complained bitterly when the colleges seemed remiss and their products disappointing. One was Peter Kenrick, coadjutor bishop of St. Louis, who, in a letter to Bishop John Purcell of Cincinnati, recommended that the bishops make a careful investigation of the colleges at their forthcoming Council of Baltimore in 1843, because, he said, "I have long since regarded [them] as anything but useful to religion. The Catholics appear to lose rather than gain by frequenting such academies, and as for the protestants (sic), they lose if you will some prejudices but they are rarely otherwise benefited by a residence in our colleges."[74] We are uncertain of Kenrick's evidence for such a severe indictment, but it can hardly have been groundless. He was obviously dismayed because the colleges, he thought, were failing the Church.

Whether or not his caustic attitude was shared by other bishops goes largely unrecorded; in any case, the pastoral letter following the Baltimore Council of 1843 was written without the faintest reference to Kenrick's harsh views. The bishops' interest in higher education, judged from this pastoral, was narrowly clerical : they asked the laity to be generous in their support of seminaries and thus assumed their duty done. Possibly Kenrick's unfavorable assessment of the colleges was the result of atypical experiences; certainly his chastisement of colleges was not prompted by the attitude of his predecessor at St. Louis, Bishop Joseph Rosati, who, in 1830, gave the colleges a generous vote of confidence : "All the Bishops would consider themselves happy to have them. Moreover, what amount of good is not done in these colleges. Therein Catholic young people are brought up in the practice of their religion, which they would not even know if they were sent to protestant (sic) schools; therein, too, protestant (sic) children lose the prejudices they are inspired with against Catholics. . . . Some of them become Catholics with the permission of their parents and those who do not will always be friends of the Catholic clergy."[75] The colleges themselves and the religious objectives dominating their programs were given unstinting approbation from other sources too, and all this without the slightest hint that service to sectarian values was an unbecoming college goal even when such subordinations actually undermined the school's chances of being a good center of learning. "I admit," the Jesuit superior of St. Louis wrote to the Society's General, "that our colleges are not doing all the good which one might desire . . . and yet without the colleges where

[73] *Sixth Annual Catalogue of the University of Notre Dame,* Distribution of Premiums Pamphlet, 1851, p. 2.

[74] Kenrick to Purcell, March 27, 1843, quoted in G. J. Garraghan, *The Jesuits of the Middle United States* (New York, America Press, 1938), III, 126.

[75] Rosati to Salhorgne, April 23, 1830, quoted *ibid.,* p. 127.

would our poor youth be and what would became of the service and support which our colleges lend to religion? . . . Such as they are, the colleges do a great deal of good. Everyone agrees that our churches in the towns do immense good. I believe before God that the proximity of the college helps a great deal to this end. . . . Considering the position in which we are, we are doing as much for the churches as the colleges in France and, I should think, more than those of England."[76]

These opinions of college goals and the colleges' success in attaining them conceal differences among various spokesmen over the comparative merits of two outlets for apostolic zeal and enterprise—the sacred ministry *or* education; they were, instead, somewhat superficial appraisals by interested and responsible persons of the amount of religious "good" the colleges could reasonably be expected to do. When all the entries were made on the balance sheet, the debits outweighed the credits : although colleges had yet to become fully efficient instruments for the Church, they were useful and warranted continued episcopal and clerical encouragement. A clerical consensus recommended a prudent delay in calling on them to account for their failures.

Three motives—seminary preparation, missionary labor, and moral formation—were apparent in the establishment of every pre-1850 Catholic college, although moving from one to another college foundation we find fluctuations in their precedential order. At Georgetown, for example, the college's missionary goals were probably less pronounced than in colleges nearer the Western frontier; yet such goals were fully accredited, for Carroll allowed for no misunderstanding when he said : ". . . on this academy is built all my hope of permanency and success of our holy religion in the United States."[77]

St. Mary's College in Baltimore, although originally commissioned as a major seminary, was during its first years little more than a missionary headquarters, and seminary priests without students to teach spent their apostolic energy on the frontier. Famous missionaries like Fathers Richard, Levadoux, Dilhet, Ciquard, Flaget, and Maréchal called St. Mary's their mother house. John Dubois, the founder and owner of Mount St. Mary's College, used the college as a base and source of support for pastoral and missionary work;[78] the St. Louis College, both before and after its transfer

---

[76] Murphy to Roothaan, November 5, 1852, quoted *ibid.,* p. 127. Jesuit colleges in France were, of course, in a rather unenviable position in mid-nineteenth century. John W. Padberg's *Colleges in Controversy: The Jesuit Schools in France from Revival to Suppression, 1815–1880* (Cambridge, Mass., Harvard University Press, 1969) is worth consulting here, for it allows us to see what collegiate models some American Jesuits were willing to imitate.

[77] Quoted in Shea, *A History of Georgetown College,* p. 11.

[78] Charles G. Herbermann, *The Sulpicians in the United States* (New York, Encyclopedia Press, 1916), pp. 124–139; and Joseph W. Ruane, *The Beginnings of*

to the Jesuits, regularly dispatched missionaries to the Western territories.[79] A long list of illustrations could be mustered to show how Catholic colleges honored their missionary functions; even in the twentieth century this outlet for apostolic zeal was considered compatible with more precisely defined academic goals and clergymen domiciled at a college were organized as mission bands to preach at parish and college missions and general religious retreats.

Georgetown's commitment to the goal of character formation was more evident than its embrace of missionary functions. The academy was intended, according to the "Proposals," to "unite the means of communicating Science with an effectual Provision for guarding and preserving the Morals of Youth."[80] During the institution's first years the college officers tried to implement the "Proposals" in a sane and sensible way, but during Bishop Leonard Neale's presidency (1799–1806) a rigorous monastic discipline was instituted, causing "many parents to withdraw their sons from the college, and although the standard of studies was raised the number of students was very much reduced during his administration."[81] Neale's enforcement of the doctrine of *in loco parentis* was so literal and rigid that a respected Jesuit historian felt compelled to remark : "The strange thing was that the ex-Jesuits' institution, intended primarily for the instruction of secular youth, was governed on the principles and in the system of a convent, while DuBourg's academy in Baltimore [St. Mary's College], though directed by Sulpicians whose work is the training of candidates for the priesthood, was conducted along very liberal lines."[82] During the period of John Dubois' direct association with Mount St. Mary's College, and thereafter also, the code of discipline was clearly intended to enforce moral and religious virtue, so Mount St. Mary's along with all other Catholic colleges of the nineteenth century took with utmost seriousness the then-current interpretation of *in loco parentis* and applied its principles with zeal and devotion.

The pre-divinity motive of early Catholic colleges is also fairly clear. A few illustrations must serve. In the case of Georgetown, John Carroll, while hoping for a seminary, started a school to prepare boys for the seminary; and in his agreement with the Sulpicians Georgetown's role was scaled down to offering a classical education for young men aspiring to the ecclesiastical state. Located near St. Mary's College (which was supposed

the Society of St. Sulpice in the United States, 1791–1829 (Washington, The Catholic University of America, 1935), pp. 95–105.

[79] G. J. Garraghan, "The Beginning of St. Louis University," *St. Louis Catholic Historical Review,* I (January, 1919), 85–102.

[80] Quoted in Daley, *op. cit.,* pp. 34–35.

[81] Easby-Smith, *op. cit.,* I, 44.

[82] William J. McGucken, *The Jesuits and Education* (Milwaukee, Bruce Publishing Co., 1932), p. 68.

to be a seminary), Georgetown did not adopt institutional goals embracing the dream, so dear to other Catholic colleges, of one day becoming a major seminary, or mixed school, where one part of the curriculum would be reserved for theological studies for candidates to the priesthood and another part for secular studies from which students were to obtain a basic education prior to entering the ecclesiastical seminary.

On rare occasions institutional aspirations were reversed, as at St. Mary's College in Baltimore, where the seminary was so poorly attended that a college division was opened in order to utilize the teachers already there. Yet, even in this case the lower division tried to restrict its enrollment to students with clerical intentions. During its first twenty-five years, Mount St. Mary's College had a history of ferment sufficient to indicate an unsettled state for institutional objectives. Conflicts between John Dubois, the founder, and the bishops of Baltimore arose when Dubois determined to preserve a seminary in association with the college despite the absence of explicit episcopal approval. These frantic years witnessed a transfer of college control from Dubois to the Sulpicians and then, when Dubois, who had entered the Society of St. Sulpice, withdrew from the Society, back to Dubois. Reinforced by the attitudes of the bishops of Baltimore, the Sulpicians were anxious to suppress the seminary at Mount St. Mary's, because they believed it superfluous, especially since St. Mary's College had too many teachers for the number of seminarians enrolled. In 1811, during the period of Sulpician control, a directive was issued "to the effect that the principal purpose of Mt. St. Mary's [is] to form boys for the ecclesiastical state, and that any boy unfitted for that state [is] to be dismissed."[83] Subsequently, and possibly because the first instructions to Dubois were ignored, another document, outlining Dubois' authority at the school and speaking directly to the college's objectives, was issued declaring Mount St. Mary's to be "a preparatory seminary and [it] must not become a secular college. Students are not to be admitted except for the priesthood."[84] Confronted by such unambiguous commands and the weight of religious authority, Dubois should have at once capitulated and redefined the college's goals to conform to the letter of these edicts. As it was, he found ways to delay an abandonment of the seminary branch during the school's Sulpician interlude, and when he again regained full control even the orders of the bishop to close the seminary went unheeded. Despite Dubois' intransigence and, on this matter, his flagrant indifference to clear directives from religious superiors, he was himself elevated to dignity and power as

[83] Ruane, *op. cit.,* p. 173.
[84] *Ibid.,* p. 174; and see Mary M. Meline and Edward F. X. McSweeney, *The Story of the Mountain: Mt. St. Mary's College and Seminary* (Emmitsburg, Md., The Weekly Chronicle, 1911), I, 148–150; and John J. Rooney, "The Old Mountain," *The Catholic World,* 66 (November, 1897), 213–221.

Bishop of New York. In St. Louis, Bishop Louis DuBourg opened a college expecting it to fulfill a variety of functions, though chief among them was the instruction of future seminarians, and all evidence points to his valiant efforts to make it an excellent Latin school. But funds for educational facilities and teachers were inadequate, so, in the end, DuBourg closed the school with an acrid remark about "that sorry school so ridiculously called a college."[85]

Almost every nineteenth-century Catholic college could be cited as illustrative of this pre-divinity motive. Few were without a close affiliation with seminaries, and in many a seminary was eventually opened in conjunction with the college itself, allowing for a student's easy transfer from the collegiate to the seminary division.

Survival and location

It would indeed be a happy circumstance if by college location we could account for the difference between institutional success and failure, and thus quickly explain why one Catholic college lived when three became statistics on collegiate mortality tables. Forty-two Catholic colleges were founded before 1850: if we are willing to credit Loras College[86] and St. Francis College[87] with continuous histories, twelve survived; or if we find a discontinuity in the operation of these two colleges rather more significant than mere hiatuses, then ten survived.[88] If we, for the moment, dismiss the historical intricacies involved in determining when a college foundation is defunct or only marking time, and credit this period with twelve permanent colleges, we find seven located away from urban areas in the quiet solitude of sparsely settled rural surroundings. Only Georgetown, St. Louis, Xavier (Ohio), Fordham, and Villanova were in or near large cities with a reasonably heavy Catholic population; the others were situated, sometimes by choice and sometimes by chance or the opportunity to procure land cheaply, in regions of the country where Catholics were few and where, on occasion, the local inhabitants showed some hostility toward the Catholic institution arising in their midst. Several impermanent colleges had the same, or similar, geographic and demographic advantages—or disadvantages—as the successful ones.

For forty years following the heavy Irish Catholic immigration to the

---

[85] Quoted in Garraghan, *The Jesuits of the Middle United States,* I, 273.

[86] See Hoffmann, *op. cit.,* pp. 1–10.

[87] See A. A. Lambing, *A History of the Catholic Church in the Diocese of Pittsbugh and Allegheny* (New York, Benziger Bros., 1880), pp. 475–476.

[88] Power, *A History of Catholic Higher Education in the United States,* p. 34.

United States (1830–1850), religious leaders begged and cajoled the Irish to remain in metropolitan areas where, supposedly, there would be safety in numbers and where, moreover, erosions of faith would be less likely.[89] Accepting the advice of the bishops and priests almost unquestionably, the newly-arrived Irish Catholics, refusing to move west, settled in large cities on the Eastern seaboard. With a concentration of Catholic people in the East, we should expect to find the best record of Catholic college survival in the seaboard states. Yet, only five of twelve permanent colleges were located in the East during the pre-1850s, and among them are St. Francis and St. Vincent Colleges, both rather far west in Pennsylvania.

From 1850 through 1870, seventy-four Catholic colleges were founded; twenty-three survived. Six now-existing colleges founded during these years were in New York State—three in New York City—while the rest were distributed among twelve states with a geographic spread from the Atlantic to the Pacific coast. Ten states with twenty successful Catholic colleges account for twenty-nine failures; New York with its six permanent institutions had five failures, only one less than Ohio, with the largest number of failing Catholic colleges in this period. In the South survival records were poor : five states with sixteen failing colleges were unable during this time to boast a single Catholic college which survived. Despite these interesting state-by-state comparisons, they hardly demonstrate conclusively the discovery of any key in geographic location to Catholic college success or failure. We must look further.

Nevertheless, the picture of the Catholic college moving west is revealing, and it bespeaks, perhaps, an inclination on the part of these frontier colleges to take at face value the missionary goals the bishops had always said the colleges should have. In the last analysis, it was probably not location at all that was critical to collegiate life or death, but a college's unequivocal acceptance of religious goals eliciting support from Catholic bishops, priests, and laymen. When a college made religious goals primary, and assigned a place of honorable mention to authentic academic objectives, greater support was forthcoming and this support, given to some colleges and not to others, was the critical factor spelling success for one and academic doom for another.

Before 1850 fewer than one-quarter of the colleges founded by Catholics survived; from 1850 through 1899 slightly under thirty percent lived; and from 1900 through 1955 thirty-six percent managed to achieve permanence.[90] These percentages may be compared to the mortality rates among nonCatholic colleges for the same period : about twenty percent

[89] See Henry J. Browne, "Archbishop Hughes and Western Colonization," *Catholic Historical Review*, XXXVI (October, 1950), 269–273.

[90] Power, *A History of Catholic Higher Education in the United States*, pp. 31–33.

lived and flourished.[91] Almost endless speculation is possible in trying to account for this steady rise in the survival rate, but no elaboration of reasons should miss the simplest explanation of all : in the first years of the nineteenth century, too many colleges overburdened a thin, impoverished Catholic population. Some colleges died well-loved but unused. As the Catholic population increased, with a relative per capita decrease in the number of Catholic institutions for higher learning, the colleges had broader foundations of resources and, learning from experience, they utilized them more efficiently. Although other reasons may be explored and justified for the historical fact of better survival records as we approach contemporary times, and a quick reference will be made to some of them, we are, nevertheless, content to accept what appears to be the most obvious explanation.

Contributing, but perhaps not determining, factors in the increasing chance, as the nineteenth century wore on, that a college would survive may be detected in the greater attention Catholics began to pay to higher studies. On the one hand, they supported colleges because they were religious centers more than schools; on the other, despite advice tendered them by their prelates—to be wary of too much learning—they sensed a need to participate in the mainstream of American life and envisioned the colleges as convenient steppingstones in this desirable direction. Thus Catholic attitudes toward higher learning suffered from ambiguities which, over the short term, helped colleges to survive, but in the long run, because of contradictory or conflicting college aims and values bred by these attitudes, colleges became somewhat sterile citadels for religion or learning. With a confirmed commitment to religion, Catholics took the word of bishops and priests for the dangers lurking everywhere in nonCatholic schools and, eschewing educational opportunities for higher study in state and non-Catholic private colleges, adopted the Catholic college as the place where commercial, vocational, and professional aspirations could be satisfied. When we see the metamorphic curriculum of the later nineteenth-century Catholic college, we shall be impressed by its new direction and its open-armed embrace of subjects previously downgraded as unworthy of an academician's time or attention.

Scholastic implementations of religious objectives remained stable, and in competition with utility-centered studies—even when practical curricula were accorded lukewarm support—inevitably came off second best. Religious deportment, moral formation, and a kindling of apostolic zeal, while not forgotten, were now equivocally defined as instrumental purposes for Catholic colleges.[92] Yet, any outright erosion of these older objectives was

[91] Tewksbury, *op. cit.,* p. 28.

[92] See John Ireland, *The Church and Modern Society* (Chicago, D. H. McBride & Co., 1896); John R. G. Hassard, "Literature and the Laity," *The Catholic World,* XXXVI (October 1882), 1–8; and Isaac Hecker, "The Next Phase of Catholicity in the United States," *The Catholic World,* XXIII (August, 1876), 577–592.

always deplored—and sometimes vigorously condemned—by managers of Catholic colleges who wanted to keep tradition pure and religious motives inviolate.[93] Their protests, however, were scantly heeded; the academic clock could not be stopped and the colleges engulfed in waves of social progress were forced to enter the modern world even amid mixed feelings about doing so.

Concurrently, the new demands on colleges either exhausted their resources, and thus the mixed-school arrangement began to disappear, or, with such a secular impress, colleges were no longer considered fit environments for seminary students. So from 1860 to 1900 we find Catholic colleges following blazed trails in higher learning and introducing professional and scientific courses to the curriculum, disposing of archaic nomenclatures designating student progress through the course of study, and abandoning their secondary school-college affiliations, on the one hand, and their pre-seminary-collegiate and seminary divisions, on the other. This action allowed the colleges to become more stable academic institutions, although the shifted emphasis did not mean that religious or diocesan clergymen questioned the superiority of theological over profane studies; rather, Catholic college policy makers sensed the impracticality, if not the impossibility, of trying to perpetuate in one institution two or three schools—secondary, college, and seminary—with clearly noncomplementary objectives. The first colleges, in trying to do too much, had had a record of failures nearly equaling their hopes; with institutional hopes more realistically curtailed, Catholic colleges were able to use their limited resources more effectively. Interestingly enough, however, in making these curtailments the colleges often felt victimized, and faced their more successful years perpetuating old ambivalences of aim and academic inhibitions, uncertain in their evaluation of the accidents of history that had saved them.

Finally, Catholic colleges began to learn from their academic forbears and applied their lessons with much-improved administrative skill. By the second half of the nineteenth century a Catholic college tradition was available for study and exploitation : presidents could profit from the errors and miscalculations of the past and, moreover, benefit from the example of successful colleges regardless of their state, private, or Catholic affiliations. It would be pleasant to be able to say that Catholic college presidents, so anxious to learn the business of college government, were indifferent to the sources of their instruction; but history refuses to support any belief that Catholic college leaders of this or later periods had any regard to lessons learned by nonCatholic colleges or universities.[94] Still, it was

93 Austin O'Malley, "Catholic Collegiate Education in the United States," *The Catholic World*, LXVII (June, 1898), 289–304.

94 Brother Azarias, "The Lessons of a Century of Catholic Education," *The Catholic World*, L (November, 1889), 143–154.

impossible to live in American society without being influenced somewhat by social surroundings and institutions, so Catholic colleges unconsciously, and sometimes consciously, imitated certain practices of nonCatholic higher education. Unfortunately, the technique of imitation was too frequently employed tardily and blindly, thus conferring on Catholic colleges the role of timid followers, unable or afraid to innovate, or what was worse, embracers of educational or administrative techniques already discarded as ineffectual by nonCatholic schools.[95]

In the end experience was probably the best teacher, for we should be uneasy with the verdict that presidents of later Catholic colleges (the president was always the central figure) were educational administrators abler than their earlier counterparts and were, in consequence of their personal superiority, capable of succeeding where others had failed. In the context of experience, it must be remembered that during its first half-century of American exposure Catholic higher education was a practice without a clearly-formed supporting theory. This void was filled by the appearance in 1850 of John Henry Newman's *Idea of a University,* and Newman's theoretical model for Catholic higher learning must have made some impression on Catholic college leaders in the United States, despite the ignominious failure of the school Newman himself founded in Ireland.[96] But if we assume that Catholic college leaders wanted to translate into action every word of Newman's remarkable little book—and this would be an exceedingly brave assumption—the direction of Catholic higher education would not have been altered much. Newman's disquisition was directed at universities, and at no time during the nineteenth century, not even after the founding of the Catholic University of America, did Catholics in the United States have an authentic university to which Newman's advice might have been applied. Even more generally, despite the honor accorded Newman's *Idea* and the regular tendency to quote his very quotable prose, on the practical level of teaching and learning, and on the essential level of higher education's objectives, Newman was paid scant heed.

[95] For the best evidence, although admittedly for a later period, see S. K. Wilson, "Catholic College Education, 1900–1950," *Catholic School Journal,* 51 (April, 1951), 121–123.

[96] See Fergal McGrath, *Newman's University: Idea and Reality* (New York, Longmans, Green & Co., Inc., 1951).

3
College government

Administrative theory

Variety in motives leading to the formation of Catholic colleges illuminates, but does not explain, administrative theory and practice current among them in the early years of their history in the United States. If the compelling reason for founding a college rested on the assumption that colleges were bastions for the religious faith of adolescents, then codes of administrative principles for conducting seminary-like schools where doctrinal orthodoxy enjoyed unassailable preeminence are easy to understand. Adherence to the objective of theological virtue—a combination of intellectual and moral values applied to a definitive denominational doctrine—confirmed a conviction that knowing and following the dogmas of the Church were the first, and possibly the only, signs of an educated Catholic. With a somewhat narrow sectarian view of the world, and a regular misinterpretation of Medieval Catholic Europe as the superior model for all organized society, Catholic colleges too often disposed of, and sometimes despised, so-called secular knowledge, because, following an ancient Christian theory of studies outmoded even at the time of Cassiodorus, such studies were thought dangerous to the integrity of sacred learning.[1] Put up with, but unloved, they were never justified for their

---

[1] The tendency to exaggerate the quality of medieval life was far too long a luxury for many Catholic historians. While there is no need to cite specific examples here, one must notice what was either naivete or arrogance in the choice of a book title like *The Thirteenth, Greatest of Centuries* by James J. Walsh. The Cassiodoran interpretation, *An Introduction to Divine and Human Readings,* translated by L. W. Jones (New York, Columbia University Press, 1946), updated educational thought and dissolved many of the old hostilities toward classical study. Still, the classics needed careful handling and circumspect excision for use in Christian syllabi until new, more liberal interpretations were made by Hugh of St. Victor (see Jerome Taylor, *The Didascalicon of Hugh of St. Victor* (New York, Columbia University

intrinsic worth. If, therefore, secular studies were of secondary and merely instrumental significance, Catholic schools with limited resources—and all rightfully claimed this unenviable distinction—could muster extremely little enthusiasm for embracing them.

Yet religious leaders responsible for educational administration were not compelled to accept the school as a religious agency, an adjunct to the pulpit. It could have been defined as a place where moral virtue had pride of place on a hierarchy of objectives. But when the primacy of doctrinal virtue was asserted as the role and purpose of a college—and when no one seriously doubted the doctrine of *in loco parentis*—a monastic-like atmosphere in the colleges was easily created and defended on the sturdiest of dogmatically assumed principles.[2]

Intellectual purposes were, doubtless, never forgotten, and to think they were entirely neglected on the level of theory is a mistake. Yet, it is fair to say, they were never given first place in these pioneer schools.[3] Most frequently the college tried to be at once a theological citadel, a training ground for morality, and a school. With so many important avenues available the college tried to follow them all; and this equivocation almost always made its failures equal its ambitions. Still, this was only one side of the picture, where the infant college essayed to be true to articles of collegiate faith, and where, although plagued by uncertainty about the means to employ, it valiantly strove to be an authentic college. The other side is confusing: the typical nineteenth-century Catholic college entered the field of higher education as a seminary;[4] its present and future were shrouded in the mysteries of maintaining in one institution programs for the preparation of priests and studies for the education of laymen.

In surrendering to urgent anxieties about the multiple problems of Catholic life in what amounted to a Protestant country, the leaders of early Catholic colleges were really their own worst enemies. They were either ignorant of, or had forgotten, the exemplary record of academic achievement provided by medieval universities, which were as Catholic in tone and doctrine as any college in the United States.[5] They had too little

---

Press, 1961), and John of Salisbury (see Daniel D. McGarry, *The Metalogicon of John of Salisbury* (Berkeley, Calif., University of California Press, 1955)). Erasmus added what was perhaps the final word in his *Liberal Education of Boys* (New York, Teachers College Press, 1946). See also Edward J. Power, *Evolution of Educational Doctrine* (New York, Appleton-Century-Crofts, 1969).

2 See Erbacher, *op. cit.*, pp. 102–108.

3 Thébaud, *Forty Years in the United States*, pp. 331–332.

4 See John Talbot Smith, *Our Seminaries: An Essay on Clerical Training* (New York, Longmans, Green and Co., 1896); Orestes A. Brownson, "Our Colleges," *Brownson's Quarterly Review*, 15 (April, 1858), 209–244; and Lloyd McDonald, *The Seminary Movement in the United States, 1784–1833* (Washington, The Catholic University of America, 1927).

5 See Lowrie J. Daly, *The Medieval University* (New York, Sheed and Ward, 1961).

confidence in their ability to shape minds, and too much confidence in their power to build morals.[6]

Had they looked more carefully at the colleges founded during the colonial period in America, they might have sensed the unavoidable disaster inherent in the direction they were taking.[7] Yet no evidence with respect to college purpose, or the technique of managing schools, exists which shows them as making such investigations or looking beyond the seminaries in the United States or abroad where they themselves had studied.[8] To try to prove that imitation, imagination, and foresight could have saved the schools long years of wasted effort and undistinguished service is none the less futile. The history of higher education in the United States is equally silent about early theoretic models among nonCatholic colleges, which demonstrated a frequent uncertainty about their purposes. It is fair to say that, during the Catholic colleges' formative period, spokesmen for nonCatholic colleges were debating the muddled purposes of *all* colleges in the country.[9]

That Catholic colleges abstained from corresponding regularly with their nonCatholic counterparts on a friendly basis is everywhere a matter of record.[10] Despite covert and sometimes overt hostility, nonCatholic institutions were not holding secret conclaves, and Catholic leaders might have learned from them. The Report of the Yale Faculty, for example, prepared in 1828, raised many important policy questions and served as an unofficial guide for a number of nonCatholic colleges for nearly a half-century, but there is no evidence in the reports, addresses, or policy documents of any Catholic college indicating so much as an awareness of the Report's existence.[11] The blind-spot hypothesis, however, is insufficient to explain why history taught American Catholic colleges so little on the level of administrative theory. To assume that Catholic college administration

[6] Thomas A. Becker, "Vocations to the Priesthood," *The American Catholic Quarterly Review,* V (January, 1880), 29–38.

[7] See, for example, John Brubacher and Willis Rudy, *Higher Education in Transition* (New York, Harper and Row, Publishers, 1958), pp. 3–116; Louis F. Snow, *The College Curriculum in the United States* (New York, Teachers College Press, 1907); and R. F. Butts, *The College Charts Its Course* (New York, McGraw-Hill Book Co., 1939).

[8] See Isaac Hecker, "College Education," *The Catholic World,* XXV (September, 1877), 814—825; and James Conway, "Catholic Education in the United States," *Catholic Mind,* II (1904), 54–61.

[9] See Francis Wayland, *Thoughts on the Present Collegiate System in the United States* (Boston, 1842); and for an historical review, see George Paul Schmidt, *The Liberal Arts College: A Chapter in American Cultural History* (New Brunswick, N. J., Rutgers University Press, 1957).

[10] For example, see Zimmer, *op. cit.,* pp. 97–101.

[11] "Original Papers in Relation to a Course of Liberal Education," *The American Journal of Science and Arts,* XV (January, 1829), 297—351. Of approximately 500 nineteenth century Catholic college catalogues I have examined, none mentions the Yale Report.

lacked theory is easy, for its history is difficult to elaborate, but mere chance, individual petulance, or institutional isolation cannot alone be blamed for the hardline followed in Catholic college administration.

Ecclesiastical government—the best general label for the way Catholic colleges were managed—begins with an assumption of undoubted confidence in the ability of its agents to define authentic policy objectives and execute them faultlessly. In the church-related college every educational program was evaluated by external criteria entirely familiar to ecclesiastics; if it failed to meet ecclesiastical hopes or norms it was either jettisoned before traditional doctrinal or canonical standards were jeopardized or it was rebuilt to accommodate *a priori* attitudes about educational directions and means. In any case, any thought that Catholic colleges were, first, educational and, second, religious agencies, was generally held to be doctrinally heterodox and pedagogically subversive.[12] Such bold assumptions about college government allowed for extreme latitude in the foundation and continuation of colleges, and we hear of few Catholic colleges whose doors were closed because either qualified clerical administrators or professors were unavailable.[13] Had administrative theory honored truer educational goals of qualification and performance, and demanded evaluative criteria drawn from the fundamental purposes of teaching and learning—in other words, if Catholic colleges had made an unqualified commitment to education rather than religion[14]—the number of Catholic colleges appearing in, and persisting through, the nineteenth century would have been reduced sharply.

As it was, a bishop, wanting the assumed benefits from a college in his diocese, elected to establish one. If clerical personnel were available in his ecclesiastical domain, he made assignments to the college staff; but if the ranks of diocesan clergy were thin, he solicited help from a religious community. And when a college was opened no one inquired about its distinctive role or asked : why a college here? The bishop had spoken with the unchallenged voice of authority and nothing was left for the faithful but to acquiesce. With the same zeal—which in other dimensions of religious action might be commended—and with the same untroubled confidence in the correctness of his judgment, he selected a principal administrator for

[12] John K. Ryan, "The Goal of Catholic College Education," *The Catholic Educational Review,* XXXII (January, 1934), 3–10; and William F. Cunningham, "The American College and Catholic Education," *Thought,* I (September, 1926), 262–278. The colleges' prospectuses, too, are clear on this point.

[13] See Orestes A. Brownson, "Our Colleges," *Brownson's Quarterly Review,* 15 (April, 1858), 218–231; and Edward J. Power, "Formative Years of Catholic Colleges Founded Before 1850," *Records of the American Catholic Historical Society,* LXV (December, 1954), 240–250.

[14] Alcuin W. Tasch, *Religious Constitutions and Institutional Control* (Chicago, University of Chicago, 1953).

the school—the president—or permitted a religious superior to appoint one if religious rather than secular clergy were to conduct it.[15]

Still, all clerics from the bishop to the simple parish priest were preoccupied with education and no one should accuse them of giving less than their best effort to support it along the lines they thought right; and this support was usually sufficient to keep the schools alive institutionally, although they were regularly at death's door intellectually. This, however, was not the result of a doctrinaire anti-intellectualism; no nineteenth-century Catholic college countenanced any conscious form of anti-intellectualism, and its principal spokesmen declaimed regularly and zealously on the virtues of the educated man.[16] But the definition of the educated man was hopelessly dated : put together as it was from abstracts of Erasmus' pedagogical theory, the parts ignored or unknown were more significant than the revelations, for shortly before Erasmus' death his codification of *pietas et litterata* was emasculated by warring Christians : Catholics and Protestants in Europe—the Jesuits, Colet, Sturm, Melanchthon, Cordier, Luther, and Calvin, for example—embraced classical humanism for their schools, but it was always a didactic classical humanism dominated by a determination for denominational supremacy or, sometimes, simple preservation. So they could not take the whole of Erasmus because Erasmus refused to serve their purpose : they took what was good for denominational proselytism and ignored the rest. Thus the nineteenth-century educational polemicist—and most Catholic college teachers were preoccupied with polemics whenever they appeared extramurally—was at pains to defend traditional values of education—and he may be praised for this—but too often he distorted or misunderstood these values. The frequently used definition of the educated man—the ultimate product of the Catholic college—found regularly in college prospectuses and catalogues, was out-of-touch with educational reality.[17] The general measure of nineteenth-century culture may be taken

[15] Edward F. Kennelly, *A Historical Study of Seton Hall College* (New York, New York University, 1944), pp. 17–31.

[16] Wilfrid Parsons, "Pioneer Catholic Universities," *Historical Records and Studies,* 31 (1940), 146–148. The *1881–1882 Catalogue of Marquette University,* p. 5, contains a typical catalogue statement: "The method of teaching in all classes insures the gradual development of both mind and morals, and is calculated to form men of deep thought, solid principles and sound religious convictions, without which education is worthless."

[17] For some examples, see Cassidy, *op. cit.,* p. 12; Thébaud, "Superior Instruction in Our Colleges," *The American Catholic Quarterly Review,* VII (October, 1881), 81–109; Thomas T. Taaffe, *A History of St. John's College,* Fordham, N. Y. (New York, Catholic Publications Society, 1891), p. 74; Meagher and Grattan, *op. cit.,* pp. 133–138; David R. Dunigan, *Holy Cross College in 1848,* unpublished M.A. thesis, St. Louis University, 1938, p. 78; Middleton, *op. cit.,* pp.21–22; Ruane, *op. cit.,* p. 140; and Roy W. Vollenweider, "Spring Hill College : The Early Days," *The Alabama Review* (April, 1954), p. 132. The following is a typical catalogue statement

from the unusual devotion these high-sounding phrases elicited, but in the last analysis, irrespective of rhetorical finesse, the education they were talking about was long out-of-date and almost hopelessly irrelevant. Still, clear doctrine, whether true or false, adequate or inadequate, easily attracted and retained adherents; its undisguised clarity demanded less from the men who were responsible for the government of colleges.

A theory of Catholic college government, then, was real enough, although less than a single printed page is needed for its elaboration. Education is a servant, religion a master; and educational policy is a by-product of doctrine and canon. Whoever is authorized to interpret theological doctrine or administer canon law is equipped to state the fundamental bases of education, and the converse, equally true, is that anyone ignorant or ill-equipped theologically or canonically must remain silent on all educational questions.[18] The educational discourse is but a paragraph in a theological tract. It was a theory again which prescribed a clerical monopoly in Catholic higher education in a most unlikely setting—the United States—yet both the theory and the monopolistic practice it generated remained in full force throughout the formative period of Catholic colleges. Its erosion, moreover, was slow and cumbersome, and even yet is incomplete.

The president

Following the tested traditions of an ecclesiastically-centered theory, Catholic colleges of the nineteenth century looked for leadership to the president of the school. In this office was vested all the authority needed for controlling every part of college life; both faculty and students were subservient to it and its occupant. This was a departure from anything the European university world had known, or practiced, in academic government; Medieval universities, dim and distant models for Catholic colleges of the United States, exempted themselves from conventional clerical discipline to elect their rectors and other university officers and, at the same time, carefully limited the authority of these officers.[19] The rector of the University of Paris, for example, held office for only two months and was then replaced;

---

for Jesuit colleges: "The course of study is substantially the form of teaching (*ratio studiorum*) followed for more than three hundred years in the Jesuit colleges in Europe, and since 1790 in our own country" (*Catalogue of Gonzaga College,* Washington, D. C., 1878–1879, p. 5).

[18] Kennelly, *op. cit.,* p. 57; Meline and McSweeney, *op. cit.,* I, 360–361, 367; and Daley, *op. cit.,* p. 55.

[19] Hastings Rashdall, *Universities of Europe in the Middle Ages* (Oxford, The Clarendon Press, 1936), I, 327–328.

with such short tenure it was impossible for any incumbent to grasp very securely the reins of control.[20] Members of the faculty—the masters— determined fundamental academic policies in what we should think was a democratic way, especially in the North of Europe; but even when this plan for faculty government had failed to cross the Alps to become established custom in Southern universities, policy-making decisions there were not relinquished to any one man or office but were exercised by students.[21] Yet the American Catholic college, regardless of its label, was not a full-fledged academic institution; it was, as we have said, a religious agency, so the policies followed in Church control applied to it as well. This policy of centering complete authority in the president's office was not unique to Catholic schools; all American colleges were administered similarly.[22] Yet there is no reason to suspect that Catholic colleges copied any existing codes of American college government.[23]

We see the president, then, hoisted to an autocratic pedestal with subjects to do his bidding. And if this policy of presidential supremacy was not borrowed from other American colleges, neither was it indigenous to Catholic schools in the United States, for it was a regularly accepted practice in the secondary schools of European Jesuits and among all other religious orders and communities engaging in the business of education. There was, moreover, a long-standing tradition of endowing seminary rectors with the same complete authority.[24] The colleges, then, had two clear sources from which to draw their ideas of government—secondary schools and seminaries—and they utilized both with unstinting devotion.

Despite the fact that Catholic colleges were only tangentially academic, men of presidential stature were never easy to discover, and the search for them was made infinitely more difficult when the pool from which they could come was necessarily clerical. To begin with, the qualifications for a president were nonacademic; his scholarly pedigree was unimportant; but his standing as a sound and solid cleric mattered, and we have no right to suppose that any priest ever occupying a presidential chair had anything less than unblemished moral and sacerdotal credentials. In 1856 James Roosevelt Bayley, Bishop of Newark, New Jersey, and founder of Seton Hall University, entered a note in his diary attesting the difficulty he and others

---

[20] *Ibid.,* p. 404.

[21] See Helene Wieruszowski, "Arezzo as a Center of Learning and Letters in the Thirteenth Century," *Traditio,* 12 (1953), 321–391.

[22] See George Paul Schmidt, *The Old Time College President* (New York, Teachers College Press, 1930); and John E. Kirkpatrick, *Academic Organization and Control* (Antioch, Ohio, Antioch College Press, 1931).

[23] Edward J. Power, "Orestes Brownson on Catholic Higher Education," *Catholic Educator,* XXIII (February, 1953), 275–278.

[24] McDonald, *op. cit.,* pp. 111—115; and Tasch, *op. cit.,* pp. 146–151.

experienced in finding the right man for a college presidency.[25] This entry, while having no special historical significance in itself, reinforced a long-standing belief that good college leadership was hard to find. Whether or not these pronouncements were only perpetuating a myth about excellence in college leadership is a tantalizing question : neither the standards of the colleges nor the stature of Catholic college presidents appointed—especially when the colleges were far from being accredited academic institutions— supplies much circumstantial evidence to support these often-repeated statements about carefully-analyzed presidential credentials.

We know John Carroll, Archbishop of Baltimore and founder of Georgetown College, voiced sentiments similar to Bayley's during the entire period of his association with Georgetown.[26] Before Georgetown opened, Carroll's vigorous search for a president led him to consider candidates both in Europe and America; finally he appointed Robert Plunkett, a man only partially fulfilling Carroll's requirements for the office. Yet we are uncertain about the reasons behind Carroll's doubts about Plunkett—and Plunkett's alleged shortcomings may have been beside the point, for Carroll had a litany of qualifications inconsistent with the needs of the position he was trying to fill.

At a time when the school was only an academy, the president of Georgetown was, according to "the general regulations" Carroll promulgated, responsible for determining the curriculum and supervising the teachers assigned to various subjects or classes; for superintending the studies and moral discipline of all students; for conferring, in public convocation, all class awards, rewards, and prizes; for conducting religious exercises, with special reference to the performance of religious duties by Roman Catholic students; and finally, for determining teachers' salaries and finding money to pay them.[27] But later Carroll appended additional responsibilities : everything having to do with "temporalities" was within the purview of presidential duty. Apparently, he meant by that term not only the maintenance of college buildings and grounds, but the examination of student performance, the visitation of classes to help teachers improve their instructional techniques, the administration of discipline both for students and professors and, on occasion—to take the last drastic step with any offenders against good order—the exercise of his expelling authority. If the list of presidential duties was long, it was because all these things were deemed too important to be left to subordinates, and to fulfill his duties expertly and fully the president must "incessantly bend his attention to the points . . . mentioned;

25 It is more difficult, Bayley wrote, "to find a good college president than to find a good anything else in this world. All that the college needs to insure its permanent prosperity is a President" (quoted from Bayley's diary in Kennelly, *op. cit.*, p. 57).

26 See Daley, *op. cit.*, pp. 60–63.

27 Baltimore Cathedral Archives, MS 9A N3, quoted in Daley, *op. cit.*, p. 55.

but though his attention should be unremitted and minute; yet it is advisable for him not to interfere personally, unless circumstances render it absolutely necessary. His authority will be so much the greater as it is seldomer (sic) exerted."[28]

Carroll's general regulations governing the president's actions did not survive as a distinctive statement in an administrative corpus defining presidential official behavior; nor were they reaffirmed in documents describing the office of president in later colleges. This lack of recognition, however, is misleading, for these documents were simply statements of conventional opinion about the management of schools and the duties of principal officers. Despite the lack of notice accorded the "general regulations" in the archives of administrative definition, their theme was honored in the administration of every Catholic college during the formative period.[29] They were reflecting an attitude rather than fostering a tradition.

The period from 1785 to 1870 saw the foundation of colleges for men, so we are for the moment excused from wondering about the qualifications for the president of a Catholic women's college.[30] In general, because most Catholic colleges were conducted by priests, the president was a priest; and, except in schools operated by religious communities of Brothers,[31] this must have been mandatory. But, again, it was an unwritten law. Neither Carroll,[32] DuBourg,[33] Portier,[34] Loras,[35] nor any other bishop with final ecclesiastical authority over colleges in his jurisdiction, ever entertained the thought that a nonclerical president was a possibility, and something more than mere whim, or inflated notions of clerical superiority, supported them : either an ancient assumption or possibly an archaically expressed canon made it both unthinkable and antiChristian for any cleric to be subject to a layman's authority.

[28] Ibid.

[29] Power, A History of Catholic Higher Education in the United States, pp. 148–150.

[30] See Sister M. Mariella Bowler, A History of Catholic Colleges for Women in the United States of America (Washington, Catholic University of America Press, 1933), pp. 96—99.

[31] See Brother Angelus Gabriel, The Christian Brothers in the United States, 1848–1948 (New York, Declan X. McMullen, 1948), pp. 132–148; and Brother Henry Ernest, The Christian Brothers College in St. Louis, unpublished master's thesis, St. Louis University, 1947, pp. 12–31.

[32] Edward I. Devitt, "Georgetown in the Early Days," Records of the Columbia Historical Society, XII (1909), 21–37.

[33] G. J. Garraghan, "The Beginnings of St. Louis University," St. Louis Catholic Historical Review, I (January, 1919), 85–102; and William B. Faherty, Better the Dream; Saint Louis: University and Community (St. Louis, St. Louis University Press, 1968), pp. 8–22.

[34] Michael J. Kenny, Catholic Culture in Alabama: The Centenary Story of Spring Hill College (New York, America Press, 1931), pp. 69–70.

[35] Mathias M. Hoffmann, Story of Loras College, 1839–1939 (Dubuque, Ia., Loras College Press, 1939), pp. 25–37.

This unwritten law of college leadership was obeyed rigorously, with protest from no one, because even cultured Catholics were untroubled by their subordination to clerical direction. The brief nonclerical adventures in Cecil College,[36] Calvert College,[37] and the Polytechnic and Commercial College of the Catholic Institute[38] allowed monopolies of clerical administration to continue unchallenged, because in these schools, all managed by laymen, the teachers were also lay and neither priest, seminarian, nor brother was ever asked to do a layman's bidding. Despite the potential hazards of pretentious clericalism, these attitudes were immune from protest, challenge, or alteration, and, sad to say, none was ever voiced or recommended. In the long run, however, the issue may be purely academic, for Catholic laymen were hardly better, if they were as well, prepared as priests to lead colleges, and we cannot believe the record of accomplishment among Catholic colleges would have been better, or even as good as it was, under lay rather than clerical management.

To debate this matter further is needless; the Catholic college president was a priest. Under the happiest circumstances he had a reputation in the Church as a powerful preacher, a man of determination, and a forceful disciplinarian capable of making his inferiors submit to his will. But outside the college walls he was expected to wear another face : fund raising, not yet a matter for experts, was, nevertheless, imperative; Catholic colleges needed money to start and complete necessary academic and domestic buildings. Catholic college presidents were praised most for the money they raised; and the presidents of the foundational period were remembered in the annals of their colleges for the buildings they financed while other accomplishments or actions bearing more directly on academic matters often went unnoticed.[39]

Within the college, presidents were expected to fulfill still another function, that of teaching; and since the president was also a college ornament, he was expected to project a scholarly image. Yet in testimonies to presidential adequacy this last point was paid scant heed, for the president who was criticized, or even removed from office, had not failed as a teacher or scholar but as a builder or disciplinarian.[40] If we consider both

[36] *Report of the United States Commissioner of Education,* 1870, pp. 508–509.

[37] Bernard C. Steiner, *History of Education in Maryland,* United States Bureau of Education Bulletin No. 19, 1894, pp. 173, 267.

[38] M. Agnes McCann, *Archbishop Purcell and the Archdiocese of Cincinnati* (Washington, The Catholic University of America, 1918), p. 75.

[39] See Timothy J. Reardon, "A Century of Catholic Progress," *Historical Records and Studies,* XVI (May, 1924), 78–86; and James Burns, "Failures of Our Higher Schools," *Commonweal,* IV (November, 1926), 140–142.

[40] See Sister M. Bernetta Brislen, "The Episcopacy of Leonard Neale," *Historical Records and Studies,* XXXIV (1945), 80–90; G. J. Garraghan, "John Anthony Grassi,

the indifference to academic qualifications in appointing a president and the multiple, almost unmanageable, demands of the office, it is indeed surprising that so many were both effective teachers and reasonably competent scholars. Nevertheless, despite the lavish praise of presidents common to institutional chronicles, the extant literature of the period is very short proof that there were many Catholic college presidents who were accorded extramural recognition for their scholarly achievements. In the last analysis, and in view of the dominant intramural stature of the president, it is indisputable that whatever progress Catholic colleges made in the nineteenth century must be attributed to the men who led them.[41]

Personalities count in any history and clearly remarkable and colorful ones occupied various presidential chairs; still, most of our information about the presidents comes from their former students, from memorial addresses, and from filio-pietistic memoirs or histories. The first source may, at times, be overly critical because of some personal encounter or unpleasant memory from undergraduate days; the others tend to flatter their subjects with delightful combinations of fact and fiction. Due allowances must be made for both, for it is unhistorical to build undeserved pedestals or to belittle with amused cynicism the men who exerted an important and lasting influence in the colleges of their generation. In this book, however, our interest is in the office itself rather than the men who occupied it.

The office, as we have said, was surrounded with ecclesiastical dignity and reverence. Its incumbents acquired their position in one of three ways : in diocesan and many religious-community colleges, presidents were appointed by religious superiors—the bishop in the former and a provincial or superior-general in the latter; in some colleges conducted by religious orders—the Benedictines, for example—the religious superior, the abbot, was ex-officio the college president and administered the office as part of his total religious functions. Eventually abbots of Benedictine monasteries with adjacent colleges delegated their academic duties to a trusted monk— the prior or sub-prior—and were thus freed from the day-to-day chores of an academic executive. Yet, even when this was done—not usually until the second or third decade of the twentieth century—abbots retained all authority proper to the president and thus weakened or fragmented delegated executive power.[42] Finally, in proprietary colleges, the president owned the land, buildings, and all collegiate facilities and administered the

---

S.J., 1775–1849," *The Catholic Historical Review*, XXIII (October, 1937), 273–292; and William P. Treacy, "A Biographical Sketch of Father Robert Molyneux, S.J.," *The American Catholic Quarterly Review*, XI (1886), 140–153.

[41] Power, *A History of Catholic Higher Education in the United States,* p. 146.

[42] The best account of Benedictine higher education in the United States is Colman J. Barry's *Work and Worship: A History of St. John's Abbey and University* (Collegeville, Minn., American Benedictine Academy, Historical Studies Number II, 1956).

school according to judgments consistent with respect for his private property.

In schools of the last category, presidents, being priests and subject to episcopal authority, were frequently disinclined to follow totally independent courses of action. Yet, bishops were often forbearing in their relations with these proprietary schools; occasionally they were simply uninformed about the decisions an owner-priest-president made and the manner in which the college operated. There were, moreover, ways to short-circuit clerical discipline, and in a pioneer land with an often loosely administered missionary Church, an imaginative president managed to find them; he kept the bishop content and handled his property in his own way.[43] But the American proprietary college was highly temporary, an expedient tolerated because substitutes were hard to find, so dwelling on it here is pointless. Diocesan and religious-order colleges belonged to more conventional patterns of collegiate organization, so if we want to see limitations on presidential authority we should turn to them. The president of a diocesan college found it absolutely essential to satisfy his bishop; not doing so meant, at the very least, his dismissal, at the most, the school's interdiction.[44] So despite all his power over internal affairs, the president of a college was somewhat hobbled, for the bishop could easily countermand any of his academic policies or even his purely technical directives; and in the last analysis the president had almost nothing to say about the clerical appointments made to the faculty. Still, we should avoid painting a picture of a tug-of-war between bishops and their presidential appointees; in the first place, college presidents were appointed because bishops sensed their allegiance to educational policies they themselves embraced; but if a bishop erred in his choice of a president, it made no matter : presidents were remarkably cautious about initiating polices unlikely to elicit the bishop's blessing.

In noting the bishop on his pedestal, we see clerical authoritarianism in action relative to one kind of Catholic college; but when we turn to another type the authoritarianism is still there, although its implementation is slightly altered. The college conducted by a religious community had an appointed president, as we have said, responsible to a superior who enjoyed unencumbered appointing authority. The college president was responsible to him, and directly to no one else. Still, the bishop's shadow was long; he spoke with the authority of the Church in his diocese and no school or college was authorized to function as a Catholic institution without his approval. Both religious superiors and regular-clergy presidents were neces-

---

[43] Private-venture college presidents could have had no better model than John Dubois; see Meline and McSweeny, op. cit., pp. 148–150.

[44] See G. J. Garraghan, "Fordham's Jesuit Beginnings," Thought, 16 (March, 1941), 17–39; Thébaud, Forty Years in the United States, pp. 331–335; Power, A History of Catholic Higher Education in the United States, p. 260.

sarily sensitive to the bishop's likes and dislikes. He could be generous with their college in various ways if it pleased him, but he could also allow it to live unloved and unsupported or, if he chose, close it and expel the religious order from his diocese. Expelling a community was an extreme exercise of episcopal authority and was used only as a last resort, but a bishop could achieve the same end by more moderate means; he could simply make the religious community so uncomfortable in his jurisdicition that it moved to another.[45]

All this was a part of the total administrative picture and a part that bespeaks some confusion of purpose, division of loyalties, and institutional instability. Yet it is a one-sided picture of the authority directed at the college from above; another side can be sketched in, a side from which the president, vis-à-vis his subordinates, both faculty and students, neither acknowledged nor felt any diminution of academic power. The limitations imposed by bishops and religious superiors were not meant to erode the president's command over internal academic affairs; if anything, they sustained it and, sometimes, because the president was always to account to his superior, made for excessive executive severity.

All incorporated Catholic colleges had boards of trustees, but in some the board was a legal reality formed only to satisfy the purposes of state, or in Georgetown's case, the federal charter.[46] Its role in total college government needs no emphasis here, but we should see it in relation to the president's position. The board was composed of clergymen, usually members of the college faculty and the religious community, although the diocesan college frequently recruited board members from the ranks of diocesan clergy who had no intimate association with the institution. Individual board members may sometimes have had a deep interest in the college's welfare, and some may have had extensive experience with colleges either in the United States or abroad, but they were advisers who spoke to the president only when he wanted to listen and were powerless to take any action or make any decision, either as individuals or as a board, not approved by him. Jesuit colleges, following the traditional practices of the Society, had, in addition to the legally imperative boards of trustees, religious consultors. These consultors —all Jesuits and probably attached to the college staff—were appointed by

[45] The clearest example of this kind of exodus led to the Jesuits' association with St. John's College (Fordham). See Thébaud, *Forty Years in the United States,* pp. 328–330; Taaffe, *op. cit.,* pp. 49–59; and G. J. Garraghan, "Fordham's Jesuit Beginnings," *Thought,* 16 (March, 1941), 17–39.

[46] Some indication of the status of the board of trustees may be gleaned from the following statement made by a trusted confrere to a Georgetown president (Benedict Fenwick to Father Grassi, December 23, 1814, quoted in Daley, *op. cit.,* p. 189): "it will be extremely difficult not to say impossible to obtain that grant of the legislature (the charter) without such a measure as those wise legislators cannot form other than suspicious ideas of a college that has no directors."

the provincial and were commissioned to render opinions to the college president (in religious language, styled rector) on matters affecting college or religious-community life. Before making certain decisions—most often those involving expenditures of money—the president was expected to hear the consultors' opinions; the procedure must be described in this way, because he was absolved from conferring with them and was in no way obligated to alter his decision after he had listened to what they had to say. Decision making was always his province, so there was no sharing of authority; but Society convention prescribed some testing of his judgment on selected persons before final action. Should the president ignore the consultor's counsel, as was his undoubted right, a consultor could put his opinions before the next higher religious superior in the Society or, if he chose, direct his appeal or complaint to the Jesuit Father General, the superior of all Jesuits, residing in Rome. This Jesuit system for getting opinion, not from the rank and file, but from trusted confrerers, was a fairly normal procedure among organized religious and in one form or another was part of administrative practice in all colleges conducted by regular clergy and brothers.[47]

In discussing the impact formally or informally designated boards had on presidential action, we should demur from concluding that their powers belonged wholly to the realm of myth, but it must be admitted that, to the extent their power was real, it was moral, depending on persuasion, not legal and therefore not regularized in policy and statute. Most college communities during the formative period were small, having usually fewer than a dozen religious persons assigned to the house, so the president, not invisible and remote from his religious colleagues, lived with them as a family, and together they tried to manage community affairs in ways befitting the perpetuation of a family enterprise.[48] It was never the president, the father of the religious family, versus the clerical faculty, and to begin with this assumption is plainly wrong; the religious community was engaged in a common undertaking; its members were committed by self-interest and solemn vow to the community's religious and educational goals, and who was better equipped to interpret and realize these goals than the father of the family? Yet, religious were also human beings and differences sometimes arose within the family. When they did, they were voiced, rectified, or suppressed behind the black, opaque curtain obscuring religious life from public view.[49]

In this context of religious-human relationships the Catholic college

[47] See Tasch, *op. cit.*, pp. 52–60.

[48] See James J. Maguire, "A Family Affair," *Commonweal*, LXXV (November, 1961), 171–173.

[49] See Raphael N. Hamilton, *The Story of Marquette University* (Milwaukee, Marquette University Press, 1953), pp. 125–134.

president performed his ecclesiastic and academic functions. He was more than an academic executive and clerically-minded commentators taking this into account speculated about the superior qualities necessary to a fully effective president. Although we do not have many such reservoirs from which to draw, Simon Bruté, a priest remembered for his long association with Mount Saint Mary's College in Emmitsburg, Maryland, and later as Bishop of Vincennes,[50] reflected a general attitude toward the office when, in 1833, he tried to codify the credentials important to the Catholic college's highest office.[51] Since Bruté's thought is free both from rhetorical and theoretic flourishes, we can take his commentary at face value, trusting it as fairly representative of conventional opinion and illustrative of common practice. Bruté begins by admitting that the list he recites adds up to an ideal and that no president can be expected to fulfill every qualification; still,

if he has good support and is not proud and sensitive he may remedy his defects and matters still go on well. Radical change is generally of doubtful experiment; more so if with persons not tried in the house that is to be delivered to them. The call for it should not be credited to the abstract, but with full details and motive—and examination of all the bearings. . . . I think the procurator, by the finances, and the prefect by his habitual vigilance and care, have much to do with the support of the house. I suspect that the duties now assigned the president can with success be subdivided. . . . [the president] has duties that can be left to the sacristan.[52]

But before this he has permitted us to see what the good president must be capable of doing. Of course, he should tend to affairs of the college, but the seminary jointly housed and administered with the college needs close attention too. Then there are priests [members of the faculty] and Sisters [in charge of housekeeping] whose spiritual welfare requires his superintendence. And now for these herculean tasks, Bruté tells us, the president must have an agreeable personality, a dignified manner, and good health; he should eschew personal ambition to embrace the principles of piety, justice, pure life, and humility, and, in addition, be a good scholar in language and literature. He should be a good divine too, Bruté continues, and by that he means the president must be capable of flawless seminary direction, an impeccable interpreter of Church doctrine, and a stern advocate for Church discipline. He should be an effective pastor of a parish congregation, a good preacher, and a pleasant conversationalist

[50] James R. Bayley, *The Memoirs of Rt. Rev. Simon William Bruté*, D.D. (New York, Catholic Publishing Company, 1876), and Herman Aldering, *A History of the Catholic Church in the Diocese of Vincennes* (Indianapolis, Carolon and Hollenbeck, 1883).

[51] Meline and McSweeny, *op. cit.*, I, 289–290.

[52] Simon Bruté's notes, quoted in *ibid,* p. 290.

in his private interviews with general visitors and parents of students. But the boys in college need understanding and management and for this the president must be at once a psychologist and a policeman. Self-possession, diligence, firmness, cooperativeness—especially with the procurator—patience, perceptiveness to "shun all extra calls," and finally, "an equitable, sane, well-supported character" complete the portrait of the perfect president.[53] Bruté adds that he has not seen this portrait translated into real life.

In less visionary language, the principal presidential responsibilities can be distilled into four categories : those of priest, administrator, educator, and disciplinarian; yet such precision entails some hazards, for an office with vague boundaries, encompassing multiple activities, almost defies delineation. One example should be sufficient to show that presidents were themselves plagued with urgent anxieties about their role : "I hope you will not take it amiss," President Mulledy, of the College of the Holy Cross, writes to Provincial Ryder, "if I beg of you to cast a look in my situation during the last year—no minister or procurator, no refectorian and I may say no clothes-room keeper, for I was obliged to watch constantly poor McElroy, whose head is so small that he is continually blundering—giving Tom's clothes to Harry, and Harry's to Mike, etc. *ad infin*. Do then send me two brothers, one who has head enough to keep the clothes room, watch dormitories, etc."[54] But if our view is broad enough we can look past the details of housekeeping and child care to see the presidents functioning as priests, administrators, educators, and disciplinarians.

Delegation of the duties in any of these categories of responsibility was virtually impossible for two reasons : first, faculty ranks were thin; with everyone fulfilling multiple roles the president was unable to enlist colleagues' help for the infrequent assignments where a delegate might have been acceptable; and second, with clerical authority the backbone of the system, the president was enjoined not to fragment his authority lest proper respect for religious superiors be undermined. Presidents may have been endowed with personal humility, lacking jealous fears for their authority as persons, but inherently the system was suspicious of any democratic erosion of legitimate authority. Presidents willing to share or delegate authority were effectively discouraged by the precedents of ecclesiastical discipline from doing so.[55]

A college president appointed pastor of a local parish or assigned to a distant mission for Sunday duty was simply practicing the profession he

---

[53] *Ibid.*

[54] Father Mulledy to Father Provincial Ryder, August 10, 1844, quoted in Walter J. Meagher, *The History of the College of the Holy Cross* (New York, Fordham University, 1944), p. 50; and see Meagher and Grattan, *op. cit.,* p. 44.

[55] See Daley, *op. cit.,* pp. 92, 169, 189.

had chosen. If freed from extramural pastoral work, he was expected to minister to the spiritual needs of the college and seminary community. Accounts of presidential activity during these frantic years always dwell on the pastoral and missionary labor of the president.[56] Should he have wanted to abandon this dimension of presidential responsibility (although evidence is lacking that any college president did) his dereliction of duty would surely have been noticed by his superiors. The chief representative of a religious agency was conscience-bound to administer the sacraments to the faithful.

Administration, though important, was fairly unsophisticated in small colleges with few students, prescribed curricula, and a faculty totally committed to extravagantly-phrased but, in practice, prosaic objectives for college education. On occasion, a president tried to clarify objectives and reorganize traditional curricula;[57] then the outcomes of administrative action were seen more than felt: seen, in the prospectus or the college catalogue, when one was published; and felt, by teachers and students, if the restatement of objectives were anything more than an attempt to attain rhetorical exactitude, or, if the curricular mechanics were anything other than tinkering with an educational apparatus assumed to be basically sound. The protein of the college course was classical, and few presidents had the temerity to modify the diet of learning tradition prescribed.

Even the most conservative president's life was seldom serene and untroubled because, as we have said, his superiors had to be satisfied. In a diocesan college this meant the bishop had to be apprised of all propositions and consulted before decisions were made. But bishops were busy men, too, so sometimes they decided to relieve themselves of close superintendence of a college by creating a board of visitors, supervisors, trustees, or governors. This board may or may not have been composed of members of the board of incorporators (a legal necessity for chartering and a way of ensuring institutional perpetuity), but no matter: it was empowered by bishops, and sometimes by other religious superiors, to shape policy for the college and even to make faculty appointments, curricular decisions, and financial commitments, thus eroding substantially the image we so far have of the president as a man with unfettered authority.

But we should not be too quick to jettison our impressions of infrangible

---

[56] All institutional histories reflect these extramural presidential activities. See, for example, Meagher and Grattan, *op. cit.,* pp. 39–44; Meline and McSweeny, *op. cit.,* I, 150–160; Middleton, *op. cit.,* pp. 22–28; and Hope, *op. cit.,* pp. 33–39.

[57] See Austin O'Malley, "Catholic College Education in the United States," *The Catholic World,* 67 (June, 1898), 289–304; Middleton, *op. cit.,* p. 32; *Report of the United States Commissioner of Education,* 1887–1888, pp. 642–643; G. J. Garraghan, *The Jesuits of the Middle United States,* III, 124; the *Forty-Third Catalogue of the University of Notre Dame,* 1887, p. 40; and Joseph T. Durkin, *Georgetown University: The Middle Years, 1840–1900* (Washington, Georgetown University Press, 1963), pp. 78–102.

presidential authority or too anxious to have him share authority with boards of trustees. When Georgetown College was founded, John Carroll decided to create a board of supervisors[58] because he lacked confidence in the first president. Thus from Georgetown's origin until 1815 the president, without full authority, was required to cooperate with a board. Yet much of this was only machinery and, at best, a safeguard, for Georgetown's history contains little evidence leading us to suppose that the board was capable of curbing the presidential will.[59] The board was an irritating reality, however, and when President Grassi and the board disagreed on the latter's legitimate role in administration and its right to define duties for the school's vice-president, a clarification of their respective powers became imperative. Grassi petitioned the bishop to dissolve the board or strip it of its power, and to allow the president to control the college free from a board's interference.[60] The bishop agreed, apparently without listening to arguments from the board, and for the next 145 years boards of trustees appeared as near-functionless ornaments in Catholic college administration. The truth is that most colleges continued to have them, possibly because legally they were important, or possibly, in imitation of administrative tables of organization found in nonCatholic colleges (although good evidence for this is lacking). But it is also true that these boards were not policy-making bodies, had no real control over the management of the institution, and that presidents were not responsible to them. In the long history of such boards, save for the Catholic University of America[61] and lay boards of trustees[62]—which never pretended to have any voice in college manage-ment—exclusively clerical appointments to them were made from among the president's administrative and faculty subordinates. At best advisory, these boards had a totally different legal and academic status from state and nonCatholic college and university boards of control.[63]

The president, we know, could have his way if he could afford it; but he had to collect money. If Catholic colleges had budgets, we could hardly expect them to be large or very detailed. But whether or not they followed anything more than crude bookkeeping techniques, or simply honored the fiscally primitive policy of spending all they had, it was extraordinary for any college to live on its income from tuition. With operating costs con-

58 Daley, *op. cit.,* p. 54.

59 Durkin, *op. cit.,* pp. 248–260.

60 Daley, *op. cit.,* pp. 169–171; 189–191.

61 John Tracy Ellis, *Formative Years of the Catholic University of America* (Wash-ington, American Catholic Historical Society, 1946), pp. 147–149.

62 See Hope, *op. cit.,* pp. 350, 392; and Faherty, *op. cit.,* p. 389.

63 Samuel P. Capen, *The Management of Universities* (Buffalo, Foster and Stewart Publishing Co., 1953), pp. 261–263; Noah Porter, *The American College and the American Public* (New Haven, C. C. Chatfield and Co., 1870), chap. 12; and H. P. Beck, *Men Who Control Our Universities* (New York, King's Crown Press, 1947).

suming usual income, unusual sources of income were needed. The president was unquestionably the man for fund-raising. The normal practice entailed preaching appeals in Catholic parish churches, soliciting bishops in the United States (if the college were conducted by regular clergy), asking for financial help from private persons within the country, and calling upon ecclesiastical agencies in Europe.[64]

Further details of fund-raising are unnecessary here, although we might add that great effort often went unrewarded. The colleges always needed money, and when a catastrophe, such as fire, destroyed a college building, their efforts were intensified. The president, again, as the central figure in the college, commanded the best audience and usually elicited the best results. However, when appeals were to be comprehensive, presidents sometimes sent representatives to speak for them. Once, at least, this was a mistake : the President of Holy Cross sent a Jesuit priest to a neighboring parish to preach an appeal for funds after fire had destroyed collegiate buildings. The pastor refused to allow the Jesuit to preach—an unlikely act if the president himself had appeared—and took the pulpit himself to say : "My dearly beloved Brethren, you are requested to tender your assistance towards the rebuilding of Holy Cross College. You have been so very liberal to me for my charitable purpose, that you ought not to be called upon. The misfortune of the College would not have been very great, if they had insured it. Yet you will give them some little thing. I do not wish to impose on your charity; but a little mite will be of a good help, and a means to see that the College is in a more respectable condition than it was before."[65] Whether this was a low-keyed, effective appeal for the college or simply a perfunctory discharge of charitable obligation is unrevealed, but college presidents always tried to be at their eloquent best when seeking financial bequests for the colleges.

There were many sides to academic administration which were unaccounted for by presidential contests with boards of trustees, elucidation of college plans to a bishop or provincial, or encounters with a public capable of helping colleges over financial hurdles. Even a pioneer college was more complex than this. Despite its apparent desire to live in its own world, the Catholic college wanted some communication with society and engaged in informal public relations activities. The president, the college's only official spokesman, employed public addresses, catalogues, and other college publications, as well as religious and public newspapers to disseminate information on college progress and need and to recruit students. Preparing the academic calendar, recruiting, admitting, placing and guiding students, developing new courses for the curriculum in order to attract students unable

---

[64] See Hoffmann, op. cit., p. 28; Burns and Kohlbrenner, op. cit., p. 46; Cassidy, op. cit., pp. 82–85; and Erbacher, op. cit., p. 74–76.

[65] Quoted in Meagher, op. cit., p. 74.

or unwilling to grapple with the classics,[66] listening to students' complaints about life in the college, these were all within the president's purview. He handled them all, one way or another, for decades without the assistance of subordinate administrators. But there were other things he could afford to ignore, apparently with impunity, because the college was unready for them : faculty committees never troubled him to define his role vis-à-vis theirs; appointments to the faculty were *pro forma,* with the president utilizing the personnel assigned to the college by religious superiors, and reassignments of clerical faculty to positions outside the college frequently being made without his prior knowledge and usually without any warning that the college was to lose them; faculty rank and promotion were unheeded; the nature of a college community was vaguely sensed by more perceptive presidents but, nevertheless, was allowed to go undefined and unrefined; the college's social responsibilities were untested; and students, allowed no part in college government, needed neither appeasing nor prudent, responsible direction before assuming their places in a world in ferment. What was left undone was probably more important than the administrative duties zealously cultivated, but Catholic college presidents tended to form an image of themselves as custodians of a *status quo* rather than as innovators or reformers.[67] On the whole, they seemed content to remain indifferent to broader issues in higher education that even in the nineteenth century were admitted to the deliberations of many good nonCatholic schools.

Undoubtedly, Catholic college presidents had little time to think about wider definitions of academic administration, and, of course, their own backgrounds of academic experience did not generate any, because, as we have said, they were expected to be full-time educators and disciplinarians. The educational function, divided between teaching in the classroom and general supervision of instruction, required the president to teach college classes as well as some important subject in the seminary, to organize courses of study, examine syllabi and approve them, recommend teaching techniques, and conduct oral examinations for the entire student body. Every public function was graced by a presiding president; every classroom needed his attention and we may suppose he visited them regularly; every misbehaving schoolboy was summoned to his court even for routine infractions of the college code.

How were presidents prepared to carry out their monumental commission as keepers of the college's academic and moral conscience? Did they not capitulate to urgent anxiety, heed the voice of hesitation to compromise

---

[66] The classical curriculum was a constant source of difficulty for students unprepared or unwilling to pursue it; see G. J. Garraghan, *The Jesuits of the Middle United States,* III, 124; M. P. Dowling, *op. cit.,* p. 62; and Orestes A. Brownson, "Paganism and Education," in the *Works of Orestes A. Brownson,* X, 551–563.

[67] Power, *A History of Catholic Higher Education in the United States,* pp. 154–155.

their responsibilities as priests, administrators, educators, and disciplinarians? The record suggests otherwise; they listened to the voice of tradition and, incorrectly estimating the magnitude of their responsibilities, tried to perform them all. Had their preparation as academicians been better, and had they understood the essential purposes of higher education more completely, they would have refused to lead such a single-handed assault on the citadel of learning. In this appraisal, questions about their professional clerical preparation need neither be asked nor answered; yet, we should ask : did the president's professional training as a clergyman fit him for administrative and educational leadership?

The kind and quality of administrative training necessary for effective academic leadership is probably a moot point—for the history of American higher education is filled with examples of successful presidents who had no special administrative training for their positions—but conversance with colleges themselves and enough academic experience to probe the deeper meaning of higher learning have been universally attested as important qualifications for men who are to direct the destines of colleges. Yet most nineteenth-century Catholic college presidents were appointed without having had previous experience, either as students or teachers, in a college : they had been educated in seminaries. Whatever administrative technique they came to possess was learned on the job and their educational insights were hammered out in day-to-day experience. The typical president was a priest in his thirties, having been ordained from six to ten years previously, and his dossier recorded as great a variety of past clerical experience as his new office would afford.[68]

Presidents trod the periphery of scholarly and pedagogical distinction; not being academically oriented when assuming office, they found their leisure hours too few to allow them to cultivate or prosecute scholarship. We search in vain for a book, article, paper, address, or academic proclamation which might have caused the attention of the academic world to center on them. Their training and experience ill-befitted academic leadership; instead it confirmed their allegiance to customary educational policies. These policies, and their accompanying practices, lay dormant, or were tolerated, until the colleges were awakened by social pressures and the example of nonCatholic colleges : bold innovation, or even a receptive attitude toward modest change, were inconsistent with institutions wanting to affect society by refusing to be part of it. Subsequently, Catholic colleges rode the bandwagon of educational progress but they were never its drivers. The gates through which the bandwagon had to pass were guarded with inflexible zeal by presidents themselves, a fact which suggests their inability to distinguish educational policy from Church doctrine or sectarian

[68] *Ibid.*

discipline.[69] Judged on administrative accomplishment alone, the record of nineteenth-century Catholic college presidents is adequate, but as educators and interpreters of a theory of Catholic higher education, their statements are better left unread.[70]

Such a harsh evaluation needs justification : why were Catholic college presidents impotent as educators? In the first place, they regularly, and perhaps naturally, subordinated their academic to their clerical responsibilities. First they were priests, then academicians. In the second place, their superiors appointed them without much attention to academic experience, scholarly aptitude, or personal ambition. Finally, presidents' tenure was brief, and with on-the-job training the only preparation available to them this may have been the critical factor.[71] In most colleges conducted by regular clergy the canonical limit of a six-year term applied, because presidents were also religious superiors. Thus, the capable and energetic president was lost to the college when his term expired, and when he was just beginning to master the intricacies of his office. During its first sixty years Georgetown had twenty-two presidents; Gonzaga College in the District of Columbia twelve from 1850 to 1890; the College of St. Francis Xavier, New York City, twelve from 1847 to 1897; the University of Notre Dame fifteen in a century; Creighton University nine in twenty-five years; Loyola in Chicago fourteen from 1870 to 1915; Marquette University seventeen from 1881 to 1948; and Boston College twenty from 1863 to 1945.[72] The average term of the nineteenth-century Catholic college president was slightly more than four years; during the same period nonCatholic colleges kept their presidents in office for a term averaging fifteen years, though, it must be admitted, the mean is raised somewhat by Charles W. Eliot's four decades at Harvard and Eliphalet Nott's threescore years at Union.

Other college officers

During its years of formation the Catholic college was managed mainly by one man; the president alone elaborated policy and executed it in day-to-day

[69] See Colman J. Barry, *The Catholic University of America, 1903–1909* (Washington, The Catholic University of America, 1950), p. 135; and Leo R. Ward, *Blueprint for a Catholic University* (St. Louis, B. Herder Book Co., 1949), pp. 312–330.

[70] If one reads the pronouncements of Catholic college presidents (even in the fragmentary form in which they are preserved—usually in institutional histories), this is the conclusion which emerges, although it must be admitted that it is clearly a subjective evaluation.

[71] Power, *A History of Catholic Higher Education in the United States,* p. 154.

[72] *Ibid.*

administration. This was a period when the titles of academic dean, dean of faculty, or dean of students, director of admissions, placement, or guidance, director of public relations or public information, and business manager all go unmentioned and unused. The unsophisticated and tiny college community was almost totally unaware of these positions—probably having slight need for them—so it is unnecessary to give them further notice here. Yet before Catholic colleges outgrew their formative years, they did make provision, in tables of administrative organization, for presidential assistants.

One of the first of these subordinate positions to emerge was the vice-presidency, an imposing title for an office nearly bereft of any precise functions and almost totally stripped of any legitimate authority. We have seen how the President of Georgetown College was irritated by the trustees' efforts to define the vice-president's function when the office was first prescribed, and how he waged and won the battle to impound trustees' authority over college affairs.[73] This victory for an infrangible presidential authority inevitably led to an atrophying of all lesser college positions, including that of professor, so from the early nineteenth century to the end of the formative period the office of vice-president was nominal and neglected. Despite their presence in the nomenclature of administrative organization, vice-presidential offices were neither accorded recognition nor status in or outside the academic community; nor was the apprenticeship potential of the office for training future presidents heeded and exploited.[74]

Another subordinate office turned out to be a more important one: it was that of the prefect of discipline.[75] Appearing fairly early in Catholic college history, the prefect, the president's right-hand man, was charged with the maintenance of good order. As colleges grew in enrollment the prefect of discipline was usually supplied with assistants who helped him carry out his policeman's role. And with the addition of a prefect, or prefects—what Orestes Brownson called "a substitute body of executive officers"—it may be said that the nineteenth-century Catholic college had

---

[73] See Daley, *op. cit.*, pp. 189–191; and for the general fear of trustees and trusteeism in Catholic institutions, see Peter Guilday, *The Catholic Church in Virginia, 1815–1822* (New York, United States Catholic Historical Society, 1924), pp. 108–110; and Hugh Nolan, *The Most Rev. Francis Patrick Kenrick, Third Bishop of Philadelphia, 1830–1851* (Philadelphia, American Catholic Historical Society of Philadelphia, 1948).

[74] A study of nineteenth century Catholic college catalogues, wherein officers of administration and faculty are cited, reveals that vice-presidents were destined for prefectures and professorships. They had the title of an administrative officer, but they spent most of their time administering discipline or teaching as class teachers and neither assignment allowed much time for administrative conditioning. For examples of administrative and faculty deployment, see *St. Louis University Catalogue, 1878–1879,* pp. 8–10.

[75] Erbacher, *op. cit.*, p. 73.

two important officers of administration : the president and the prefect of discipline. The original use of the term *prefect* in an academic context is unrecorded and it was Brownson again who objected both to the term itself and to the crude exercise of power the prefect was allowed : he averred it was "as arbitrary as that of the district school, without the same checks on its excessive exercise."[76] The office of prefect, he wrote, "in its relation to the business of teaching in our colleges, does not involve that aptitude on the part of its incumbent for imparting instruction which its classic significance implies. If the office, so modified, were to be generally revived and reintroduced, the title of boatswain of a cruiser, or the provost-marshal of a brigade, would be a better title than that of Prefect."[77] In any case, neither the criticisms of Brownson nor of anyone else impaired the prefect's authority over college boys or, if he were aware of such criticisms, caused him any anxious moments. His authority came with an annual appointment; he was responsible to the president and to no one else, and the best prefect was one who could control the boys and bend them to the college's disciplinary code without intruding on the president's time. The prefect's qualifications for supervising the discipline of young men were apparently unimportant as long as he was strong, fearless, alert to the clever intrigues of young men, and unequivocally loyal to the letter of presidential edict.

The prefect's conception of good order was broad and literal : he watched the boys go to bed, checked to see that they remained there, and awakened them in the morning in time for daily Mass. From him they obtained permission to leave the college grounds, although in some colleges boys were never allowed away from the college unless accompanied by a prefect. His eyes watched them while they studied and played; he read their letters home and censored all incoming mail. While eating, washing, and playing the boys were constantly under the prefect's watchful care; and he usually controlled their wardrobe and took custody of any pocket money they had. If the prefect of discipline needed assistants, they were usually recruited from the ranks of teachers, and on rather rare occasions the prefect of discipline himself may have been a class teacher.[78]

We find frequent references to the office of procurator—a combination of treasurer and business manager—but this officer usually belonged more properly to the religious community than to the college. In addition, as college enrollments increased, it was sometimes necessary to assign a member of the clerical faculty to the post of college chaplain. At first, the president acted also as pastor of souls, but when he could no longer do everything expected of him he found a delegate to care for the students' day-to-day

[76] Orestes A. Brownson, "Our Colleges," *Brownson's Quarterly Review,* 15 (April, 1858), 216.

[77] *Ibid.,* p. 217.

[78] Erbacher, *op. cit.,* pp. 102–111.

spiritual welfare, the chaplain. To this college officer the boys could bring a variety of troubles and usually be confident that their revelations, doubts, and anxieties would be held in confidence.

With these officers, all clearly sustained by delegations of presidential authority, the table of administrative organization in the Catholic colleges of the formative period was complete.[79]

[79] *Ibid.,* pp. 69–78.

4

Catholic college faculties

Duties and qualifications

Throughout most of the nineteenth century Catholic colleges placed considerably more emphasis on a teacher's duties than on his capacity for fulfilling them. Yet this narrow theory of teaching could, for the most part, be implemented with relative impunity since the teacher's role was largely routine; he was expected to follow a prepared syllabus without deviation, and in the last analysis he was a hearer of lessons rather than a professor of a subject. If the colleges had been real institutions of higher learning, such testimony, coming from almost every account of a college's history, would have been devastating indeed, but, as it was, the colleges were not authentic schools of higher education, and a teaching corps capable of conducting elementary and secondary studies was probably sufficient.[1]

Still, such a corps was not easily organized, or, once organized, retained; not even the Catholic elementary and secondary schools of the early United States were staffed with well-qualified teachers, so it may be unreasonable to expect more from the higher than from the lower schools.[2] On the other

[1] See Edmund J. Goebel, *A Study of Catholic Secondary Education During the Colonial Period up to the First Plenary Council of Baltimore, 1852* (New York, Benziger Bros., 1937), pp. 5–25; *Catalogues of the Colleges of the Society of Jesus in the United States, 1857 to 1896*, University of Detroit Archives; G. J. Garraghan, "The Beginnings of St. Louis University," *St. Louis Catholic Historical Review*, I (January, 1919), 85–102; G. J. Garraghan, "Fordham's Jesuit Beginnings," *Thought* 16 (March, 1941), 17–39; G. J. Garraghan, "Marquette University in the Making," *St. Louis Catholic Historical Review*, II (April, 1920), 417–446; G. J. Garraghan, "Origin of Boston College," *Thought*, 17 (December, 1942), 617–656; Irenaeus Herscher, "The History of St. Bonaventure University," *Franciscan Studies*, 11 (September, December, 1951), 365–424; and Mathias Hoffmann, "The Oldest College in Iowa," *The Iowa Catholic Historical Review*, VII (1935), 3–14.

[2] See Richard J. Tierney, *Teachers and Teaching* (New York, Longmans, Green &

hand, expectations are really beside the point, for our interest is in the history of these schools rather than what we should have expected them to be. Thus, tendencies to apologize for lack of teaching quality in the colleges, because lower schools had poor teachers too, is not only unhistorical but largely irrelevant. Of this much we can be fairly certain : Catholic colleges of the formative period were beset with the same faculty problems that earlier colleges of the country had faced.[3] They, along with their earlier counterparts, had students who needed to be taught, and they secured the services of available teachers without examining too closely either their credentials as teachers or their pedigree as scholars.

We know, too, that native sources of teacher supply were quickly exhausted as the colleges continued to multiply; it was always difficult to make supply equal demand because the career of a college teacher, since he was almost certainly a cleric, was highly temporary. In the early Catholic college there was hardly any place for a layman dedicated to teaching : neither the regimen of the college nor the remuneration for his services encouraged a young man to seek an academic career. In addition to this, the Catholic college was, as we have said, determined to be a religious agency first and a school second;[4] thus, the usual qualifications for a teacher in a Catholic college began by demanding clerical status. Without a well-organized seminary system,[5] there were too few priests to fill available ecclesiastical positions, so the colleges had to make their way through most of the nineteenth century without a full complement of qualified faculties.[6]

Sometimes they turned to Europe, as earlier American colleges had also done, to recruit clergymen and clerical teachers, for both ecclesiastical schools and universities in Europe were more capable of satisfying the needs of Catholic colleges than were American nonCatholic universities. Although at the time of Georgetown's founding several American colleges were already operating on a fairly sound basis, there is no hint that John Carroll or any other person responsible for the future of a Catholic college turned to them for teachers. Instead they looked toward Europe and importuned their

---

Co., 1915); and J. A. Burns, *Catholic Education: A Study of Conditions* (New York, Longmans, Green & Co., 1917), pp. 68–75, 162–168.

[3] See Noah Porter, *The American Colleges and the American Public* (New Haven, Charles C. Chatfield & Co., 1870), chapter 4; Mary L. Smallwood, *An Historical Study of Examinations and Grading Systems in Early American Universities* (Cambridge, Mass., Harvard University Press, 1935), pp. 44–56; and Francis Wayland, *Thoughts on the Present College System* (Boston, Gould, Kendall and Lincoln, 1842), pp. 36–40.

[4] Orestes A. Brownson, "Catholic Schools and Education," *Brownson's Quarterly Review*, 3 (January, 1862), 66–85; and the Pastoral Letter of 1866 in Guilday, *The National Pastorals*, pp. 189–191.

[5] Michael J. Kelly and James M. Kirwin, *History of Mt. St. Mary's Seminary of the West* (Cincinnati, Keating and Co., 1894), pp. 9–19.

[6] See Erbacher, *op. cit.,* pp. 79–83.

friends and acquaintances there to encourage young clergymen to come to America and seek positions as teachers in Catholic colleges. We know how Carroll conducted recruitment campaigns for teachers during the entire period of his association with Georgetown; inevitably he concentrated on Europe, England especially.[7] Quite frequently he was disappointed, for neither his friends nor the persons whom they contacted shared Carroll's vision of service in an American Catholic college "as an opportunity for infinite service to the cause of God and his Church."[8]

In conducting his search for a president, an activity occupying a considerable part of his time between Georgetown's founding and the beginning of teaching, Carroll generated an attitude toward college teaching destined to prevail throughout the foundational period—one that saw the president not only as the chief administrator of the school but the principal teacher as well. Thus, despite Carroll's efforts to recruit a good faculty to supplement the work of the principal teacher, he left an indelible impression that the president was the single-handed conductor of all college business. But while Carroll's attitudes toward both college administration and teaching tended to achieve permanence as a collegiate way of acting, they at the same time conceal his determination to have a highly competent staff of teachers at young Georgetown. And on this point Carroll was atypical. His own academic experiences as a student and teacher in Europe had left him with a profound understanding of the responsibilities of an academic institution, and it is probably fair to say that he was never fully satisfied with the appointments made either to the presidency of Georgetown or to its faculty. Still, his correspondence shows him to have been a realistic man, fully aware that some of his aspirations would have to be compromised in the pioneer college.

In chronicling the endeavors of Carroll to staff Georgetown, and in assessing his attitudes toward the duties of a college faculty, we run the risk of overemphasizing the institutional side of Georgetown's development. Clearly Georgetown's history alone is incapable of giving us all the data we need to reconstruct the early history of Catholic colleges in the United States. But another aspect of this is worth our attention : Georgetown was regarded as the principal Catholic college of the United States during the entire formative period, not just because it was the first college founded, but also because it was probably the best school; and Catholic colleges subsequent to Georgetown looked to her for their model.[9] Perhaps Carroll

[7] Daley, *op. cit.*, pp. 60–65; and Guilday, *The Life and Times of John Carroll*, pp. 790–800.

[8] Quoted in Daley, *op. cit.*, p. 61.

[9] For example, see Walter J. Meagher and William J. Grattan, *The Spires of Fenwick: A History of the College of the Holy Cross, 1843–1963* (New York, Vantage Press, 1966), pp. 103, 120–121.

anticipated this, and it may explain his scrupulous attention to the school's progress even when his association with Georgetown became somewhat remote.[10]

Because Carroll's ideals were high, he was often critical of the men appointed to conduct the school's affairs. In some respects Georgetown's first historians did Carroll a considerable disservice by perpetuating the myth that he was fully satisfied with the school's day-to-day operations,[11] but recent, careful histories have been more revealing.[12] For example, Carroll was especially critical of Bishop Leonard Neale, whom he had appointed to the presidency, and referred to Neale as being incapable of governing a college.[13] All in all, he thought the appointment was a mistake; but in view of Neale's episcopal status it would have been extraordinary to correct the error. Neale, we know, had an antediluvian attitude toward college study; he regarded college life as a time for the inculcation of good monastic discipline, appropriate, perhaps, to a seminary or monastery, but inconsistent with academic standards and ideals. It was Carroll himself, not the teachers or the students at Georgetown, who speculated about the value of a college course, dominated by routine pedagogic techniques and rigid institutional canons restrictive of personal freedom, for young men expected to take their places in the world, either as clerics or laymen, and combat all kinds of errors, vices, and moral challenges.[14] He advanced the educational proposition, one unheeded by Catholic colleges during the greater part of the nineteenth century, that youth cannot be equipped to take a responsible place in the world by being insulated scholastically from the realities of life.

Even if Carroll's personal academic standards had been low, he would have had difficulty in obtaining teachers for Georgetown; and thus he is doomed to appear historically in a picture of faculty qualifications bordering on inadequacy and, sometimes, incompetence. In pre-Civil War Catholic colleges, whether conducted as diocesan institutions or as a religious community's apostolic endeavor, about thirty percent of the teachers were imported from Europe;[15] in the long run this may have been a mistake, for it served to portray the Catholic college as a foreign enclave at a

---

[10] Guilday, *The Life and Times of John Carroll,* pp. 795–798.

[11] See John Gilmary Shea, *A History of Georgetown College: Memorial of the First Century* (New York, P. F. Collier, 1891), pp. 15–18; and James S. Easby-Smith, *Georgetown University* (New York, The Lewis Publishing Co., 1907), I, 36–40.

[12] Daley, *op. cit.,* pp. 112–113.

[13] *Ibid.,* p. 114.

[14] Guilday, *The Life and Times of John Carroll,* pp. 800–801.

[15] Cassidy, *op. cit.,* pp. 83–84; Power, *A History of Catholic Higher Education in the United States,* p. 90; Thébaud, *Forty Years in the United States,* pp. 331–332; and *A Sketch of Gonzaga College From Its Foundation in 1812 till the Celebration of the Diamond Jubilee in 1896* (Washington, Gonzaga College, 1897).

time when a high premium was being given to native Americanism.[16]
Yet, on the other hand, it would be demoralizing to consider the stature
of Catholic college faculties of this period if they had been without cadres
of reasonably competent teachers and scholars emigrating from Europe
to staff the colleges.[17] In staffing colleges, religious communities usually
had the best resources. Besides, they could borrow men capable of teaching certain classes from other provinces or religious houses—something
a bishop could seldom do for a diocesan college—or transfer religious
confreres from Europe to brief assignments in their colleges. This historical
fact explains why almost every bishop who founded a college tried
at some time or another to interest a religious community in assuming its
control. Occasionally a religious community accepted a bishop's invitation
when the prospects for supplying teaching personnel from the diocese were
bad, but in general, especially with the Jesuits, religious orders were reluctant
to assume responsibility for a college unless they knew they could solve
the problem of academic manpower.[18] Even with these good intentions,
they often involved themselves in scholastic adventures which drained their
resources of teaching personnel and required them to spread the talents of
their best men too thinly.[19]

While, in retrospect, some of these examples of a qualified teaching
faculty for colleges may be impressive, and from time to time we may find
a person associated with the colleges expressing opinions on the subject
which justify our confidence in the assumption that Catholic colleges had
minimum standards of faculty competence, dwelling on this phase of
faculty history is patently unprofitable. In the first place, even Carroll's
determined exertions to have good teachers at Georgetown was an
unemulated exercise, and in the second place, since most early colleges
were really houses of religious doctrine and moral formation, they were
insensitive to standards that should have obtained in authentic institutions
of higher learning. With these preconceptions affecting a college's academic
personality, what college could demand from its priest-teachers high scholarship or even conventional pedagogical qualifications? It is clearly impossible

[16] See Orestes A. Brownson, "Native Americanism," in *Works,* X, 32–52; and
John Tracy Ellis, *The Life of James Cardinal Gibbons, Archbishop of Baltimore,
1834–1921* (Milwaukee, Bruce Publishing Co., 1952), II, 71–80.

[17] See Thomas Hughes, "Educational Convoys to Europe in the Olden Times,"
American Ecclesiastical Review, XXIX (1903), 24–39; and Erbacher, *op. cit.,*
pp. 79–80.

[18] See G. J. Garraghan, *The Jesuits of the Middle United States,* III, 247–248.

[19] See, for example, Anon., *A Catholic History of Alabama and the Floridas* (New
York, P. J. Kenedy and Sons, 1908), pp. 297–300; Willis G. Clark, *History of
Education in Alabama,* U. S. Bureau of Education Bulletin No. 8, 1889, pp. 188, 193;
and Michael J. Kenny, *Catholic Culture in Alabama: The Centenary Story of Spring
Hill College* (New York, America Press, 1931), pp. 68–73.

to conduct any teacher-by-teacher historical evaluation of early Catholic college faculties, or to muster much direct evidence pointing to lack of faculty quality; yet there is an abundance of circumstantial evidence implying that most teachers in Catholic colleges did not match the qualifications of professors in nonCatholic colleges of the country, and that they took their legitimate academic role somewhat less seriously than their nonCatholic counterparts.[20]

This was due, we should think, to a number of assumptions inseparable from the Catholic attitude distilled in this country toward higher learning.[21] If higher education was less than a serious intellectual business, scholarly pedigree and a relentless pursuit of truth, using scholarly implements, were pointless; if, moreover, the academic objective of the college was to prepare boys for ecclesiastical life, the usual requirements of higher learning could be modified to suit this more limited purpose. Such attitudes explain why so many clerical teachers in the Catholic college were preoccupied with clerical duties away from the college, and while they were at the college conducting classes could be more interested in the boys' moral and religious development than in their learning.

Still, some teachers, usually European imports, the evidence suggests, both understood the purposes of higher learning and were equipped to lead boys along proper academic avenues.[22] Why did these teachers miss becoming true ornaments of Catholic academic life? Two factors reduced their effectiveness: a majority of imported teachers found idiomatic English unmanageable and were thus separated from their students by a serious language barrier;[23] even in the absence of this barrier, the experience of European teachers was so different from the situation they met in American colleges that their truer, and sometimes more rigid, academic orientation rendered them ineffective with boys whose intellectual ideals were more pragmatic than classical. On a broader level, the committed European teacher with good academic credentials felt out-of-place in the American Catholic college: he could not understand it, nor could his colleagues and students fathom a scholarly determination born and nurtured in European universities. On the whole, despite good credentials and the college's willing-

---

[20] Compare Erbacher, *op. cit.*, pp. 79–83, with Charles F. Thwing, *A History of Higher Education in America* (New York, D. Appleton-Century Co., 1906), chap. 14.

[21] See Francis P. Cassidy, *Catholic College Foundations and Development in the United States: 1677–1850* (Washington, Catholic University of America, 1924), p. 94.

[22] See Thébaud, *Forty Years in the United States*, pp. 331–332.

[23] *Ibid.*, p. 331; Arthur J. Hope, *Notre Dame, One Hundred Years* (Notre Dame, Ind., University of Notre Dame Press, 1943), p. 26; and Oswald Moosmüller, *Bonifaz Wimmer, Erzabt von St. Vincent in Pennsylvanien* (New York, Benziger Bros., 1891), p. 78.

ness to publicize the appointment of European scholars to their staffs,[24] such teachers in early Catholic colleges enjoyed only limited success.

When the colleges organized their first curricula, as we shall see,[25] they tended to limit the languages taught, except for Latin and some Greek —although the less said about Greek the better—in order to conduct what they believed was a pure classical course. When modern languages were introduced—French, German, and Spanish—they were listed as extras, or subjects for study outside the regular requirements of the curriculum.[26] But it was not long before the pressures from a college's clientele recommended that modern languages be included in the regular curriculum. And then, because the colleges had so many foreign teachers on their faculties, men entirely fluent in their native tongues, they announced with pretensions of academic superiority that these languages were being taught by teachers to whom the language was native.[27] In this they again missed the real academic point, and mistakenly assumed that because a person spoke a language he had impeccable qualifications to teach it as a college course.

If college managers were too often insensitive to lack of quality, incomplete scholarship, unready students, and poorly formulated educational objectives, some teachers did not share their immunity. A few, we know, resigned in despair; others, sensing inevitable frustration in the colleges' erratic academic climate, simply refused appointments to Catholic college faculties.[28] Still others, forsaking the college, remained in seminary teaching where, with somewhat better-prepared, more serious and professionally-minded students, they were able to salvage their academic ideals. These were hard years for college teachers, and there were no signs anywhere of a change in the teaching atmosphere : certain religious communities engaged in the business of education despairing of better times ahead, simply abandoned their schools and colleges to turn to more fruitful religious labor.[29]

[24] For example, see Erbacher, *op. cit.*, p. 80.

[25] See pp. 122–152.

[26] While this was usually true of the early colleges, it should be noted that modern languages were freed from the impediment of an extra charge toward the close of the period. St. Louis University offered French and German at no extra charge, according to its *Catalogue of 1879–1880*, p. 22. German, for example, was a required course at the College of the Sacred Heart (Wisconsin) (*Catalogue of 1881–1882*, p. 11) and at Canisius College (*Catalogue of 1895–1896*, p. 6). Latin was the language of instruction in logic, metaphysics, and ethics classes at Loyola College (Baltimore) (*Catalogue of 1889–1890*, p. 3).

[27] Kenny, *op. cit.*, p. 70; and Erbacher, *op. cit.*, pp. 94–95. The *1889–1890 Catalogue of Sacred Heart College*, Denver, carried this statement: "German, Spanish, French, and Italian are taught, each by a Professor whose vernacular it is" (p. 3).

[28] Power, *A History of Catholic Higher Education in the United States*, p. 91; Thébaud, *Forty Years in the United States*, pp. 331–332; and Meline and McSweeny, *op. cit.*, pp. 159–161.

[29] Herbermann, *op. cit.*, pp. 50–54; Edward A. Fitzpatrick, "The Foundations of

An eye-witness account of teaching-learning standards in Catholic colleges of the 1840s has been left us in a memoir by the famous and learned Jesuit, Augustus Thébaud. He reports on conditions at St. Mary's College in Kentucky, but, at the same time, invests his description with a degree of generalization which implies that St. Mary's practices were common in other Catholic colleges of the country. At St. Mary's most faculty members were French and had brought their French educational experience and teaching techniques with them; they had, he said, a decided preference for a thorough training in Latin grammar, which meant not only a study of Latin language and literature, but a sturdy confidence in the educational value of long Latin compositions, which, on a purely pedagogic level, involved students in translating themes from English to Latin. When St. Mary's teachers discovered their students were incapable of meeting such traditional standards of linguistic exactitude, they improvised and, in the end, considering the students' general lack of preparation for college work, did the best they could.

To bridge the gap between student readiness to learn and curriculum expectations frequently became impossible, even with the introduction of effective remedial techniques. At that point these teachers, Thébaud reports, refused to acknowledge or be influenced by nonCatholic college methods of curricular organization, and adamantly prescribed preparatory studies which were to be coupled with their college course. They were totally ignorant, he says, of the four-year college course which led to graduation in nonCatholic colleges; when they were forced by circumstances to look for models to follow outside their own institution and beyond their own educational traditions, they imitated St. Joseph's College in Bardstown,[30] only twenty miles away, where the "custom was to receive all boys who presented themselves, classify them as well as possible, keep them as long as they could, and grant them their degrees when they refused to stay."[31]

This example of college operation, at first horrifying to Jesuits unwilling to sacrifice French notions of academic seriousness or to jettison the entire teaching tradition of the *Ratio Studiorum,* nevertheless offered the best chance of an accommodation with educational reality. In the end St. Mary's did its best and organized a college course that, according to Thébaud, never lasted more than three years. He adds : "the programme of studies printed in our prospectus was sufficiently long and fair; but it was understood that

St. Mary's College," *Catholic Educational Review,* XXVII (March, 1929), 124–134; A. Hauber, *Oaks and Acorns: St. Ambrose College* (Davenport, Ia., St. Ambrose College, 1951), pp. 9–19; Walter H. Hill, *Historical Sketches of St. Louis University* (St. Louis, Patrick Fox, 1879), pp. 5–10; Faherty, *op. cit.,* pp. 8–12; and Hoffmann, *op. cit.,* pp. 25–36.

[30] See W. J. Howlett, "The Early Days of St. Joseph's College at Bardstown, Kentucky," *Illinois Catholic Historical Review* (April, 1922), pp. 372–380.

[31] Thébaud, *Forty Years in the United States,* pp. 331–332.

this should be carried out when possible."[32] Thus we learn two things from
Thébaud's candid account : first, something about the standards set for a
college course in the 1840s, and second, the hazards of putting complete
confidence in the colleges' announcements about their courses of study, the
standards enforced, their academic objectives, or their faculty qualifications,
because such public statements were often a camouflage for the actual
conditions.

Distinguishing the collegiate ideal from the reality and recognizing that
by hardly any stretch of the imagination could these schools be called true
institutions of higher learning, bishops and religious superiors felt dispensed
from applying rigorous tests of quality to the men assigned as college
teachers. They were, of course, more selective in appointing presidents
than mere teachers; in the long run, content to assign men to college
faculties who could administer discipline judiciously, they were almost
totally indifferent to scholarly aptitude or ability, which could, under the
circumstances, be labelled academic affectation or pedantic ornamentation.[33]

Our first impression of nineteenth-century Catholic-college faculties is
that most teachers were priests. This was the ideal, of course, and most
bishops and religious superiors assigned priests to college teaching whenever
possible.[34] Sometimes, however, the ideal was out of reach, so bishops and
superiors did the next best thing; they used seminarians—young men studying for the priesthood in seminaries connected with colleges—to staff college
classrooms.[35] When neither priests nor seminarians were available, they considered, as a last resort, appointing laymen to faculties. But this was always
emergency action, for laymen, whose credentials of doctrine and spirituality
were assumed to be doubtful, could be utilized only in English instruction
or other equally unimportant subjects.[36] Normally it was expedient to
appoint seminarians, obviously superior to laymen in that they were doctrinally orthodox, morally sound, willing to follow directions of superiors, and
inexpensive. Mount St. Mary's, for example, probably owed its continued
existence to the fact that seminarians, supported through seminary studies by
bishops, could be assigned to college teaching duties without adding to the
instructional costs of the college.[37] During its years as a diocesan college,
Spring Hill regularly used seminarians as college teachers, as did Mount St.
Mary's of the West, and practically every other Catholic college associated

[32] *Ibid.*

[33] See Kenny, *op. cit.*, pp. 180–182.

[34] See Erbacher, *op. cit.*, pp. 73–80; Cassidy, *op. cit.*, pp. 82–97; and Power,
A History of Catholic Higher Education in the United States, pp. 92–93.

[35] See *Sketch of Gonzaga College*, pp. 7–9; Garraghan, *The Jesuits of the Middle
United States*, I, 304; and Kelly and Kirwin, *op. cit.*, p. 93.

[36] See Meline and McSweeny, *op. cit.*, I, 360–361; and Daley, *op. cit.*, p. 74.

[37] Meline and McSweeny, *op. cit.*, I, 159–161.

with a seminary.[38] In at least one college, Gonzaga, in Washington, D. C., seminarians formed the entire college teaching complement and were thus supported through their seminary studies.[39]

Faculty quality in formative-period Catholic colleges therefore left much to be desired. But if the schools were elementary and secondary rather than collegiate in character, it was probably a fair enough arrangement to use seminarians as teachers when academically-prepared priests were unavailable. And surely one must remember the financial relief the colleges enjoyed by resorting to such measures. Yet what can be praised, or tolerated, as a realistic response to the exigencies of the pioneer period, can also be blamed when these institutions outgrew their formative periods, became more fully collegiate in rank, and were better equipped financially to recruit qualified teachers. Their failure to improve the quality of their faculties is a matter of record; they chose instead to convert temporary expedients into regular practice and then, in order to satisfy their public, and possibly their own institutional consciences, created a theoretic justification to support the action taken.[40] They began by questioning the importance of academic degrees for college teachers (believing, no doubt, that the seminaries, not of status legally to grant degrees, were satisfactory substitutes for a university preparation of college teachers), then doubted the worth of actual teaching experience, which, if realistically applied as a qualification would have eliminated most seminarians from college faculties, and finally refused to honor reasonable and balanced teaching loads for their teachers.[41]

If spokesmen on faculty standards accurately represented the mentality of the colleges, they were undisturbed when teachers disappeared from school to supply missions on holidays, at week-ends, and in vacation periods, for they refused to admit that such extramural spiritual duties interfered with teaching quality. One commentator, writing about the faculty at Spring Hill College, says the teachers never "'permitted them [the outside activities] to interfere with their educational work.'"[42] And he goes on to maintain that, while modern college association officers would be greatly disturbed by the lack of leisure early college teachers had for class preparation and research—being assigned as many as five hours teaching a day—this heavy burden did not trouble a nineteenth-century Catholic college teacher. The same writer alleges that the old-time teacher came from a "sturdier race," and that an infusion of zeal and spirit nerved him "to double or treble

---

[38] See Kelly and Kirwin, *op. cit.,* pp. 180–185; Kenny, *op. cit.,* pp. 68–73; and Erbacher, *op. cit.,* pp. 79–82.

[39] *Sketch of Gonzaga College,* p. 33.

[40] See, for example, James F. Loughlin, "The Higher and Lower Education of the American Priesthood," *The American Catholic Quarterly Review,* XV (January, 1890), 101–122; and Ward, *op. cit.,* pp. 273–282.

[41] Kenny, *op. cit.,* pp. 180–182.

[42] *Ibid.,* p. 180.

the work of our moderns with impunity."[43] And then he avers that because teachers in these colleges dealt with the fundamentals of education, with principles and truths not requiring determined study and research, they were able to conduct their classes without the kind of preparation needed by less fortunate members of the nonCatholic academic community. And finally, he invokes the strength and light of God's grace, which somehow transformed marginally-qualified teachers to a state of intellectual omniscience. In the end, apparent shortcomings are metamorphosized into virtue: "the results speak loudly for the effectiveness of their methods; and facts are stronger than theories."[44]

In the last analysis, however, faculty standards, qualifications, and duties needed more than rhetorical justification, and the historian can only be amused by statements that, while not so intended, confirm the weaknesses of nineteenth-century Catholic college faculties. What they lacked —and even the most spirited defenses affirm some lack—was, some say, counteracted by the deep absorption students had in their studies, "and the loss of distinguished professors occasioned no interruption in the courses nor of the quality of teachings."[45] These romanticized versions of Catholic college life must never be taken at face value, for neither the determination of the best teachers, the rigid moral environment of the schools, nor the high assessment of student motives for study can make these accounts innocent of wishful thinking. And while commentators may be spared reprimand for their piety toward institutions with which they had close associations, they cannot, on the other hand, be absolved from charges of faulty judgment: there must always be a distinction between good public relations and authentic history.

Besides priests and seminarians, the categories obviously preferred as teachers, colleges sometimes assigned religious brothers to direct the studies of boys not yet ready for college classes, but who were allowed to remain at the college because there were no other schools.[46] These courses were clearly elementary. When brothers were unavailable for, or were incapable of, elementary teaching, some colleges announced, as did Notre Dame in 1864, that younger students were being taught by "highly competent female teachers."[47] The female teachers were religious sisters who, during the formative years, before Catholic women's colleges came into existence, maintained an academic relationship with colleges in this way. Yet brothers

43 *Ibid.*, p. 182.
44 *Ibid.*
45 *Ibid.*, p. 259.
46 See Brother Constantius, "The Christian Brothers in the United States," *Catholic Educational Review*, I (April, 1911), 313–323; and Brother Angelus Gabriel, *The Christian Brothers in the United States, 1848–1948* (New York, Delcan X. McMullen, 1948).
47 *Twentieth Catalogue of the University of Notre Dame*, p. 13.

founded colleges of their own—fifteen during the formative period (although none before 1859), of which four were permanent[48]—and, in general, their schools never needed to apologize for their quality to colleges founded and conducted by bishops or religious communities of priests. Brother-conducted colleges, it must be admitted, suffered from the fact that Catholic people automatically invested priest-teachers with superiority over all other teachers, so that making a brothers' college flourish was a hard task. In addition, brothers' colleges lacked the abundance of resources available to colleges wherein priests and seminarians were members of the religious community.[49]

Neither religious brothers nor sisters exerted any significant impact on the standards or quality of teaching during the formative years of Catholic colleges, and, as a matter of fact, neither did laymen, although the latter were more numerous on college faculties than either of the former. Following Erbacher's data on faculty composition,[50] we find twenty-six laymen among 240 teachers in twenty-five Catholic colleges in 1850. About one lay teacher for each college is an unimpressive statistic, yet it must be weighed against a per college teaching staff of fewer than ten. The number of lay teachers in thirty-three Catholic colleges in 1855 rose to fifty-five, with a total teaching complement of 313; thus the lay-clerical ratio was slightly altered. By 1860, thirty-three colleges had a total faculty of 303; sixty-three were laymen.[51] In 1872, with the formative period nearing termination, fifty-five Catholic colleges employed the services of 677 faculty members, of whom eighty were laymen;[52] and in 1882, fifty-six Catholic colleges reported a total faculty of 714; 427 were religious, 225 were unclassified, sixty-two were laymen.[53] As the years passed in the formative period, Catholic colleges must have been successful in adding clerical personnel to their teaching staffs, because, although the gross number of laymen on Catholic college faculties increased, the ratio of laymen to clerics decreased.

The old assumption, then, that the solution to the faculty issue in Catholic colleges was found in the appointment of lay teachers is only partially valid.[54] During the formative period, although conditions changed in later periods and laymen eventually played a more important part in college teaching, the layman's role was insignificant; so the period began and so it ended. One can hardly avoid the conclusion that laymen were

[48] See Power, *A History of Catholic Higher Education in the United States,* pp. 333–336.

[49] See Thomas J. Donaghy, *Conceived in Crisis: A History of La Salle College, 1863–1965* (Philadelphia, La Salle College, 1966), pp. 10–33.

[50] Erbacher, *op. cit.,* p. 79.

[51] *Ibid.*

[52] *Report of the United States Commissioner of Education, 1872,* pp. 762–781.

[53] *Report of the United States Commissioner of Education, 1882,* pp. 596–630.

[54] Erbacher, *op. cit.,* p. 79; and Power, *A History of Catholic Higher Education in the United States,* p. 95.

welcomed to Catholic college faculties only when clerics were unavailable, and we doubt whether qualifications often entered the picture. Still, during these frantic years clerical supply was short, so we may suppose that almost every college of the formative period had at least one layman on its faculty. It would be desirable to know something about his status once he had an appointment.

To begin with, one must use the term *faculty* liberally when applying it to Catholic-college teachers during this period; and in this connection there is no reason to suppose that lay teachers were the objects of personal discrimination : their treatment was nearly identical, except where clerical duties were involved, with that accorded clerical colleagues. Bound by the same regulations with respect to official duties and all the activities both inside and outside the college (although not having made religious vows), they were required to live in the school and conform to all religious exercises and obligations. A lay teacher, moreover, was permitted to leave the college only with permission; his candle was to be extinguished by nine o'clock in the evening; alcoholic beverages and tobacco were forbidden. Violation of any regulation concerning his deportment brought a fine (a deduction from his salary) or summary dismissal.[55] Under no circumstances could he claim tenure : whenever a clerical replacement was available his position was pre-empted; in any case, he was retained on the college staff only as long as was necessary. And, yet, despite the unenviable status and poor conditions associated with laymen, the history of later faculty development in Catholic colleges of the United States is mainly a chronicle of the appointment of qualified laymen to teaching positions, although to believe that such appointments were a reflection of formative-period policy is to indulge in fanciful anticipation.

Undoubtedly, however, the seeds of the later progress are found in the first period, where the colleges discovered, usually to their dismay, that using laymen was unavoidable.[56] Still, although bowing to the inevitable, they rejected total capitulation and withheld from laymen a faculty status equal to that of priests and seminarians. Policy was more important than the personalities involved : the nature of the Catholic college—a religious agency first and foremost—prescribed an unenviable role for the lay teacher. Besides, administrators felt uncomfortable with subordinates over whom they lacked complete control; and parents who sent their sons to college were unhappy with nonclerical teachers. All in all, this was a bad omen, and qualified laymen (always few in number in these colleges) were usually and understandably hesitant about attaching themselves to institutions where they would always be regarded as subordinates and where opportunities

[55] *Ibid.*

[56] See G. J. Garraghan, *The Jesuits of the Middle United States,* III, 247–248; and Ward, *op. cit.,* pp. 280–282.

for professional advancement were either unlikely or impossible. Some laymen were former seminarians who used college teaching as an exit from the seminary; others were prospective seminarians wanting to sample life in a religious community before taking a more final step toward clerical life. History records few instances of laymen free from personal vested interests seeking appointments to faculties of nineteenth-century Catholic colleges.[57]

The few who did brighten the picture somewhat, and give us further information about faculty standards, duties, and the status of lay teachers. As late as 1884, the situation so far reported remained largely undisturbed if we may judge from the testimony of Charles Warren Stoddard, who in this year considered accepting a teaching position at Notre Dame. Apparently knowing enough about Catholic colleges to make him cautious, Stoddard framed some preliminary questions and began by asking about his duties as professor of English Literature. He wanted to know how many classes he would be expected to teach, how many students each class would have, and how old the students would be. In addition, he asked what would be expected of him when he was not engaged in class teaching, or, as he put it, "would he be his own master?"[58] And when vacation periods came would he be permitted to leave the school to visit, travel, or do as he pleased? Suspecting a rather rigid regimen in the college, he inquired further what hours were expected, "when to rise, when to go to Mass, when breakfast, recreate, etc.?"[59] Near the end of a long list of questions, he asked if he would be free to write friends, and to receive letters from them, without any of the correspondence being inspected by the "Rev. President or the Rev. General, or anyone but myself?"[60] After exhausting this line of inquiry about his duties as a teacher and the general conditions of life at the college, he felt it only fair to tell the Notre Dame officers of administration something about himself and to give them some insight into his confirmed habits: "I have been," he wrote, "for some years what is known as a free liver. I have taken wines and liquors with my friends whenever I felt like it and have sometimes taken more than was good for me . . . I am a smoker—but I have never in my life chewed. I have been through the pipe and cigar stages, and now smoke only cigarettes."[61] Finally, he indicated his willingness to prepare for the "chair" of English Literature and, assuming he would have freedom to pursue his own interests unencumbered by school

---

[57] Erbacher names a few; see Erbacher, *op. cit.*, pp. 81–85; also, Henry A. Brann, "St. Mary's College, Wilmington, Delaware," United States Catholic Historical Society, *Records and Studies*, VII (June, 1914), 81–84.

[58] Charles Warren Stoddard to Fr. Daniel Hudson, September 12, 1884, University of Notre Dame Archives.

[59] *Ibid.*

[60] *Ibid.*

[61] *Ibid.*

policy, to accept an appointment to the Notre Dame faculty; but he was careful to add that he "could accept nothing outside of [teaching] in your University." [62]

Stoddard, we must realize, was considering a faculty appointment to Notre Dame after it, along with most Catholic colleges, had adopted the nonCatholic college practice of specializing professorships. Thus, in the 1880s we find teachers spending their time upon one subject. But throughout the formative period this was not the way faculty time had been utilized. Teachers were assigned to a matriculating class and they stayed with this class, often being its only teacher, for the entire college course.[63] In the earliest colleges, of which Georgetown is a good illustration, only clergymen were allowed to be class teachers, because they alone were expected to be permanent appointees; laymen were used to handle the "extras," or classes outside the regular curriculum, such as rudiments, drawing, fencing, music, and, sometimes, English.[64] In such roles the weight of responsibility was light and it was really unnecessary to make searching inquiries into laymen's academic qualifications if their functions were to be only on the fringe of teaching. To put it succinctly, the layman teaching "extras" was no better than his subject and a lack of respect for what he taught was reflected in his salary.

John Carroll, whose attitude toward faculty standards was unexcelled by anyone of his status, assigned the layman teaching English at Georgetown to a low rung on the academic ladder and he justified this action with something besides the low status of English teaching : "But as it cannot be expected that the meer (sic) teacher of English will be a candidate for H. Orders, it is proposed to give him £80 [then about $200] per annum.[65] Even Carroll, we see, with better than average ideals of college teaching, was captive to the clerical myth that a college teacher must be either a prospective or an ordained priest. At this point, early in Catholic college history, we may be right in believing that we have found the origin of the double standard applicable to clerics and laymen on Catholic college faculties.

If lay teachers lacked certification for full faculty membership in these citadels of learning and were thus barred from teaching subjects in the regular curriculum or conducting a class through college study, their talents could nevertheless be utilized for things outside teaching where the presence of clerical dignity was unnecessary or unseemly. At Mt. St. Mary's in Mary-

62 *Ibid.*

63 William J. McGucken, *The Jesuits and Education* (Milwaukee, Bruce Publishing Co., 1932), pp. 233–234; and Faherty, *op. cit.,* p. 114; for exceptions to this practice, see G. J. Garraghan, *The Jesuits of the Middle United States,* III, 210; and Taaffe, *op. cit.,* p. 73.

64 Power, *A History of Catholic Higher Education in the United States,* p. 97.

65 Daley, *op. cit.,* p. 56.

land, for example, a certain Ernest Lagarde, listed as a member of the 1869 faculty, was commissioned by the president to collect past-due bills from former students. According to the record, about thirty-five thousand dollars were due from such sources, and Lagarde, spending an entire summer as a bill collector, returned with only seventy-five dollars to show for his efforts.[66]

Laymen, however, if they found no place in Catholic colleges either as professors in the classical course or in outside functions, such as bill collecting, were more frequently employed as teachers of commercial subjects. Commercial curricula were introduced as adjuncts to regular college studies;[67] and despite what clerical college managers thought about commercial and English courses (it is an understatement to say they were unimpressed by them) the colleges were unable to discontinue such courses once started, or to refuse to introduce them, if only because so many students wanted precisely such training from college study.[68] The colleges, then, unable to ignore such practical curricula, added or continued them, but separated them carefully from classical studies.[69] This put further strain on already limited teaching resources. In Jesuit colleges, where the Society's rules prohibited its members from teaching commercial subjects, this inevitably meant employing laymen as teachers.[70] Still, commercial courses lacked

---

[66] Meline and McSweeny, *op. cit.,* II, 85.

[67] Meagher, *op. cit.,* p. 36; and *Catalogue of St. Francis Institute, 1882–1883,* p. 1.

[68] Taaffe, *op. cit.,* p. 74; B. J. Lenoue, *The Historical Development of the Curriculum of the University of Notre Dame* (Notre Dame, Ind., University of Notre Dame, 1933), p. 30; and see Erbacher, *op. cit.,* pp. 90–91.

[69] G. J. Garraghan, *The Jesuits of the Middle United States,* III, 247–248; Taaffe, *op. cit.,* p. 74; Meagher, *op. cit.,* p. 56; and Daley, *op. cit.,* p. 225. College catalogues give a fairly precise picture of the commercial course: *Catalogue of Xavier College, 1879–1880,* pp. 12–13; *Catalogue of Marquette College, 1881–1882,* p. 5, where the commercial course is described as "necessarily inferior to the classical;" *Catalogue of St. John's College* (Fordham), *1890–1891,* pp. 12–13; *Catalogue of Gonzaga College* (D. C.), *1889–1890,* p. 6, wherein students who are unable to handle the classical course are allowed to take the commercial; *Catalogue of Spring Hill College, 1889–1890,* p. 66, where degrees were withheld from commercial course students; *Catalogue of St. Ignatius College* (Calif.), *1889–1890,* p. 6, where degrees were awarded only from the classical course; *Catalogue of Santa Clara College, 1889–1890,* p. 4, where only a certificate was given for commercial courses; *Catalogue of Canisius College, 1889–1890,* p. 2, where a commercial course was worth a certificate but not a degree; *Catalogue of St. John's College* (Fordham), *1890–1891,* p. 12; *Catalogue of St. Ignatius College* (Chicago), *1895–1896,* p. 20; *Catalogue of St. Louis University, 1895–1896,* pp. 27–29; *Catalogue of Marquette College, 1895–1896,* p. 11; *Catalogue of Detroit College, 1895–1896,* pp. 24–27; *Catalogue of St. Ignatius College* (Cleveland), *1889–1890,* p. 3; and *Catalogue of St. Louis University, 1879–1880,* pp. 20–22. St. Francis Institution handled the issue this way, according to the *Catalogue of 1881–1882,* p. 5: "There are two distinct Courses of Instruction—the *Classical* and the *Commercial,* though for the present, both Courses are taught jointly."

[70] See R. N. Hamilton, *The Story of Marquette* (Milwaukee, Marquette University

collegiate caliber, so laymen responsible for teaching them were denied the status of faculty members.[71] At many Catholic colleges—St. Louis is a good example—the financial burden added by the employment of lay teachers for commercial subjects led religious superiors and college presidents to examine the impact on the college of eliminating commercial courses altogether.[72] Some colleges took a calculated risk, simplified their curricula, and offered only the classical course;[73] others discovered the commercial course, despite the financial burden of paying nonclerical teachers, too important and too profitable to drop.[74] No college was able to ignore the effect of losing up to half its students as the aftermath of the deletion of the commercial course. How long could so-called academic purity be sustained? In the end, usually around 1880, Catholic colleges found they could cope with the fiscal burden imposed by broader programs of study. With this issue resolved late in the developmental period, they admitted the commercial course to full collegiate status and, as a corollary, laymen became fully accredited members of Catholic college faculties.[75] But before the advent of this period, a few laymen had labored for nearly a century with inferior and unenviable standing in Catholic colleges. For the most part, however, they had been unusually silent about their subordination—if, indeed, they recognized it—and with characteristic docility had ratified that dogmatic assumption in Catholic educational tradition that clergymen alone are fully commissioned educators of youth.

Natural bias against laymen in foundational-period Catholic colleges goes a long way toward explaining why their role was always limited and unimportant. And in this context it was never easy for laymen, almost accidentally associated with the colleges, to encourage students to follow academic careers. Apart from his own somewhat tarnished image, the lay teacher had other good reasons for demurring from recruiting lay colleagues. Yet this is only part of the picture, although admittedly an important part. Few Catholic laymen were qualified, according to then-current definitions,

Press, 1953), p. 273; and G. J. Garraghan, *The Jesuits of the Middle United States,* III, 247–248.

71 This is clear from the designations given to instructional personnel in the catalogues, where commercial teachers are listed as accessories. See Faherty, *op. cit.,* pp. 114, 293; and Donaghy, *op. cit.,* p. 18.

72 G. J. Garraghan, *The Jesuits of the Middle United States,* III, 247–250.

73 Erbacher, *op. cit.,* pp. 90–91.

74 G. J. Garraghan, *The Jesuits of the Middle United States,* III, 120; David R. Dunigan, A *History of Boston College* (Milwaukee, Bruce Publishing Co., 1947), p. 148; Irenaeus Herscher, "The History of St. Bonaventure University," *Franciscan Studies,* XI (September, December, 1951), 387–390; Thébaud, *Forty Years in the United States,* p. 350; and Kenny, *op. cit.,* p. 211.

75 Lenoue, *op. cit.,* p. 25.

to be class teachers,[76] and the colleges, in any case, could not afford them.[77] In this respect Catholic colleges were traveling familiar avenues : earlier American colleges had been faced with identical faculty problems and solved them much in the same way, by appointing ministers and prospective ministers to their staffs. By the time Georgetown College was founded nonCatholic colleges had made considerable progress in assembling professionally-qualified faculties, and in order to keep them intact were paying salaries from £150 to £200 a year; but Georgetown, according to Carroll's stated plan for faculty, was prepared to offer only £60 to £80 a year.[78] Such stipends failed to attract and retain men who expected to earn a living from college teaching; only clergymen with stole fees as subsistences or persons with additional sources of income could afford the luxury of an academic career. Throughout the formative period the salary picture remained unmodified. After the Civil War Mt. St. Mary's College paid a priest-teacher of metaphysics, ethics, and senior English a salary of twenty-five dollars a month; the professor of theology in the seminary attached to the school received a monthly salary of fifty dollars. A lay teacher at the same school at the same time was paid seven hundred dollars a year; and one year when enrollment decreased, his salary was reduced, without any notice, by two hundred dollars. His resignation, the only alternative in such a case, resulted in a restoration of the deduction, and the teacher stayed on at the college.[79]

Discouragements facing laymen interested in teaching in Catholic colleges had their origin, as we have said, partly in the lay and clerical attitudes toward education wherein teaching was an extension of the pulpit. The climate of Catholic colleges was simply unreceptive to lay teachers; yet, apart from this climate, other vexing obstacles regularly appeared : laymen were expected to gamble on their income and thus on the prospect of feeding and clothing their families decently. A decline in enrollment was regarded as justification for reducing salaries or, in some cases, dismissing unneeded teachers at a time of the school year when chances for other teaching employment were slight. But if some unexpected circumstance led to a sharp increase in student enrollment and teachers were asked to handle more than their normal class load, additional remuneration for extra work was out of the question. Risks were imposed on the persons least able to take them, but lay teachers had no choice. It is unnecessary, then, to discuss either the relevance or existence of tenure policies or disputes over their

[76] Faherty, *op. cit.,* p. 114.

[77] Erbacher, *op. cit.,* pp. 74–76.

[78] Daley, *op. cit.,* p. 39.

[79] Meline and McSweeny, *op. cit.,* II, 36–41. If the layman's salary appears to be comparatively high, one must remember that clerical teachers always received room and board as a perquisite. Laymen did not usually get such benefits.

application : according to college statutes no lay or clerical teacher had any legal claim on his position, and since laymen were considered entirely expendable they were always the first to go.[80]

The picture thus sketched of faculty qualifications and duties in colleges of the formative period differs from that in the usual institutional history —which tends to sell objectivity at discount and heaps praise on every move a college made—and it differs, too, from Erbacher's monograph wherein a less critical summary is given. Catholic college teachers, he wrote, "were on the whole excellent men. They had received a good education themselves, frequently abroad, and were well prepared for their tasks to which they devoted their entire life. There were many scholars among them, not only in theology and philosophy, but also in the languages and sciences, and not a few wrote textbooks which have come down to our own day and are still found in some classrooms. The laymen who taught at these colleges were generally highly trained men. About one third of them possessed an academic degree, usually the degree of Master of Arts."[81]

It is possible, of course, to accept Erbacher's assertion that Catholic college teachers were excellent men and, at the same time, entertain grave misgivings about their capacities as college instructors. Among religious communities, it is true, teachers with European educational backgrounds were common, but, as Thébaud pointed out,[82] some foreign teachers were unable to use English effectively, which should cast a doubt on their qualification for teaching boys who knew only English. Europe, moreover, did not continue indefinitely as a general training ground for Catholic college faculties, and we find that, with the exception of the promising seminarian or young priest sent abroad to complete his studies, most Catholic college teachers were young priests who remained at the college after ordination, or seminarians who had spent their entire teaching career thus far at the very college where they were both studying and teaching.[83] Besides, it is apodictically clear, most teachers, whether religious or lay, seldom spent any great length of time in college teaching. According to institutional histories, always excellent examples of apologetic literature wherein deficiences are never admitted if they can be explained away, impermanence was the most serious obstacle surrounding faculty growth and quality : three years was an extraordinarily long tenure for a priest at any

---

[80] See Erbacher, *op. cit.,* p. 80; Willis Nutting, "Catholic Higher Education in America," *New Blackfriars,* 32 (July, 1951), 340–344; Alexander Sigur, "Lay Cooperation with the Magisterium," *The Jurist,* XIII (July, 1953), 268–297; and Samuel K. Wilson, "Catholic College Education, 1900–1950," *Catholic School Journal,* 51 (April, 1951), 121–123.

[81] Erbacher, *op. cit.,* p. 82.

[82] Thébaud, *Forty Years in the United States,* pp. 331–332; and *Tenth Annual Catalogue of the University of Notre Dame, 1864,* p. 13.

[83] Power, *A History of Catholic Higher Education in the United States,* pp. 92–93.

college unless he belonged to the religious community, and a seminarian hardly ever devoted more than two years to teaching.[84] Even members of religious communities, although sometimes permanently attached to the community's colleges, may have been shifted regularly from one college to another and, indeed, from one function to another. With the exception of a handful, lay teachers appeared and disappeared annually.

Even in the most sympathetic interpretation of Catholic college history, our powers of imagination and invention are taxed to find men who could be termed scholars among over-worked and under-educated faculty members. The books noticed by Erbacher are small change in the history of American publishing; and the image of the colleges' modernity is tarnished by a report that some textbooks were still used a full hundred years after they were written.[85] Other testimony fails to confirm the classical nature of these books. And on the point of laymen being highly trained men, with about one-third having an academic degree,[86] all kinds of polite demurrals are possible. If we assume, however, that this statistic is accurate, we are left to interpret the meaning of a Master of Arts degree at a time when it was commonly conferred without any attention whatever to graduate courses, literary study, or scientific accomplishment. Most colleges in the early United States awarded master's degrees, but they did so without the formalities of course work, examinations, or dissertations.[87] An assertion that the possession of a master's degree by a Catholic college teacher bespoke high training or guaranteed teaching qualifications would have to be buttressed with some additional justification, and even then it borders on wishful thinking.

Unduly harsh criticism of the college teaching climate is understandably generated by applying contemporary standards to the colleges of the nineteenth century; not only is this unfair, but it also blemishes the record of dedicated accomplishments in these colleges. In their own day the colleges did good work in educating students along avenues that otherwise would have remained closed, and due credit for this should be acknowledged in any history. If the colleges performed useful, although not always high-quality, service, praise belongs to the teachers who daily met their classes. It was they who transformed arid texts and prescribed methods into learning situations; along with their teachers young men grappled with mysteries of learning and were encouraged to ponder the duties of life and religion. On the whole, the teachers during this formative age of Catholic colleges rescued the age from complete darkness.

[84] Erbacher, *op. cit.*, p. 82.

[85] *Ibid.*, p. 80.

[86] *Ibid.*, p. 81.

[87] See the *United States Catholic Almanac: or, Laity's Directory, for the Year 1833* (Baltimore, James Myers, 1833), p. 56, for a description of the master's degree at St. Mary's College in Baltimore.

The colleges' greatest failure was trying to do too much and thus overburdening their faculties to a point where effectiveness was sacrificed. Orestes Brownson, the most perceptive lay Catholic of the nineteenth century, had something to say about this, and we should pay close attention to his analysis. The colleges, he wrote, "assume responsibility of conducting education from its rudiments to the immediate preparation for one of the learned professions."[88] Besides, the schools furnished room and board, were committed to lead the students in the direction of moral and religious virtue, and made promises, in the "case of youth of tender age, of a much more assiduous care."[89] All students, Brownson observed, were put in the same mold, and regardless of age were made to conform to the same regulations. This system demanded too much of teachers, for in addition to their pedagogic duties they were expected to assist prefects in maintaining college discipline. Brownson withheld an indictment of Catholic college teachers for what were really faults of the system, but he also refused to acknowledge their alleged scholarly qualities. Under the circumstances, he willingly conceded, they were doing more than should have been expected of them; teachers' qualifications, he thought, were unimpressive but adequate. Yet he was uneasy about a clerical faculty's commitment to religious discipline rather than to scholarly achievement; in other words, he found fault with a theory of teaching which subordinated a teacher's intellectual functions to religious goals and made classroom teaching an incidental part of a priest's profession.

Despite the obvious necessity that clerics should adhere to the profession of theology, Brownson wrote : "This diversion makes the education of youth a matter of secondary interest, and any reflecting man cannot fail to perceive that instruction so given is to a degree merely perfunctory, and falls short of what it should be."[90] Brownson was attacking not only a Catholic college theory of teaching but the very foundation of its teaching system—the clerical teacher—and his criticism must produce in the historian two levels of response. Theoretically he was justified : in practice, Catholic colleges of the nineteenth century would never have survived without clerical teachers, and Brownson's comments must be regarded as inapplicable. They bespoke an idealism the colleges could never afford.

On the other hand, from behind the flight of acrid barbs aimed at the colleges from the stance of a public man and a father with sons in Catholic colleges,[91] Brownson gave Catholic college teachers well-deserved praise, saying that any benefits a student derived from Catholic colleges were due

[88] Orestes A. Brownson, "Our Colleges," *Brownson's Quarterly Review*, 15 (April, 1858), 218.
[89] *Ibid.*
[90] *Ibid.*, p. 231.
[91] Meagher and Grattan, *op. cit.*, pp. 64–65.

to the skill, ability, and energy of the teachers and not to the colleges' supposed administrative and disciplinary integrity or to their hierarchical involvement with the Church. "We owe to the men, not the system," Brownson wrote, "any success the Catholic college has enjoyed."[92]

Faculty rights and responsibilities

This chapter began with an assertion that Catholic colleges paid more attention to faculty duties than qualifications, and the dogmatic tone can be sustained long enough to add that rights were always subordinated to responsibilities. If we chose to elaborate the rights of nineteenth-century Catholic college faculties, we should quickly discover the inevitable brevity of our intended discourse, for the colleges of the formative period were devoid of provision for, and paid no heed to, such things as tenure, rank, promotion, or a teacher's academic freedom to speak to the president and his administrative lieutenants in clear educational language about the intellectual needs of a college community or the legitimate and decent claims of a wider knowledge in the higher learning.

Under severely regimented conditions in the college, with its prescribed curriculum, usually approved by a Roman congregation or a European religious community's teaching code—such as the *Ratio Studiorum*—[93] even minimal conceptions of academic freedom were absent. The teacher was expected to teach a course without deviation from approved syllabi containing tested tenets of knowledge selected for their compatibility with religious doctrine. Both the content of a course and its pedagogy were prescribed. For the most part, the progress of students was determined by the president or some other college officer, but not by the class teacher.[94] Materials of instruction, scant as they were, were selected and the textbook, the keystone of college teaching, was adopted without a teacher's advice or consent. This practice was subjected to modest change as decades passed, and some liberalizations were introduced, but even in the mid-twentieth century some Catholic colleges, believing supervision of textual materials was essential, required teachers to submit their proposed textbook adoptions to the president or the province prefect of studies—the educational adviser to the

[92] Orestes A. Brownson, "Our Colleges," *Brownson's Quarterly Review,* 15 (April 1858), 235.

[93] Thébaud *Forty Years in the United States,* pp. 351–353.

[94] See *Marquette College, A Quarter Century* (Milwaukee, Marquette College, 1906), p. 15; Hamilton, *op. cit.,* pp. 273–275; Erbacher, *op. cit.,* p. 96; Daley, *op. cit.,* p. 228; and *Detroit College Catalogue, 1880,* p. 4.

religious superior or provincial—for his approval. The gates of reading were never left unguarded.

But to return to the old-time college, where there were no specialists : a teacher's preferred area of instruction was disregarded; he was assigned to any class needing a teacher.[95] What the teacher wanted was a trivial matter, and whether or not he was fit to conduct the classes assigned to him was a decision someone else made. The teacher was subservient to the system's leaders : he was expected to follow directions.

Tenure was an unused term of uncertain meaning : a teacher stayed at a college as long as he was needed; when the demand for a teacher's services disappeared, so did the teacher.[96] This, of course, posed no special problem for religious members of the college community; their vows of religious obedience made tenure inconsistent with even the most liberal interpretations of collegiate statutes. If members of a religious community could claim a legal right to their position, which had canonical legitimacy only for fully accredited pastors of parishes, the entire structure of religious assignment and reassignment in keeping with vows of obedience would be destroyed. No religious faculty member argued his right to remain in a college office, and none spoke of tenure, although many disliked the reassignments tendered them. What they disregarded as unimportant for themselves, or for their religious family, was, they tended to think, also unnecessary for lay helpers who from time to time came to the colleges to fill a temporary need.[97] Had leaders of Catholic colleges thought seriously about tenure, they would surely have been more concerned about appointments and would have looked more carefully at a candidate's qualifications. As it was, with no precedents for tenure in American colleges, Catholic presidents were completely dispensed from making such critical and far-reaching decisions. In the long run, the absence of tenure policies (and we have no real reason to expect them) may have been a blessing in disguise, for the colleges were often compelled to appoint obviously unqualified teachers. That they did not remain long in the colleges was good; but had tenure protected them, the colleges would surely have suffered more serious damage than from the impermanent and temporary arrangements they chose to follow.

Faculty rank—professor, associate, assistant, and instructor—was almost completely unknown in these early colleges, as it was in most American colleges of the day, so presidents were freed from forming policies concerning rank or determining criteria for appointments to a certain rank and the promotion of faculty members from one rank to another. All were

95 Faherty, *op. cit.,* p. 293.

96 Power, *A History of Catholic Higher Education in the United States,* p. 99.

97 James J. Maguire, "A Family Affair," *Commonweal,* LXXV (November, 1961), 171–173.

professors, or none were : and senior members of a college faculty neither expected nor received any academic courtesies consistent with their seniority, although senior religious persons were accorded a deference and a dignity within the closed circle of religious community life. But this had little to do with their place on a college faculty.

Being on a college faculty implied no status outside the college, for the ordinary citizen could hardly be expected to attach more value to things of the mind than the colleges themselves did; such membership, moreover, implied no more than that here was a teacher commissioned by superiors to conduct classes. Yet, Catholic colleges automatically enjoy immunity from direct criticism here : they simply followed ordinary conventions of American higher education which, for the most part, accorded faculties few rights and privileges and easily overlooked such presently critical items as rank, tenure, and promotion policies.[98]

After testing policy and administrative indifference to faculty quality, freedom, and status, we should recapture, if possible, the professional expectations of faculty members themselves. This, however, must always be done in the context of a system that put a premium on a teacher's versatility and determined his value according to his ability to fulfill day-to-day college needs; not the least of these needs, as we have said, was keeping good order. Discipline was the prefect's domain, but for the routine of administering discipline faculty members could be conscripted as they were needed. Already we have an image of a Catholic college considerably more solicitous of a student's moral and religious development than of his intellectual growth, and this is a valid image. For teachers, this emphasis was translated into long hours of watchfulness over student behavior, which in turn demanded residence in the college. The college hall was the students' home; usually it was the faculty's home too.

Student recollections give us additional information on the consumption of faculty time. One student reported that he was sent to Mt. St. Mary's College, Maryland, in 1825, arriving April 12th (an unlikely time to begin a college course, but no matter), and "On the evening of that day my attention was attracted to two young seminarians loading muskets with buckshot. I was informed that they patrolled the premises all night . . . to prevent anything like malicious intrusion, or the entrance of anyone not entitled to the Seminary [college] grounds."[99] In addition to blocking intruders, we may suppose, they also discouraged older students from slipping away from college to rendezvous with young ladies, visit nearby taverns, or find a decent meal at a neighboring home. Records of faculty assignment to menial duties in and around the college are incomplete

[98] See J. E. Kirkpatrick, *The American College and Its Rulers* (New York, New Republic, 1926).

[99] Meline and McSweeny, *op. cit.*, I, 139.

and fragmentary; these are evidences so easily obliterated by time, yet it is quite clear that teachers had many such duties, including that of standing guard, and were expected to fulfill them to the letter. On the whole, we should think, they performed everything expected of them without much murmuring against a system that treated them with so little professional respect.

If the excessive authoritarianism of administrative tactics in early colleges discouraged the faculties from responsible involvement in college life, members of those faculties must bear some share of the blame. They were accessories after the fact, because their perception of a faculty was as faulty as the president's or the bishop's; and since they were being deprived of a proper role in college affairs, they should have been the first to speak. The record is barren of evidence that any did; yet we should be surprised if Catholic colleges of this time were unable to boast of at least one eccentric on their faculties. It is unfair, therefore, to assert that not a single professor sensed the deprivations inherent in college policies, but this was clearly a matter whereupon faculties as a whole lacked a common sentiment. They took things as they were, and accommodated themselves so docilely to administrative control that they scarcely dared hope for the best. Not even nocturnal assignments to guard the college grounds or never-ending domestic commitments to immature college boys shook them from their lethargy. The historical picture, then, must be fairly balanced : administrators were unquestionably myopic but members of Catholic college faculties were short-sighted too. The denominational orientation of the colleges and the religious profession of presidents and a majority of the faculty explain the lack of academic vision, but such factors do not at the same time supply a historical justification for it.

Attitudes toward college teaching

In an earlier chapter we sampled the attitudes of prominent clerical Catholics with respect to higher learning in general;[100] it is necessary now to assess the effects of this attitude on college teaching. Catholic colleges, we know, if we can take at face value the curricular descriptions they themselves provide, tried their best to be classical schools, and only as a last resort allowed nonclassical commercial and English courses to infect the purity of their curriculum.[101] When contamination was inevitable (presidents always

[100] See pp. 11–35.

[101] Easby-Smith, *op. cit.*, I, 31–33; Meagher, *op. cit.*, pp. 35–36; Dunigan, *op. cit.*, pp. 34–50; *Report of the United States Commissioner of Education, 1887–1888*, pp. 642–643; and W. J. Howlett, "The Early Days of St. Joseph's College at Bardstown, Kentucky," *Illinois Catholic Historical Review* (April, 1922), pp. 372–380.

guarded the gates against curricular change as best they could) faculty ranks were necessarily broadened to include teachers with nonclassical credentials. These new teaching positions were usually filled by laymen.[102] But before this happened on any large scale, the colleges were content to accept a theory of teaching which enjoined them to mine from specified texts everything teachers and students were expected to know. The colleges bent every effort to remain true to humanistic traditions as they understood them, and even when that orientation was disturbed, they assumed, as pedantic humanists centuries before them had dogmatically asserted, that everything worth knowing was contained in classical literature.

Anyone reasonably competent in classical studies—and every clergyman was expected to have credentials here—was qualified to stand before a college class and take it over frequently-traveled roads with a full confidence that these led to a safe and decent education. Whatever needed to be taught was ready and waiting, having earlier been extracted from classical texts. This view of knowledge made it easy for teachers to hear lessons, and it allowed them and their superiors to neglect dedicated and determined scholarship, on one hand, and provisions for such scholarship, on the other.[103] This, we should think, was neither an oversight bred of incorrect appraisals of scholarship nor the embracing of anti-intellectualism, but the natural consequence of a sincere belief that the totality of worthwhile knowledge was already within man's grasp.

If we couple this attitude, which had authentic foundations in neo-humanism, with an aversion to uncommitted scholarship—that is a rejection of any teaching not serving a high religious purpose[104]—we discern a basic approach to college teaching. And as long as this approach was honored, the colleges were faced with insurmountable obstacles to academic progress and faculty development.

But even if attitudes toward knowledge and the teacher's role in connection with it had been considerably more academic, the situation in the colleges would not have been greatly different, because the students enrolled were generally incapable of going much beyond the spoon-feeding techniques implicit in the college program of studies. What need had these Catholic colleges for scholar-teachers?

Again, we can consult Brownson for further information on the state of Catholic college teaching. In 1862 he was invited by President Sorin to join the Notre Dame faculty. This speaks well for Sorin's liberalism and

---

[102] For example, in the 1880 regulations of the Jesuits' Missouri Province, no Jesuit was permitted to teach commercial subjects; see Power, *A History of Catholic Higher Education in the United States*, p. 98.

[103] See Erbacher, *op. cit.,* pp. 92–101.

[104] Cassidy avers that Catholic educators believed knowledge for its own sake was worthless (*op. cit.,* p. 94); and Middleton, *op. cit.,* pp. 21–22.

breadth of vision, because even then Brownson was *persona non grata* in many ecclesiastical circles, and his *Review* articles were anathema to some bishops.[105] Nevertheless, Father Sorin was willing to appoint Brownson and, we should think, would have been happy to have this controversial figure, thought of by some as an American Newman, teaching at Notre Dame. Still, there was a strange ambiguity in Sorin's attitude, for Brownson, despite his history and credentials, was to be treated as any other member of the faculty and, apparently expected to play the usual role of mother and disciplinarian, as well as instructor, to college boys. Brownson unquestionably weighed the invitation with care, but in the end decided that Notre Dame would demand more than his health and energy could bear.[106] Brownson's contacts with the colleges were sufficiently close for him to realize the vast array of nonacademic duties expected of the lay teacher. Although he may not really have believed that Notre Dame would utilize him for prefecting, teaching, bricklaying, landscape gardening, and stable-cleaning, he knew that some Catholic colleges kept lay teachers busy at such things. In the absence of clear assurances about the limitations of his duties, he declined the proferred appointment.

The Catholic college was an extension of the religious community, and codes of conduct and administrative control justified by religious constitutions were applied to it without noticeable modification. Thus, when John Carroll framed an administrative code for Georgetown College—one honored with the force of ecclesiastical law by later Catholic colleges—he relegated the teacher to a position of complete subservience to the president and religious superior. It mattered not whether teachers were clerical or lay; the same law applied to all. Among Carroll's democratic ideas about college government, a faculty's appropriate role goes unnoticed; he made the president the final authority on all internal matters, but showed some political astuteness in advising presidents to involve professors prudently. The president, he wrote, "will find great advantage in this; and in general his government will be made easier for him by his testifying in, and where it may be done, consulting concerning all business relative to the conduct of education, with the head professors who will be flattered by such attention."[107]

A quick reading of Carroll's edict leaves a good impression of liberality and sensitivity to sound college government : here is a man who wanted to engage professors in the total business of education. But a closer second reading generates some misgivings about Carroll's attitude and the depth of his commitment to faculty participation in the academic operations of a

105 Orestes A. Brownson, "Editor's Remarks," *Brownson's Quarterly Review*, 22 (1873), 1–2.

106 Orestes A. Brownson to Fr. Edward Sorin, January 6, 1863, University of Notre Dame Archives.

107 Quoted in Daley, *op. cit.*, p. 55.

college: the president is to ask for participation when he wants it on matters "where it may be done." He is, however, happily absolved from seeking faculty advice and testing faculty reaction except when he wants it. Otherwise, avenues of communication are closed. Even when they are open, because the president chooses to open them, consultation is a ploy intended to flatter professors. Flattery was at best a weak foundation on which to build administrative-faculty relationships.

It is clear enough that such relationships were superfluous; a good president free from any restrictions faculty intervention might impose was the governmental structure aimed for: "All that the college needs to insure its permanent prosperity is a President."[108] Even in proprietary colleges —where one might anticipate erosions of strict religious discipline—attitudes were the same. A former owner-president who summed up his experience in this field was Bishop John Dubois, who spoke with some authority about the approved role of the college teacher in a letter to his successors at Mt. St. Mary's. He began by stating his conviction that only with religious communities at the helm could Catholic colleges survive, because, he said, teachers received such enormous salaries that colleges would be rendered bankrupt paying them. Even then, with good salaries, lay teachers could not be depended upon; they would sell their services to the highest bidder and would always be moving from one college to another. He could neither understand nor approve this freedom of movement. But then he touched on a really critical point: "No subordination and harmony can prevail among professors not united by the vow of obedience, and of course no subordination among the children constant witnesses of the misunderstanding among their teachers;—nor can piety prevail as in a pious and religious order."[109]

Here is a former college president, bishop of the great and influential diocese of New York, no doubt aware of such colleges as Columbia, but incapable of believing that a good education could be obtained in a school whose faculty was not governed by the statutes of a religious community and administered by the edicts of a religious superior. And Dubois was stating a typical thesis shared by several generations of Catholic clergymen. John Hughes, the militant and capable bishop of New York, one of Dubois' successors, was even more explicit in jettisoning any theory countenancing administrative-faculty government for Catholic colleges. For a college, he said, "a republican form of government will never answer." Ideas, he thought, were destroyed by analysis and comparison, and the president of a college might be left with a decision arrived at by a common consent to which he was opposed. "The government [of a college] is as the human body and it will never do for the hands and the feet to enter into the

108 James R. Bayley, quoted in Kennelly, *op. cit.*, p. 57.
109 Quoted in Meline and McSweeny, *op. cit.*, I, 360–361.

deliberations of the head, otherwise they will oppose sometimes and having opposed, they will either not obey at all, or if they do, it will be with such symptoms of reluctance as will still manifest opposition." [110]

Neither Dubois nor Hughes displays much knowledge of college life or history, although both bishops were deeply involved in the founding and management of Catholic colleges; and Hughes' crude physiological metaphor served only to perpetuate and solidify an arrogant administrative attitude toward college faculties. Speaking from within the sheltered atmosphere of ecclesiastical life, and understanding the colleges only in terms of religious objectives, neither Dubois, Hughes, nor, for that matter, their episcopal confreres for the next half-century, who adopted the same thesis, could have articulated any other sentiments. And this was a bad omen for faculty development in Catholic colleges. Administrative authority in the college and ecclesiastical authority in the monastery were cut from the same fabric of religious traditions; as long as this tradition remained intact nineteenth-century Catholic colleges were untroubled by democracy.

Although some Catholic ecclesiastics in the later nineteenth century had a balanced and sane approach to a religious authority proper enough in the religious house, but illogical in its application to academic policies, it would be a mistake to think that their views were heeded. Perhaps the best sign that Catholic colleges were not irrevocably caught in a doctrinaire trap in which it would be impossible for them to utilize faculty talent in planning and executing policy is found in the writings of John Lancaster Spalding. What he had to say about Catholic-college teachers is worth quoting, despite the undoubted fact that the statement was made in an administrative climate determined to disregard it. The teacher, Bishop Spalding wrote, "should be trusted and cheered in his work. To make him a slave to minute observances, the victim of a system of bureaucratic regulations, is to take from him the joy and delight he should find in his work and to superinduce in him a servile disposition. To degrade him to the level of a machine is to make him unfit to mould and inspire free men." [111] Needless to say, Spalding spoke a language that Catholic colleges of the nineteenth century would only vaguely have understood.

[110] Quoted in *ibid.*, p. 367.
[111] John Lancaster Spalding, *Opportunity and Other Essays* (Chicago, McClurg, 1900), p. 121.

5

In the classroom

Curricular history is important because it reflects what educated men were willing to justify as worthwhile knowledge and intellectual values. Higher education's curriculum tells us something about the objectives of higher learning, for even in the least sophisticated college the subjects studied were always instruments for attaining instructional goals, sometimes clearly stated, but more often vaguely sensed. The college curriculum was forged with an implied assurance that it would produce a decently educated person.[1]

The first American colleges tried to respect two commitments: one to a humanistic educational tradition; the other to a preparation of ministers for church service. Put another way, their commission, as they understood it, was to produce a class of learned men, and even more exactly, a class of learned men for the Christian ministry. The way to fulfill this commission, they assumed, was to use materials of instruction consisting largely of the classics, along with logic, geometry, and physics, to which were added, for more practical clerical use, such ancient languages as Greek and Hebrew, and some dogmatic theology. This curricular system, transplanted with relatively few modifications from the English universities of Oxford and Cambridge, was honored by a majority of nonCatholic colleges until the close of the eighteenth century.[2] Any changes made had been dictated by pressing social needs, or, in some instances, by the refusal of students to pay allegiance to educational tradition; but these infractions of tradition did not effectively undermine the classics, then accepted as the best means for stimulating mental growth and development. The dominant curricular theory of the age was committed to the processes rather than the products of learning;

[1] See "Original Papers in Relation to a Course of Liberal Education," *The American Journal of Science and Arts,* 15 (January, 1829), 297–351.

[2] F. A. P. Barnard, *Annual Report of the President of Columbia College* (New York, Columbia College, 1872), p. 31; and Louis F. Snow, *The College Curriculum of the United States* (New York, Teachers College Press, 1907), pp. 2–21.

regardless of a student's personal objectives for enrolling in a college course, he was required to submit to an educational diet uniform in all its proportions.[3]

The humanistic tradition was unquestionably strong and, in America, voices favoring its revision were weak. Yet, even if stronger and more persistent voices had demanded curricular change in higher education, they would have been ineffective, for academic audiences were entirely comfortable with the dogmatic assumption that colleges were places for an elite, and more especially for an elite with objectives hitched to denominational religion. In the eighteenth century—despite the chairs of medicine and law, of science and languages at a few colleges—organizing groups of educators, or college officers, willing to circle the same tree of reform was virtually impossible.[4]

These curricular postures were taken and defended in the American colonies for two centuries; but after the War of Revolution changes began to occur and sometimes the demand for change outran the colleges' ability to keep pace. Now and then strong voices of dissent were challenged, as in the famous Report of the Yale Faculty,[5] and curriculum updating had to mark time. Yet, during the period when Catholic colleges first appeared in the United States, the college world was in ferment. The college course seemed open for inspection and ready for change; this should have been a happy time for Catholic colleges : they could have used the two-century experience of their native counterparts to introduce a college course free from outworn assumptions and capable of meeting the needs of students in nineteenth-century America. Instead, history tells us, they closed their eyes to change and imported even older ideas on college study from the archives of European educational practice.[6]

In the first place, ignoring what should have been an easy lesson to learn, Catholics began their school system from the top down.[7] This was a

---

[3] See George Paul Schmidt, "Colleges in Ferment," *American Historical Review*, LIX (October, 1953), 20.

[4] Edward Everett, "University Education," *North American Review*, 10 (January, 1820), 115–137.

[5] "Original Papers in Relation to a Course of Liberal Education," *The American Journal of Science and Arts*, 15 (January, 1829), 297–351. For analyses of the Report, see R. F. Butts, *The College Charts Its Course: Historical Conceptions and Current Proposals* (New York, McGraw-Hill Book Co., 1939), pp. 118–125; George Paul Schmidt, *The Liberal Arts College: A Chapter in American Cultural History* (New Brunswick, N. J., Rutgers University Press, 1957), pp. 55–58; and Richard Hofstadter and C. DeWitt Hardy, *The Development and Scope of Higher Education in the United States* (New York, Columbia University Press, 1952), pp. 15–17.

[6] Cassidy, *op. cit.*, pp. 13–43; Erbacher, *op. cit.*, pp. 5–9; Garraghan, *The Jesuits of the Middle United States*, I, 293–294; and Thébaud, *Forty Years in the United States*, pp. 330–335.

[7] See Guilday, *The Life and Times of John Carroll*, pp. 790–791; and Sr. M.

mistake earlier colonists had made, and it was an educational error Catholics seemed anxious to imitate. So when we look at curricula in the first Catholic colleges, we are often left with the impression that they were colleges only in name, chiefly because they offered basic along with somewhat more advanced studies and admitted to their classrooms any boy who wanted even the most rudimentary learning. And it took a long time before such expedients were rooted from accepted practice, for as late as, say, 1877 some Catholic colleges still refused to separate rudimentary classes from classes which, by that time, were more appropriately collegiate in caliber.[8] In the second place, Catholic colleges interpreted their educational responsibility as being neither complete nor liberal; their chief goal was preparatory. A young man could finish his education in the seminary, but college educational limits were set by the uneasy compromise perpetuated between the ultimate goal of terminal studies (training outside the college) and the transitional goal of preparatory studies, which shaped and dominated the college course. Intrusions of practical studies, inevitable because students would be helpless without them, further complicated instructional processes and goals, but Catholic colleges effectively repudiated such studies on the level of theory while handling them perfunctorily on the instructional level.[9]

If Catholic colleges in the formative period had simply followed American higher education's contemporary traditions, which gave less attention to the preparation of clerics, the historian's task, if not more pleasant, would, at least, have been easier. He could have shown that their curricula were duplications of current practice along with a few concessions to denominational preference. But this was not how it happened. There is no evidence that Catholic colleges were moved to contemplate the curricular theories distilled in three significant documents which for decades had guided, and disturbed, nonCatholic colleges: the Harvard "Laws" of President Dunster, 1642; the "Programme" of the first provost of Pennsylvania, 1756; and the Report of the Yale Faculty, 1828.[10] In the final analysis, Catholic colleges were out of step with the march of higher education in the United States: surprising as it may be, their curricula did not contain the knowledge considered of most worth by the educated community; when, in their academic enclaves, educational reality compelled them to give way a little, they offered students courses to prepare them for divinity studies rather than divinity studies themselves; on the other side of the coin, they refused to acknowledge the relevance of practical curricula and resisted

---

Salome Tlochenska, *The American Hierarchy and Education* (Milwaukee, Marquette University, 1934).

[8] Meagher, *op. cit.*, p. 33.

[9] See Middleton, *op. cit.*, p. 33.

[10] See Snow, *op. cit.*, pp. 2–21.

them as long as possible.[11] Such colleges, moreover, had an array of non-academic functions, ranging from the moral formation of students to institutional commitments for missionary work,[12] so there was little determination and less time to concentrate on intellectual goals unrelated to the purposes of preparatory schooling.

Curriculum of the formative period

It was hard for Catholic colleges of the formative period to state the objectives of their courses, whatever may have been their own institutional hopes or those for higher education in general. In this respect they shared a common disadvantage that time alone could not erode. Prior to 1870 all Catholic colleges began their academic history as combinations of elementary and secondary schools.[13] And even when upgrading added a college course of studies to a secondary-school foundation, the elementary side of teaching was difficult to abandon. Thus, despite the colleges' unwillingness to offer an educational curriculum suited to a wide ability range—and, perhaps, a clear inability to do so—Catholic colleges, often being the only schools in their geographic region, were inevitably forced to admit students who came through their gates without being able to control their quality. What weak and varied student backgrounds in formal learning, to say nothing of multifarious motives for study, could do to a college course of studies needs no elaboration here. And the colleges, inevitably capitulating to the pressure for entry rather than selecting students fitted for an academic course, nevertheless sensed the need to state some admission standards in order to maintain an appearance of respectability, and usually framed their admission criteria in such a way that few, if any, would be excluded.[14]

[11] See Georgetown's statement in the *Report of the United States Commissioner of Education, 1887–1888*, pp. 642–643.

[12] Erbacher, *op. cit.*, pp. 64–68.

[13] Many examples are possible; for three, see G. J. Garraghan, "The Beginnings of St. Louis University," *St. Louis Catholic Historical Review*, I (January, 1919), 85–102; Meline and McSweeny, *op. cit., I*, 59–73; and J. W. Riordan, *The First Half Century of St. Ignatius Church and College* (San Francisco, Crocker Company, 1905), pp. 69–111. It should be noted that elementary studies were especially tenacious: in the *Catalogue of St. John's College* (Fordham), *1895–1896*, p. 16, the announcement appeared that no one under twelve years of age was admitted; and the *Catalogue of Gonzaga College* (Spokane), *1895–1896*, p. 7, stated that no one under nine years of age was admitted.

[14] Charles L. Souvay, "Around the St. Louis Cathedral With Bishop Dubourg, 1818–1820," *St. Louis Catholic Historical Review*, V (April, July, 1923), 149–159; Erbacher, *op. cit.*, p. 83; *Catalogue of St. Louis University, 1869–1870*, p. 15; Francis

Elementary studies in these colleges handled the rudiments in a traditional way, and there is little to be learned from dwelling on them; but the features of secondary teaching give us better information about the life of learning. Every effort was made to use European models and to conduct secondary studies not materially different from those in the old, tradition-dominated classical schools that had come into existence following the religious revolt of the sixteenth century. The handiest model for Catholic schools was the Jesuit *Ratio Studiorum*; its long history of success in Europe recommended it to the managers of Catholic colleges who after reading the *Ratio,* remained uncertain about broader objectives in higher education. Although European Jesuit colleges were preparatory schools with a single-minded commitment to a high standard of classical study, American Catholic colleges selected them as exemplary prototypes and ignored the fact that imitating them would be, at best difficult, at worst impossible.[15]

John Carroll, the ex-Jesuit founder of Georgetown, designed the school with his own Jesuit experience and the Jesuit plan of studies uppermost in his mind.[16] Besides, Georgetown became an authentic Jesuit college after 1814,[17] and for at least the next half century offered other Catholic colleges the best model of curricular organization and purpose at a time when they desperately needed a plan to follow. They could not turn to nonCatholic colleges for inspiration and example, because their consciences would not allow it, so they tried to conform to what was assumed to be orthodox practice by copying Georgetown. Before 1835 this could not have been easy, for even Georgetown was unable to offer a precise model, but after that date its curriculum was codified and stood as a beacon for Jesuit and non-Jesuit colleges alike.[18]

In their determination to find national models from which American Catholic colleges were derived, historians have sometimes settled on France, the home of the College of St. Omer, which, according to Cassidy,[19] was the prototype for the first American Catholic college, and he detects, also,

---

X. Talbot, *Jesuit Education in Philadelphia: St. Joseph's College, 1851–1926* (Philadelphia, St. Joseph's College, 1927), p. 40; *Sketch of Gonzaga College,* p. 13; *St. Joseph's College Catalogue, 1857–1858,* p. 7; *Xavier College Catalogue, 1863–1864,* p. 4; Middleton, *op. cit.,* pp. 21–22; Meagher, *op. cit.,* pp. 57–62; Meline and McSweeny, *op. cit.,* I, 55; and *First Prospectus of Spring Hill College,* October 29, 1830.

[15] For a lucid elaboration of Jesuit educational ideals and practices, see Allan P. Farrell, *The Jesuit Code of Liberal Education* (Milwaukee, Bruce Publishing Co., 1938; and Thébaud, *Forty Years in the United States,* p. 331, for an admission that traditional college curricula were too demanding.

[16] Daley, *op. cit.,* pp. 42–43.

[17] See John McElroy "Reestablishment of the Society in the United States," *The Woodstock Letters,* XVI (July, 1887), 161–168.

[18] See Daley, *op. cit.,* pp. 222–224.

[19] Cassidy, *op. cit.,* p. 12.

a permanent French influence,[20] which, in turn, is disallowed by Thébaud who, in his *Forty Years in the United States of America,* wrote that the Jesuits conducting American colleges were forced to forget all their French notions and their own *Ratio Studiorum.*[21] We may agree with Thébaud's evaluation of influence to the extent that distinctive French curricula and methods were sometimes forgotten, and with his statement that the *Ratio* was neglected in American Catholic colleges, if we mean that precise studies and method recommended in the *Ratio* went unused, but the spirit of the *Ratio* was entirely evident in Georgetown's curricular organization and nomenclature.[22] The famous Brownson, on the other hand, in an analysis of Catholic college origins, was certain that foreign example and influence were lacking: "From the little resemblance that it bears to any other system of either near or remote antiquity, we should be led, for quiet's sake, to consider it indigenous to the soil on which it flourishes."[23] While Brownson's summary dismissal of foreign influence, not unconnected with his ardent proAmerican bias, may well be debated, he was probably right in maintaining, despite numerous examples imported from abroad, that American Catholic colleges were never abject followers of any precise foreign model. Still, his interpretation must not be allowed to trap us in the fallacy that these colleges were autonomous institutions completely free from European, or more exactly, Roman ecclesiastical directions. Before opening colleges American bishops petitioned Rome for advice and some- times for detailed directions on the management of such schools; religious communities followed prescriptions from their Roman headquarters for their American projects. No evidence supports the view that American Catholic colleges were founded and nurtured independently of European educational and ecclesiastical influence. Yet, despite this influence, the American Catholic college was different from anything Europe had produced.

The European classical school—frequently called a college—was closely associated with the university, while the American Catholic college had a working relationship with the seminary; when, as a second historical step in curriculum development classical studies became a clear part of Catholic

[20] *Ibid.,* p. 83.

[21] Thébaud, *Forty Years in the United States,* p. 331. Thébaud's disclaimer would seem to be too strong, for in his study of Jesuit colleges in France, John W. Padberg, *Colleges in Controversy: The Jesuit Schools in France from Revival to Suppression, 1815–1880* (Cambridge, Mass., Harvard University Press, 1969), pp. 142–163, describes educational practices which were common also to nineteenth-century American Catholic colleges. It should be understood, I think, that the attribution of a clear national character to Jesuit education, which, in any case, was the model American Catholic colleges followed, is always somewhat inaccurate.

[22] Daley, *op. cit.,* pp. 90, 220–224.

[23] Orestes A. Brownson, "Our Colleges," *Brownson's Quarterly Review,* 15 (April, 1858), 212.

college curricula, they were regarded as unimportant in themselves, but exceptionally important as stepping-stones toward professional theological study. Yet Catholic colleges, despite their determination to keep intact an affiliation with seminaries, adopted somewhat broader goals which included the preparation of secular youth who, in time, came to the colleges in pursuit of paraprofessional and professional credentials. In a word, Catholic colleges could ill afford the luxury of a classical preparatory curriculum; and when this became clear they added to the classical curriculum courses in English studies, as well as commercial and scientific subjects. In doing so they were making further concessions unavoidable : yet an English course, imperative in a country where a limited worth was attached to classical language and literature, could demonstrate its value even for boys preparing for the priesthood.[24] Commercial subjects were another story, however, for they could be justified only on purely secular grounds; in the end the colleges put up with them because they produced revenue, but tried to keep them on the fringe of curricular respectability.[25] This official indifference to commercial courses must have mystified parents who sent their sons to college for exactly such studies, and they regularly appealed to the colleges to continue commercial courses and abstain from discouraging students who chose to pursue them. A mother whose son was at Holy Cross College wrote to the president recommending limiting her son's studies to English, except for a French course or so : "I think it will be quite quite (sic) useless for him to recommence Greek or Latin, or any of the higher studies, as he does not manifest any capacity for them, and it only retards his progress in others for which he is deficient."[26] Asking that the boy be allowed to study English grammar, geography, and arithmetic, she added the hope that he would master these subjects because, in a year or so, he would probably be apprenticed in a trade.[27]

During the first fifty years of Catholic college history, the colleges found commercial courses repugnant to their devotion to loftier objectives; they allowed such courses a place at the school because students wanted them, but refused them status as college curricula. And it is hard to argue that they should have had collegiate standing, for with penmanship, arithmetic, and bookkeeping the principal ingredients, the caliber of such programs was low. But low standards were not the crucial issue : what really bothered

[24] Roy W. Vollenweider, "Spring Hill College : The Early Days," *The Alabama Review* (April, 1954), p. 132.

[25] This lack of status persisted for a long time and is evidenced in the following catalogues years later; *St. Louis, 1889–1890,* p. 23; *Canisius, 1889–1890,* p. 2; *Santa Clara, 1889–1890,* p. 4; *St. Ignatius* (Calif.), *1889–1890,* p. 6; *Spring Hill, 1889–1890,* p. 66; *Gonzaga* (D.C.) *1889–1890,* p. 6; *St. Ignatius* (Chicago), *1895–1896,* p. 20; and *Marquette, 1895–1896,* p. 11.

[26] Meagher, *op. cit.,* pp. 36–37.

[27] *Ibid.*

them was the fact that "the study of the classics [did] not enter at all, the time being wholly given up to English and the study of business forms."[28] Dwelling on commercial subjects at this stage is premature, because, as we have said, they were unrecognized in the college course, and it was not till early in the twentieth century that such courses achieved both status and permanency. In the formative period, commercial subjects were academic expedients, to which some active opposition was aroused, and religious superiors responsible for all religious institutions in their jurisdictions, could write to a college president—as a Jesuit provincial once did—suggesting the college "confine [itself] to the classics. The English or commercial course is humbugging, but *ne quid nimis*."[29]

The efforts of Catholic colleges to remain classical schools were continually eroded : commercial subjects refused to disappear and scientific courses, deemed essential for publicity, had to be added, although before 1860 science took the form mainly of lectures on scientific subjects, accompanied, sometimes, by simple laboratory demonstrations accounted by the students to be very pleasing.[30] Materials for these scientific demonstrations were stored in scientific cabinets, which, by twentieth-century criteria, would be thought amusing artifacts from thin museum collections.

The college curriculum could meet challenges from commercial and scientific subjects and keep its equilibrium, but English posed a much more serious problem. If the colleges were to be true to classical traditions, English study should have been proscribed. But this was not done. Nor can we take at face value the assertions of superiors and presidents that English study was unimportant and should be deprived of a regular place in college studies. Despite its claim for classical purity and its hopes for classical excellence, the early American college was destined to promote English studies. The "mere humbugging," perhaps a desperate reaction, was more of a rhetorical plea than a firm statement of policy, for to picture the Catholic college as an exclusively classical school is to distort the facts. As early as 1820, English was recognized as having an authentic place in college curricula, and a prefect of studies spoke enthusiastically about the cultivation of the vernacular as a worthy objective for a college course.[31] And he was not talking about literal translation, but asked for "grammatical and pure English. Read good books and acquire the harmonious language of Addison, the numbers of Pope, the majesty of Milton."[32] In setting a tone for teaching at this time, his instructions to Georgetown's teachers went

---

28 Taaffe, *op. cit.*, p. 74.

29 Meagher, *op. cit.*, p. 36.

30 See David R. Dunigan, *Student Days at Holy Cross College in 1848* (St. Louis, St. Louis University, 1938), p. 78.

31 Daley, *op. cit.*, p. 224.

32 *Ibid.*

even further : "It surely cannot be doubted that the vernacular language is always the most important. Without this knowledge every other branch of education would be almost useless." [33] Thus in part following the example of Georgetown, but also sensing the educational outlook of prospective students, Holy Cross, Notre Dame, St. Louis, along with most other Catholic colleges, gave English study a position of relative importance in their curricula. However, their justifications of English study were seldom as fundamental as the Georgetown prefect's, and for public consumption they usually preferred to have their prospectuses advertise their intellectual attachment to the classics. St. Louis may be regarded as typical : there the school's second founder, Charles F. Van Quickenborne, although realizing that with a faculty of four and a cadre of poorly prepared students neither a complete secondary nor college course could be offered, deferred to his advisers and permitted publication of a curricular prospectus emphasizing the traditional classical courses. This somewhat pretentious announcement notwithstanding, the St. Louis college was only a well-equipped grammar school until 1832. Latin was not taught at all; students were assigned either to higher or lower English : in the former, already able to read, students grappled with grammar; in the latter they learned the A B C and reading.[34]

The colleges were optimistic : if unable to offer complete classical courses, because of inadequate faculties, they could at least qualify as English schools, but this, too, frequently swamped them in wishful thinking and, again, allowed their failures to equal their ambitions. In the days before native-born priests, seminarians, and laymen formed faculties, English must have been nearly as great a linguistic mystery as Greek to some teachers. Yet the colleges offered English courses, sometimes taught by men who, though adequate enough in French, spoke hardly any English;[35] or fluent in German, their native tongue, found communication in English extremely burdensome.[36] In colleges of the South, justifications for English study were usually ignored, and the concessions Northern and Western schools made to English teaching were made instead to French. Still, we must allow for a few exceptions : St. Mary's College in Baltimore included both Spanish and French in the college course, although English, it is said, was not neglected.[37] But neither Georgetown nor Fordham offered German, Spanish, or French in their early curricula, and when such language studies

[33] *Ibid.*

[34] G. J. Garraghan, "The Beginnings of St. Louis University," *St. Louis Catholic Historical Review*, I (October, 1918), 100.

[35] Hope, *op. cit.*, p. 36.

[36] Moosmüller, *op. cit.*, p. 78; Charles A. Brady, *Canisius College: The First Hundred Years* (Buffalo, Canisius College, 1969), p. 72; and Thomas E. Harney, *Canisius College: The First Nine Years* (New York, Vantage Press, 1971), p. 87.

[37] Ruane, *op. cit.*, p. 140.

did occupy college youth they were studied as extras or accessories.[38] At Spring Hill College, although instruction was in English, the French influence was strong enough to command for the French language a regular place in general communication : French and English took turns weekly as the language of the playground, refectory, and dormitory.[39]

Save in public announcements about curricular objectives and means, where a display of confidence was expected, Catholic colleges were uncertain of their qualifications to offer either classical or English courses, uneasy about the extent to which students really wanted the one rather than the other, and confused in their interpretations of liberal and practical education. When curricula were classical, possibilities for liberal learning were present, but remarkably few students seemed to be liberally motivated. In some cases they resisted mastering fundamentals which could have been used either liberally or practically, as they wished. In some schools, because students were determined to have useful learning, but were unable to afford college fees, it became necessary to institute manual-labor arrangements so that a boy could earn his room, board, and tuition working on the college farm or in the college workshop. With productive labor finished, he could return to his studies. A manual-labor school, alleged to have been the first in the United States, was maintained at Notre Dame for orphaned children who wanted to learn a trade.[40] Perhaps the manual-labor school was separated from the college, although complex institutional organizational structures were little known in the nineteenth century; it is easier to imagine it as a college appendage. Villanova, we know, opened a manual-labor school in connection with the college in 1850, and admitted orphan boys over sixteen years of age.[41] Mt. St. Mary's in Emmitsburg encouraged students to keep chickens, garden, and, in addition, develop some skill in one of the useful arts;[42] and at Spring Hill College, after Jesuits assumed control, boys were expected to contribute one day a week working on the college farm.[43]

Early Catholic colleges rejected the principle that knowledge for its own sake was worth the effort of study,[44] but it is unlikely that any ever made any long-term commitment to manual-labor education. Their expectation that knowledge would lead to use was supported by more sophisticated elaborations, such as, for example, the one contained in Villanova's early prospectus (about 1850) : "a classical and scientific, or purely mercantile

---

[38] This was still so in 1878–1879, according to *Georgetown College Catalogue*, p. 4; and *St. John's* (Fordham) *College Catalogue*, p. 6.

[39] *Prospectus of Spring Hill College, 1832*, p. 3.

[40] Hope, *op. cit.*, pp. 62–63.

[41] Middleton, *op. cit.*, p. 33.

[42] Meline and McSweeny, *op. cit.*, I, 37–38, 78–81.

[43] Kenny, *op. cit.*, p. 134.

[44] Cassidy, *op. cit.*, pp. 93–94.

education will be given to children, or the one will be so blended with the other, as to qualify the pupil to embrace any of the learned professions, or to apply himself to business. It is hoped that experience will show that proper attention is paid to the young gentlemen who may be sent to this institution."[45]

As Catholic colleges matured, they tried to prune elementary subjects from their curricula, and most, we think, were happy to welcome the advent of higher standards. But jettisoning the rudiments was a luxury all could ill afford, so some colleges kept a program of mixed studies, which began with reading, writing, and arithmetic and ended with fairly careful instruction in technical rhetoric. At Notre Dame, for example, a department for "minims" (elementary studies) was retained without interruption for several years after the college curriculum was firmly organized,[46] and at Georgetown, in 1815, enough young children were present to organize a class for reading, writing, and general preparation for classical study.[47] Later still, in 1827, the college register named a new student "aged 8 [who] could read words of two syllables,"[48] and in 1829 noted that a boy "aged 19 was received and placed in the second class of Rudiments."[49] In the same year, a student from Brazil "aged 9 . . . entered the college and not knowing sufficient to be admitted to the class of rudiments was put under the care of Brother Clarke until he should have learned to read."[50]

When Catholic colleges felt prepared to eliminate their elementary studies classes, they were about ready to organize and upgrade the college course. During the formative period the tendency was to equate higher learning and classical curricula and, as a corollary, to downgrade English study to a secondary or preparatory level. So the more academic the colleges became, the less attention they paid to English. This has led to some confusion amongst historians : on the one hand, college spokesmen denounced English as unworthy of a decent education; on the other, they affirmed the undoubted value of skill in the vernacular. Unless we understand that the educational program conducted by the colleges was divided into secondary and college grades, four years to the first and three to the second, these pronouncements put us in a quandary. The truth was that most college officers regarded English as a necessary secondary-school subject, but rejected it for the college course; and this might be taken as a matter of fixed policy from which few schools departed. One that did, Spring Hill College, defined its preparatory course as essentially classical,

---

45 Middleton, *op. cit.,* pp. 21–22.
46 Hope, *op. cit.,* p. 221.
47 Daley, *op. cit.,* p. 184.
48 *Ibid.,* p. 226.
49 *Ibid.*
50 *Ibid.*

omitted English as a subject for study, but recognized it as a medium of instruction.[51]

If the seven-year course, with its dual system, is important to an understanding of Catholic college attitudes toward English studies, it is equally important in the comprehension of the role entrance requirements played in colleges of the formative period. In the colleges' first years, students were needed badly, so no attempt was made to impose standards which would admit only the best students; again since the colleges never lost sight of their apostolic function, it was impossible to state admission criteria solely in intellectual or academic terms.[52] No Catholic school closed the door in the face even of a stupid boy seeking moral uplift and, more hopefully still, spiritual salvation; at the same time, a school with all levels of education in its program found it easy to justify the admission of almost any boy. In this context of educational and spiritual necessity, high standards were reserved for the rhetorician's pen, but on the level of day-to-day college operation were paid scant heed. Had strict entrance requirements been set, we should probably have criticized the schools for their unrealistic pretensions; as it was, they were trying in their own way to meet the needs of the time. If conditions had not changed for the better, Catholic colleges might have continued their undemanding way through history oblivious to demands for higher standards. But conditions did change. Lower schools began to dot the educational horizon, and colleges were less frequently asked to perform the work of an educational omnibus; Catholics in the United States, moreover, had greater need for authentic college products.[53] Catholic colleges responded the only way they could, by essaying to become better schools. And one dimension of academic quality was the provision of more capable and better prepared students.

During the formative period, the first entrance credentials were simply stated and easily ascertained by a reading examination.[54] If a boy could read, he would be assigned to a grade in the classical course; if deficient in reading skills, he could be assigned to a class in rudiments, or to a tutor, to remedy his shortcomings. Thus, the reading examination, administered by the college president or the prefect of studies—a forerunner of the academic dean—is associated with Catholic colleges from early in their formative years until the advent of the twentieth century. Notre Dame, for example, abandoned the reading entrance examination only in 1901.[55]

[51] See Roy W. Vollenweider, "Spring Hill College: The Early Days," *The Alabama Review* (April, 1954), p. 132.

[52] Erbacher, *op. cit.,* p. 83.

[53] See Isaac Hecker, "College Education," *The Catholic World,* XXV (September, 1877), 814–825; and John R. G. Hassard, "Literature and the Laity," *The Catholic World,* XXXVI (October, 1882), 1–8.

[54] Erbacher, *op. cit.,* p. 83.

[55] Hope, *op. cit.,* p. 271.

What was distinctive about entrance procedures for the colleges of this period must, again, be related to the six- or seven-year course maintained by most Catholic schools. Entrance qualifications of new applicants for secondary study were tested, but if a boy remained at school to complete his preparatory course, his qualifications for the more advanced demands of the college curriculum were simply taken for granted. Almost as a matter of policy, entrance officers rejected the idea that anyone was initially unfit for a place in their school; and they preferred to give boys a chance either to fail in class or otherwise to prove their moral unsuitability for membership of a Catholic college community. It may often have been difficult to remain in college, because of the multiple restrictions placed on student freedom, but it was surely not hard to enter. The standards demanded at the reading examination were flexible; presidents and prefects of studies interpreted them to meet the individual case. Sometimes they misjudged a student's aptitude and assigned him to a class for which he was unready; then it was up to the teachers to correct the error: he was moved down the curriculum ladder to a point which his achievement fitted.

The first unstructured years of Catholic college curricula are admittedly hard to follow; courses of study varied from institution to institution and within the same institution at different times. Varieties of curricular patterns continued, of course, because Catholic colleges matured separately; each school had its own pattern of growth. Only in a general way, then, can we discuss the common features of curricular development, realizing that these features became prominent at different times from school to school. The best evidence that a college had achieved relative curricular maturity was the conferral of degrees. The first Catholic college to award the academic degree of bachelor of arts was Georgetown, in 1817,[56] and shortly thereafter Georgetown upgraded its curriculum and regularized its course of study; as such it served as a model for other Catholic colleges and made their years of development somewhat easier. St. Louis, in 1838,[57] Fordham, in 1846,[58] and Notre Dame, in 1855,[59] appear to have organized a college curriculum whose completion could be recognized by a bachelor's degree; Holy Cross, in 1856, Spring Hill, in 1859, Mt. St. Mary's, in 1853, and Villanova, in 1865, separated lower from higher courses and aimed the college curriculum toward a bachelor's degree.[60]

Although some differences still existed in courses, standards, and breadth of curriculum from one formative period school to another, there were common features, inspired mainly, we should think, by the example

[56] Shea, *A History of Georgetown College,* p. 52.
[57] Faherty, *op. cit.,* pp. 56–57.
[58] Taaffe, *op. cit.,* p. 52.
[59] *Tenth Annual Catalogue of the University of Notre Dame, 1855,* p. 4.
[60] Power, *A History of Catholic Higher Education in the United States,* p. 78.

of Georgetown. While it would not be historically accurate to make Georgetown's history speak in detail for that of all Catholic colleges, clearly
Georgetown was the leader to whom her sister institutions looked for
guidance. Knowing this, we can describe curricular developments at Georgetown, beginning with the stated curriculum of 1820, and add to the
description salient examples of curricular formation, and reformation, at
other Catholic colleges of the genre.

Georgetown began granting bachelor's degrees in 1817, and sensing a
need for public recognition of her academic program, if degrees were to
have meaning, essayed to strengthen and regularize her curriculum. This
reconstruction took about three years. Thus in 1820 Georgetown had what
amounted to a six-year college course leading to a bachelor's degree,
although secondary-level studies were still in evidence for the first half of
the course. If a student elected to remain at the college to study advanced
mathematics and philosophy he won a master's degree.[61] This six-year
course leading to the bachelor's degree deserves our consideration, because
this curriculum, with only slight modifications and some internal reorganization, dominated Catholic college degree programs for the next half century.
This was the curriculum, too, that, almost from the beginning, maintained
an intellectual affinity with the Jesuit *Ratio Studiorum,* although it is probably impossible to find minute observance from the *Ratio* in it.[62] The spirit
of the *Ratio* was followed, and spirit alone, perhaps, could have been
followed, for the *Ratio* was never meant to guide combinations of secondary
and collegiate studies. It was intended solely for secondary schools. Moreover, the *Ratio* aimed at pure classical style and linguistic exactitude. Such
goals were too high for Catholic college curricula of the United States.
Still, the *Ratio* was a perceptive educational document : the colleges learned
from it and were guided by its broad educational precepts.

Georgetown's academic year of 1820 began on September 15th and
ended July 31st; for the first time the year was equally divided into two
sessions.[63] Yet in determining their academic calendars, Catholic colleges
refused to imitate Georgetown on these commencement and termination
dates and we find the colleges organizing their school years, with or without
a break between sessions, according to student need, parental wish, the
sacerdotal duties of teachers, climate, and various other things.

Since Georgetown's curriculum of 1820 occupies such a distinctive role
in Catholic college history, further information about it is desirable. Six
classes were organized, with one year allotted to each class : these, in order
upwards were Rudiments, Third Grammar, Second Grammar, First Grammar, Humanities, and Rhetoric. At the outset this plan (and the employ-

---

[61] Daley, *op. cit.,* pp. 213–214.
[62] *Ibid.,* p. 220.
[63] Shea, *A History of Georgetown College,* p. 58.

ment of these nomenclatures) was mainly a restructuring of old programs :
rudiments suggest elementary study; the three grammar classes remind us
of secondary schools; only the last two years suggest higher studies. With
the exception of the rudiments class, however, probably maintained exclusively for students with faulty preparation for the third-grammar year and
undoubtedly elementary in its principal features, the other years of study
were consistent with extant standards of college curricula. It is obviously
unfair to apply present-day criteria of curricular content and standards to
colleges of the early nineteenth century. Yet the rudiments class is a conundrum, for college history assures us that a good sign of college maturation
was a repudiation of elementary studies. This was something Catholic
colleges of the formative period were seldom able to do.

In any case, Georgetown's 1820 curriculum, leading to the bachelor's
degree, began with Rudiments—for which the stated prerequisite was
reading ability—with intent to expose the young scholar to English and
French grammar, as well as studies in arithmetic. At the end of the year
he was expected to read and write English correctly. Third Grammar
continued the study of English and French; some of the easier French
authors were read, and toward the end of the year the syllabus added Latin
grammar. In Third Grammar, Latin grammar and literature moved into a
prominent place in the curriculum; they may even have become its
dominating feature. In Second Grammar the curriculum revolved around
Latin; students completed Latin compositional exercises, read Caesar, and
capped their year's study with French authors and geography. First Grammar was more imposing and the list of student tasks was long and arduous;
Latin selections from Cornelius Nepos, Sallust, and Livy were studied;
Cicero's minor works were introduced, and some of Ovid's *Elegies* were
read. Besides this concentration on Latin authors, the study of French was
retained, and Greek was introduced. By the end of the year, according
to hopes expressed for student accomplishment, students should be reading
parts of Scripture, the satires of Lucian, and the history of Xenophon, all
in Greek or Latin. As if this were not enough, the students were encouraged
to pursue leisure-time studies in history and algebra.[64] In what proportions
idealism and realism were mixed in the codification of this program is
impossible to say, although it is difficult to believe that the syllabus was
followed to the letter : it was an ideal to be aimed for rather than a goal
regularly in reach. But at least the stated demands of the curriculum left
little to be desired in terms of hard work and academic respectability.

The study of humanities turned on Latin almost exclusively, for, it
was assumed, the boys had a sufficient introduction to Greek. They studied
Cicero again, concentrating now on his orations, and read Virgil, Horace,
and Livy in Latin, and parts of Homer in Greek. To this sturdy scholastic

[64] *Prospectus of 1820.*

diet, which, Daley says, "makes the paper buckle with its weight," were added history, algebra, geometry, and some studies in mythology. By the time students were ready to enter the final, sixth year, they were, if the curriculum described was followed faithfully, inured to hard work and unlikely to be troubled by what faced them next in the Rhetoric class : rhetoric's arsenal of technical rules was waiting to be mastered, and students were expected to write and speak well, faithful to the oratorical tradition of humanistic education. But this was not all. They continued with Cicero's orations, and the works of Homer, Virgil, and Horace, to which were added studies in history and mathematics. Whatever unevenness appeared in the curricular requirements from year to year, with the middle years apparently more demanding than later years, may be due to the curriculum's description rather than to any real discrepancy in the advance of academic standards. At the end of the course we find a surprising appendix : a class in book-keeping was taught for the convenience of students who wished to learn it.[65] Yet in keeping with conventional practice, bookkeeping, along with drawing, music, and dancing, was taught outside the regular curriculum.

So far there was no mention in the school's course of religious study. It was taken for granted, so special notice was unnecessary. Mentioned or not, religious study was there : all students took a catechism course taught at four o'clock on Saturday afternoons; and, we should think, considering the religious nature of the school, the entire curriculum was liberally infused with religious teaching and perspective.

Curriculum builders in the early colleges, especially at Georgetown, were guilty of exaggerations, and agreeing with Daley is not easy when he writes of the 1835 curriculum, which was a reconstruction of the 1820 course, saying "one can summon courage to read through the course of studies at this time only by realizing that the college students of 1835 not only read but followed this syllabus."[66] Although it may be prudent to defer reaction until we are familiar with the 1835 syllabus, it is difficult to imagine either a curriculum or students with all the quality Georgetown's chroniclers assume. We know standards outlined in college-program descriptions were often amended in practice;[67] we know, too, that Catholic college teachers (and Georgetown's teachers fitted this mold), were unequipped to lead students through a demanding intellectual course in the classics; moreover, from what we know of students' preparation for college study and the nature and kind of scholarly motives inspiring them, it is hard to take the standards implied in this curricular description seriously or even to accept the curriculum at face value. With these disclaimers on the record, we can turn to the course of studies adopted by Georgetown in 1835.

[65] Daley, *op. cit.,* pp. 221–222.
[66] *Ibid.,* p. 222.
[67] The best witness here is Thébaud, *Forty Years in the United States,* pp. 351–353.

Although using the same nomenclature for the first-year course—Rudiments—the curriculum of 1835 quickly departed from the standards of 1820 : rather than allow students in their first year to travel the road of English study and end with a fair ability to read and write English, the new curriculum took them immediately into the study of Latin and Greek grammar. In order to sharpen their grammatical tools, students made grammatical studies of Cicero's letters and tested their standards of written expression in composition. Complementary studies in English grammar were conducted to reinforce Latin, and the history of the Old Testament and geography were added. Although we are uncertain about the amount of time devoted to each branch of study, the best evidence supports an assumption that classical elements in the curriculum were given pride of place.

Next came Third Humanities with the letters of Cicero, Plato's *Phaedrus,* and the authors of *Graeca Minora.* On the more routine side of instruction, exercises in Greek, Latin, and English grammar were required and compositions were assigned in all three languages. The nature of composition writings was different from what we should now expect; a good composition was usually the rewriting of a story from memory, retaining as many classical allusions as possible, and remaining strictly faithful to the theme and detail of the classic. Originality was ignored; a classical style was given less credit than literary and linguistic exactitude. With this definition of good writing in mind students were absolved from rigorous scholarly standards. When they finished writing Latin, Greek, and English themes, often mainly exercises in translation from one to another language, they turned, so the syllabus says, to Bible history and North American geography. Perhaps geography was intended to be a diversion from arid classical study. Second Humanities, the third year, was largely a continuation of exercises in language and composition, with the Roman historians—Nepos and Caesar—added to what remained unread of *Graeca Minora.* Ancient history appears for the first time and the geography of South America and Europe is given a place in the curriculum.

First Humanities adhered to Latin authors : Sallust, Cicero's minor works, Virgil's *Eclogues* and parts of the *Aeneid*; Lucian and Xenophon represented Greek writers. Latin prosody now demanded student attention, and compositions in Latin, Greek, and English were conventional assignments. Studies in mythology, the history of Greece, and the geography of Asia and Africa completed the fourth-year course of study. With this much classical background, students were ready for Poetry—the fifth year—when they studied Cicero's orations, selected parts of Livy, Virgil, and the Roman poets Catullus, Tibullus, and Propertius. Selections from Horace, Xenophon, Thucydides, Theocritus, and Homer were read and, from time to time, prose and verse compositions were required in Greek, Latin, and English.

The Poetry-year curriculum was embellished by studies in ancient geography and the history of Rome.

Now the end of the long course was in sight—only two years to go—and students must have strengthened their resolve to finish what was so well begun. The Poetry year was followed by Rhetoric—the sixth course—which, being true to its title, demanded not only conversance with the principal orators of antiquity but a full knowledge of the technicalities and subtleties of rhetoric as well; the techniques of the former and the instruments of the latter were to be used in the ever-present prose and verse compositions. The curriculum directed students to Quintilian's *Institutio Oratoria,* Cicero's *De Oratore* and *De Inventione,* along with something from Juvenal, Persius, Horace, Livy, Demosthenes, Homer, and Sophocles. No one could charge a student who had stayed this long at Georgetown with illiteracy in the classics. But he was not finished yet, as he would have been had he followed the course of 1820. A seventh year, Philosophy, stood between him and graduation : this year's studies exposed students to courses in logic, metaphysics, ethics, natural and experimental philosophy. "As the students in this class are supposed to be good scholars," the prospectus read, "the Lectures on Logic, Metaphysics, and Ethics are delivered in the Latin language." [68] At this point the student was ready for the elusive bachelor's degree. But more was available for students who wanted more : the prospectus of 1831 had promised to perpetuate classes in "Bookkeeping for the convenience of those who wished to learn it," [69] and to offer Italian, Spanish and German if students wanted to study these languages. Besides, there were classes in music, drawing, and dancing for the student who had extra time on his hands. These were the extras, so often met before and later in Catholic colleges, for which students paid additional tuition charges.

The advantage of greater maturity allowed Georgetown to outdistance its Catholic college partners in the development of prescriptive curricula for the bachelor's degree; and we must not expect her imitators to keep pace. They were, however, aware, even at a distance, of Georgetown's curricular upgrading and made brave efforts to follow suit, although several years elapsed before their curricula were either as long or as strong as the one at the "mother" school. In reviewing the historical picture of formative-period curricula, it is unnecessary to describe curricular developments at every Catholic college, or even to describe in detail the curriculum at each of the ten permanent Catholic colleges founded before 1850, for they shared common objectives, an educational doctrine subordinating learning to religious aims,[70] and a strong tendency to imitate one another. Thus,

[68] *Prospectus of Georgetown College, 1835.*

[69] *Prospectus of Georgetown College, 1831.*

[70] This remained true for decades. See the following college catalogues for the year 1878–79; St. Louis, Xavier, St. Mary's (Ka.), Detroit, St. Ignatius (Chicago),

we find, curricular practices initiated at Georgetown at the beginning of a decade are usually duplicated at other Catholic colleges by the end of it. As often as not the art of imitation failed to produce the desired results because of great variations in educational resources and academic climate from school to school; yet a model was available and the colleges tried to be true to it.

The depth of the commitment to imitation is confirmed by a few examples from nineteenth-century Catholic colleges. St. Louis, far from Georgetown, especially in the early 1800s, and in a less settled part of the country, was unable to replicate Georgetown's 1835 curriculum until about 1855,[71] and by that time, of course, Georgetown herself had moved forward to more advanced stages of development. Still, sensitive to models rather nearer than the *Ratio Studiorum,* to which Jesuits regularly paid verbal allegiance, St. Louis instituted a Latin curriculum around 1831, and by 1832 was ready to state a fixed program of studies for what was called a college course. But a preparatory class was kept for the most practical of reasons : fifty pupils were waiting to enter it. According to the school's own description of its course, given to the Jesuit General in 1882,[72] this preparatory class was divided into five sections, each with its own teacher, and the boys were led through the alphabet, spelling, reading, and geography. Three grammar classes were built on this elementary foundation; together they enrolled eighty-nine students. Assuming that the General knew, without being told, what grammar studies entailed, the curricular statement pertaining to the three grammar years was perfunctory and avoided detail. Boys were instructed in composition, but, of course, if we grant that that instruction had the usual quality expected of Jesuit pedagogy, grammatical and literary achievement preliminary to composition must have been impressive; it was, at least, as good as it could have been in a three-year course. The fifth and last year, called Rhetoric, had an 1832 enrollment of thirteen students. The obvious missing element from the St. Louis curriculum, and one freely admitted by the author of the *Descriptio,* is a preoccupation with Latin : only eight students were engaged in Latin study. Nothing at all was done in Greek, but a class of French was taught daily and one in natural philosophy was offered on the afternoons of recreation days—Tuesdays, Thursdays, and Sundays.[73]

With both the example of Georgetown fairly clear and the traditions

---

Georgetown, St. John's (Fordham), Loyola (Baltimore), Boston College, Gonzaga (D. C.), Spring Hill, Immaculate Conception (La.), Santa Clara, Canisius, and Las Vegas (New Mex.).

[71] Faherty, *op. cit.,* p. 114.

[72] "Descriptio et status Collegii Sti. Ludovici," mense Januario, 1832, in Carraghan, *The Jesuits of the Middle United States,* I, 293–294.

[73] *Ibid.*

of the Society inspiring a determination for educational quality, St. Louis' managers were disinclined to mark time with this abbreviated course of study. So by 1838 a six- or seven-year college course was organized and publicly announced as the avenue to a bachelor's degree. Its year-by-year specifications need not engage us, for they followed the same pattern as Georgetown's 1835 curriculum, but the general content should be of interest. The course of study at St. Louis led, the public releases said, to a competent knowledge of Greek, Latin, and English and entailed a thorough study of classical grammar and literature. Besides these, geography, ancient and modern history were mentioned as important studies, along with branches of moral philosophy, ethics, and metaphysics; the long course was completed by studies in natural philosophy, mathematics, and rhetoric.[74] Should a student decide to go beyond the bachelor's to the master's degree, the prospectus told him how it might be done : "the degree of A. M. is given to the alumni who, after having received the degree of A. B., shall devote two years to some literary pursuit."[75] Students without a bachelor's degree from St. Louis, but with a degree from another institution, could qualify for a master's degree by producing evidence of at least a two-year period of literary study.

While this is not the place to examine the credentials of Catholic colleges for offering degrees beyond the bachelor's, it should be noted that it was common practice among American colleges, including Catholic colleges, to grant master's degrees in this way, without any formal courses, and most colleges chose to follow this custom almost from the time of their founding. There is, then, neither academic audacity nor presumption in St. Louis' plan.

During its years as a diocesan college, Fordham (St. John's) conducted a course of studies with the usual mixture of elementary, secondary, and higher studies. But with the advent of Jesuit control in 1846, and the experience the Jesuits from St. Mary's College, Kentucky, brought with them to New York, it was possible almost at once to institute a more regular and demanding college curriculum. The famous Augustus Thébaud was Fordham's first Jesuit president; under his direction the requirements for a bachelor's degree were stated as follows : "the aspirant [for the bachelor's degree shall] be able to read with ease the works of Cicero or Livy, Virgil or Horace, Demosthenes or Homer, and to stand examination in arithmetic, algebra, geometry, and trigonometry."[76] This statement of college requirements was unquestionably affected by the 1832 edition of the *Ratio Studiorum,* but probably even more directly by the example of Georgetown.

---

[74] "The Record Book of the Proceedings of the Board and Faculty of St. Louis University," in *ibid.,* III, 209.

[75] Hill, *op. cit.,* pp. 56–57.

[76] Taaffe, *op. cit.,* p. 72.

At the end of the first year of Jesuit control, the school's curriculum was subjected to scrutiny and a clearer and more definite organization was proposed : now a six-year program was arranged consisting of three grammar classes, wherein rudiments were taught when necessary, and classes of Humanities, Rhetoric, and Philosophy.[77]

Spring Hill College made oblique reference to its course of study in a prospectus printed in the October, 1830, edition of the *United States Catholic Miscellany* by announcing two professorships of English, two of French, two of Latin, one of Spanish, one of mathematics, and one of Greek. The professorship of Greek, it should be added, was held sometimes by Bishop Michael Portier, the Ordinary of Mobile and the school's President, and sometimes by the Bishop's vicar-general. Without full-time teachers, since neither the office of bishop nor vicar-general was discharged perfunctorily, Greek classes could hardly have been taken very seriously. In addition to a clear concentration on language study in the Spring Hill curriculum, it was announced that due attention was paid to geography, astronomy, history, rhetoric, belles-lettres, and the elements of physics and chemistry.[78] Precise curricular organization at Spring Hill in 1830 is too much to expect, and it is hard to know whether or not the professorships promised in the prospectus were active.

At Xavier College in Cincinnati teaching began with a dual curricular organization, classical and commercial, but the first prospectus clearly subordinates commercial to classical study. This is entirely in keeping with conventional practice. Xavier could hardly be termed unconventional because she followed St. Louis in almost every educational detail, except in the organization there of an evening school, a striking innovation for this time. Yet, Xavier College's evening study was not intended for regular college students; it was, rather, for the teaching of "the German language [to some] who have expressed their wish to attend at night . . . and also a Book-Keeping class, will be opened . . . and will be taught every evening towards candlelight." [79]

For final illustrations of curricular progress through the formative period, we may turn to Notre Dame, which began, so one of her historians says, "as a tidy French boarding school." [80] The first prospectus, issued in 1851, was sketchy and offered few details about studies beyond Father Sorin's statement that "bookkeeping, as its importance requires, has received a double amount of labor." [81] This extraordinary attention to commercial

[77] For an evaluation of Fordham's studies before the Jesuits assumed control, and indirectly those at Mt. St. Mary's in Maryland—because Mt. St. Mary's was the model for St. John's—see Thébaud, *Forty Years in the United States,* pp. 351–353.

[78] Kenny, *op. cit.,* pp. 69–70.

[79] *First Prospectus of Xavier College.*

[80] Hope, *op. cit.,* p. 66.

[81] Lenoue, *op. cit.,* p. 21.

courses is surprising, and may even be misleading, for it is unlikely that the Congregation of the Holy Cross or its resident religious superior, Edward Sorin, envisaged Notre Dame as a commercial college. Yet, in an effort to achieve academic security, Notre Dame tried to attract students and temporarily, at least, chose to extol the virtues of a commercial education. In 1854 the course of studies was reorganized or, more accurately, organized with college study in mind. Ten departments were mentioned, and for the first time in Catholic college history we see a departmental organization of studies taken seriously. The following subjects were fitted into departmental categories : Christian doctrine, logic, metaphysics, geometry, algebra, Greek, Latin, elocution, grammar, analysis, modern history, geography, spelling, composition, letter writing, public reading, natural philosophy, chemistry, bookkeeping, arithmetic, penmanship, French, and German. In addition, and outside the departmental structure, manual-labor-school students studied such trades as tailoring, carpentry, shoemaking, blacksmithing, and baking. Some extracurricular instruction was offered in music, painting, and drawing.[82]

In 1855, Notre Dame's collegiate course was set at six years,[83] but a precise separation of college from preparatory studies was deferred until 1864.[84] The 1855 course, however, remained materially unchanged until 1873, and was given its most complete description in the *Catalogue* of 1864 : "This course, designed to impart a thorough knowledge of the Greek, Latin, and English languages; of Mental and Moral Philosophy, of pure and mixed Mathematics, and of Physical Science, is completed in six years."[85] Approaching what later became the unit measure for college studies, Notre Dame announced that students aiming for the bachelor's degree should have six units of Latin, six of Greek, four of English, four of mathematics, two of philosophy, and two of natural philosophy. Although no requirements for modern foreign languages were listed, the *Tenth Annual Catalogue* of 1855 had introduced a statement on the subject that was repeated for the next quarter century : "The study of French can be pursued at this University with unusual facilities, as it is universally spoken in the Society who has charge of the institution, many of whose members are fine French scholars. German, Spanish, and Italian are also taught, but with Music and Drawing, all these languages form extra charges."[86] Alongside the collegiate course and the extras stood the commercial course, now clearly stipulated as a study for students not seeking a college degree.[87]

[82] *Ibid.*, p. 23.
[83] *Tenth Annual Catalogue of the University of Notre Dame, 1855,* p. 4.
[84] *Twentieth Annual Catalogue of the University of Notre Dame, 1864,* p. 13.
[85] *Ibid.*
[86] *Tenth Annual Catalogue of the University of Notre Dame, 1855,* p. 5.
[87] *Ibid.*

In one of its catalogue statements, Notre Dame confirmed an attitude common among Catholic colleges approaching the end of their formative periods in curricular development and collegiate organization : "The course of study has been methodized anew, has been greatly enlarged, and is, it is believed, rendered fully adequate to the demands of the advancing culture of the Northwest; the corps of Professors and Tutors was never before so numerous and efficient to which may be joined the scarcely less important consideration that each succeeding year has witnessed large and expensive additions to the material facilities for imparting a thorough and complete education."[88]

The road through the formative period had been long and hard; some colleges had fallen by the wayside; others were deficient in attaining the practical goals of achievement they themselves had set; but for the most part, Catholic colleges surviving the formative period were ready, during the 1860–1870 decade, to separate preparatory from collegiate courses, to offer bachelor's degrees after a regular six- or seven-year course, to subordinate clearly commercial studies to classical curricula, and to answer the roll of colleges in company with respectable institutions of the land. Hazards to success were still on the road ahead—some were old, some new— but the colleges could look to the future taking satisfaction in the fact that hard work, sacrifice, and determination had enabled them to come so far. By 1870 the identity of Catholic colleges was assured; their stability, while less certain in individual cases, could in general be assumed; they had succeeded in becoming schools and now they charged themselves with the obligation of becoming authentic agencies of higher learning.

Classroom methods of the formative period

The broad instructional program of early Catholic colleges—with courses for boys ranging in age from eight to twenty-six—makes generalizations about classroom methods a complicated business. No doubt good teachers adapted their techniques to the age and educational level of their students whenever they could, but a vote of confidence in the common sense of teachers able to create situations favorable to learning enlightens us little on the details of their pedagogy. And if we add the possibility of poorly-prepared teachers, who lacked both learning in the subjects they taught and motivation for teaching, to the practice common in most colleges of appointing a class teacher to stay with the students through the entire college course,[89] we have an historical thicket with few avenues of light.

[88] *Ibid.*

[89] All early prospectuses make the place of the class teacher incontestable. See

Catholic college teachers were likely to honor tradition, both in the content of schooling and in its pedagogy, so we should expect to find that, to the extent of their familiarity with classical technique, they adopted it for the classes they were directed to teach.[90] Modifications of the older pedagogy were inevitable—as were departures from it—but neither were made in the conviction that the classical technique itself was inappropriate.

Time alone had obliterated and fragmented much of classical pedagogy, and Catholic colleges had few scholars capable of reconstructing it, so, at best, it had to be mined from documents and constitutions wherein the educational obligations of religious societies were stated.[91] Once these excavations were made, however, they were implemented mainly by teachers who, wanting to teach their students the way they themselves had been taught, had reached the college classroom by a route of study in an American Catholic college. In this system traditional methods associated with classical and humanistic teaching atrophied, despite the appearance of European-educated teachers because, along with their lack of rapport with students, they found difficulty in remembering and adapting details of classroom technique their mentors had employed in very different circumstances.

Anxieties about remaining true to the past were too great to allow any hasty relocation of pedagogical loyalty, so teachers and prefects of study searched the files of their own religious communities to find plans of studies and teaching guides for use in American schools. The best of these old plans, and the one most often used, the Jesuit *Ratio Studiorum,* could be followed only here and there.[92] Its original purpose had been to deploy teaching techniques in connection with Greek and Latin language and literature for students already familiar with both languages, but too often the *Ratio* proved to be of little help to overworked teachers unable to make any assumptions about the scholastic skill their students brought to school with them.[93] Had the pedagogic problem been given the attention it deserved, the schools should have admitted that what they had as a residue from their European and classical heritage was, pedagogically speaking, almost useless for the classrooms of American colleges, and started anew to create sets of pedagogical principles that would lead to accuracy of knowledge rather than literary exactitude and imitations of classical style. Neglecting this, the schools were forced to utilize instruments of instruction ill-suited to the subjects studied and the students being taught.

for example the 1878–1879 catalogues of Georgetown, St. John's, St. Louis, and Xavier.

[90] Erbacher, *op. cit.,* p. 94.

[91] Ward, *op. cit.,* pp. 273–292.

[92] Robert Schwickerath, *Jesuit Education, Its History and Principles* (St. Louis, B. Herder, 1904), pp. 287–289.

[93] Burns and Kohlbrenner, *op. cit.,* p. 269; and Meagher and Grattan, *op. cit.,* pp. 165–167.

At the elementary level—and every Catholic college of the formative period had some involvement here—teachers were hearers of lessons; the boys took their books, tablets, and exercise manuals, when they had any, prepared their lessons and recited them when called upon by the teacher.[94] Because classes were small and the skills of learning were fairly obvious when mastered, complex examination procedures were underdeveloped : our knowledge even of the routine testing devices used is extremely limited. At the secondary and college levels the methods employed and the tests used form a larger part of the permanent record.[95]

In many details of class management Catholic colleges employed practices common in American colleges, for both collegiate systems shared a common heritage. Had Catholic colleges wanted to be entirely different from their counterparts in the United States, they would have found it difficult to define a separate and distinctive approach to teaching; so despite their denominational allegiance, which made for some differences in goals and content, and a vigorous determination to ignore nonCatholic colleges around them, they had inevitably to stand on the same general pedagogical platform.[96] Yet, while this was true, they made the most of minor differences. What must appear most unusual and distinctive, for instance, among Catholic colleges was their enthusiastic embrace of a class-teacher method, where a teacher began with a class in its first secondary or college year and stayed with it through the entire college program.

Sometimes a class had only one teacher for the full seven-year course, but there were other ways in which the system could work : in some colleges class teachers were freed from rudiments, and in others they were not promoted with their classes beyond the Poetry year.[97] In the former plan, students met their permanent teacher in Third Grammar or Humanities; in the latter, the teaching of advanced classes, Rhetoric and Philosophy, was left to so-called specialists.

The class-teacher arrangement, although introduced in American Catholic colleges during Georgetown's early years, was an imitation of a teaching practice developed by the Jesuits in 1548, so Georgetown must not be credited with its invention. But Georgetown gave it currency in this country and with Georgetown's recommendation plus its Jesuit credentials, the method was adopted in most nineteenth-century Catholic colleges. Departures were made from the class-teacher method when circumstances

---

[94] William P. Treacy, "Some Early Catholic Grammar Schools," *United States Catholic Historical Magazine,* I (1887), 71–73.

[95] Goebel, *op. cit.,* pp. 161–165, 220–221.

[96] Sister St. Mel Kennedy, *The Changing Academic Characteristics of the Nineteenth-Century American College Teacher* (St. Louis, St. Louis University, 1961), pp. 25–26.

[97] Taaffe, *op. cit.,* p. 70; and Garraghan, *The Jesuits of the Middle United States,* III, 210.

required, and we know that where methods of teaching were concerned the colleges could be flexible in adapting teaching procedures to the skill and versatility of their teachers.[98] Still, revisions of what were regarded as sound technique were always justified as expedients and were intended to be temporary. Class teachers were an ideal. Who other than a class teacher could know students' strengths and weaknesses better, or suit the appurtenances of learning to them?

Flaunting convention was always unseemly, so whether or not they liked the class-teacher method, Catholic colleges accepted it and were generally opposed to suggestions of any change going beyond an incidental tampering with the system. One early Catholic college countenanced innovation but only briefly : shortly after the beginning of its Jesuit period, Fordham jettisoned the old method and introduced the specializing professor. Thereafter, in following their curriculum, students moved from teacher to teacher, and may have had as many different teachers as subjects. Why Fordham took this bold step is unrecorded, although the example nonCatholic colleges offered in connection with the specialist teacher was apparent, and Fordham's leaders may have seen some virtue in the practice. In any case, the rarified air of distinction made Fordham uncomfortable; after a year as an innovator she returned to her old teaching ways, because, so one of her historians said, too much student time was wasted in passing from the class of one teacher to another.[99]

If the college was so jealous of student time, it might have found other ways to economize—surely Fordham was not following Quintilian's ancient admonition to "lose time rather than save it"—so the reason given for returning to the old practice may have been misleading : more likely, although this speculation lacks evidential support, the Fordham Jesuits were told by their superiors to restore the class teacher. In any case, an historical association of class teachers and Catholic colleges is entirely valid, and this compatibility resisted the erosions of time and educational innovation until the colleges' curricula changed so much that class teachers were out of the question.[100] On the level of method Catholic colleges were in the unenviable position of reacting to educational circumstances rather than taking a hand in shaping them.

In all college classrooms recitation and repetition were popular techniques, and every teacher put great confidence in them; discussion was a little-known method, and lecturing not common.[101] What possible good could come from allowing students to talk about their studies? They had been sent to school to learn, not to exchange opinions! And the lecture, too

---

[98] Hoffmann, *op. cit.,* pp. 136–137.
[99] See Taaffe, *op. cit.,* p. 73.
[100] Kennedy, *op. cit.,* pp. 112–117.
[101] Erbacher, *op. cit.,* pp. 92–101; and Meagher and Grattan, *op. cit.,* pp. 165–167.

advanced a method to use in connection with immature students, was reserved either for the most advanced college classes or the seminary. The heart of instruction was the insistence on reading, a logically consistent priority for an educational philosophy taking at face value the assertion that the classics were inexhaustible sources of all worthwhile knowledge. It is therefore important to know what reading entailed and how it was taught. Once boys finished elementary studies they were ready to read and, according to official pronouncements, were expected to read the classical languages. However, since they were not good Latinists—and the less said about Greek the better—it was necessary for the teacher to give them some help and prepare them for the reading assignment. He began by outlining the narrative; then he explained various grammatical constructions used, passed to comments on style, elaborated the meaning of novel words and phrases, and, finally, sent the students to their reading books.[102]

This technique of teaching reading, widely used in college classical curricula, especially in Jesuit schools, had the undoubted validation of tradition : it was the Jesuit method of prelection all over again.[103] When the teacher finished his discourse, introducing students to the classic or an assigned selection from it, they were ready to read. This meant they studied the literary selection and noted its grammar, style, message, and meaning. If they had studied hard, they could recite by heart everything the teacher had told them plus some details they themselves had wrestled from the text. With one classic finished, they turned to another; the process went on and on, save when composition was part of the syllabus. Then, in their writing, students were expected to reproduce a classical story they had read, and a good composition was one that remained true to the original both in the details of the story and in imitation of style. No thought was given to originality in student writing. Still, this method had two assumed values which had nothing whatever to do with personal writing style : the first, that Latin usage would improve with practice and that composition was unquestionably good practice; the second, that in following a classic almost to the letter—at least, as closely as memory allowed—students were forced into classical writing styles : good writing, so a dogmatic assumption ran, is always a matter of writing the way classical authors had written. In addition, although no defense of these teaching practices is to be found in the literature on Catholic-college teaching, the discipline involved in such study, and produced by such minute observance to models, must have been tremendous. And it would be presumptuous for contemporary methodologists to discard these pedagogic techniques with scorn, for they were clearly consistent with the goals of education Catholic colleges had set for themselves.

[102] Shea, *A History of Georgetown College*, pp. 86–89.
[103] Allan P. Farrell, *The Jesuit Ratio Studiorum of 1599* (Washington, D.C., 1970), pp. 66–67, 127–128.

In the classroom, where daily, weekly, and monthly repetitions were conducted, every addition to knowledge was related to what students had already learned, and nothing was to be forgotten.[104] Besides, repetitions were interclass as well as intraclass : once a week, usually on Saturday, the entire student body, with the exception of boys in rudiments, was assembled to repeat and review its accomplishments. The week's work was summarized by classes, and a prize or reward was given to the class that made the best showing. At the end of the month, a somewhat more formal convocation was held, attended by the president, and sometimes by outside visitors, for students to display how much they had mastered during the month. We know few details of these formal, and somewhat elaborate, repetitions, but competition among classes and students was keen, and what is more, was encouraged as a matter of instructional policy. Students were awarded prizes, titles, extra days of recreation, or places of honor at college banquets for excellence in these scholarly displays of erudition.

According to methodological precepts in force in Catholic colleges, the textbook was important; it was the chief instrument of instruction, although it required interpretation, and the students needed the guidance of a teacher. But there were some subjects for which texts were either unavailable or inadequate. Then the teacher could lecture; and some teachers, deploring the conventional dependence on texts, indicated a preference for classroom lectures which, they thought, would add vitality and zest to teaching and learning.[105]

Considering the limitations on teachers' freedom of action in Catholic colleges, however, these private convictions were seldom translated into teaching technique. If, or when, they were, too little is known of the lecture technique in Catholic colleges to permit an evaluation. Again, to judge from the general state of teaching and of teachers' credentials, it would be surprising indeed to discover elaborations of scholarly research or critical and objective interpretations of the classics or classical commentaries in these lectures. In scientific subjects, the lecture, making use of the thin resources of the scientific cabinet and involving a demonstration, was probably used because it was the only technique available; and in philosophy, especially as philosophical teaching moved beyond a recapitulation of fundamental precepts to involve student thought in burning religious, social, and political questions of the day, lectures were unavoidable.[106] Still, they may have been more apologetic than critical in tone and content, and more concerned with sustaining orthodox than independent thinking. The

[104] Meagher and Grattan, *op. cit.*, p. 167; and Dunigan, *op. cit.*, pp. 155–157.

[105] Henry A. Brann, "St. Mary's College, Wilmington, Delaware," United States Catholic Historical Society, *Records and Studies*, VII (June, 1914), 82.

[106] Talbot, *op. cit.*, pp. 118–127.

lecture, moreover, was always a good way to communicate information or ideas unavailable in textbooks—especially in the absence of respectable library resources—and this may have been its best, or only, recommendation. In any case, although employed, the lecture technique never dominated the Catholic college classroom of the day, and this was sometimes regretted : a priest-teacher at Mt. St. Mary's College confessed that "the Latin authors are too narrow in their scope . . . [and] I have rarely succeeded in making students learn anything differing from the text-book which they have in their hands."[107]

Adherence to dry-as-dust texts had few dedicated champions among teachers in Catholic colleges; yet respecting texts and unable to dispense with them, they were directed to employ them as instruments for a decent education. The ideal was expressed by John Carroll, who again must be praised as the greatest man we meet in the history of Catholic higher education. His remarkable insights and his breadth of pedagogical vision were almost unbelievable. In 1791, essaying to set standards for teaching at Georgetown, he considered the question of teaching method and tried to give his confreres the benefit of his wisdom and experience. He began by asserting that "one of the most essential necessities for success in educational work is the possession of natural, thorough, and effective methods of teaching."[108] Such methods were to be applied uniformly by teachers in all classes. "In this respect,"Carroll continued,"Georgetown enjoys peculiar advantages. Her teaching is guided by the principles laid down in the famous ratio studiorum . . . It is a noteworthy fact that many of the recently-devised methods of teaching, such as the natural, the inductive, and similar plans, are in reality mere repetitions of the devices recommended long ago in the ratio studiorum and practiced with varying degrees of fidelity in the colleges of the Society of Jesus."[109]

Carroll's pedagogy was Jesuit pedagogy (he may be forgiven for traces of superiority in his endorsement of it), and, since we know how much Georgetown influenced not only American Jesuit colleges but all Catholic colleges, it became a prescriptive technique in every American Catholic college. Still, Carroll was unwilling to rest solely on the past or to disallow amendments to ancient teaching codes; his fundamental respect for teaching was too great for him to think that texts alone were enough : "What is learned from the living voice of the teacher is acquired more thoroughly and more completely" than from texts; the classroom teacher, moreover, can guide the work of emulation, direct the friction of mind on mind, and explain difficult points not covered in the text. These teaching directions, he said, along with "repetition in public of the whole lesson are some of

107 Meline and McSweeny, *op. cit.*, II, 71.
108 Quoted in Easby-Smith, *op. cit.*, I, 31.
109 *Ibid.*, p. 32.

the more important agencies at work during the hour of class, which cannot be supplied out of class, and so an hour of class lost is a distinct and in some sense irreparable loss."[110] Indictments for narrowness should be avoided here, for Carroll completes his thought on the importance of class-room teaching by saying that whatever is neglected in the classroom is "not only a loss to mental training, it is a serious menace to the regularity of college discipline" as well.[111]

Carroll was setting an ideal, one undoubtedly followed faithfully when conditions warranted and when teachers were qualified, but there were frequently unbridgeable gaps between the ideal and the real. Even some cur-ricular goals were at variance with Carroll's idealism and blocked its implementation. The living voice of the teacher, the friction of mind on mind, were easily-buried pedagogic values when facility in Latin was made the chief product of study at the college level. Long hours of study with relentless attention to linguistic detail discounted an announced allegiance to a broad education, and, in addition, on a level of day-to-day teaching made teachers supremely conscious of the value of translation as a teaching-learning technique for Latin excellence. In the end, whatever policies relative to method were stated, the practical goals of study made them ineffective and invisible. Even the much-heralded composition writing, as a means for mastering style, turned out to be little more than a series of exercises in translation. And English study, despite much praise and justifica-tion, was subordinated as a helpmate to Latin study. English was a medium of instruction in the curriculum, and attention was paid to it for its medial use; but the inherent values of English study were either denied or missed. English was a tool used for learning something more valuable—Latin—and methods of English teaching were distilled in this context.[112]

Classroom practice had an elusive quality : in Catholic colleges, it was said, teachers followed an approved teaching code, but the historian is seldom able to find his way inside the classroom to confirm or reject this assumption; and if independently-minded teachers decided to ignore the code they would, in all probability, have been silent about their innovations. Now and then a former student praised the inventiveness of a teacher and implied an excellence bred of pedagogical eccentricity, but the memories of graduates, when it comes to college-day recollections, are not sufficient to keep us on safe historical ground. We know what Catholic college teachers were expected to do in their classrooms, and we have a fair idea of the textbooks they used. We know, too, that these texts needed the approval

110 *Ibid.*, p. 33.

111 *Ibid.*

112 For example, see "Descriptio et status Collegii Sti. Ludovici," mense Januario, 1832, in Garraghan, *The Jesuits of The Middle United States,* I, 293–294.

of college and religious superiors before adoption. But we must admit that in closing the classroom door teachers preserved, and concealed, more than their anonymity. At one point, however, that of the examination, both the content to be mastered and the teacher's method of instruction were partly revealed. We learn from this, also, that some use was made of globes, maps, and scientific exhibits as materials for teaching in addition to the ever-present textbook and classical anthology.[113]

Examinations, then, give us some insights into teaching that otherwise would be difficult, or impossible, to obtain : they were used mainly as a basis for promotion from one class to another, and, although it was conventional for students to spend an entire year in a class, examinations were administered three times a year in order to allow particularly successful students to accelerate their progress through the college course. Scheduled near Christmas, Easter, and Pentecost, with the president and all teachers present, these oral examinations were conducted with the class teacher acting only in the capacity of an observer, for normally he was disqualified from interrogating his own students and sometimes he was barred from the examining room. The class teacher, using results from compositional exercises, determined a student's rank in class; his colleagues decided whether or not a student merited promotion.

Fragmentary records of the materials used as bases for oral examinations are extant.[114] They indicate a general requirement that students should have an almost faultless knowledge of the classical authors, the grammatical texts, and the rhetorical treatises studied. Sometimes students were asked to read and explain classical selections, say, something from Homer; or they were given selections from the Bible, from a book of sermons, or a mathematical text and asked to repeat what they knew about them. A good memory was an undoubted advantage in these examinations, but more than memory was essential, so we are told, for a mark of excellence. Unquestionably, the oral examination ordeal motivated students to prepare and review their lessons with unusual care and in great detail; the examination proceedings were so formal and so awesome that boys must surely have been sternly disciplined by their experiences of them. The examination system, and, in fact, the entire teaching, aimed at repeating what was already known. It relied on the humanistic doctrine that everything worth knowing was buried somewhere in the classics, and paid scant heed to interpretation, to finding inspiration for the contemporary world, to developing the student's own style of written or oral expression or his

---

113 Erbacher, *op. cit.*, p. 95.

114 See Daley, *op. cit.*, pp. 226–230; *Marquette College, A Quarter Century, 1881–1906* (Milwaukee, Marquette College, 1906), p. 15; and W. J. Maxwell, *Loyola University* (Chicago, Loyola University Press, 1919), p. xviii.

ability to think for himself. Originality of thought and expression was ignored; the good student was one who knew his texts faultlessly and could reproduce them from memory on the proper cues from oral examiners.

Toward the end of the formative period, oral examinations began to give way to written tests prepared and finalized in a highly complex way by an appointed examining board. The examining board consisted of the class teacher—now allowed a part in assessing the achievement of his students—the prefect of studies, and another member of the college faculty. Examination questions were prepared first by the class teacher—usually about twice as many as could be used—and submitted to the prefect of studies. The prefect evaluated the questions, accepted the ones he liked, amended the text or the sense of others, and sent them on to the examiner —the disinterested teacher—who now had his chance to help shape the examination. When he finished his editing and revising, he returned the questions to the prefect of studies who made final amendments. Now the examination was ready. On examination day the students and the examiner assembled in the examining room and waited for the prefect of studies, who held the questions in his custody, to deliver the test. The examiner then administered the examination. With the examination over, the examiner collected the papers and turned them over to the class teacher for correction and scoring. A student's success or failure, after all this complicated process, was decided by the class teacher. Such a cumbersome system must have had some virtue, but what this virtue was is mysterious; the test began with the class teacher and appraisals, it would appear, depended solely on his judgment. Still, the prefect of studies felt that he must be involved and an outside teacher was needed, no doubt, to add a tone of objectivity to the whole business. Sometimes teachers and administrators in Catholic colleges found it easy to make mountains of molehills.

Somewhat apart from strict examinations, but part of the total evaluative system nevertheless, were competitions in composition writing. Compositional exercises, as we have pointed out, determined a student's rank in class, and this was no trivial matter in colleges giving so much attention to competition. Composition topics were assigned to a class by the teacher of the next higher class; it was then the duty of the teacher of the lowest class to assign theme topics to the highest class. And themes were written in several languages, usually English, Latin, and Greek or French. Plainly, only one composition was written, accompanied by two translations, but good translations could be obtained only by careful work, and the amount of student labor involved must have been considerable. A board judged the compositions on their aggregate merit. If, by chance, two or more students wrote compositions of equal merit, a "write-off" was scheduled; but at this stage, in order to keep the identity of the competing scholars concealed from the students, all students were assigned themes to write, but only the compositions of the two students competing for places of honor were read and appraised.[115]

There were other ways, too, to keep students on their intellectual toes. At Georgetown, for example, in 1826, a more scientific system of assessing student progress was invented : the points system. Each day, for student recitations and other classroom work, points were allotted by the teacher; he kept a record of the points and at the end of the month the student with the largest total was awarded a "ticket of eminence."[116] This plan for bringing competition down to a day-by-day level was remarkably durable, for it was still used, with only minor adjustments concerned with merit-point standards, at the University of Detroit in 1880. There, students meeting the standard won badges of distinction awarded in a monthly student-faculty convocation.[117]

Generalizations about student-faculty relationships are somewhat hazardous, especially in a system putting such inordinate value on authority. And when these relationships were tested in situations where teachers were clerics, entitled to due clerical reverence, it is hard to know where faculty influence began and ended and where clerical dignity and student obeisance to priestly status stopped and started. Students reverenced their teachers probably more as clerics than as academic men, but for the most part they sensed their teachers' clear interest in them, in itself a good omen for a sound relationship. It is hard to believe, despite the codes of conduct that fill the house literature of any college, that the atmosphere was either artificial or unfriendly. Generally, we think, boys had a good time at college and liked their teachers, although sometimes distrusting them when teachers were commissioned to act as prefects.

We have now seen something of the methods of teaching and the materials of instruction used in nineteenth-century Catholic college classrooms. A final word may be added in connection with opportunities for learning outside the classroom. For the most part, the Catholic college campus was an intellectual and cultural desert; located either far from an urban area or shut off from urban facilities if in a city, it afforded boys little opportunity to enrich themselves culturally or intellectually. Now and then a priest or missionary preacher might be invited to lecture on some phase of religious life; on occasion a political figure found his way to the Catholic school; but men of culture, artists, authors, even businessmen, were seldom seen on campus and almost never presented to the students. This would not have been so bad had the colleges supported their class study by providing a good library, but this too was overlooked. Nothing at all is heard of libraries in connection with class teaching; and we doubt whether the

---

[115] Daley, *op. cit.*, p. 227.
[116] *Ibid*, pp. 227–229.
[117] *Detroit College Catalogue, 1880*, p. 4.

libraries with their thin holdings—even in 1872 only one Catholic college had as many as 30,000 volumes, seventeen had fewer than 4,000 volumes, and sixteen, apparently unwilling to reveal their library inadequacies, refused to answer the Commissioner of Education's query—[118] could have maintained any meaningful relationship to instruction. Library books were on religious and theological subjects, and since the majority were written in Latin the boys found them either unpalatable or unusable.

[118] *Report of the United States Commissioner of Education, 1872*, pp. 762–781. While this Report is probably the best general source of information on college libraries of this genre, college catalogues made frequent references to libraries. A few illustrations may prove interesting. "The College Library contains thirty thousand volumes, amongst which are many rare and curious works. There are one hundred volumes printed between the years 1472 and 1520; three manuscripts anterior to the year 1400, and others of later dates" (*Georgetown College Catalogue, 1879–1880*, p. 16). The same year Xavier College reported 14,000 volumes in its library (*Xavier College Catalogue, 1879–1880*, p. 6). *St. Ignatius College* (Chicago) *Catalogue of 1878–1879*, p. 8, notes the addition of "some valuable (books) during the course of this year. Charlevoix, S. J.—History of Paraguay, two vols, folio, 1657; . . . Calhoun, John C.—Speeches and Life, 10 vols., 8vo., 1843; . . . Sheridan (Rt. Hon. R. B.)—Speeches, three vol., 8vo., 1842; . . . abridgement of the Debates in Congress, vols., 1879. Rev. John McKenna, N. Y., has donated a well-preserved copy of the Bible in Chinese, besides another work, also in Chinese, entitled "Conversations between two Friends."

St. John's (Fordham) *Catalogue of 1881–1882*, p. 3, reported 20,000 volumes in the library and noted that 5,000 of these were eligible for circulation. In the catalogue for Fordham a decade later, p. 4, the total number of volumes in the library had increased to 30,000 and 6,000 volumes were said to be "especially adapted to the needs of the students." *Santa Clara College Catalogue, 1889–1890*, p. 24, reports 12,000 volumes, "some four centuries old and well preserved," in the college library.

Gonzaga College (D. C.) *College Catalogue for 1889–1890*, p. 17, contains an extract from the student by-laws governing library use: "1. All students of the College may become members of the Library Association; but no one not an actual student shall be allowed, under any circumstances, to take out a book. 2. Two books may be taken out every week: One from the Religious, the other from any of the remaining departments (Literature, History, Science, Fiction); but no more than two books may be retained at a time. 3. Each student is responsible for the book inscribed under his name; hence, should any be lost, he is bound to make up for the loss. In case the lost book forms part of a set, the cost of the entire collection may be required. 4. Any one defacing books or their covers, or injuring them in any other way, will be fined according to the extent of the damage done."

St. Peter's College library, according to the *1889–1890 Catalogue*, p. 5, contained 2,200 volumes; Loyola College, in Baltimore, claimed 30,000 volumes in its library, according to its *1889–1890 Catalogue*, p. 3. Creighton College had 5,000 volumes in its library, of which 1,000 could be used by students (*Catalogue of 1889–1890*, p. 5). Xavier's library had grown to 16,000 volumes, according to the *Catalogue of 1889–1890*, p. 8.

Gonzaga College in Spokane reported that "the library numbers several thousand volumes" in its *1895–1896 Catalogue*, p. 6. In the *1895–1896 Catalogue*, St. Ignatius College in Chicago claimed 20,500 volumes (p. 10); Loyola (Baltimore) claimed 40,000

The bare rooms used for classes were probably more attractive to students than inaccessible libraries with theological tracts and ecclesiastical tomes, few of which spoke in languages students understood. Still, the Catholic college was not altogether a bleak place : the recollections of its students, even in the nineteenth century when conditions were most primitive, are usually positive and encouraging. If the products of these schools chose not to castigate them for their classrooms, teaching techniques, and generally uncultured atmosphere, we find no contemporary commission for doing so.

the same year (p. 5), of which 2,000 "are carefully selected for the immediate use of the students, who have, besides, their society libraries." Boston College's library contained 4,000 volumes in 1895 (*Boston College Catalogue, 1895–1896,* p. 11).

Creighton College claimed a professors' library of 7,000 volumes and a students' library of 1,600 volumes in its *1895–1896 Catalogue,* p. 4.

6

The undergraduate

Administration, faculty, curricula, all necessarily belong to a portrait of nineteenth-century Catholic colleges; but unless dimensions sketched from the students' side are added our knowledge of life in these colleges remains incomplete. Histories of American higher education ordinarily describe how students fared in a generally repressive collegiate atmosphere; yet, for the most part—if what we know about early colleges is reliable—college life, except for a few obvious details, remained substantially unchanged for more than a century. Collegiate government structure, set before the advent of the nineteenth century, put a student in his place, and neither this structure nor the efforts of students to organize their own power much altered their standing until the late 1960s. Whether this old system should be praised or blamed, considered useful or wasteful, is not a question for history; still, it remained an undoubted fact that once a student entered college he was powerless to alter his living conditions or effect any permanent changes in college centers of power.

A pragmatic theory of college government perpetuated this notion : colleges must be citadels of learning wherein younger generations are fed a wisdom validated by the experience of former generations. And capitulating to student pressure or surrendering control of colleges to the very persons they were expected to teach, stood, in the conventional wisdom, as the basest kind of academic heresy. Despite college officers' contemporary willingness, as far as public statement goes, to abandon the traditional doctrine of *in loco parentis*—a theory that a college stands in the parents' place and is responsible for students in their stead—the fact of its abandonment may be debated; or, it may be asserted, colleges have substituted another theory allowing them to interpret contemporary social values and make these interpretations prescriptive in college life. Again, affirming or rejecting such action rests outside the ambit of history, although an historian, employing historical reflection, should be able to show that earlier anxieties surrounding student life, although somewhat modified by the inevitable stream of time, were generated within the same context of frustration and desperate student hope that idealism would in the end be the victor, and that not only college life, but all social life, would be more worth living. The idealism of youth, with few exceptions, has appeared under different guises to plague the colleges, their administrators, and their faculties. It is too much to say that the natural enemies of college students are their teachers and deans, but by reading college history one way we might be led to such conclusions. Perhaps in only one kind of college, the nineteenth-century Catholic college, was this student idealism so repressed or impotent that its effects on student life went unobserved. With this challenge to the old Catholic college we can begin an historical reconstruction of undergraduate life in Catholic colleges during their formative period.

The undergraduate's duty

Most colleges of the early nineteenth century were dour places; yet there were none to rival Catholic colleges in their capacity to exercise dogmatic control over their clientele or elicit from it an uncritical affirmation, and thus conduct themselves according to the will of ecclesiastics without heeding their public, faculty, or students. If Catholic college faculties were impotent forces in college life[1]—in determining goals and conditions to reach them— students could hardly be expected to fill the vacuum. Upon entering college their duty was to honor academic and disciplinary regulations; the code was articulated in precise, easily-understood language : a student's responsibility was to follow it to the letter. While some complaint was inevitable, and some minor insurrections form a small part of the permanent record,[2] students, for the most part, were sufficiently docile before their clerical taskmasters to do what they were told.

The *status quo* was perpetuated with relative ease because : first, doctrinal and ecclesiastical authority appeared to confirm the schools' actions, and a devoted Catholic would consciously avoid eroding or undermining legitimate authority (the indoctrination of episcopal and clerical omniscience had been too effective for that); second, the schools tended

---

[1] See chapter four. A study of the prospectuses of the period tends to confirm the conviction that with so many things expected of a faculty, it could hardly do anything with excellence. For examples of diverse assignments, see *St. Louis University Catalogue, 1876–1879*, p. 8; *1889–1890*, pp. 54–57; and *St. John's* (Fordham) *College Catalogue, 1881–1882*, pp. 16–18.

[2] Shea, *A History of Georgetown College*, p. 166; and Dunigan, *A History of Boston College*, pp. 111–112.

to be class schools, in company with the other colleges of the country, and strong social and parental pressures kept a class image intact; finally, except for prospective clergymen studying in the schools (their scholastic goals were clear and naturally enough they embraced the values of the clerical system), the students themselves were so heterogeneous in age, preparation for study, and intellectual ability, as well as motivation for college work, that common purposes among them seldom emerged.[3] If the ideal was ever to reform college life through student initiative, then the students themselves were their own worst enemies.

At Boston College in 1865, according to a former student's report, "fifty scholars ranging in years from twenty-six to eleven made up the entire membership. . . . The first pupils were all shades of industry and idleness."[4] While by this time Catholic colleges were talking about entrance standards, and a few were administering examinations to select students who would enter college halls, they were in general broadly-based schools with students ranging from grown men to mere boys, and the examination was an ineffective barrier to the admission of students, young or old, who lacked a real vocation for college study.[5] The old rudiments classes were kept intact to the end of the formative period,[6] and we should not expect much from elementary-school boys vis-à-vis the administrative establishment, save for innocent pranks and the extravagant excursions of youth.

Still, if entrance examinations were discounted, another limitation could be imposed on enrollment—that of age, although even here the colleges gave an impression of latitude. In the early years of the formative period, Georgetown College had set age eight as the minimum age for admission, providing the boy could read and write.[7] Spring Hill's first prospectus spoke of limiting enrollment to boys under twelve years old,[8] and Notre Dame welcomed children of elementary school age.[9] St. Louis[10] and Villanova,[11] during their first years, were little more than good grammar

---

[3] Erbacher, *op. cit.*, pp. 83–86; and, it should be noted, this heterogeneity was a lasting feature. See *St. John's* (Fordham) *College Catalogue, 1895–1896*, p. 16—no one under twelve was admitted—and *Gonzaga* (Spokane) *College Catalogue, 1895–1896*, p. 7 where a rule excluded any student under nine years of age.

[4] Henry C. Towle, "Pioneer Days at Boston College," *The Stylus*, 11 (June, 1897), 332–338.

[5] *Georgetown College Catalogue, 1879–1880*, p. 4; and *St. John's* (Fordham) *College Catalogue, 1881–1882*, p. 15.

[6] Talbot, *op. cit.*, p. 40; *Sketch of Gonzaga College*, p. 13; *Marquette College: A Quarter Century, 1881–1906*, p. 13; *St. Joseph's College Catalogue, 1857–1858*, p. 7; and *Xavier College Catalogue, 1862–1863*, p. 4.

[7] Daley, *op. cit.*, p. 69.

[8] Kenny, *op. cit.*, p. 70.

[9] Hope, *op. cit.*, p. 65.

[10] Garraghan, *The Jesuits of the Middle United States*, I, 292.

[11] Middleton, *op. cit.*, p. 36.

schools, so they readily admitted young boys. Even by 1870, the St. Louis catalogue still felt a need to state age requirements : "No student will be received under the age of ten, nor over that of sixteen, unless he is considerably advanced for his studies."[12] Mt. St. Mary's (Maryland) was officially designated as a *petit séminaire* for extended periods during its first years, and despite its managers' efforts to upgrade the course to maintain college standing, its classes were often predominantly elementary in character.[13] The College of the Holy Cross used ages eight and fourteen as minimum and maximum ages for admission and at the same time announced a distinctive course differing "from all other colleges in New England, in as much as it [combined] an English high school and a Latin school with a collegiate course."[14] At St. Joseph's College in Philadelphia in 1851 "the average age of the first collegians was something less than 12 years;"[15] and Gonzaga College in Washington, D. C., offered a program to students who were very young.[16] The age of admission ranged from ten to sixteen both at St. Joseph's College,[17] Bardstown, Kentucky, and Xavier College[18] in Cincinnati.

In practice, academic entrance requirements were neglected. Some colleges, as a matter of policy, restricted attendance to Catholic students,[19] although public announcements of exclusiveness were usually avoided; others were more liberal and publicly promised to welcome any student regardless of his profession of faith.[20] Such was the case at Spring Hill where, in the first prospectus, we find this statement : "Though the regency of the College be Catholic, yet no influence will be exercised upon pupils bred in the principles of other Christian Denominations. Good order, however, will require them to attend the public exercises of morning and evening prayers, and the Divine service of the Sabbath."[21] But the attitude at Boston College was even more liberal : "Students that are not Catholics will not be required to participate in any exercises distinctively Catholic;

[12] *St. Louis College Catalogue, 1869–1870*, p. 5.

[13] See John M. Rooney, "The Old Mountain," *The Catholic World*, 66 (November, 1897), 212–230.

[14] "The Catholic College of the Holy Cross," *The Metropolitan Catholic Almanac, and Laity's Directory*, 1844, pp. 88–89; and *The Boston Pilot*, August 3, 1850.

[15] Talbot, *op. cit.*, p. 40.

[16] *Sketch of Gonzaga College*, p. 13.

[17] *St. Joseph's College Catalogue, 1857–1858*, p. 7.

[18] *Xavier College Catalogue, 1862–1863*, p. 4.

[19] *New York Freeman's Journal*, XII (August 1851),; and *The Catholic Telegraph, Cincinnati*, XXII (July, 1853), 5.

[20] Erbacher, *op. cit.*, p. 84. *St. Louis University Catalogue, 1878–1879*, p. 13, illustrates the liberal position : "Pupils of every denomination are admitted, provided they are willing to attend, in respectful manner, the public exercises of religious worship."

[21] *First Prospectus of Spring Hill College*, October 29, 1830.

nor will any undue influence be used to induce a change in religious belief."[22] Both Spring Hill and Boston College were Jesuit institutions and both, we may suspect, were following the liberal tradition inaugurated at Georgetown on this matter of accepting nonCatholic students. Article IX of Georgetown's 1798 prospectus had spoken of a need for uniformity in the religious practice of Catholic students, but had generously dispensed students of other faiths, who, while welcome at the school, were to be housed separately from Catholic students. In all respects, save religion, the prospectus said, students, without regard to religious preference, would be treated alike.[23] Yet this generous spirit was by no means widespread; Holy Cross College, a better example of the generality, was, according to an 1865 advertisement in *The Boston Pilot*, "established solely for the education of Catholics."[24]

Throughout the greater part of the formative period, entrance standards, as we have said, were largely inoperative, although from time to time they received notice in college publications. Toward the end of the period, however, Catholic colleges began to feel the effects of competition, and in a struggle for respectability found it necessary to be more assertive on the question of admission requirements.[25] Thus, around 1870 we discover significant reforms, which are illustrated by Erbacher.[26] He represents Manhattan College's entrance requirements as being typical of standards enforced in all Catholic colleges.[27] And while this view may be somewhat optimistic, it does contain elements to recommend it. In 1866 Manhattan College had two tracks in its college program: English-Mathematical and Classical. For admission to the former students were expected to have academic skills attested to by a knowledge of: Brown's *English Grammar,* Graham's *Synonymes,* Robinson's *Arithmetic,* Mitchell's *New Intermediate Geography,* Mitchell's *Ancient Geography,* Grace's *Outlines of History,* and Bridge's *Algebra* and *Geometry.* Mastery of these books should have given students a working knowledge of grammar, skill in composition, competence in intellectual and practical arithmetic, information on the geography of Asia and Africa, a broad view of history, and some insights into algebra and plane geometry. With this background they were ready to enter the English-Mathematical course, although we are uncertain how this knowledge was tested and are tempted to believe that at Manhattan College, and at other schools where similar requirements were in force, the entrance

---

[22] *Boston College Catalogue, 1868–1869,* p. 4.

[23] Easby-Smith, *op. cit.,* I, 41–42.

[24] *The Boston Pilot,* April 8, 1865.

[25] Edwin C. Broome, *A Historical and Critical Discussion of College Entrance Requirements* (New York, Columbia University Press, 1902).

[26] Erbacher, *op. cit.,* pp. 87–91.

[27] *Ibid.,* p. 83.

examination was oral and was administered either by the president himself or his chief academic lieutenant, the prefect of studies.[28]

Entrance to the collegiate classical course was guarded by stronger gates, according to the stated requirements of Manhattan College : Andrew's and Stoddard's *Latin Grammar,* from the beginning through prosody, along with Andrew's *Exercises* in composition; *Viri Romae* and *Caesar* were represented and the student was expected to be familiar with four books from each; Virgil's *Eclogues* or Sallust's *Jugurtha* were listed and the student was expected to know one or the other; the same was true of Fisk's or Valpy's *Greek Grammar,* as far as prosody; Boise's *Greek Composition;* and one book of Xenophon's *Anabasis.*[29] This much students were to bring with them as intellectual experience.

The importance of these new requirements lies less in the subjects and the books mentioned, because we know they changed from college to college,[30] than in the fact that the schools were beginning to state their entrance requirements in terms which allow us to believe that more attention was at last being given to the academic side of college life than to the moral and purely devotional.[31] The colleges, having outgrown their missionary preoccupations, were no longer so anxious to admit only Catholic boys who needed religious training. But while it is accurate enough to advert to this changing emphasis and some reduction in enthusiasm for religious objectives, it would be unfair to accuse the colleges of consciously or unconsciously neglecting students' religious training or life. Religious objectives were always important, and in the long run they supplied Catholic colleges with their identity and integrity.

As far as entrance requirements are concerned, a Catholic college was still in its formative period until it had jettisoned its old preferences for specific subject matter, represented by particular books or classical selections, and had substituted a general trust in the secondary school course. Throughout the 1870s and on into the 1880s, we begin to find the colleges stating entrance standards in a different way : if the prospective student had completed a secondary school course, or preparatory studies in schools either related to Catholic colleges or independent of them, he would have credits, or units, in one modern foreign language plus Latin; in addition, such studies as English grammar, history, geography, arithmetic, and algebra were expected, and in each of his subjects he should have a passing grade of sixty and a cumulative average of seventy-five.[32]

[28] Brother Constantius, "The Christian Brothers in the United States," *Catholic Educational Review,* 1 (January, 1911), 319.

[29] *Ibid.,* and see Erbacher, *op. cit.,* p. 83.

[30] For example, see Meagher and Grattan, *op. cit.,* pp. 132–138.

[31] *Boston College Catalogue, 1898–1899,* pp. 47–53.

[32] Donaghy, *op. cit.,* p. 20.

Since so many Catholic colleges were committed to the six- or seven-year course almost to the end of the formative period (1870),[33] a student's transfer from the lower (preparatory) to the higher (collegiate) course was made with ease. A successful student in intramural preparatory studies was welcomed to the higher course. But a student from another preparatory school applying for admission created some unforeseen problems. Which class should have him? And what confidence could college authorities have in his moral and religious aptitude? In the first case, they made their unique promotion tests do;[34] for the latter, they depended on testimonials regarding the student's character issued by the institution from which he came. If transferring from extramural secondary schools to college study was some-times done, it was by no means a popular practice, and even less popular was the now common tendency of students to transfer from one college to another. Once enrolled at a college, the student remained there if he intended to obtain a degree; but exceptions were possible, and the 1862 *Catalogue of Seton Hall College* shows how they were limited : "No pupil will be received from another College without unexceptionable testimonials, and none will be retained whose manners and morals are not satisfactory."[35]

Only one part of the transfer picture is disclosed by looking at the secondary school movement upward to the college; the other part, from the college to the seminary, was much more satisfying to a Catholic academic community. We know these transfers usually took place within one institu-tion, where the college and seminary were coordinate or mixed schools, but they also occurred from colleges without seminary attachments to an independent seminary or to a college-seminary institution.[36] These transfers, once recognized, can be passed over, for they are part of the story of professional developments in Catholic higher education and are deferred to a later chapter. Still, one small item related to transfer students needs further exploration : what about the boy who spent a few years at one college and then, for his own good reasons, decided to move to another? Where would he be placed in the college course? Would he be a student of Humanities, Poetry, Rhetoric, or Philosophy? His class standing depended on the results of a promotional examination administered to all students at the beginning of each annual term. When they returned to school in the late summer or early fall, after their vacation months at home, they were tested to determine if they were ready for the next higher class.[37] Transfer students were examined with the regular students and thus found their proper class. This strange practice of leaving the college student at an

[33] See *Report of the United States Commissioner of Education,* 1872, pp. 762–781.

[34] *Xavier College Catalogue, 1878–1879,* pp. 7–8.

[35] *Seton Hall College Catalogue, 1862,* p. 6.

[36] Hoffmann, *op. cit.,* pp. 108–112.

[37] Donaghy, *op. cit.,* p. 21.

academic loose end for the summer, uncertain about his promotion, had one obvious merit : it enabled colleges to classify transfer students easily and with a minimum of effort.

The boys were now in college, and whether they were really in a college course of studies or only at preparatory steps made no matter, for their general regimen was identical. The day of academic duty followed this pattern : up early, around five a.m. in warm weather and five-thirty in winter, the boys were directed first to wash. At the most primitive colleges their ablutions were taken out of doors at the pump when weather permitted or, on winter mornings, in improvised wash rooms indoors. Properly scrubbed, they marched on to morning prayers and then Mass, and after Mass to the study hall for a period with their books. When breakfast was ready they filed to the refectory for bread and coffee—apparently the breakfast menu never varied—and after the day's first meal were treated to a short recreation period. Classes began around eight o'clock and continued until about eleven-thirty, when another recreation interval was allowed. Dinner came next, followed by a visit to chapel and then recreation for an hour and one-half. At Georgetown, in the 1820s, "the studyroom was locked (during the first hour of recreation), and no one was allowed to have a book of any kind—a very good rule, but in our case a useless precaution; for I don't think any of us were given to private study."[38] Mid-day recreation was followed by a half-hour study period; then afternoon classes began and continued until four o'clock. Now a light lunch was served, usually a piece of bread, followed by another recreation period of ninety minutes. Praying the rosary followed recreation, then evening study, which, in turn, was followed by supper—a light repast, often nothing more than bread and tea, for the noon meal was the main one.[39]

Five periods of recreation—in all, about five hours—were scheduled in the order of the day, and we may wonder how the boys used this time or, how, with so much time on their hands they kept out of mischief. Because so many harmless diversions were forbidden—for example, card playing and ball games were taboo[40]—the ordinary way for boys to use their free time was to take long walks around the college grounds or to play simple games in the playground. Hardly any fun was organized, but we shall try to reconstruct the boys' diversions later. Recreation followed supper in the daily schedule and continued until eight o'clock; then night prayers in chapel, and off to the dormitory and sleep.[41]

Notre Dame in 1843, Villanova in 1850, and Spring Hill in 1870,

---

[38] Shea, *A History of Georgetown College,* pp. 62–63.

[39] *Ibid.*

[40] *Catalogue of Boston College, 1879–1880,* pp. 5–6; *Catalogue of St. Joseph's College, 1860–1861,* pp. 7–9; and Meline and McSweeny, *op. cit.,* II, 94.

[41] Shea, *A History of Georgetown College,* pp. 62–63.

followed a daily schedule remarkably similar to Georgetown's 1820 regimen. Sunday, of course, was always a full holiday from classes, and Tuesdays and Thursdays were half-holidays. With these days accounted for, the rest of the week's schedule looked like this : boys started their day at 5.30 a.m., except at Spring Hill, where it began a half-hour earlier. Daily Mass for all students was at 6.30 at Notre Dame and Villanova, but at 5.25 at Spring Hill. A study period followed Mass, and then breakfast at 7.00, except at Spring Hill where it was served about 7.30. Classes began some time between 7.30 and 8.30. Recess was at 10.00, then there were classes again until dinner at 12.00. Classes resumed at 1.30 or 2.00, with a recess and lunch about 4.00, and then classes again until 5.00. Spiritual exercises and recreation preceded supper at 6.30 at Notre Dame and Villanova, but at 7.15 at Spring Hill. Intervals of recreation and study followed supper, and the boys were in bed at 9.00 at Notre Dame and Villanova, but at 8.30 at Spring Hill.[42]

The college day was long, but the year was long too; its commencement varied from school to school, usually some time toward the end of summer or early fall, and, interrupted by three or four vacations, it lasted until late spring or early summer. Yet vacation periods did not always mean that the boys could leave school; sometimes they could not even go home for Christmas.[43] Although precise data are unavailable, for the colleges were careless about maintaining such records, we are led to assume that the college year before 1850 was somewhat shorter than in later years. We know that in 1871, at the very end of the period of formation, fifty-five Catholic colleges were in existence, and forty-two reported the number of weeks in their school year in response to a query from the United States Commissioner of Education : one college had a thirty-nine week session; fifteen scheduled their courses over a forty-week period; twelve colleges had a forty-two week year; three colleges ran their studies for forty-three weeks; eight colleges for forty-four weeks; one college for forty-five weeks; one college for forty-six weeks; and one college kept the students in session for a full fifty-two weeks.[44]

Another side of a college student's life is reflected in the number of colleagues he had in class. For the most part, we should think, college enrollments were small, although, again, we must admit that our data are not entirely dependable, for the schools were inclined to report all their students in college study, when, clearly, half or more were really engaged

[42] See Hope, *op. cit.,* pp. 66–67; Middleton, *op. cit.,* p. 36; and *Spring Hill College Catalogue, 1870–1871,* p. 8.

[43] In the 1880s, the College of the Sacred Heart (Wis.), St. Mary's (Ka.) and Gonzaga (Spokane) insisted that boys stay at school during all vacations. (*Catalogue of Sacred Heart College, 1881–1882,* p. 5; *Catalogue of St. Mary's College, 1889–1890,* p. 11; and *Catalogue of Gonzaga College, 1889–1890,* p. 4).

[44] *Report of the United States Commissioner of Education,* 1872, pp. 762–781.

in preparatory subjects. Yet the fact that students were regarded by the colleges as part of their college population if they attended the institution, irrespective of their level of study, tells us something about their attitude toward students.

Erbacher collected data from eighteen of the twenty-five colleges during the years 1850 to 1865 and reported average enrollments as follows : 1850, 123 students per college; 1855, 131 students per college; 1860, 140 students per college; and 1865, 173 students per college. The total increased from 2,213 students in 1850 to 3,455 in 1865.[45] We can try to interpret these data by making two assumptions : first, that the course in which these students were enrolled lasted seven years, and second, that there was an equal distribution of students in the seven classes (a dubious assumption this, at best, because the heavier enrollments were usually in the rudimentary years). These would give about seventeen students per class in 1850; eighteen to a class in 1855; twenty to a class in 1860; and twenty-four per class in 1865. And if we assume further that only the last three years of the course were really collegiate in caliber and standards, we should have an average college enrollment of fifty-one in 1850; fifty-four in 1855; sixty in 1860; and seventy-two in 1865. In 1872, fifty-five Catholic colleges reported enrollment data to the United States Commissioner of Education : college students numbered 1,918; 4,004 were listed as elementary and secondary school students; 1,867 were unclassified.[46] The last category must have been a mixture of seminarians, students continuing studies beyond the bachelor's degree, and students in elementary and secondary studies not properly classified. Interpreting these data, we arrive at about thirty-five college students for each institution and, if we assume an even distribution among three college years, we end up with about eleven students to a class. Even if we say, for argument's sake, that all unclassified students were on some level of college study, we have only seventy college students per school or about twenty-three to a class. The 1872 reports cast some doubt on the authenticity of Erbacher's sources and, therefore, his summary of enrollment; they suggest, moreover, a college system sparsely populated with mature students rightly categorized as dealing with college curricula.

This obvious conclusion is valid despite the fact that the total student population at any one college may have been fairly large. And among this population were boys from states other than the one in which the college happened to be located; on occasion, students from foreign countries were listed on the student register too. During its first decade, Holy Cross, for example, reported students from New Hampshire, New York, New Jersey, Maine, Connecticut, Rhode Island, Pennsylvania, Maryland, North Carolina, South Carolina, Georgia, Canada, Mexico, Peru, Argentina, and

---

[45] Erbacher, *op. cit.,* p. 85.
[46] *Report of the United States Commissioner of Education,* 1872, pp. 762–781.

Turkey. One lonely Filipino earned this note on June 13, 1848 : "Entered this day, Francisco Cembrano, aged 18 years. He is from Manila (sic) Philippine Islands, near China, Nathan Cook of Salem, Mass. his guardian."[47]

The clearest record of standards for awarding degrees in the early Catholic colleges comes from Thébaud's recollections,[48] and he found almost nothing to praise. Students, he said, were given degrees when they refused to remain longer in college. While Thébaud unquestionably related his own experiences with complete candor, it must be emphasized that he was acquainted with the colleges in their early pioneering days, and it is unlikely that they operated according to his description for very long. When they settled on and made a required curriculum the only avenue to a degree, students were expected to follow it and were then awarded the degree of bachelor of arts. Degrees were granted in long and lavish ceremonies, for they were highly prized even in institutions that had a way of placing high value on nonacademic accomplishments. No doubt many students, for one reason or another, were unable to finish the course and thus never obtained a degree. But, Thébaud's testimony excepted, there is no convincing evidence to support the conclusion that Catholic colleges dishonored academic degrees or awarded them in perfunctory fashion. Their degrees, we should think, were entirely respectable, and making due allowances for the age, came only as a result of considerable effort and demonstrable ability on the part of the recipient. While the same standards did not protect the integrity of master's degrees, Catholic colleges, it must be admitted, were only following the practices of the best colleges of the country when they awarded master's degrees to students who testified to a continuing interest in literary topics after graduation from the college.[49]

Discipline

Nineteenth-century Catholic college students were charged with two principal responsibilities : attending to studies and contributing to good order. The syllabus outlined a student's responsibilities to the former; a code of disciplinary regulations, administered by a corps of prefects under the superintendence of a prefect of discipline, ensured attendance to the latter. Since we have already sampled the academic side of undergraduate life,

---

[47] Meagher, op. cit., p. 46.

[48] Thébaud, Forty Years in the United States, p. 331.

[49] Hill, op. cit., pp. 56–57; and St. Louis University Catalogue, 1878–1879, p. 12 : "Subsequently the degree of A. M. can be obtained by devoting a second year to the study of Philosophy in the Institution, or two years to a learned profession."

we may turn to the day-to-day contacts with regulations intended to bind the student to ideals of good order.

Regardless of a student's age or level of academic accomplishment, he was expected to comply with the general law of behavior set down by college officers. One code governed the behavior of all students; it applied with the same force to Philosophers (except at Fordham in 1896 where they only were allowed private rooms)[50] as to students in rudimentary years. Perhaps it is unnecessary to say that students enjoyed little freedom, for, constantly under the watchful eyes of their prefects, they could leave the school grounds only with written permission from their parents and a direct warrant from the president. The entire day was regimented, and they were made to account for any neglect of routine duties prescribed in the order of the day.[51] The ideal Catholic colleges honored was that good discipline is guaranteed when rules covering every eventuality are promulgated and given uniform application; no exceptions were countenanced and appeals to reason were discouraged. Of course, the colleges, traditionally committed to teaching students the fundamentals of a decent education, including those of moral formation, adhered to a conviction that habits of will are inculcated by doing consistently what is right. The validity of arsenals of rules and regulations was dogmatically assumed.

As illustrative of the kind of personal restriction in force in Catholic colleges of the nineteenth century, the regulation concerning pocket money may serve. First instituted at Georgetown in 1814,[52] it was duplicated in one way or another in every Catholic college for the rest of the formative period : "As long experience has convinced the directors that a profusion of pocket money is very prejudicial not only to good order, but even to study and application, they therefore request that parents will not be too indulgent of their children, in allowing more than one dollar per month at most and whatever is allowed must be deposited in the hands of the procurator of the house."[53] While sound in principle and intention, the rule went too far in making no allowance for older boys who should have had some experience in handling their own funds, and it neglected entirely the educative possibilities involved in allowing students to make some of their own decisions. If boys were seldom allowed to leave school, their spending propensities would naturally have been limited; but no matter, the regulation disbarred students from controlling their own property and thus deprived them of good practical lessons.

Individual responsibility, although praised in the rhetoric of policy

---

[50] *St. John's* (Fordham) *College Catalogue, 1895–1896,* p. 14.

[51] James Fitton, *Sketches of the Establishment of the Church in New England* (Boston, Patrick Donahoe, 1872), p. 309.

[52] Daley, *op. cit.,* p. 243.

[53] *Ibid.*

statements, was actually discounted. Colleges created for their students environments in which immaturity was prolonged, probably because of their imperfect conception of an academic community; they chose rather to imitate the monastic establishments with which they were more familiar. Old monastic schools had aimed at preparing boys for full religious participation in monastic life, and in some respects Catholic colleges reproduced this ancient model; but in departing from a monastic regimen, their next best example was the seminary, and student life in college was guided by seminary prototypes. Now and then questions were raised about the employment of such archaic disciplinary rules and techniques, judged even by critics to be proper enough to monasteries or seminaries but inapplicable in a college—John Carroll alluded to this when he questioned the capacity of Leonard Neale to govern Georgetown,[54] and Orestes Brownson was uneasy about the colleges' tendency to regard every student as a potential monk[55]—without any perceptible alteration in college life. Being responsible and devout citizens of the Church seemed to mean something different from being responsible and sensitive citizens of civil society; to seek the former was good, the latter was much less important; so codes of conduct governing religious life were assigned pride of place in the colleges. Self-discipline, to judge from the statements made about it, was eagerly desired; still, we must admit, the means to ensure self-discipline were organized in a most curious way.[56]

Colleges located in or near cities had both boarders and day students, and their regulations took due notice of this. Of course, day students had a freedom away from the college not enjoyed by boarders, and it was always possible that they might contaminate boarders by introducing attitudes inconsistent with college rules. So day students had to be watched with special care and, in some cases, segregated from boarders. This, we should think, was no easy matter; in the end it must have been counted a failure. Nevertheless, day students were different and rules governing their conduct had a special codification.[57]

The records of all Catholic colleges of the period reflect a general preoccupation with disciplinary regulations both for boarders and day students. One of the most complete sets is found in the *Boston College Catalogue for 1879–1880,*[58] and pertains directly to day students, who at the time were a majority in Boston College's student body. While it is true

[54] *Ibid.*

[55] Orestes A. Brownson, "Our Colleges," *Brownson's Quarterly Review,* 15 (April, 1858), 216.

[56] Erbacher, *op. cit.,* pp. 107–108.

[57] For example, day students were forbidden to mail letters or do any errands for boarders as late as the 1880s (*Georgetown College Catalogue, 1881–1882,* p. 22).

[58] *Boston College Catalogue, 1879–1880,* pp. 5–6.

that this code of behavior belongs to what we have labeled the period of development, it was actually a continuation and amplification of regulatory codes in force at the college for the fifteen years previous. The statement begins with rules governing the student's entrance to the school on the morning of a class day : he is to "repair immediately to the cloakroom, where [he] will deposit . . . books, overcoats, etc.; thence proceed directly to the gymnasium, where [he] will remain until time for Mass."[59] Some students—they must have been nonCatholics—were exempt from Mass attendance, so they were obliged to remain in the gymnasium and not "to leave the gymnasium for the school-room, unless accompanied by the teacher."[60] Once in the classroom, students were enjoined to remain unless granted permission to leave, and then they were "to return without unnecessary delay." Places for recreation and play were identified as the gymnasium and the court. "All the rest of the premises are 'out of bounds,' except when the Prefect gives permission to walk by the Church, or, to members of the Debating Society, to recreate in their own room."[61] Then followed a short litany of prohibitions : tobacco was forbidden; playing ball, "snow-balling, pitching, and all games that endanger the windows are prohibited;" no boisterous conduct is allowed in "the corridors or classrooms at any time," and even in the gymnasium and on the playground "behavior should be decorous. In fine, any conduct unbecoming the gentleman will be regarded as violation of the College rules. Flagrant offenses, such as are detrimental to the reputation of the College, or are obstructive of the good order of the pupils, are grounds for expulsion," the code warned; but for the more ordinary faults, such as tardiness, poor preparation for lessons, or childish pranks, "detention after school, or some lines to be copied or committed to memory, are usually found sufficient penalty."[62] Then the cooperation of parents was solicited : they were asked to insist on home study, to inform the school if boys were kept at home or if they were withdrawn from school, to be alert for the receipt of the student's monthly progress report, "and not to pass over without inquiry marks falling below seventy-five." Both parents and students were advised that since "religious motives [are] habitually appealed to, little need has been experienced of frequent or severe punishment." Finally, the announcement warned parents and students alike that their books and clothing must be kept in the safe places provided by the college and that the "College will not be held responsible for a loss which could only occur through negligence."[63]

[59] *Ibid.*
[60] *Ibid.*
[61] *Ibid.*
[62] *Ibid.*
[63] *Ibid.*

Perhaps there are few grounds for debating the reasonableness of these rules, and taken as out-of-context samples of discipline they look innocent enough. Yet their tone is both defensive and arbitrary and bespeaks an atmosphere of study where minute observance of rule was the mast to which the educational flag was nailed. There were, moreover, no exceptions for older, more mature boys able to decide some things for themselves.[64] All students were treated as mere children. Yet, on the whole, day students were probably envied by their colleagues who lived in the college most of the year. Boarders, unable to escape to the less repressive atmospheres of home and community, were confined in college where their every move was watched and remembered.[65] This atmosphere may be caught from codes of discipline for boarders imposed, for example, by St. Joseph's College, Bardstown, Kentucky, and promulgated in its *Catalogue of 1860–1861.*[66]

Beginning with the statement that students who board at the college "are at all times under the superintendence of Prefects," it goes on to warn that no one "is received as an extern" unless his home is in the vicinity of the school. Younger students, the announcement continues, are separated from older ones, with each group having "its own playground, study-hall, dormitory, refectory, and chapel."[67] But this reputed division of boys according to age groups must be interpreted generously, for the facilities of St. Joseph's College in 1860, and for some time thereafter, could not have accommodated many grades of students in separate refectories or chapels.[68] What the regulation really meant to say, since the college was a mixed school with seminary and college branches,[69] was that boys in college studies—from elementary instruction to the higher levels—were grouped together separately from seminarians, who had their own living quarters, recreational facilities (restricted parts of the college grounds), study halls, and places to pray. St. Joseph's, like other Catholic colleges of the day, cloistered seminarians and thus prepared them to minister to the faithful in a secular society by insulating them almost completely from that society during their years of divinity study.

The regulations have set the scene somewhat optimistically, and are now ready to go on to other matters. We find that a physician—an

---

[64] Erbacher, *op. cit.*, p. 105, says "Older students were put more on their honor," but I look in vain for evidence of this.

[65] Erbacher, *ibid.*, claims that "A number of institutions took special care lest watchfulness degenerate into espionage and destroy the confidence of students," but, again, I am unable to confirm his view by the testimony of college regulations.

[66] *St. Joseph's College Catalogue, 1860–1861,* pp. 7–9.

[67] *Ibid.*

[68] W. J. Howlett, "The Early Days of St. Joseph's College at Bardstown, Kentucky," *Illinois Catholic Historical Review* (April, 1922), pp. 372–380.

[69] B. J. Webb, *A Centenary of Catholicity in Kentucky* (Louisville, Charles A. Rogers, 1884), p. 439.

"experienced Physician" at that—visits the premises daily, for "the greatest care and attention is bestowed on the sick."[70] And, almost ominously, the document proclaims : "public exercises of Religion are those of the Catholic Church, but students of all denominations are admitted—provided they be willing to assist at all daily exercises of Religious Worship."[71] The rule was unequivocal, but it had a local application which should not be taken as too firm an indication of general practice in Catholic colleges. We know of some unevenness in regulations pertaining to religious duty and discipline, although Catholic students everywhere lived according to one code demanding regular attendance at all religious devotions; some colleges allowed nonCatholic students freedom to frequent their own churches or to attend religious services as they pleased;[72] others, with the permission of parents, made boys participate in Catholic ritual;[73] while still others simply assumed that any student enrolled would conform to the religious discipline of the place regardless of his denominational affiliation.[74] Of course, this action should be freed from any implications of secret or improper pressure, for the colleges having such rules followed them, making it perfectly clear in their prospectuses what was expected of all students.

Every Thursday of the academic year at St. Joseph's was a day of recreation and classes were suspended; the first Wednesday of every month was set aside for awarding "Badges of Honor," which were conferred on the most deserving students from each class; and, in addition, printed certificates were awarded students who, during the month, had distinguished themselves by their diligence and good conduct.[75]

From this point on the regulations assume a distinctly negative tone : no student could "go to town" unless accompanied by a prefect and then he had to have the special permission of the president; all books circulated among students needed the approval of the prefect of studies—thus the censorship process was unrelenting. Students' outgoing letters were subject to a prefect's inspection, and we may well doubt whether he was searching for grammatical or syntactical inconsistencies; students were forbidden to circumvent the prefect's supervision by having their own boxes at the post office, and they were warned not to commission anyone in town to receive or forward their letters.

Reports of student progress, the regulations state, are sent home "during

[70] *Catalogue of St. Joseph's College, 1860–1861,* pp. 7–9.

[71] *Ibid.*

[72] *Catalogue of Boston College, 1868–1869,* p. 4.

[73] Easby-Smith, *op. cit.,* I, 40–41.

[74] *First Prospectus of Spring Hill College,* October 29, 1830.

[75] *Catalogue of St. Joseph's College, 1860–1861,* pp. 7–9. Saturdays were usually free days, although a few colleges used the first Saturday of the month "not for class recitations, but for certain literary and religious exercises" (*Boston College Catalogue, 1895–1896,* p. 15).

the months of April and December;" in addition to informing parents or guardians of academic proficiency, such reports would also advise them of health and conduct. Should any student violate the rules, he knew he would be punished "in a mild but effectual manner." And if this punishment proved ineffective and the student remained refractory "or immoral, he will be sent back to his parents or guardians." The student who left school before the annual examination at the end of the year, "forfeits all right to an Honorable Certificate," apparently a nineteenth-century equivalent to withdrawal in good standing.

Finally, the regulations inform parents that if they desired to withdraw their sons, they must "give timely notice to the President, settle all accounts, and forward money to defray traveling expenses." The implication was clear, although no evidence of its enforcement is known, that the college would retain the boy in its custody until parents settled the account. For boys who remained at school, parents were told, money must be supplied for clothing and other necessary items, because "no advances are made by the institution. To meet such expenses a sufficient sum should be deposited with the Agent."[76]

Twenty years later, 1879–1880, Georgetown College repeated regulations for boarders that had been in force for a half century. They are relatively brief, but general enough to cover most situations, and, moreover, are typical of such codes of conduct in Catholic colleges for the formative period. We add them to give a fuller account of student life and the rules governing it. By now we know the colleges well enough to expect a regulation forbidding students to leave the campus without presidential permission and enjoining them, even with permission, to return by six o'clock in the evening. Assuming all students were boarders, the regulations permitted students whose parents lived in the District "to visit them on the first Saturday of each month and to remain with them until Sunday evening."[77] The normal way of college life was boarding; trips home for week-ends were discouraged without any clear justification, and this limitation on student freedom stands as another example of arbitrary laws in vogue for decades at almost every Catholic boarding college. The remnants of such regulations remained in Catholic colleges for men well into the twentieth century and obtain still in some Catholic colleges for women.

Georgetown's prefects could not read all incoming mail, but, according to the rules, they could "reserve to themselves the discretionary power of opening all letters to students, not known to be from parents or guardians."[78] And they were strict about the circulation of ephemeral books and papers : any judged to be immoral rendered their custodian liable to expulsion.

[76] Catalogue of St. Joseph's College, 1860–1861, pp. 7–9.
[77] Catalogue of Georgetown College, 1879–1880, p. 13.
[78] Ibid.

Besides, the college rules prohibited the use of tobacco in any form, and the code advised students that they "were required to abide by the College regulations" on this and other matters. There were, Georgetown's announcements said, no distinctions "in the reception of students on the ground of religious belief, but all boarders are required to be present at the public exercises of religion."[79] As a minimum all students were compelled to attend Mass on Sundays and other important feast days; this regulation, we see, was a retreat from earlier, more liberal pronouncements allowing non-Catholic boarders to absent themselves from Catholic worship.[80]

Only the most obvious violations of rules were anticipated and mentioned in the colleges' public literature, but codifications for house use, written in meticulous detail, were distributed to all students. They were expected to know the rules and follow them to the letter. A perusal of such student rule books suggests two conclusions: first, that college officers responsible for the formulation of such texts revealed, both in writing the rules and administering them, a woeful lack of depth in child and adolescent psychology. We should not hope to find scientific perceptions in what are now highly complex fields of knowledge, but we have a right to expect something better than a complete flight from common sense. The second conclusion is this: the indexes of prohibited activities were so long that we tax our imagination in discovering what students might freely do. A complete list of forbidden actions would be burdensome here, although the foremost proscriptions must be mentioned: card playing, swearing, drunkenness, striking instructors or prefects, and locking them in their rooms head the list; dancing, attending theaters, playing games of chance, horse-racing,

79 *Ibid.*

80 See Easby-Smith, *op. cit.*, I, 40–41. Loyola College in Baltimore had a brief set of rules included in the catalogue, supplemented by a fuller set circulated intramurally. Loyola's student code read as follows: "As no play is allowed in the streets about the College, the Students must not assemble in the morning before 8 o'clock, at which time the doors are opened. All must be present at $8\frac{1}{2}$ o'clock, when, at the sound of the bell, all play immediately ceasing, the Catholic Students go in ranks to the Church to hear Mass; and those who are not Catholics repair to one of the class-rooms for study. Schools commence at 9 o'clock. At $10\frac{3}{4}$ there is a short recess, and at noon one of 30 minutes. The session terminates at $2\frac{1}{2}$ o'clock, P.M.

In case of absence from School or late attendance, a note from the parent or guardian, accounting for such absence or lateness, is required. A note is also required when parents wish their children to leave before the end of the class.

All must be clean and neat in person and apparel, polite and obedient to the Officers of the College, and respectful to their companions.

No play is allowed in the House. Improper conduct in coming to School and returning from it, the use of tobacco in the College, and the introduction of books or papers foreign to the course of studies, are forbidden.

Any injury done to the walls or furniture of the House, besides subjecting the offender to punishment, will be repaired at the expense of his parents" (*Loyola College Catalogue, 1878–1879*, p. 5).

dueling, and carrying weapons were all universally taboo. Using liquor was normally forbidden, although occasionally, at one college or another, we find exceptions could be made, with the guarantee that it would be taken in moderation by an industrious and prudent student.

This was one side of discipline; another side was displayed mainly in regulations published concerning student dress. The colleges, no doubt sincerely concerned with moral and character formation, took this part of their job seriously; yet, they often give the impression of attaching greater importance to the cut and color of a boy's coat than to the inculcation of moral habits. They gave inordinate attention to nonessentials and in disciplinary matters had a way of making mountains out of mole hills.

At this point our view of college life must become sowewhat episodic. Student reports said some critical things about college environments for study and living, yet despite regimentation, students had a natural loyalty to dimly understood ideals of Catholic learning from which, they thought, the colleges sometimes departed. When this happened, students were moved to complain, although they usually deferred any public airing of their views until their degrees were safely in hand. One student recollection is quoted in Dowling's book : [81] there was, this young man found, an absence "of anything like a college spirit. The boys seemed to be devoid of interest in the place, to say nothing of enthusiasm." They studied, but when classes were dismissed they ran, happy to be rid of them, "like workmen glad to get away from the scene of hard toil." At first he blamed the students for their lack of devotion to study and their inability to face any loyalty to the college, but concluded finally that it was not their fault. "There was a certain atmosphere about the place that was chilling and depressing. If it was not actually repelling, it certainly was not attractive."[82] This student was unable to account for the unhealthy climate he sensed. With the advantage of a longer perspective, we may be able to help him.

We know the colleges' penchant for prescribing everything to do with student life; clothing, for instance, was a matter for college officers' attention. In the 1860s, students at Fordham were told to pack their trunks with "three suits of clothes for summer and three for winter; at least six shirts, six pairs of woolen and six pairs of cotton socks; six pocket-handkerchiefs; six towels; four cravats; four pairs of shoes or boots, one pair of overshoes; one cloak or overcoat; a silver spoon, fork, drinking-cup, marked with his name."[83] At the College of the Holy Cross in 1848, the clothing regulations prescribed the uniform for all public occasions : it consisted "of a black coat or jacket, black vest, grey pantaloons for winter, and white for summer."[84]

[81] Dowling, *op. cit.*, p. 187.

[82] *Ibid.*

[83] *Catalogue of St. John's College, Fordham. 1862–1863*, p. 4.

[84] Dunigan, *Student Days at Holy Cross College in 1848*, p. 54.

Seminary students wore different uniforms, apparently to distinguish them easily from college students; their jackets were green with blue pantaloons.[85]

Before 1850 few exceptions were allowed to the rule that all students wear uniforms; after 1850, however, uniforms began to disappear. Georgetown had set the precedent with its regulations of 1798 : to check the natural propensities of youth to extravagance and to prevent just complaints from parents on the matter of college dress, the rule commenced, "all boarders shall wear an (sic) uniform dress, to be furnished by the college on the cheapest terms, unless their parents should choose to take that trouble themselves, in which case they must scrupulously conform to the due quality, colour, and form."[86] Despite the colleges' apparent willingness to enter the clothing business, in addition to their multifarious duties related to instruction and discipline, historical records indicate that not many parents chose to be relieved of "that trouble themselves." While many colleges followed Georgetown's example and offered to supply, at a student's expense, uniforms for official wear, this was, we should think, an unprofitable side of their total enterprise. Nevertheless, a tradition was securely established for wearing uniforms, and from a college point of view it had three obvious recommendations : first, when away from school boys were easily identified by their mode of dress; second, uniformity in such externals as clothing insidiously undermined any tendencies toward individualism and generated an allegiance to a spirit of religious communism. In schools where conformity was a watchword, divergent thinkers and unique dressers were put in the same category and both were discouraged. Besides, most college officers, probably conditioned by the drabness of their own clerical dress, thought students outfitted in uniforms looked nice. Finally, in spite of the undoubted fact that nineteenth-century colleges were upper-class schools, wide variations existed in the financial capacities of families with sons in college, so that competition for excellence in clothing and the escalation of attendant expenses was effectively obviated by the rule directing every boy to wear a uniform.

Besides their uniforms, boys at early Georgetown were instructed to supply two knives and forks for table use, a mattress and a pillow, two pairs of sheets and two pillow cases, three blankets and a counterpane or rug.[87]

In hardly any other areas of college life was there more student reaction than on this matter of uniforms. Older students hated them, if we may judge from the thin records extant, and younger students came to believe such regulations were oppressive. So, as we have indicated, after 1850 Catholic colleges reviewed and considered amendments to their clothing

85 *Ibid.,* p. 55.
86 Quoted in Easby-Smith, *op. cit.,* I, 40–41.
87 *Ibid.*

regulations. Without acknowledging any deficiencies in the wisdom or good-
ness of former rules, they began to allow, as St. Joseph's College did in
1860, "new students . . . to wear out the clothes they bring with them."[88]
When used clothing was discarded, uniforms were demanded as a means "to
prevent extravagance in dress."[89] But this relaxation of a strict, old code
was usually interpreted as repeal of a despised rule; and students, hearing
what other American colleges were doing about modifying or jettisoning
clothing regulations altogether, believed they had won a point. Now, for
the first time, student eruptions appeared and a tug-of-war began between
the will of college authorities and the determination of students to be
treated like mature persons. At Boston College in the 1870s students objected
even to the uniforms drill companies were directed to wear, and when the
college, in an effort to still student dissent, revived the old rule that
"henceforth it will be of obligation to procure the college uniform,"[90] the
entire Rhetoric and Poetry classes refused to return to school. Since the boys
had yet to enroll for the term to which the restored rule applied, the college
was powerless to expel them and was left without students in its two
higher classes. The strike was joined by some students in First Humanities
as well. Almost half the college's student body refused to reenter school
while the regulation with respect to dress remained in effect. For the first
time of which we have any clear record, a Catholic college capitulated to
the wishes of its students and allowed the regulation to go unenforced.[91]

Most colleges were spared Boston College's tactical disadvantage, and
were thus freed from the humiliation of rescinding any of their rules. They
could usually find the ringleaders of student revolt and remove such
unworthy members from the college community. This was an effective,
although extreme, measure for enforcing discipline. Yet college officers,
with the possible exception of a few narrow-minded prefects, were neither
mean, small, nor unfriendly men who enjoyed penalizing students, so they
eschewed such extreme action whenever possible. Plenty of instances prove
their unusual forbearance. At the same time, we are aware, other disciplinary
action could be taken, with good hope for success, but without undue
severity.

The stated philosophy of discipline in every Catholic college accepted
physical chastisement as a necessity, but refrained from endorsing it as
universally valid or as a regularly employed therapy. Beating boys with the
old-fashioned instrument of learning—the rod—was a last resort; the official
theme was moderation. Still, a historian would be naïve to take at face
value all protestations about the mildness of discipline. A prefect thinking

---

[88] *St. Joseph's College Catalogue, 1859–1860,* p. 9.
[89] *Ibid.*
[90] Dunigan, *A History of Boston College,* p. 111.
[91] *Ibid.,* pp. 111–112.

a boy needed a beating gave him a thorough one, and was satisfied he had performed a high disciplinary duty. Prefects, moreover, were seldom asked to justify their handling of boys, or made to apologize for their enthusiasm or diligence in demanding conformity to college rules. Rules were to be obeyed, and prefects used the most effective means at their disposal. But there were other ways to enforce rules, too, and prefects, most of whom must have been basically Christian gentlemen, used them. Extra study was a penalty employed sometimes by class teachers and prefects; memorization of lines (selected from the classics) was deemed useful therapy, and had the additional advantage, college officers thought, of aiding mental development. Then we meet the highly popular practice of confining the student in solitary, a practice that in retrospect looks colorful and effective, for being deprived of the company of one's friends was, indeed, a severe penalty. But the precise operation of this disciplinary measure is unclear : as used today, detention rooms are maintained in almost every school in the land to penalize students for minor offenses and infractions of the rules : all we have from farther back are the names by which such rooms were known. In Catholic colleges they were variously dubbed, although the terms "jug" or "sky parlor" appear with regularity in literature on student life. A mere reference to the "jug" was usually sufficient to strike terror into the heart of an entering student, for its notoriety had no respect for campus boundaries; he had undoubtedly heard lurid tales about the severity of punishments it meted out. In addition, he feared the reputation of a "jug rat" (a student who spent an abnormal amount of time in confinement), thinking it would impair his standing with fellow students. The novice soon discovered, however, that the "jug" was not a bad place, nor was a reputation as a "jug rat" something disgraceful; rather than costing him status, it even added an aura of heroism.[92]

Smoking, always a serious offense unless the student could produce a prescription from a physician or a bishop's written permission, was penalized by the memorization of 300 lines; other violations of the college code were sometimes penalized by having to do without meals, eating the main meal on one's knees, or reciting several decades of the rosary in chapel. We may cull from Mt. St. Mary's "jug" book for the year 1868–1869 some violations and their prescribed penalties : "for laughing in class, write 250 lines of Caesar. For talking in ranks, go to the lockup during breakfast. For cutting benches in classrooms and refusing to give up the knife, 150 lines from Caesar and go to the lockup during dinner. For running downstairs, 100 lines of Sallust. For shooting stones through the study-hall window, 250 lines of Caesar."[93]

[92] See Shea, *A History of Georgetown College,* p. 157.
[93] Meline and McSweeny, *op. cit.,* II, 82.

Regulations concerning pocket money and its use were universally stated in college regulations; even the pocket money allowed had to be used circumspectly, for many things were on the list of prohibited purchases for students. Candy and tobacco led the list; if students were caught with either, prefects confiscated them as contraband. Such losses alone were bad enough, but when students discovered that the prefects consumed the contraband in the quiet of their room, "the poor, vanquished raider confined to the lock-up adjoining, getting only the smell of his labor and money,"[94] the practice, indeed, bordered on being intolerable. Students made a game of outwitting their prefects; they purchased in secrecy and cached their goods in places prefects were unlikely to look. Often they were remarkably successful. But in the end, of course, discipline won, and bold culprits who had become adept at the art of outwitting prefects were, to use the terminology of the day, "given their trunk." The principal deterrent to expulsion, discounting for the moment the Christian forbearance of the president, was an unpaid bill. At Notre Dame, for example, a certain youth "thumped" a teacher who had disciplined him for unauthorized swimming in St. Joseph's River without a swimming suit. Expulsion was the only obvious solution. Yet the president seemed unwilling to expel the boy until forced to do so by the teacher's threatened resignation. Since the boy's account was settled in full, such drastic action was easier.[95]

Threats to teachers' life and limb were never great in Catholic colleges; other deterrents to violence aside, most students were young and small, easily dominated physically by teachers and prefects. The little fellows found it wise to do as they were told, for any failures put them in jeopardy and prefects had all kinds of punishments ready for them. They minded injunctions to stay within the prescribed limits of their playground, to stand and sit erect, and to observe meticulously the rule forbidding students to blow their noses with their hands. For older boys problems of control were greater, but somehow the colleges rose to the occasion and were remarkably successful in maintaining good order without inciting rebellion among the students.

The Catholic college way of life in the nineteenth century, like life in other colleges of the country, was for students to live in college halls. But Catholic college halls had few private rooms, so most students were assigned to common sleeping rooms. This arrangement gave students unusually fine opportunities to perpetrate innocent but irritating pranks. Except for scheduled hours of sleep these quarters were off limits, but such precautions were largely ineffective in preventing boys from using the cover of darkness to play pranks on fellow students and prefects. The latter, of course, were the real targets of these nocturnal diversions : short-sheeting,

94 *Ibid.*
95 Hope, *op. cit.,* pp. 97–98.

putting bread or cracker crumbs in a bed, overturning beds with sleeping boys in them, bringing livestock to the dormitory, concocting some odoriferous potion from the ingredients of the scientific cabinet, all gave students a great deal of fun and infuriated their prefects.

At certain intervals, usually once a month, boys were directed to write their parents.[96] These letters were usually composed under the watchful eye of a prefect; in any case, he read them before mailing. Occasional letters, however, scarcely satisfied young men's appetites for contact with the outside world, so they ignored proscriptions about leaving school grounds and frequently strayed away looking for fun and feminine companionship. No uniform penalty can be found for such crimes, and colleges were probably more lenient in reprimanding them than they were with others considered more dangerous to good order. At one college, for example, a room reserved for debating society use was declared off limits to society members for a month because someone spat tobacco juice on the floor. Wine, stolen by students from the kitchen, was put to conventional use, although boys were treated severely if caught and could be compelled to miss several meals to pay for their fun. In order to find more comfortable and less demanding surroundings, boys sometimes feigned illness and checked in at the infirmary, where, in proportion to the seriousness of their claimed sickness, they were waited on by infirmarians and generally offered better than the usual bill of fare. College disciplinarians discovered these ruses and invented ways of clearing hypochondriacs from the hospitals. Literature judged immodest was, of course, confiscated and immediately destroyed; boys caught with such material were confined for a month of Tuesdays, required to kneel in the refectory during meal time, and deprived of their Sunday dinner.

We wonder what they missed when meals were withheld. Dining in Catholic college refectories, where places at table were assigned according to various criteria—sometimes height, merit, or age—is a subject which defies entirely trustworthy historical description : neither student nor college accounts can be taken at face value. Students conventionally employed choice and pejorative adjectives to describe the quality of the food; naturally enough college announcements stressed its wholesomeness and careful preparation. In any case, the boys, we know, often made foraging tours into town and countryside looking for food to buy or an invitation to dine out. And they report their successes in finding tasty food, including cider, sauce, pie, and cheese. But even at the college table their extraordinary hunger may have compensated for the culinary shortcomings of unimaginative cooks; students themselves speak of returning from the playground to devour a dozen slices of bread, without butter or molasses, washed down with tea. But they tell, also, of going to breakfast to "eat bread soaked in

[96] Power, *A History of Catholic Higher Education in the United States,* p. 130.

turpentine or the burning fluid [kerosene],"[97] of goose that was nothing but skin and bone, of soup that was dishwater, and of meat "tough enough to break a fellow's teeth."[98]

Menus are hard to reconstruct, yet we are tempted to think the college table was reasonably well set, despite the regularity of student complaint. Breakfasts were always light, except possibly on Sundays and religious feast days, when departures were taken from the usual bread and coffee. The main meal served at noon included meat dishes, except on Fridays and other days of abstinence; lunch, a repast of bread and milk or tea, was served around four in the afternoon; and supper, another light meal, was scheduled for some time between six and seven-thirty. Boys were discouraged from eating between meals and permission to dine away from college was an extraordinary privilege. Despite what must have been coarse fare, students at a Catholic college never starved, although they were always hungry.

Student life in the colleges was sometimes dull, and, as we have said, discipline was unrelenting; an overabundance of rules put every boy in jeopardy, and he was frequently unable to predict whether they would be interpreted strictly or liberally. He knew college boundaries should not be crossed without authorization; lessons were to be finished fully and on time; essays and compositions should be the products of his own labor. There were times for laughing, but laughing at the wrong place or time could be a serious offense; and certain periods of silence were prescribed for all, periods which in due course led the boys to invent an ingenious sign language. Singing was discouraged, as was whistling; wasting food was a high crime; the list could go on and on. Yet this was only one, though probably a predominating, side of college life; there was another, where boys enrolled at rural colleges were allowed to fish and hunt and generally use the recreational resources provided by nature. And in a few colleges the courtesies of gentility allowed older students to have a glass of wine with a feast-day dinner or a cup of egg nog at Christmas and New Year's day.[99] On the whole students adjusted to their environment, complained regularly, and sometimes bitterly, about their situation, but took good times with bad and lived in anticipation of the termination of their college careers. Student common sense, and the natural resiliency of youth, contributed to a Catholic college record remarkably free from revolt and flagrant challenge to the disciplinary code and its administration. Yet the few exceptions to sanguine student temperament may be worth noting.

At Georgetown College in 1850, members of the Philodemic Society,

[97] Healy Diary, quoted in Dunigan, *Student Days at Holy Cross College in 1848,* pp. 155–159.

[98] *Ibid.*

[99] Daley, *op. cit.,* pp. 248–249.

believing they had just grievances against their prefect, met to discuss them. Whether or not they planned any action against the prefect is unknown; nevertheless, the prefect, hearing of the meeting, responded by suspending all Society activities for a month. The members vented their wrath at this penalty by refusing to participate in public reading at supper, and later incited a small disturbance in the study hall and dormitory. Three students, suspected as principal plotters, were expelled; but their fellows, unwilling to see three boys penalized for the acts of the entire group, stood by them. Forty-four students made an exodus from the college to establish headquarters in a Washington hotel. From there they dispatched a communiqué to Georgetown's President, James A. Ward, in which conditions for settling the dispute were outlined. All students involved in the foray, they began, must be readmitted in good standing, and be absolved from penalty or threat of punishment. In addition, they insisted, the offending prefect must be dismissed from the college staff. Unless these conditions were met, they would not consider returning. They wanted the President's reply by eleven o'clock the next day.[100] Wheels of compromise moved slowly, and college authorities temperamentally opposed to capitulation to student pressure employed delaying tactics, but in the end—after ten days of negotiation— the students won their points : the prefect was allowed to resign from the staff and the students, with their amnesty safely in hand, returned to Georgetown.

Two years later, in 1852, Georgetown was again the scene of student revolt. This time, however, the general code of discipline, rather than a prefect, was their target. Not surprisingly, the boys thought rules governing their conduct were too harsh and, since they were emerging from a period—following the first revolt—where the enforcement of college law had been somewhat relaxed, sought to retain and extend what they chose to regard as emancipation from authority. In any case, to surrender without protest was unthinkable. So when the prefects began to administer discipline according to pre-1850 prescriptions, students were determined to fight back. The fuse was lighted by a prefect's assignment of lines to be memorized as a penalty for the infraction of some minor rule. The boys threw stones and inkstands around the study hall, broke furniture and windows, and showed other manifestations of resentment against the authorities of the college. They hoped, apparently, to repeat their victory of two years earlier by forcing the president to reform disciplinary regulation along lighter and more humane lines.[101] The President, however, refused to heed their threats of violence or of withdrawal from college; instead, he promptly expelled six students, identified as ringleaders, and notified their parents of this action by telegram—the first time a Catholic college used telegraphy for such a

---

[100] Shea, *A History of Georgetown College,* p. 166; and Daley, *op. cit.,* pp. 286–288.
[101] Shea, *op. cit.,* pp. 178–179.

purpose.[102] In the college's response in this instance to student protest we see a more general attitude coming into force in Catholic colleges : rules must stand, despite what students think or like; if they refuse to abide by college law they have one freedom in reserve—they may leave the college at once. This philosophy of discipline, thus clarified, was practiced for another century : in Catholic colleges rule and authority must withstand, at almost any cost, fragmentation and erosion by student feeling.[103]

Diversion

Any chronicle of student diversion in Catholic colleges is bound to be inadequate, because no full and dependable record of the way boys consumed leisure hours is available. What testimony exists, moreover, is always exaggerated or minimized by personal involvement, and sorting fact from fiction is almost an unmanageable task. Yet we want to know something about the lighter side of college life, and must therefore accept the need to scan pictures of it blurred both by the extremities of student complaint and the extravagances of college publicity.

It would be plainly wrong to concentrate on the enjoyment boys felt in circumventing school regulations or on depicting them as lawless youth disrespectful of authority, but we must remember that appropriate mixtures of student exuberance, pietistic codes of conduct, and literal-mindedness on the part of prefects of discipline made breaking college rules an exciting and attractive student enterprise. Leisure hours were used for planning and executing schemes to confound prefects and amuse fellow students. Tiring of flaunting college regulations, boys turned to other forms of recreation.

Admittedly, facilities for games, dramatics, and leisure-time reading left much to be desired, but the colleges always thought a distinction between an educational and an instructional day was worth making. The former extended from rising to retiring; the latter was coterminous with the schedule of study and classes. Thus, some effort was made, especially in extracurricular religious activities, to integrate the two and make both days contribute to overall objectives the colleges hope to achieve. Educationally this made good sense. Still, obstacles to the implementation of this policy very nearly made it inoperative.

For the first fifty years of their life in America, Catholic colleges thought athletics merely a waste of time; sport was something to be frowned on or

---

[102] Power, *A History of Catholic Higher Education in the United States,* p. 134.
[103] Erbacher, *op. cit.,* p. 102.

forbidden. In some schools organized games were proscribed by disciplinary regulations and students who ignored the rules were fined. One student, referring to the Catholic college climate of the late nineteenth century, said : "We had no gymnasium, no play-ground, no football team, no opportunity, in fact, for anything in the line of athletics except an occasional baseball game."[104] Football was taboo at all early Catholic colleges, as were other organized sports, and it was not until the post-Civil War period that the schools recognized the need young, growing, and energetic men had for physical exercise in games and contests. Even then they approached what should have been good, clean fun in an oblique way and affirmed the worth of sport, not for its own sake, the physical benefits therefrom, or the sheer fun of it, but because it could help maintain discipline.

Intercollegiate athletics appeared tardily in Catholic colleges, usually because facilities were inadequate, often because transportation from school to school was a problem too difficult to solve, or because they were uneasy about having their boys come in contact with students from other, especially nonCatholic, schools. When, after many false starts, the colleges entered into intercollegiate competition, they continued to preserve their exclusiveness and sought opponents from among Catholic colleges. Even then they usually restricted their participation to the game of baseball, which, at best, could involve only a few of the students. This much could be done without a coach and without equipment, except what was supplied by the participants themselves. Sometimes the colleges appointed a student coach, or assigned a faculty moderator, who may or may not have had any interest in athletics, to supervise athletic discipline.

Formal intramural competition was either totally ignored or poorly organized; college authorities simply neglected to recognize this side of college life : there was nothing in their own seminary educational backgrounds that would have recommended more attention to organized recreation. There were, of course, some informal excursions which must have been fun : at some schools the boys hunted, fished, went boating, used nearby streams for swimming, and winter's snow and ice for sleighing and skating. In Southern colleges fencing was popular among the students. And we must not neglect to mention that in 1814 Georgetown College appropriated five hundred dollars for the construction of a handball court.[105] Wrestling, a sport that should have been known and appreciated by classically-minded teachers and students, lacked official recognition and was engaged in only as a pastime on the playground when boys had nothing else to do, or on those occasions when they had personal disputes to settle. Indeed, an interest in athletics among Catholic colleges, both intramural

---

[104] Dunigan, *A History of Boston College,* p. 110.
[105] Daley, *op. cit.,* p. 245.

and intercollegiate, did not really develop until the advent of the twentieth century; it most surely did not figure large in their formative period.

Language, literary, dramatic, and debating societies occupied students' out-of-class intellectual, recreational, and political interests. The last-named were especially popular, for the older students took politics seriously, and by their actions proved that, although their teachers were content to live in political ivory towers, they were not. And literary societies usually prepared the ground for the first libraries in Catholic colleges; without them, Catholic schools would have been deprived in even minimal library resources for decades. In some colleges several literary and library associations actively competed in selecting good books and compiling large collections. Eventually these libraries merged with the official institutional library, but their remnants remain : even now we are able to find books in Catholic college libraries clearly marked as having belonged to one or another library association.

Religious associations of all kinds were common in early Catholic colleges; even a small school had as many as a dozen, and it appears they were popular with students and their programs were taken seriously. Journalism must also be listed as an out-of-class student activity. Under close supervision students prepared daily and weekly college announcements, kept bulletin boards, and were enlisted to help publish the annual prospectus; in this way, it was hoped, they would become acquainted with the fundamentals of journalism. Student newspapers were never found in the first colleges[106] because they were too expensive : they were regarded also as too dangerous an instrument to put into student hands. With an instinctive admiration for military careers and a latent approval of militarism's authority and order, Catholic colleges encouraged the organization of drill companies, and often listed them as extracurricular activities. Fraternities were conspicuous by their absence in all Catholic colleges; how students felt about them and whether or not they missed such associations is little known, although college officers, as a matter of inflexible policy, strictly prohibited their appearance on campus.

Support

At the beginning of the chapter we spoke of the duties an undergraduate had to the college he attended and set that discussion of duty within the context of the educational regimen. But duty had still another side : it was left almost entirely to students to supply colleges with the necessary financial support.

[106] Hamilton, *op. cit.,* p. 99.

In a country with a small and generally impoverished Catholic population endowments and gifts from private persons were rare, and public sources of financial aid were generally stopped up either by legal obstacles or by the barriers of prejudice. Georgetown, in 1833, received a federal grant of city lots[107] valued at about $25,000, mainly because a year earlier Columbian College had been awarded a tract of federal land. The proposed statute authorizing the grant to Georgetown was opposed on the grounds that Catholic institutions were not qualified to receive disbursements from public resources, but in the end a congressional sense of equity prevailed and the bill was approved. Two years later Senator Thomas H. Benton of Missouri introduced a bill calling for a land grant from the national domain amounting to a township, or 23,040 acres, to St. Louis University.[108] Benton's bill, trapped in committee for three years, was debated on the Senate floor in 1838 only to be returned to committee and never heard of again. St. John's College (now Fordham) received a money-grant of $2,500 from New York State in 1849[109] and at about the same time St. Bonaventure College received similar financial help.[110] Other Catholic colleges may have benefited similarly, but evidences of such transactions, if, indeed, they occurred, are no longer extant.

To get their start Catholic colleges, for the most part, had to depend on their own resources and this took a great deal of ingenuity. John Carroll used the revenue from the sale of Jesuit land to purchase the site for Georgetown and to erect its first buildings;[111] Bishop Louis DuBourg deeded property to the Jesuits when they agreed to take the college in St. Louis;[112] and Bishop John Purcell made an outright gift of his Cincinnati college to the Jesuits in order to convince them of the need to found Xavier.[113] These are but a few examples of how bishops were willing to assist Catholic colleges, and they could be multiplied, not only with respect to founding, but at times subsequent when the colleges found themselves desperately in need of funds. Yet those same factors which contributed to the economic disadvantages of Catholic colleges applied also to the bishops, so there were times when the bishop could not save a college from financial disaster. Then the college had to find another source of money or close its doors. We should not expect to find many evidences of desperate action among records open to the public eye, for Catholic college accounts were handled with diligent

107 Easby-Smith, op. cit., I, 70.

108 Garraghan, The Jesuits of the Middle United States, III, 206–210.

109 Malcolm T. Carron, The Contract Colleges of Cornell University (Ithaca, Cornell University Press, 1958), p. 6.

110 Irenaeus Herscher, "The History of St. Bonaventure University," Franciscan Studies, 11 (September, December, 1951), 365–424.

111 Daley, op. cit., pp. 39–40.

112 Faherty, op. cit., p. 19.

113 Garraghan, The Jesuits of the Middle United States, III, 166.

confidentiality; still, Walter J. Meagher, the capable historian of Holy Cross, reports that on one occasion the President, not knowing where else to turn, appealed to the students. With the help of the Second Humanities class he was able to collect $500.[114]

Even the best expedients were undependable, so in the last analysis the only reliable and regular source of income for Catholic colleges was tuition. Before 1821 all Catholic colleges collected tuition from their students, but in this year an issue arose threatening the financial security of Jesuit colleges. Washington Seminary, opened September 29, 1820, as a school for Jesuit theology students, almost at once found itself in financial jeopardy. A plan was devised for conducting a day school "with classes up to syntax" for boys who would be taught by the theology students. Tuition collected from the boys could then be used to support Washington Seminary. But the Jesuit General repudiated this arrangement, saying that "he could not in conscience tolerate the practice as being openly at variance with the religious poverty enjoined by the Jesuit rule."[115] The directive was clear : Jesuit schools were to be free, and Washington Seminary's elementary adjunct either had to comply or close.

Both the Society's rule and its long teaching tradition endorsed free instruction; European Jesuit schools, moreover, had flourished by following the rule. The Jesuit General wondered what was so different about the schools in the United States. Provincials, presidents, and consultors did their best to explain indigenous American prejudices against free schools, pointing out that without either endowments or tuition income the demise of Jesuit colleges was certain. Still, the General refused to rescind his order restraining Jesuit schools from charging fees for instruction, so Washington Seminary's day school was doomed. It closed September 25, 1827.[116] But this was only one school, and an elementary school at that; there was no immediate cause for alarm and the colleges might have continued their extra-rule practice of collecting modest fees for teaching had it not been for the General's decision to send a personal representative to the United States to visit Jesuit schools.

The General's representative, Peter Kenny, arrived in the United States, probably early in 1830, with "instructions to see that the regulations of Father General [Fortis] were rigorously carried out." After inspecting Georgetown, Kenny reported to the General that "the alleged prejudices against free schools did not exist or if they had existed were no longer in evidence; and that the existing legislation in regard to tuition-money should not be modified."[117] This statement alone, made from the protected precincts

114 Meagher, *op. cit.*, p. 79.
115 Garraghan, *The Jesuits of the Middle United States,* I, 34.
116 *Sketch of Gonzaga College,* p. 33.
117 Garraghan, *The Jesuits of the Middle United States,* I, 304.

of Georgetown College, shows how much casual observers, partly insulated from reality, can really miss. But Father Kenny could miss more than the deep-seated prejudice against free schools and what he missed was right under his nose : Georgetown's tuition charge, like that at St. Louis, was five dollars, although it was camouflaged as a fee "for fuel and servants. No charge for tuition." [118] Servants, however, were unknown at Georgetown and fuel was little used; if Kenny had asked, any Jesuit would have been bound to admit that the five-dollar charge was for instruction.

Blind at Georgetown, Kenny saw clearly enough when he reached St. Louis, and he immediately dispatched a report to the General telling him of the tuition St. Louis was charging, "which, though a mere pittance, is still real tuition-money deriving from a legal contract and is far in excess of the expenses incurred on their (the day scholars') behalf, if the teachers be left out of the account." Again the real point of tuition was missed, for it was plainly impossible to leave the teachers out of account; income from teaching was their only source of support.

Nothing in the St. Louis situation allows us to suppose either that the Jesuits there were unaware of the rule on gratuitous teaching or unwilling in principle to follow it. Five years before Father Kenny came to St. Louis, President Charles Van Quickenborne had written to the General applauding his "resolution . . . not to permit money to be received from teaching boys at Washington," and soliciting instructions from him : "If your Reverence sees anything that we do here against holy poverty, let me know and I will change it immediately." [119] But after the college was opened, he wrote the General again, and now he had some questions :

Is it lawful to require from parents who send their sons to school in St. Louis or St. Charles a fee in money with which to meet the cost of building? In St. Louis many subscribe on condition that they pay for the education of their children. I answered—if they wish, they may—I should receive the money as a donation or alms. You certainly cannot live, if you receive nothing, and if you labor for us, it is our duty to support you. Is it lawful to receive such donations or alms? All the consultors have answered affirmative to both.
Since in these parts there is need of a fire in school, is it lawful to demand something in payment for the wood?
Also for the making and use of the benches.[120]

An explicit adherence to the rule obviously meant the end of Jesuit colleges in the United States. In 1833, President Verhaegen told the General that the annual salary of one lay professor accounted for all the nominal fees paid by one hundred students. In addition, free instruction was a detri-

[118] Daley, *op. cit.,* pp. 281–282.
[119] Garraghan, *The Jesuits of the Middle United States,* I, 305.
[120] *Ibid.*

ment to Catholic education, because parents, clinging to their antipathies against free teaching, and confusing free schools with pauper schools, preferred nonCatholic, tuition schools. This tuition issue, then, never just a private Jesuit matter, solicited the attention of the Ordinary of St. Louis, who petitioned the Holy See in May, 1832, to dispense St. Louis Jesuits from the rule forbidding compensation from teaching.[121]

A dispensation was granted, January 13, 1833, authorizing the Jesuit General to determine the exact terms of its application. Acting on this authority the General issued instructions applying the dispensation to Jesuit schools unable to support themselves or to such schools as might be affected by anti-free-school prejudices. On February 1, 1833, in *Orinatio de Minervali,* additional instructions about the dispensation were given. According to Garraghan, this document

enjoins that tuition-rates are to be adjusted to those obtaining in other reputable day-schools of the country; that poor boys are not to be turned away or in any way neglected through inability to pay; that lawsuits are never to be instituted to recover tuition-fees; and that the income derived from tuition-fees is to be spent on the support of the Jesuits and on school equipment, including furniture and libraries, and that no part of said income may be lawfully expended for the subsistence of the Jesuit teachers in the contingency that expenses under this head can be adequately met from other sources.[122]

With the tuition question settled for Jesuit colleges, they, like other Catholic colleges, and like American colleges generally at this time, used income from instruction as a principal means of support.[123] Although neither generality nor reliability can be asserted for any summary of Catholic college charges for room, board, and tuition during the formative period, a few examples of those from various colleges may prove interesting. The first prospectus of Georgetown stated that the "pension for tuition" was ten pounds sterling a year; board and room were extra, of course. In 1798, the Georgetown prospectus was more exact : article twelve set out the terms of payment, "which is always to be made half-yearly in advance, [and] are here annexed :"

---

[121] *Ibid.,* p. 307.

[122] *Ibid.,* pp. 308–309.

[123] We should note, however, that charging tuition was by no means a universal policy among Jesuit colleges. St. Joseph's College in Philadelphia, founded in 1851, began to operate as a free school in 1889 (*St. Joseph's College Catalogue, 1895–1896,* p. 5); and Creighton College, using the $147,500 endowment of Mary Lucretia Creighton, operated as a free school for some time (*Creighton College Catalogue, 1881–1882,* p. 6; *1889–1890,* p. 8; *1895–1896,* p. 3).

	Dolls.	Cts.	
For Board,	100:	0	
Tuition,	26:	67	
Mending linen and stockings,	4:	0	
Washing,	6:	0	
Doctor's fees, remedies and nursing,	3:	0	
Firewood for schools,	2:	0	
Pew in church for Catholic students,	1:	0	142:67
Entrance money,	4:	0 [124]	

Article thirteen provided the terms for students who lived in the house reserved for nonCatholics :

For the boarders in the separate house, the board will be 132 dollars. The other articles, viz. tuition, &c the same as above.—This difference in the prices of the two boards will be easily accounted for by the necessity of renting a house for this express purpose and furnishing it with servants and necessary articles.[125]

In 1827 the following charges were announced for Mt. St. Mary's College :

Board and Tuition, payable half-yearly in advance	$150
Washing and Mending, and mending materials	12
Extra Charge for French	20
Spanish	20
Drawing	25
Music, vocal and instrumental	40
Use of the Piano	8
Use of Bed and Bedding	10
Charge for Pen, Ink, and use of English Reading Books, Doctor's salary, unless parents prefer the alternative of a bill in case of sickness	5 [126]

Catholic college charges, it appears, despite the great variations among them, were slightly higher than those at nonCatholic schools, so for good or ill the undergraduate in the Catholic college made a greater investment in his own education, and his duty to himself, to say nothing about his duty to the college, should have been that much the greater.

[124] Easby-Smith, *op. cit.,* I, 40–41.
[125] *Ibid.*
[126] Meline and McSweeny, *op. cit.,* I, 187–188.

STUDENT FEES AT TEN CATHOLIC COLLEGES, 1870–1900[127]

COLLEGE	YEAR			
	1870	1880	1890	1900
Georgetown	$325	$ 50[b]	c	$380
Mt. St. Mary's	300	300	$300	300
Notre Dame	300	300	300	300
Holy Cross	250	200	60[b]	260
Spring Hill	225	300	90[b]	65[b]
St. Louis	250	60[b]	60[b]	60[b]
Villanova	250	250	250	225
Fordham	300	60[b]	60[b]	325
Xavier (Ohio)	60[a]	60[a]	60[b]	60[b]
St. Vincent	180	c	c	260

[a] Day students only
[b] Tuition charge only
[c] No report for the year

STUDENT FEES AT TEN NONCATHOLIC COLLEGES, 1870–1900[128]

COLLEGE	YEAR				
	1870	1880	1890	1900	c
Harvard	$25	$150	$150	$150	$350
Yale	90	140	125	155	545
William and Mary	45	40	b	35	108
Columbia	100	150	150–200	150	400
Dartmouth	60	90	b	100	450
University of Georgia	60	a	a	a	160
Brown	75	100	100	105	400
University of Michigan	a	20	20–35	30	190
University of Wisconsin	18	a	a	a	350
University of Pennsylvania	35	150	100–200	50–200	450

[a] Tuition free for residents of state
[b] No report for the year
[c] Estimated annual living expenses (room, board, and incidentals)

[127] *Report of the United States Commissioner of Education, 1870,* pp. 506–516; *1881,* pp. 595–606; *1889–1890,* pp. 1600–1609; *1899–1900,* pp. 1924–1943.
[128] *Ibid.*

II
The period of development: 1870-1940

7

Professional education

Toward the end of the eighteenth century, when the first Catholic college appeared on the American scene, the college-going public was temperamentally ready for a shift in higher educational perspectives away from a determined and dedicated allegiance to what passed for classical learning to a utility-centered program consistent with the recommendations made by John Locke several decades before and endorsed with varying degrees of enthusiasm by such American thinkers as Benjamin Franklin and Thomas Jefferson.[1] With increasing frequency, parents, students, and parts of the general public were disinclined to accept at face value the old pronouncements either that higher learning had nothing to do with professional skill—because of its liberal goals—or that it had everything to do with it—because the classical curriculum with its capacity for training the mind was a complete preparation. But if these Americans, all with a keen interest in higher education, could occasionally find the higher ground of college purpose and call for new and different college programs, we must quickly admit that their pleas for reform fell on almost totally deaf ears: the men who controlled the colleges were unready for any change in college direction. And there were some good justifications for their defense of the *status quo*. In the first place, the deeply rooted traditions of apprenticeship training were everywhere in evidence: religious ministers, with only a few notable exceptions, were prepared for their vocation through fairly lengthy and reasonably close associations with ministers and preachers who had occupied the pulpit for some time;[2]

[1] See Edward J. Power, *Evolution of Educational Doctrine* (New York, Appleton-Century-Crofts, 1969), pp. 251–271; Thomas Woody, *Educational Views of Benjamin Franklin* (New York, McGraw-Hill Book Co., 1931); and Roy J. Honeywell, "A Note on the Educational Work of Thomas Jefferson," *History of Education Quarterly,* IX (Spring, 1969), 64–74.

[2] Mary L. Gambrell, *Ministerial Training in Eighteenth Century New England* (New York, Columbia University Press, 1937), pp. 140–150.

fledgling lawyers read the law, helped prepare legal documents, and did odd jobs around the court when it was in session, under the guidance of men already admitted to the bar, and this was the accepted method of legal training;[3] prospective doctors apprenticed themselves to practicing physicians and while in their company hoped to learn whatever was necessary about medical remedies and therapeutic practices.[4] The engineer, the navigator, the surveyor, the schoolmaster, all entered their professions in much the same way : they learned under the direction of accredited professionals or they followed the even more ancient art of learning-by-doing. In any case, the force of tradition appeared to be strong enough to keep professional training outside the schoolhouse door.

Undoubtedly some respected opinion ran counter to the assumptions that kept the apprenticeship system intact, and this opinion was by no means American in origin or of especially recent vintage. Legal scholars of the Great Renaissance had seen the relationship between codes of law and the need to interpret and apply these codes to their own genre, and what the humanists detected in their careful studies was recalled by succeeding generations.[5] Grammar, rhetoric, and logic had an obvious and undeniable contribution to make to the interpretation and administration of law; and where could these subjects be learned better than in the schools? There was, moreover, a theory or philosophy of law standing as the bedrock to precedent and practice and most of this remained unrealized in the poorly-defined and inconsistent measures used for the training of men for the courts. Legal theory should have had special meaning for Americans interested in the law, for their ideas of democracy and freedom perforce affected the entire corpus of jurisprudence. Yet, what was later so obvious, that legal study in the new country, with what amounted to a new form of government, could no longer afford the luxury of outmoded and ineffective legal training, was, in effect, ignored, and legal education was made to mark time for almost another half-century. Beginning in the 1780s, Tapping Reeve, a remarkably successful attorney and judge in Litchfield, Connecticut, who had regularly accepted apprentices for legal training, found his practice reduced by the effects of war and political insecurity, so he accepted a larger number of apprentices and established what amounted to a law institute.[6] Thus, the first American step was taken toward removing legal education from the vagaries of individual tuition

3 E. G. Dexter, "Training for the Learned Professions," *Educational Review,* 25 (January, 1903), 31–37.

4 W. F. Norwood, *Medical Education in the United States before the Civil War* (Philadelphia, University of Pennsylvania Press, 1944), pp. 140–147.

5 See R. R. Bolgar, *The Classical Heritage and Its Beneficiaries* (Cambridge, Cambridge University Press, 1954), pp. 290–295.

6 John S. Brubacher and Willis Rudy, *Higher Education in Transition* (New York, Harper and Row, Publishers, 1958), p. 109.

and at the same time the cornerstone was laid for a para-academic approach to the study of law. Reeve's example was followed often enough to allow the historians of legal education to write into their histories two avenues of preparation for the bar, but before considering these further, we must record two demurrals in connection with the law institute. First, although Reeve's school was both important and respectable in the annals of legal education—and graduated such American leaders as Henry Clay, John C. Calhoun, and Horace Mann—its insistence on quality was paid scant heed by the institutes following in its footsteps. These law institutes, competing with the apprentice system, found it difficult or impossible to alter much, or depart from, the practices recommended or dictated by apprenticeship. For the most part, they offered quick, perfunctory courses, collected the fees from their students and sent them to the bar examination, if the colony or state had the good fortune to have one. What they did, with only a rare exception, hardly counted as legal education. Second, what appeared as a bold stride in the direction of improved standards for studies under the auspices of incorporated legal institutes was really only a faint copy of the highly professionalized studies of the law that since the advent of medieval universities had been well-known in European academic centers. And the modern universities in Germany, France, and England, benefiting from the humanists' contribution to education in the specialties—law, medicine, and philosophy—had made considerable progress in establishing the boundaries of a science and theory of law and had done good work in producing legal scholars.[7] So the American law institute cannot be given credit for breaking any new ground along these lines.

The tale chronicling the forward progress of studies in the law from the primitive and usually unsatisfactory apprenticeship arrangements to custody in college schools of law is marked by false starts, compromises, outright imitation, and finally relative success. It is, moreover, a story too involved for these pages;[8] but in the end, around the middle of the nineteenth century, we find courses in law securely established in the principal universities of the United States. The administrative relationships between the colleges and the professional schools were not always praiseworthy, for even in the best colleges the law school retained its independence and was little affected by collegiate affiliation. Eventually, however, due primarily to the forceful leadership of a few dominant presidents, the schools of law were brought to heel.

Law became an established study in the colleges by following one of two rather different routes : we know, for example, that chairs of law were created at the College of William and Mary, the University of Pennsylvania,

[7] Bolgar, op. cit., pp. 290–295.

[8] See J. G. Rogers, "The Standardization Movement in American Law Schools," Educational Record, 13 (July, 1932), 220–223.

and Columbia University before the end of the eighteenth century and these chairs eventually produced a sub-structure of separate departments, schools, or colleges;[9] and we know also that Yale and a few other colleges acquired institutes of law and converted them into their own law schools. This latter course, it can be said, was made respectable and attractive by Yale when it arranged to embrace the Litchfield Institute as an academic appendage.[10] But much still remained to be done, and here we should note Harvard's early nineteenth-century example, which was followed by other colleges, of requiring the equivalent of a college education for admission to the department of law.[11]

In medicine, as in law, the proper balance between the school and the practitioner's office was hard to find in the primitive professional climate of early America. European universities were deeply involved in scientific medicine by the advent of the eighteenth century. Nevertheless, they were constantly engaged in a running battle with a conventional wisdom which refused to pay heed to the just claims of empirical knowledge. Long before the medieval universities appeared on the scene, the medical authorities were established—Hippocrates and Galen—and hardly any physician or medical faculty professor could afford to be an innovator, either by introducing new texts or departing from the old ones, regardless of the empirical data he might have. So within the field of medicine itself the priorities were obscured by old prejudices, inordinate confidence in the authorities, or an open-armed embrace of empiricism; new methods of training the medical doctor marked time while the profession itself ironed out its internal problems.[12] American medical opinion could afford to ignore the debates of the European medical societies and in doing so continued with a minimum of interruption the ancient art of preparing doctors according to the broad rubrics of apprenticeship. The outlines of a medical apprenticeship were clear : a medical student attached himself to a recognized doctor, studied under him, accompanied him on his rounds, nursed patients, noted the advice, and watched the therapy he prescribed. What was not so clear, however, was the commitment the physician had to instructing his apprentices and, moreover, the length of time necessary for their training : the conscientious student might stay with his mentor for nearly a decade and absorb an abundance of medical knowledge and practical skill, whereas an apprentice with lower standards might easily assimilate the more obvious precepts of the medical fraternity, perfunctorily grasp the techniques of therapy, and leave his teacher after a period of six

9 Brubacher and Rudy, *op. cit.,* p. 198.

10 *Ibid.,* p. 204.

11 Charles W. Eliot, *Harvard Memories* (Cambridge, Mass., Harvard University Press, 1923), p. 135.

12 Bolgar, *op. cit.,* pp. 290–295.

months or so. But these difficulties were of long standing : Galen himself, who spent twelve years in a medical apprenticeship, complained of the quickness and superficiality of the medical training of some of his confreres.[13]

Around the middle of the eighteenth century, especially after science had a chance to make an impression on some American educational leaders, and even while some students were still going to Europe to study medicine, chairs of medicine were established at the stronger colleges. The University of Pennsylvania, largely due to Benjamin Franklin's influence, took the lead and was followed a few decades later by Harvard, Dartmouth, Yale, and Brown.[14] At about the same time, however, although the old-fashioned apprenticeship system remained intact, physicians accustomed to having apprentices articled to them decided to expand their teaching practice, so they abandoned their individual teaching efforts and incorporated medical institutes wherein students could be trained for the profession of medicine.[15]

Generalizations about the medical institute must be stated with some degree of caution : for the most part, we should think, the independent medical institute was a money-making venture paying little attention to the standards of medical practice; it took students wherever it could find them, collected their fees, offered them a few perfunctory lectures on the science and art of the profession, and then turned them out as medical doctors on an unsuspecting public. Yet, the picture had a brighter side; here and there a medical institute took its work seriously, tried to control the quality of its students, offered them a respectable professional curriculum over a definite period of years, mixed a theory of medicine from the textbooks with careful internship experience, and set reasonably high standards in the examinations administered prior to conferring the medical degree. This was all praiseworthy and positive, and a good omen for things to come. But for a hundred years from 1750, not more than a half-dozen such institutes managed to withstand the keen competition which they experienced from low-grade institutes and the old-time apprenticeship system.

The improvement of the standards of medical education was, in the end, a contribution made by the colleges. After the Civil War, and, again, due to the leadership of a few unusual men at the helm of the better colleges, standards for medical education were raised by requiring a college education for admission to a collegiate medical school, and by demanding that the medical schools themselves organize their courses in an academic manner, taking into account both the scientific accretions to the corpus of theory

---

[13] T. Puschmann, *Handbuch der Geschicte der Medizin* (Jena, 1902), I, 374–378.

[14] Richard Hofstadter and C. DeWitt Hardy, *The Development and Scope of Higher Education in the United States* (New York, Columbia University Press, 1952), pp. 80–85.

[15] Norwood, *op. cit.*, pp. 180–185.

and the significance of empirical data.[16] At last, and in the collegiate medical schools, the knowledge contained in the books was wedded to experience gained from the laboratory and the sick room. Although much remained to be done, the first steps had been taken to sever medicine from the realm of myth, magic, old-wives' tales, dogmatic assumption, and on-the-job training.

Moving away from complete confidence in apprentice training for the most honorable professions took some time; the first signs of this trend appeared, for law and medicine, in the last decades of the eighteenth century or the early years of the nineteenth and, probably because of their persistent social significance, the upgrading of a professional education in these fields attracted a good deal of attention. But another branch of higher education, theology, was due for some reconditioning too.

We know how difficult it is to determine whether the earliest colonial colleges were merely professional theological schools with some liberalizing courses attached to their curricula or whether they were, in fact, liberal arts colleges associated unequivocally with a religious denomination and thus a dependable source from which the congregations might draw their ministers.[17] Whatever the historical truth is, the curricular mixtures of theology and humanism were generally so unrefined as to make that truth relatively unimportant : a graduate from a colonial college was neither a theologian nor a humanist. In the early years of the nineteenth century Andover Theological Seminary tried to redress what appeared to be a deficiency in higher learning and defined its scholastic objectives along lines that should have made it a professional theological school : admission requirements stated that a prospective student must have, first, a vocation for the ministry, and, second, a college degree. On these bases Andover built a three-year divinity curriculum.[18]

But the Andover innovation, attractive as it was to the clerical fraternity, had to make its way through the thicket of apprentice practices which for centuries had dominated the practical training of ministers. All this took time and it took, too, once again, the good offices of the established colleges. The day of the independent theological school had hardly begun before the colleges entered the field of professional theology by adding schools of theology to their conventional structure, either by founding them or affiliating those already in existence.[19]

Thus, as we approach the period when the first Catholic colleges in

[16] See D. H. Fleming, *William Welch and the Rise of Modern Medicine* (Boston, Little, Brown and Co., 1954), pp. 79–83.

[17] See George Paul Schmidt, *The Liberal Arts College: A Chapter in American Cultural History* (New Brunswick, N. J., Rutgers University Press, 1957).

[18] Brubacher and Rudy, *op. cit.*, p. 201.

[19] See P. Lindsley, *Plea for a Theological Seminary at Princeton* (Trenton, N.J., 1821), pp. 14–15.

what is now the United States were founded, we find a kind of higher learning which, although it might be uncertain about the academic standards it should impose for matriculation, was committing itself at once to a broad humanism and a narrow professionalism. American higher education was trying its best to serve two masters, knowledge and society; and it accepted this monumental commission without the experience, the sophistication, or the resources to manage the contending forces at work within its own limited structure.

Catholic colleges and the professions

Our consideration of the early American Catholic college thus far has not discovered in it any of the appurtenances of a professional school. Yet it is easy to be deceived by the appearances of history. If we look for signs of legal, medical, engineering, or pedagogical curricula among the Catholic colleges of the early years of the nineteenth century, we shall surely be disappointed, for their embrace of professionalism and their conception of a true professional education did not take a form measurable in this way. On occasion, of course, the early colleges included in their curricula some commercial subjects, and some of them went out of their way to extol the virtues of bookkeeping, but they downgraded such subjects and refused to allow them professional standing.[20] The Catholic attitude toward the

---

[20] B. J. Lenoue, *The Historical Development of the Curriculum of the University of Notre Dame* (Notre Dame, Ind., 1933), p. 30; and Walter J. Meagher, *The History of the College of the Holy Cross* (New York, Fordham University, 1944), p. 36. Classical curricula were accorded pride of place on Catholic colleges' scales of values—as they were generally in American higher learning—and eroding this attitude was slow business. Students in the commercial program at St. Louis University could get bachelor of science degrees by adding an additional year of study (*St. Louis University Catalogue,* 1879–1880, p. 23). In the *Marquette College Catalogue, 1881–1882,* p. 5, the commercial course is described as being "necessarily inferior to the Classical." *St. Ignatius College Catalogue* (Calif.), *1889–1890,* p. 6, allowed for degrees only in classical studies; and Santa Clara permitted a certificate for commercial study (*Santa Clara College Catalogue, 1889–1890,* p. 4); as did Canisius (*Canisius College Catalogue, 1889–1890,* p. 2). *Gonzaga College* (D. C.) *Catalogue, 1889–1890,* p. 6, mentions a dispensation allowing certain students to take the commercial course. At St. Ignatius College in Cleveland the classical course took six years, the commercial course but three (*St. Ignatius College Catalogue, 1889–1890,* p. 3). The commercial course at Fordham in 1890 was a five-year course and the college *Catalogue,* 1890–1891, p. 12, says a degree was granted but does not name the degree. Certificates rather than degrees were still awarded for the commercial course at Marquette and St. Ignatius (Chicago) in 1896 (*Marquette College Catalogue, 1895–'896,* p. 11; and *St. Ignatius College Catalogue, 1895–1896,* p. 20).

professions was a severely limited one, and this limited attitude was imposed mainly by the Catholic clergy themselves, who, for good reasons or bad, accorded to their own way of life a superior professional status. What lay outside the boundaries of the sacerdotal occupation was necessarily secular and therefore either inferior or unworthy. By preaching and example the Catholic clergy helped create an attitude similar to their own among the lay members of the Church. The uneasy compromises between the secular and the sacred, the persistent ambiguities that had long before evolved in Christian life over what had merit and what had none were perpetuated in American Catholic communities. A ringing endorsement of the hierarchy's policy from almost every pulpit—do not educate your children beyond their proper station in life[21]—gave this policy the force of defined doctrine and helped set directions for the lay way of life.

This dogmatic exhortation about the educational goals suitable for lay Catholics allowed for but one exception : while Catholics were admonished to study a syllabus of duty to their religion, and clearly to eschew the learned professions and even the benefits of a decent lower education, they were importuned to cultivate religious vocations among the young and thus to send a chosen few to Catholic centers of higher learning where they could prepare for the priesthood.[22] What the bishops really meant when they expressed their educational philosophy in pastoral letters originating in Church councils was that boys should aspire to a better life by using the means of formal education only when the school they chose was the seminary and the profession they sought was the priesthood. Such self-serving statements of educational policy, although admittedly having elements of benefit for the institutional Church, did nothing for the future of Catholic higher education and may, in fact, have retarded its development by several decades. In the first place, despite John Carroll's determination to have a school which would have as its principal objective the preparation of boys for the seminary,[23] there is no sound reason for believing that many members of the Catholic clergy were optimistic about the possibilities of a domestic education for a native clergy. The source of clerical supply was Europe, and so it remained for some years, and the local clergy, itself of European origin, conveniently assumed that this picture would remain unchanged. From the beginning, then, even Carroll's progressive policy of taking the first steps toward the founding of ecclesiastical schools met with some determined opposition. And, though this was the course eventually adopted and

[21] Peter Guilday, *The National Pastorals of the American Hierarchy* (Washington, National Catholic Welfare Conference, 1923), p. 215.

[22] Sister M. Salome Tlochenska, *The American Hierarchy and Education* (Milwaukee, Marquette University, 1934), pp. 221–240.

[23] Peter Guilday, "The Priesthood of Colonial Maryland," *The Ecclesiastical Review* (January, 1934), pp. 8–17.

Catholic colleges did grow out of schools that were founded for professional reasons, it is nonetheless true that the Catholic college, as a place either for liberal learning or professional training, was made to mark time while the Catholic clergy debated the merits of a native education for a native clergy.[24] So if we begin by questioning the wisdom of these intransigent tactics of opposition to Carroll's plan, we must remember at the same time that the first real effort to establish a higher professional school for the preparation of priests in this country—St. Mary's in Baltimore—failed because there were too few students to justify a continuation of the program.[25] It was this failure which advanced the argument a stage further, for when for want of students the seminary had to suspend operations, the school's managers decided to admit students with secular intentions and offer them some of the elements of liberal learning. But, this, too, met with opposition, especially from Carroll, who saw St. Mary's practice as a threat to the future of the Georgetown Academy.[26] At this second stage, then, with various admixtures of motives and turns of clerical politics, with one lesson learned from the inability of St. Mary's to conduct seminary classes, because too few students were educationally prepared for them, and another from the limited enrollment at Georgetown, another beginning was made to establish a professional theological education on a solid foundation. After several false starts, and a few ignominious failures, this meant the creation first of minor seminaries, which would admit boys for elementary study, and then later, when the boys were ready, the expansion of the same school into the role of a major seminary.[27]

Thus, in historical perspective, we see Catholic colleges in the United States, although breaking no new ground as far as professional education was concerned, beginning in about the same way, and with the same narrow objectives, as had guided the founding of American colleges a century and one-half before. It is unnecessary, possibly even counterproductive, to reargue the purposes of colonial higher education here; we have said before, while recognizing legitimate areas for disagreement and debate, that the stated purposes of these colleges was to furnish ministers for the pulpit.[28] When such narrow goals were no longer satisfying to the better colleges, they sought to broaden their objectives by becoming fairly

[24] Peter Guilday, *The Life and Times of John Carroll* (New York, Encyclopedia Press, 1922), pp. 450–452.

[25] Joseph W. Ruane, *The Beginnings of the Society of St. Sulpice in the United States, 1791–1829* (Washington, Catholic University of America, 1935), p. 39.

[26] Guilday, *The Life and Times of John Carroll*, p. 466; John Gilmary Shea, *The History of the Catholic Church in the United States* (New York, J. G. Shea, 1886–1892), II, 378–382.

[27] Lloyd McDonald, *The Seminary Movement in the United States, 1784–1833* (Washington, Catholic University of America, 1927), pp. 125–139.

[28] See pp. 48–53.

orthodox schools for the cultivation of liberal learning. These realignments of objectives took some time, for changing the college course was never done in a day, and, we should think that, by the time Georgetown was founded, a theory of higher education which could make the Yale Report of 1828 an entirely natural expression of academic opinion was quite widely acclaimed. Or to put the matter another way, and to say it somewhat more bluntly, the better colleges in the United States had by this time committed themselves to liberal learning and had set aside as unworthy of undergraduate, nonprofessional education the archaic denominational goals of the first colleges.[29] This is the example the managers of the early nineteenth-century Catholic colleges might have seen fit to copy, but either by accident or design they refused to look in any direction for guidance save to the old tomes containing the guidelines and the directives for seminary training. It would probably be incorrect to assume that this was an over-sight, that their failure to test the waters of American higher education before becoming immersed in them was bred of clerical myopia or plain stupidity, for the kinds of schools Catholics established were exactly the kinds of schools they wanted.

Hence, it would seem plainly wrong to attribute the shortcomings of early Catholic colleges to the naïveté of their managers; they may have misread the need for higher learning in the Catholic community, and for this they can be subjected to historical indictment, but they did have a clear vision of what higher education should be : higher schools for Catholics were to commit themselves to the preparation of priests.

Studying only the documents of Catholic college history from the time of Georgetown's founding to 1850 and feigning an unawareness of the existence of any other kind of higher learning on this Continent, we should be compelled to conclude that, indeed, only Catholic colleges existed and that apart from them the colonies and the first states were intellectual wastelands. While the Yale Report was being written in 1828, twelve Catholic colleges had been established, although only nine were still operating —St. Thomas Aquinas College, St. Thomas, Kentucky, closed its doors in 1828; the New York Literary Institute ceased to exist in 1813; and Louisiana College suspended operations in 1825[30]—and none offers any evidence that the kind of ferment which led to the Yale Report—the challenge professional curricula threw down before the classical course—existed among their managers also.[31] Even after 1828, when the Yale Report (published in 1829) was the common currency of academic discussion and debate, no Catholic college spokesman adverted to it, either to endorse or denounce

[29] Hofstadter and Hardy, op. cit., pp. 48–49.

[30] Edward J. Power, A History of Catholic Higher Education in the United States (Milwaukee, Bruce Publishing Co., 1958), pp. 256–259.

[31] Ibid., pp. 53–54.

it, and no Catholic college felt compelled to take its ringing endorsements of the classical course at face value or, what is worse, to admit of their existence.

Indeed, it would have been easy for the managers of Catholic colleges to follow in the wake of classical education—the wake having been made by the writers of the Yale Report—for almost from the beginning of such colleges in the new country their official pronouncements had paid lip service to liberal learning, and with some good reasons. Whatever may have been the real objectives of Catholic institutions, and we argue here that they were primarily ecclesiastical, it was close to obvious that the teachers in the colleges had credentials of scholarship limited almost solely to a classically oriented curriculum. Even when the colleges were seemingly insensitive to their public image, they had enough pride to insist on putting their best foot forward in public : besides, by staying close to the classical course they were fairly certain of the support of a tradition which for the past several centuries had recommended classical teaching with unstinting devotion. Several decades later, as in the report Georgetown prepared for the United States Commissioner of Education in 1887, the Catholic colleges could speak in glowing terms of a "course calculated to develop and train all the powers of the mind, rendering it able to understand and appreciate all branches of learning. It serves as a foundation for special training in any branch which the student, with his mind matured and trained, may decide to take up." [32] When the writers of the Yale document sought to stabilize the direction of a superior education by clearly identifying its foundations, they used language which has a familiar ring when we see it again in the statements issuing from the Catholic schools. The interesting thing to observe, however, is not so much the similarity of language and the identity of sense, but that by 1887 the apparently convincing arguments in the Yale Report, now over sixty years old, were really out-of-date and out-of-step with the principal currents of American higher learning.

In a way, though, this debate over the parallels between the Yale Report and later Catholic college announcements about the foundations of liberal learning is either irrelevant or beside the point. Catholic colleges of the early or formative period were not, in fact, especially concerned about liberal learning—they were intent, as we have said, on paying it lip service— for their mission, they thought, lay in other directions : first, they wanted to prepare priests, or, failing this, to give prospective priests their preliminary

[32] *Report of the United States Commissioner of Education,* 1887–1888, pp. 642–643. While, it is true, this report was written to serve a special purpose, it stated a position which Georgetown and most other Catholic colleges had assumed almost from their founding. Georgetown's catalogues, for at least a decade, had used the same language, and because Georgetown was a model we find similar statements in the catalogues of other Catholic colleges.

education; second, they sought to protect the faith and morals of Catholic youth, and this objective was honored even when the schools found it necessary to admit boys with Protestant religious allegiances; and finally, assuming that the first two purposes had been pressed forward with enthusiasm, they tried to be effective missioners in a country where, it seemed to them, the need for faith was greater than for learning.

Thus, despite our failure to detect in such colleges evidence of clear professional standards and aspirations, the first Catholic college managers were ready to admit within the privileged sanctuaries of their own common rooms that their highest purpose, and sometimes their only reason for persevering in institutions where success came so hard, was to prepare some young men for the ecclesiastical life. So even without the usual appurtenances of a professional school, the commitment of the Catholic college was clear : it essayed to stay within the familiar precincts of classical education and thus prepare boys for seminary study either in a seminary attached to the college, in one that would soon be established in the college, or in one somewhere in this country or in Europe.[33] The arguments used by the authors of the Yale Report could have had a special meaning and relevance for the Catholic colleges, if they had known them, for the kind of general literary competence at which that document aimed was of considerable use to the future student of theology.

An assertion that the Catholic college never became a professional divinity school in the same way that professional schools of law and medicine did should be listened to, because it is plainly accurate. The early Catholic college was permeated with a professional tone, but frequently, although the tone was enough to give the school a special character, it never evolved much beyond a vague commitment to higher theological study. And in the end, by the time the Catholic college began to mature in the later part of the nineteenth century, professional divinity curricula had been largely excised from the college program. This was done, it must be admitted, not so much for academic reasons as for justifications of moral and clerical formation : young men preparing for the vocation of the priest, it was assumed, would be better prepared for their life in the Christian ministry if they were educated away from lay students. So, again, we find the Catholic colleges following an academic route tried and rejected by the older nonCatholic institutions of the land. Beginning with the

---

[33] See Ruane, *op. cit.*, pp. 81–85; Mary Meline and Edward F. X. McSweeny, *The Story of the Mountain; Mt. St. Mary's College and Seminary* (Emmitsburg, Md., The Weekly Chronicle, 1911), I, 30–31; Mathias M. Hoffmann, *Story of Loras College, 1839–1939* (Dubuque, Ia., Loras College Press, 1939), pp. 73–80; Michael J. Kelly and James M. Kirwin, *History of Mt. St. Mary's Seminary of the West* (Cincinnati, Ohio, Keating and Co., 1894), pp. 69–73; and Sebastian A. Erbacher, *Catholic Higher Education for Men in the United States, 1850–1866* (Washington, Catholic University of America, 1931), pp. 64–65.

Andover experiment, the Protestant theological schools had decided to sever their old relationship with the colleges; but this movement failed, and in the end Protestant divinity education was returned to the colleges. The professional education of the minister was set once more within the broader perimeters of general education in a heterogenous academic community. But the Catholic colleges, apparently seeing little merit in this maneuver, undertook finally to separate the theological curriculum as it pertained to professionally minded students from the general superintendence of the college community. Perhaps Georgetown was again in a position to establish the model, for in 1869 its school of theology was removed from the Georgetown campus and located at Woodstock, Maryland.[34] Still, our sources tell us, the authority to grant degrees in theology, an authority awarded to Georgetown by papal decree in 1833, remained with Georgetown, and legally the Woodstock school had the standing of an academic satellite.[35]

It should be clearly stated, however, that Georgetown, in allowing the professional school of theology to leave its campus, was not removing a theological perspective from its curriculum for undergraduate students. But this is a part of the history of undergraduate curricula which must be chronicled elsewhere.[36] It may be said here, however, without intruding too heavily on historical material appropriate for another chapter, that the separation of the seminary from the Catholic college was simply geographic, for the impress of the seminary model on undergraduate curricula was too great ever to be ignored. When the time came for Catholic colleges to distinguish clearly among the parts of their teaching syllabus which were elementary, secondary, and higher in scope and standards —this movement had its inception with Georgetown in 1851[37]—and to adopt, with some misgivings, the nomenclature and divisions of the non-Catholic colleges of the land—freshman, sophomore, junior, and senior— it became imperative for them to abandon the old amorphous seven-year classical program which ignored real differences between elementary, secondary, and college boys. This left them with a secondary curriculum —this is what the classical course was destined to become (it was what it had been for three centuries)—but without a college course, and they were in a quandary about where to get one. Temperamentally and philosophically they found the models then extant in American higher learning distasteful, if not actually heterodox or immoral, so they turned for guidance to the only schools available to them—the seminaries.

The seminary course was clearly professional, although disguised by

[34] Joseph T. Durkin, *Georgetown University: The Middle Years, 1840–1900* (Washington, Georgetown University Press, 1963), p. 115.

[35] *Ibid.,* 224–226.

[36] See pp. 250–251.

[37] *Georgetown College Catalogue, 1851–1852,* p. 3.

some trappings of liberal learning, and naturally enough it was tailored for young men with religious vocations. No Catholic college president or prefect of studies seriously believed that the seminary curriculum could be transferred intact to the college, for it was a special kind of education protected by the myth that only someone in orders could master its intricacies. Still, its orthodoxy was guaranteed, which was a definite argument favoring its imitation; moreover, it was the only clear model available. In addition, it was admittedly hard to rebut the dogmatic assumption that what was good educationally for the prospective priest must also be good for the students in the secular college program. Who could be sure that some of the boys on the college side of the black curtain would not one day be touched by the clerical vocation? So when it became necessary to find a new curriculum for the college course, the studies were excavated from the mines of ecclesiastical syllabi. With undoubted confidence in the literary foundation provided by the secondary curriculum which had been completed in preparation for the college program or which was conducted along with it, the new college course could become predominantly philosophical and theological. The core of the new curriculum in Catholic colleges, then, as we move into the period of development, was one found in the seminaries; and with some modifications in title and with minor adjustments in content, the curriculum of the Catholic colleges turned out to be a feeble version of the seminary course. What it retained from its investiture in the divinity school, for this was probably easier to transfer than standards or moral sensitivities, was a strong professional flavor. For decades philosophy courses in Catholic colleges were taught which managed to ignore philosophy's capacity to wrestle with the burning issues of everyday life in society, in favor of its service as a tool for the science of theology. Theology, as a college study, discarded this professional flavor, for the theology intended for the lay Catholic was always to be a continuous effort to accept rather than to understand, and under these auspices theology lost the scientific status so long claimed for it. In actual fact, the courses were expected to give the students enough ammunition to defend their beliefs and the Church before all who should challenge them or it. Theology became an exercise in apologetics, and the most renowned teachers of theology as well as the most sought after pulpit preachers were apologists.

In leaving this phase of professionalism in Catholic higher learning, without invading the field of seminary history, itself a separate study,[38] we are convinced that a certain kind of religious professionalism never left the Catholic colleges, and with this in mind it should be easier for us to understand why, with further development and greater maturity in Catholic higher learning, it was relatively easy for the colleges to become enamored of professional education of other kinds.

[38] See McDonald, *op. cit.,* pp. 88–89.

Catholic colleges entered the arena of legal and medical education at earlier stages in their institutional development than their counterparts in America. But when they did, they had no intention of introducing Catholic thought to the rudiments of these professions; what they wanted most of all from the professional schools they encouraged as part of their own administrative and academic structures or adopted from the broad fields of independent professional institutes was the prestige of having their undergraduate curricula associated with the more honorific courses leading to the traditional learned professions. Still, in historical perspective, it is hard to believe that the managers of these schools were right in thinking the road to academic respectability lay in the embrace of departments or colleges of law and medicine, for even the most optimistic evaluation of American Catholic higher learning in the nineteenth and early years of the twentieth century is unable to lean very heavily on either the number or the excellence of professional schools. In any case, by about the middle of the nineteenth century the Catholic colleges, somewhat uncertain about their future as schools committed to transmitting a cultural legacy, but yet unconvinced of their legitimate role in the business of professional education, tried to benefit from a momentum pushing professionalism into the vanguard of American educational consciousness. Catholic colleges, moreover, entered the field of professional teaching when it was fairly easy to do so : the standards later associated with colleges of law and medicine were yet on the distant horizon, so no question was asked about the quality of the established or affiliated schools, and there were hardly any criteria for answering such a question if it had been asked. Such issues were raised, of course, in the 1870s, after Charles W. Eliot began a systematic upgrading of the professional curricula at Harvard, and after the professional associations in law and medicine began to show some concern for the public image of the members of their professions.[39] But when the first Catholic colleges tested the waters of medical and legal education they were absolved from setting any rigid standards for themselves and were relatively immune from any criticism that what they were doing in either field failed to meet the tests of accepted educational practice. If, on occasion, an outside or an inside critic should make some caustic remark about the standards of professional schools associated with Catholic colleges, he could always be rebutted with the statement that most, if not all, of the collegiately related professional schools were doing about the same thing and had similar standards.[40] In a word, the early professional schools, regardless of the

[39] Norwood, *op. cit.*, pp. 172–178; A. Z. Reed, *Present Day Law Schools in the United States and Canada* (New York, Carnegie Foundation for the Advancement of Teaching, Bulletin No. 21, 1928), pp. 85–101.

[40] T. C. Smith, "History of the Medical Department of Georgetown University," *Transactions* of the seventy-fifth anniversary of the Medical Society of the District of Columbia, February, 1894.

college with which they were associated, were almost totally free agents. As we have said, it was easy to enter the field of professional education, and in embarking on this new venture the optimism of the Catholic colleges was one-dimensional : they hoped to gain prestige from these associations. To their credit they demurred from making a moral or academic case for their professional ventures.

Medical schools

The principal limitation on professional horizons for Catholic colleges was imposed by their charters. In keeping with the tendency of state legislatures prior to the Dartmouth College decision to award broad academic privileges in college charters, the older Catholic college enjoyed the greatest freedom of action in instituting professional curricula and granting the highest professional degrees. The charters for Georgetown College and St. Louis University, for example, were university charters, whereas, in the case of the colleges founded after 1820—and especially after 1850—such charters awarded the colleges a restricted authority for granting university degrees and sometimes, as in the cases of the University of Notre Dame and Boston College, the charter was worded in a way such as to discourage the granting of M.D. degrees.[41]

Such limitations were not applied to St. Louis, however, for that Jesuit university was authorized by its charter of 1832 to conduct programs and award the degrees normally conducted and awarded by universities of the world. As early as 1835, therefore, and prompted perhaps by the generous language in its charter, perhaps by a determination to make the college grow, St. Louis University entered into a compact with the St. Louis Medical Society whereby both parties agreed to work toward the establishment of a medical school in the near future. What was proposed in the agreement of 1835 was fulfilled by 1842, for in the latter year instruction commenced in the St. Louis University medical department, although in 1839 the college awarded an honorary M.D. degree to a St. Louis dentist, B. B. Brown, and may thus have gained the distinction (whatever it may be worth) of having granted the first M.D. degree west of the Mississippi River.[42]

The history of the Catholic colleges' first venture into medical education

---

[41] Arthur J. Hope, *Notre Dame, One Hundred Years* (Notre Dame, Ind., University of Notre Dame Press, 1943), p. 59; and David R. Dunigan, *A History of Boston College* (Milwaukee, Bruce Publishing Co., 1947), pp. 111–115.

[42] William B. Faherty, *Better the Dream: Saint Louis University and Community, 1818–1968* (St. Louis, St. Louis University Press, 1968), p. 62.

is shrouded in some obscurity; yet, we know, for example, that the first faculty had six members, the first students numbered twenty-nine, and at the end of the first year the university conferred six M.D. degrees.[43] It is unclear whether or not the students who enrolled in the department of medicine were themselves college graduates, although, since hardly any medical school in the land, and no medical institute, asked for a college degree as a condition of entrance, it may fairly be doubted that the department at St. Louis University was prepared to depart very far from accepted practice. St. Louis University historians tell us that the medical department "was enjoying facilities for medical instruction of the highest order,"[44] and that after 1844 the standards were upgraded to provide the following avenues for obtaining the degree of doctor of medicine : three years of study under a professor along with three years of medical lectures; or attendance at two full courses of lectures at the St. Louis University medical department with an option of transferring credit earned from lectures at another recognized medical school, or of counting four years of medical practice as the equivalent of one course of lectures; or taking an examination in all recognized medical fields, writing a thesis on some medical topic in either English, French, or Latin, and giving proof of both age (every candidate for a degree had to be at least twenty-one) and solid moral character.[45] But they tell us also that in 1848, 1849, and, again in 1855 the medical faculty recommended the severance of the medical school from St. Louis University. In 1855, the contract between the college and the medical faculty was abrogated and, Hill says, "by mutual consent [the medical department's] connection with the St. Louis University finally ceased, but without any unfriendly feeling or hard thought on either side, since the peculiar circumstances of the times seemed to compel the medical department to adopt that course."[46]

What were these peculiar circumstances? It is unlikely that they were at all related to the quality of instruction in the medical school, the students enrolled, financial considerations vis-à-vis the college and the medical department, or the internal structural relationships between the medical department and the University. There is, at least, no evidence to suggest administrative ruptures or personal animosities within the academic community of which the medical department was a part, although admittedly somewhat on the outer fringe. Apparently the members of the medical faculty, who were probably responsible for the solvency of the

---

[43] *Ibid.*, p. 83.

[44] Gilbert J. Garraghan, *The Jesuits of the Middle United States* (New York, America Press, 1938), III, 204.

[45] Faherty, *op. cit.*, p. 84.

[46] Walter H. Hill, *Historical Sketches of St. Louis University* (St. Louis, Patrick Fox, 1879), p. 73.

school and stood to profit or lose financially depending on its fortunes, had some evidence (perhaps only a hope) that the medical school's chances of prosperity would be better independent of a Catholic college. Possibly the faculty believed that good students would hesitate to enroll in a medical department associated with a Catholic school, at a time when, to say the least, the academic reputations of American Catholic institutions were poor. Religious prejudices were current and in the heyday of Know-Nothingism it is probably true that the medical department's association with a Catholic college was not an asset.[47] In addition, antiCatholic elements in the community began to capitalize old fears. Democratic institutions, especially colleges and hospitals, they said, were jeopardized whenever they were controlled either directly or remotely by the Jesuits. These verbal scares and this common scandalmongering might have been overcome—and both the university's officers and the medical faculty began by ignoring them—except for the unforgivable carelessness of the medical faculty in allowing parts of human cadavers used in the dissection laboratories to be left as trash in a yard adjacent to the medical building. Boys found these human remains, spread the story of their discovery about, and soon the exaggerated tale was current that the Jesuits at St. Louis University were torturing and killing Protestant men and women. The Jesuits had to be punished, and a mob soon gathered to seek revenge. It broke into the medical building and destroyed all the equipment.[48]

Despite the relative ease with which these tales of atrocity could have been dispelled, the logical and honest disclaimers never caught up with the original misrepresentations, and for the next several years the medical department was the object of scorn and distrust. It was against this background that the medical faculty voted to disassociate from St. Louis University. At first the University was unwilling to accede to the wishes of the medical faculty and refused its request both in 1848 and 1849, but in 1855, with no indication that tensions had lessened or hostilities moderated the request for disaffiliation was honored.[49]

From the medical department's side of the picture, if religious prejudice was an insurmountable obstacle to the progress of medical education, it is easy to understand why severance was sought; but if the reasons for having a medical department associated with St. Louis University were sound in the first place, it is hard to understand from the college's perspective how this secession, even in the face of tension and hostility, was countenanced at all. The answer is probably this : although we are uncertain about the actual articles of agreement between the medical faculty and the university, the university was absolved from suffering any financial

[47] *Ibid.*, and Garraghan, *op. cit.*, p. 204.
[48] John O'Hanlon, *Life and Scenery in Missouri* (Dublin, 1890), pp. 92–93.
[49] Faherty, *op. cit.*, pp. 103–104.

loss incurred by the medical department or from responsibility for any debts it contracted; in short, the medical department retained considerable autonomy and was entitled to insist on disassociation from the university. It is, then, with reservations about the nature of the relationship between the medical department and St. Louis University that we assign to the school in St. Louis the distinction of having been the first Catholic college to embrace professional medical education.

St. Louis University's experience with medical curricula, however, did not prejudice it from trying again, forty-eight years later, in 1903, to organize medical curricula as part of the school's program.[50] At that time, probably because it was easier to adopt a medical school than found one, St. Louis University merged the Beaumont and Marion-Sims Medical Colleges into its university structure. And by then the priorities in American higher education were such that a medical school could no longer enjoy the luxury of autonomy or of mere affiliation with a university; the new medical college at St. Louis University became a full-fledged member of the academic community.

Yet, despite St. Louis University's determination to have a medical school, its second venture into medical teaching was hardly crowned with instant success, if we may judge from Flexner's report on it. In 1909, Flexner examined the medical school and commented that students were admitted with "less than a high school education,"[51] to a school with two hundred and forty-three students and a teaching staff of one hundred and twenty-one, although only six professors devoted full time to the college. Tuition fees—$26,630.00 in 1909—were the principal source of income, although during the seven-year period since the school's creation the university itself had contributed about forty thousand dollars from its general funds.[52] Flexner liked the laboratory facilities at the school and approved the provisions being made "for research in several directions;" but found fault with the clinical side of teaching : "The material, while fair in amount, is scattered and under imperfect control. The hospital use is not organized, equipped, or conducted with a view to the requirements of modern medical teaching."[53] Flexner's famous report gave medical colleges two options, either to raise their standards or cease teaching; St. Louis University took the report seriously and chose the former option as its later history attests.

Apparently without concerning itself about St. Louis' experience with

[50] Abraham Flexner, *Medical Education in the United States and Canada* (New York, Carnegie Foundation for the Advancement of Teaching, Bulletin No. 4, 1910), p. 255.
[51] *Ibid.*
[52] *Ibid.*
[53] *Ibid*

medical education, or even consulting the managers of the St. Louis University, Georgetown had decided to annex a medical department in 1849. No evidence exists to suggest that Georgetown would have taken a step in this direction on its own, although it is known that Georgetown's president, James Ryder, and his consultors, were anxious to upgrade the institution and improve its public image as a school of university status. Had it not been for the fact that the Columbian University Medical College, located in the District of Columbia, was operating along fairly restrictive policy lines, an appeal to Georgetown by some physicians interested in engaging in medical teaching that it should consider an affiliation request from a medical department might not have been made. As it was, four physicians, after first testing whether or not they might affiliate to the University of Virginia and apparently being refused, approached the President of Georgetown.[54]

Whether or not there were prior discussions with the authorities at Georgetown, and if there were, whether or not encouragement had been given, goes unrecorded. In any case, in a letter of late November, 1849, these Washington physicians—Noble Young, Flodoardo Howard, C. H. Liebermann, and Johnson Eliot—disclosed their plan to establish a medical college in Washington, D.C., and asked Georgetown to extend to their school its authority to grant the M.D. degree. The letter plainly stated the physicians' desire to have the medical school accepted as part of George-town College and not as a merely convenient appendage for degree purposes, although they claimed what they called "the usual privilege of nominating the professors"[55] for the medical department at a time in collegiate history, especially in Catholic colleges, when this was the usual privilege only of the president of the college.

Other versions of the origin of Georgetown's medical department differ slightly from the one given here. Durkin, in his *Georgetown University: The Middle Years, 1840–1900,* omits the name of C. H. Liebermann as one of the founders,[56] and John Gilmary Shea in *A History of George-town College,* a book commemorating Georgetown's centennial, calls Dr. Joshua A. Ritchie, an 1835 graduate of Georgetown, the medical department's founder.[57] But Ritchie's name is absent from Durkin's account, which makes us suspect that Dr. Ritchie was only an intramural promoter for the medical department. Both the idea and the impetus for professional medical curricula at Georgetown came from the doctors outside the college faculty.

---

[54] Power, *op. cit.,* p. 244; and James S. Easby-Smith, *Georgetown University* (Chicago, Lewis Publishing Co., 1907), I, 316.

[55] *Ibid.*

[56] Durkin, *op. cit.,* p. 29.

[57] John Gilmary Shea, *A History of Georgetown College* (New York, P. F. Collier, 1891), p. 169.

In this connection, considering that Shea was writing a history mainly for alumni, he may be pardoned for having tried to associate this new department, and what he considered to be an upgrading of the college's status, with the efforts of an alumnus. Without calling into question Shea's credentials as an historian we can take exception to his braggadocio remark that "the Medical School began under some difficulties and had many drawbacks before success was established; but it was not possible for anything connected with Georgetown College to fail."[58]

On November 28, 1849, Georgetown College accepted the proposal of the four doctors along with the conditions it contained.[59] Shortly thereafter the President of the College ratified the nominations made for the medical department's first professors. The swiftness of the decision is indeed surprising and makes us wonder if the administrators of Georgetown fully understood the obligation they were assuming for the school by their quick and open-armed embrace of a professional curriculum. This was their first experience with medical education, a fact which at least modified the charge of hasty action without sufficient reflection about the general effect of a medical curriculum on the college or its eroding influence on undergraduate studies. Their preoccupations at this point were principally nonacademic. They thought instead of the financial burdens imposed by the addition of such a school, and appended a clause to the agreement which stated that the medical department should free Georgetown from such conditions or burdens.[60] In this financial respect they were deadly serious, for in 1850 the first appropriation for the new school came from the doctors' own pockets to the tune of one hundred dollars each.[61]

In May, 1851, seventeen months after the initial proposal had been made to Georgetown—and with about 151 students in the undergraduate college, some of them still in elementary or secondary classes—the first students were admitted to the new medical school.[62] Housed in a leased building, with a six-bed infirmary and a dispensary under construction next door, the medical department listed a faculty of eight professors who were responsible for a curriculum of two courses, each of which lasted about four months.[63] Our sources are silent about the number of students enrolled for the first session, and they are silent also about the employment of eight professors in a department with only two courses for a program of studies covering only two years.[64] Similarly, we are totally ignorant of the require-

58 *Ibid.*
59 Durkin, *op. cit.*, p. 29.
60 *Ibid.*
61 *Ibid.*, p. 84.
62 *Ibid.*, pp. 29–30.
63 Power, *op. cit.*, p. 245.
64 See Durkin, *op. cit.*, pp. 29–30; Easby-Smith, *op. cit.*, I, 316–318; and Shea, *A History of Georgetown College*, pp. 168–171.

ments for admission to the department. Thirty years later in the *College Catalogue for 1880–1881* seventeen rules and regulations were listed which were to govern the medical student through his course. Such items as curricular requirements ("three (3) full courses of lectures"), class attendance and recitations (both obligatory), the nature of examinations and their administration, awards and prizes along with other details were covered, but still not a word related to admission standards appeared anywhere. This oversight was repaired, however, in the *Georgetown College Catalogue for 1890–1891* where a section entitled "Requisites For Admission" appeared, stating that in accordance with the "recommendations of the American Medical Association, a preliminary examination is required for admission. This is for the purpose of ascertaining whether the candidate can profitably pursue the technical study of medicine, and of preventing those not qualified from wasting time and money. The applicant will be examined upon the ordinary branches of an English education." And then the statement went on : "A preliminary examination will not be required of those who are graduates of a college, a high school, or an academy." Despite such minimal precautions Flexner's report on Georgetown in 1909 noted that entrance requirements were "less than a four-year high school course."[65]

A Dr. Thomas C. Smith, who was associated (either as a professor or as a student) with Georgetown's medical department during the early years, allows us to look quickly, but not too critically, at the quality of the school, although he is careful to append the remark that the description he gives of medicine at Georgetown could have been made without amendment about any other extant medical college.

[I do] not violate any confidence when [I say] that the examination preliminary to graduation in the earlier years of the college was a mere farce when compared with that of recent periods. The examination was oral. It is true that a thesis was required of each graduate, but to say that any one of these contained an original idea, or demonstrated familiarity with the subject discussed, would be an act of charity only excusable on the ground that so little was known definitely that it would have been dangerous to be too critical.[66]

What Smith neglects to say, but what may be gleaned from other sources, is important too : for most of its early history, at least until 1876, the medical department at Georgetown offered courses at night during the summer in order to accommodate students who were unable to enroll during the regular academic year. Night school medical study was finally suspended

[65] Flexner, *op. cit.,* p. 201; *Georgetown College Catalogue, 1880–1881,* pp. 43–45; and *Georgetown College Catalogue, 1890–1891,* pp. 76–77.
[66] See T. C. Smith, *op. cit.*

at Georgetown in 1895 as a concession to better standards,[67] although in the best universities night medical courses had been dropped twenty years earlier.

An infirmary was connected with the department almost from the beginning, but hospital affiliations allowing for internship training were not available until 1878. The old laboratories were so poorly equipped that one observer was astonished to think how a professor of chemistry could teach an adequate course in chemical science without the normal laboratory instruments and materials at his command.[68] So at Georgetown from 1851 to 1878 medical education neither advanced beyond nor fell behind the standards familiar to the medical institutes of those or earlier days. But 1878 was a year to remember, for then Georgetown's medical school began to make important reforms in its teaching.

Before the reform of 1878, which became operational in the 1878–1879 term, the full medical curriculum had required two years' study. Each academic year lasted five months. From this time onwards the course was extended to three years and the months of study were raised to seven.[69] Other reforms related to teaching were instituted too : classes were taught in anatomy, physiology, chemistry, and materia medica, and every student was required to attend; examinations were demanded for every course and a student's performance on the examination governed his progress through the curriculum; lectures were reduced to two or three a day, rather than four or five, as in the old plan, and were clinical as well as didactic; and, finally, weekly recitations were held for each class.[70] By reducing the number of daily lectures the faculty intended to free students for out-of-class preparation and independent study, an unusually liberal attitude for a nineteenth-century college faculty whose respect for tradition might easily have been translated into a heavier schedule of lectures. The results of the experiment with independent study are unknown, although we may suppose, since the system remained in vogue, that the faculty at Georgetown judged them to be good.

In addition to regular work in the classroom or lecture hall, medical students at Georgetown were required to spend time in the laboratories and dissecting rooms and to devote some time to the practical side of medicine by working in the school infirmary or in the clinics of Providence Hospital or The Children's Hospital. The common, though voluntary, practice of associating a prospective physician with a licensed doctor of medicine for a period of up to three years is not mentioned in the medical school's records of this period, so we are left to believe that the acceptance or

---

[67] S. C. Busey, *Personal Reminiscences and Recollections* (Washington, Dornan Co., 1895), p. 348.

[68] Power, *op. cit.,* p. 245.

[69] *Georgetown College Catalogue, 1878–1879,* p. 17.

[70] Durkin, *op. cit.,* p. 88.

otherwise of such a pupilage was left to the student himself : he practiced medicine on his own, if he wanted to, after the receipt of his degree, or he apprenticed himself to an established doctor, if he were so inclined. Yet on this point, Georgetown's school is neither to be praised nor blamed, for there was nothing in the codes of medical education, or for that matter in the statements of policy from the American Medical Association, founded in 1846, to encourage medical schools to organize regular internships.[71]

We are not surprised when the historians of Georgetown College tell us that the medical school was a teaching institution indifferent to medical research.[72] Here again, Georgetown was content to stay within the familiar precincts of medical education, and in doing so she kept company with all other medical schools in the United States. Her emphasis could hardly have been different, for the Georgetown medical faculty lacked a research orientation. Its members, for the most part full-time physicians and part-time teachers, simply lacked the interest, the capacity, and the instruments for engaging in research. They essayed to fulfill the school's stated purpose : to teach; but even in this respect their success in producing qualified physicians must be judged as modest. The graduating class from the medical school in 1877 numbered two students; there were four in 1878; six in 1879; five in 1881; seven in 1882; and four in 1883.[73] During the thirty-year period between 1870 and 1900 the medical department never graduated more than thirty medical students in a single year; the average number, our sources tell us, was twenty-three, and during this same period the enrollment never exceeded eighty.[74] Yet size is evidence of almost nothing and we are led to believe that despite its relatively small enrollment the medical school's standards were good : in 1877, as we have said, two students received the M.D. degree from a total student body of forty; in 1878 the enrollment was forty; in 1879, thirty-eight; in 1881, forty-one; in 1882, thirty; and in 1883, twenty-seven.[75]

The upgrading of the medical school's curricula and standards in 1878 set a pattern for the next decade, during which the school seemed to prosper, for in 1891 enrollment was reported as being over one hundred students. Besides, a department of bacteriology was added; a department of pathology was planned; clinical opportunities for the students were augmented by an arrangement with Providence Hospital; and the laboratories were enlarged and "equipped with all the latest improved appliances, regardless of cost."[76] Still, the last decade of the nineteenth

[71] Norwood, *op. cit.,* pp. 192–198.

[72] Durkin, *op. cit.,* pp 90–91.

[73] *Ibid.,* p. 89.

[74] *Ibid.*

[75] *Ibid.;* and *Georgetown College Catalogue, 1880–1881,* p. 60.

[76] Durkin, *op. cit.,* p. 197; and *Georgetown College Catalogue, 1890–1891,* pp. 76–77.

century proved to be one of remarkable gains in professional education in the United States, including medical education, and Georgetown's optimistic assumptions about keeping pace with the best medical colleges of the land were in jeopardy. First, there was the eye-opening letter from Dr. Austin O'Malley in December, 1891, which was severely critical of the standards of medical education in the United States, and of Georgetown in particular, and of the unprogressive management of the medical school under the administration of its Dean, Dr. George Magruder.[77] Then there was the ferment within the medical school itself and a running battle with the president of Georgetown about capital expenditure.[78]

O'Malley, who held a faculty appointment in Georgetown's medical school, had taken a leave of absence for postgraduate study at the University of Berlin. While in Berlin he took time to write to Georgetown's president to tell him that all the departments and most of the courses in Georgetown's medical school were unworthy of respectable medical education and, moreover, that the dean was not only unprogressive but was subservient to a military-medical clique that had managed to dominate the medical school. This military approach to medicine, O'Malley averred, was dangerously unscientific and, in addition, was antagonizing the best qualified professors on the faculty. The dean's attitude and his parlor approach to the profession earned the enmity of good doctors who might be enlisted as professors at the school, and his arrogance, O'Malley said, caused directors of clinics and supervisors of operating rooms to deny Georgetown students and faculty members the privilege of using them. Whether or not O'Malley's letter precipitated any action on the part of the president is unclear; at any rate, it gave him something to think about and the parting remark—"There is much down there (at the medical school) I feel sure you never heard of"[79]—may have alerted him to look more closely at the conduct of the dean and his faculty.

Shortly after O'Malley wrote his letter, Dean Magruder petitioned the president of Georgetown for additional funds to enlarge the laboratories and build new ones. The place, he said, was overcrowded for the students then in attendance, and since there were plans to enlarge the student body, instructional facilities would soon be entirely inadequate.[80] The dean apparently overlooked the fact that he could have placed a limit on the number of new students admitted to the school. The president responded to Magruder's petition for funds in typically administrative and virtually unanswerable fashion : there was no money available, so the petition would have to be refused.[81] If O'Malley was right when he alleged that Magruder

[77] Durkin, *op. cit.*, p. 198.
[78] *Ibid.*, pp. 200–201.
[79] *Ibid.*, p. 109.
[80] *Ibid.*, p. 200.
[81] *Ibid.*, p. 199.

was a bad doctor, he was wrong when he thought that the dean was unprogressive or unimaginative, for Magruder countered the president's bald refusal of funds with the proposition that if the college would advance the sum of ten thousand dollars to build the necessary facilities the members of the medical faculty would reimburse the college by a payment of $1,500 a year for a period of five years.[82] Even this was unacceptable to the president. Magruder then offered the president a moratorium on medical faculty salaries to help the college build the necessary facilities, but for some reason or other the president was equally cool in his response to this plan. He suggested instead that he would allocate ten thousand dollars for the cost of the proposed improvements if the medical faculty would agree to pay an annual interest of five percent for five years on the ten thousand plus a like interest rate on thirty thousand dollars, which the college had already invested in the medical school.[83] The president wanted to find some way to add to the medical school's facilities, but to do so without cost to the college. The medical faculty refused this arrangement, but offered to pay a flat $1,500 for a period of from three to five years, if the president would invest for a similar period ten thousand dollars for necessary improvements in the medical buildings. And this was the compromise finally agreed to.[84] But while it was an arrangement relieving Georgetown of financial responsibility for the medical school, it also served to turn the medical school into a nearly autonomous unit in the Georgetown complex. It had long been a matter of policy that the medical school should not be a burden to the college, so the doctors on the medical faculty, having invested their own money in the school, supposed they were entitled to be an independent corporation affiliated to Georgetown only for degree-granting purposes. They did, in fact, form such a corporation and for a number of years asserted their independence. To some extent they were abetted in doing so by the unwillingness of Georgetown to have financial involvement. Yet, the legal independence of the medical school was unacceptable to Georgetown, and all signs of such independence were finally suppressed by the president of the College in 1893.[85]

In the 1890s Georgetown's medical school abandoned its night school courses and became exclusively a day school, added a fourth year to its curriculum, making it one of the few four-year medical schools in the United States, and even, although somewhat timidly, approached the issue of coeducation. In 1898, Louise Taylor applied to the medical faculty for admission, apparently to pursue the course leading to the degree of doctor of medicine, but the medical faculty, insufficiently liberal to admit

82 *Ibid.*, p. 201.
83 *Ibid.*
84 *Ibid.*
85 *Ibid.*, p. 203.

females on the same basis as males, compromised by offering her private courses in anatomy.[86] The records are silent on what became of Miss Taylor after she finished her special courses.

In another era the issue of coeducation might have been a central one, but as it was the Georgetown medical school was confronted with a more critical question : the Catholic University of America, interested in professional education and unwilling to wait for a medical school of its own to mature, made a determined effort to appropriate the Georgetown medical school. While it may be wrong to assert that the Catholic University of America was directly involved in this affair, for neither the bishops who comprised the board of trustees nor the Rector of the University, Bishop John J. Keane, appear to have favored a pirating of Georgetown's professional schools, the name of the University was unavoidably connected with a venture, promoted by the Apostolic Delegate to the United States, Archbishop Francis Satolli, to separate the medical school from Georgetown and attach it to the Catholic University.[87]

The Catholic University was anxious for recognition as a true university, so it emphasized its commitment to graduate study by avoiding opening undergraduate colleges and by promoting the development of professional schools of law and medicine. In some respects Georgetown stood as an obstacle to the development of professional education at the Catholic University, if only by attracting some students who might otherwise go to the new university and by soliciting resources from Catholics willing to contribute money to Catholic professional schools. That this was the position was recognized both by the Jesuits and the managers of the Catholic University. Thus, Georgetown was directed by its European Jesuit superiors to underemphasize both its professional and postgraduate departments and to give them as little public notice as possible.[88] On the other hand, it was understood that the Catholic University would eschew the field of undergraduate education.[89] Clearly, the Rector of the Catholic University had been determined to open schools of law and medicine, but just as

---

[86] *Ibid.*, pp. 202–203. *Georgetown University Catalogue, 1890–1891*, pp. 76–92, is quite complete in its description of the medical course. Methods of instruction are mentioned, recitations are stressed, courses are sketched, clinical opportunities are outlined, library resources are noted, written class examinations are specified, and graduation requirementse are stated. The catalogue states, in addition, that "There will also be held two trials before a Moot Court, composed of members of the Law Faculty, in which students of the Third Class (seniors) will be examined as expert witnesses; the senior students of the Law Department acting as attorneys for the prosecution and defense."

[87] Patrick Henry Ahern, *The Catholic University of America, 1887–1896* (Washington, The Catholic University of America Press, 1948), pp. 101–102.

[88] Durkin, *op. cit.*, pp. 250–253.

[89] Colman J. Barry, *The Catholic University of America, 1903–1909* (Washington, The Catholic University of America Press, 1953), pp. 65–69.

clearly unwilling to go through the process of building up part-time and night school faculties as Georgetown had done.[90] Then, somewhere behind the façade of ecclesiastical politics Satolli began to work for the proposition that the medical school and the law school at Georgetown should be transferred to the Catholic University. Acting either on his own authority or on advice from Rome, Satolli approached the Dean of Georgetown's medical school with the proposition that the transfer be made. In a letter of March 1, 1894, the Delegate noted that approval for a transfer had already been given by the Jesuit General and that the Pope envisaged a relationship between the medical school faculty and the Catholic University identical to the one then extant between the medical school and Georgetown. He implied that the transfer was the wish of the Holy Father and he further expressed the opinion, which, he said, was shared by the Pope, that much good would accrue to the University, the Church, and science itself by bringing about a transfer of the medical school.[91]

The Georgetown Jesuits, if we may judge from the president's first reaction, were unhappy about the prospects of abandoning the medical school, yet they appeared willing to bow to the demands of authority.[92] The dean and faculty of the school, however, refusing to countenance the transfer, made their views known in a letter from the dean to the delegate, wherein the dean wrote: "I have frequently and carefully considered the subject and am now positively of the opinion that a purely sectarian medical school would not prosper in this country. Consequently I would not be willing to serve as a member of such a Faculty. As there are but few Catholics in the Medical Faculty the wishes of the Catholic University or even his Holiness Leo XIII, would not have the slightest influence upon them."[93] This stand taken by the faculty directly involved served to harden Georgetown's attitude on the question of transfer and the Jesuits began to oppose the proposal openly; but the critical opposition came not from the Jesuits, who stood to lose a school, but from the lay members of the medical faculty. When it became perfectly clear that such a forced transfer would in the end be a transfer of nothing, for the faculty refused to be a pawn between two Catholic institutions, the entire idea was abandoned.

With the stability of Georgetown's medical school assured, the foundation was laid for medical education in selected Catholic colleges. Georgetown proved that medical education under Catholic auspices could succeed despite external pressures, internal erosions, and clerical politics. From this point on, the history of professional medical education in

[90] Ahern, *op. cit.*, p. 102.
[91] *Ibid.*, pp. 101–102.
[92] Durkin, *op. cit.*, p. 251.
[93] Ahern, *op. cit.*, p. 103.

Catholic institutions of higher learning was mainly a matter of adding a few medical schools to the list. Still, even in these happier circumstances, Georgetown's medical school had yet to demonstrate its credentials of adequacy. In 1909, when Flexner collected data for his famous report, he found evidence at Georgetown suggesting that the medical school was "a university department in name only."[94] Students were admitted to medical studies with "less than a four-year high school course" as a foundation, and they were taught by a staff of seventy-four professors none of whom gave "full time to the medical school, except the dean, who had the chair of hygiene and is treasurer of both medical and dental schools."[95] Enrollment in 1909 was eighty-nine. Depending on tuition fees, the medical school had an annual income of about $11,000 from which to pay expenses, to equip laboratories, and maintain clinical facilities. Yet Flexner found "well stocked [laboratories] for pathology, bacteriology, and histology, a fair equipment for experimental physiology, and an ordinary chemical laboratory."[96] Facilities for clinical use were inadequate and "several miles distant."[97] Using Flexner's report as a guide, Georgetown gradually improved its medical school to the point where, toward the close of the period of development, it could take its place alongside the best medical colleges of the land.

Undaunted by its rebuff from Georgetown, the Catholic University tried again to organize medical education. This time, in 1902, it planned to start its own school away from Washington, either in New York City or in another metropolitan area. This second attempt was similarly abortive.[98]

In 1892, John A. Creighton offered to donate a hundred thousand dollars for the creation of a medical department in Creighton College. This benefaction was accepted by the school's board of trustees and the medical college was opened the same year. Its first class enrolled thirty-six students and eight years later, in 1900, the total enrollment in the medical school was 143.[99] Following the example of Georgetown, the Creighton medical school organized a four-year curriculum for medical education in 1896.[100]

Flexner visited Creighton medical school in 1909 and gave it a passing mark. He found entrance requirements demanding less than a "four-year high school education," a student body of 175, and forty-nine teachers,

[94] Flexner, *op. cit.,* p. 201.

[95] *Ibid.*

[96] *Ibid.*

[97] *Ibid.*

[98] Peter E. Hogan, *The Catholic University of America, 1896–1903* (Washington, The Catholic University of America Press, 1949), pp. 58–59.

[99] M. P. Dowling, *Reminiscences of the First Twenty-Five Years at Creighton* (Omaha, Burkley Printing Co., 1903), pp. 138–143; and Power, *op. cit.,* p. 247.

[100] Flexner, *op. cit.,* p. 260.

only one of whom devoted "his entire time to medical instruction." Laboratories, he said, were "adequate to instruction," but both the library and the museum were small. Quiz-compounds, which Flexner took as a sign of weakness, "are sold on the premises." Hospital associations for teaching were limited, but available; clinical laboratories were lacking.[101]

Another medical school was that established in Niagara University in 1898. The medical faculty numbered twenty-eight and the school enrolled a few students, but the historical record removes Niagara from the lists of medical education after 1900.[102]

In the twentieth century, Marquette University, Fordham University, Loyola University in Chicago, and Seton Hall University embarked on medical education. Marquette began by affiliating the Milwaukee Medical College in 1907 and later, in 1913, purchased the defunct school of the Wisconsin College of Physicians and Surgeons. In the latter year medical education came under the direct control of the university.[103] In 1905 Fordham opened a medical school which closed in 1921.[104] In 1909 Loyola University (in Chicago) agreed to affiliate the Illinois Medical School and in 1910 made a similar arrangement with the Bennet School of Medicine. In 1917 Loyola University purchased the Chicago College of Medicine and Surgery and then brought the three affiliated schools into the university structure as a single medical school.[105] In 1956 Seton Hall University added a college of medicine to its expanding educational structure.[106]

Following the detailed historical progress of medical education in Catholic universities down to the 1970s is too cumbersome a task for these pages (and, in any case, is better left to a special study,) yet enough should be said here to dispel any doubt about the quality of medical schools which are organically related to Catholic universities. Without exception they are respectable schools with excellent reputations, enviable ornaments of the universities to which they are related.   .

[101] *Ibid.*, p. 261. Flexner's finding with respect to admission standards was all the more damaging because such standards had not been modified for the past fifteen years. *The Creighton University Medical College Catalogue, 1895–1896*, p. 8, had set the admission code : "A certificate of good moral character from a reputable physician. A diploma or certificate from a recognized college, school of science, academy, normal school or high school, a teacher's certificate or other evidence equivalent to the foregoing, of satisfactory preliminary education. Students unable to meet these requirements are admitted on passing examinations proving them to be possessed of an education equal to the above."

[102] Power, *op. cit.*, p. 247.

[103] Raphael N. Hamilton, *The Story of Marquette* (Milwaukee, Marquette University Press, 1953), p. 70.

[104] Power, *op. cit.*, p. 247.

[105] Flexner, *op. cit.*, pp. 211–212.

[106] Power, *op. cit.*, p. 248. In the mid-1960s this college became the New Jersey College of Medicine and Dentistry in Newark.

Law schools

Catholic colleges, with their old propensity for both seeking a professional education and inadvertently following the trends in nineteenth-century American higher education, found it somewhat easier, as we have seen, to concentrate on professional theological training than on other kinds of professional education; but when resources allowed they were anxious to enter other professional fields as well. This, we know, explains the entry of a few Catholic colleges into medical education where the chances of enhancing a college's status were good, but medicine was costly and, in time, following the Flexner Report, a rather hazardous undertaking which could put the reputation of the entire institution in jeopardy.[107] Law, it seemed, promised better possibilities for success together with fewer threats to an academic reputation, and this Catholic college preference for law was justified by sound reasons.

In the first place, managers of Catholic colleges never really doubted the humanism of their educational philosophy and they supposed, correctly we should think, that this humanistic orientation, plus an abundant ethical heritage, could make important contributions to the law. We know, if we read the history of legal education during the years of the Great Renaissance, how much the study and practice of law were affected by rhetoric, logic, and linguistic exactitude;[108] and there were good reasons for believing that law in the United States could profit from some immersion in these disciplines also. Whether or not Catholic colleges had a fuller humanistic legacy than other American colleges is debatable, yet the mere possession of this heritage served as a motive force behind their excursions into legal education. Clearly the American tradition was for lawyers to become public men and public men would shape public policy : if Catholics wanted to affect public policy, they should forthwith delegate their colleges to involve themselves in the preparation of students for the legal profession. In the second place, and on a plainly practical level, legal education was one of the least expensive kinds of professional training; Catholic colleges looked over their balance sheets and decided they could afford law schools.

If, however, the catalyst of Catholic thought was to be introduced into judicial proceedings and political forums by means of Catholic-educated lawyers, it was necessary for Catholic colleges to create law schools of recognizable worth and scholarly standing and thus give their graduates the benefit of whatever luster might be attached to the name of their *alma mater*. In a field where enviable reputations were hard to win,

[107] See Brubacher and Rudy, *op. cit.,* p. 205.
[108] Bolgar, *op. cit.,* pp. 290–295.

Catholic colleges were at a special disadvantage : their own scholarly reputations, by almost any appraisal of academic status, were low; and they lived in a nineteenth-century climate that, if not actually hostile to Catholic institutions, was extremely suspicious of them. Besides, the Catholic legal scholar who might be recruited to teach in a college of law was rare and hard to find; those who made a reputation for themselves in the practice of law, if we assume that they had some qualities to recommend them for the classroom, were usually unwilling to make the financial sacrifice teaching in a Catholic law school would require. So, in the end, the best motive for creating the Catholic law school was, in effect, ignored and the cultivation of Catholic legal thought was left to the hazardous effect of a course in legal ethics (a course commissioned to communicate the best ideals of Catholic legal philosophy), being handled by a clerical professor of moral philosophy. The actual classroom instruction in legal principles and techniques was conducted by professors whom the school was able to hire. This meant, of course, a faculty of laymen; it meant also a part-time faculty, with judges, practicing attorneys, and others connected with the law filling most of the positions.[109]

Announcing the opening of a course in law was simple, and the first Catholic colleges performed this feat with all the right academic flourishes; but staffing the school with qualified professors who might give it an instant reputation was something else. Frequently this meant appointing non-Catholic teachers to the law faculty and then living with the anomaly intrinsic in such a practice : the school was founded, all the announcements always said, to teach law in the Catholic tradition of equity, justice, and humaneness,[110] in other words, to promote a Catholic philosophy of law and graft it to the precedents from the case books; but in its day-to-day operations the school's character was determined by its wisest and most prominent teachers who were hardly ever equipped either intellectually or emotionally to carry out this commission.

The ambitions of the first Catholic law schools were seldom realized. Whatever the prospectus said, they were usually small schools with about a dozen students, most of whom could attend lectures only at night, and one or two teachers who left their judicial chambers or their law offices for a short time in the evening to meet their classes. Such arrangements hardly counted as law schools. These first steps into the business of legal education were, it must be admitted, more in the nature of law institutes and legal lectures.

---

109 Hope, *op. cit.,* pp. 151–152; Faherty, *op. cit.,* pp. 313–316; and Durkin, *op. cit.,* p. 94. It should be noted that every catalogue from a Catholic college law school mentioned with pride the presence of a large part-time faculty.

110 See Shea, *A History of Georgetown College,* pp. 203–204; *Catalogue of Georgetown College, 1851–1852,* p. 18–19; and St. Louis *Republican,* July 15, 1843.

At St. Louis University, for example, where Catholic legal education had its beginnings in 1843, neither a school of law nor a law course was established, but a series of lectures was delivered by Judge Richard A. Buckner, a retired judge from Kentucky.[111] The Judge, having family connections in St. Louis, proposed to the President of St. Louis University that a course in law be instituted; the President agreed and Buckner was appointed Professor of Common and Chancery Law. With such a situation as lecturing on law at the University would afford, the Judge could move to St. Louis. For the next four years legal education at St. Louis University consisted of whatever lectures the Judge chose to give; and the lectures were given, not to students specializing in the law, for there were none, but to students pursuing regular undergraduate college work. However inauspiciously, legal education was thus introduced in some sort into Catholic colleges, but at St. Louis University, at least, it stopped in 1847, because Judge Buckner died in December of that year.[112] In 1908 St. Louis University re-entered the field of legal education and this time founded a regular law school.[113]

Between 1843 and 1869 various Catholic colleges tested their ability to maintain some kind of legal course, either legal lectures, departments or schools of law, but none enjoyed success or permanence, and none made a sufficient impact on the history of legal education in Catholic colleges to warrant further notice on these pages.[114] In 1869 the prospect for Catholic legal education changed with the opening of what was to be the first permanent Catholic law school in the United States at the University of Notre Dame. The school opened with four professors and about a dozen students who were expected to follow a two-year course to the degree in law.[115] Three of these students took Notre Dame's full course and graduated from the law school in 1871.[116] As part of a student's educational preparation for the Notre Dame law school, a foundation in the liberal arts was demanded, but the regulations governing admission practices during the school's infant years are unclear : the educational preparation for law, and the foundation in the liberal arts referred to, may not have implied college-grade study.[117] Certainly the degree of bachelor of arts was not required for admission to the Notre Dame law school, for as late as 1926 two years of college study were still being demanded for admission to law and only in 1928 was this requirement raised to three years.[118]

111 Faherty, op. cit., pp. 90–91.
112 Ibid., pp. 88, 106.
113 Ibid., p. 245.
114 See Power, op. cit., pp. 252–253.
115 Hope, op. cit., p. 151.
116 Ibid.
117 Catalogue of the University of Notre Dame, 1872, p. 24.
118 Catalogue of the University of Notre Dame, 1928, p. 56.

In 1870, the president of Georgetown College made the following announcement at the annual commencement exercises : "I am happy to announce . . . that we are about to enlarge the functions of the institution by the establishment of a law department. This action completes our course as a university."[119] No doubt Georgetown was interested in its internal development as a university and took the step toward law as one means of ensuring its status as a qualified member of the American academic fraternity. But there were other reasons too, and they may have been more convincing than Georgetown's aspiration to take its place among the better schools of the country. Only two institutions in the District offered opportunities for legal study : one was an independent, one-man law institute; the other was a law department attached to Columbian College.[120] Georgetown could thus enter the field of legal education, for which a need could be demonstrated, and at the same time enhance its reputation. The market seemed to be right for a law department at Georgetown. A faculty of law professors could be recruited from among the public officers working and living in Washington, and the capital expenditures for a law school were expected to be low.

The first faculty at the Georgetown law school attracted prominent persons, including one Supreme Court Justice, Samuel F. Miller, an assistant United States attorney general, J. Hubley Ashton, a judge of the District's Supreme Court, Charles P. James, and Gen. Thomas Ewing, once a legal consultant to President Lincoln.[121] These men held professorships in the law school during its first years, although their association with the school was part-time, and others of similar prominence were added as the school matured.

This ornamental faculty taught a total of fewer than thirty students, most of whom were also part-time, during the first half-dozen years of the school's existence, but the law school's enrollment should be balanced against the enrollment of other parts of the college in order to get a realistic picture : the graduating class in the college numbered twenty-one in 1874 and dropped to seven in 1877.[122] So, taking these data into account the law school was holding its own. Fifteen students graduated from the law school in 1877 and eighteen in 1880.[123]

From its opening in the fall of 1870 to 1897 the course leading to the bachelor of law degree covered a two-year period. The prospectus announced that the lectures were held in the evenings, after the usual office hours, and

[119] Easby-Smith, op. cit., I, 421.

[120] G. E. Hamilton, "History of the Law School at Georgetown University," College Journal, 39 (March, 1911), 308.

[121] Catalogue of Georgetown College, 1871–1872, p. 15; 1875–1876, p. 19; 1887–1888, p. 24; and 1891–1892, p. 39.

[122] Durkin, op. cit., pp. 76–77.

[123] Ibid., p. 77.

that "the degree of Ll.B. [was] conferred on students who have been present for at least two years at the course of study prescribed and who, having attended the exercises of the school for one year, shall pass a satisfactory examination."[124] This regulation, admittedly hard to interpret, must have demanded the equivalent of two years of legal study, one year of which was in residence. And, at this point, we should be interested to know what was studied by the prospective lawyer and how the instructional techniques were deployed, for once we see what was done at Georgetown we can be fairly certain that her practices were duplicated by every other Catholic law school for the next half-century.

By the time Georgetown entered the business of legal education, the case-study method of teaching was fairly firmly established in most law schools of the country,[125] so it is no surprise that the professors at Georgetown taught their students in the way they themselves had been taught, and this meant using the case method. Teachers and students concentrated on the books containing legal opinions on real cases and from these legal opinions they abstracted basic legal principles. Logical processes of deduction and induction were put to use and we are reluctant to condemn this method without a fair hearing for it had a number of good points to recommend it. But in the end, whatever the quality of the logical steps involved and however well a student might know the law exhumed from the cases, this was still a narrow approach to law, an approach, as its friends said, which could make law really a science.[126]

To argue that a student in a law school could be prepared for his chosen profession without having a solid grasp of legal details would be puerile, yet it is easy to see that a greater breadth in legal education could remove the study of law from the limitations of its lair in rule, regulation, and technique. Cultural or, at least, nontechnical courses promised to widen the horizon of the prospective lawyer and, in the end, make him a more completely educated attorney. Georgetown's legal program tried to combine the best features of technical and cultural law. The former was essential and Georgetown chose to add the latter—so that we find such subjects as Comparative Law, History of Law, International Law, Political Science, Legal Ethics, and Philosophy of Law in the curriculum.[127]

We find, also, a determination to stay close to classical studies, for in 1890 the *Georgetown University Catalogue* indicated that a course in

---

[124] *Catalogue of Georgetown College, 1870,* p. 46.

[125] James B. Scott, "The Study and Teaching of Law," *Educational Review,* 28 (September, 1904), 130–151.

[126] A. J. Harno, *Legal Education in the United States* (San Francisco, Bancroft-Whitney Co., 1953), pp. 83–84; and Joseph Redlich, *The Common Law and the Case Method* (New York, Carnegie Foundation for the Advancement of Teaching, Bulletin No. 8, 1914), pp. 15–38.

[127] Durkin, *op. cit.,* p. 97.

Latin was available for law students. Noting that many law students "find themselves embarrassed on the very threshold of their studies by want of acquaintance with the Latin language," the establishment of a professorship of Latin was announced for "the express purpose of giving instruction in that language to such students of the Law School as may desire to avail themselves of the opportunity thus afforded." Studying Latin was not, we note, made compulsory. But the recommendation was persuasive : "Students who, from any cause, have not acquired a classical education will find this added feature of the course of great practical advantage and value in the study and practice of law."[128]

In the classroom the students heard lectures on the law books and submitted to frequent quizzes, given by junior professors, to test their understanding of what they had been taught; repetitions, a favorite Jesuit teaching technique, were introduced too, wherein a question-and-answer routine made the student reveal both what he knew and what he had forgotten or had never learned. Any deficiencies were noted and the student was expected to correct them before the next repetition.[129] As part of the same passion for mental exercise the moot court was established and students were able to demonstrate their knowledge of law along with their ability to speak and think on their feet.[130]

A respectable legal curriculum was too heavy for a two-year course, and this was soon recognized by the Georgetown faculty, but any thought of extending the course and requiring another year for the bachelor of law degree was premature; the faculty therefore did what appeared to be the next best thing : it added a one-year postgraduate course in law, com-

[128] *Georgetown University Catalogue, 1890–1891,* pp. 108–109.

[129] G. E. Hamilton, "History of the Law School of Georgetown University," *College Journal,* 39 (March, 1911), 308. The system of classroom instruction in force for years at Georgetown is described in the *Catalogue of 1890–1891* (pp. 110–111): A lesson, averaging from thirty to forty pages of the text-book, is assigned in advance, which the student is expected to master as thoroughly as he can before the recitation hour. The lecturer then goes over the ground covered by the text, explaining what is obscure or difficult, pointing out the application in practice of the principles treated of, and illustrating, by examples, their application in actual cases. Then follows the "Quiz," in which the lesson is gone entirely over again in the shape of questions, requiring the students to reproduce in their own language all that it contains, with practical applications of the doctrines learned to supposed cases put by the lecturer. The student thus has three opportunities of becoming familiar, theoretically and practically, with each topic treated of in the course: *once* by careful study of the text, *a second time* by the discussion of it in the lecture, *and once again,* by himself reproducing and practically applying the principles thus taught, in his answers to the "Quiz." This system has been found, after careful and painstaking tests, most satisfactory to both teacher and student, and productive of the highest standard of proficiency in study. It is believed to be absolutely the best.

[130] *Georgetown College Catalogue, 1880–1881,* p. 63.

prised of subjects for which the two-year course had no time. After completing this third-year a student would be granted the degree of master of law.[131]

These two programs—a two-year course leading to the LL.B. and a three-year course to the LL.M.—were continued at Georgetown until 1897, when a three-year course leading to the LL.B. was required of all students in the law school.[132] What Georgetown did either in its undergraduate course or in its professional schools other Catholic colleges were also apt to do, so, although in those other colleges which adopted a legal curriculum the dates would certainly be different, the same general patterns that were found earlier at Georgetown could at a later time be found in them.[133]

But before we leave Georgetown's law school, its relationship to the Catholic University of America should be given brief notice. We know already how an abortive attempt had been made to appropriate the Georgetown medical school to the Catholic University, and now we shall see how the same tactics of academic piracy were visited on the Georgetown law school. In 1894, when it seemed imperative for the Catholic University to enter the professional fields in a strong and decisive way, the Apostolic Delegate to the United States, Archbishop Francis Satolli, working on behalf of the Catholic University, proposed to the law faculty, as he had to the medical faculty, that it should sever its relationship with Georgetown and become part of the Catholic University.[134] The docile attitude of Georgetown's Jesuit administrators in the first instance has already been demonstrated and we know that for the medical school, at least, it took some time before a strong negative response could be fashioned. The dean of the law school, G. E. Hamilton, speaking for the faculty, answered directly and with dispatch :

. . . Speaking, therefore, for myself and all the Professors, I wish to assure you that the contemplated transfer will never be consented to or permitted by us to be carried into effect. It cannot be carried into effect whether the President and the Directors of Georgetown University or the Jesuit organization, is willing or unwilling. It cannot be carried into effect by direct mandate from Pope Leo XIII.

The Law Department if the University of Georgetown was organized by the graduates of the Academic Department, and through love for the old and

[131] *Georgetown College Catalogue, 1878–1879,* p. 15.

[132] *Georgetown University Catalogue, 1897–1898,* pp. 118–121.

[133] Georgetown's lead could be followed on most things, but there was one advantage other schools could not duplicate—access to a magnificent legal library. The *Georgetown University Catalogue,* 1890–1891, p. 102, described this unique Georgetown feature: "The Law Library at the United States Capitol, in charge of the Dean of this Faculty as official librarian, contains over 50,000 volumes. . . . This magnificent collection is freely open to (Georgetown) students for seven hours daily."

[134] Ahern, *op. cit.,* pp. 102–104.

honored institution. The Faculty serves not because of monied considerations or salaries, but because of their affection for, and interest in, the University of Georgetown; and the proposition of transfer is not only impractical but borders close upon an offense.

. . . The transfer is, therefore, out of the question.[135]

The dean's letter closed this episode in the history of Georgetown's law school; in some respects it served to open a new era for professional education at the Catholic University.

In 1895, the managers of the Catholic University, now seeing that, if professional schools were to be established in their institution, they would have to establish them themselves, organized a department of law within the school of social sciences.[136] But this was a temporary, and apparently an unsatisfactory, arrangement, for it tended to hide law away among a variety of other studies and thereby detracted from its professional and academic standing. So in 1898 a separate school of law was organized with two curricula : one was a three-year undergraduate course leading to the degree of bachelor of law; the other was a graduate program offering master's and doctor's degrees to students who had already earned their undergraduate degrees in law. The degree of *doctor utriusque juris*, the prospectus said, was also offered.[137]

The ambitious approach to legal education made by the Catholic University was unquestionably praiseworthy and it was guided by the idea that legal study should be something more than a mere preparation of lawyers for the courts. This much could be done by other law schools, but the Catholic University wanted to be different; and rather than try to teach law as a practical art or trade (a kind of indoctrination in legal methods and practices) it wished to reflect in its teaching the philosophy of the University and illuminate the courses with "ethical, historical and political science, based on immutable principles of reason and justice, and governing the conduct of men in view of their relation to God, the state, and one another.[138] Whether or not the teaching at the law school ever achieved these high purposes is hard to say. Possibly the new approach to law at the Catholic University (although its newness must be measured against evidences of the same theory in the testimonials from Georgetown)[139]

135 *Ibid.*, p. 102.

136 *Ibid.*

137 *Catalogue of The Catholic University of America, 1895*, p. 11. This degree, it should be noted, had its origin in the medieval university of the thirteenth century and had combined studies in canon and Roman law. At the Catholic University, apparently, this ancient combination was to embrace, in addition, contemporary law.

138 Barry, *op. cit.*, pp. 170–174.

139 G. E. Hamilton, "History of the Law School of Georgetown University," *College Journal*, 39 (March, 1911), 308–310.

was denied a fair test, for in 1908 the trustees of the University decreed that the law school be closed. A variety of reasons were offered for excision of legal studies from the curriculum : professors of law were not available to staff the school, capable students were hard to recruit, and money could not be found to support the kind of law school the Catholic University wanted. Yet, while the law school was suppressed, legal education continued in an informal way at the Catholic University through the lectures of William C. Robinson, the former dean of the law school, who was retained on the Catholic University faculty.[140]

Guided by the example and experience of St. Louis University, Notre Dame, Georgetown, and the Catholic University of America, departments and schools of law began to find their way into Catholic colleges in the early years of the twentieth century. To give details of founding and institutional development for all the various law schools in Catholic colleges is obviously impractical in this book. We are content to indicate that once the pattern of development was set by the principal Catholic colleges, the law schools organized in the others were fair imitations of it. Law was incorporated in the following colleges in the nineteenth century : Notre Dame, 1869; Georgetown, 1870; and the Catholic University, 1895. In the twentieth century the schools following added a legal curriculum : Creighton, 1904; Fordham, 1905; Marquette, St. Louis, and Loyola (Chicago), 1908; Duquesne and Santa Clara, 1911; San Francisco, De Paul, and Detroit, 1912; Gonzaga, 1913; Loyola (New Orleans), 1914; Loyola (Los Angeles), 1920; St. John's (Jamaica, N. Y.), 1925; Boston College, 1929; St. Mary's (San Antonio), 1934; Seton Hall, 1951; and Villanova, 1953.[141]

Among schools of law especially, although a similar image was projected by medical schools associated with these colleges, a degree of independence or autonomy was attained by Catholic college law schools which made them the wonder of the academic community. The age-old portrait of the Catholic college president dominating his school contains more elements of truth than fiction except where the law school is under consideration; and this erosion of presidential authority in the Catholic colleges was taking place at the very time when college and university presidents in other American colleges were affirming their duty to control both the liberal arts and the professional school sides of university life.[142] In their long association with Catholic colleges, schools of law were seldom brought to heel by the authority of the president, the board of trustees, or the dean of the liberal arts college, nor were these officers ever able to prove to professional faculties that professional schools, especially schools

---

[140] Barry, *op. cit.*, p. 174.
[141] Power, *op. cit.*, p. 253.
[142] Brubacher and Rudy, *op. cit.*, pp. 346–350.

of law, should become fully integrated components of the total college environment. It was always easy for administrators in Catholic colleges to control the college faculty, because it was easy to replace persons who taught grammar, French, or history, for example, but professional schools were never easy to staff. In determining policies for schools of law and medicine particularly, the faculties of these schools enjoyed a position of independence envied by teachers in other departments. The administrator whose mere whim was law in the college of arts and sciences was regarded as an intruder in professional schools, and his influence was as insignificant in the latter as it was supreme in the former.

Other types of professional education

By the end of the nineteenth century theology, medicine, and law had a firm foothold in the Catholic colleges of the United States and further developments along these lines were fairly clearly prescribed by the demands of the professions themselves, the imposition of educational standards by professional associations, and by the thrusting ambition and rivalry among collegiate professional schools.[143] From this time on, except possibly for professional theology, the college was never entirely a free agent in the codification of curricula for the senior professions and this curtailment of independence served to reduce the number of institutions, especially those under Catholic management, embarking on professional curricula in these studies. Had there been fewer extra-institutional restraints, a considerably higher percentage of Catholic colleges, we may assume, would have tried to create schools of medicine and law. As it was, the demands of respectable professional education in the prestigious professions were out-of-reach for most Catholic colleges, so they had to be content, on the one hand, with the further cultivation of their theology curricula and, on the other, with an adoption of college curricula for the less honorific junior professions.

Preparation for these junior professions was an issue to be reckoned with on the level of higher learning, and in an area where much less was prescribed about what was acceptable and what was not, Catholic colleges could range more freely in adding curricula in such fields as engineering, architecture, nursing, education, dentistry, pharmacy, music, social service, industrial relations, social science, foreign service, physical education, journalism, and speech.[144] Yet the entry of Catholic colleges

143 Hofstadter and Hardy, *op. cit.,* pp. 181–184.

144 Speech programs were often given special attention in Jesuit colleges. For example, Detroit College offered five special classes in elocution, voice culture, gesture, and practice (*Detroit College Catalogue, 1895–1896,* pp. 28–29); and Mar-

into the arena of education for the newer professions was by no means as leaders of a new educational movement, but as followers in fields already cultivated by other colleges in the United States. The frontiers of collegiate education for the newer professions were opened in 1824 by Rensselaer Polytechnic Institute. In this school for theoretical and practical science, teachers could be prepared who, in turn, would teach aspiring students the secrets of applying science to husbandry, manufacturing, and domestic economy.[145] Thus the age of technical education began, in which schools would concern themselves with the question of making science useful. To this end new educational means were introduced at RPI : laboratory methods of instruction were instituted to capitalize on the practical side of knowledge and to put theory to work, and a variety of evening and extension courses were organized in a curriculum that would bring this kind of practical tuition within the reach of any students ready to profit from it.[146] The remote and sometimes indifferent college classroom populated by sons of the upper classes was beginning to lose its luster and the idea that liberal education for the gentleman was the only kind of instruction worth anything was now being indicted more and more. While attitudes toward higher learning began to change, always with some damage to the traditional doctrine of liberal learning, RPI continued its assault on the conventional liberal curriculum. In 1835 courses in civil engineering were added, and in 1849 the school broadened its technical perspectives even further by becoming a general polytechnic college.[147] Yet even while this pioneering institution embraced the objectives of technical education, it refused to forsake all the goals of liberal learning and made room in its total curriculum for courses that would contribute to the students' mental and physical culture.

Standard liberal arts colleges read the signs of the times, and reasoned that if RPI could institute technical curricula and add to them the elements of liberal culture, they could modify their own courses of study to introduce some of the appurtenances of technical instruction. Thus, in 1845, Union College announced a course in civil engineering;[148] Harvard and Yale, in 1847, organized the Lawrence Scientific School and the Sheffield Scientific

quette instituted elocution as a special course in 1895 (*Marquette College Catalogue, 1895–1896,* pp. 32–33).

[145] P. C. Ricketts, *History of Rensselaer Polytechnic Institute* (Troy, N. Y., Rensselaer Polytechnic Institute, 1930), pp. 41–59.

[146] Walter P. Rogers, *Andrew D. White and the Modern University* (Ithaca, Cornell University Press, 1942), pp. 115–123.

[147] Franklin Greene, *Rensselaer Polytechnic Institute* (Troy, N. Y., P. C. Ricketts, 1933), pp. 13–14.

[148] *Union College Catalogue, 1856,* pp. 23–24.

School respectively;[149] in 1852, Dartmouth opened the Chandler Scientific School and Brown organized a department of practical science.[150] In 1855, the University of Pennsylvania established a department of mines, arts, and manufacture.[151] The Massachusetts Institute of Technology, opened in 1865, provided additional impetus for the rapidly growing movement in higher learning, a movement greatly indebted to and abetted by the Land-grant College Act of 1862.[152] With the advent of the twentieth century, forty-two technological colleges were engaged in the business of higher education, which in the United States was beginning to wear a new face. Against this background of educational evolution and with several avenues already clearly marked out, Catholic colleges took their first cautious steps toward educating students for the new professions.

Although most Catholic college presidents and prefects of studies disliked professional education and refused to admit that their schools were affected by it, professional education nevertheless played a fairly prominent role in the Catholic colleges. There is no foundation for the belief that Catholic colleges were unequivocally devoted to liberal learning and that for the first half century of their existence in the United States they were uniformly successful in driving the awful apparition of professional education from their academic portals. They regularly embraced clerical training and the fondest hope of most Catholic colleges was some day to become renowned centers for theological studies; but even when they could not become great theological schools and had to settle for educating a native clergy as best they could, their curricula were always flexible enough to squeeze in a few commercial courses and thus try to educate some of their students for the challenges of the business world. Admittedly, the commercial courses in the majority of Catholic colleges, at least for the first seventy-five years of the nineteenth century, were unsuccessful in achieving full collegiate status; but no matter, they were part of the college course of studies and by putting up with them the colleges gave them recognition.[153] Yet, while it is entirely clear that commerce could find its way into the Catholic college curriculum and add an element of professionalism to it, it is also an obvious part of the historical record that the elevation of commerce studies to the standing of separate pro-fessional schools or departments in the Catholic college was a slow and painful process. This temporizing with commercial subjects and an apparent uncertainty over how to handle them was due in part to the nature of the

[149] R. H. Chittenden, *History of the Sheffield Scientific School* (New Haven, Yale University Press, 1928), I, 24–26, 45–47.

[150] *Ibid.,* pp. 45–47.

[151] See Brubacher and Rudy, *op. cit.,* p. 62.

[152] R. G. Axt, *The Federal Government and the Financing of Higher Education* (New York, Columbia University Press, 1952), pp. 59–60.

[153] Power, *op. cit.,* pp. 85–87.

commercial curriculum itself, which, in fact, could be integrated without too much difficulty into an existing liberal arts curriculum and, moreover, offered no great challenge to the reality of the situation in which Catholic colleges found themselves. In theory they eschewed professionalism—all their public announcements verify this—but in practice, in the day-to-day operation of their school, they realized that some students had come to them, not to be nurtured as humanistic scholars, but to be educated for the world of business.[154] If the Catholic college refused to tailor some program of studies for such students, the students would either go else-where or neglect college study altogether. Thus, elements of institutional self-preservation dictated the compromises which in the end allowed the commercial course a high degree of security in the Catholic college, despite the fact that its very existence ran counter to the announced educational philosophy of the institution wherein it found a home. This inconsistency proved in time to be troublesome and had a permanent effect on the educational standing of the commercial course, department, or school in the life of American Catholic colleges. Commerce was an educational step-child, to be put up with and kept, but always to suffer from lack of genuine love.[155]

That was one side of the issue; another side is clearly reflected in the problem of finding teachers for commercial subjects. Traditionally, and sometimes by edict, clerical teachers were excused from any involvement in nonclassical subjects, so if commercial courses were to be offered laymen would have to be appointed.[156] But the nineteenth-century Catholic college did everything in its power to prevent laymen from invading its faculty and, supposedly, distorting the conventional image of the Catholic college as a school where teaching was the distinct domain of clerics. This resistance was the product of theory, a theory capable of eliciting dedication and devotion, and it was supported by the public pronouncements and private convictions of almost every nineteenth-century Catholic bishop. Yet, if

[154] Lenoue, *op. cit.*, p. 30.

[155] For the development of commercial curricula in the last years of the nineteenth century, see *St. Louis University Catalogue, 1879–1880*, pp. 20–22; *Xavier College Catalogue, 1879–1880*, pp. 12–13; *St. John's College* (Fordham) *Catalogue, 1890–1891*, pp. 12–13; *Detroit College Catalogue, 1895–1896*, pp. 24–27; and *St. Louis University Catalogue, 1895–1896*, pp. 27–29. At St. Louis this statement prefaces the four-year course of study described in the catalogue: "This curriculum offers to those who do not wish to avail themselves of a regular classical training the means of acquiring a good English or Commercial education. It embraces Book-Keeping, a full course of Arithmetic, with the elements of Algebra, and to a complete Grammar course, it adds the study of Style, the principles and practice of the minor species of Composition, especially Letterwriting, and a course of Religious Instruction. It is completed in four years, and prepares students for commercial pursuits" (p. 27).

[156] Power, *op. cit.*, pp. 97–98.

this theory of clerical academic supremacy was sometimes subjected to reasonable doubts, it could always be supported by practical arguments. How could a Catholic college pay laymen salaries and still remain solvent? Such was the conundrum facing the Catholic college whenever it thought seriously about upgrading the commercial course. The obstacles to the development of professional schools of business and commerce, then, were almost insurmountable and so they remained until internal attitudes began to change and until the pressures from outside the college during the early years of the twentieth century became too heavy to ignore.

Interestingly enough, the arguments discouraging the introduction of new curricula into the undergraduate college were never used against the infant schools of law and medicine which had affiliated to Catholic colleges during the last half of the nineteenth century. Some of the reasons why this was so may be found in the traditional standing of these higher professions : almost without regard to the cost to a conventional philosophy of education, these schools were worth having because they could add luster to the college's name. But there was another side to the matter, one that had nothing to do with the teaching traditions of Catholic schools, traditions, as we have said, which made it imperative for clerical teachers to man the classrooms : the first schools of law and medicine in American Catholic colleges were established with clearly defined limits to the financial responsibility the college would assume for them.[157] Thus, the cost of employing lay professors in law and medicine was a burden for the professional school, not the college, to bear, and it was left to work out its fiscal problems in the best way it could. This special treatment, if, indeed, we are right in so labeling it, was not available to the commercial course, department, or school. Obviously the principles of professional education were sufficiently flexible, even in the Catholic college, to permit both an enthusiastic embrace of law and medicine (with financial autonomy) and the adoption of a dour attitude of doubt and denial whenever any one of the newer professions sought to establish itself and affirm some degree of independence in the college community.

After the first decade of the twentieth century, however, the inroads made by the newer professional studies in the nonCatholic colleges of the country raised the issue both of competition and completeness : if Catholic colleges neglected programs for various kinds of professional education, they would surely lose prospective students to colleges conducting such programs; and without the professional departments and schools that now began to appear on the campuses of the most respectable American institutions, Catholic colleges would seem to be incomplete. So, again, thinking more of the public image a Catholic college might project than of the legitimate educational needs of students, the managers, with their usual hesitations,

[157] See Durkin, *op. cit.*, p. 29.

and with some false starts, adopted a policy of opening satellite schools for professional training, always withholding from these schools the genuine blessing of academic standing and prominence and regularly subordinating them in facilities, faculty, and finances to what was yet regarded as the heart of the college, the curriculum in the liberal arts.[158] So when the new schools of engineering, education, and nursing appeared on Catholic college campuses they shared a common fate : they stood in the shadow of the liberal arts, as possibly necessary, yet nevertheless intrusive, studies to be kept in a properly subordinate position; and the students enrolling in these professional schools were relegated to the rank of second-class academic citizens. These attitudes of arrogance were always unhealthy, but they helped the colleges pay lip service to their educational traditions, which somehow had resisted the educational evolution of the modern world; and these same attitudes, moreover, proved their durability by becoming perennial doctrines in the Catholic college. Only a few of the new professional schools escaped the academic doubts and recriminations that were kindled and kept alive by the proponents of the liberal arts and this escape was accomplished not by demonstrating how much action-oriented education could achieve and thus receiving the blessing of the established liberal disciplines, but by asserting their independence and thus further separating themselves from the liberal educational tradition. Dentistry, more clearly technical and more properly wedded to schools of medicine than to liberal arts, found its route to independence a fairly easy one, but dentistry proves no point among Catholic colleges because only eight schools of dentistry were able to survive in the Catholic academic atmosphere.[159] Nor do the twelve existing schools of engineering make the point any clearer,[160] although it must be admitted that both in dentistry and engineering the improved status of these professions outside the college community helped their academic standing immensely.

What really counted in the end was not the value the college attached to the newer professional subjects, but the status these newer professions achieved outside college walls. And in this instance we have once again the unhappy duty to report that even for determining the worth and the promise of parts of its own curriculum the college was usually an extremely poor judge and was all too frequently incapable of rendering an informed opinion. Catholic colleges allowed science, education, and social science entry into their curricula, but for long decades they refused to take any of these subjects seriously or endow them with the resources that their social standing and importance demanded.[161]

[158] Erbacher, *op. cit.,* pp. 87–91.
[159] Power, *op. cit.,* p. 253.
[160] *Ibid.*
[161] See Leo R. Ward, *Blueprint For A Catholic University* (St. Louis, B. Herder Book Co., 1949), pp. 331–341.

Worst of all was their record with teacher education, where they refused to heed even the obvious needs of a developing system of Catholic elementary and secondary schools, and even after being forced to lend their support to the important business of educating teachers, their efforts were perfunctory because they were still dominated by the conviction that the highest objectives of a Catholic college were to be found outside the urgent requirements of life in society. Pedagogy was below them and their liberal ideals; it would have to be content with a studied indifference.[162]

Thus, at the end of the seventh decade of the twentieth century, the ten existing schools of education in Catholic colleges,[163] are still seeking full academic recognition in their local university communities; and departments of education in Catholic colleges which have not seen fit to create separate professional schools suffer similar academic deprivations. This truculent attitude toward Education on the college's part, even in the face of a pressing need for professionally-prepared teachers, led to experiments with teacher education in diocesan teachers' colleges. Reversing a clear trend that had been in operation for almost fifty years—a trend recommending an integration of professional and liberal education—these diocesan teachers' colleges moved away from the regular colleges to prepare their students as teachers in the lower schools. The pioneer institution in this Catholic teachers' college movement was founded in connection with St. Francis Seminary near Milwaukee, Wisconsin, in 1871, and was named the Catholic Normal School or Teachers' Seminary.[164] Two courses were organized : one, three years in length, was open to prospective common-school teachers; the other, five years in length, was committed to preparing students for secondary-school teaching. For the next seventy years a majority of teachers in Catholic lower schools were prepared for their pedagogic work in the forty-two Catholic normal schools or diocesan teachers' colleges.[165] After 1936, although the Catholic liberal arts colleges refused to accord Education full standing—still doubting its academic stature—professional Education courses were admitted to their curricula, and slowly but surely the normal school faded into the background.

Still, even with the colleges seeming to preempt the field of teacher education, the teachers' college under Catholic auspices and separate from the regular liberal arts college or, by the mid-twentieth century, the university, refused to withdraw from its professional involvement in the

162 Francis M. Crowley, "Catholic Teacher Education," *Catholic School Journal,* 51 (April, 1951), 118–120; and T. F. O'Leary, *Inquiry into the General Purposes, Functions, and Organization of Selected University Schools of Education* (Washington, Catholic University of America, 1941).

163 Power, *op. cit.,* p. 253.

164 *Ibid.*

165 John R. Hagan, *The Diocesan Teachers College* (Washington, Catholic University of America, 1932); and Power, *op. cit.,* p. 253.

preparation of teachers. As late, therefore, as 1955, three Catholic diocesan teachers' colleges were still in operation, and in the same year twenty-one normal schools admitted students solely for teacher education.[166] Most of these normal schools, it must be agreed, were conducted by religious communities of Sisters and were intended only for members of the religious community. Yet, even as such, they proved by their very existence the inability of Catholic colleges and universities to establish departments, schools, or programs of Education capable of driving these short-cuts to professional Education out of business.

[166] *Ibid.*

8

Catholic undergraduate colleges
for men

By the year 1870 the formative period for Catholic colleges in the United States was drawing to a close: the older colleges, beginning with Georgetown and going on through the "venerable ten," had become sensitive not only to the changes taking place in American higher education but for the need to alter their own educational strategy as well, and the newer colleges founded later in the first period, or even during the period of development, were anxious to imitate the procedures of their academic forbears. The colleges had begun their educational careers in the United States with the assumption intact that first and foremost they should be schools for the preparation of priests; they had bent every effort to make themselves into proper places for the training of young clergymen who on finishing their course in the college could proceed to a seminary. Even when this objective became obviously inappropriate for all students who might enroll in a Catholic college, it was justified, nevertheless, by a pedagogic conviction that all students should be taught tested and worthwhile knowledge. What knowledge had better credentials than the traditional content of the divinity course? Obviously, an educational theory for higher learning centered on divinity studies allowed the colleges to ignore completely any and all legitimate demands prospective women students might make on them. Catholic colleges for men stood deaf and impervious to justifications for coeducation until the twentieth century was well advanced, and even when it became clear that such restrictive policies deprived women of their educational rights amendments to them were adopted painfully and reluctantly.

Catholic colleges of the formative period, we know, were able to control the education of many of their students from the first levels of elementary teaching through to the more advanced stages of college instruction. Criticism of them on this point, however, is undeserved, for if they had

238

refused to respond to the need for teaching rudiments to boys who enrolled they would at once have proved their inadequacy as educational institutions. The early colleges were elementary and secondary as well as higher schools because they had to be, and much of their early history seems chaotic and confused because by force of circumstances these schools were compelled to teach what students needed to learn. Sometimes this meant teaching reading,[1] but more often it meant organizing secondary-school curricula,[2] for, clearly, these schools were acting out an early history before American high schools became a reality. In fact, the Catholic college regarded the first three years of its course as a Catholic substitute for Latin-grammar schools and academies, the natural and ordinary preparatory schools for nonCatholic colleges of the country.[3]

A curricular history of the formative period need not be repeated here in order to provide a foundation for an historical study of undergraduate colleges for men during the seventy years following 1870. We know why Catholic colleges were six- or seven-year schools for the first half of the nineteenth century,[4] but we need to see how, during the period of development, they sought to reconstruct their programs of study along lines eventually parallel with those pioneered by nonCatholic colleges. For this our best sources are the prospectuses of the Catholic colleges, which, it should be said, were written with a care and style befitting the literary education in which their schools took so much pride. One may be tempted, on occasion, to debate the merits of the requirements of the college course or the philosophy of education reflected by the college catalogues, but never to denigrate the excellence of their literary qualities.

Catholic colleges wanted to be classical schools, but during the early

---

[1] G. J. Garraghan, "The Beginnings of St. Louis University," *St. Louis Catholic Historical Review*, 1 (October, 1918), 100; Hope, *op. cit.*, p. 221; D. B. Warden, *A Description of the District of Columbia* (Paris, 1816), pp. 106–108; and Daley, *op. cit.*, p. 226.

[2] See, for example, G. J. Garraghan, "The Beginnings of St. Louis University," *St. Louis Catholic Historical Review*, 1 (October, 1918), 85–102; Meline and McSweeny, *op. cit.*, I, 59–73; and Joseph W. Riordan, *The First Half Century of St. Ignatius Church and College* (San Francisco, Crocker Co., 1905), pp. 68–83.

[3] Preparatory or high school classes were kept in the college for a long time and were common even in the last years of the nineteenth century. *St. Louis University Catalogue, 1895–1896*, p. 30, carried this announcement, typical of a number of colleges, about preparatory instruction: "The object of this Class is to introduce younger pupils to the study of the first principles of Grammar chiefly by class-drill; to form them to habits of attention and application, and thus prepare them for one of the regular Courses of Instruction. Requirements for entering this class are :— 1st. The Applicant must know how to read, write and spell creditably. 2d. He should know Arithmetic as far as Long Division included."

[4] See pp. 122–140.

years of their life this hope went unrealized;[5] now, in the first years of the developmental period, they thought the time was ripe for them to become what they had always wanted to be, so we see signs of change without seeing at the same time many evidences of modernity. Even the American high school with its definite preparatory commitment had little effect on Catholic colleges, for they chose to regard the high-school education, which some of their students had had, as a substitute for elementary, not secondary, instruction. The best to be expected, then, in the way of reducing the length of the college course from the conventional seven years was not to eliminate the three years that had been part of preparatory education, but one year only, the year of rudiments. The willingness of the Catholic college to distinguish between elementary- and college-level study is clear once we pass the mid-point of the nineteenth century, but nothing much can be said about distinctions between, or separations of, secondary- and college-level curricula until several more decades had passed.

New dimensions

Neither in the traditions of Catholic education nor, for that matter, in the chronology of school development in English America was it possible for Catholic college managers to find the model for the college plan they adopted.[6] Catholic education in Europe had noted the difference between secondary and higher schools and there were plenty of European prototypes which might have guided the founders of American Catholic colleges. It is impossible to believe that they were totally unaware of traditional school organization, so we are left to conclude that they made a conscious effort to ignore it. Yet, much closer to home, sometimes at their very doorstep, Latin-grammar schools, academies, public and private, Catholic and non-Catholic high schools demonstrated convincingly how educational levels could be organized and how it was unnecessary for the college to assume that it alone was capable of superintending all formal teaching.[7] Of course,

---

[5] See Erbacher, *op. cit.,* pp. 64–68; Agatho Zimmer, *Changing Concepts of Higher Education in America Since 1700* (Washington, Catholic University of America, 1938), p. 99; William J. McGucken, "Jesuit Influence in University Education," *Historical Bulletin* (March, 1940), pp. 51–52; and the *Catalogue of Detroit College, 1886–1887,* p. 9 : "The Classical Course is designed to impart a thorough liberal education. In the accomplishment of this purpose the ancient classics hold first place, as the most efficient instrument of mental discipline."

[6] Orestes A. Brownson discussed origin and models in "Our Colleges," *Brownson's Quarterly Review,* 15 (April, 1858), 211–212 and Cassidy, *op. cit.,* pp. 83–87.

[7] See Elmer E. Brown, *The Making of Our Middle Schools* (New York, Longmans, Green and Co., 1902), pp. 323–330, 398–400.

Catholic colleges were suspicious of all nonCatholic secondary schools and they generated a special antagonism toward the public high school because it was either a secular school, devoid of religious perspective, or because it embraced the religious attitudes of Protestant sects.[8] In either case the public high school was anathema, and all other kinds of nonCatholic secondary schools were informally interdicted as well.

Still, the question remains unanswered : why was so little confidence shown in Catholic secondary schools, sometimes connected with parishes and sometimes under the jurisdiction of religious communities? Such schools were unquestionably orthodox, so other reasons must have been given for doubting them and refusing to accept them as educational steppingstones to the colleges. No doubt some parish secondary schools were incapable of conducting respectable preparatory (classical) studies, and the colleges were aware of this;[9] yet independent secondary schools, directed by Catholic brothers or priests, were undoubtedly graduating students whose accomplishments were equal to those of students just finishing the third or fourth year in a Catholic college. All this, it seems, was ignored, for somewhere in the code of Catholic higher education was lodged a dogmatic assumption which affirmed the necessity of maintaining continuity in a college course of studies. A student was expected to begin and end his college course, which combined secondary and higher studies, within the walls of one institution, and no other procedure could be countenanced.[10] Thus, it was difficult or impossible for a student to enter college at mid-course, having had his secondary schooling in a separate high school or academy; it was also almost impossible for students to move from one college to another. No trust was shown for lower schools and little enough, we might think, between one Catholic college and another.

Before 1893, the year when the Report of the Committee of Ten was issued,[11] the possibilities of articulation between Catholic high schools—or any high school for that matter—and Catholic colleges should have been apparent, and the need for such articulation should have been imperative. Yet little or nothing was done. After the Report, when public and private high schools alike turned slowly away from preparatory objectives toward terminal ones, and when they began to minimize college preparation because they were committed to preparing their students for life, the relations

[8] Burton Confrey, "Backgrounds for Our Secularized Public Schools," *Thought,* 5 (December, 1930), 452–473.

[9] John T. Murphy, "Catholic Secondary Education in the United States," *The American Catholic Quarterly Review,* XXII (July, 1897), 449–464; and Edmund J. Goebel, *A Study of Secondary Education During the Colonial Period up to the First Plenary Council of Baltimore, 1852* (New York, Benziger Bros., 1937), pp. 161–175.

[10] Cassidy, *op. cit.,* pp. 88–89.

[11] National Education Association, National Council of Education, *Report of the Committee of Ten on Secondary School Studies,* 1893.

between high schools and colleges became strained. From that point the Catholic college could find ample justification for having a preparatory course integrally related to college studies and it repeated this justification whenever its long course was challenged.[12]

But in the long run the six- or seven-year college course was doomed : in the first place there was always the question of respectability and reputation; Catholic colleges were never able to afford the luxury of being totally different from other colleges in the country. They hoped to be different in some important respects—mainly in their theological foundations—and sometimes they were convinced that what they were doing was both different and better than the work of their institutional confreres. But intramural convictions about superiority, or even academic respectability, were insufficient; Catholic colleges had in the end to adhere to the general direction American higher education was taking, and that direction was always unsympathetic to the long course.[13] In the second place, about the time Catholic colleges entered their developmental period regional accrediting associations made their first appearance in the United States;[14] these associations were unwilling to endorse the seven-year course, or even its six-year counterpart, so Catholic colleges interested in obtaining accreditation were virtually forced to jettison the preparatory years in their curriculum. Outside pressures, then, rather than internal, self-generating reforms recommended a four-year college course, and Catholic colleges, while seeking the blessing of an accrediting association, were disposed to keep their hands on preparatory instruction, and they did so by organizing the first three or four years of their regular curriculum into a separate preparatory, or high, school which they maintained on their own campus.[15]

Yet, even before the Report of the Committee of Ten altered the direction of American secondary education and by its action forecast some reconstruction of collegiate admission requirements and curricular assump-

---

[12] Thébaud, *Forty Years in the United States,* pp. 348–352; Austin O'Malley, "Catholic Collegiate Education in the United States," *The Catholic World,* 67 (June, 1898), 289–304; and William J. McGucken, *The Jesuits and Education* (Milwaukee, Bruce Publishing Co., 1932), p. 122.

[13] Nicholas M. Butler, "The American College," *Education Review,* 25 (January, 1903), 10–20; and National Education Association, "Length of the Baccalaureate Course and Preparation for the Professional Schools," *Proceedings,* 1903, pp. 496–500.

[14] Calvin O. Davis, *A History of the North Central Association of Colleges and Secondary Schools, 1895–1945* (Ann Arbor, Mich., the Association, 1945).

[15] See Colman J. Barry, *Worship and Work: Saint John's Abbey and University, 1856–1956* (Collegeville, Minn., American Benedictine Academy, 1956), p. 231; and for further evidence on the separation of studies, the following college catalogues: *Canisius, 1889–1890,* pp. 13–16; *St. Peter's, 1889–1890,* pp. 8–11; *Holy Cross, 1889–1890,* pp. 7–11; *Boston College, 1889–1890,* pp. 11–13; *Fordham, 1890–1891,* pp. 10–11; *Loyola* (Baltimore), *1889–1890,* pp. 8–9; and *St. Louis, 1895–1896,* p. 30.

tions, Catholic colleges were uneasy about being out-of-step with what appeared to be the normal curricular patterns of higher education in the United States. Such outside influences were always remote, because Catholic colleges kept aloof from their nonCatholic counterparts and if given a free choice would have ignored them completely; but this was plainly impossible. If the colleges refused to indulge in normal academic intercourse, that was their business; but students, parents, professors, and society as a whole were sensitive to college policies, so any hope Catholic colleges might have entertained of total independence was doomed from the outset. Thus, there was a certain inevitability about their subsequent capitulation to the normal ways of academic organization, but it is clear, also, from any perusal of the record that Catholic colleges tried with might and main to defer the inevitable. They refused to be like other colleges; this was a matter of policy, they thought. But they were never able to strike out in their own direction, not caring what other schools in the United States were doing. This tug-of-war between wish and necessity left them in the middle of curricular and organizational dilemmas.

Trying to resolve these dilemmas by modest experiments which would keep their fundamental image intact, they endeavored to shorten the college course further than had been tried earlier. Reducing the length of the college course from seven to six years was a concession, but, as we have said, this alone was hardly enough to affect the basic thrust of the college course. By the early 1870s, however, mere tinkering with the old program was insufficient; something more drastic needed to be done if the colleges were to represent themselves before their public as vital and responsive institutions. Against their better judgment, but forced to act, nevertheless, several Catholic colleges reported to the United States Commissioner of Education in 1872 some of the curricular changes they had been making.[16] Among these reported changes one thing stood unchanged : the college was to retain custody of secondary school studies. So in this 1872 report, we find that one Catholic college had organized a two-year college course; twenty-three offered a four-year course, without distinguishing high school from college studies; two had a five-year course; five a six-year course; and four a seven-year course.[17] The twenty remaining Catholic colleges either refused to answer the Commissioner's query or chose to ignore it; in any case, what, if anything, was being done to update their curricula goes unrecorded in this survey. It is probably fair to assume, given the Catholic attitude toward the new department or bureau of education in the Department of the Interior,[18] that the colleges failing or refusing to report were still honoring the six- or seven-year curriculum. Whether they were or not,

[16] *Report of the United States Commissioner of Education, 1872,* pp. 762–790.
[17] *Ibid.*
[18] Burns and Kohlbrenner, *op. cit.,* pp. 174–175.

Catholic colleges in general made plain their determination to keep the high school as the first part of the college course. Various tactics to perpetuate this wedding of what should have been two distinct curricula were calling the preparatory part of the course humanities, or the academical, but not really separating the curriculum into lower and higher studies; or organizing a preparatory school, with its own administrative head and faculty, and melding its curriculum with the college course of studies. Although the first tactic was probably more popular than the second during the final years of the nineteenth and the first decade of the twentieth century, its prospects for becoming a standard way of organizing Catholic higher schools were never good. It was a poor compromise destined for certain rejection. The latter tactic was much more successful and, although in many respects a compromise, rather than a straightforward effort to meet the curricular issue forthrightly, in the long run it bore good fruit because it established as a working principle the separation of high school and college curricula. From the colleges' point of view such a compromise was acceptable because it allowed them to retain almost total control over the education of their students, and with two schools, the college and the high school, on the same campus and under the direct control of the same high administrative officers, the presumed integrity of higher education could be protected. From the public's point of view and from that of an accrediting association, this separation fulfilled the letter of the law : high school and college curricula were distinct.

Catholic colleges relinquished the high school course with extreme reluctance, clinging to it until the 1940s when they finally consented to a complete break.[19] Yet the old plan for keeping the high school and the college together was academically indefensible after the second decade of the twentieth century. We must look elsewhere to find the reason for keeping the two schools together and the old system intact, and when we do we again become aware of the indelibly religious nature of the Catholic college and the fact that it was first an instrument of the Church and only afterwards a school. The high school years, either in a school standing independently of a college or in the long college course, were the most fertile years for cultivating vocations to the religious life as priests, brothers, or in the case of Catholic women's colleges, sisters.[20] With demonstrations of this fact always at hand, Catholic college managers were horrified by the thought that the principal source of clerical supply might be allowed to

[19] See William F. Cunningham, *General Education and the Liberal College* (St. Louis, B. Herder Book Co., 1953), pp. 23–28.

[20] John T. Murphy, "Catholic Secondary Education in the United States," *The American Catholic Quarterly Review*, XXII (July, 1897), 449–464; and Thomas A. Becker, "Vocations to the Priesthood," *The American Catholic Quarterly Review*, V (January, 1880), 29–38.

escape their control; so they made every effort to rescue their preparatory departments from the spiritual erosions of the American college way of life.

From the years of their first founding until almost 1890 Catholic colleges in the United States maintained the stability of a curriculum pattern which allowed students in the first year of secondary instruction to have the same academic classification as students in the last year of the college course. All students, regardless of their scholastic accomplishments, were labeled by the same phrase : all were "college students." [21] Yet, the calendar refused to stand still and, as we have said, the colleges were unable to live comfortably with their past; it shortly became obvious that some reorganization would have to be made in curricula. Experiments with reorganized curricula were conducted over a thirty-year period from 1890 to 1920, and when we look for leadership among the colleges for this movement toward curricular reform we find that for once Georgetown was not in the vanguard setting the pace; its place of traditional leadership was relinquished to St. Louis University. While it would be a mistake to suppose that St. Louis was the birthplace of the four-year college course, for nonCatholic colleges had been operating along these lines for almost two hundred and fifty years,[22] yet it was in St. Louis University that the first Catholic tests were made with the regular four-year college course and it was at this institution that a four-year model acceptable to other Catholic colleges was shaped.[23] Once again we see how it was possible for Catholic colleges to follow paths of reform in higher learning without ever being trail blazers.

The St. Louis plan, as the four-year curriculum for Catholic colleges come to be known, was intended to be a model for Jesuit colleges in the United States, and so it became, but its influence went far beyond the Jesuit circle of colleges to affect every Catholic college seriously concerned with keeping abreast of curricular trends in American higher education. In the first place, the St. Louis plan separated the high school from college courses of study, and high school students, if they were retained on the college campus, were deprived of their collegiate designation. This abrupt separation was a new experience for Jesuit educators and it did some violence to their educational plan as outlined in the respected *Ratio Studiorum;*[24] yet they had had some practical preparation for departures

[21] Power, *op. cit.,* p. 110.

[22] See Edward C. Eliot, *Rise of a University* (New York, Columbia University Press, 1937), II, 211—212; and Charles K. Adams, "The Next Step in Education," *Forum,* 10 (February, 1891), 629–630.

[23] G. J. Garraghan, *The Jesuits of the Middle United States,* III, 505–510; and *St. Louis University Catalogue, 1880–1881,* p. 13.

[24] See Allan P. Farrell, *The Jesuit Code of Liberal Education* (Milwaukee, Bruce Publishing Co., 1938), pp. 423–426.

from the *Ratio,* for it is probably true that in American Jesuit schools the letter of their educational code had often been sacrificed to the demands of expediency, although they tried with unstinting devotion to remain true to its spirit.[25]

Once the principle was accepted that the college course should be four years in length (although it must be admitted that some colleges anxious to follow the St. Louis plan found it impossible to design a four-year program), the nomenclature designating the various years had to be decided on. St. Louis University adopted the names of Humanities, Poetry, Rhetoric, and Philosophy for the four college years, making them correspond to the freshman, sophomore, junior, and senior years in nonCatholic colleges.[26] Apart from number and nomenclature, however, the St. Louis plan was only a timid step toward curricular reorganization; there were no bold efforts either at St. Louis or anywhere else either to change the content of the curriculum or to introduce elective courses from which students might choose those subjects that caught their fancy.[27] The college course pretended to be classical, and in a few colleges this was perhaps more than pretense, but the most striking feature of the Catholic college course of study was its inflexibility rather than its classical qualities. Only one avenue was open to the degree of bachelor of arts and all students were required to follow it.

Latin and Greek retained their honored positions in the teaching syllabus during this entire period of experiment with curricular organization, for no one doubted that what was then being taught was proper to the

[25] Thébaud, *Forty Years in the United States,* p. 331.

[26] G. J. Garraghan, *The Jesuits of the Middle United States,* III, 505–510. Although St. Louis' class nomenclature was common, followed exactly at places like Holy Cross (*Catalogue, 1889–1890,* pp. 7–11), Canisius (*Catalogue, 1889–1890,* pp. 13–16) and Xavier (*Catalogue, 1879–1880,* pp. 9–10), it was often modified: Boston College used First Grammar, Humanities, Rhetoric, and Philosophy (*Catalogue, 1889–1890,* pp. 11–13) as did St. Peter's (*Catalogue, 1889–1890*). Loyola (Baltimore) (*Catalogue, 1889–1890,* pp. 8–9) used Classics, Belles-Lettres, Rhetoric, and Philosophy.

[27] Timothy Brosnahan, "President Eliot and the Jesuit Colleges," *Sacred Heart Review* (January, 1900), pp. 8–12, stated the general objections. Catalogue statements are illustrated by that of *Loyola* (Baltimore), *1895–1896,* p. 10: "This course, which serves as a foundation for special training in any branch which the student, with his mind matured and trained, may decide to take up, is obligatory on all; to render it in any considerable degree elective, would be to defeat its very end and aim;" and by that of *Creighton, 1895–1896,* p. 4: "Recognizing that the students are not the proper judges of the preparatory studies they should pursue, the officers of the College do not intrust them with the selection of their studies, except under certain well-defined restrictions. Parents should not encourage their sons to seek dispensations from certain branches, since youth are prone to ask exemption from the very studies which are most necessary, at the same time that they may be the most distasteful."

college course. How it should be packaged was the only question. Along with the strict requirements for studying Latin and Greek, the Catholic college adopted another feature : the academic lockstep. The college course was presumed to take four years to complete; all students should partake of the same educational diet and all should master the curriculum's various parts at the same pace. This, however, was a departure from the traditional Jesuit plan which provided for promotion from one class to another when a student's achievement merited promotion,[28] and while this departure was a procedure recommended mainly because it respected good order, it was vulnerable to challenge on educational grounds. The challenge, we know, was seldom, if ever, made.

We have noted the Catholic colleges' valiant efforts to follow traditional precepts of classical education and, though they never mentioned the Yale Report,[29] they endorsed it by their day-to-day operations and willingly assigned pride of curricular place to the classics. What they wanted most to do, however, they rarely accomplished. A full complement of classical courses was too heavy a load for the students and, as often as not, for the faculty as well. Georgetown's spokesmen use some glowing terms about the curriculum elaborated in the college's prospectus;[30] and its literary image is imposing; yet, from other sources, we know that stated curricula were visions of what might be done rather than accurate descriptions of the scholastic standards students fulfilled.[31] If this was true at Georgetown, the premier Jesuit college and the trail blazer for all Catholic colleges in the United States (and evidence points in that direction), then it was also true of all other Catholic colleges. We should be well advised to make due allowance for the rhetorical skill of prospectus writers. What this means is that Catholic colleges, while maintaining a theoretical adherence to classical education, were seldom capable of fulfilling their advertised expectations.

Students were either unable or unwilling to follow the classical course, because, despite ardent recommendations, it failed the pragmatic test of utility. When boys in Catholic colleges were aiming for the seminary and ultimately for the priesthood, the values of the classics were easy to market, but as Catholic colleges evolved in history, and as the colleges were upstaged by major and minor seminaries established in various dioceses, the colleges' responsibility for and involvement in clerical education and training was

[28] McGucken, *The Jesuits and Education*, p. 279; and Daley, *op. cit.*, p. 220.

[29] "Original Papers in Relation to a Course of Liberal Education," *American Journal of Science and Arts*, 15 (January, 1829), 297–351.

[30] Daley, *op. cit.*, pp. 220–224; and J. Fairfax McLaughlin, "The Beginning of Georgetown College," *The Catholic World*, XLVII (February, 1888), 610–619.

[31] J. A. Burns, "Early Jesuit Schools in Maryland," *Catholic University Bulletin*, XIII (July, 1907), 361–381; and Edward I. Devitt, "Georgetown in the Early Days," *Records of the Columbia Historical Society*, XII (1909), 21–37.

eroded.[32] Secular-minded students began to come to the campus at about the same time that an American interest in science was being whetted, so Catholic colleges were compelled, sometimes against their better judgment, to dilute their classical program by shaping a curriculum that was partly classical and partly scientific.[33] This was only one way to handle the issue created by an expanding interest in science. Another way was to design two or more curricular tracks. Some colleges, disposed to follow this latter alternative, could by artful maneuvering end up with two, three, or four fairly distinct college courses of study : classical, scientific, commercial, and pre-divinity.[34]

Science and technology were becoming facts of American life, and though they by no means dominated it they were earning more and more attention and had already found their way into the academic arena, especially in polytechnic colleges and land-grant schools.[35] Yet Catholic colleges were unable, in many instances, to see why they should become involved in science, not merely because their basic interests were in another direction, but because at bottom they doubted whether science could be a friend of organized religion. This meant that science courses might be taught, sometimes as a separate curriculum, but they were things to be put up with, always undernourished and unloved. We may put commercial curricula in the same category, although theologically they were regarded as neutral rather than potentially hostile like science. They were worth, perhaps, a timid embrace.

Despite its dogmatic affirmations about liberal learning and discipline of the mind, the Catholic college had, almost from its beginning in the United States, paid heed to demands for practical learning, and such demands centered frequently on commercial subjects. The first steps allowing commercial courses a place in the curriculum were taken with considerable hesitation; their status was downgraded by calling them 'extras,' by not counting them toward the requirements for a degree, or by pointedly indicating that they were taught by laymen.[36] But these equivocations were challenged more and more by increasing student pressure for courses that would enable them to leave college with saleable skills. So the next step toward giving the commercial program an independent curricular position was taken when the colleges, while still refusing to grant degrees for study

[32] See Lloyd McDonald, *The Seminary Movement in the United States, 1784–1833* (Washington, Catholic University of America, 1927), pp. 128–132.

[33] Power, *op. cit.,* p. 85; and David R. Dunigan, *Holy Cross College in 1848* (St. Louis, St. Louis University, 1938), pp. 78–80.

[34] Erbacher, *op. cit.,* pp. 87–91.

[35] See Earle D. Ross, *Democracy's College: The Land Grant College Movement in the Formative Stage* (Ames, Ia., Iowa State College Press, 1942), pp. 136–151.

[36] *Catalogue of St. Louis University, 1858–1859,* p. 5; and *Twentieth Annual Catalogue of the University of Notre Dame, 1864,* p. 13.

in a commercial curriculum, consented to recognize it with a commercial diploma.[37] This policy remained fairly general until about 1860. Thereafter, many colleges, at last recognizing the inevitable, designed their curricula to make room for at least two routes to the college degree : the classical and the commercial. The origin of the new policy is somewhat obscure : Spring Hill College is credited with having separated commercial from classical curricula in 1859 and, at the same time, agreeing to grant degrees for study in either curriculum;[38] St. Louis University, however, seems to have been the first of the Jesuit colleges to put into operation what was to become a uniform Jesuit plan with respect to commercial curricula, and this was in 1862. According to the Jesuit plan, all Jesuit colleges would retain or establish commercial curricula; such curricula would be strictly separate from classical programs; and Jesuits themselves would be excused from teaching commercial curricula except when philosophy was part of the course.[39]

Despite this recognition as part of a collegiate instructional program, the commercial course was still incapable of meeting all the tests Catholic colleges wanted to impose on curricula, so commerce lingered in an academic limbo until about 1920, when the last theoretical obstacles simply disappeared and commerce was at last accorded full academic standing. Yet if we consider the expectations Catholic college managers had for commercial programs of study and the way they allowed such programs to be organized when they finally countenanced them, it is easy to see why commercial curricula had remained academic nomads in Catholic colleges. Notre Dame was as friendly to commercial subjects as any Catholic college and saw, probably more clearly than most, the fiscal advantages to having them in the teaching syllabus, but the 1863 Notre Dame prospectus describing the course came precariously close to damning it with faint praise. The announcement began by saying that the commercial course was intended for students "who cannot or will not avail themselves of a regular classical

---

[37] G. J. Garraghan, *The Jesuits of the Middle United States,* III, 237; D. R. Dunigan, *The History of Boston College,* p. 148; Mark V. Angelo, *The History of St. Bonaventure University* (St. Bonaventure, N. Y., Franciscan Institute, 1961), pp. 63–64; and Thébaud, *Forty Years in the United States,* p. 350. A student who completed the commercial course at St. Louis University could take an additional year of study and be awarded a bachelor of science degree. (*St. Louis University Catalogue, 1879–1880,* p. 23) Certificates were awarded to students who finished the commercial course in these colleges: St. Ignatius (Calif.), Santa Clara, Canisius, Fordham, St. Ignatius (Chicago), and Marquette. (*St. Ignatius College Catalogue, 1889–1890,* p. 6; *Santa Clara College Catalogue, 1889–1890,* p. 2 *St. John's* (Fordham) *College Catalogue, 1890–1891,* p. 12; *St. Ignatius College Catalogue* (Chicago), *1895–1896,* p. 20; and *Marquette College Catalogue, 1895–1896,* p. 11).

[38] Kenny, *op. cit.,* p. 211. Commercial degrees, however, are not mentioned in *Spring Hill's College Catalogue, 1889–1890,* p. 66.

[39] G. J. Garraghan, *The Jesuits of the Middle United States,* III, 122.

training, [by giving them] the means of acquiring a good English or Commercial education. It embraces Bookkeeping, an ample course in Arithmetic, with the elements of Algebra; and to a complete Grammar course it adds the study of Style; the principles and practices of the minor species of composition, especially Letter-writing, and a course of Religious Instruction. It is completed in four years and prepares students for commercial pursuits."[40] It would, indeed, be hard to imagine how a course so described could compete effectively with the classical course for a place of honor among college studies. We know it did not so compete and we know, too, how it was compelled to mark time for another sixty years before its credentials were recognized as being valid.

This Notre Dame statement relative to the place of commerce in the curriculum tells us something more about Catholic college curricula, however, and it does so in a way that makes its significance easy to miss. A course of religious instruction was being offered, and this, despite what we might conclude from any contemporary study of Catholic college programs of study, was an innovation. The traditional approach to the curriculum had allowed for plenty of religious or theological study, so much may be taken for granted, but separate courses in doctrine, catechetics, or theology were not organized for the college student. Spiritual studies were built into the total teaching program—every course or year of study had its religious side—in such a way as to obviate special courses. But this artful device for integrating a theological perspective with literary and linguistic requirements always assumed that the fundamental thrust of the curriculum would be classical. When this assumption lost universal validity with the introduction of commercial curricula, separate courses in religious doctrine had to be offered. And now for the first time, and somewhat tardily, considering the historical ground Catholic colleges had covered, we find courses in religion being introduced almost as afterthoughts to curricula barren of classical credentials.[41] Eventually, these separate courses in religion, successful in their impact, were built into an inflexible core and became, surprisingly enough, the distinctive genius of Catholic college teaching. Yet, with the record of history properly illuminated, we discover that theological or religious course requirements never figured in the original deposit of academic faith bestowed on Catholic higher learning.

After the Civil War, as we have seen, Catholic colleges began to broaden their curricula; science and commerce were added to the so-called classical course, but this was only part of the picture. The most significant

---

[40] *Nineteenth Annual Catalogue of the University of Notre Dame, 1863,* p. 11.

[41] For the order of studies in commercial courses in which the separate course in religion was prominent, see *St. John's* (Fordham) *College Catalogue, 1890–1891,* pp. 12–13; *St. Louis University College Catalogue, 1895–1896,* pp. 27–29; *Detroit College Catalogue, 1895–1896,* pp. 24–27.

changes occurred in connection with the classical course itself : instead of organizing the content of the curriculum into a total teaching syllabus for one year and ignoring, as had been the common practice, any curricular claim a separate subject might have, the colleges began to think along subject lines. When they did, they began to assign particular subjects to particular teachers and thus, a full century after the nonCatholic colleges had instituted specializing professorships, the Catholic colleges began to add them as well. In the quarter century following the Civil War, announcements published by Catholic colleges indicated the separate subject status of French, Spanish, German, Gaelic, geography, chemistry, and astronomy.[42] This was a time for curricular enrichment; it was a time, too, for making important additions to the classical curriculum in such a way that, though the classical course would surely be changed, it could be spared destruction. For the most part, however, this was wishful thinking, for classical curricula had already met their Waterloo; after their disintegration whatever allegiance was paid them was to their name alone.

Still the traditional degree was that of bachelor of arts and so it remained for years to come, although in trying to protect the integrity of the classical course, new degrees were used to designate collegiate accomplishments in non-classical fields of study. Some Catholic colleges offered the degrees of bachelor of science, bachelor of engineering and, for students who took everything in the classical course but the classical languages—substituting for them one modern language—the degree of bachelor of philosophy.[43] The direction was clear : Catholic colleges were going to offer multiple curricula along with appropriate degrees, but progress along these lines was slow. In 1872, for example, Catholic colleges awarded one hundred and forty-nine bachelor's degrees; ninety-eight were bachelor's degrees in arts.[44] Yet after 1910 this business of adding new degrees was accelerated greatly and Catholic colleges, keeping pace with other institutions of higher learning in the United States, were prepared to offer curricula leading to any recognized degree.[45]

With a multiplication of curricula and the adding of new subjects to them, the old college-wide plan for organizing and administering the curriculum became obsolete. Departments were organized and into this departmental structure both teachers and subjects were fitted. And with this movement, it became necessary for students to plan their course of study : what subjects should they study to fulfill the stated requirements for academic majors and minors? This question clearly anticipated the controversy over the elective system and, though Catholic colleges escaped the

---

[42] *Report of the United States Commissioner of Education, 1872,* pp. 762–790.
[43] *Ibid.*
[44] *Ibid.*
[45] For litanies of degrees available, see *The Catholic Almanac,* 1910.

full impact of electivism, they were by no means entirely immune from it either. Catholic college response to the issue of electivism, related as it is to a theory of liberal education, is handled in the next section.

Ferment and change

Neither presidents nor prefects of study were disposed to add new dimensions to the doctrine of liberal learning which had been inherited from Catholic higher schools in Europe. The Jesuit teaching tradition and the Jesuit code of liberal education were at once the most visible guides for a college course of studies. In view of the origins of Catholic higher education in the United States and the fact that Georgetown's founder was himself a Jesuit,[46] it was natural for a Jesuit educational legacy to have prevailed, and, what is more, as far as most Catholic colleges were concerned, to have become prescriptive. It is clear, once nineteenth-century attitudes toward higher learning are known, that Catholic colleges could adopt a theory of liberal learning, Jesuit in elaboration and application —even though some colleges were entirely free from the Society's influence— without at the same time embracing the day-to-day teaching practices recommended, or required, by Jesuit pedagogy. All this was natural enough, for as we review educational history we find the educational consequences of religious revolt and reform represented in two distinct, though not always clearly separate, teaching codes. Protestant liberal, or humanistic, education was guided by the educational pronouncements of Melanchthon and the pedagogical organizations of Sturm;[47] Catholic liberal, or humanistic, education was defined and organized by the Jesuits.[48]

American Catholic colleges, then, had a common source of scholastic inspiration. As we have said, this source was Jesuit, so it was entirely possible for Jesuit attitudes toward liberal learning to have an impact on the Catholic colleges of the United States which bore little relationship to the actual number of Jesuit schools extant.

Anyone who wanted to know what Catholic colleges should teach, how long the course should be, what emphases should be given in instruction, and what the goals of higher learning should be, could read the *Ratio Studiorum* and therein find all the important answers.[49] Whether or not,

---

[46] B. U. Campbell, "The Life and Times of John Carroll," *The United States Catholic Magazine,* V (November, December, 1846), 676–682.

[47] R. R. Bolgar, *The Classical Heritage and Its Beneficiaries* (Cambridge, Cambridge University Press, 1954), pp. 356—360.

[48] *Ibid.*

[49] See Edward A. Fitzpatrick, *St. Ignatius and the Ratio Studiorum* (New York, McGraw-Hill Book Co., 1905), pp. 263–275.

once having the answers, the reader, if he were a Catholic college president, could apply them to his particular problems or translate them into daily practices and environments for learning was another matter, because the *Ratio* presumed, once the spirit of its message was caught, an artful adaptation of its spirit to the peculiar circumstances of a school, the students who enrolled, and the social climate of the country where the school was located.[50] Thus, in spite of its dogmatic tone, this epistle of educational purpose was not always a prescriptive handbook. The Jesuits understood this probably better than most other Catholic college managers, and knowing the spirit of their ancient document and acting in firm response to it, they could nevertheless allow their schools to react in some measure to current social forces. Outside the Jesuit circle this distinction between the spirit and the letter of an educational creed was only partly understood, so when there were questions about what should be done, the letter of the law was given pride of place; therein lay the danger to constructive thinking and prudent judgment about the limits and goals of liberal learning. Apart from pedagogical practices recommended in the *Ratio,* to which the Jesuit teacher tried to be true, one of the strangest anomalies in nineteenth-century Catholic college history was the determination of nonJesuit Catholic colleges to follow the curricular paradigm of the *Ratio* more vigorously than the colleges of the Society.

Yet, while this observation should stand intact, it would be inaccurate to portray Jesuit colleges as being either oblivious or indifferent to the academic advice of their Jesuit predecessors. In practice they did not stray very far from the general precepts of liberal learning which tradition and experience had imposed. Thus, we find definitions of college purpose and ringing endorsements of liberal education in the last years of the nineteenth century which, if we were ignorant of their dates and depended only on internal criticism of the documents, would surely be assigned to the first years of Catholic college history in the United States. One such document, representative of the Catholic college position on the nature of higher study, was prepared by writers at Georgetown in 1887 and was submitted to the United States Commissioner of Education for inclusion in his *Report* for that year.[51]

The statement began by acknowledging that its curricular descriptions and affirmations were extracted from Georgetown's policies, and went on to admit that these policies were usually followed by Jesuit colleges in the United States.[52] What was not alleged in the statement, but may be added by the historian, is that Georgetown's policies on liberal learning had the

---

[50] "Descriptio et status Collegii Sti. Ludovici, mense Januario, 1832," quoted in G. J. Garraghan, *The Jesuits of the Middle United States,* I, 293–294.

[51] *Report of the United States Commissioner of Education, 1887–1888,* pp. 642–643.

[52] *Ibid.*

full endorsement, and wherever possible the careful imitation, of all Catholic colleges in the United States. While the statement was by no means a decree or an edict, it was, nevertheless, a forthright assertion of educational convictions and no Catholic college of this genre would have wanted to alter any of its details or disavow its conclusions. And even as late as 1887, as we read on in the statement, a decided preference was expressed for the seven-year program, including both preparatory and collegiate departments, although the writers of the statement must have known of the St. Louis experiment with the four-year course and, moreover, of the wide variations among Catholic colleges in the length of their courses, as reported to the Commissioner of Education in 1872.[53] Such information, however, could not deter them from saying what they thought the ideals of liberal education should be and apparently these ideals prescribed a course of studies a full seven years in length. This Catholic interpretation of the design for liberal learning arose unquestionably out of sincerely-held convictions, but these convictions were always bolstered by a love for the past and a yearning to preserve the values recommended by the voice of tradition. In the case of the Georgetown authors, since the course they endorsed was plainly an adaptation of the Georgetown curriculum of 1835, there were fairly obvious elements of self-justification.

"The plan of studies [at Georgetown] is based on the idea that a complete liberal education should aim at developing all the powers of the mind, and no one faculty at the expense of the others."[54] Here, on the level of broad purposes, the authors might simply have cited the Report of the Yale Faculty and left it at that, for what they wrote had been stated many times before. Whether or not they were aware of the Yale Report is, for us, a mystery; yet, their indifference to or ignorance of it is probably beside the point, because they intended to say how liberal goals should be achieved, and what they had to offer along these lines is nowhere part of the Yale document.[55] The first years of the course—their terms lack precision here, although they really meant to say three years—are when the memory receives "the principal share of attention," and students are engaged in "mastering the rudiments of Latin, Greek, and mathematics, and in acquiring accuracy in the use of [their] native tongue."[56] This three-year involvement with the rudiments contains the cornerstones on which more advanced studies may stand, so it is important to cultivate judgment "by means of translations from one language into another, and by the study

[53] *Report of the United States Commissioner of Education, 1872*, pp. 762–790.

[54] *Report of the United States Commissioner of Education, 1887–1888*, p. 642.

[55] "Original Papers in Relation to a Course of Liberal Education," *American Journal of Science and Arts*, 15 (January, 1829), 297–351.

[56] *Report of the United States Commissioner of Education, 1887–1888*, p. 642.

of mathematics."[57] Accordingly, as judgment is more and more exercised, the role of memorization is reduced in scope.

When students are able to read Latin and Greek with some facility, the statement continues—and the assumption is fairly clear that this should take three years, although some students may progress faster, or others more slowly—they begin the really serious part of their college study and are introduced to the best selections of ancient and modern literature. This study of the humanities should take one year and when the student is finished, his literary taste should be cultivated. The fifth year of the college course (conventionally dubbed Poetry, although such class nomenclature was eschewed by the Georgetown writers) is a year for training the student's imagination : "the nature of poetry is explained, the technicalities of verse-making are mastered, and the great poets are carefully studied." Rhetoric follows poetry and in this sixth year "critical powers are exercised and developed;" the authors are subjected to scientific analysis, the statement avers, the principles of oratory are elaborated, "and the speeches of the world's greatest orators are read and discussed." The seventh year is the time for disciplining the reasoning faculties and to this end logic, metaphysics, ethics, mathematics, and natural science are prescribed for students. Of these, metaphysics is assigned pride of place and justified by the statement that "a thorough knowledge of it is regarded as of the utmost importance, since it serves to arrange all the student's knowledge systematically, and gives him the ability to grasp firmly the principles of any special study to which he may wish to devote himself."[58]

The capstone of the course, then, is metaphysics and its broad objectives are stated as clearly as we have a right to expect, but the total program is more extensive than this one branch of philosophy and its objectives are likewise more enticing : "This course is calculated to develop and train all the powers of the mind, rendering it able to appreciate and understand all branches of learning. It serves as a foundation for special training in any branch which the student, with his mind matured and trained, may decide to take up."[59]

With such undoubted confidence in the quality of the course thus described, and with its implied guarantee that the mind formed and developed within the boundaries of liberal learning could organize and assimilate any vocational, professional or specialized knowledge it might later encounter, it is easy to see how this flag of liberal learning could be nailed to Georgetown's educational mast, and, moreover, how any suggestions of changing its obligatory character could be rejected summarily. Electivism would erode the true genius of liberal learning and, in the end,

[57] *Ibid.*
[58] *Ibid.*
[59] *Ibid.*, p. 643.

would destroy this perfect plan of education, for how, asks the writer of this document, can a student, before his mind is developed, judge what studies will be most beneficial to him?[60] The point is clear : if the plan is perfect, what possible justification can be advanced for change?

Still, Georgetown wants to be in step with the age, and to keep her image from being tarnished by any seeming indifference to new branches of study or to progress in the old disciplines. Her heart, it is true, is in the past, but her head, the statement is careful to imply, is strictly in the present. "She watches [accretions to knowledge] with a keen eye, and while jealously guarding the stores of the past, she will not suffer her students to be deprived of the more glittering treasures of modern culture."[61] So additions to knowledge which satisfy her tests of importance are put into the curriculum and are "taught with a philosophical analysis intended to guard the student against that confounding of mere information with learning, which is the danger of modern education." But with a curriculum already filled with irreplaceable subjects, it is necessary to allow some important parts of learning, such as natural history, to be handled outside the regular curriculum in student societies. Natural science is a field of knowledge whose importance is admitted by the author, or authors, of this statement, yet because Georgetown's curriculum is unable to bear the full weight of a complete scientific study, instruction in natural science is allowed to intrude only to the extent "supposed desirable for the completion of a perfect general education, such as a highly cultured man of any profession would wish to possess."[62]

This was a statement of firm policy and every Catholic college essayed to honor it. But it was a forlorn hope. The policy was out-of-date a full quarter of a century before it ever found its way into the Commissioner's *Report*. Catholic colleges which saw more clearly the impossibility of making the calendar stand still tried again to alter their curricula without at the same time capitulating to what were considered the greatest evils of modern education. Change along three or four lines seemed possible : a reduced emphasis on the classics; a further development of an English curriculum; the organization of the college course into a four-year curriculum; and the addition of prescribed courses in religion to all curricula.

Although most colleges continued to adhere, if their prospectuses faithfully represent their educational theory, to the traditional assumption that a complete, decent and liberal education was possible only in a classical course, the classics were fast losing favor. It is never an easy thing for any institution to believe sincerely in the efficacy of certain means and then,

60 *Ibid.*
61 *Ibid.*
62 *Ibid.*

because of the nature of its social role, to have to adopt other means or, at least, to retreat from or compromise the means in which it has made an act of faith. Yet this is precisely the dilemma Catholic colleges were faced with. On the level of theory, the virtue of the classical course had the status of a dogmatic assumption; on the level of practice, however, members of Catholic college faculties were expressing reasonable doubts about the educational worth of the old course. One professor had the temerity to state publicly that in his entire career he had never met "a single American pupil who read one line of Latin without being obliged to do so by his professor." [63] His remark bespoke some lack of understanding of the fundamental justification for the classics, and so far as the merits of a classical education were concerned was beside the point; yet it revealed that there were some faculty members at least who could not avoid using the criterion of utility even in this context. Certainly this was the criterion the colleges' public wanted to use. Neither the college going public nor, for that matter, the educated community outside the translucent boundaries of monasteries or religious community houses was willing any longer to accept the age-old justification for classical learning—that it made minds and men—nor were they enthusiastic about courses in Latin and Greek for their own sake once the assumption about the doctrine of mental discipline was abandoned. Educational acts of faith, they could see, were now being made in connection with applied mathematics, physical science, the useful arts, and all the branches of positive and practical knowledge which could contribute to the material progress of society.[64]

Catholic colleges were fully aware of a lack of real enthusiasm for the classical course wherein they put so much of their trust. They knew, too, they were fighting a losing battle, but they were unwilling to surrender. True, they might have to alter their courses somewhat and prune a few of the elements of their old allegiance, but they would, they hoped, be able to salvage something. A typical expression of this attitude is recorded for us by the Jesuit President of St. Louis University in a letter to the Jesuit General : "It will take time to convince the youth of America, even in a well-organized college like that of St. Louis, that the study of the ancient languages is of any use to them; we shall never be able to get along without teaching a special course for such as are preparing for a career in business." [65] While this statement was not meant to be a call to arms, it was, nevertheless, indicative of a tactic the Catholic colleges intended to

[63] G. J. Garraghan, *The Jesuits of the Middle United States,* III, 124. For ample justification of the classics, see for example, *Boston College Catalogue, 1895–1896,* pp. 8–9; and *Holy Cross College Catalogue, 1895–1896,* p. 17.

[64] See M. P. Dowling, *Reminiscences of the First Twenty-Five Years at Creighton* (Omaha, Burkley Printing Co., 1903), p. 62.

[65] G. J. Garraghan, *The Jesuits of the Middle United States,* III, 124.

employ : they would cling to as much of the classical course as possible while adding more up-to-date subjects to the curriculum, but endeavoring all the while to convert the college student, once enrolled, to an enthusiastic belief in the virtues of the classics. It is hardly necessary to say that this tactic failed, but its failure can never be charged to a lack of energetic persuasion on the part of Catholic colleges. It would be plainly an exaggeration to suppose that every professor took to the stump for the classics, but the fundamental policy of the Catholic colleges was clear : the classics were the road to a decent education. Breaking ranks on this question of college purpose was rarely done in an educational age, and in colleges, where the realities of academic freedom were still a long way over the horizon.

Opposition to the classics arose among persons who were unable to see their worth, or who believed other subjects had a more legitimate claim on the college curriculum because of their intrinsic utility. Debaters expressing such arguments scored points easily enough, but there was another direction of attack which was more serious because those who made use of it were in a better position to influence Catholic educational thought. In 1851, Abbé Théodore Gaume published his famous polemic, *Le Ver rongeur des sociétés modernes ou le Paganisme dans l'éducation,* wherein he attacked classical education as a dangerous threat to modern society.[66] The Abbé, apparently, had rediscovered some old doubts and anxieties about the pagan classics which had been vented by the Church Fathers, but he eschewed compromise and balance as recommended by Saints Jerome and Augustine and preferred instead the irrational solution of, say, Tertullian. Neglecting several centuries of Christian educational tradition which had found ways of coming to terms with the classics, Gaume counseled an immediate flight from them and advocated a Catholic college curriculum filled with the works of the Fathers and other Christian authors.[67] The issues that Gaume raised were dead ones but some of his readers brought them back to life and began to attack the classics because they were pagan, and, moreover, because they were dangerous to the faith and morals of Christian students. How much real notice was taken of Gaume's acerbic writings is hard to assess; but the classical curriculum was now assaulted on both flanks : on the one, it lacked utility, on the other, it was unChristian. Little wonder then that the classical course's days in the Catholic colleges were numbered. Yet it refused to die quickly or without a struggle.

In the end, however, the classical course disintegrated most of all

[66] Théodore Gaume, *Le Ver rongeur des sociétés modernes ou le Paganisme dans l'éducation* (Paris, 1851), pp. 3–4, 289.

[67] See Orestes A. Brownson's review of the book, "Paganism in Education," in the *Collected Works of Orestes A. Brownson,* X, 551–563.

because it was necessary to make room for other courses and, despite the convincing prose of the Georgetown writers in their document for the Commissioner of Education wherein they stated a formula for a perfect liberal education, such room was really being made as early as 1890. The new course, with full college credentials, and retaining only those elements from the classical curriculum which could not under any circumstances be discarded, was an English course. We see it most clearly in the *Forty-Third Catalogue of the University of Notre Dame,* in 1887, but its dimensions came to be general among the Catholic colleges. Notre Dame described the new course with extraordinary optimism : "A change is coming over American colleges with respect to the teaching of English. Till a very recent period the higher branches of Rhetoric and Literary Criticism did not receive all the attention they deserve. The last decade has witnessed a marked improvement in this point, and the importance of the higher study of English is rapidly being recognized at all the great educational institutions of this country and Europe. It has been remarked by a great authority that 'when once the English Language and English and American Literature become recognized as a regular educational course, the advantages will be so great as to constitute nothing short of a national benefit.' "

"The Faculty of the University of Notre Dame recognizing the fact that exclusive study of the ancient languages and pure science is not in itself sufficient for a liberal education, have determined to institute a course which shall provide for a more than ordinarily thorough acquaintance with the English language and with English and American Literature. At the same time, all that is more serviceable in the Classical and Scientific courses will be made an indispensable requisite." [68]

The English course, following Notre Dame's leadership, began to appear more regularly in Catholic college prospectuses, and by the advent of the twentieth century it was difficult to find a Catholic college where curricular reorganization, including departures from a rigid classical scholastic regimen, had not taken place. Still, in any hierarchy of curricula, the classical course appeared first on the list and the colleges were anxious to show their educational values in the distinctions they made between degrees granted for the various curricula. The majority of colleges continued to reserve the bachelor of arts degree for the classical course; only students who had taken both Latin and Greek could qualify for the traditional B. A. English, Scientific, and Commercial curricula had their own degrees or certificates which, in the ordinary judgments made around the colleges, were deemed somewhat less worthy than their more ancient counterpart. Another quarter of a century was needed to bring about any alteration in the balance, and even when bachelor's degrees were given nominal equivalence in the colleges' literature, some pains were taken to show

[68] *Forty-Third Catalogue of the University of Notre Dame, 1887,* p. 40.

that the statement meant less than it appeared to; the bachelor of arts degree continued to hold pride of place and for it students would have to involve themselves in classical studies.

Curricular updating, as we have said, was accompanied by structural changes : preparatory and collegiate curricula were separated and Catholic colleges ended up with a four-year college course. Yet the abbreviation of the college program, the introduction of practical studies, and the departure from the classics, all changed the nature of the Catholic college. In a word, the old curriculum had been counted on to do two things : to expose the student to the content of a decent liberal education, and to form him morally and religiously. It was taken for granted, as long as the college course remained mainly classical, that separate subjects in religious doctrine and theology were unnecessary, because the classical course was capable of integrating these important studies into its total perspective. It was assumed, moreover, that the new studies, English, scientific, and commercial, were incapable of such integrating functions. Thus a curricular requirement was introduced which made mandatory for all Catholic students the study of courses in religion in each of their college years. Traditionally, secondary education had included doctrinal studies only during the first three or four years of the nine-year course, and this was true both in Protestant and Catholic secondary schools. But now, Catholic colleges in emphasizing the structure of college studies by separating them from preparatory courses, felt compelled to pluck from the preparatory curriculum separate courses in religion heretofore reserved for the first years of the secondary school.

By following its own curricular instincts the Catholic college of the later nineteenth century had generated all kinds of ferment and created multiple dilemmas for itself which took more than a half-century to resolve. Yet, to complicate academic life even more, the Catholic college was now exposed to the ugly apparition of electivism, and the elective issue was not of its own making.

Myths have invaded the history of the elective struggle in American higher education and (as is usual with myth) have distorted its true dimensions. First, although electivism was surely popularized and extended under the leadership of Charles W. Eliot, he was not its inventor : indeed, the origin of the elective idea would be hard to find in the history of learning, but its American birth was probably presided over by Thomas Jefferson.[69] Long before Eliot became the spokesman for what was sometimes represented as a new educational idea, the foundations of electivism had had a theoretical elaboration in attitudes Jefferson had expressed toward higher

[69] Herbert B. Adams, *The College of William and Mary* (Washington, United States Bureau of Education, 1887), pp. 39–40, 50, 56; and P. A. Bruce, *History of the University of Virginia* (New York, Macmillan Co., 1920), I, 223–241.

learning at the College of William and Mary and the University of Virginia. Second, the idea that electivism was a nonCatholic plot to intimidate and destroy higher learning and that the principal, sometimes the only, defenders of true education were the Catholic colleges, should be summarily abandoned. Actually, Catholic colleges were able to maintain a posture of relative indifference to electivism because as a matter of policy they refused to be affected much by the direction their nonCatholic counterparts chose to take. Opposition to electivism was voiced mainly, not by Catholic college spokesmen, but by professors and presidents who were convinced of the values of the old education, of the classics, and of prescriptive curricula, from places like Princeton, Columbia, and Amherst.[70] Thus, the picture of Catholic colleges standing at the gates fighting a last-ditch fight against the evils of the elective system is pure illusion; the sound of a Catholic voice was heard only when the policies of electivism seemed to threaten the vested educational interests of Catholic colleges.

While it is unquestionably true that Catholic college presidents and professors alike were uneasy about the prospects of an elective curriculum, and from time to time inserted curricular dicta in their educational pronouncements,[71] they conducted nothing even faintly resembling a campaign against electivism. Thus the literature on educational policy coming from Catholic authors of this period allows this issue to lie fallow and fails to prove that electivism was for them a burning question of the day. Yet electivism did have one Catholic opponent who appears to have represented Catholic thought on the subject, Timothy Brosnahan, S.J., and he ought to be given a hearing here.[72] At the outset, however, it should be made plain that he was speaking more for himself than for the Catholic colleges : in no sense was he designated as their spokesman, although they were entirely willing to endorse the hard line he chose to take.

In 1899, Harvard's president, Charles W. Eliot, published an article in *The Atlantic Monthly* advocating an application of the elective principle to American secondary schools.[73] In this article, Eliot sought to justify electivism and in doing so referred to Jesuit colleges and branded their curricular policies as archaic. Particularly offensive to Brosnahan, as it

[70] C. M. Fuess, *Amherst: Story of a New England College* (Boston, Little, Brown and Co., 1955), pp. 80–90; and R. F. Butts, *The College Charts Its Course* (New York, McGraw-Hill Book Co., 1939), pp. 131–143.

[71] *Creighton College Catalogue, 1889–1890,* p. 4; and *Loyola College Catalogue* (Baltimore), *1895–1896,* p. 10. Also Ruth Everett, "Jesuit Educators, Modern Colleges and the Elective System," *Arena,* 23 (June, 1900), 647–653.

[72] Brosnahan's academic career took him to a number of Jesuit colleges, where he was well known as a scholar and writer. At the time of his controversy with Eliot, he was professor of Ethics and Natural Law at Woodstock College, Maryland.

[73] Charles W. Eliot, "Recent Changes in Secondary Education," *Atlantic Monthly,* LXXXIV (October, 1899), 433–434.

turned out, was Eliot's paralleling of Moslem and Jesuit education. After stating that a prescriptive code for Moslem learning was set forth in the *Koran,* Eliot added :

Another instance of uniform prescribed education may be found in the curriculum of the Jesuit Colleges, which has remained almost unchanged for four hundred years, disregarding some trifling concessions to natural sciences. . . . Nothing but an unhesitating belief in the divine wisdom of such prescriptions can justify them; for no human wisdom is equal to contriving a prescribed course of study equally good for even two children of the same family between the ages of eight and eighteen. Direct revelation from on high would be the only satisfactory basis for a uniform prescribed school curriculum. The immense deepening and expanding of human knowledge in the nineteenth century, and the increasing sense of the sanctity of the individual's gifts and will-power have made uniform prescriptions of study in secondary schools impossible and absurd.[74]

In a religiously sensitive age it is easy to see how Eliot's equating of Moslem and Catholic policies could provoke strong rejoinders, and by pointedly implying that Jesuit policies of curricular uniformity were obvious absurdities he almost certainly provoked polemical combat. A public questioning of the soundness of Jesuit school policy was one thing, and it was taken seriously enough, but even the most sensitive Jesuit could hardly believe that Catholic colleges could be helped or hindered much by what the president of a secular college had to say about them. Eliot's article might have been ignored, even by the combative Brosnahan, had it not been for apparently complementary action on Eliot's part with respect to the admission of Catholic college graduates to the Harvard law school. For some time prior to 1899 Harvard had published a list of colleges, including a number of Catholic colleges, whose graduates could matriculate without examination as regular students in the law school. But in the Harvard University catalogue of 1898–1899 this list was revised and only two Catholic colleges, Georgetown and Notre Dame, remained on it.[75] Graduates from other Catholic colleges could be admitted as special students, but in order to graduate with the bachelor of laws degree they would have to attain a standing fifteen percent higher than the minimum standards required for graduation.

By taking this action, or by allowing it to be taken by the law faculty, Eliot demonstrated his lack of confidence in the academic standards of all but two Catholic colleges. Since Eliot had criticized Jesuit colleges for their curricular rigidity and his critique could be taken to apply to most Catholic colleges because of their tendency to follow Jesuit patterns, it was quickly

[74] *Ibid.*
[75] *Harvard University Catalogue, 1898–1899,* p. 525.

assumed, although not necessarily correctly, that Eliot was equating the highest standards of college education with electivism. Unless a college adopted the elective system, so Catholic opinion ran, it would be excised from Harvard's approved list. But what was overlooked at this point was also important : Georgetown, unquestionably the citadel of Jesuit educational policy for the United States and unequivocally opposed to electivism in any form, remained on the list; and Notre Dame, though somewhat less clearly beholden to Jesuit educational philosophy, yet equally opposed to an elective system, retained its coveted Harvard accreditation.

Brosnahan had no time for electivism because he was certain that students were incapable of making the right educational choices; moreover, he was confident that parts of the Catholic college curriculum had met the acid test of time and had proved their usefulness by producing decently educated men. Despite his untroubled confidence in the efficacy of classical curricula, Brosnahan willingly conceded the importance of modern subjects to a nineteenth-century college curriculum and, he said, the Jesuit colleges had made this concession too : ". . . instead of one hundred per cent. of this time being given to Latin and Greek as in the schools of the seventeenth century, only about fifty-three per cent. is given to these studies today. Three hundred years later, then, forty-seven per cent. of class time is conceded to modern studies. Evidently there has been some change in the last 'four hundred years' . . ."[76] While it is obviously difficult to translate class time into percentages, as Brosnahan had done by using the Georgetown curriculum of 1899 as a paradigm, he succeeded in making his point : the Jesuit colleges had not been impervious to change, for, even without allowing electivism to prevail, they had introduced "concessions" to the growth of modern knowledge. He argued that Catholic colleges could obtain the benefits of change and progress without resorting to Eliot's elective plan, and time has proved him right, for Catholic colleges never accepted the practice of the free elective or the underlying educational theory of equivalence of studies. Besides, in refuting Eliot, Brosnahan scored some clever debater's points which endeared him to his Catholic public. Eliot had written how the Jesuit system had not changed in four hundred years; Brosnahan had no difficulty in proving that in 1899 the Jesuit plan for education, formulated in 1599, was only three hundred years old; and by comparing the curricular offerings of the Catholic colleges of the early nineteenth century with those of 1899, he could demonstrate that change was a common fact of Catholic college life. Finally, and at his polemical best, Brosnahan discounted Eliot's allegation that the Jesuit colleges had been too slow in entering the contemporary world. Yet in doing so he

[76] Timothy Brosnahan, "President Eliot and the Jesuit Colleges: A Defense," *Sacred Heart Review* (January, 1900), p. 11. This article has been reprinted in a variety of journals.

either did not know, or suppressed his knowledge, that electivism was not invented by Eliot. Brosnahan should be permitted here to speak for himself :

But a complete change from the uniform described course is a policy of recent date. Until the school year of 1872–1873 there were prescribed studies for each of the four college years at Harvard. About that time it was discovered that no 'human wisdom was equal to contriving a prescribed course of study equally good' for all Seniors. Thereafter this conviction gradually grew in extension until it comprehended at successive intervals the Junior, Sophomore and Freshman years. About fifteen years ago, then, after two centuries and a half of successful work in the field of education, Harvard recognized that 'direct revelation from on high would be the only satisfactory basis for a prescribed school curriculum,' and the present elective system that characterizes that institution was finally introduced. Fifteen years is a very short time in the history of an educational movement, yet within that brief span of years the elective system has become to its advocates an educational fetich, which whoso does not reverence is deserving of anathema. Nevertheless, it would be too much to expect that it should have been adopted before it was invented. In so far, therefore, as it is a reproach to Jesuit Colleges not to have accepted that system, the 'four hundred years' dwindle to fifteen. It would consequently have been more exact, though less telling, to have said that: For the last fifteen years the curriculum of Jesuit Colleges has remained practically unchanged.[77]

Following the article, "President Eliot and the Jesuit Colleges," where he made a more convincing case for the responsiveness of the Jesuit colleges in altering content while keeping the Jesuit pedagogy intact than he did against the elective system, Brosnahan turned to the issue that was most responsible for triggering the controversy in the first place : law school admissions.[78] To illustrate why Catholic colleges formerly on Harvard's accredited list should be reinstated—because the quality of their instruction was entirely respectable—Brosnahan took Boston College as his model, and anyone wanting to absorb details of the 1899 Boston College curriculum can get them from this document. Brosnahan chose Boston College for his model because it was a good school and he was wise enough and, moreover, a sufficiently skilled controversialist, to know how to select the best weapons. But there were other reasons too, and they are reasonably related to the merit of the debate. Boston College, only a few miles from Harvard, had an advantage of proximity which made comparison both natural and convenient; besides, according to Brosnahan, Eliot had singled out Boston College as a place where improvements might be made and in a press inter-

[77] *Ibid.,* pp. 14–15.
[78] Timothy Brosnahan, *The Courses Leading to the Baccalaureate in Harvard College and Boston College,* n.d., n.p., pp. 3–4.

view had said, referring to Boston College graduates, that they knew why their school was not on the list, "and they know the only way [it] can be put on that list. It is for them to improve their course of study."[79]

Brosnahan used forty printed pages to denounce the Harvard policy of requiring students from nonaccredited colleges, who were supposedly educationally disadvantaged at the time of their admission, to perform fifteen percent better than the minimum standard demanded for graduation[80]—and it must be admitted now that Brosnahan succeeded in finding and capitalizing on the weakest point in Harvard's policy—to criticize Eliot and his˙elective theory along lines elaborated in the earlier article, and to compare the college courses at Harvard and Boston College. Enough has been said about the first two points, but the last deserves further examination. Brosnahan was at pains to reject both the educational assumptions of Harvard's president and his imprecise advice about improvement which, he concluded, was unavoidably connected with his theory of electivism. But let Brosnahan testify now for himself :

And yet we must improve our studies according to the model that is shown us. What we want, in view of the partial exposition I have made of the Boston College curriculum, is a little less 'must,' and a little more 'why.' We can not accept an *ex-cathedra* decision on the matter. Former assertions of the president of Harvard regarding Jesuit schools have raised no presumption in favor of his accuracy. An hour or so spent in comparing the catalogues of Boston College and Harvard College, adding thereto some information which is the common property of any one about Boston, leads us to call in question the accuracy of his latest pronouncement regarding Boston College. While willing to admit that the course of Boston College—or of any other college—could be improved, we see no reason whatsoever for suspecting that it is in any way inferior to the collegiate course or courses at Harvard, and furthermore, we have solid reasons for believing that it is superior —that it gives a true mental training.[81]

Catholic college involvement in the elective controversy was always marginal, even while Brosnahan was heaping coals on the fire, for with their confidently sanguine attitude about the validity of their curricular assumptions concerning what knowledge had worth and what had little or none they could afford the luxury of indifference to the froth and foam of academic debate. On the relatively few occasions when it seemed appropriate for Catholic spokesmen to take a stand, they quoted with approval the acid phrases of men like Princeton's McCosh, who in his long academic career never found time to say one good thing about electivism : "I should prefer a young man who has been trained in an old-fashioned

---

[79] *Ibid.,* p. 8.
[80] *Harvard University Catalogue, 1898–1899,* p. 525.
[81] Timothy Brosnahan, *The Courses Leading to the Baccalaureate . . . ,* pp. 38–39.

college in rhetoric, philosophy, Latin, Greek, and mathematics, to one who had frittered away four years in studying the French drama of the 18th century, a little music, and similar branches."[82] Besides, even without an untroubled confidence in the correctness of their curricular views, Catholic colleges were absolved from entering into combat because there were others who were proclaiming the arguments they so liked to hear. Yet, most of the complaints registered against the evils of electivism, even the most balanced ones, refused to make any allowance for the wisdom of the unusual student. After all, there was nothing in the theory or practice of electivism demanding that students fritter away their college years; the honorific elements of the traditional classical course were maintained in the greatly expanded curriculum and students could elect them. But this point was almost too clear to be noticed.

While, as we have said, Catholic colleges could remain aloof from the principal battles over electivism, they were effectively barred by the accidents of educational evolution from ignoring election as an academic reality. Even Brosnahan, while denouncing electivism as an unmitigated evil, unknowingly, perhaps, but convincingly, nevertheless, countenanced it after imposing what he assumed were necessary safeguards : Catholic colleges had opened their curricula to new subjects and since no student could take everything, he selected from among the new subjects those he judged best; multiple curricula were organized and students were allowed to say as they entered the school whether they would study the classical, the English, the scientific, or the commercial courses; and, in addition to what could be built into the curriculum, cocurricular activities offered additional opportunities to exercise some freedom of choice. Thus, with the hesitations and ambiguities which, by now, we know so well, Catholic colleges, on the one hand, entered the twentieth century clinging to their old allegiances and refusing, on a policy level, to wear a new educational face, but, on the other, responding reluctantly to the inexorable demands of a modern world ready to pass them by, altered curricular edicts and liberated their curriculum from captivity to the classics just in time to win back seats on the bandwagon of contemporary higher learning.

By the first decade of the twentieth century, with some form of electivism accepted in practice but rejected in policy, it became possible for the colleges to face some old conundrums with administrative equanimity : the long course with its class teacher and year-long syllabus was beating a rapid retreat to obscurity; a new nomenclature for the college years was adopted; new subjects were added when good excuses could not be found for keeping them out. The old college had changed, and old ways, regardless of their nostalgic adornments, were abandoned. The colleges were now

[82] William M. Sloane, *A Life of Dr. James McCosh* (New York, Charles Scribner's Sons, 1885), p. 201.

ready to accept without reservation the professional schools' curricula about which, formerly, they had had so many anxieties. Moreover, they were willing to experiment with the semester system of curriculum organization wherein, rather than study a subject for an entire college year, the student started and completed a course in half the college year.[83] On their own, these were good omens and they tended to assure the stability of Catholic colleges in the difficult years ahead. But almost equally valuable as a rudder for collegiate stability and for steering the college directly into the realities of the future was the adoption of postgraduate study on a formal and reasonably respectable academic basis.

With relatively few exceptions, nineteenth-century Catholic colleges had conferred masters' degrees, but the postgraduate curriculum, if there was one, and the courses themselves, were haphazard or worse. As long as graduate degrees were granted on the basis of primitive educational customs and without any heed to scholarly accomplishment or institutional reputation, the future of Catholic colleges was in jeopardy. But in the last years of the nineteenth century reforms were initiated and the colleges, using their resources to the best advantage, tried to offer postgraduate studies of real worth to their students, keeping them consistent with their judgments of academic quality. Thus, about midway in the developmental period, we see Catholic colleges raising their academic sights by expanding, liberalizing, and upgrading their undergraduate courses and by infusing their academic atmosphere with the perceptions of scholarship through postgraduate study.[84] Upward extensions of the traditional college were everywhere in evidence and along with them the case for higher quality teaching and learning was given a fair hearing. Catholic college managers now clearly understood the meaning, the difficulties, and the promises of higher learning better than their predecessors; the higher learning, they saw, wore a new face. And this new face revealed dimensions previously strange to the leaders in Catholic colleges : the age of the university was just beginning; the Johns Hopkins and its imitators were making educational news; William Rainey Harper, in addition to the important things he could say about the university, was talking about a junior college.

Without distinguishing themselves particularly in the junior college movement, Catholic educational leaders, nevertheless, took some part in it. Some Catholic college plans were predicated on the hope that by starting

---

[83] See *Report of the United States Commissioner of Education, 1872,* pp. 762–790; *Catalogue of Georgetown University, 1890–1891,* p. 37; *Catalogue of St. Louis University, 1889–1890,* p. 40; and *Forty-Sixth Catalogue of the University of Notre Dame, 1890,* p. 49.

[84] For examples of postgraduate courses, see *St. Louis University Catalogue, 1879–1880,* p. 24; *1889–1890,* p. 26; and *St. John's* (Fordham) *College Catalogue 1890–1891,* p. 11.

as two-year schools they could eventually muster the strength to qualify as fully-fledged four-year colleges. In a more highly competitive and critical educational climate it was hazardous to begin with the full four-year format, but with the two-year college an acceptable part of higher learning's structure the way was open for new foundations whose aspirations were more modestly stated. Then too, a few Catholic schools decided that their commission could genuinely be exercised best by remaining two-year colleges, so they accepted their status without any immediate aspirations about a four-year course.[85]

New uncertainties

The structure and curriculum of Catholic colleges have occupied us long enough and it is important now that we should see the student in the collegiate setting time, accident, and design had prepared for him. Chapter six reviewed the disciplinary codes and their application, as well as the day-by-day scholastic regimen, for the long period of formation, and since the period of development was characterized by an adamant resistance to change, we should not be surprised to know that student life during the developmental period was little different from what it had been before. At any rate, the differences appear to be of no great significance, for the doctrine of *in loco parentis* was still honored and enforced. We can be satisfied therefore with what has already been said about this dimension of student life.[86]

In the old college students had entered by way of the elementary curriculum and, although at the time of admission many were able to read, they were still exposed to the rigors of rudimentary study. During the

---

[85] "Recent Developments in the Catholic College," *Catholic School Journal,* 30 (March, 1930), 96–98; William H. Conley, "The Community College," *National Catholic Education Association Bulletin,* 46 (May, 1950), 15–24; and Edward A. Fitzpatrick, *The Catholic College and the World Today* (Milwaukee, Bruce Publishing Co., 1954).

[86] Examples of the application of traditional disciplines are almost endless in the college catalogues. *St. Mary's College Catalogue, 1889–1890,* p. 12, stated that one professor would leave Chicago, and another St. Louis, on the first Monday of September to accompany students en route to St. Mary's. Regulations governing student conduct stated in *St. John's* (Fordham) *College Catalogue, 1890-1891,* p. 6, retain the tone of earlier years. What was new pertained to military drill, which was required of all, except students in Latin philosophy, on three days of the week. The rule was considered good, for it was still in force in the *Catalogue of 1895–1896,* p. 18. Cadet undress uniforms were required of all students in the middle and lower classes (*St. John's* (Fordham) *College Catalogue, 1890–1891,* p. 6). Military drill was obligatory at St. Joseph's College too (*St. Joseph's College Catalogue, 1895–1896,* p. 9).

period of development, change in admission regulations and standards came only slowly, but eventually the elementary years were lopped from the college course, to be followed shortly by a similar disfranchisement of preparatory studies. When the college stood alone and without entangling elementary or secondary alliances (this, we know, became fairly common after about 1875), it was possible for the first time to speak with some exactitude of standards for college admission. In Catholic colleges these were always two-dimensional, with moral aptitude playing an equal role with scholastic accomplishment and intellectual promise, and sometimes a more important one. Yet, despite its ability to project a truer image of a college curriculum by 1875, the Catholic college retained its unwillingness to exclude deserving Catholic boys whose academic promise was dim. Although most colleges made general statements about their entrance standards, they both phrased and applied them in such a way that any boy they chose to admit could qualify.[87] They were not looking for scholars or for students who would some day startle the intellectual world with their accomplishments; they wanted young men who could be molded along conventional lines toward the objectives of individual, social, and religious responsibility. That they chose to fulfill these goals by preserving their ancient affinities with the classical course will never cease to amaze us.

By 1890, however, the colleges were ready to put a new leaf in their prospectus and they listed the preparatory studies boys should have completed for the various courses—classical, scientific, English, commercial— now available for the college student.[88] Even so, these statements are easily misinterpreted, for rather than an indication of strict admission requirements they were more often guidelines for preparatory schools to follow in constructing their own curricula. Entrance to the classical course was guarded by requirements in Latin and Greek literature, and normally the college statement specified the classical selections the boy should know.[89] Sometimes he was tested on this knowledge before the college accepted him, but the tests were often perfunctory and the standards of accomplishment demanded ranged from high to low according to the impression

[87] Henry C. Towle, "Pioneer Days at Boston College," *The Stylus*, 11 (June, 1897), 332–338.

[88] *Xavier College Catalogue, 1890*, p. 14; *Catalogue of Detroit College, 1891*, p. 11; *Catalogue of Georgetown University, 1890–1891*, p. 16; *Catalogue of St. Louis University, 1891–1892*, p. 22; and *Forty-Sixth Catalogue of the University of Notre Dame, 1890*, p. 30.

[89] See Brother Giles Mullen, *Latin and Greek in College Entrance and College Graduation Requirements* (Washington, Catholic University of America Press, 1926), pp. 18–21; 111–121; *Gonzaga College Catalogue* (Spokane), *1889–1890*, pp. 6–7; *Sacred Heart College Catalogue, 1889–1890*, pp. 2–3; *St. Ignatius College Catalogue* (Cleveland), *1889–1890*, p. 4; and *Spring Hill College Catalogue, 1889–1890*, p. 6.

a boy made either on the college president or the prefect of studies.[90] Requirements for admission to nonclassical curricula were stated too—the colleges were less serious about them, behind their equivocal evaluations of their worth—and they usually mentioned such subjects as English grammar, practical arithmetic, geography, history, algebra, and geometry.[91] The colleges were willing to live with these admission standards for the next half century, when, well toward the end of the period of development, they began to adopt, as nonCatholic colleges had done some decades before, regional or national college entrance examinations.[92] Before this, though, the private entrance examination had declined in status and, with more trust being accorded to the quality of high schools, Catholic colleges were guided mainly in their admissions judgments by what they saw on an applicant's secondary school transcript.

But this was only one side of the coin and whatever past academic accomplishment might predict about future scholarship, there were the twin issues of moral quality and religious orthodoxy to be considered too. Thus, before a Catholic college took a chance with a prospective student, it wanted to know a good deal about his moral and religious habits. While certitude on these points was often elusive, the colleges wanted to be convinced that no boy admitted would ever be a threat to good order or religious uniformity. Home town pastors, as it turned out, played a major part in college entrance decisions, for what they had to say, or refused to say, about an applicant carried far greater weight with college presidents

[90] The following statements on admission are typical: "Every candidate for admission, who is not personally acquainted with some member of the Faculty, must produce proper testimonials of good moral character. If he comes from another College, he will be required to present a certificate of good standing in the Institution which he has left."

"While no one is refused on account of the religious opinions he may entertain, still all are expected to conform, in a respectful manner, to the ordinary exercises of public prayer" (*Marquette College Catalogue, 1889–1890,* p. 7). "No one will be admitted unless he has a good moral character. Any one coming from another Institution will be required to produce a satisfactory recommendation from the Principal of such Institution" (*Santa Clara College Catalogue, 1889–1890,* p. 12). "Candidates, as they present themselves, are examined by the Prefect of Studies, and placed in the Classes for which they are found qualified" (*St. Peter's College Catalogue, 1889–1890,* p. 5). Gonzaga College noted that the best time to come to college was at the beginning of the year, but added that "students are accepted anytime" (*Gonzaga College Catalogue* (Spokane), *1889–1890,* p. 6).

[91] *St. John's* (Fordham) *College Catalogue, 1890–1891,* pp. 12–13; *Gonzaga College Catalogue* (Spokane), *1895–1896,* pp. 7–9; *Loyola College Catalogue* (Baltimore), *1895–1896,* pp. 4–5; *Boston College Catalogue, 1895–1896,* pp. 10–11; *St. Joseph's College Catalogue, 1895–1896,* pp. 6–7; *Marquette College Catalogue, 1895–1896,* pp. 25–31; and *Canisius College Catalogue, 1895–1896,* p. 8.

[92] See Edwin C. Broome, *A Historical and Critical Discussion of College Admission Requirements* (New York, Macmillan Co., 1903).

than any academic evidence that might be mustered.[93] The college of the developmental period was more rigorously Catholic, less liberal in its willingness to admit nonCatholic students (except possibly in its professional schools of law and medicine), and more convinced of its denominational and apologetic role, if this was possible, than had been its counterpart of the formative period. Such a college, of course, had to be cautious in flying its banner of denominational exclusiveness too blatantly, for if it stated an admissions policy implying the application of religious tests, its charter might be put in jeopardy.[94] Yet the same results could be obtained by less extreme measures : nonCatholic students were unwelcome, but no college prospectus said so in plain language. Despite their determination, however, to be denominationally and academically single-minded, the Catholic colleges of the developmental period never became narrow sectarian schools. This was due partly to attitudes of optimism and equality implicit in a restlessly expanding frontier society, but it was due, too, to the sensitive consciences of Catholic colleges which, despite their undoubted orthodoxy, refused to deny learning opportunities to decent, serious students regardless of their religious faith. These colleges, moreover, because of their reverence for tested conventions of teaching and learning, and because they forthrightly announced a profound interest in the moral formation of students, were frequently preferred over some nonCatholic private and state colleges by parents who accepted and approved the educational policies of Catholic colleges without at the same time countenancing the denominational doctrines on which they stood.[95] Never being overburdened with students, then, and looking always to tuition fees for support, Catholic colleges, without altering their denominational badge or retracting one word in their fundamental policy, could allow nonCatholic students to matriculate.

Even with such liberal inconsistencies occasionally affecting admissions criteria, these schools were still fully Catholic and their students were, with only a few exceptions, of one mind with respect to religious faith. Such homogeneity on basic questions of value bespoke a conservative collegiate climate wherein the burning questions of the day could be viewed from the

[93] Canisius College used language almost identical to that of every Catholic college : "Candidates for admission who are not personally acquainted with some member of the Faculty must present testimonials of good moral character" (*Canisius College Catalogue, 1895–1896,* p. 7). Various phases in Canisius' history are touched on in Charles A. Brady's *Canisius College: The First Hundred Years* (Buffalo, Canisius College, 1969).

[94] See S. W. Brown, *The Secularization of American Education* (New York, Russell and Russell, 1912), pp. 29–31; and Charles N. Lischa, *Private Schools and State Laws* (Washington, National Catholic Welfare Conference, 1924–1928).

[95] See Erbacher, *op. cit.,* pp. 9–31; Middleton, *op. cit.,* pp. 21–22; G. J. Garraghan, *The Jesuits of the Middle United States,* III, 125; Meline and McSweeny, *op. cit.,* I, 55; and Meagher, *op. cit.,* pp. 57–62.

antiseptic platform of principle or in which, because the colleges' policy was always to immunize students from life, they could simply be ignored. If neither attitude held much promise of long-term progress, the college atmosphere was nevertheless effective in maintaining a remarkable sanguinity among Catholic college students. Although the years covered by the period of development were fairly quiet ones in all American colleges, Catholic college students distinguished themselves by cultivating an aloofness from the social and educational realities of life. Their mentors deliberately sought the tranquility guaranteed by noninvolvement, and Catholic college students, unquestionably affected by an environment of learning where the past was more important than the present or future, demonstrated their capacity for absorbing what they were taught. Apart from coeducation and athletics, two great issues involving and affecting college life, the period of development is devoid of any sign that students wished to alter a collegiate atmosphere inherited from the previous period. And, furthermore, both the great issues mentioned had their origin and resolution without any apparent reaction from the students themselves. Either they began by being indifferent or were taught to be indifferent about such things.

American colleges began as educational citadels for men and so they remained for two centuries until Oberlin College, in 1833, broke the patterns of the past and admitted girls with the full status of college students.[96] Antioch College, in 1853, and the State University of Iowa, in 1856, followed suit,[97] and thus began a slow process of chipping away at a tradition so hoary that no scholar could remember its birth. Historical accuracy recommends that we notice the nineteenth-century origin of separate colleges for women in the United States, but the same concern for accuracy demands an admission that these schools, even when called colleges, were incapable of competing with colleges for men in terms of academic standards, curricula, or degrees.[98] Such schools, creditable enough as institutions providing a finishing or a polite education, never belonged in any company of respectable colleges, and whatever they became later, are better left unmentioned in any serious chronicle of early nineteenth-century American higher learning.

Higher education for women, on the Catholic side of the picture, is noteworthy only for its absence, save for a few convent schools and academies, until the very last years of the nineteenth century and then, as we shall show in the next chapter, Catholic colleges for women began

[96] Robert S. Fletcher, *History of Oberlin College* (Oberlin, Ohio, Oberlin College Press, 1943), I, 205–210.

[97] Lynn White Jr., *Education of Daughters* (New York, Harper and Row, Publishers, 1950), pp. 50–60.

[98] Louise S. Boas, *Women's Education Begins* (Norton, Mass., Wheaton College Press, 1935), pp. 15, 18–25.

by following well-blazed trails marked out by pioneer, nonCatholic womens' colleges.[99] Even more fallow, during the entire nineteenth century, is the field of Catholic coeducation, for not a single Catholic college for men ever contemplated cultivating it.[100]

This total rejection of higher learning for women by Catholic colleges was not short of justification at the time. First, there was an appeal to principle, which, while seldom expressed publicly, stated that women were by nature incapable of serious higher study. Catholic clerics, presidents and professors, probably guided by the Church's traditional but unofficial attitude toward the natural inferiority of women, were unable to find any convincing testimony proving that women either needed or could profit from higher learning. Unless better evidence was forthcoming to change their minds, the doors of Catholic colleges should remain closed to the daughters of Eve. Even persons willing to admit more myth than truth in the ancient tale that women were morally and intellectually men's inferiors, were asked a practical question, as it was called, to clinch and close the matter : Would a college education make women better wives and mothers? To the Catholic priest-professor who could proclaim without any sign of mirth that the best diploma for a woman was always a large family and a happy husband, the answer to this question was an unequivocal 'no.'[101] Yet differences of opinion among reasonable men on the preceding points were always possible and debating them seldom produced the clear-cut policies of educational exclusiveness Catholic colleges eventually adopted. The final justification, however, was always convincing. If Catholic colleges for men admitted women to their classrooms, they would also have to make provision for living accommodation, and women living on the campus in company with men, regardless of the safeguards imposed, would destroy good order, discipline, intellectual concentration, and morality.[102]

Nothing so far said supports the implication that the issue of coeducation put nineteenth-century Catholic colleges into a state of ferment; they never seriously contemplated the prospect of liberalizing their admissions policies to the point where they would actually have to use the arguments available to them. Although nonCatholic colleges might want to experiment with coeducation, or even try to justify it along lines set forth in the 1867 *Report of the United States Commissioner of Education,*[103] Catholic colleges wrapped themselves in an impervious cloak of immunity until 1909. But before we turn to the events of 1909 which, in the end, succeeded in

[99] See pp. 294–302.

[100] Power, *op. cit.,* pp. 139–143.

[101] See Hamilton, *op. cit.,* pp. 124–130.

[102] See Sister Leo Joseph Devine, *A Study of the Historical Development of Coeducation in American Higher Education* (Chestnut Hill, Mass., Boston College, 1965), pp. 160–174.

[103] *Report of the United States Commissioner of Education, 1867,* pp. 385–387.

expurgating old antipathies and opened the way for a selective adoption of coeducational policies, we should know that Catholic colleges in the United States were acting on their own judgment when they resisted coeducation for more than a hundred years. The edicts governing and disciplining Catholic institutions, despite the ominous inferences that might be extracted from them, were formally silent about the potential evils of educating boys and girls in the same classrooms; but after the Church took an official stand (more easily interpreted as a proscription than a condemnation of coeducation) in an encyclical letter of 1929, *The Christian Education of Youth*,[104] Catholic colleges became more active than ever before in suppressing their monumental fears about coeducation, and began to welcome young women to the campus. Perhaps the Roman Pope was not speaking directly to American Catholic colleges for men when he wrote the encyclical, but if he had any message for them, they were not listening. Yet, despite this twentieth-century trend toward coeducation, the majority of colleges for men were unready to discard either their own hard-won traditions or the Pope's episcopal counsel, for, as late as 1955, only fifteen of eight-four traditionally male colleges had rewritten their admissions policies to allow for the matriculation of girls.[105] Fifteen years later, with the case against coeducation even less convincing, the list of men's colleges adopting coeducation was lengthened to twenty.

Whether we approve or decry the erosion of a tradition which for so long seemed entirely reasonable to Catholic colleges for men, we should know that without the clear demonstrations women were able to give that higher learning had its uses for members of their sex, Catholic colleges would have made no move at all toward coeducation. Even with these demonstrations, victories for coeducation were painfully slow. Without intending these consequences for higher education, although men with clearer pedagogical perceptions could easily have predicted them, the Third Plenary Council of Baltimore in 1884 had laid the foundations for collegiate coeducation in a Catholic context. That council legislated a complete system of parochial elementary schools,[106] but while paying lip-service to the quality of elementary school instruction and to the teacher's central place in formal learning processes, it completely ignored the obvious insufficiency of qualified teachers and, moreover, the absence of teacher-education institutions that might produce them. These things the council left to chance.

When wise men were myopic and failed to take responsible action, it was left to the ingenuity of others less important, if not less wise, to fill this educational vacuum. In 1874 a Catholic replica of the chautauqua,

104 Pius XI, *The Christian Education of Youth,* 1929.
105 Power, *op. cit.,* p. 143.
106 Peter Guilday, *The National Pastorals of the American Hierarchy,* pp. 243–247.

whose purpose was to give Sunday-school teachers intensive training in pedagogy and Catholic doctrine, had been instituted, a full decade before the bishops met in Baltimore to shape Catholic educational policy for the next century. There is no evidence that the prelates were aware of this, and, in any case, it was ineffective and obviously incapable of supplying any large number of teachers. This chautauqua, always an agency struggling to escape demise, amounted to nothing until it was absorbed by the Catholic University Summer School in 1910.[107] But before this the pressing need for teachers in the lower schools had been met forthrightly, although inadequately, by the Columbian Summer School at Madison, Wisconsin, established in 1895, the Winter School of New Orleans, founded in 1896, and the Maryland Summer School, opened in 1900.[108] These schools were the Catholic counterparts of the lectures on schoolkeeping delivered before any audience by itinerant professors or those pronounced in the primitive normal schools that had made educational news in the 1820s and 1830s.[109] But they were plainly out of step with a more enlightened educational age.

For twenty-five years, then, after the bishops made their famous laws on parochial education and enjoined all Catholic parents to enroll their children in Catholic schools, Catholic colleges for men acted as if parochial schools, on the one hand, and Catholic girls who might be educated to teach in these schools, on the other, did not exist. In 1909, James McCabe, president of Marquette University, sought to redress these plainly unacceptable educational conditions by opening an eight-week summer session wherein religious women could pursue college studies.[110] At this stage, coeducation in Catholic colleges was approached both as an expedient and as an experiment; male students would never remain in college during the summer months, and when they returned for the regular term the Sisters would be back teaching in their parish schools. The Catholic attitude was perfectly clear even at this late date, and President McCabe must have shared it : only an imperfect moralist or an educator who had taken leave of his senses would countenance any combination of men and women in a Catholic college classroom. Marquette, in allowing religious women free access to its halls, had no intention of advocating or sponsoring coeducation. Yet, even the most carefully controlled experiments sometimes get out of hand, and this was precisely what happened to President McCabe's progressive plan.

Intermingled with the Sisters who registered for Marquette's summer session in 1909 were a number of lay women who, having misinterpreted

107 Power, *op. cit.*, p. 141.

108 *Ibid.*

109 John R. Hagan, *The Diocesan Teachers College* (Washington, Catholic University of America, 1932), pp. 25–41.

110 See Hamilton, *op. cit.*, pp. 124–130.

the school's advertisements, decided to take advantage of the new educational opportunity now offered. And the school's officers, being unable to see any other prudent course of action at the time, or failing to find any rubric allowing them to deny admission to these lay women, decided to accept their registrations.

The accidents of imprecise communication, then, put lay women in Marquette's classrooms, and the Jesuit Provincial, the religious superior responsible for Marquette, upon hearing that they had invaded a Jesuit college, thereby overturning more than three centuries of educational tradition, wrote to Marquette's President recommending that all summer session classes be canceled.[111] But at this point, President McCabe, showing some mettle as an educational innovator, and recognizing the erosion of old allegiances even among some elements of Marquette's Jesuit community, disappointed too at having to abandon the summer course and worried about the legal implications of cancellation, did not immediately carry out the Provincial's recommendation. Instead, he appealed to higher authority, asking that the issue of summer school attendance for women be submitted to the Jesuit General for a ruling. The Provincial, by now probably uncertain about what should be done with a school session already in progress, acceded to the President's proposal, so the whole issue was sent to Rome. Rome moved slowly, a blessing in disguise no doubt, for this gave proponents of coeducation—even the modest coeducation Marquette had invented—time to justify a departure from strict Jesuit educational policy dictated by the pressing need for qualified teachers in the rapidly multiplying parish schools. And, moreover, because coeducation stood now as a disputed question over which sincere advocates for one side or the other could disagree, it was possible for Marquette to continue its experiment through the summers of 1910 and 1911, and thus give coeducation the additional strength of an educational practice presently in force. The text of the debates to which the Jesuit General listened before he made a decision may never be fully known; in any case, even without it, we know that the decision, coming in the spring of 1912, was favorable; Marquette was allowed to continue its summer-school plan.[112] But before 1912, and without any document of approbation in hand, President McCabe, once having tested coeducation, appeared to become a convert to it; for apparently without the prior approval of superiors in the Society he brought about an affiliation of the Wisconsin Conservatory of Music to Marquette University.[113] Several Conservatory students were women, so in a highly technical sense they became Marquette students and Marquette became selectively coeducational even for the regular school year.

111 *Ibid.*
112 *Ibid.*
113 *Ibid.*

Whatever Father McCabe's motives, and whether or not his action in committing Marquette to coeducation before the General had spoken was premature, the University was faced now with a new problem : could it grant the Jesuit A. B. to a woman?[114] And this question seemed to have an importance quite irrespective of the course of study—summer session or regular year—which a woman had followed. But now a policy change in another Catholic college occurred—De Paul University in Chicago became fully coeduational in 1914[115]—and Marquette was spared whatever embarrassment it might have felt at being the first Catholic college to promise conferral of its academic degrees on young women.

On the level of policy the major obstacles to coeducation semed markedly smaller in the light of Marquette's and De Paul's modestly progressive plans; yet as a result of their actions no one should be led to suppose that Catholic colleges in general were anxious to become coeducational schools. Both cautious and hesitant, some allowed women to matriculate as part-time, summer-session, or special-program students, whereas others, heeding either the voice of tradition or the practical difficulties of their own campuses, maintained intact all the conventional barricades against the admission of women. This spectrum of different attitudes to coeducation remained a fact of Catholic college life until the end of the period of development, although departments of education, schools of nursing, and special postgraduate and graduate studies—all generated during the later years of this period—stood as constant reminders of legitimate claims women could make on institutions of higher learning. Yet the historian should not argue, nor does he, that every Catholic college for men must, if it is to be true to the best ideals of higher education, embrace policies of coeducation. Nothing in educational history or theory could justify such an arrogant stance, although history does tell us that coeducation entered the Catholic college surreptitiously and, once there, was justified along professional and vocational rather than liberal lines. It tells us, moreover, that the moral issue—a determination to preserve the college from becoming a harem—was always the central and deciding one whenever coeducational policies were debated. And, finally, it tells us that Catholic colleges accepted coeducation in principle, not merely as a useful expedient, and allowed it to work both ways—colleges for men admitting women and colleges for women admitting men—only in the final period of their historical evolution in the United States.[116]

Despite its classical credentials, sport, and more importantly sport for sport's sake, was always given a cool reception in Catholic colleges. Yet, though officially unwelcome, it earned the allegiance of students, and

114 *Ibid.*
115 *De Paul University Catalogue, 1914,* p. 7.
116 Devine, *op. cit.,* pp. 239–244.

necessity being the mother of invention, they found ways to use it happily and effectively for their own ends. There are enough references, among student reminiscences, to the lack of athletic facilities, the proscriptions of the use of playgrounds and gymnasiums, and the danger to good decorum if students were to be allowed to cultivate attitudes of frivolity and play-addicted sloth, to convince us that the colleges were unwilling to befriend sport. [117] If they could not keep students from playing, they could at least ignore their penchant for sport and refuse to recognize it by withholding both time and facilities, and, even when the first college teams were organized, they could adopt an attitude of indifference, if not of actual hostility. There is really no need for detail here. The policies of the old period remained in full force : if boys wanted to play baseball, handball, tennis, or anything else they did so on their own during time carved out from a busy and closely supervised order of the day. They could, in addition and in some colleges only, swim, fish, boat, and hunt when such activities clearly did not interfere with the schedule of college life.[118] For the most part, this indifference to the real genius of sport and the contribution it could make to a decent, liberal education was never revised out of the Catholic college legacy : we look in vain for progressive programs, both varied and vital, among colleges of the developmental period, and when we change our perspective to update it to the period of awakening, we find, reconfirmed and unchanged, this traditional indifference to sport.

Missing the genuine educational values of sport was one thing; exploiting sport for publicity and profit was another. In the long run Catholic colleges were culpable on both counts. But missing the former and capitalizing on the latter could apparently be done without undue sensitivity to the logical contradiction involved; sport encouraged and husbanded for publicity and profit came dangerously close to professionalism, and the most adroit of debaters would have to be nominated to prove that it had any educational significance. Even then such spokesmen could be truly convincing only when they conducted a dialogue for the deaf.

In the last quarter of the nineteenth century, Catholic colleges adopted baseball and made it their representative game, hoping thereby to attract attention to themselves, attention most desperately needed. As we follow this college sport down through the years, we find the colleges living their best athletic moments when their baseball club, with carefully recruited players, could compete with a major league team and come out of the fray with complimentary press notices.[119] Second only to this was the pride felt

[117] David R. Dunigan, *A History of Boston College,* p. 110; and Daley, *op. cit.,* p. 245–246.

[118] Power, *op. cit.,* pp. 136–137.

[119] See F. Wallace, *The Notre Dame Story* (New York, Rinehart, Irwin & Clarke, 1949).

when one of their students went directly from the college diamond to the major league stadium to exhibit his fielding, hitting, or pitching prowess.[120] But these episodes of undiluted joy could not go on forever and in this respect collegiate organization became baseball's worst enemy : Catholic colleges changed their college year, to conform, no doubt, to the calendars of other colleges, and the season when baseball might be played was converted into a long summer-vacation period. In the end, baseball was doomed to the status of a minor sport.

With baseball now obsolete, the colleges, still seeking the rewards an athletically-minded public might bestow, turned to the infant sport of football. During the period between the two great wars—World Wars I and II—football had its heyday in the Catholic college; almost without exception the colleges for men fielded teams of talented players rather than competent students seeking exercise or diversion, and in a few of the colleges whose dedication to football was most intense these players were never asked to distract themselves with class attendance.[121] An accident of history had turned the spotlight of football fame to shine on Notre Dame,[122] and Catholic colleges from coast to coast lived with the great hope that history might somehow be repeated. Their hopes, it should be reported, were sometimes nearly rewarded, for there were enough near misses in this business of grasping for football fame to make the contest seem worthwhile. But in the long run this ardent athleticism did the colleges more harm than good. Apologists for Notre Dame, Fordham, Georgetown, Detroit, St. Mary's, or Santa Clara may argue convincingly that their football era is more to be praised than blamed : [123] it catapulted these schools to national prominence, although their exploits were described by sportswriters rather than educational journalists; it welded together a potentially indifferent group of alumni and motivated them to circle the same tree of support; and, finally, and at long last, it allowed Catholic colleges to rid themselves of the deep feelings of inferiority which had plagued them throughout

---

[120] Durkin, *op. cit.*, pp. 237–244; Faherty, *op. cit.*, pp. 253–256; and Meagher and Grattan, *op. cit.*, pp. 179–184.

[121] Howard Savage, *American College Athletics* (New York, Carnegie Foundation for the Advancement of Teaching, 1929), pp. 13–20.

[122] William F. Cunningham, "The Liberal College," *Journal of Higher Education,* 6 (December, 1935), 254–260.

[123] See M. A. Bealle, *The Georgetown Hoyas: The Story of a Rambunctious Football Team* (Washington, Columbia Publishing Co., 1947), pp. 42–52; Allan P. Farrell, "Catholic Colleges and Public Relations," *Catholic Mind,* 46 (January, 1948), 56–61; "Fordham University; One Hundred Years Old," *Catholic Action,* 23 (October, 1941), 20–21; Richard Sullivan, *Notre Dame* (New York, Henry Holt and Co., 1951); Wilfred Schoenberg, *Gonzaga University: Seventy-Five Years, 1887–1962, passim* (Spokane, Gonzaga University Press, 1963), pp. 348–349; and Angelo *op. cit.*, pp. 91–93.

most of the period of development. They could point with pride to obvious demonstrations of achievement in a highly competitive, vigorous, and often savage contest among men. But the cost of all this was heavy. Failing to recognize their athletic kudos as the small change of academic history, Catholic colleges lived too long with their sporting illusions and allowed the really important sides of their enterprises to mark time while they chased the rainbow of athletic fame. How long this fruitless hunt would have lasted if the colleges had been allowed to follow their own intimations of greatness no one can say, but they were not allowed to follow them—not, at least, with impunity. World War II decimated the male enrollment in all colleges; young men returning from war to continue their college studies were too busy and too intense to follow the usual frivolities of undergraduate life; and, most of all, competition for the entertainment dollar began to leave college football stadiums only partially filled. Football became more popular, it is true, but it also became far more expensive to field a good team, to play the game according to the standards of the professional football leagues. The face of American entertainment had changed and the change left too little room for college football. Only two dozen or so colleges with the most solid football reputations could afford to maintain their pre-war athletic priorities; the others, including dozens of Catholic colleges, either abandoned football as an intercollegiate sport or whittled it down to modest dimensions.[124]

Catholic colleges, however, deeply convinced of the worth of some kind of athletic publicity, and warned away from football by their balance sheets, traded football for basketball.

Throughout the period of development, then, Catholic colleges repeatedly tested the treacherous waters of athleticism and as repeatedly came dangerously close to being swamped; yet this involvement with athletic policy never succeeded in convincing top level Catholic college administrators of the educational significance of the gentlemanly sports. Thus, the picture of college athletics at the end of the period of development was devoid of any marks of sport for sport's sake, and liberal education in its sporting dimensions, despite the kind things Catholic college spokesmen liked to say about the intellectual side of liberal learning, was always sold at discount. In Catholic colleges, according to the established doctrine of the developmental period—yet without any clear evidence that the Carnegie report was influential—sport was strictly for spectators, and so it remained, without any clear indications that this fundamental doctrine was likely to change, as the colleges moved through their period of awakening.

[124] Hunter Guthrie, "No More Football for Us," *Saturday Evening Post,* 224 (October, 1951), 24–25.

Management and hostility

The years corresponding to the Catholic colleges' period of development were, for the nonCatholic colleges of the country, a time for administration-faculty tensions: experience had proved the undoubted worth of the great man at the helm of the academic ship, but colleges and universities were becoming so complex that one-man rule was, of necessity, being diluted by a variety of new administrative officers.[125] If the college president had to countenance some delegation of his monumental authority over college affairs to subordinates—vice-presidents, deans, business managers, and deans of discipline—members of the faculty were no less anxious to erect boundaries around what they considered to be their special domain and to protect it from intrusions by this new breed of college officers. The last half of the nineteenth century introduced to American higher education a variety of administrative prototypes and these models, as the schools matured further, became so deeply embedded in the structure of higher learning that the limitation of their powers, or even their effective control, became virtually impossible. No confidence is violated in labeling the twentieth century the age of administration or in acknowledging that the figure of the professional academic manager became common on college campuses. Perhaps professors' fears had some foundation in fact.

Yet, during most of the period of development, Catholic colleges, as compared with their American counterparts, preferred to remain out of fashion and regularly rejected administrative inflation. Some new officers were no doubt needed and they were carefully, almost reluctantly, added to administrative tables of organization, but other offices were apparently allowed to atrophy. The old college had a president, a vice-president, and a prefect of discipline; the nineteenth-century Catholic college found it possible to do without a vice-president or, if one were appointed, to prune the office of powers to the point of impotence. But it kept the prefect of discipline, who was a master of morals, and quite frequently added a prefect of studies, who in later years, really with the advent of the twentieth century, was entitled dean.[126] It would be wrong, of course, to deny the office of dean to the colleges of the nineteenth century, for in the few schools where professional curricula of law and medicine were established, deans were appointed to superintend these special studies; but

[125] See Paul C. Reinert, *Faculty Tenure in Colleges and Universities from 1900 to 1940* (St. Louis, St. Louis University Press, 1946), pp. 95–127.

[126] Darrell F. X. Finnegan, *The Function of the Academic Dean in American Catholic Higher Education* (Washington, Catholic University of America Press, 1951), pp. 68–69; *St. John's* (Fordham) *College Catalogue, 1881–1882*, pp. 16–18; and *St. Louis University Catalogue, 1878–1879*, p. 8; *1889–1890*, pp. 54–57.

outside professional education the Catholic college dean was a rarity. During the last four decades of the developmental period, however, all this was changed, with deans, department heads, chairmen, or directors, admissions officers, registrars, and business managers making their appearance. Yet, such administrative broadening as did occur was set within the narrow limits of a clerical definition of presidential authority, and administrative evolution was perforce required to pay heed to the reality of vows of obedience. Catholic college presidents continued, as before, to be religious superiors and could therefore face their administrative subordinates and members of the faculty demanding submission to two kinds of authority—religious and educational.[127] Thus, during this entire period, deans, department heads, and other administrative officers occupied unenviable positions and their exercises of authority were always more apparent than real. We must wait for the period of awakening if we want to see fundamental changes in the administrative picture of the Catholic college.

The unwillingness of presidents to allow any erosion of their basic authority could be justified by the most practical of excuses : Catholic colleges, never wealthy and generally without any endowment other than a religious community's endowment of men, had to husband their resources with more than ordinary perspicuity. And since the president could be praised or blamed for a college's success or failure, he was unwilling to allow anyone but himself to make mistakes. We have seen something of the mortality rates among early colleges and we know that even a Catholic college was susceptible to bankruptcy.[128] In one way or another everything a college did was related to fiscal policy and management; little wonder then that presidents wanted to keep a tight rein on every movement of the academic enterprise. When a president examined the financial state of his college, what did he find?

He found, as had his predecessors, that the principal source of college income was the tuition students paid, and he knew, if his college was Jesuit, that he would have no difficulty whatever in obtaining the dispensation made available to Jesuit schools by the papal instruction of January 13, 1833.[129] This dispensation from the Jesuit rule, pertaining to gratuitous teaching, we remember, could be granted if, on the one hand, students refused to attend free schools or, on the other, if schools were unable to support themselves without tuition fees. Catholic colleges outside the Jesuit circle were, of course, always free to charge fees for their instruction, and these fees, which had remained practically unchanged for the half-century before the Civil War, doubled by 1870 and then remained relatively

[127] James J. Maguire, "A Family Affair," *Commonweal*, LXXV (November, 1961), 171–173.

[128] Power, *op. cit.*, pp. 31–35.

[129] G. J. Garraghan, *The Jesuits of the Middle United States*, I, 307–308.

constant until the end of the century; during the next forty years, that is, up to the end of the period of development, they almost doubled again.[130]

Table I[131]

ROOM, BOARD, AND TUITION IN SELECTED CATHOLIC COLLEGES, 1870–1900

COLLEGE	1870	YEAR 1880	1890	1900
Georgetown	$325	$ 50 (b)	(c)	$380
Mt. St. Mary's	300	300	$300	300
Notre Dame	300	300	300	300
Holy Cross	250	200	60 (b)	260
Spring Hill	225	300	90 (b)	65 (b)
St. Louis	250	60 (b)	60 (b)	60 (b)
Villanova	250	250	250	225
Fordham	300	60 (b)	60 (b)	325
Xavier	60 (a)	60 (b)	60 (b)	60 (b)
St. Vincent	180	(c)	(c)	260

(a) day students only   (b) tuition only   (c) no report for the year

Table II[132]

TUITION IN SELECTED NONCATHOLIC COLLEGES, 1870–1900

COLLEGE	1870	YEAR 1880	1890	1900	*
Harvard	$ 25	$150	$150	$150	$350
Yale	90	140	125	155	545
William and Mary	45	40	(b)	35	108
Columbia	100	150	150	150	400
Dartmouth	60	90	(b)	100	450
University of Georgia	60	(a)	(a)	(a)	160
Brown	75	100	100	105	400
University of Michigan	(a)	20	20	30	190
University of Wisconsin	18	(a)	(a)	(a)	350
University of Penn- sylvania	35	150	200	200	450

(*)   college estimate of board, room, and other expenses in 1900
(a)   free tuition for state residents
(b)   no report for the year

[130] *Report of the United States Commissioner of Education, 1870*, pp. 506–516; *1899–1900*, pp. 1924–1943.

[131] Compiled from *Report of the United States Commissioner of Education, 1870*, pp. 506–516; *1881*, pp. 595–606; *1889–1890*, pp. 1600–1609; *1899–1900*, pp. 1924–1943. There were varieties of special charges. At Xavier, for example, instruction in vocal and instrumental music varied from fifty cents a lesson to fifty cents a month. In every case, the teacher was paid directly by the student. *Xavier College Catalogue, 1878–1879*, p. 8.

[132] *Report of the United States Commissioner of Education, 1870*, pp. 506–516; *1899–1900*, pp. 1924–1943.

The preceding tables, showing room, board, and tuition charges in ten Catholic colleges for the years 1870, 1880, 1890, and 1900, and tuition charges only in ten nonCatholic colleges for the same years, illuminate a side of college life where reliable data are hard to find, especially for the years before 1900.

Income from tuition was used to maintain religious faculties, to pay the salaries of lay faculties—and laymen were becoming more common in Catholic colleges—to build and maintain classroom buildings, to purchase books for libraries, and, indeed, to build the libraries themselves, now regarded as essential supplements to college teaching and a public testimony that colleges had reached a stage of academic maturity. With so many calls on their money, it is, indeed, clear why the colleges were always so close to the thin edge of poverty. The total dependance of Catholic colleges on tuition income, one must remember, had clear, although not always sinister, implications for admissions policies. On one hand smaller numbers meant less expense; on the other, diligent efforts to expand enrollments might, at least temporarily, give income a lead over expenditure.

Despite a preoccupation with financial questions which refused to be silenced—and questions rigidly impervious to evolutionary forces, because they refused to go away—Catholic undergraduate colleges had other sides worthy of our attention. In the first years of the developmental period, the Catholic college was a small place with few students and only a handful of teachers; but a broadening of the college course, changes in attitude about the kinds of boys who might profit from higher learning, an insidious orientation to utility curricula which the colleges were incapable of resisting, and the final divorce of college study from predivinity or divinity training, combined to alter the face of Catholic higher learning. With more students studying different courses, the small old-fashioned college faculty was pretty well out of date, so faculties were enlarged by adding religious teachers whenever possible and, when this was impossible, by appointing lay professors. The ground for lay professors had been broken when commercial courses made their first appearance and now it could be cultivated by allowing laymen to teach in a number of academic fields formerly thought to be the special province of the priest-professor. By the end of the period of development, when laymen equaled or outnumbered clerical professors, only two academic departments—theology and philosophy—remained sealed off, normally strictly forbidden to teachers not in holy orders.[133]

Apart from the strange academic mysticism surrounding the departments of philosophy and theology, which seemed to suggest that their teachers needed a brand of inspiration and scholarship supplied only by the sacrament of holy orders, laymen were allowed free range in all other

[133] See Hamilton, *op. cit.*, pp. 273–275.

departments and could now entertain reasonable expectations of following an academic career in a Catholic college. And these expectations might well be fulfilled so long as they were limited to faculty rank; as we review the record of administrative appointments throughout the long period of development, looking for the name of a single layman—except in the professional schools—we look in vain, for there were none. Two hypotheses may be advanced to explain their absence : either laymen were incapable of holding positions of responsibility and trust—but this is hardly convincing when we see how far nonCatholic colleges, both state and private, were able to go depending only on the qualities of leadership with which laymen were endowed—or they were excluded from them by inflexible policies unnecessarily preserved from an archaic clerical tradition. Possibly Catholic academic men were less capable than their Protestant counterparts, and this point may not be entirely void of truth if we are impressed by the evidences of intellectual poverty on most Catholic college campuses, although it is hard to see why this environmental defect should have infected Catholic laymen without any possibility of remission while Catholic clerics were totally immune from it. Clearly such fanciful rationalizations of history lead only to dead ends : laymen in Catholic colleges were excluded from all higher administrative positions, and even from leadership in departments, because the managers of Catholic colleges so decreed. Such decrees, final and not subject to appeal, lay outside the boundaries of permitted debate and effectively attenuated a layman's ambitions.[134] The policy of this period, as the policy of the earlier one had done, described laymen as second-class academic citizens, useful, even necessary, but unloved, and this remained their status until the advent of the period of awakening. What effect the status of academic stepchild had on the scholarly ideals of the lay professor, his energy, efficiency, and dedication in the classroom, or his image before the students he was expected to teach and inspire, can only be a matter of conjecture. Yet the calendar kept moving and better days were over the distant horizon.

Standing between natural enemies—the students—on one side, and religious and academic betters—the clerical fraternity—on the other, lay members of Catholic college faculties were not slow to discover that any discussion of faculty rights, self-imposed responsibilities and duties, dedication to a disinterested scholarship, or academic freedom, during this still bleak developmental period, was an exercise in futility and entirely pointless. On these issues the Catholic college historian should try to be silent, for in discussing them he only makes their state to appear worse than in fact

[134] See John J. Meng, "American Thought: Contributions of Catholic Thought and Thinkers," *National Catholic Education Association Bulletin,* LIII (August, 1956), 113–120.

it was. Still, academic freedom may be singled out and some good things said about it, even in the colleges of this era, although one must recognize that Catholic colleges could be exceptionally generous in allowing scholars conventional freedom because there were so few producing scholars on the faculties and little likelihood that anyone would soon put such policies to a test; besides, no professor wanted to stray outside the boundaries of educational or denominational orthodoxy, due, in part, no doubt, to the provincialism of his own education and his deep determination to remain true to his faith.[135] In the context of academic freedom, then, although it must be admitted that no Catholic college chronicle recounts denials or adumbrations of it, the banners nailed to the Catholic college mast appear unimpressive and colorless.

Why laymen accepted appointments in Catholic colleges of this era, or remained once appointed, is a question for which we have no satisfactory answer. Perhaps they found solace in looking over the academic fence to their confreres in nonCatholic colleges to find that their misery, indeed, had company.[136] Yet, when they looked more closely they identified the one sign of status in nonCatholic college faculty organization which they thought they wanted : this was academic rank. In the old Catholic college either all were professors or none were, and this lack of faculty distinction according to rank had made for some uneasiness, because either for reasons of education, college degree, or teaching experience one teacher or another thought some deference should be accorded him. The introduction of the rank system in the first years of the twentieth century, however, created more problems than it solved and instead of making for harmony between a lay faculty, now beginning to feel its mettle, and a religious faculty, where academic status and clerical privilege were regularly confused, it brought to the surface the old antipathies clerics felt toward laymen invading the academic sanctuary, on the one hand, and sharpened the anti-clerical dispositions of lay professors, on the other.[137] Adopting a rank system appeared to be a progressive move and it put Catholic colleges in step with other good schools of the country, but, in fact, it led to an undeclared war between two factions on the faculty—clerical and lay—who, apart from this issue and the hostility it bred, should have been, considering their fundamental allegiances, enterprising and co-operative co-workers. In the end, however, both the rank system and the hostilities it generated

[135] See Edward B. Rooney, "The Philosophy of Academic Freedom," in Hunter Guthrie and Gerald G. Walsh (eds.), *A Philosophical Symposium on American Catholic Education* (New York, Fordham University Press, 1941), pp. 116–128.

[136] See Nicholas M. Butler, "University Administration in the United States, *Educational Review,* 41 (April, 1911), 342–343.

[137] John J. Kane, "American Catholics and Scholarship," *The Catholic World,* CLXXXII (December, 1955), 166–172.

gained a degree of permanence and fed an undercurrent of divisiveness on Catholic college faculties that may not yet have disappeared.

The trouble started, not with the merit or demerit of rank itself, but with the assignment of rank. In most Catholic colleges which adopted a rank system there were two levels, assistant professor and full professor; in some, three levels of rank, associate professor being added to the two above; in a few, four levels of rank—the three levels above plus that of instructor. Somehow clerical members of the faculty, whether or not their credentials were superior to those of laymen, ended up as professors while most laymen could manage only an assistant professor's rank.[138] Laymen should have perceived rank's lack of real significance, for it carried with it neither academic nor financial emoluments, and they should not have allowed their pique such an impulsive range; yet, umbrage was their only defensive weapon and they used it without discrimination. Being neither wise nor scholarly—and extramural college structures were usually mysteries to them—they missed what was the basic element in their grievance : the college, not being a religious house of studies, a monastery, or a seminary, should have had but one faculty, one set of rules, and one set of standards to be administered to all without regard for any considerations other than academic. But this was not the case and clerical administrators, whether presidents or deans, awarded rank at whim. Alternatively, on the basis of a medieval code which had proscribed laymen from sitting in judgment on clerics, the plan for administering rank directed laymen to seek promotion from committees of clerical administrators, sometimes with a lay faculty representative added, but excused religious members of the faculty from following this route to academic preferment.[139]

Sensing that their fundamental academic rights were being abused in a clerically-dominated college, laymen sought some relief by organizing, clandestinely at first and then in the open, lay faculty associations which were intended to give them a united front for negotiating with the college administration. But these associations were almost totally ineffective except for their success in keeping the black curtain tightly drawn between them and the religious faculty. This, clearly, was the wrong direction to take, either for their own good or the welfare of the college.

Men who think their situation is desperate grasp at almost anything they think will help and with lay faculty associations having time and again proven their sterility, some lay faculties went outside the college walls to seek an affiliation with labor unions.[140] Despite the fact that the social

[138] See John D. Donovan, *The Academic Man in the Catholic College* (New York, Sheed and Ward, 1964), pp. 96–97.

[139] *Ibid.*, p. 183.

[140] Theodore Maynard, "The Lay Faculty Again," *Commonweal*, 22 (May, 1935), 64–66.

encyclicals with their explicit endorsements of labor's right to organize[141] were more or less regularly taught and praised in their classrooms, the colleges, without exception, anathematized these affiliations to trade unions and summarily dismissed the ringleaders from their faculties.[142] Such decisive action kept the rank and file in line and drove home a lesson that lay faculties had taken a long time to learn : laymen on Catholic college faculties were expendable.

Still, laymen were needed in Catholic colleges and, so administrators reasoned, it would be better to have them as friends than enemies. Thus, due either to craftiness or enlightenment, and finding it difficult to maintain a good social image while denying the clear lessons recent papal encyclicals had taught, some Catholic college presidents decided to support and encourage the lay faculty associations and gave them some measure of attention. While it was never easy for these associations to become much more than company unions, they gave laymen a platform for venting their frustrations and occasionally directing appeals to the president. Most of their appeals were non-academic, having to do with salary, tenure, and retirement. The first was outside the pale of negotiation and so it remained, because lay faculties either could not or would not use the critical weapon in collective bargaining—the strike; the colleges were uneasy about the second—tenure—and chose to withhold it until the advent of the period of awakening when, clearly, professors were in a better position to claim tenure and the colleges were in a better position to afford it; the third, retirement income, had to wait until the next period too, and for good reasons. Catholic colleges hardly able to pay the salaries of active members of their faculty could not have been expected to pay retirement benefits as well and for the greater part of the period of development, Catholic colleges, along with most other colleges of the land, had to ignore the issue. No special blame attaches to them for this, but when The Carnegie Foundation for the Advancement of Teaching organized its retirement plan for college teachers in 1905,[143] Catholic colleges were extraordinarily cool toward it. Because of their clear religious control, Catholic colleges were not eligible for membership in the Carnegie plan as it was originally stated,[144] but there is no evidence that they thought it a good plan either with or without their membership. Timothy Brosnahan, S. J., a man we have met before on the elective question, decided once again to speak for Catholic colleges, this time to denounce, on the one hand, the whole Carnegie

---

[141] Leo XIII, *Rerum Novarum,* 1891: and see Currin V. Shields, *Democracy and Catholicism in America* (New York, McGraw-Hill Book Co., 1958), pp. 107–113.

[142] *The Detroit News,* April 5, 1949.

[143] See Henry S. Pritchett, "The Policy of the Carnegie Corporation for the Advancement of Teaching," *Educational Review,* 32 (June, 1906), 83–93.

[144] *Ibid.*

retirement plan, and, on the other, to call into serious question the need for any such thing as retirement for college teachers. College teachers, it appeared to him, should be allowed to manage their own affairs and it would be unfair to put "them in a position of dependency to another body of incorporated presidents, who either directly or through affiliated presidents have the power, even if they should not have the inclination, of keeping them in intellectual and religious subjection."[145] Brosnahan found a bogy man to exploit and he used his best polemical skills to retard retirement plans among Catholic colleges; actually, however, they needed little help in holding the line of inaction on this issue, for, as we have said, retirement plans calling for contributions from both colleges and faculty members were, fiscally, out of the question. The future held better things for Catholic faculties, but the future was a long time in coming; in some colleges, unfortunately, it is still on the way.

Before we leave period-of-development undergraduate colleges and their multiplicity of problems, all part of the painful experience of growing up, a word should be added about two additional sides of college life : methods of teaching and the development of college libraries. We have seen the methods of the old college with its class teacher and at times we were certain we were looking at an elementary schoolmaster at his desk. It is pleasant, indeed, to report that Catholic colleges made steady progress in improving both the quality of their curricula and the quality of their teaching. A good deal of classroom time was still spent in drill and repetition—make haste slowly and leave nothing out was taken to be good pedagogical advice—but once the fundamentals were mastered and the student moved into the newer subjects, the scene much more closely resembled a contemporary classroom. The class teacher was gone; specializing professors handled the studies for which they were equipped either by education or experience; textbook recitations gave way to interpretive lectures; the classroom routine was liberalized and dry-as-dust dictations were replaced by class discussion : all good omens of still better things to come. The most striking methodological innovation, however, occurred in science teaching, where the laboratory technique finally came of age.[146]

Still, students depended heavily on their teachers; docile and submissive, they were disposed to do what they were told and to learn what they were taught. Success and failure were dutifully reported by the professor after

[145] Timothy Brosnahan, "The Carnegie Foundation for the Advancement of Teaching: Its Aims and Tendencies," *The Catholic Education Association Bulletin,* 7 (August, 1911), 22–23.

[146] See Durkin, *op. cit.,* pp. 132–134; Faherty, *op. cit.,* pp. 331–336; and Robert J. Sheehan, "A Brief History of the Development of the Natural Sciences, University of Notre Dame," *Proceedings of the Indiana Academy of Science for 1954,* 64 (1955), 228–233.

he had judged the merit of classroom work and examinations by percentage marking systems : 100 percent was perfect; seventy-five percent was a pass; failure was ascribed to students who scored lower than sixty percent, in some colleges, or fifty percent, in others.[147] Marking systems, however, were always too highly personalized, whatever college regulations may have stated, to give us any information about the generality of scholarly standards. New-fangled objective examinations, while not outlawed, were suspected of being incapable of assessing the kind of achievement that really counted; they were favored much less than the essay examination which, spokesmen said, could penetrate the mere provision of information to test a student's ability to think. Whether this was a correct or an incorrect appraisal of objective examinations makes no matter here, but we should be aware that the essay-type test was accorded pride of place in Catholic college examination procedures.[148]

Few Catholic colleges ever had an overabundance of physical facilities, so during the period of development, as before, they found it necessary to improvise wherever improvisation was remotely possible. They may even have been responsible for the idea of the multi-purpose college building. Classrooms could be converted into dormitories, and vice versa, within a twenty-four hour period; refectories could be used for lecture halls; gymnasiums could be used as chapels; and storerooms could be made to fit the description of libraries. In the old college, we know, neither curricula

---

[147] There were variations, of course, Xavier Colleges used the merit-note system, with 20 merit-notes being the standard for each class exercise. At the end of the term the notes were added and awards were made to the students with the highest totals. (*Xavier College Catalogue, 1879–1880,* p. 7) Loyola College (Baltimore) appealed to parents to inquire about any mark falling below seventy-five. (*Loyola College Catalogue, 1878–1879,* p. 6) Boston College graded memory lessons from 10 down, translations from 20 down, and compositions from 30 down. Monthly averages were published. Mid-term examination results were added to the student's total and thus his performance score for a half-year was ascertained. (*Boston College Catalogue, 1889–1890,* p. 7) Gonzaga College (Spokane) used a 100-point system —not percentages—on which to base its evaluative judgments. (*Gonzaga College Catalogue, 1895–1896,* p. 10).

[148] *St. Ignatius College Catalogue* (Chicago), *1880–1881,* pp. 15–24, carried sample examination questions. Forty theses, all in Latin, were to be defended in logic and metaphysics. Ten questions in English covered the calculus. Forty theses, in Latin, needed defense in moral philosophy. Eight questions in English covered mechanics. The examination terminated with ten questions, in English, on astronomy. At Fordham (*St. John's College Catalogue, 1881–1882,* p. 5) candidates for the B. A. had to pass exams in natural, mental, and moral philosophy, evidences of religion, philosophy of history, and in higher mathematics. While written exams were apparently not demanded in Latin, Greek, and general literature, the student was expected to give evidence of "having attained a specific standard." See also, Durkin, *op. cit.,* pp. 24, 52, 233; LaSalle College, *Student Handbook, 1945–1965;* and Boston College *Catalogues,* 1920–1940.

nor teaching methods dictated library study, search, or research, and the college could thus be absolved from doing much, or anything, about library space or the acquisition of books. Resources could surely not be squandered on a separate library building and books should not be purchased for a faculty or student body who would not read them. Plenty of good reasons could be found for justifying a lack of attention to plainly inadequate library facilities and services.

Shortly before the end of the nineteenth century, however, Catholic college curricula and methods of teaching began to change and these changes, coupled with demands from outside accrediting agencies for library improvement and the setting of standards for adequate college libraries, motivated Catholic colleges, first, to set aside some space in a college building for library purposes—where books could be shelved and students could read and study—and, then, when financial conditions were right, to construct a college library building.[149]

Now, in the 1970s, these old libraries, built sometime in the past one hundred years, are plainly obsolete and only a few colleges continue to use them for their original purpose. Of course, such libraries were built for what were then the colleges' current needs and their obsolesence should not surprise us. What were those needs? Being colleges, not universities, these schools could be content in the beginning with a modest total of books, probably a few thousand, most of which were theological or classical works in Latin; moreover, they could give little attention to the acquisition of new books. Before 1882, in fact, when Notre Dame's President allocated five hundred dollars for the library book budget, Catholic colleges were without any plan or appropriation for keeping their libraries up to date or adding to them.[150] This situation was not quite so bad as it sounds. If students had textbooks and the notes teachers gave them, why should they repair to the library? And considering what books these libraries housed, this question made good sense.

Even when use of a library came to be justified, this justification was limited to course-related reading and study, which should always be done on the library premises and, in the nature of things, had to be done there, for no Catholic college countenanced lending privileges until Notre Dame, again, adopted this innovation in 1873.[151] Trusting learning too little, and

---

[149] Faherty, op. cit., p. 367; Hope, op. cit., pp. 168–169; Durkin, op. cit., pp. 81, 103, 153; Meagher and Grattan, op. cit., p. 209; and Wilfred Parsons, "Notes on the History of Georgetown Library," Catholic Library World, 11 (December, 1939), 67–71.

[150] Hope, op. cit., p. 223.

[151] Ibid. Book borrowing was carefully controlled after its introduction to the Catholic college library. The following regulation stated in the Gonzaga College Catalogue (D. C.), 1889–1890, p. 17, was typical: "Two books may be taken out

erudition not at all, Catholic colleges were careful to discourage students from reading too much or reading too widely : living literature could make no claim on the libraries, and if dangerous books, for some reason or other— possibly for the homework of the polemicist—had to be kept in the library, they were always hidden from student view behind iron gratings and locked doors. Only the librarian himself could enter such rooms and then only to secure a special book for a reader who had petitioned for and received the bishop's approval. Now, on this point, the colleges were only following the clear directives of the Church, and for this they should not be subjected to ridicule. Modifications of the Church's book policy—the *Index of Forbidden Books*—were not seen during the period of development and the colleges, themselves, showed no signs of uneasiness about living with this policy, although in some instances the president sought and obtained from the bishop a delegation of episcopal authority allowing him to grant or withhold approval on written applications to read otherwise forbidden books. Sparingly used by students and faculty (and this pleased the person in charge of the books, because he liked to keep them new), these libraries needed neither full-time librarians nor a library staff. What is more, it was plainly unnecessary to keep them open all hours of the day and night : a few hours a week would do nicely. The college library, then, by no means the worst side of the picture, does the Catholic college of the period of development little credit; yet, on the other hand, if we bear in mind what the colleges were, the libraries were as good as they had to be.[152]

All in all, this period of development, however much it may pain us to read its history, was undoubtedly inevitable in the evolution of Catholic higher learning in the United States. In any case, its history cannot be rewritten.

---

every week : one from the Religious (section), the other from any of the remaining departments; but no more than two may be retained at a time."

[152] Considerable information on library growth can be found in college catalogues. For this book, the following were consulted : *St. Ignatius College Catalogue* (Chicago), *1878–1879*, p. 8; *1889–1890*, p. 24; *1895–1896*, p. 10; *Loyola College Catalogue* (Baltimore), *1889–1890*, p. 3; *1895–1896*, p. 5; *Santa Clara College Catalogue*, *1889–1890*, p. 24; *St. Peter's College Catalogue*, *1889–1890*, p. 5; *Gonzaga College Catalogue* (Spokane), *1895–1896*, p. 6; *Xavier College Catalogue*, *1879–1880*, p. 6; *1889–1890*, p. 8; *St. John's* (Fordham) *College Catalogue*, *1881–1882*, p. 3; *1890–1891*, p. 4; *Creighton College Catalogue*, *1889–1890*, p. 5; *1895–1896*, p. 4; *Boston College Catalogue*, *1895–1896*, p. 11; and *Georgetown College Catalogue*, *1879–1880*, p. 16.

9

Catholic women's colleges

For a country so young, unusual interest was shown in the establishment of colleges during the years separating the Constitution's ratification from the War between the States; yet, while this interest is easily attested, its source, we know, was mainly lodged in denominational convictions which chose to concentrate on the services higher learning could perform for organized religion;[1] and its direction, without exception, was blinkered by an allegiance to traditions concerned only with the education of males.[2] Had this allegiance been restricted to the level of higher education, proponents for women's educational rights might have seen rays of hope, but, as it was, not only the higher but the lower schools, too, were vigorously protected from the invasion of the fair sex. Such attitudes, undoubtedly originating in Europe and transplanted in America, were nurtured in Puritan New England where code and convention stated in clear language that a girl whose rudimentary training allowed her to read the Bible had all the education she needed.[3] A literate woman was rare; girls who essayed to reach the standards of a decent education were rarer still, and the few who reached them had done so by an unremitting application of private effort. Lacking extrinsic motives for study, however, even the natural curiosity of an intelligent girl was dulled by the social environment in which she lived; in the long run, it paid few dividends. Southern ladies, it is true, were expected to have a polite education—one befitting their social station, which was always different from that of the ordinary woman in the North or South—so they repaired to native or European finishing schools to acquire the polish and perception expected.[4] None of this counted

[1] See Donald Tewksbury, *The Founding of American Colleges and Universities Before the Civil War* (New York, Teachers College Press, 1932), pp. 81–83.

[2] Thomas Woody, *History of Women's Education in the United States* (Lancaster, Pa., Science Press, 1929), II, 137–140.

[3] *Ibid.*, I, 129.

[4] I. M. E. Blandin, *History of Higher Education of Women in the South Prior to 1860* (New York, Neale Publishing Co., 1909), pp. 9–15.

for effective education, and even if it had, social status was so much more effective in limiting opportunity that only a handful of persons escaped from the bounds.

Good excuses for the scant heed paid women's education are hard to find, but the best, possibly the only one—which today would be rejected with derision—and undoubtedly the most convincing to an age supremely confident of its fundamental assumptions, ran like this : Neither a woman's nature nor her life's role as wife and mother requires the good offices of formal instruction; in fact, too much education—and too much was probably defined as any—might prove to be either a distraction from or an impediment to the fulfillment of conventional duties. Faced by this imposing principle, speculation about other justifications for the absence of women's colleges from the American scene until nearly the middle of the nineteenth century is a waste of time. Male education in America started at the top, with colleges, and filtered down to lower levels; female education started at the bottom and worked up. And what needed to be done was not accomplished in a day or even in a decade.

Beginnings

Catholic colleges for women took nearly a half-century longer to develop than their nonCatholic counterparts, but this historical datum should occasion no surprise, for, in any perspective, Catholic institutions, being what they were in a country being what it was, were inevitably destined to follow in the historical wake of more initially representative social institutions. Yet, even taking this time-lag at face value, one is bound to see how much ground had been gained : one hundred and fifty years separated the respective founding of Harvard and Georgetown; forty-one years after Elmira Female College was established the College of Notre Dame of Maryland appeared.[5] Thus, any assumption that the Catholic women's college movement, was marking time or countenancing dilatory tactics in the face of clear educational necessity is plainly indefensible. Catholic women's colleges moved swiftly, perhaps too swiftly, to stake their claim in the almost totally uncultivated field of women's higher learning, but neither their good motives, on one hand, nor an undeniable need for higher education for women, on the other, could immunize them against the stark realities, the ever-present difficulties, or the imponderable dilemmas of college life in America. Hard lessons were there to be learned; their studentship was never easy.

[5] Sister Mary David Cameron, *The College of Notre Dame of Maryland* (New York, Macmillan Company, 1947), pp. 35–38.

Education for women in America, as we have said, started at the bottom and worked its way to the top; Catholic women's education used the same ladder. The point of departure was New Orleans where, in 1727, a community of Ursuline Sisters from France, responding to the French Governor's invitation, opened a girls' school and called it the Ursuline Academy of New Orleans. Nine Ursuline nuns, along with one novice and two postulants, conducted this school, for long prominent as an educational center in Louisiana, and offered a course of studies consisting of reading, writing, arithmetic, catechism, sewing, and fine needlework.[6] The careful and dependable Goebel says the Ursuline Academy "may be rightfully regarded as the 'mother school' of Catholic secondary education for girls in the United States."[7]

So beginning in the South, and now following no particular geographic route, although naturally enough staying close to centers where Catholics settled, these elementary and secondary schools for Catholic girls began to multiply across the country. The Visitation Congregation opened a convent school at Georgetown, D. C., which, in 1832, enrolled a hundred girls in an English-speaking curriculum, an innovation for the age, consisting of literature, language and music. As the academy matured, mathematics, philosophy, and chemistry were added, which is proof of the absence of languor among school foundations managed by Catholic religious women.[8] Mother Elizabeth Seton's Sisters of Charity founded St. Joseph's Academy at Emmitsburg, Maryland, in 1810,[9] and the Sisters of Loretto were active in developing secondary education for girls in Kentucky at the same time.[10] Religious of the Sacred Heart, in St. Louis in 1827, opened the Young Ladies Academy and described the following secondary school curriculum in its prospectus:

English and French-Reading, Writing, Grammar, Arithmetic, Sacred and Profane History, Geography, use of the Globe, projection of Maps, Mythology, Poetry, Rhetoric, Natural Philosophy and domestic Economy, Sewing, Marking, Lace,

---

[6] J. A. Burns and Bernard J. Kohlbrenner, *A History of Catholic Education in the United States* (New York, Benziger Bros., 1937), p. 30.

[7] Edmund J. Goebel, *A Study of Catholic Secondary Education During the Colonial Period up to the First Plenary Council of Baltimore, 1852* (New York, Benziger Bros., 1937), p. 32.

[8] Bernard J. Kohlbrenner, "Catholic Girls' Secondary Schools: Their Origin and Formative Years," *Thought*, 10 (September, 1935), 196–210; Marion J. Brunowe, *A Famous Convent School* (New York, The Meany Co., 1897); and Hugh Graham, "A Prospectus for the First Catholic Girls' Academy in Illinois," *Mid-America*, XV (October, 1932), 110–112.

[9] Annabelle Melville, *Elizabeth Bayley Seton, 1774–1821* (New York, Charles Scribner's Sons, 1951), pp. 208–209.

[10] B. J. Webb, *The Centenary of Catholicity in Kentucky* (Louisville, Charles A. Rogers, 1884), pp. 31–43.

Muslin, Tapestry and Bead Work; Painting on Velvet and Satin, drawing, Painting in water colors and crayons; Shell and Chenille work, Artificial Flower making Filigree, Hair work, and crystallized Parlor Ornaments; Music, vocal and instrumental.[11]

This curriculum, evidencing the steady evolution taking place in girls' schools toward a more clearly academic orientation of studies and even bespeaking some imitation of curricula conventional in men's colleges, seems to have been representative of curricula in Catholic schools for women. It demonstrates how difficult it was for such schools to live with the existing tradition of women's education, to offer reasonably respectable studies along elementary and secondary lines, and at the same time to cultivate aspirations for college standing, without succumbing to institutional schizophrenia. Their most obvious failures must be attributed to overambition : they simply tried to be too many things to too many people. With an undisguised seriousness of purpose they tried to combine liberal and domestic studies in the same course, and with a disarming humility took the curricular theory and practice of colleges for men as their models. While their preoccupation with ancient dicta was clear—especially with those telling them why female education on any level should be devoted to equipping a girl for her principal station in life—they were similarly sensitive to the capacity of a woman's mind and the need it has for genuine formation. Although the mixture of rhetoric, for example, and filigree, in the same curriculum, must strike us as anomalous, if not actually contradictory, women's schools were apparently able to live with such mixtures and to capitalize on them. A bold new movement in Catholic women's education, one which threw overboard the conventions which had always recommended domestic training in preference to mental development, would surely have died from lack of support. So, consciously or unconsciously, Catholic schools for women followed the only avenue available to them : making concessions to domestic training and the polite arts in their course of studies, they introduced enough solid learning to make their places respectable schools. And if we wanted to compare the first years of the women's colleges with those of men during their formative period (which is easy enough to do), we should find that the colleges for women do not suffer by such a comparison.[12]

Yet, even in 1870, when Catholic colleges for men were just entering the second period of their evolution in the United States, it was too early

---

[11] See Goebel, *op. cit.*, p. 87.

[12] See Mary B. Syron, *A History of Four Catholic Women's Colleges* (Detroit, University of Detroit, 1956), pp. 16–21; and M. J. Considine, *A Brief Chronological Account of the Catholic Educational Institutions in the Archdiocese of New York* (New York, Benziger Bros., 1894), pp. 18, 23, 31, 54.

to talk seriously about Catholic colleges for women. Huge Catholic immigration in the 1840s had sharpened the priorities of all Catholic agencies commissioned to serve the Church in this missionary land. Schools, we know, received their share of attention, and schools for girls were not neglected. Dioceses became active in education and encouraged parishes to open schools; religious communities for women devoted nearly all their energy to the education of girls; girls' academies appeared on the scene; but almost without exception, at least until the late 1870s, the curricula of these schools were predominantly practical and the "emphasis gravitated towards the purely elementary studies and the arts."[13] Still, two moderate departures from standard practice catch our eye : among the frills of a syllabus for girls we may find the occasional course in Latin, logic, or ethics, and from varieties of teaching methods cull a few techniques which took some account of the educational doctrine of individual differences. In reporting on the work of the infant women's academies in 1834, *The Catholic Almanac* told its readers : "each department [of the academies] is subdivided into classes to suit the capacity, age, and proficiency of the young ladies."[14] And, taking a page from the Jesuits' book of method, Sister-teachers used emulation as a principal device for generating motives to learn. Rewards and prizes were offered to students for extraordinary achievement and their accomplishments were recognized by important men from outside the school. Thus, Archbishop John Hughes' appearance at Mount Saint Vincent-on-the-Hudson to present medals for achievement in domestic science[15] was neither an accident nor an isolated incident; the schools wanted their girls to know how excellence would be rewarded.

One hundred and fifteen Catholic girls' schools—all but three were directed by religious communities—were founded in the years between 1829 and 1852.[16] These schools provided the scholastic foundations for Catholic women's colleges which made their first appearance about a half-century later. With the exception of Trinity College, all early Catholic women's colleges matured from academy foundations and in this respect they differed from the first nonCatholic colleges for women preceding them.[17] This difference should not, however, blind us to the penetrating influence which nonCatholic women's colleges exerted on their Catholic counterparts. Indeed, it ought to surprise us into noticing it particularly, for in taking nonCatholic women's colleges for their model, Catholic colleges

[13] Goebel, *op. cit.,* p. 228; and Sister Margaret Marie Doyle, *The Curricula of the Catholic Women's College* (Notre Dame, Ind., University of Notre Dame, 1932), pp. 13–24.

[14] *The Catholic Almanac,* 1834, p. 97.

[15] See Doyle, *op. cit.,* p. 27.

[16] Power, *op. cit.,* p. 183.

[17] Sister M. Redempta Prose, *The Liberal Arts Ideal in Catholic Colleges for Women* (Washington, Catholic University of America, 1943), pp. 14–16.

for women were reversing an article of educational faith which for more than a century had dominated the thinking of Catholic colleges for men. Colleges for men refused to learn from their academic forbears; colleges for women, however, were anxious to absorb any lessons history could teach. This being the case, it is important that we learn something more about nonCatholic colleges for women, although the full litany of their history need not be recited.[18]

A persistent antipathy for the education of women was almost universal in eighteenth- and nineteenth-century America. Catholic schools had no monopoly of inertia in this respect. NonCatholic educators were equally keen to preserve the *status quo*. Despite these intransigent attitudes toward the education of their sex, however, some women were brave enough to tackle the issue squarely. The names of Emma Willard and Catherine Beecher in particular stand out; both were responsible for introducing trenchant arguments in support of the cause of women's education. Emma Willard stressed the contribution female academies could render to society if they paid less attention to frills and polite accomplishments and concentrated more on educating their students intelligently. Private schools for girls, she averred, should be in the vanguard of the teacher-education movement.[19] Catherine Beecher, in an educational career spanning nearly fifty years, tried her best to promote women's colleges and refused to weaken her educational crusade by attempting to do as much for lower-level schools for girls. Along with her sister, Beecher founded the Hartford Female Seminary in 1828.[20]

The female seminary, however, was not an authentic college and there was hardly anything Miss Beecher could do to make it one; it stands in American college history as a halfway-house between high schools and colleges.[21] Without all the characteristics of the junior college of later years, it nevertheless reminds us of one. But these seminaries contained some prophetic anticipations of women's higher learning, and the better ones —Troy Female Seminary, Adams Female Seminary, and the Ipswich Academy—broke ground for the colleges.[22] They sometimes broke ground for other innovations as well, for Louise Boas, in her account of Wheaton Female Seminary, reminds us of the occasional appearance of a young man as a student in these schools and goes on to add : "[the fact] that

---

[18] Louise S. Boas, *Women's Education Begins* (Norton, Mass., Wheaton College Press, 1935);and Woody, op. cit. Both books explore the history of these colleges in detail.

[19] Eleanor Flexner, *Century of Struggle* (Cambridge, Mass., Harvard University Press, 1959), pp. 24–25.

[20] Catherine E. Beecher, *The True Remedy for the Wrong of Women* (Boston, Phillips, Sampson and Co., 1851), pp. 52–55.

[21] Woody, *op. cit.,* I, 310.

[22] See Anna Brackett (ed.), *Education of American Girls* (New York, G. P. Putnam's Sons, 1874), pp. 203–210.

boys could prepare for college at girls' schools speaks well for the Latinity of the teachers, who were for the most part women."[23] Yet, clearly, if boys were preparing for college in these schools, female seminaries must have been preparatory, not collegiate, institutions. With few exceptions, so they remained.

The first experiments with coeducation—Oberlin College in 1833 (in 1841 Oberlin conferred bachelor's degrees on three women), Antioch College in 1853, the University of Iowa in 1856, and the University of Michigan in 1870 admitted women—tended to blunt the forward thrust of the women's-college movement, but, as it turned out, coeducation was practiced mainly in the Midwest—and even there by no means generally— with the colleges of the East and the South refusing to liberalize their admissions policies and open their doors to girls. The die was cast: if women were to have higher learning, they would have to found their own colleges.

Elmira Female College, probably the first of the real colleges for women, was chartered by the New York State Board of Regents in 1855.[24] With a six-year curriculum, including two years of preparatory study, Elmira offered the bachelor of arts degree; and now, because in this college higher education for women was stripped of its domestic elements, its curriculum could resemble that of a men's college without being a mere replica of it.

Distinctions between the curricula of good colleges for men and the better colleges for women had to be no more than temporary, in any case, for with their varied curricular backgrounds, which could on occasion elicit amusing critical commentaries on their courses and degrees—a newspaper editor had a lot of fun with such degrees as M. P. L. (Mistress of Polite Literature), M. M. (Mistress of Music), M. I. (Mistress of Instruction), M.P.M. (Mistress of Pudding Making), M. D. N. (Mistress of the Darning Needle), M. S. B. (Mistress of the Scrubbing Brush), M. C. S. (Mistress of Common Sense), and M. W. R. F. (Mistress of a Well Regulated Family)[25]—and their preparatory departments (reminiscent of the confusion among earlier men's colleges), women's colleges were forced to mature rapidly if they wanted to maintain an image of educational respectability. Not able to afford the time to determine their own educational direction in the matter of curricula, women's colleges regularly imitated colleges for men. In doing so they were convinced of the trustworthiness of their standards, no minor matter in a competitive educational society. Whether

---

[23] Boas, *op. cit.,* p. 15.

[24] A. J. Brumbaugh, *American Universities and Colleges* (Washington, American Council on Education, 1948), pp. 16–17.

[25] Quoted in Vera M. Butler, *Education as Revealed by New England Newspapers Prior to 1850* (Philadelphia, Temple University, 1935), p. 147.

or not they thought of the curriculum in colleges for men as in any way ideal, schools for women were apparently content to follow it; so we find the classics working their way into the curriculum of women's schools at a time when in men's colleges their status was already in doubt.[26] At Elmira, for example, an elective course in Greek was offered in the junior year.[27]

The founders of women's colleges were, for the most part, and naturally enough, women, for if they themselves procrastinated on the issue of higher learning it would be difficult, indeed, to see why men should carry the fight for them. In a few notable instances, however, the natural patterns of founding were breached and men appear in prominent founding roles : one such was Matthew Vassar who started a college for women in 1861, but his institution had to mark time until the end of the Civil War; by 1865, however, Vassar College had a faculty of about thirty and an enrollment of three hundred and fifty.[28] Vassar's founder had put part of his considerable fortune into the school, expecting that in both curriculum and aim it would be *sui generis*; he meant, of course, that Vassar College should educate girls in the best traditions of literary learning but that in doing so both womanly grace and refinement should be protected and improved.[29] Imitation of men's colleges, in this instance, was not recommended. Knowing what Vassar wanted for his money and his school, we should be interested in finding out what he got : first, treading familiar paths, the school opened a preparatory department, continuing it until 1888, with the specific purpose of giving girls who matriculated the proper foundations for college study. Second, and still within the common precincts of college practice, entrance requirements were set clearly presuming a classical background : students were expected to know Latin grammar and syntax, two orations of Cicero, two books of Caesar, a little French, and some other generally-stated literary skills. Third, the curriculum was divided into two parts, one classical, the other scientific. Although the scientific course was seldom praised for its quality, Vassar's classical course had a good reputation and was often considered the equal of similar courses offered in good colleges for men. Arnold's *Prose Composition,* six books of the *Iliad,* Plato's *Phaedon,* and selections from Livy, Cicero, Horace, and Tacitus were staples in the syllabus.[30] So, in the end, despite Vassar's determination to have a school course designed especially for women, his high ambitions were redirected and the college became a carbon copy of conventional higher learning.

[26] Mabel Newcomer, *A Century of Higher Education for American Women* (New York, Harper and Row, Publishers, 1959), pp. 50–51.

[27] Robert Fletcher, *The Beginnings of College Education for Women and of Coeducation on the College Level* (Oberlin, Ohio, Oberlin College Press, 1937), p. 41.

[28] Woody, *op. cit.,* II, 181.

[29] Boas, *op. cit.,* p. 243.

[30] Woody, *op. cit.,* II, 181–182.

Smith College, founded in 1875, with its three curricula—classical, literary, and scientific—evidently shared Vassar's original expectations of a distinctive education for women, but succeeded only in duplicating, both in entrance requirements and curricula, the men's colleges of New England.[31]

Before a quarter-century had passed—from Elmira's founding to the origin of Wellesley College—colleges for women had relinquished their fond hopes of being different and toned down their promises to offer a kind of higher learning tailored to a woman's special needs. No doubt the continued existence of these needs could have been proved; no doubt, too, the colleges, if they had persisted, could have done something to satisfy them; but in terms of public support the battle appeared futile and common sense dictated capitulation to the educational prescription signed and sealed by men's colleges. Meeting educational reality face to face, Wellesley College, using its founder Henry Fowle Durant as spokesman, announced an ambition to "offer to young women opportunities for education equivalent to those usually provided in colleges for young men. The institution will be Christian in its influence, discipline, and course of instruction."[32] At last, the shibboleth for a higher learning of supreme quality was acknowledged to be the over-all curriculum of colleges for men; and this admission both allowed colleges for women to forget many of their old convictions about special courses and permitted them the luxury of singlemindedness as they moved forward in history to make their mark on higher education. Yet, Wellesley, in admitting the worth of the curriculum of men's colleges and willingly adopting it, was not preaching any abandonment of the women's college movement. Only women were to be appointed to the faculty; only girls were admitted as students; the unchallengedly feminine atmosphere of the school was seen as the means to womanly taste, refinement, and character, whereas only a few short years before such femininity had been defined solely in terms of divergent objectives.[33]

Perhaps these colleges were eminently successful in creating a climate wherein female virtues could be inculcated and enhanced, for this is a point where, if proof is possible, it is hard to find. But in another aspect of college life—the establishment of an exclusively female faculty—they appeared to be asking for trouble. Their determination to salvage something from crushed hopes is understandable, although their belief that this salvaging might be done by means of an exclusive faculty is not entirely praiseworthy. By 1875 the handful of women's higher schools of a half-century earlier had expanded to two hundred and nine,[34] although hardly

[31] Boas, *op. cit.*, p. 247.

[32] Alice Hackett, *Wellesley: Part of the American Story* (New York, E. P. Dutton, 1949), p. 39.

[33] *Ibid.*, pp. 40–41.

[34] Woody, *op. cit.*, II, 185.

more than a dozen were authentic colleges. Yet all these schools needed teachers and, if the teachers were to be women, where were the schools to find them? Some, of course, came from graduating classes in the older women's colleges and some from the coeducational colleges of the Middle-west; but all too often others came without any legitimate college background at all.[35] Women's colleges, then, were in the extraordinarily uncomfortable position of trying to improve their image, and of seeking to maintain a reasonable equivalence with colleges for men, with faculties strong in missionary zeal for women's emancipation but weak in the usual implements of scholarship and lacking in the ordinary academic qualifications.

Recognizing their weaknesses, on the one hand, does not absolve us from forthrightly acknowledging their strengths, on the other; and women's colleges had as many of the latter as they had of the former. Beginning by eschewing professional or vocational curricula and for a long time steering clear of a field where well-educated women could have made a highly significant contribution—that of teacher education—colleges for women concentrated on mental discipline, general culture, moral values, and religious virtue.[36] In all, they performed well enough to distinguish themselves clearly from female academies and seminaries, institutions of the educational level from which they themselves had climbed, and to disabuse a college-bound female population of the notion that their only route to educational salvation lay in becoming co-eds in a male institution. After all, they were now chartered, degree-granting institutions; their students, having met the stiffer entrance requirements of classical preparatory courses, were mature young women in search of a higher culture; their curricula, whether classical, scientific, or literary, were respectable facsimiles of those in good colleges for men; and innovations adopted in men's colleges in the name of better education or higher standards were speedily incorporated into their own educational code. This was the first stage in women's higher learning and it formed a fairly stable foundation on which Catholic colleges for women could build.

Progress

We have noted the singlemindedness of nonCatholic colleges for women : resolutely they rejected professionalism and vocationalism to keep to the strict and narrow line of liberal learning. Although, admittedly, their success in remaining true to the grand ideal was usually marred by falls

[35] Newcomer, *op. cit.*, p. 19.

[36] Quida (pseud.), "The New Woman," *North American Review,* CLVIII (May, 1894), 614; and Woody, *op. cit.,* II, 138.

from this high norm, on the level of policy they refused to equivocate or to admit that they should be regarded as service institutions either for lower schools or for family life. Catholic colleges for women, however, right from their beginnings, were deprived of the luxury of even hoping for a precise, single purpose; instead they were faced with the extraordinarily difficult task of trying to educate women along liberal lines and at the same time to fit them for service to the Church as teachers in the schools prescribed by the Third Plenary Council of 1884. Other colleges for women were often denominational schools and, it may be assumed, their educational efforts were intended to serve broadly-defined religious objectives; but they were never, as were Catholic women's colleges, regarded as servants of the Church, on the one hand, and training schools for the education of parochial school teachers, on the other. Liberal ideals were almost bound to suffer under the heavy strain of such a commission.

The period of delay between the pronouncements of the Third Plenary Council and the founding of the first Catholic college for women in 1896—the College of Notre Dame of Maryland[37]—meant that most Catholic elementary school teachers were conducting schools without any of the benefits higher learning might bestow. But criticism at this point should be moderated by the knowledge that most elementary schools in the United States were in the hands of teachers whose learning was similarly limited. Still, it is extremely hard to believe that Catholic teachers as poorly prepared as were the vast majority could apply pedagogic practices new to them without some considerable loss of the educational impact hoped for. With their usual hesitation about trying anything new, Catholic colleges for men ignored the whole matter of teacher education and chose to pretend that the legislation of 1884 was unreal. Twenty-five years later they still found it difficult to see where they had any legitimate responsibility even for extension, part-time, or summer school teacher preparation:[38] we have already seen how the summer-session idea at Marquette was opposed in 1909.[39] Girls' schools were more active and, to their credit, saw more clearly where the great pedagogical imperatives lay; but, not being colleges, these Catholic academies and female seminaries could accomplish only a small part of the titanic work before them. Despite the argument of clear necessity, the first Catholic women's colleges were accepted into the circle of Catholic higher learning reluctantly and their role in teacher education

[37] Cameron, op. cit., p. 56.

[38] See John L. Spalding, "Normal Schools for Catholics," The Catholic World, 51 (April, 1890), 78–87; Isidore J. Semper, "The Church and Higher Education of Girls," Catholic Educational Review, 29 (April, 1931), 215–225; and Sylvester Schmitz, The Adjustment of Teacher Training to Modern Educational Needs (Atchison, Ka., The Abbey Student Press, 1927).

[39] R. N. Hamilton, The Story of Marquette University (Milwaukee, Marquette University Press, 1953), pp. 120–130.

was seldom perceived or appreciated outside the walls of the women's colleges themselves.

The best justifications for Catholic higher education for women, then, are to be found within the context of teacher preparation, and whether the women's colleges liked it or not, and frequently they did not, they had to accept educational realities which tolerated, rather than emphasized, the liberal aspects of the curriculum of a woman's college.

With these insights into the fundamental questions of the motivation for and the founding of Catholic women's colleges, we are able to move on to some of the early institutions themselves and observe the pace of their historical evolution. The College of Notre Dame of Maryland, founded in 1896, as we have said, was the first, to be followed in quick succession by the College of St. Elizabeth, Convent Station, New Jersey; Trinity College, Washington, D. C.; St. Joseph's College, Emmitsburg, Maryland; and the College of New Rochelle (originally named the College of St. Angela); all these were founded before 1905.[40] Fourteen additional Catholic colleges for women were founded in the decade after 1905; thirty-seven between 1915 and 1925; and nineteen between 1925 and 1930. In 1955, one hundred and sixteen Catholic colleges for women were operating in the United States and in 1970 Catholic higher learning for women was represented by the even larger total of one hundred and thirty-seven.

The formative period for Catholic women's colleges, if we date the formative period from the founding of the first college, was only about twenty years in duration, although if we consider the academy years as foundational years for these first colleges, we should have to take a somewhat longer view. Perhaps the longer view, irrespective of historical niceties, is the more satisfying, so without engaging in overmuch detail we shall try to follow the evolution of ground-breaking institutions from their academy beginnings to a time when their place as colleges was both recognized and secure. Time and the absence, in these first women's colleges, of any sufficient sense of making history, have obliterated a great deal and left the records incomplete. This is something outside the boundaries of our control; the historian can no more than do his best to keep the record fair and accurate.

Where Catholic colleges for men were in the habit of launching their infant educational enterprise by using the imposing title of college in the institution's name, schools for women, whatever their institutional expectations may have been, were always more humble in their public utterances. And while it was often difficult to distinguish secondary and college features in the early men's schools, a difficulty complicated further by the theoretical affirmation that higher learning really encompassed seven years, the issue

[40] Edward J. Power, *A History of Catholic Higher Education in the United States* (Milwaukee, Bruce Publishing Co., 1958), p. 183.

of definition among early Catholic women's schools seldom arises: they began as secondary schools and remained so for a long time without introducing any truly advanced subjects to their curricula. The College of Notre Dame of Maryland is a good illustration of a school staying within what appeared to be comfortable pedagogic boundaries; in an early prospectus—Notre Dame started as an institute in 1863, with six boarders and twenty day students[41]—the school accepted a commission "to develop the mental, moral and physical powers of the pupils; to make them refined, accomplished and useful members of society."[42] Reaffirming and expanding the terms of these objectives, "The Prospectus and Catalogue of St. Joseph's Academy for Young Ladies," (later St. Joseph's College) stated in its 1875–1876 edition:

The Sisters who conduct the establishment consider themselves conscientiously bound to respond to the confidence which parents and guardians place in them, by giving their pupils a christian and virtuous education, strictly attending to their intellectual development, cultivating that refinement of manners which will fit them for society, and giving them that physical care which they would receive under the parental roof.[43]

These were objectives appropriate for academies but, as we shall see at once, women's schools could mature to collegiate rank without altering the main balance of their generally-stated purposes. Thus, the College of New Rochelle, in its catalogue of 1911–1913, was able to retain and develop the traditional aims of Catholic female education and apply them specifically to higher learning:

[At this college, women's higher education] means such stimulation and promotion of the physical, intellectual, and moral growth and development, as shall result in complete womanhood. The college ideal of its graduates is that of a woman of culture, of efficiency and of power—a woman capable of upholding the noblest ideals of the home and of the Church, and possessed of the training that shall make her an efficient worker in society and in the professional world.[44]

And at Trinity College, where there had been no academy years to blur purposes or impose institutional traditions, because Trinity began as a college, the prospectus was able to promise an

embrace of all the branches taught in the best colleges of the same grade, for women, with the addition of the science of Religion, Domestic Economy, and

[41] *Ibid.*, p. 184.
[42] *Catalogue of Notre Dame of Maryland, 1876,* p. 4.
[43] *Catalogue of St. Joseph's College, 1902–1903,* p. 41.
[44] *Catalogue of St. Angela's College, 1906–1908,* p. 7.

other branches deemed useful in fitting a woman for her proper sphere in the Home and Society. Together with science and religion—knowledge and love of God—love of country will be instilled; a laudable pride in its glorious history and fidelity to its Constitution and laws inculcated at all times.[45]

Statements of purpose, then, will not teach us much about the changes taking place in Catholic women's schools, so we must look elsewhere for signs of revision and maturity. When we do, we come face to face with curricula. But before these schools, during their academy years, said anything about courses of study, they wanted their public to know something about the physical attractions and the creature comforts of the place. So doing what colleges for men had done before them, they described their surroundings, and we can turn to the 1876 prospectus of Notre Dame of Maryland for an illustration :

[The building is] constructed and furnished with every accessory and appointment for comfort, convenience and safety. It is thoroughly ventilated, well heated by hot water, lighted by gas, and each story is provided with excellent spring water, speaking tubes, electric bells and clocks. As security against fire, there are two fire plugs in each story with hose attached; to call assistance at any moment of danger, an electric alarm has been placed in the tower.[46]

Having received assurances about the physical well-being of their daughters, parents were then told what the girls would study. Apparently by way of a concession to polite education, modern foreign languages were given some prominence in the curriculum; French and German were given special notice as vehicles of refinement, and the proud claim was repeated —it had been made first by colleges for men—that the teachers of these languages were teaching their native tongue.[47] The prospectus, moreover, promised degrees to qualified students. We should be careful, however, about accepting these degrees as being representative of college accomplishment. The schools themselves did not intend to imply that they were college degrees, but only awards, such as Minor Mistress of English Literature —bestowed on students who had taken a regular course in English, along with three years' study of one foreign language—or Major Mistress of English Literature—given to students who, in addition to the English course, had pursued the study of two foreign languages for three years. The speaking of foreign languages was prized too and appropriately rewarded by the invention of still further "degrees" : a student capable of the fluent use of one foreign language, bolstered, of course, by estimable accomplishments in the regular curriculum, was dubbed a Minor Mistress

45 *Prospectus of Trinity College, 1899,* p. 8.
46 *Catalogue of Notre Dame of Maryland,* 1878, p. 4.
47 *Ibid.,* p. 5.

of Liberal Arts; the "degree" of Major Mistress of Liberal Arts demanded fluency in two foreign languages.[48]

Two years later, in 1878, this academy took another step in the direction of higher learning by adding to its curriculum a subject which for four hundred years held pride of place in all Western colleges and universities : "a short course of Latin is introduced merely to give the pupil an idea of the construction of the language, how it compares with the modern languages, etc., to which the school gives more attention. . . . If a pupil prefers a more extensive course in Latin, instead of French or German, she will receive private instruction."[49] The classics were catching the attention of the managers of these schools, and hopes of engaging regular teachers in Latin were bright; but the Sisters were not entirely blinded by the brilliance of this possibility. Indeed, they had other developments in mind. They promised, by means of more or less regular lectures delivered by professors from nearby Johns Hopkins University and the University of Maryland, to teach chemistry, literature, natural philosophy, and history. Latin lingered in a curricular limbo until 1885, when it was able to displace modern foreign languages; by 1895, a year before the school achieved full college status, Latin study was required of all students.[50] It may be possible, then, to see the evolution of women's schools from academy standing to collegiate status by paying particular attention to the position which the study of Latin occupied in their curricula. The more visible Latin became, the closer the school was to the level of higher education.

The general tendency among Catholic women's academies aiming at college standing was to establish their new status by making a quick, sharp break with their past. Yet there were enough exceptions to this general pattern of development to arouse our interest in women's schools where academy and college curricula were mixed. St. Joseph's College prospectuses may here offer us some inside information. In 1875 the academy's curriculum was publicly set out and this curriculum was apparently considered to be entirely adequate, for it remained basically unchanged until the school adopted a clear college program. This is what the prospectus of 1875 had to say :

The Course of Instruction in this Academy embraces Orthography, Reading, Grammar, Rhetoric, Prose and Poetic Composition, Plain and Ornamental Writing, Practical and Rational Arithmetic, Book-keeping, Principles of Algebra and Geometry; Ancient and Modern Geography, with the use of Globes; Astronomy; Sacred and Profane History, Biography and Mythology; Logic; Moral and Natural philosophy; Chemistry; Botany; Mineralogy; Conchology, Latin, French, Spanish, Italian and German Languages; Music on the Piano, Harp and Guitar, Vocal

[48] *Ibid.,* pp. 4–5.
[49] *Ibid.,* p. 8.
[50] *Catalogue of Notre Dame of Maryland, 1895,* p. 11.

Music, Drawings; Painting in Water Colors and Oil; Plain and Ornamental Needlework.[51]

To this rather full course of study, which no student was expected to complete in its entirety—a fact which made some kind of election inevitable—the following five years witnessed the addition of metaphysics, logic, and ethics. The school had not yet, however, accepted the full embrace of liberal learning and perhaps stilled some apprehensions that its curricula were moving away too far from the practical and useful with the following statement: "the branch of Domestic Economy receives due attention in the young ladies' course of study."[52] If the phrase domestic economy sounded stilted and formal, the catalogue was quick to admit that among the many acquirements of this course was "learning how to prepare a cup of coffee."[53] No doubt the school thought domestic science important and worthy of the notice it was accorded, but young women who were beginning to think about being useful outside the home could, after 1890, find something else in the curriculum too. Calisthenics, stenography, and typewriting were appended to an already long list of subjects.[54]

Yet all this was intended for the high school student; something more had to be added if the gap between academy and college was to be bridged. At St. Joseph's, in 1880, this was accomplished by creating a postgraduate course, anticipating by twenty-two years a regular college program, wherein students were allowed to "devote their time to a more thorough course of Reading and Belles Lettres, or to pursue some specialty in the Musical or Arts Department with the view of attaining perfection."[55] This postgraduate course, open to students either from the academy itself or from other high schools, waited another decade before achieving independent standing at St. Joseph's, when it was separated from high-school study and organized as a formal two-year curriculum. The first year of the two-year postgraduate course engaged students in classical literature, conic sections, differential calculus, history, mental philosophy, higher chemistry and physics, Latin, German or French, and Greek. The second year was even more imposing: comparative literature, differential and integral calculus, biology, history of education, Latin, Greek, French or German were all separate subjects. In the classical syllabus the works of Livy, Horace, Cicero, and Persius were studied; prose composition was part of the Latin and Greek courses; and of the latter the writings of Demosthenes, Sophocles, Euripides, and Homer were firmly part.[56] Without college status and also

---

51 *Catalogue of St. Joseph's College, 1875–1876,* p. 6.
52 *Ibid., 1880–1881,* p. 3.
53 *Ibid.*
54 *Ibid., 1890–1891,* p. 6.
55 *Ibid., 1880–1881,* p. 5.
56 *Ibid., 1899–1900,* pp. 15–16.

without any legitimate legal authorization to grant degrees, St. Joseph's awarded both A. B. and A. M. degrees,[57] although the meaning of each degree and the differences between them are now unclear.

Without the persistent traditions which had lived for about a century in men's colleges, Catholic colleges for women were able to escape from their mixed high school-college years freer from anxieties about rejecting their past than was true of their male counterparts. Never being fully committed to the seven-year college program, which perforce included preparatory studies, and being less dogmatic about the true avenues to a generally-acknowledged higher learning, they could lay aside their high school and academy involvements, without forgetting them completely, in order zealously and vigorously to exploit their new opportunities in higher education. At the same time, being absolved from the burden of a fairly full classical syllabus, they could seriously consider the newer subjects which in the last years of the nineteenth century were claiming places in college curricula, and moreover, give a friendly welcome to varieties of vocational and liberal curricula just coming over the horizon. With more courses in the curriculum, women's colleges found the departmentalization of subjects appealing and began by accepting departmental organization, specializing teachers, and greater specialization for students,[58] where their male counterparts impulsively rejected such innovations until, in order to maintain respectability, they were forced to accept them. Only with one subject—religion—did colleges for women find it imperative to live in the past : girls' high schools had always had religion courses, so Catholic women's colleges followed the academy precedent here and without a single exception installed religious study in the curriculum and made it mandatory for all Catholic girls.[59]

Appearing on the scene of American higher learning after accrediting associations were established as academic watchdogs and, also, after criteria for college admission were stabilized, Catholic women's colleges were spared the agonies suffered by their brother institutions of first stating and then refining their admissions procedures. Women's schools, once reaching college level, could simply accept what by then were fairly conventional admissions criteria and assume that their students were reasonably well prepared to master the curriculum put before them. Still, Catholic women's colleges, displaying some lack of confidence in certificates issued by the College Entrance Examination Board, and even in high school and academy transcripts, were prepared to supplement either or both with local written examinations covering English, Latin, a modern foreign language,

[57] *Ibid.,* p. 6.
[58] Doyle, *op. cit.,* pp. 101–122.
[59] *Ibid.*

mathematics, history, and science.[60] For the most part, however, entrance requirements were never burning issues in the history of these colleges, so dwelling on them now would be profitless.

Catholic women's colleges, founded, chartered, and fully populated, had to fix their instructional compasses. The academic lives of institutions of their own kind had been short, so traditions were seldom available for exploitation or guidance; yet guidance was much needed and they took as their best models the curricula both of Catholic colleges for men and of nonCatholic colleges for women. Both were worth study; neither merited slavish imitation. Although Catholic women's colleges must have been tempted simply to borrow all the curricular practices of Catholic colleges for men, because these practices appeared to have the blessing of a Catholic way in higher learning, their good common sense prevented them from making such a grave mistake; and they never seriously considered themselves to be mere replicas of nonCatholic colleges for women, if for no other reason than that their denominational orthodoxy ruled out that alternative. Still, they could borrow without copying, and, in the end, they did. Catholic colleges for men were caught in a curricular ferment toward the end of the nineteenth century, so what was praiseworthy and what was not, what should be followed and what discarded, was far from clear. Yet Catholic women's colleges, despite disturbing uncertainties that they were always on the right instructional track, took from colleges for men the spirit of service to the Church and to the Catholic community at large; from non-Catholic women's colleges they borrowed the ideals of the kind of liberal learning best suited to a woman's nature. In cold type, however, curricula of Catholic women's colleges rarely reflected this meld, and we shall have to look elsewhere to discover their distinctive features.

Early Catholic women's colleges adopted curricular statements which, as we read them now, have a routine, conventional sound. The College of Notre Dame, for example, in its first announcement of a four-year college course, described three curricula—regular (a combination of classical study and domestic economy), literary, and scientific—leading to the bachelor of arts, literature, or science degrees respectively.[61] At the College of New Rochelle, we see sharper signs of feminism in a course for college students described as liberal and centered on literary and linguistic studies. A four-year requirement of English study was, at once, an obvious rejection of pedagogic belief in the supremacy of classical studies and clear evidence of a determination to be educationally up-to-date. And the English course had intellectual meat: first-year English consisted of advanced rhetoric, history of the language, and history of literature; drama belonged to the second year; advanced composition and poetics to the third; and in the fourth

[60] Power, *op. cit.*, p. 190.
[61] *Catalogue of Notre Dame of Maryland, 1895–1896*, p. 3.

year advanced rhetoric earned another look, together with a course in American literature. Departments of English, languages, mathematics history, economics, and domestic economy were in evidence, but subjects without affinity to these departments were available too : education, chemistry, biology, and astronomy.

In the College of New Rochelle's literature special notice was given to the department of domestic economy where, in addition to a conventional general course, special courses were offered in elementary cooking, fancy and invalid cooking, general sewing, and laundry work. Laundry work was recommended as a "good, practical course in the washing and ironing of plain and starched pieces; the doing of fine laces; the removal of stains." [62]

Trinity College, accepting what appears now to be a proper division of curricula, offered three college programs of study—classical, scientific, literary—each four years in length, leading to one degree, that of bachelor of philosophy. The pride of place assigned to the degree of bachelor of arts and confirmed by decades of academic tradition was thereby shaken. Shaken, too, was the old assumption that a college degree could be reached by only one curricular route : Trinity College referred to the possibility of students taking elective courses and hesitatingly recommended a five-year program for its girls. But whether the college course was to be four or five years really made no difference to basic policy, for at Trinity "the system of instruction . . . is partly the once universal college method and partly the elective method." [63] Without endowing the elective method with singular virtue, the managers of Trinity could, nevertheless, see its pragmatic worth, and they found no insurmountable problem in organizing curricula enabling students to study required courses (the once universal college method) and concurrently enrolling for other subjects as well. [64]

St. Mary's College, Notre Dame, Indiana, liberalized both curricula and degrees in Catholic women's colleges even more when, in 1905, a plan was announced offering bachelor of arts degrees for the study of classics or English, bachelor of science degrees for general science or botany, bachelor of philosophy degrees for history or political science, and bachelor of literature degrees for studies in literature. [65]

The multiplication of degrees, although this alone may not have changed the essential thrust of the curriculum, called into question two of the basic tenets of traditional liberal learning, namely, that only one route leads to the bachelor's degree and that only one kind of bachelor's degree —the one in arts—counts. While no evidence extant suggests a conspiracy among Catholic colleges for women to undermine the bachelor of arts

[62] *Catalogue of St. Angela's College, 1906–1908,* p. 35.
[63] *Prospectus of Trinity College, 1899,* p. 14.
[64] *Catalogue of Trinity College, 1901–1902,* p. 20.
[65] *Catalogue of St. Mary's College, 1905–1906,* p. 8.

degree or the traditional classical curriculum, these colleges obviously recognized American higher learning's new face and plainly understood the need for rethinking old assumptions. Waiting for the articulation of a new theory of liberal learning—one taking into account almost half a millenium of intellectual progress—and without any clear directives to follow other than traditional justifications for the classical course, which could no longer be taken at full face value, Catholic women's colleges were guided by a code of pragmatism. They offered the courses, the curricula, and the degrees recommended by their own educational experience. This did not lead to a rejection of the classics, nor did it demand either attacks on or defenses for the classical course. So we find Catholic women's colleges entering the twentieth century without any of the polemical bitterness which had characterized Catholic men's colleges for the past half century. Still, although they may perhaps be praised for eschewing an educational controversy in which they were poorly practiced, their fundamental pragmatism left them open to some academic dangers. Being, in effect, liberal, vocational, professional, domestic, and artistic in their educational aims, they accepted more academic responsibility than they were prepared to handle.

They paid lip service to liberal learning, for they knew of the Catholic colleges' long record of friendship toward any course wherein knowing had precedence over doing, and, moreover, they had no wish to betray a century's devotion to the classics evidenced in the history of Catholic men's colleges; yet they found the strict classical course plainly unacceptable as an educational instrument for their girls. The curricula were built which gave the classics their due and, as we have already said, Latin study was always taken as a sign of a school's attainment of collegiate rank; but neither classical languages nor classical literature were allowed to dominate the course. No doubt the cultural doctrine affirming that the classics contained everything most worth knowing was still in force, and the managers of Catholic women's colleges wanted to honor it as best they could; but, for the most part, they themselves were not classically educated and were hardly the best advocates for a scholastic plan whose real genius they only faintly perceived. In the end, then, whatever their educational instincts may have recommended, they were incapable of endorsing the doctrine fully. But a coolness toward the classics, along with some equivocation about the cultural doctrines supporting them as educational means, was a poor substitute for a theory of higher learning. What alternatives were open? It is probably true that, neither forming a theory of their own nor borrowing one from extant systems of higher education, Catholic women's colleges marched into the twentieth century intuitively confident of the good they could do in the education of women, yet plagued by uncertainties about the principal focus their academic endeavor should provide. Without the benefits of precise theory, most Catholic women's colleges turned out to be what the exigencies of their location, on the one hand, and their students, on the other, prescribed for them. Fate, sometimes friendly, allowed a few Catholic women's colleges to become highly effective institutions. For others, if we read the historical record correctly, it remained fickle and withheld both distinction and effectiveness.

These ambiguities and uncertainties affected other issues as well. Electivism, we know, fell on fallow curricular fields in Catholic colleges for men, and, apart from Brosnahan's spirited defense of a required curriculum and his similarly strong condemnation of elective systems, earned very little notice.[66] Yet, neither colleges for men nor women were immune from some of the more reasonable claims advanced by spokesmen for election, and subsequently, even in the face of indifference to the need for change and of strong protests about the evils in modern education, electivism of a modest type became a fact of Catholic college life. Colleges for women, less adamant that colleges for men—possibly thinking their gamble a smaller one—adopted a watered-down elective plan. Of course, some studies were always required, but it was a rare college for women which refused to allow its students some choice of subjects in their total course of study. Yet, even while countenancing choice for their own students, the official stance opposed electivism.[67] Of one thing the historian of Catholic women's colleges can be fairly certain : whatever they did for or against electivism, their influence on the broad elective struggle taking place in later nineteenth-century American higher education was of no great consequence.

All, or most, Catholic colleges had had some preparatory links to the long college course or to what they called academical departments, so the fact that Catholic colleges for women grew from earlier high schools should not be used against them. These lower school relationships were brief in the case of Catholic women's colleges and, for the most part, the schools were anxious to get rid of them in order to advance more quickly their ambitious plans for higher study. Yet, in a few instances, while the college course was embryonic and still not quite independent, the schools tried to maintain a general purpose curriculum—high school and post-graduate—from which an enterprising girl could obtain either a bachelor's or a master's degree. We have earlier confessed an inability to ascertain the differences, if any, in requirements for the two degrees, but this question can be ignored, for we are less interested in the original postgraduate course, attached to the high school, than in the later postgraduate course, added to the college curriculum. Catholic girls' colleges, struggling with

[66] Syron, *op. cit.*, p. 89; and Doyle, *op. cit.*, pp. 82–125.

[67] *Ibid.*, and Sister M. Mariella Bowler, *A History of Catholic Colleges for Women in the United States of America* (Washington, Catholic University of America Press, 1933), pp. 113–114.

four-year college standards, avoided involvement with graduate-level studies for the first quarter-century of their American experience, but the time came quickly—too quickly in some colleges—when the need for or desirability of advanced degrees for educated women became clearer. If Catholic women's colleges wanted to be complete educational institutions, they too would have to embark on postgraduate and graduate education. The list of schools which did so embark is long, for most Catholic women's colleges organized postgraduate departments, in anticipation of later development into graduate schools, within two or three decades after achieving full collegiate standing. Only the extraordinary Catholic girls' college, or one with extremely limited resources, turned a deaf ear to recommendations for an upward extension of its program.

Some colleges opened nondegree-granting postgraduate departments, but this tactic was abandoned after a short time because without the promise of a degree students would find postgraduate study strikingly unattractive.[68] During the first thirty years of the twentieth century Catholic women's colleges organized various postgraduate programs, the most popular of which was Education, and almost endless variety was evidenced in the way these studies were administered, supported, taught, and recognized. At best, however, postgraduate work was marking time until better things should come; the aim was a graduate school. Again, when graduate schools were organized, their existence was impressive only from the outside: any reasonably perceptive college visitor would have found it extremely difficult to know which courses in a curriculum were clearly graduate in standards and caliber, and which professors were equipped by experience, training, and scholarship either to plan or teach such courses.

The haste in establishing graduate study in Catholic women's colleges is illustrated by Trinity College's history, where, in 1900, undergraduate students were first admitted, and where, in 1904, a graduate department opened with four graduate students. In 1905 Trinity conferred four master of arts degrees.[69] While the graduate program was maintained—it was suppressed in 1932—advanced students were invited to study in departments of Greek, German, Latin, English, sociology, history, and philosophy. These subjects, the college believed, were its principal strengths, and during the twenty-eight years of graduate study at Trinity, fifty-one master's degrees and at least four doctorates were conferred.[70] At the College of New Rochelle, a graduate division was established in 1913, in which both master's and doctor's degrees were to be awarded. Although only ten years

---

[68] Sister M. Eleanore, *On the King's Highway: Story of the Sisters of Holy Cross of St. Mary's, Notre Dame* (New York, Appleton-Century, Crofts, 1931), pp. 315–316.

[69] *Historical Sketch of Trinity College, 1879–1925* (Washington, Sisters of Notre Dame, 1926); and *Catalogue of Trinity College, 1906–1907*, p. 65.

[70] Syron, *op. cit.*, p. 91.

old, having been authorized by the University of the State of New York to confer academic degrees for the first time in 1904, the college printed a prospectus ambitiously announcing ten graduate courses in the department of English, and a variety of graduate courses in the departments of history, economics, sociology, physics, chemistry, and mathematics. The promises of graduate study at this college went mainly unfulfilled, for during the years of graduate involvement—graduate programs were canceled in 1932— only ten master's and no doctor's degrees were conferred.[71]

In the first years of the twentieth century, then, Catholic women's colleges showed surprising energy in upgrading their curricula by inaugurating graduate study. No secrets are revealed when we say that these developments were almost always premature : the colleges were simply neither ready to bear the scholarly weight of advanced study nor able to afford the financial demands advanced studies would make on their impoverished treasuries. Catholic colleges for women, however, were quick to appreciate the requirements of higher learning, and, once seeing they were on the wrong track in trying to become complete universities, they abandoned graduate school ambitions, except for graduate study in Education. It took them slightly more than a quarter-century to learn this important lesson. Just one Catholic college for women, after 1932, determined to swim upstream to establish a graduate school : St. Mary's College of Notre Dame founded a school of theology, open to lay and religious women, in 1944, offering both master's and doctor's degrees.[72] In 1970 this graduate program at St. Mary's was still in operation.

When the maintenance of respectable, college-wide graduate programs appeared to be out of reach for the vast majority of Catholic colleges for women, they responded to plain educational common sense and suspended such programs, except, as we have said, in a few subject areas where their qualifications for such special studies were judged acceptable. Nor should it be assumed that these colleges were driven from the field of graduate study by watchdog accrediting associations; they themselves initiated the steps toward retrenchment. But, if graduate school hopes had to be relinquished, other areas of study outside the regular undergradute course, yet short of graduate standing, could be cultivated. Professional curricula, departments, and schools began to appear in Catholic women's colleges around the time decisions were being made to limit graduate study severely.[73] Most popular among professional studies, again, was Education, and professional Education was usually available, either in departmental

[71] Sister Mary Bernice O'Neil, *Evaluation of the Curricula of a Selected Group of Catholic Women's Colleges* (Washington, Catholic University of America Press, 1942), pp. 106–108.

[72] *Catalogue of St. Mary's College, 1943–1944*, pp. 17–18.

[73] Doyle, *op. cit.*, pp. 122–125.

or school structure, on graduate as well as undergraduate levels, either in a regular session or during summer school. In addition to Education, professional studies in pharmacy, nursing, journalism, and domestic science made regular appearances in the curricula of these colleges.[74] Yet, for all the activity along such lines, it would be wrong to assume that Catholic women's colleges were obsessed with professionalism, even less that their accomplishments qualified them to challenge what were by now fairly fully integrated professional studies in Catholic colleges for men. Professional curricula in women's colleges, irrespective of their intrinsic merits, were seldom preferred by Catholic female students to similar curricula in colleges for men, and this false image of inferiority showed no sign of being erased.

Still, there were avenues these colleges could explore which remained closed to their male counterparts : one was the summer school, wherein opportunities of varying quality were offered to the teaching Sister to continue and, perhaps after long years of summer study, to complete her course for the bachelor's degree.[75]

Catholic women's colleges had cherished the fond hope of one day becoming universities, as we have said, but when they tested the realities of American educational life more fully they abandoned such aspirations to begin looking for more achievable goals. Junior colleges and Catholic women's colleges had appeared on the American educational scene almost simultaneously, but for the first twenty years or so after the women's college movement had gained momentum, the junior college plan was simply a comfortable resting place for a women's college. Such a women's college started as a junior college, in fact, whatever nomenclature it employed, but always affirmed its junior college standing as temporary. Its real aim was to mature into a four-year degree-granting school. And most Catholic women's colleges achieved their aim, although (and this point should now be stressed) some were never blinded by overmuch allegiance to original aims. Finding their resources better suited to two- rather than four-year college programs, a few Catholic women's colleges decided to abandon academic pretense and lower their educational sights to conform with institutional resources : they became junior colleges. This was one way in which Catholic women's junior colleges were organized, yet it was a way neither common nor popular. The vast majority of Catholic women's colleges, irrespective of their potential for stability and growth, refused to countenance any retreat from commissions formerly accepted. They were, and would remain, four-year schools. Yet, after 1930, competition in higher

[74] *Ibid.*, pp. 123–124; and Bowler, *op. cit.*, pp. 111–112.

[75] See Thomas E. Shields, *The Education of Our Girls* (New York, Benziger Bros., 1907); and Sister Bertrande Meyers, *The Education of Sisters* (New York, Sheed and Ward, 1941).

education, keener than ever before, made the establishment of a four-year school a monumental task; and, even assuming that a four-year school could be founded, predictions of success were hazardous. At this point several new Catholic women's schools, again reading the signs of the times, settled for two-year status. Starting as two-year colleges, and finding their work on the junior college level effective and rewarding, they determined to remain junior colleges without any announced expectations about becoming four-year schools.

Manners and morals

In Catholic colleges for men, models for student life, for the inculcation of manners and the discipline of morals, were taken from seminaries; in colleges for women, models were transplanted from the convent. Thus, although some codes governing the conduct of female students might have differed on minor details from those applicable to males, the theory of student life was identical in both institutions. Every effort was made to admit only docile, orthodox students who, exposed to the code of internal discipline, would remain docile and orthodox. College officers, standing *in loco parentis,* were deadly serious about the responsibility they had assumed for the care and education, the manners and the morals, of students in their custody. Parents were assured of the safety of the buildings, the healthfulness of the climate in the region where the college was situated, the availability of medical services and of everything pertaining to the physical well-being of their children; they were promised, moreover, the rigorous and vigorous protection of student morals along with a quality of classroom instruction aimed at improving both the mind and the will. The theory has already been stated in full, and its repetition here is unnecessary; but a few details of its special application in Catholic women's colleges may repay notice.

First, in order to sense the tone of discipline, it should be said that codes of conduct in girls' schools were uniform : they applied to all girls, all schools, and all levels of instruction. It made no matter whether a girl was in a nineteenth-century academy or in an early twentieth-century Catholic women's college, because not one letter in the text of disciplinary regulations had been changed.[76] And sets of rule books, explaining in fine detail a litany of prohibited activities, were always distributed to students when they entered the college's gates. Needless to say, supervision was minute and unrelenting; rules were made to be followed. Regulations

[76] Syron, *op. cit.,* pp. 77–83.

pertaining to dress were stated far more fully than in colleges for men : only garments fashioned from acceptable materials were permitted; fine and expensive clothing was forbidden; ruffles on washable clothing were taboo. Plain ear-rings and brooches could be worn, but all other jewelry was banned. Parents and correspondents were notified of the rule against sending candy to students and a common statement in the prospectus read : "novels, pamphlets, newspapers, sent to the pupils, are not delivered."[77] All incoming and outgoing mail, the girls knew, was subjected to careful scrutiny.[78]

Until the late 1930s prescriptions concerning dress were common, and in some Catholic women's colleges students were required to wear uniforms. The 1923–1924 catalogue of the College of Notre Dame of Maryland told prospective students that blue or black dresses with white collars were mandatory; hemlines should measure ten inches from the floor; sweaters, sleeveless dresses, and low-cut evening gowns were summarily forbidden. This hard line on dress was justified by an argument heard before : "The College desires to occupy the students with the acquisition of virtue, knowledge, and usefulness in general, rather than to excite emulation in following fashions or gratifying inclinations to vanity."[79] With the colleges' discouragement of fancy and expensive clothing for their students went a concurrently dim view of visitors who, it was supposed, would distract the girls from their academic study and their attachment to the school's disciplinary routine. The colleges began by prohibiting all male visitors —they simply refused to take responsibility for them—even though such visits from boys, if permitted, would have been subjected to the most assiduous control. But twenty years into the twentieth century, they relented somewhat and allowed the girls to have male visitors on Saturday and Sunday afternoons, providing, of course, the name and pedigree of the callers were made known to the Sister prefect of discipline at least a week earlier. At some colleges, such visits needed the prior approval of parents as well. St. Joseph's College published this edict on the matter : "No visits are received or made by pupils unless authorized by parents in writing. Epistolary correspondence is subject to the same regulation and is liable to the inspection of the Mother Superior."[80]

Colleges for men were never entirely successful in keeping their boys in the college grounds, nor were they, for that matter, any more successful in isolating them from female companionship. Still, they tried. When the period of awakening came, Catholic college men began to enjoy freedom of movement outside college walls and were allowed to seek the company

---

[77] *Catalogue of Notre Dame of Maryland, 1876,* pp. 6–7.
[78] *Ibid.,* p. 7.
[79] *Catalogue of Notre Dame of Maryland, 1923–1924,* pp. 45–46.
[80] *Catalogue of St. Joseph's College, 1890–1891,* p. 11.

of young ladies. Girls' schools, however, were somewhat more progressive, although they had begun by discouraging all male-female relationships, simply rewriting the old codes of discipline that had prevailed for decades in the men's colleges. A women's college could hardly afford to bury away its students from men, for clearly Catholic attitudes were sympathetic to a girl's natural motivations toward marriage and family life. Still, since girls were not to be allowed to wander around outside the college boundaries, the colleges decided to encourage periodic visits from young men, probably from a nearby Catholic men's college, for afternoon teas and dances. The girls could invite young men, the Sisters could inspect them, and these daylight parties could be conducted under the watchful eyes of the prefects. Eventually, of course, class dances and banquets were approved and college social life took a step toward sophistication, for these affairs were always held in the local community's best commercial establishments.

The requirements of recreation were attended to; a few Catholic women's colleges prescribed daily exercise periods, which could range all the way from timed hikes around the college grounds to supervised physical education activities.[81] But whatever was done along these lines had to be organized and supervised to ensure that neither the college's prized intellectual aims nor its moral goals should ever be jeopardized. While it would be unfair to characterize the life of a girl in a Catholic women's college as dull, it would be an exaggeration to call it gay. The code of conduct was not meant to encourage gaiety, so the girls were guided, and sometimes driven, to adopt a puritan demeanor. Most girls, it turned out, learned to be good actresses.

In schools where religious virtue, moral deportment, and intellectual consistency counted for so much, it would not have been surprising to find admissions regulations inflexibly excluding all but Catholic girls. Some Catholic colleges for men, we know, specifically rejected denominational exclusiveness; the vast majority were willing to accept any good boy regardless of his religious beliefs, providing he could pay his tuition. No evidence exists to suggest religious exclusiveness in Catholic women's colleges either : from their first founding they willingly, although perhaps unenthusiastically, accepted nonCatholic students. The policy of St. Joseph's College was typical of most Catholic women's colleges and, moreover, remained so until the late 1940s : "The Institution is a Catholic one; yet members of every denomination are received. For the maintenance of good order, all the boarders are required to attend the public services of Religion as well as to observe the Regulations adopted for their improvement."[82] Whether this statement was planned obfuscation or merely faulty syntax may be

[81] Sister M. Celestine Casey, *Loretta in the Rockies* (Denver, Loretta Heights College, 1943), pp. 116–121.

[82] *Catalogue of St. Joseph's College, 1876–1877*, p. 8.

debated, although it appeared to prescribe the attendance of all students, regardless of their religious connections, at Mass and other devotions. The regimen of religious practice included required participation at daily Mass and active involvement in varieties of other devotional exercises, such as night prayers, periodic recitations of the rosary, semi-annual religious retreats, and prayers before and after meals in the refectory. Apparently nonCatholic and Catholic students were expected to observe the regimen in its entirety, so this part of the statement is fairly clear. But what did observing "the Regulations adopted for their improvement" mean? Perhaps this rule's author only meant to say that all students, leaving out of account religious differences, were expected to abide by the laws of the college. But another interpretation is consistent with the language of the rule, and in some colleges another interpretation was made fact. A student's duty toward religion included not only practicing the faith but learning more about its doctrines and justifications as well, and the latter part was accomplished best by taking regular courses in religion. Convincing evidence of this is indeed scanty; nevertheless, we may fairly assume that in some Catholic colleges for women every student was required to study Catholic doctrine. More frequently, however—and this was a situation much easier to defend—Catholic women's colleges were in the habit, like the majority of Catholic men's colleges, of requiring nonCatholic students to take fairly neutral courses in religion, such as evidences of Christianity or Biblical studies. Both Catholic colleges for men and women were hostile to any proposal excusing nonCatholics from the curricular requirement of religious study and they refused to consider reforms along these lines. On the question of mandatory religious study, then, the period of Catholic college development ended as it began, without discernible change.

Catholic women's colleges adopted fully and unapologetically the doctrine of *in loco parentis,* and this doctrine remained fixed and immovable during the first half of the twentieth century; yet, understandably, parents would want to know about their daughters' progress at college and, since visits were discouraged, regular reports on student diligence and deportment were sent home. Such reports were made monthly, quarterly, or half-yearly, but whenever rendered, they told parents about a girl's academic standing—marks for achievement went through the changes already noted in colleges for men—her deportment, and her religious conduct. Trying to leave nothing unsaid, they also recorded a student's achievement in such things as cooking, baking, darning, mending, sewing, and tapestry making. In addition to reports to parents, the colleges made a public record of student achievement by printing premiums and honors in college catalogues. Such premiums, naming the students who received them, were given for academic excellence, domestic science, and conduct. A premium was the highest honor, but other categories of recognition were published too : honorable mention was bestowed on students for academic excellence and sometimes for "polite and amiable deportment;" various "rewards" were assigned for "general improvement."[83]

Catholic colleges for men were traditionally unresponsive to exhortations to admit women to their classrooms, and once Catholic colleges for women appeared, colleges for men could argue, first, that the higher education of girls could be handled better in schools especially designed for them and, second, that admitting girls would generate acrimony and rivalry among Catholic institutions. By informal common consent, colleges for men and women tried to avoid stepping on each other's academic toes. Besides, the plain fact was that neither wanted students of the opposite sex. And this attitude of mutually anxious non-involvement prevailed for a long time. We have seen, however, how Marquette University and then De Paul University ignored convention to become partly or fully coeducational.[84] The growth of this movement towards coeducation, as it became more noticeable, offered a real threat to women's colleges and their position was plainly less happy. Using almost every means available, including, at times, episcopal authority, they tried to block or obstruct the coeducational movement in Catholic men's colleges. Success here, however, was almost always overmatched by failure : coeducation might be retarded; it could not be halted. In the end, it appeared, Catholic women's colleges would have to do their best with what they had, or, rather, they would have to develop schools of character and quality which, despite the presence of coeducation, would be attractive to Catholic girls. This direction, it is pleasant to report, was the one most Catholic women's colleges chose to take; it is also pleasant to report that it paid dividends. In the end, however, coeducation proved to be too strong an adversary, and many women's institutions were seriously weakened by this progressive educational step.

Another course of action, however, was open to women's colleges : they themselves could become coeducational and by admitting men could enter the lists of competition with colleges for men. For the most part, and for most women's colleges, this was neither an acceptable nor a reasonable alternative to remaining what they were—schools for girls. By 1955 only seven Catholic colleges for women had adopted coeducational admissions policies and by 1970 ten additional colleges for women had decided to admit men. Coeducation among Catholic women's colleges, then, was seldom more than a minority idea, an alternative more often rejected than embraced.

[83] *Catalogue of Notre Dame of Maryland, 1876*, p. 7.
[84] See pp. 275–277.

Academic management

For the first half-century following their founding in the United States, Catholic women's colleges remained outside the main stream of American higher learning. They were seldom compelled to compete with other colleges; their graduates could find a friendly and comfortable environment either as teachers in parochial schools or as wives and mothers in Catholic homes. Indifference to academic dispute was a luxury they could afford. Besides, it was almost natural to them, quite apart from the question of whether or not they could afford it. Such colleges had grown out of earlier female academies which, in turn, had had their foundations in the religious convent; as much as, possibly even more than, a Catholic men's college, the Catholic women's college reflected religious rather than academic ideals. The religious community of Sisters responsible for the college was determined to stamp its special character of life and religion upon its students and these qualities of life and spirituality were wedded to the living traditions of religious life and the community's rule, not to textbooks, scholarly status, or academic pedigree. Every Catholic women's college paid allegiance to religious ideals, although each used its own language to describe them. The Ursulines, who controlled the College of New Rochelle, adopted the principle that an Ursuline philosophy of life should be instilled in the students and, to achieve this objective, certain subjects, and later, certain departments, were reserved, where only Ursuline Sisters could be assigned as teachers. In order, moreover, to ensure the currency of Ursuline ideals throughout the college, only Ursulines could occupy the positions of department heads or directors.[85]

The department system, already part of the collegiate academic structure when Catholic women's colleges appeared, was adopted quickly, a fact which spared them the anxieties so common to Catholic colleges for men two decades earlier. Religious women proved their ability to apply the machinery of academic administration to their colleges : deans, department heads, registrars, business managers, all made their debuts shortly after these colleges were established; yet, even with an up-to-date academic organization the colleges were still subject to the control of religious rather than academic policies. Eyes and ears were closed to regional and national debates about the management of colleges, the deployment of curricula, and the optimum employment of faculties, for decisions on such matters were made by mother superiors who seldom wandered far from their convents and almost never participated in educational dialogues with their peers. College leadership came from the closed system of religious preferment :

[85] Syron, *op. cit.*, pp. 108–111.

the president of a Catholic women's college held her office *ex officio* : her claim was based on the fact that she was a religious superior and she occupied the president's office as long as she remained the religious superior. Even more so than in colleges for men, the superior-president's word was law, and it made no matter whether the question to be answered was academic or religious. Wise presidents were tempted to ask advice on difficult issues, but their advisers were seldom persons either acquainted with or involved in the business of higher learning. From inside the college, trusted, older Sisters might be consulted; from outside, a bishop, a local priest, or a president of a nearby Catholic men's college might be asked to illuminate issues; on purely business matters, a respected Catholic banker, lawyer, or judge might be called to the councils.[86] Final decisions, however, were always made at the top, without regard for the opinions or attitudes of faculty members, and it is not surprising that such decisions regularly demonstrated a serious degree of mental inbreeding. The higher administrators of Catholic women's colleges insulated themselves from the fundamental ferment of the academic world and, at the same time, tried their best to copy its administrative machinery. Yet, despite valiant efforts to copy administrative procedures which they only partially understood, Catholic women's colleges proved, in the long run, to be less comfortable with modernization than colleges for men, and their inability to compete successfully in the volatile market of higher learning in the 1950s, 1960s, and 1970s may rest mainly on this fact. Women's colleges were exceptionally well-managed in terms of the prudent use of physical and financial resources; had they been less diffident about becoming involved in educational debate and had their commitment to religious goals been controlled by a constant appraisal of what a religiously-related education might legitimately aim for, we might have been able to commend them as freely for their academic management as for their use of financial resources.

Where Catholic women's colleges could embrace the relatively up-to-date curricula of the twentieth century, and almost from the first days of their founding offer degree programs capable of satisfying fairly diversified student tastes—and this without succumbing to a totally elective system— they were far less successful than, say, their male counterparts (who were backward in meeting the curriculum of the twentieth century face to face) in recruiting and deploying teachers to cope with these multiple new courses. During their formative period Catholic men's colleges capitulated to the inevitable and allowed laymen to join their faculties; it may even be fair to say that progress in men's schools can be measured by the increase of laymen on faculties. But in colleges for women, the policy of religious exclusiveness on the faculty prevailed long after it had been jettisoned by

---

[86] Bowler, *op. cit.,* pp. 96–100.

colleges for men and long after any reasonable justification could have been advanced for retaining it. College professors in Catholic women's colleges were drawn from the ranks of religious Sisters assigned to the school. Their backgrounds in higher learning, their academic degrees and teaching experience—nothing need be said here of scholarship—were strikingly unimpressive; their teaching duties ranged over a variety of unrelated subjects; and their nonteaching duties—prefecting and spiritual direction— were similarly heavy. Classroom instruction had a necessarily routine quality and the textbook, long the essential tool in American schools, became the principal teacher in Catholic women's colleges. Still, Sister-teachers could be good pedagogues : drill, repetition, recitation, and examination dominated instructional technique; lectures were rare, and rarer still were outside assignments where the resources of libraries, always weaker than in men's colleges and with fewer prospects for improvement, were of little help.

Aimed especially at the lower schools, yet affecting colleges for women as well, was the Sister Formation Movement, which proved to have a wholesome and salutary effect on faculties of religious women.[87]

With burdensome academic and nonacademic duties around the college, and with the submissiveness expected of good nuns, faculty members had a more than enviable public record of harmonious activity and commitment. Lay women could have part-time or temporary appointments or, in some extracurricular functions, could be assigned fairly responsible, permanent duties, but full faculty status was withheld. Such outsiders had no real chance of interesting their colleagues in improving the lot of faculties; their attempts would almost certainly have fallen on deaf ears. Indeed, without learning or teaching experience outside the college where they were now professors, Sisters were not likely to support any movements for faculty reform or for any definition of faculty rights and responsibilities. The whole business of faculty participation in the management of college affairs was at once a mystery and a dead issue; with the exception of a handful of Catholic women's colleges, it has remained so.

Since the faculty was so submissive and there was an almost total unwillingness to think of college teaching as anything more than hearing lessons—despite what the better teachers themselves may have accomplished in their own classrooms—and as a regular routine for supervising moral and religious formation, the absence of faculty rank need cause no surprise. Most Catholic women's colleges were entirely indifferent to faculty rank until after 1940, and even then rank was assigned in a bewilderingly unprofessional way. By 1970 assignments of rank were common in Catholic

[87] See Sister Elizabeth Ann, I.H.M., in *Planning for the Formation of Sisters,* Proceedings of the Sister Formation Conferences, 1956–1957 (New York, Fordham University Press, 1958), pp. 247–250; 285–287.

women's colleges, but criteria for the various academic ranks remained unclear. Perhaps these colleges would never have adopted any rank system at all had accrediting associations not insisted on gradations of faculty and had the colleges themselves been somewhat more successful than they proved to be in keeping lay women out of their faculties. Try as they might, Catholic women's colleges were unable to ignore the academic world in which they lived and that world also refused to ignore them. They had therefore to give some thought to reputation : standards of academic quality required appropriate credentials for college teachers and when Sisters were not available or lacked such credentials, lay women and, less frequently, laymen, received faculty appointments. Without going into the details of lay-faculty life in these colleges—its vicissitudes were similar to those described in colleges for men—lay women and men held an uncertain tenure and exerted an influence on college policy which was inconsiderable at best.

This picture of faculty standards and standing in Catholic women's colleges, however, had a brighter side : with a religious faculty, the principal and often staggering expense of higher education was considerably modified, for this faculty served without salary. Thus, the cost of attending a Catholic women's college was low : tuition, on the average, amounted to about one-half the charge in a Catholic men's college; and since Sisters were better housekeepers and domestic managers than priests or brothers, charges for room and board were always lower too. There was always, moreover, an obvious attachment to the rubric of Christian charity among these women's colleges. They refused to score their prospectuses with crotchets about fees having to be paid in advance; and, if the full details of their bookkeeping were known, we should no doubt find that thousands of deserving girls were educated in these schools, although neither they nor their families could afford to pay room, board or tuition charges.

In reviewing seventy years of Catholic women's college history in the United States, we must remember that they appeared at a time when the idea of female higher learning was accepted unevenly and reluctantly by influential portions of the American Catholic community. We should bear in mind, moreover, that they had to follow a lead given by nonCatholic colleges for women, without all their advantages, and with some disadvantages from which their nonCatholic counterparts were excused. The rapid expansion and growth of Catholic higher learning for women coincided with the decision of some Catholic colleges for men, for decades oblivious to the legitimate educational needs of women, to experiment with coeducation. In this competitive situation educational foundations for women found some additional motivation, although more significant than competition for the growth of Catholic women's higher education was the fact that religious communities for women attained a fairly high degree of stability around the beginning of the twentieth century and were thus capable of undertaking such monumental responsibilities as the higher education of girls. Notice should also be directed again to the influence of the legislation of the Third Plenary Council of 1884 and the unequivocal position it took with respect to the parish school. Religious communities for women responded to the challenges implicit in this legislation in various ways : one way which affected the future of higher learning was to found and conduct colleges which would prepare Sisters and lay women for teaching positions in parish schools.

Catholic colleges for men by 1970 were so different from what they had been during their formative period that the less said about the formative period the better, but this is not the case with women's colleges. Their formative period—1900 to 1920—is so much closer to their present that its motives and policies linger on and influence policies in the 1970s; yet, of course, these old policies and motives are more up-to-date than any which might be extracted from the early history of a Catholic men's college. In any case, and without breaking completely with the past, Catholic women's colleges in the seventh decade of the twentieth century were symbols of the progress that can be made by sheer determination, dedication and little else, for without the advantages of public notice—advantages often exploited by Catholic colleges for men and coeducational colleges in attracting benefactions—and almost totally devoid of endowments,[88] these colleges for women have used resources available to them to make important and lasting contributions to American Catholic higher learning.

[88] Sister M. Francesca Brownlee, *Endowment and Catholic Women's Colleges* (Washington, Catholic University of America, 1932), pp. 34–35.

10

Catholic colleges
in the age of the university

By 1875, after more than two centuries' experience with higher learning and with the multiple benefits of urbanization, industrialization, political stability, and economic affluence to add sinew, American higher education should have become a clear, commanding, secure, mature force in American life. Whether or not the exact opposite was true may be debated; yet there is plenty of evidence of a loss of confidence in higher learning at a time—in the 1870s—when secondary schools were just beginning to make their great assault on a no man's land between elementary schooling and college study.[1] Old, good friends of the colleges were chagrined to see college curricula becoming increasingly irrelevant to the mainstream of life; even the best academic polemicists were incapable of making outworn arguments convincing to more practically-minded persons who now refused to encourage attendance at or support of schools which for so long had been accorded pride of place among the country's educational institutions.[2] Colleges resisted change; society thrived on it. Schools which since the War of Revolution had refused to live in and be part of society could hardly expect to have much influence upon, much less to exploit, the social and economic developments everywhere taking place around them.

Whatever theoretical validity the proposition may have that the objectives of higher education can be defined and recognized by rational

---

[1] The ratio of college students to the total population had been declining: in 1838, one of every 1294 boys attended college; in 1869, the ratio was one of every 1927. Hundreds of colleges were faced with sharp losses in enrollment (see *Annual Report of the President of Columbia College*, 1870, pp. 40–62).

[2] George Paul Schmidt, "Intellectual Crosscurrents in American Colleges," *American Historical Review*, XLII (October, 1936), 46–67; see also, A. F. West, "Must the Classics Go?" *North American Review*, 138 (February, 1884), 152–159; and C. King, "Artium Magister," *North American Review*, 147 (October, 1888), 376–381.

processes which remain unaffected by time or circumstance, the history of colleges in the United States illustrates one context in which it proved impossible. It took American colleges a long time to concede that society, if not their master, was at least their guide, that students were essential to their existence, and that social influence was an important precondition for the ensuring of financial stability.

To reshape the image and redirect the curricular emphasis took time and even when attempts were made to accelerate the process, so much ground had been lost by decades of inaction that instant success was almost too much to expect. Shortly after the Civil War the colleges sensed that something was amiss and on the strength of intuition they made a great decision : they resolved to fulfill society's expectations. Allowing some time for this resolution to percolate within their own councils, the colleges, by 1875, were ready to meet the educational needs of their time by reconstructing their curricula, making room, in effect, for scientific and technical subjects; but they intended to keep enough of their traditional subjects of instruction to satisfy their own sense of integrity.[3] What they meant when they talked about reconstruction was not change but compromise and in the end the projected reforms failed because the college community was incapable of recognizing what needed to be done. Society wanted progress and the advance of the technology of science to help men live better lives; all this depended on pushing back the frontiers of knowledge and finding behind them the things that would be of use. But these American colleges had little aptitude for any kind of research outside the conventional boundaries of language and literature and, moreover, lacked both faculties and facilities for working on the frontiers of knowledge.[4]

Some colleges, we know, anticipating this shift in belief as to what knowledge was of most worth, organized professional schools and departments;[5] others around this time were founded as professional or technological schools;[6] and not to be left out of account were federally-sponsored land-

[3] George Paul Schmidt, "Colleges in Ferment," *American Historical Review,* LIX (October, 1953), 19–42; and see Thorstein Veblen, *The Higher Learning in America* (New York, B. W. Huebsch, 1918).

[4] John W. Burgess, *The American University* (Boston, Ginn and Co., 1884); H. T. Ely, "The American Colleges and German Universities," *Harper's Magazine,* LXI (July, 1880), 253–260; and James McCosh, "What an American University Should Be," *Education,* 6 (September, 1885), 44–45.

[5] Richard Hofstadter and C. DeWitt Hardy, *The Development and Scope of Higher Education in the United States* (New York, Columbia University Press, 1952), pp. 88–94.

[6] Russell Chittenden, *History of the Sheffield Scientific School* (New Haven, Yale University Press, 1928), I, 81–83; D. R. Fox, *Union College* (Schenectady, Union College, 1945), pp. 21–23; and L. B. Richardson, *History of Dartmouth College* (Hanover, Dartmouth College Publications, 1932), I, 420–428.

grant colleges commissioned especially to engage in scientific and practical study for the advancement of agriculture.[7] Some schools were always productive, responsible agents for the new education and the critic of American higher learning should remember them when he generalizes about the shortcomings of later nineteenth-century colleges. Yet such schools were always too few in number to make much difference, let alone lead a renaissance; the weight of tradition was against them and they had their hands full maintaining their own quality without worrying about leading an educational crusade. Some colleges, moreover, while intending to satisfy the new scientific interest, were engaging in activities for which they had little or no "preparation, and this caused no little trouble : schools which accepted the munificence of the land-grant act might, for example, appoint a minister or philosopher to teach their courses in agriculture.[8] This transparent violation of academic trust caused the rural public, from the outset skeptical about the benefits alleged for scientific and theoretical husbandry, to lose confidence in agricultural education, and they were understandably reluctant to embrace scientific farming when its secrets were so easily revealed that a former professor of divinity, philosophy, or language could overnight become a teacher of agriculture. Teaching deficiencies, most obvious in land-grant schools, were apparent elsewhere as well; professors of the classics or philosophy suddenly claimed expertness in science and technology and the professional schools giving them a platform jeopardized their images in a way most difficult to repair.

Had the colleges alone borne the disdain of the public and the more responsible elements of the academic community for this educational fraud, their reward would have been no more than just, but collegiate irresponsibility, easily misread, generated a widespread distrust of intellect. It would be pleasant, indeed, to be able to exonerate American colleges of responsibility for the indictment of intellectualism, but the record of their pretensions and their arrogance in bedecking their curricula with the dress of science when they lacked qualified teachers of science is always there to testify against them. They promised more than they could deliver, and with the skill of the most adroit sophist converted failure into achievement by means of rhetorical trickery. The confident assertion that America's lack of faith in intellect had its origin in a native pragmatism bred and nurtured on a rough frontier should therefore be modified enough to accept, as an accretion, the crude forgery the colleges worked on the public. America, trusting the only intellectual agency she knew, the college, was at first misled; and once fooled by the college's academic sleight of hand, was not

---

[7] See Earle D. Ross, *Democracy's College: The Land Grant College Movement* (Ames, Ia., Iowa State College Press, 1942).

[8] W. O. Thompson, "Spirit of the Land-Grant Institutions," *Proceedings of the Association of Land Grant Colleges*, 45 (1931), 103–108.

easily fooled again. If Americans became anti-intellectual it was due not to a native perversity, not even to wealth, but to the simple fact that having been repeatedly shortchanged by false intellectuals they finally refused to make an effort to distinguish pseudo- from real-intellectualism. In higher education's long history few examples of a learning that was no better than nominal stand out so clearly or so flagrantly as those of nineteenth-century American colleges. Offering any course or program of study which seemed attractive, and ignoring both order and quality in learning, they equipped their teachers with textbooks and commissioned them to teach anything in the curriculum. By turning back the calendar to the mere beginnings of formal education, they sinned against the very thing they should by then have been capable of promoting—intellectual responsibility.

The colleges' miserable failure in responding to society's legitimate demands for scientific and technological education may find excuses of a sort, but even good excuses were insufficient to satisfy society's yearnings for progress. Besides, the evolution of knowledge could not be made to stand still waiting for the colleges to catch up. The age of the college in America, from 1636 to 1875, in a country where colleges had been both symbols and citadels of intellectual achievement, was almost over, and a new institution with clearer commitments to scientific progress, as well as better qualifications for securing it, was being recommended as a reasonable alternative to the old college. Had private industry grasped the initiative at this time to create its own agencies for scientific research and technological development, the age of the university might never have dawned; but, as it was, private industry, preoccupied with its own problems of production and distribution, chose to look elsewhere for an institution capable of bringing out the treasures from scientific mines. Once again, as the United States had done so often before, European models were studied, and now the German university, in the heyday of its illustrious career, appeared to fulfill the necessary specifications as a model for transplantation and imitation.[9] American students for a half-century had been making the academic grand tour, and whenever they encountered the German university they were both awed by its commitment to research and impressed by the quality of its work. They returned home to give glowing accounts of German higher learning and, in a few places, to experiment with German-type university studies.[10] But even the best of these experiments was incapable of removing the crusts of indifference set upon the American college and done to a turn by decades of total involvement with classical curricula; what was needed was an entirely new

[9] Charles F. Thwing, *The American and the German University* (New York, Macmillan Co., 1928), pp. 40–44.

[10] *Ibid.*, pp. 42–43.

approach, broad and unrestrained, which would allow for a total dedication to scholarship in an institution whose first and foremost commitment was to its nurture, an institution, in fine, prepared to fill the place in learning left forfeit by the American college. The day when the college occupied the center of the stage was over; the era of the university was just beginning, and with the Johns Hopkins University in 1876 the first American university was founded.[11]

Taking German higher education as its model, the Johns Hopkins University abandoned the traditional commitments the American colleges had to the liberal education of gentlemen and replaced them with unequivocal allegiances to specialization, research, and scholarship. Gone, too, was the undergraduate, for the Johns Hopkins, taking its university commission seriously, admitted only those students already in possession of bachelor's degrees.[12] The college, thereafter, stood in the shadows of higher learning, still sending its most serious graduates on to the new university, but its old luster was gone. While this innovation—the enrolling only of graduates of the four-year college in the university—turned out to be temporary, it was an additional warrant that henceforth higher learning would be a serious business, not for boys, but for mature men. Besides, and genuinely, everyone at the university was a student : formally designated students were, of course, working for their advanced degrees, but members of the faculty, already in possession of their doctorates, were professional scholars who refused to take a vacation from learning. This deadly serious approach to higher education became a source of inspiration for the better American colleges—for those determined to follow in the Johns Hopkins' footsteps—so places like Harvard, Yale, Columbia, Michigan, Wisconsin, and Cornell began to establish and reorganize their graduate, or university, studies.[13] In so doing, they jettisoned their old notions of fitting in additional subjects to their undergraduate curricula and thus, without painful effort, crossed the threshold of university education. Instead, they recruited more highly specialized professors, opened laboratories with the apparatus for research, stocked libraries with technical books and journals, and capped their progressive performances by organizing graduate schools which should perch at the top of each institution's structure. Special, not liberal, education became the watchword of the graduate school; with specialization the order of the day, elective curricula were given wide range.

In the university new goals and means replaced old ones and colleges

[11] See John C. French, *History of the University Founded by Johns Hopkins* (Baltimore, Johns Hopkins Press, 1946).

[12] Daniel C. Gilman, *Launching of a University* (New York, Dodd, Mead and Co., 1906), pp. 134–136.

[13] Richard J. Storr, *The Beginnings of Graduate Education in America* (Chicago, University of Chicago Press, 1953), pp. 128–132.

which made the necessary effort to bring in the specialized higher learning suddenly appeared with different faces. But their revitalization, on the one hand, and their commitments to scholarship, on the other, were as yet incomplete, for in 1875 the man standing at the helm of the academic ship was still the minister-president, and in an era when the president's word was law, progress could easily be impeded by presidents who refused to embark upon, or to take seriously, the procedures necessary for academic reform. The president was a stumbling block, and so he remained until the colleges hoping for university standing became sufficiently secular to fill the president's chair with a man of science rather than a man of God. The steady, orthodox hand of a minister-president had written edicts to guide the faculty and students of the old college, but in university-oriented schools these prescripts sounded redundant and reactionary, for such schools wanted, and needed, not the testimony of a minister but the skillful guidance of an enlightened, far-seeing administrator. Thus, unlike the old-time college president, the pioneers of the new education were not clergymen but secular, scientific men with broad experiences and interests. Andrew D. White of Cornell, Daniel Coit Gilman of Johns Hopkins, Charles W. Eliot of Harvard, G. Stanley Hall of Clark, David Starr Jordan of Stanford, and F. A. P. Barnard of Columbia—men who directed their schools into the paths of university development—were alike in their coolness to religious orthodoxy, their advocacy of thorough, responsible scholarship, their scientific backgrounds, and their command of administrative techniques.[14] These men and these schools blazed the trail which other colleges, anxious also to become full universities, followed, although sometimes (as in the case of Yale and Princeton, where clerical presidents were not abandoned until, in 1899, Yale appointed Arthur Twining Hadley, and, in 1902, Princeton installed Woodrow Wilson) with timidity and hesitation.[15]

New universities, like the Johns Hopkins, Clark, and Chicago, and old colleges, like Harvard, Yale, and Columbia, where graduate schools were added, appeared before the public as zealous, competent custodians of a higher learning anxious to be responsive to society's needs, and with this commitment nailed to their educational masts they were fully authorized to ask for the public's support. Later, when they were able to demonstrate that their promises of accomplishment were above the level of vague hope and, moreover, that the products of their scholarship and research did make a difference in American life, they could solicit and obtain endowments large enough to stagger the imagination.[16] After all, it was by prudent and productive employment of their resources that they had proved they could be universities; the gifts and endowments obtained for university

14 See Hofstadter and Hardy,. *op. cit.,* pp. 33–34.
15 *Ibid.,* p. 34.
16 *Ibid.,* p. 32.

expansion and research were used effectively, prudently, sometimes dramatically, and always with some social purpose.

The most obvious obstacle in the road of university progress, which, of course, did not at once affect the recently established universities, was the structural problem of attaching a graduate school to an existing college and insulating the former from the contaminating, ascholarly area of undergraduate studies. This latter was always a problem to the better schools, which saw no way of relinquishing their undergraduate colleges even in the face of their more serious commitment to advanced graduate study. The autonomy sought for graduate schools and graduate faculties, which allowed them to live in the larger academic community without being part of it, while real enough in some institutions, was forever imperiled by divided loyalties and conventional allegiances. Varieties of administrative constructs were tried in order to keep graduate schools pure and graduate faculties dedicated to scholarship, while at the same time allowing undergraduate departments to continue their traditional objectives of transmitting and conserving knowledge. But even the best plans beset administrators with almost insoluble problems which, we have since learned are perennial and may, in fact, be indigenous to mixtures of college and university studies in one institution.[17]

Yet, irrespective of internal issues which arose to convince university presidents that their lives were never meant to be serene, the college-university reaffirmation of its relationship to life in society and the compelling proofs it could make of this fact redressed many of the grievances American society had against the old college. The age of the college ended on notes of complaint and distrust; the age of the university began with optimism and hope. American Catholic colleges were destined to seek their fortunes now, not in the old world of the college, but among the broadening horizons of respectable universities. They, too, if they valued their reputations, would have to test the waters of advanced learning, which time and again would bring them to the apron of university status.

---

[17] Abraham Flexner, "The Graduate School in the United States," *Proceedings of the Association of American Universities,* 1931, pp. 110–115. Endeavoring to avoid the confusion of college and university purposes, *Holy Cross' Catalogue of 1895–1896,* p. 17, stated its collegiate creed: "Keeping in view the essential distinction between collegiate and university education, as that of a general as distinguished from a special or professional education, the branches of our Course have been selected as the best means of developing harmoniously all the intellectual powers of the student."

Modesty and presumption

The university revolution proved in the long run to be a blessing in disguise for Catholic colleges, for now they too would have to meet the standards of relevance, efficiency, and competence generally expected of institutions of higher learning. What they needed, and sometimes wanted, to do, however, was never easy, and their stages along the road to university standing were accompanied by fluctuations in mood, by urgent anxiety over imperative compromises, and by an understandable hesitancy in accepting what appeared to be secular trends in American higher learning.

From their beginnings, Catholic colleges, although consciously avoiding the most direct influences of their nonCatholic counterparts, perforce shared in the general evolution of American higher learning. Immunity from the changes and pressures of life, whatever its attractions, was patently impossible and immunity from the growth of educational needs was likewise out of the question. So the curriculum of Catholic colleges for men passed through several fairly distinct periods of instructional emphasis before it finally assumed a definite collegiate caliber and shape. Catholic colleges for women, as we have seen, were in some respects fortuitously positioned to benefit immediately from the lessons history had taught their academic forbears, but in other respects, because they had so many models from which to choose, the charting of their course was both complicated and confusing. From schools with a preponderance of elementary curricula, Catholic colleges slowly built courses of study of secondary scope and depth; subsequently secondary and college studies were mixed in an amorphous seven-year program (except in women's colleges); finally, college curricula were installed and a four-year college program adopted. Yet long before the last step was taken in the direction of maintaining separate college curricula, some Catholic colleges had ambitiously promised master's degrees to their students; the more ambitious ones talked about becoming complete universities. This brave talk, however, could not disguise the narrowness of their academic intentions, because, whatever their prospectuses may have claimed for college courses, on the one hand, and advanced degrees, on the other, Catholic colleges were unwilling to think of themselves as schools with primarily intellectual commissions. Their preoccupation with other objectives was always too great to allow them the freedom to fulfill university ambitions, for if religious and moral values were uppermost in their institutional minds and if intellectual accomplishment was tolerated but unloved, the necessary conditions for achieving university status were obviously absent.

Prior to 1890 Catholic colleges in the United States lacked faculties, facilities, students, and resources for embarking on genuine university studies. Nevertheless, in the two decades before 1890 a number of Catholic colleges announced graduate programs, although as a matter of actual historical fact such programs were merely extensions or continuations of undergraduate courses.[18] During these long, bleak years antedating the university revolution, Catholic colleges, in company with their nonCatholic confreres, described postgraduate and graduate study in quantitative rather than qualitative language. They, along with most other colleges of the country, graciously conferred a master of arts degree on any student who remained at the college for a year following the receipt of his bachelor's degree. What students did during this extra year remains largely a mystery, for their course was not planned nor were any professorial mentors assigned to guide them over the obstacles of advanced study. The serious student read books of interest to him, or whatever he could find in the college library; sometimes he attended the lectures of professors whose reputations were good, or simply took the courses he had been unable to take during his undergraduate years. If students decided to seek their advanced education in a college other than the one from which they had taken their bachelor's degree, they were apparently allowed to do so, although it must be said that most colleges regarded such persons as academic nomads and discouraged their presence on the premises. Daniel Coit Gilman's recollections bear on these points, for he himself had tried to find something to do in a year of indecision following his graduation from Yale, and the situation he described, while probably not typical of all colleges, and certainly not of Catholic colleges, reveals the general lack of interest in formal college programs of study beyond the undergraduate years.[19]

It was easy for Catholic colleges of the developmental period to be indifferent to the quality of postgraduate instruction, for, preoccupied as they were with the essential elements of a classical curriculum in which communication of a cultural inheritance was imperative, neither innovative teaching nor research was believed to be worth even cursory attention. Yet, more significantly, it is difficult to prove that the managers of these Catholic colleges where postgraduate study was apparently encouraged had any clear idea about the new educational responsibilities they assumed when they proclaimed the availability of graduate study and graduate degrees at their colleges. Catholic college presidents, prefects of studies, and deans—when

---

[18] For example, these announcements: *Georgetown College Catalogue, 1878–1879*, p. 4; *St. John's* (Fordham) *College Catalogue, 1878–1879*, p. 5; *Xavier College Catalogue, 1878–1879*, p. 6 *Prospectus of the College of St. Francis Xavier* (New York), *1879–1880*, pp. 3, 6; *St. Ignatius College Catalogue* (Chicago), *1880–1881*, p. 9; and *Creighton College Catalogue, 1881–1882*, p. 5.

[19] See Gilman, *op. cit.*, p. 9.

they finally appeared—were, for the most part, home grown; their definitions of higher learning were limited by what they themselves had experienced in a Catholic college and seminary a few short years before; hardly a one had ever visited the campus of a nonCatholic college, and none had studied at a genuine university. When Catholic college presidents listed their schools among the institutions offering graduate instruction, their intentions were unquestionably good in that they hoped by taking this action to bring prestige to the campus, but even if such meritorious motives be admitted, it is hard for them to escape the charge that fundamentally their action was irresponsible and uninformed. Mindful of academic inbreeding and recognizing the deficiencies of nineteenth-century Catholic colleges, which go a long way toward explaining the overambition of their managers, the historian is still unable to absolve presidents from an indictment for stupidity in having led their schools down roads they had no possible justification for taking. It was hardly a secret that Catholic colleges were only just finding the necessary strength to appear before their public with reasonably respectable undergraduate curricula, and suddenly they were commissioned to confer graduate degrees as well. This was a point noted by persons sensitive to the reputation Catholic colleges had for academic quality. An anonymous author in *The Catholic Advocate* wrote with an unusual degree of candor when he admitted that "rudimentary Greek and Latin Grammar schools, [are] kept by Jesuits and others, which in sheer mockery of the name, are called universities. But these titles decieve no one, and provoke no comment, out of respect to the spirit of humbug which is so prevalent with us. If a young man, upon leaving one of these institutions, has sufficient education to enable him to construe words grammatically, we must be satisfied."[20] And Augustus Thébaud, with over forty years' experience in American Catholic colleges, also tells us of their premature ambitions and points to a most compelling reason why Catholic colleges should have, at this time, been consolidating their positions rather than trying to look for new academic worlds to conquer. The main weakness, he avers, was in the quality of teaching where the deficiency was so great

that in all colleges except those of our Society, the professors of the lower classes, and even occasionally of the collegiate course, were seminarians who at the same time followed a theological course for the purpose of preparing for ordination. How could they do both well? In the Jesuit colleges, though this was not so glaring a feature, because it is altogether opposed to our constitutions, still often the superiors thought that necessity compelled them to leave our constitutions inoperative on account of the small number of our novices and juniors.

Moreover, neither in the colleges directed by the Sulpicians or secular priests, nor in those controlled by the Jesuits, could there be found men willing to devote their whole lives to teaching. The need for priests in parishes and missions was

[20] *The Catholic Advocate,* January 28, 1871.

in fact so imperious that candidates for the priesthood looked to parochial and missionary work as the paramount object of their lives.[21]

With or without good teachers, and with or without advanced curricula, Catholic colleges paid scant heed to counsels of caution and marched confidently forward, granting degrees representative of university studies. And there were few good reasons why, in 1875 or so, they should not have been doing so because on even weaker grounds, and in accordance with the conventions of nineteenth-century higher education, they had been doing so since about 1817.[22] In 1833, *The Catholic Almanac* described how graduate degrees were conferred at St. Mary's College in Baltimore : the degree of master of arts was awarded to students "of the College, who, two years, at least, after having received that of Bachelor of Arts, will apply for it to the President and the Faculty, provided they can prove, that from the time they left the College, they have been engaged in literary, or scientific pursuits, and can produce certification of moral deportment."[23] St. Mary's standards, however, should not invite scorn; the school was simply following accepted canons and even then could have pointed to Harvard, where similar procedures were in force.[24] Yet, for some time after non-Catholic colleges had begun a stricter observation of the differences between honorary and earned degrees, Catholic colleges persisted in ignoring them. Seton Hall College, as late as 1900, and probably the last Catholic college to retain this old tradition, declared in its prospectus that "graduates in the Classical course who shall have subsequently spent two years in scientific, professional or literary studies, may on application to the Faculty and on presentation of satisfactory testimonials, be admitted to the degree of Master of Arts."[25]

In seeking to discover when graduate degrees were first awarded in Catholic colleges, we are treading the mere periphery of certitude. Caution is imperative because with the colleges' penchant for secrecy—or, at least, their hesitancy about maintaining written records—positive assertions would be difficult to support with incontrovertible evidence. What sources we have say Georgetown first granted a master's degree in 1817,[26] probably the first Catholic college to do so, and that Mt. St. Mary's College conferred a

[21] Augustus J. Thébaud, *Forty Years in the United States of America* (New York, United States Catholic Historical Society, 1904), II, 350–351.

[22] Sebastian A. Erbacher, *Catholic Higher Education for Men in the United States, 1850–1866* (Washington, Catholic University of America, 1931), pp. 10–72.

[23] *Catholic Almanac; or, Laity's Directory, for the Year 1833,* p. 56.

[24] Colonial Society of Massachusetts, *Collections,* "Harvard College Records," vol. 15, pp. 26–27.

[25] *Catalogue of Seton Hall College, 1900,* p. 16.

[26] John M. Daley, *Georgetown University: Origin and Early Years* (Washington, Georgetown University Press, 1957), p. 204.

doctorate in 1851,[27] but the less said about this the better. In any case, the record appears to confirm a belief that Catholic colleges abandoned timidity when it came to granting advanced degrees and frequently did so within a year or so after they were founded. Neither the college course nor wine, it appeared, was assumed to improve with age. Yet paging through such early prospectuses as are extant leaves us without clues about advanced degrees; these publications say nothing about them, although commencement broadsides say they were conferred. Graduate degrees, we should think, were always limited to the master's, for the doctorate goes unmentioned (save for the tale about Mt. St. Mary's) as an earned degree at any Catholic college, except the Catholic University of America, before 1895.

The period of silence about graduate degrees came to an end around 1860 and from then on Catholic colleges notified students of their availability in various college publications. It was still too early, however, to refer to programs for graduate study, because the colleges had yet to devise them. But what could be said was said, and a few illustrations may have historical worth. St. Joseph's College of Bardstown, Kentucky, used its catalogue of 1857–1858 to make this announcement : "On completing the Classical Course the Degree of A. B. is conferred on all whose success in examination entitles them to that distinction; and after two years creditably spent in some literary pursuit, the graduate can, upon application, receive the Degree of A. M." [28] In 1860, following this formula, St. Joseph's College awarded three master's degrees.

In 1838 St. Louis University, braving publicity earlier, had announced that "the degree of A. M. is given to alumni who, after having received the degree of A. B., shall have devoted two years to some literary pursuit." [29] And for the next twenty years master's degrees were awarded on these terms. In its catalogue for 1861–1862, however, St. Louis University changed its advanced degree requirements slightly : "On completion of the Classical Course, the degree of A. B. is conferred upon all those who, on examination, are found deserving of that distinction. Subsequently, the degree of A. M. is obtained by devoting a second year to the study of Philosophy in the Institution, or two years in a learned profession." [30] Apparently following the new code, St. Louis University awarded one master's degree in 1861 and two in 1862.

Catholic colleges, however, did not move forward on a common front with respect to graduate degree requirements. This is attested by the

27 Edward J. Power, *A History of Catholic Higher Education in the United States* (Milwaukee, Bruce Publishing Co., 1958), p. 207.

28 *Catalogue of St. Joseph's College, 1857–1858,* p. 7.

29 Walter H. Hill, *Historical Sketches of St. Louis University* (St. Louis, Patrick Fox, 1879), p. 57.

30 *Catalogue of St. Louis University, 1861–1862,* p. 10.

record of Xavier College in Ohio where, in 1862, ignoring what St. Louis had already done, this rule governed advanced degrees : "On completing their classical course, the degree of A. B. is conferred on all who prove deserving of that distinction, and after two years creditably spent in some literary pursuit, the graduate is entitled to the degree of A. M."[31] Xavier College waited until 1878 to upgrade its requirements for graduate degrees to equal those set by the modest rules St. Louis University had published in 1862.[32]

In 1871, although formal programs of graduate study were still lacking, forty-two master of arts degrees were conferred by eleven Catholic colleges out of a total of one hundred and forty-nine degrees of all types granted by all the Catholic colleges of the country.[33] The graduate degree-granting colleges, with the number of master's degrees granted in parenthesis, were : Spring Hill (2), St. Ignatius, now the University of San Francisco (1), Notre Dame (2), Santa Clara (2), Rock Hill (6), St. Louis (1), Fordham (6), St. Francis Xavier of New York (11), Xavier of Ohio (1), Villanova (4), and Georgetown (6).[34] Any inclination to criticize these Catholic colleges for prematurely involving themselves in the business of granting degrees for which they lacked formal programs of study is discouraged when we realize that such degrees had for a long time been awarded by the most prominent colleges in the United States on the same informal basis.[35] The first earned master's degrees were conferred by Harvard in 1874, by Yale in 1876, and by Princeton in 1879.[36] Catholic colleges, it is true, may have been unworthy of the advanced degrees they granted, but they were hardly out of step with conventional academic procedures; and it did not take them long, once Harvard and Yale and other good schools began to develop graduate curricula, to organize their own formal programs of graduate study.

Again we find Georgetown in the vanguard of a Catholic college movement seeking greater respectability and meaning for its master's degrees. Georgetown, in 1877, established the first formal Catholic college graduate program,[37] although some historians have claimed the right of precedence either for St. Louis University[38] or the University of Notre Dame.[39] Yet St. Louis' own announcements give no support whatever to a

[31] *Catalogue of Xavier College, 1861–1862*, p. 5.

[32] *Catalogue of Xavier College, 1878–1879*, p. 6.

[33] *Report of the United States Commissioner of Education*, 1871, pp. 762–781.

[34] *Ibid.*

[35] *Ibid.*, 1870, p. 418.

[36] Walton C. John, *Graduate Study in Universities and Colleges in the United States*, U.S. Office of Education, Bulletin No. 20, 1935, pp. 5–6.

[37] *Catalogue of Georgetown University, 1877–1878*, pp. 4–5.

[38] Hill, *op. cit.*, p. 56.

[39] Arthur J. Hope, *Notre Dame, One Hundred Years* (Notre Dame, Ind., University of Notre Dame Press, 1943), p. 167.

belief in the existence of graduate curricula before 1879;[40] and the post-graduate course at Notre Dame, announced in 1873,[41] appears to have been just that and no more—in other words, a postgraduate course devoid of the essentials of graduate study. This is how Notre Dame described its course :

The want of such a course has been for a long time felt by students desirous of continuing to perfect themselves in those studies which require several years of close attention. The Postgraduate Course is now open, and we invite our Graduates, and such others as are able, to enter it and avail themselves of the advantages it affords of prosecuting their studies to a successful conclusion. The students of this course occupy themselves with Philosophy, History, and Natural Sciences. Law and Civil Engineering may be optional studies of the course.[42]

It would need an exceptionally generous interpretation of this statement to make it qualify as the preamble to a formal graduate program, and even then one would be faced with the necessity of discovering where law and engineering would fit as part of graduate study. By introducing professional studies into its postgraduate course, Notre Dame was probably only blurring the distinctions then being sought between undergraduate and graduate curricula, on the one hand, and graduate and professional curricula, on the other.

If Georgetown's graduate program announcement of 1877 is less than a clear manifesto for university studies, with its broad curriculum in moral philosophy, history of philosophy, special branches of science, and civil, political, and international law, it is, nevertheless, considerably clearer in its commitments than anything so far stated by other Catholic colleges.[43] Although a preference for the term postgraduate is still evident, George-town's prospectus for the year 1877–1878 reveals the school's intention to embark on studies which should have been called graduate. Equivocation is gone : master's degrees must be earned and students must follow a pre-scribed course of studies; in addition, they must prove their worth as prospective scholars by preparing a discriminating, scholarly dissertation. It is in these regulations that we find for the first time any mention of that scholar's masterpiece, the dissertation, among descriptions of postgraduate programs in Catholic colleges. Georgetown's pioneering statement is brief, so we can allow it to speak for itself :

The degree of Master of Arts, in course, is conferred upon Bachelors of Arts who have passed satisfactory examinations in the post-graduate course of Ethics and Natural Philosophy.

[40] *Catalogue of St. Louis University, 1878–1879*, p. 3.
[41] *Thirteenth Catalogue of the University of Notre Dame, 1873*, p. 57.
[42] *Ibid.*
[43] *Catalogue of Georgetown University, 1877–1878*, pp. 4–5.

The candidate for the degree of Bachelor or Master of Arts, is required to compose an essay on some Literary, Scientific or Moral subject, which, if accepted by the Faculty, must be left in the archives of the College.

Honorary degrees are conferred, at the discretion of the Faculty, upon those who unite proficiency in the Classics with an eminence in Literature or Science.[44]

As Georgetown moved forward to assimilate graduate studies into its total academic syllabus, Fordham (then called St. John's College) followed quickly in its wake to alter and upgrade the requirements for postgraduate study. For some time Fordham had been offering master's degrees,[45] so there was no change in that respect; but since Georgetown was making notable alterations in the requirements for the postgraduate course, Fordham believed it wise to do the same. In 1878, Fordham granted ten master of arts degrees under the following regulation : "Graduates who desire a fuller mental training may, in the Post-Graduate class, pursue the study of Natural Law, and of the other branches of higher education. This second year [a second year of philosophy study] is of the greatest importance to a young man. At the end of the year the degree of Master of Arts is conferred, after a satisfactory examination."[46] Nothing, we note, is said about a dissertation and nothing about the subjects which are to form the student's syllabus of study. But all this is taken care of in the following year's prospectus, where the work of the academic year's two terms is carefully outlined with appropriate notations for the subjects to be studied and the books to be read. The curriculum, it must be admitted, was narrow, for the only field of study wherein a student might seek a master's degree was philosophy, although complementary studies in "Natural Science and Modern Languages" were permitted.[47] But in this one graduate field, at least, Fordham made a respectable beginning. Theses are mentioned : "students are obliged to defend their theses, both in Class and before the Faculty, against some of their own number, or against professors and others appointed to attack them."[48] These disputations, the articles say, are usually conducted in Latin; dissertations and essays, also required of students in this advanced course, are prepared in English; and, during the second term, "Essays on three different subjects, already treated in class, are written, and the best is awarded a gold medal worth fifty dollars."[49]

Yet, while Georgetown, Notre Dame, and Fordham were slowly working their way toward more advanced curricula and respectable master's degrees,

---

[44] *Ibid.*

[45] Thomas G. Taaffe, *A History of St. John's College* (New York, Catholic Publication Society, 1891), p. 52.

[46] *Catalogue of St. John's College, 1877–1878*, p. 4.

[47] *Ibid., 1879–1880*, p. 12.

[48] *Ibid.*

[49] *Ibid.*

most Catholic colleges were content to stay within more familiar precincts of postgraduate study. Innovation had yet to become popular; Catholic colleges preferred to resist change and the College of the Holy Cross here serves as a good illustration of this perennial feature of Catholic higher learning. In 1877, despite what a few Catholic colleges had done or were about to do, Holy Cross thought it a good idea to restate the terms on which it would grant master's degrees : "if [the student remains] longer in the College, and [pursues] the Higher Branches of Rational and Natural Philosophy, or, if he [enters] a learned profession, after completing the above course of College Studies [for the A. B.], he may receive the Degree of Master of Arts."[50]

Holy Cross, then, was marking time en route to a more scholarly graduate study and while she did so St. Louis University tried a rather novel experiment. In the college catalogue for 1881–1882, St. Louis University set out the rules for a postgraduate program which, this announcement said, had been in operation for two years.[51] But the rules had hardly been stated when observers began to wonder whether St. Louis was inaugurating graduate or postgraduate programs or only a lecture series. And this was legitimate confusion, for as we study the regulations now we are unable to fathom the school's intentions : anyone could enroll for the lectures; persons already possessed of bachelor's degrees could aspire to master's degrees; persons involved for the first time in higher studies could earn the coveted bachelor's degree. According to St. Louis' 1881–1882 catalogue of courses and programs, this lecture series, introduced in October, 1879, with sessions on mental and moral philosophy, anthropology, and history, was well received. The printed notice scheduled the series to begin around the middle of October and continue until about the middle of April, with lectures being delivered three times a week from 6 :30 to 7 :30 p.m. A month-long Christmas intermission interrupted the lectures. Assuming that some interested persons might attend the lectures for purely cultural reasons, without either bachelor's or master's degrees in mind, the school promised to "vary the treatises for the benefit of those who may desire to attend for more than one term."[52] At the end of the course—a course meant one series of lectures, or about twenty meetings—"such members of the class as have given satisfaction by regular attendance may apply for the degree of Bachelor of Philosophy, which will be granted on condition that they pass an examination on theses to be selected from the matter developed during the course, and present an original and creditable paper on a given subject."[53] On this basis either an A. M. degree (if the student had an

[50] *Catalogue of the College of the Holy Cross, 1877–1878,* p. 8.
[51] *Catalogue of St. Louis University, 1881–1882,* p. 22.
[52] *Ibid.*
[53] *Ibid.*

A. B.) or a bachelor's degree was awarded, for the rule is quite explicit :
"Application for either degree is at the option of the members of the class,
and must be made in writing at least two weeks previous to the close of
this course." [54]

The charges to students for what St. Louis called a postgraduate
course were modest, although at this point conventional terminology was
abandoned and the catalogue lists thirty dollars as the cost for "Season
Tickets for the Entire Course," and a ten dollar diploma fee for the Ph.B.
or the A. M. degree. A suspicion that the college had the general public in
mind rather than serious degree-seeking students is borne out by the rule
that boarders would not be enrolled in the program. But toward the end
of the catalogue statement there is some reassurance that St. Louis was
after all making a commitment to advanced instruction, although its standard was equivocal : "Graduates of the University, or of any College of the
same grade, students and graduates of Law or Medicine, and gentlemen of
literary or scientific culture will be admitted to the above course." [55] But
the implications of every side of the program confirmed one unwritten rule :
women were not invited to the lectures.

Despite the brave talk that this course was really fulfilling a pressing
educational need and that the lectures were well-attended, the lecture hall
was seldom overcrowded, and in the year following the cost of season tickets
was reduced from thirty to ten dollars.[56] In 1884 the lectures were maintained as before, with the addition to the catalogue description of lecture
topics in the two discrete fields of general physics and history. The next
year the list of general subjects for lecture or graduate treatment was
expanded to include anthropology, biology, and psychology, and the professors responsible for the program saw fit to insert in the college bulletin
some sample examination questions for the guidance of students who might
want to fulfill the examination requirement for degrees.[57] Although there
are no dependable data revealing the number of students who took degrees
as a result of this program, the records indicate that one hundred and
twenty-six persons enrolled and bought season tickets for the lecture course
in the six sessions held between 1879 and 1886.[58] Twelve professors from
the St. Louis University participated in the lecture series during these
years and they numbered among their listeners twenty doctors of medicine
from the St. Louis community. Even better attendance was evident for the
academic year 1886–1887 : with eighty-five season tickets sold, it was hard

[54] *Ibid.*
[55] *Ibid.*
[56] *Ibid., 1883–1884,* p. 24.
[57] *Ibid.*
[58] *Catalogue of St. Louis University, 1879–1880* to *1885–1886.*

to label St. Louis' extraordinary venture into graduate studies a failure.[59] Yet the University consultors to the Rector recited their reasoned doubts about the quality and purpose of such a program. They must have sensed the St. Louis experiment was clearly out of step with graduate study developments taking place elsewhere in the country. If they looked toward the Johns Hopkins University, or even to Notre Dame or Georgetown, they could sense the dangers to university reputation inherent in their own graduate lecture program. The consultors took a responsible stand, which they believed to be in the best interests of the university's future, and told the President that the lecture program, despite its apparent popularity, had achieved "little good [and that] had been done at a great cost of labor."[60] They argued, moreover, that all St. Louis' degrees were being cheapened by the degrees offered from the postgraduate course, which "was feeding a fashion among non-Catholics chiefly."[61] Consultors to a Jesuit superior must be heard but their advice can be ignored, and in this case it was fairly easy for the President to overrule his consultors because the lecture series showed plenty of signs of financial, if not necessarily academic, vitality. So this St. Louis novelty in graduate study was continued for some years until, faced with the legitimate demands of carefully organized and fully academic graduate work, it finally died of old age.

Despite the intransigent opposition of some Catholic colleges to any alteration in their traditional approach to advanced degrees or to attractive novelties like the graduate lectures at St. Louis University, and despite the obvious academic inadequacies indigenous to many Catholic colleges, the advance of graduate study was too determined to be halted or diverted by the hostility inevitable amongst administrators and faculties still devoted to classical curricula. Georgetown seemed to have surrendered her place in the vanguard of Catholic college progress about the end of the Civil War and other schools threatened to become the model for Catholic higher learning in the United States; but what looked like surrender was only a temporary accident of history. Georgetown proved to be both willing and able to lead, and in respect to graduate study she proved this time and again. But it was proved most convincingly in the action Georgetown took in 1891 "to justify the recognition of the graduate classes as a permanent department of University training."[62]

Beginning with the admission, veiled, it is true, but there nevertheless, that the forty-year history of graduate degrees at Georgetown was less than praiseworthy—partly because it was disorganized and partly because it

[59] *Catalogue of St. Louis University, 1887–1888*, p. 29.

[60] Gilbert J. Garraghan, *The Jesuits of the Middle United States* (New York, America Press, 1938), III, 438.

[61] *Ibid.*

[62] *Catalogue of Georgetown University, 1891–1892*, p. 30.

lacked continuity—and that the traditional procedures would never do now, the school prepared a clear prospectus for graduate study, which included vital information about objectives, courses, admissions policies, degrees, fees and expenses.[63] And to add even greater luster to what she had planned, Georgetown, for the first time, designated a graduate faculty responsible for teaching and directing the programs of study leading to advanced degrees. Graduate study, the Georgetown catalogue said, was intended "for those graduates who desire to continue and extend to the highest attainable degree their education in the Arts and Sciences, whether it be for the mere love of learning, or to qualify themselves as professors, or finally with a view to a more complete preparation for some one of the learned professions, by devoting themselves to liberal studies cognate to the career aimed at, but of a more elevated scientific character than can be attained in the ordinary professional schools of the country."[64] The courses pursued by students, who held bachelor's degrees from Georgetown or "institutions of like standing," were intended to be taxing enough to test the academic energies of any student; yet, and this may have proved to be a problem for the future, the student could handle them as preparations for the "study of Law and Medicine . . . or pursue the postgraduate branches simultaneously with the study of these professions in the schools of Georgetown University."[65] Even at this stage, it seemed, the best of the Catholic colleges was unsure about the proper role of postgraduate study and could offer it as a part-time scholastic occupation along with the study of law or medicine. In this context, there cannot have been much doubt of the taxation of a student's energy. Perhaps, however, most students were spared the grueling experience of simultaneous graduate and professional study, choosing instead to do one or the other.

In enrolling for the postgraduate course, students were committing themselves to a required course in rational philosophy; "the other courses are elective; but at least three distinct subjects must be chosen, involving a minimum of eight hours' attendance at lectures per week."[66] For students who selected scientific subjects and needed practical experience, laboratories were kept open eight hours daily.[67] And as a concession to modern studies, along with an advertisement that a critical literature in these languages was available for review, French or German was required, with a note appended that both were desirable. Yet most of a student's work was probably done in the classroom, where he listened to lectures, received direction and

63 *Ibid.,* pp. 30–32.
64 *Ibid.,* p. 30.
65 *Ibid.,* p. 31.
66 *Ibid.*
67 *Ibid.*

guidance about outside reading, took tests, participated in repetitions, and presented his written papers.

Apparently degrees at master's level other than that of master of arts were projected for the postgraduate department, although they are not named. This much only was said : "The requirements for other degrees are analogous to those for the Master of Arts."[68] These requirements therefore included one year of "study and satisfactory examinations in three courses."[69] Theses, monographs, essays were considered part of the examination, and, according to the catalogue, they were to "be assigned at progressive stages of the lectures."[70] The implication is evident that a dissertation was part of the requirements for a master's degree, and we know that dissertations were written; but the postgraduate regulations themselves say nothing about them. Not wanting the advantages of postgraduate study at Georgetown to go unnoticed, the catalogue statement sets them out : we discover that "students have the privilege of consulting their professors beyond the class hours,"[71] and, moreover, were permitted, under the direction of their teachers, to use the library, the physical and chemical cabinets, and the museum. Besides all this, prizes amounting to twenty-five dollars were awarded to the best student in each course and to the best student in all courses. A prize-winning student could come close to paying his tuition fee and book expense, because the charge for tuition was listed at sixty dollars, the diploma fee at ten dollars, and, it was said, "text-books will not ordinarily exceed \$8 or \$10."[72] To these expenses the student would need to add about three hundred dollars for "room, board, and washing."[73]

Six professors were assigned to the postgraduate department, although it is unclear whether or not they had other instructional duties in the college as well.[74] In any case, they were responsible for the following fields of knowledge : Metaphysics and Ethics, Literature, History, Mathematics, Physics, and Chemistry; and some of these fields were divided into the courses following : Metaphysics, Natural Theology, Ethics, General Literature, English Literature, French Literature, Theory of Historical Writing and Introduction to History, Constitutional History of Greece, Rome, England, and the United States. In Mathematics, Physics, and Chemistry distinct course titles were not used.[75] Laboratory experience was mentioned as part of the requirement for the work in Physics and Chemistry, and, in

[68] *Ibid.*, p. 32.
[69] *Ibid.*
[70] *Ibid.*
[71] *Ibid.*
[72] *Ibid.*
[73] *Ibid.*
[74] *Ibid.*, p. 34.
[75] *Ibid.*, pp. 34–36.

addition to all this, a category of supplementary courses was mentioned and described as a "series of lectures on subjects of general interest [which] will be arranged as opportunities arise during the year."[76] What must have been meant was that the school would invite outside lecturers on various topics and that graduate students could attend these lectures.

Although Georgetown was the first of the Catholic colleges to engage in advanced studies at this new, higher level, and is thus separated from other Catholic colleges whose historians occasionally assert this enviable precedence for their own schools, it would be an overstatement to maintain that Georgetown, in 1891, was much more than over the threshold of graduate studies. One of her most careful historians, indeed, admits as much.[77] If a separate postgraduate faculty was a good omen for the future success of graduate commitment,[78] Georgetown, in pioneering such a development, did not make an immediate success of it. Yet a first step it was toward better things to come, and once again Georgetown was the pace-setter: a graduate school was organized in 1895.[79]

Despite the undoubted fact, confirmed easily by comparisons between descriptions of the new program of advanced studies and older ones that distinctions between graduate, postgraduate, and undergraduate curricula and standards were yet to be made with clarity and precision, Georgetown's establishment of a graduate school did provide an academic foundation upon which authentic graduate study could build. Some of the old-fashioned terminology used and courses organized for postgraduate departments were retained in Georgetown's graduate school prospectus of 1895–1896, but what was new counted for more than what was old. First, the graduate school, with a graduate dean, was accorded an autonomy inconsistent with anything before seen in Catholic college postgraduate organizations; and, while this autonomy, naturally enough, was subject to institutional limitations—for the graduate school was still a part of Georgetown University, not an autonomous institute as the schools of medicine and law had been only a few decades before—it provided a latitude of action which enabled graduate departments to do their own serious thinking about the aims set for the graduate school at Georgetown. Second, the inspirational rhetoric and the academic moralizings so characteristic of postgraduate announcements were less apparent; the talk about perfection in liberal studies was toned down, partly because it appeared to be an inordinately ambitious claim and partly because other legitimate scholastic goals could now be seen more plainly. In the place of pious exhortation

---

[76] *Ibid.,* p. 36.

[77] Joseph T. Durkin, *Georgetown University: The Middle Years, 1840–1900* (Washington, Georgetown University Press, 1963), pp. 253–255.

[78] *Catalogue of Georgetown University, 1891–1892,* p. 34.

[79] *Catalogue of Georgetown University, 1895–1896,* p. 25.

appeared a more simply academic, although not necessarily an easier, goal :
"The aim is to surround the graduate student with every facility for
advanced work, and every incitement to independent inquiry—in a word,
to inspire him with the genuine spirit of scholarship."[80] Two new and
exceedingly important dimensions are added to the purpose of graduate
work by this straightforward sentence—independent inquiry and scholarship :
neither had been given much attention, in fact, neither had been fully
understood, by Catholic college postgraduate professors in years past.
Perhaps both independent inquiry and genuine scholarship were still only
pious hopes and whether or not Georgetown was capable of cultivating
either at this time may be debated. What is important to the history of
Catholic college graduate school development was that at last these central
elements to university study were recognized and made part of a graduate
school's academic code. Once again, and on this higher level, Georgetown
could be imitated by her sister institutions around the country. Yet, although
the generative force of Georgetown's example may go unquestioned, we
still need a clearer picture of what in Georgetown's graduate school was
capable of being imitated.

Five departments formed Georgetown's graduate school : philosophy,
language and literature, history, natural science, and fine arts.[81] Graduate
courses were slightly more numerous than in the last year of postgraduate
organization. Now there were seventeen in all : three in philosophy, five in
language and literature, two in history, five in natural science, and two in
fine arts. The breadth of these courses, set out in detailed catalogue descriptions, is frightening to the advocate of competent scholarship, and raises,
moreover, some question about the depth of study a student might reasonably be expected to achieve. But if here we are treading familiar ground,
seeming at times to recapitulate the intention of postgraduate departments,
we must notice that in addition to the superior aims declared for graduate
study—independent inquiry and scholarship—the horizons of that study
are expanded beyond the traditional master's degree. For the first time in
any Catholic college graduate department with its origin in the old college
we find a regular program leading to the earned degree of doctor of philosophy. This degree was offered, and a degree program for it was instituted,
at Georgetown in the academic year, 1895-1896.[82]

Despite the clarity of purpose in the announcement of Georgetown's
graduate school, fluctuations in mood, compromises and false steps were
associated with its attainment. In the first place, and probably to satisfy
the academic appetites of prospective students, the school's prospectus,
although it appeared to refer solely to full-time study, inserted the amend-

80 *Ibid.,* p. 26.
81 *Ibid.,* pp. 25-29.
82 *Ibid.,* p. 26.

ment that classes convened both during the day and in the evening.[83] The implication was clear and students read it correctly : they could follow their daily pursuits in commerce, government, or industry and still be enrolled in Georgetown's graduate school. The catalogue makes no attempt to justify the amendment : the assumption that day and evening classes were designed with the working student in mind is probably correct. So, at the outset, the full-time study requirement was compromised. And the catalogue, despite its affirmation that graduate school study required the full attention of the student, carried a somewhat disturbing invitation to students in the schools of law and medicine to complement their professional curricula with graduate study.[84] This invitation had been made before when postgraduate courses were all Georgetown had to offer, and apparently it was hard for the officers of the school to reject a generous policy which had encountered no opposition.

In addition to these issues, to which the historian must pay some heed, the provisions necessary for academic specialization as an instrument of scholarship go almost unnoticed in Georgetown's code. This, too, attracts his attention. Of course, Georgetown was faced with a problem which almost put her in the position of having to disguise her graduate programs : the Catholic University of America was in its infant years and the managers of Georgetown were strictly enjoined against competing with the new school.[85] Sometimes, it would appear, developments in graduate study were halted altogether by Jesuit superiors; at other times these same superiors counseled Georgetown to proceed with caution in her graduate school and to avoid any public announcements which would look like competition for the new institution.[86] In this context it is easier to understand why Georgetown's graduate school stance was sometimes indecisive and why public announcements were markedly reticent. Even if Georgetown had not been disadvantaged by the privileged position the Catholic University of America was supposed to have with respect to graduate studies, some of the difficulties might still have been present, for Georgetown, we must remember, was blazing a new trail for Catholic colleges and it was not always easy for her to find the right route and mark it correctly.

A few of the marks she left along the path for other institutions to follow are worth recording—some of them policy directions, others purely matters of administrative regulation. Graduate study is intended for students who either want learning for its own sake (and the implication is clear that this is a sufficient reason) or for the purposes of professional advance-

83 *Ibid.*, p. 30.
84 *Ibid.*, p. 25.
85 Durkin, *op. cit.*, pp. 217–218.
86 *Ibid.*, pp. 221–222.

ment. Whatever the student's motive, "The courses, if pursued to the full extent recommended, are ample enough to tax the energies of any student. Yet the minimum work exacted is not too much to be profitably combined, in some cases, with the required attention to purely professional studies."[87] Admission requirements were modest, asking only that prospective students should be graduates of Georgetown "or of institutions of like standing."[88] Residence requirements varied according to the degree sought—either one or two years—but with respect to board and room the catalogue made it clear that students taking only graduate work at the school could "live within the College walls or not, as may suit their convenience," but students in the schools of law or medicine who were also taking graduate work were "expected to live outside of the College."[89] Apparently college accommodation for students was limited and generally reserved for students outside the professional schools, so Georgetown wanted to be sure that professional school students would not use the pretext of graduate study just to get a room in the college dormitory.

Studies were to begin with the opening of the academic year on "the first day of October" and to close "on the third or fourth Tuesday in June."[90] Academic schedules were flexible in the nineteenth century, so it was unnecessary for the catalogue to be any more explicit.

With these somewhat routine items out of the way, the catalogue statement gets down to the business of academic regulations. The courses are named and described and the student is told what he may expect his studies to be : "Class work is carried on by lectures, direction in reading, and intimate personal and practical guidance on the part of the professor, and on the side of the student by repetitions, written papers, and the preparation of original theses and investigations."[91] The aim of graduate work, the prospectus says, is to inspire and equip students for scholarship. And this goal of scholarship is marked out by the requirement that every student select, with the dean's concurrence, "at least three courses, involving attendance upon lectures for eight hours a week."[92] One course was always to be rational psychology, a course required before under the name of rational philosophy,[93] so the student's choice was really limited to two courses, not three, as stated in the catalogue. Three courses a year was the standard and a student could obtain his degree by adhering to it, but if he wanted to go beyond the minimum requirement, as his curiosity or

[87] *Catalogue of Georgetown University, 1895–1896,* p. 25.
[88] *Ibid.*
[89] *Ibid.*
[90] *Ibid.*
[91] *Ibid.*
[92] *Ibid.,* p. 26.
[93] *Catalogue of Georgetown University, 1891–1892,* p. 30.

scholarly motivation might at times dictate, he could do so without jeopardizing his chances of taking a degree, because however many courses a student might take he was expected to stand for examination only in three. One of the three courses for examination had to be rational psychology.

Aids to study are mentioned, but, as before, they are listed as the libraries, museums, the scientific collections, the lectures of the professors, and the privilege of consulting teachers outside the classroom. Something new is added, however, for now there is a Graduate Library of Literature, "a special collection intended for seminar work and already comprising some thousands of volumes,"[94] available for the graduate student's use. It is, indeed, surprising that with such a new and unique addition to the list of scholarly appurtenances no one bothered to count the number of volumes in this special library.

Missing from the requirements are the previous statements about a reading knowledge of French and German for either the master's or the doctor's degree, except for students enrolled in courses of French and German literature, where a knowledge of such languages is a condition for admission to the course. A student may qualify for the master's degree by fulfilling a year's residence, assuming he has a bachelor's degree, "with attendance upon lectures, presentation of papers, and satisfactory examinations"[95] in the three courses for which he is held responsible. For the degree of doctor of philosophy "two years of residence and application to selected and duly authorized graduate courses are required." In addition, the candidate has to pass a general examination, "present a thesis bearing upon his special department of study, and convince the committee appointed by the Faculty of his distinguished merit to receive this degree."[96]

Regardless of the number of courses taken, tuition for the academic year is $100; room, board, and washing will cost the student about $300 a year.[97]

By launching a graduate school Georgetown, then, evidenced an interest in completing its own university program in such a way as to put it on equal footing with other good schools of the country. The first part of its prospectus allows us to believe that allegiance to scholarship was clear and unequivocal, but toward the end of the statement about graduate work there are signs of retrocession from the meritorious standards hoped for. Georgetown was, after all, not quite certain which branches of learning ought to qualify for graduate school standing and appeared willing to leave further development of the program, not to the internal

[94] *Catalogue of Georgetown University, 1895–1896*, p. 26.
[95] *Ibid.*
[96] *Ibid.*
[97] *Ibid.*, p. 27.

processes of scholarly maturation, but to the opportunities offered or the demands suggested from outside. Students were invited to write to the school about areas of study not mentioned in the prospectus and the assumption may be made that if a sufficient number of students wanted "additional branches of learning" Georgetown's graduate school would offer them.[98] Then there is a section titled "practical suggestions," which turns out to be nothing more than an exercise in alerting prospective students to various uses—some of them devoid of scholarship and the quality of independent inquiry—to which graduate school study might be put. Journalism is a possibility, the prospectus says, but we look in vain for any program in journalism; college professors may become qualified by taking the degrees offered; "students of the Church" can make themselves ready for the seminary by taking such courses as ecclesiastical history and developing a facility in Latin "by conversation in groups formed for this purpose;"[99] finally, students interested in continuing their education in technical schools and eventually earning the degrees of Civil, Mechanical, Electrical, or Mining engineering can take preliminary courses in the graduate school, transfer to technical schools, and thus "take the degrees of C. E., M. E., and E. E. in two years, instead of four."[100] What may have been meant as attractive afterthoughts intended to interest students with professional rather than scholarly goals, put in doubt the commitment Georgetown was either willing or capable of making to the high standards of university scholarship.

With this model before them, one in which various combinations of studies were possible, some with and some devoid of scholarly pedigree, it was possible for Catholic colleges to follow Georgetown in constructing graduate programs and inaugurating graduate schools in which the fundamental conditions for advanced study and legitimate university standards might earn all too little attention. But Georgetown was not the only model Catholic colleges had to follow : nonCatholic universities had their graduate schools, and Catholic colleges, if they had chosen to do so, could have imitated them; and then there was the Catholic University of America, a school whose original commission pointed clearly toward university rather than college education, which because of its formal Catholicity and its integration with ecclesiastical government was a far more acceptable model than any so-called secular school. Because of its singular position in Catholic higher learning, and because of the tone it set for university study, we must take a closer look at this new institution, a creature of the Church in the United States—the Catholic University of America.

[98] *Ibid.,* p. 30.
[99] *Ibid.*
[100] *Ibid.*

The Catholic University of America

Catholics in the United States were preoccupied with questions of religious stability, so for the first three-quarters of the nineteenth century their debates centered on how the Church could be strengthened in America and how adherents to it could best be served by its multiple ministrations.[101] It would be claiming too much to say that they were convinced of education's central role in the formation of good men; yet they did regard schools as being important instruments for religion, always assuming that such schools would be strictly orthodox and subject to the control of a vigilant clergy. We have seen how the first colleges were organized and how their objectives were construed, and by now we know why Catholic colleges of the formative period were generally incapable of leadership in American higher learning. Even their efforts at self-improvement during the developmental years were half-hearted and inadequate, because there was no real conviction that academic excellence or scholarship should ever be allowed to compete with moral formation and spiritual orthodoxy. With attitudes like these, the slow and painful progress of Catholic colleges toward university standing is easily understood; and it is also easy to see why their first attempts at university studies were combinations of modesty and pretension. As we have said before, however, it was simply impossible for Catholics to make the calendar stand still and, when the full realization of this fact made its impact, they began to look for ways to make their schools of higher learning both more respectable, when compared with other colleges of the country, and more serviceable to them and the Church.

In 1876 the validity of the education offered by the old college was still believed in, but now with some hesitation about its monopoly of means. Various kinds of new colleges—technical, professional, agricultural—began to appear and with their appearance demonstrated their usefulness to a population interested not just in the totality of knowledge promised by the ancient classical course but in the techniques required by technology. Catholic attitudes toward higher education changed more slowly than those of the great majority of their countrymen, probably because of their nurtured conservatism, but they did change, and the time was at last ripe for some adjustments in their higher schools. What should these changes be? Should Catholic colleges become professional schools? Should they jettison their traditional allegiance to the classics? Should they become more academic and so, possibly, less moral and religious?

---

[101] See John Lancaster Spalding, *Means and Ends of Education* (Chicago, A. C. McClurg and Co., 1897), pp. 219–223.

If these questions had been answered by lay members of the Catholic population, the course chosen by Catholic higher education in the last years of the nineteenth century might have been different; but, as before, they were answered not by laymen but by ecclesiastics. And the entrance of the Catholic college into the new world of university-oriented higher learning was guided by clerical prescriptions concerning the kind of advanced education Catholics ought to have. So whatever pronouncements were made relative to university study under Catholic auspices, preferential treatment was always accorded to statements asserting the need for a university curriculum in which theology and philosophy should have pride of place.[102] Modest and diffident suggestions were sometimes offered about a kind of higher learning modeled on European universities: why not, for instance a university limiting its curriculum only by the boundaries of human knowledge?[103] But such a model was too ambitious for the cautious policies of the American hierarchy and they refused to consider it seriously. What they wanted, and what they were willing to settle for, was a school concentrating on the advanced theological training of priests; and they expected to call such a school a university. The general debate over university schools took its slow course and while it did the American prelates marked time; they refused to be hurried. In one sense, of course, they were right, for if the new school or schools being discussed were to be seminaries, then existing colleges and seminaries were already filling the most pressing needs. Additional schools of the old type were by no means imperative.

It was still unclear just what, if anything, should be done to create a new university, and if a new university were created, what its principal commitments should be. On one side of the debate, the proposition was advanced, as we have intimated, that any new school should concentrate on advanced theological curricula;[104] on the other side, arguments could be heard in support of a university along the lines described by John Henry Newman.[105] Yet both positions had some obvious weaknesses: why was it necessary to create a new school in order to offer a more advanced course in theology? This could be accomplished with much less cost and effort (as well as a wider diffusion of opportunity) by upgrading a few of the existing diocesan seminaries. Why was it necessary to contemplate the establishment of a university when so many Catholic colleges—Georgetown,

[102] See, for example, "On the Higher Education," *The Catholic World,* XII (March, 1871), 721–731; "College Education," *The Catholic World,* XX (September, 1877), 824–830; and "What is the Outlook for Our Catholic Colleges?," *The American Catholic Quarterly Review,* VII (July, 1882), 385–407.

[103] Thomas A. Becker, "A Plan for the Proposed Catholic University," *The American Catholic Quarterly Review,* I (October, 1876), 655–679.

[104] Power, *op. cit.,* p. 204.

[105] See John Henry Cardinal Newman, *The Idea of a University* (New York, Longmans, Green and Co., 1927).

Fordham, St. Louis, and Notre Dame, for example—were just starting to cross the threshold of university status? Would not such action irreparably weaken these schools? After all, how abundant were Catholic resources for supporting universities and why should a new school be created to do what existing schools could easily be made capable of doing? If one could make convincing the argument that diocesan priests needed neither learning nor erudition—that the seminary had given them everything necessary in the way of theological education—and that members of religious orders who might have need for advanced study because of their association with the colleges could easily obtain such education in European or American universities, and, moreover, that, as far as lay Catholics were concerned, the existing colleges were all they needed, then the case for a new school —a university it was called, for want of a better name—was almost indefensible.

Looking at the question of higher education with an understanding only of their own professional needs, and heedless of the legitimate educational aspirations of laymen, the American Catholic clergy could think of a new university only along lines that would be of direct benefit to them. And with this rationale as a guide, the future of a new school, whether it was to be an authentic university or only a high school of theology, was indeed precarious. What complicated the whole issue even more and tended to distort commitments to learning in the Catholic University of America when it was founded, was the uncertainty and confusion in the American Catholic mind about the nature of a university. Undoubtedly some prelates and clergymen, and a few interested laymen, had read Newman; but Newman's *Idea of a University* did not become a classic for decades afterwards, so when they read it they found considerable difficulty in accepting it as a constitution for higher learning. There was, moreover, almost nothing in their own educational experience to confirm the scholarly allegiances Newman endorsed in his incomparable prose. If, as we have suggested, the Catholic college presidents and deans who were only now thinking of upgrading their schools along university lines were uncertain about the meaning of a university, it is easy to understand why the seminary-trained bishops, who were, after all, the persons to make the decision about a new Catholic university, had some difficulty in fathoming its significance.[106]

Whether or not a Catholic University should be established was hardly a burning issue of the day when the prelates assembled in Baltimore in 1884 to convene the Third Plenary Council. And left to their own inclinations, both because few of them thought it necessary to do anything about the talk of a university and because no firm proposal was before them, they

[106] John Tracy Ellis, *The Formative Years of the Catholic University of America* (Washington, American Catholic Historical Society, 1946), pp. 67–86.

would probably have left the matter untouched. But during the first days of the Council, Mary Gwendoline Caldwell, a wealthy young heiress of New York City, offered three hundred thousand dollars to the bishops if they would adopt a plan to establish a National Catholic School of Philosophy and Theology.[107] Miss Caldwell's proffered benefaction was probably not her idea alone, for John Lancaster Spalding, Bishop of Peoria, Illinois, long an advocate of a Catholic university, is known to have recommended the project to her. And in order to make the whole plan more palatable to the prelates who either misunderstood universities or had some misgivings about them, the institution was to center its efforts on philosophy and theology at first and then, when conditions were right, to add other faculties with a view to becoming a complete university. Miss Caldwell offered her money, but not without some conditions : the school was to be established in the United States (while this might have appeared obvious, Bishop Spalding knew only too well the prelates' penchant for supporting schools in Rome and he did not want the money wasted on some ill-conceived Roman venture); it should be controlled by the Catholic bishops of the United States; it should always be an independent institution without any association with other Catholic colleges, universities, or seminaries; enrollment was to be limited to clerical students who had completed their elementary courses in theology and philosophy (provision for lay students, at least under these conditions, were ignored); the school was never to be surrendered to the control of a religious order and its professors should come preferably from the secular clergy and the laity; other faculties could in time be affiliated to the original ones of theology and philosophy "with a view to forming a Catholic University;" the benefaction was to be used only for its stated purpose and the location of the school, once determined, was not to be altered "without the greatest reasons;" and, finally, Miss Caldwell was to be recognised as the founder of the institution. The letter wherein this offer was made, and the conditions for complying with it as set forth, was dated November 13, 1884.[108]

Miss Caldwell's generous proposition undoubtedly impressed prelates who were unwilling to allow such a large sum to slip through their grasp. Yet the argument advanced by Archbishop Michael Heiss of Milwaukee was still very much to the point : a Catholic university was premature and it was unnecessary to create a new school for purposes that could easily be fulfilled by improving the larger, or provincial, seminaries.[109] As long as the bishops conceived of the university only as a place for the advanced training of diocesan priests, Miss Caldwell's proposition was in jeopardy. Their attitudes had to be amended and at this stage John Lancaster

107 *Ibid.*, p. 96.
108 The letter, with the conditions mentioned, is quoted in *ibid.*, p. 97.
109 Power. *op. cit.*, p. 225.

Spalding, again the right man at the right time, essayed to perform this difficult task. His role was not an easy one, for in supporting the idea of a new university, he had to tread a precarious path between opponents of a university, advocates of existing seminaries who would willingly consider strengthening the seminary system, and the determined defenders of Catholic colleges. The two latter were arguing from the sanctuary of vested interest, as well they might, while spokesmen for the first—the anti-university clan—were either afraid of a university or believed one to be completely unnecessary. Finding a way between these three conflicting positions was, as we have said, a task requiring the nicest diplomacy, but Spalding, confident that he was equal to it, undertook to do so in his sermon on the "Higher Education of the Priesthood," delivered before the Council on November 16, 1884.[110]

He began by stilling fears among the prelates who regarded the new school as a threat to Catholic colleges and by assuring his fellow ecclesiastics that the mission of the diocesan seminary was to train its students for the practical work of the ministry. But something more than the colleges and the seminaries was needed if the narrowness and one-sidedness of the priest's professional education was to be supplemented by more liberal, broader intellectual objectives. Spalding's justification for a university-type school was incomplete, for he centered his whole case on the need for the higher learning of clerics and entirely neglected the education of lay Catholics, but this emphasis was perhaps necessary : the case for the university would have been weakened by admitting before the Council that university studies of worth might in time stray far from the boundaries imposed by the disciplines of theology and philosophy. But it would have been weakened also by acknowledging that within the existing seminaries there was a latent desire to become centers of intellectual culture. And it was this that interested Spalding most. Thus, it was necessary for him to say from the pulpit some hard things about the seminaries. Quite bluntly he told his audience, many of whom were responsible for the character and quality of diocesan seminaries, that the seminary was "not a school of intellectual culture, either here in America or elsewhere, and to imagine that it can become the instrument of intellectual culture is to cherish a delusion."[111] He documented his conclusion by pointing to the seminary's methods of teaching which, he said, "are not such as one would choose who desires to open the mind, to give it breadth, flexibility, strength, refinement, and grace."[112] Seminary textbooks, he went on, were too frequently written in a "barbarous style," and seminary professors "wholly intent upon giving

---

[110] The text of the sermon is in Spalding, *op. cit.,* pp. 212–216.
[111] *Ibid.,* p. 212.
[112] *Ibid.*

instruction" were too often dry, mechanical, and totally indifferent to the kind of pedagogy which might kindle a spark of real intellectual curiosity.[113] But faulty or indifferent methods of teaching were not the worst features of seminary instruction : the professor "not possessing himself a really cultivated intellect . . . holds in slight esteem expansion and refinement of mind, looking upon it as at best a mere ornament."[114] This evaluation of the seminary system, he said, rather than being a criticism of the ecclesiastical seminary, was simply a way of pointing "to the plain fact that it is not a school of intellectual culture, and consequently, if its course were lengthened to five, to six, to eight, to ten years, its students would go forth to their work with a more thorough professional training, but not with more really cultivated minds."[115]

The American Church needed its seminaries, and Spalding knew that any recommendation to scuttle the system or to change its fundamental direction would meet with determined opposition. His university project had enough enemies as it was, so any determined assault on the seminaries would have been imprudent, for, in the end, it would have achieved only a nettled indifference, if not an outright animosity, toward what he hoped to achieve. The prospects for a university, it might seem, were not made brighter by declaring against the deficiencies in the seminaries; yet Spalding was determined to convince his brother prelates that, whatever the seminaries were, or however excellent they might become, they were not intended to be universities, and it was a university that American Catholics needed. "It is only in a university," he said, where "all the sciences are brought together, their relations adjusted, their provinces assigned . . . so long as we look rather to the multiplying of schools and seminaries than to the creation of a real university, our progress will be slow and uncertain, because a university is the great ordinary means for the best cultivation of the mind."[116]

Despite Spalding's affirmation about the need for a university, where culture and intellect would be cultivated, the urgency of his appeal was toned down, for he knew that a university could not be created in a day. It had to be started modestly, beginning, as Miss Caldwell had proposed, with a curriculum of theology and philosophy, and from its first foundations be shaped gradually toward academic completeness. At the same time, the projected institution, despite the brave talk about its becoming a university in the conventional sense, was supposed to be an additional rung on the ladder of clerical education, and even Spalding's manifesto does almost nothing to alter this fact. The committee of the council to which the

113 *Ibid.*
114 *Ibid.*, p. 213.
115 *Ibid.*
116 *Ibid.*

university issue was channeled was the committee on clerical education; in this committee a motion (in which the suggested university was called a principal seminary) was proposed and seconded to defer the entire matter to a subsequent plenary council. But whether the failure of this notion to gain committee approval was due to the bishops' determination to have a principal seminary, assuming they had been convinced by Spalding's arguments for higher studies, or whether they feared that a negative vote would keep them from getting their hands on Miss Caldwell's benefaction, is a moot point. In any case, the committee's vote to consider the possibility of establishing some kind of higher school cleared the air and allowed for a positive approach to the whole question. Now supposedly, a principal seminary or a university could be decided on its merits. A sub-committee of the conciliar committee on clerical education was formed to conduct a detailed study of the matter and commissioned to report its recommendations before the Plenary Council adjourned. After two weeks' study the committee submitted its report recommending the acceptance of Miss Caldwell's gift; the Council confirmed the committee's report and incorporated in its decrees sent to Rome for approval a plan for the founding of the Catholic University of America. Thus, it is fair to claim December 2, 1884, as the date for the founding of the Catholic University, although papal approval was delayed until October 22, 1885, and canonical institution did not come until April 10, 1887. The university opened its doors to students on November 13, 1889.

American Catholics were thus committed by their hierarchy to a Catholic university, but it should be pointed out at once that the term university was clothed in considerable ambiguity. When the Baltimore council forwarded its decrees to Rome, and when those decrees were approved in Rome, the language used should have made the advocates of a real university foundation uneasy, for the phrase 'principal seminary' was always used in place of the term 'university.' The hope was stated, it is true, that from this 'principal seminary' a "perfect university of studies" might some day grow, and the projected curriculum, while encompassing three or four years of study in theology, canon law, and philosophy as a beginning, did allow for the subsequent development of curricula in "the natural and other sciences." [117] Proponents of a university could find some comfort in these phrases, and the implication that such language would hardly have been used in connection with normal seminary studies. There was another implication, that a fully graduate school was intended : only students who had finished "the usual course of studies" were to be accepted. Still, the constitution for the new school was unclear and, in view of the old animosities surrounding the original plan for a Catholic university,

[117] See Ellis, *op. cit.*, pp. 114–115.

the road ahead for the infant institution was threatened by hostility and difficulty.

The major difficulty, of course, lay in the fact that the bishops of the Third Plenary Council were uncertain about what they were approving when they voted the decree for a principal seminary for the United States. A few undoubtedly, following Spalding, intended to support something more than a high school of theology, but, given the later nineteenth-century episcopal mentality, it is probably fair to conclude that the majority had approved what they thought would be a higher seminary, not a university. But to complicate the issue even more, many of them either refused to admit of any distinction between the two, or if they did so admit (timidly and reluctantly) they were unable to understand why Catholics should be interested in supporting a university. The prelates plagued by these anxieties found comfort in the opinions of some American nonCatholics : the New York *Times* devoted an editorial to the subject of a Catholic university and asked what such a university would teach. A university, the *Times* writer assumed, should include science as well as theology in its curriculum, but "The Church of Rome is generally regarded as hostile to modern science." Yet even without that hostility to certain branches of knowledge, why should a Catholic university be interested in teaching purely secular subjects? This, the editorial writer said, would be "like establishing a Presbyterian school of mines or a Methodist agricultural college."[118] The *Times* advised Catholics to husband their resources more wisely and forget about a university. And this is precisely what a number of influential Catholic bishops wanted to do.

Some kind of school was going to be founded, nevertheless, and whether it was only a principal seminary or a university it would still have to be located somewhere. The debate over the school's purpose could mark time while the issue of location was settled. Every section of the country was recommended for the new school; propositions were advanced for purchasing existing colleges—Seton Hall and Mt. St. Mary's were most frequently mentioned in this connection—but such plans were vetoed by the school's principal benefactor and since she had not yet transferred any money to the bishops her voice was strong. Finally, early in 1885, the university committee, which had been appointed by the Council to handle the details of founding, selected Washington, D. C., as the site for the new school.

It would be pleasant, indeed, to be able to report that once the location of the school was decided its forward progress was uninterrupted by uncertainty and unimpeded by episcopal opposition, but the record shows otherwise. Eastern bishops, dissatisfied with the location of the university,

118 New York *Times,* December 13, 1884.

sometimes refused to have anything to do with the proposed school and prohibited collections within their dioceses for its support. Some, perhaps, believing that the university would be of little benefit to their dioceses, or doubting whether the university would fulfill the objectives they had assumed would be appropriate to a principal seminary, conspired to establish competing schools. And the ideas about competing schools were not all invidious or irrelevant: the United States, it was maintained, was simply too large a country to be served by one university located in Washington; at least two additional universities, one for the Middlewest and one for the West, should also be planned. Yet, if we accept for the moment the merit of a multiple university plan, it must nevertheless be admitted that planning for two additional universities before the original one had been solidly founded was premature. Moreover, it was never entirely clear that such plans were anything more than subversive (if plausible) distracters which would so overload the concept as to bring about its abandonment in entirety, the already ratified university plan going down with it. In any case, some members of the university committee took these plans seriously enough to recommend that an appeal be directed to the Pope, asking him to declare a moratorium on the founding of additional Catholic universities in the United States for twenty-five years. Prospects that the university plan would attain realization were already so poor that its best advocates feared any competition at all.

With the university's location settled, after strong opposition had been overcome, the next logical step could be taken: the selection of a president or, to use the archaic ecclesiastical term, a rector. The university committee's first and natural choice was John Lancaster Spalding, more than any other person responsible for the university idea in the first place. But Spalding, for his own reasons, refused the position and Bishop John J. Keane, of the diocese of Richmond, was selected. No doubt Keane's qualifications for such an important position were fully weighed by the committee, and must have seemed to them good; but they were not generally apparent. He himself admitted to knowing nothing about a university.[119] Yet he took his appointment seriously and in the short time at his disposal tried to learn as much as he could about university affairs. Ellis says Keane spent a "good part of the next two years . . . inspecting universities in America and Europe and taking counsel with university administrators whenever the opportunity presented itself."[120] Much of the opposition to Keane came, of course, from persons unfriendly to the university, for whom whoever was named to the rectorship would have been unacceptable. If it was easy to point to Keane's obvious lack of familiarity with academia, easy to score debater's points against him on this ground, members of the episco-

119 Power, *op. cit.*, pp. 228–229.
120 Ellis, *op. cit.*, p. 181.

pate critical of Keane's appointment should have been more sensitive to appointments they themselves had made to college presidencies and seminary rectorships, for neither in their record of appointments nor, for that matter, in the record of appointments made to Catholic college presidencies since the founding of Georgetown, had familiarity with the institution which they were to govern been considered a critical credential. Keane's appointment was well within Catholic academic conventions.

Being an unpopular choice among those who might have helped the new institution most did not lighten the load for the new Rector when he began to seek financial support for the University, when he set about the highly involved task of writing the statutes which should govern it, or when he endeavored to recruit a faculty of scholars worthy of the anticipations nurtured for the infant school. Money was always hard to get, but it became a good deal harder when bishops of large dioceses refused to endorse fund raising within their sees for the University's benefit. The Pope, of course, had given his official encouragement and endorsement to the University, but bishops, when they wanted to, could find ways to observe the letter of the law while breaching its spirit, and they could halve the annual collection receipts for the University, keeping one part for the schools and seminaries in their own dioceses. Statutes, troublesome too, were eventually hammered out in such a way as to be acceptable both to the American bishops and Rome. Recruiting a faculty for the new school was probably the most difficult job facing Keane and his task was complicated further by the fact that, for an American school with an advertised American image, he had to look for prospective professors and promising scholars in Europe.

At the time the Catholic University was founded American Catholic higher education was about a hundred years old, and for about a half-century Catholic colleges had been tinkering with graduate degrees. But in actual fact these institutions had produced few university scholars and the recruitment of a faculty for the new University from the ranks of native clergymen and laymen was patently impossible. Umbrage could be taken about this, and doubtless members of the American clergy resented being reminded that from among their ranks persons qualified for a university professorship were extraordinarily hard to find; nevertheless, if Keane was to remain true to the standards set for the University, he had to look beyond the boundaries of the United States for a faculty.[121] But, again, why this should have caused the American prelates so much concern is a minor mystery. For decades the colleges had been staffed by foreign-born priests and brothers, and most Catholic colleges conducted by religious orders were still anxious to recruit teachers from their houses in Europe.

[121] See John J. Keane, *Catholic American*, November 24, 1888.

Tapping Europe for college teachers had been, and to a great extent still was, the American Catholic college way. Yet the prelates made an issue of what they thought was an anomaly and criticized Keane and the University for proceeding under false colors. How could a school be American if it was filled with European teachers? Keane, however, was perfectly honest about the predicament he was in with regard to faculty talent : at first teachers would have to come from Europe, but "as fast as we can find Americans of the necessary calibre to fill the professorships they will be appointed." [122] Five European professors were appointed to the original faculty and Keane characterized them as first-class scholars. But the best scholars may not have been willing to leave European centers of learning to engage in a pioneer venture, and there was some substance, no doubt, to the remark Cardinal Manning is said to have made : "Bishop Keane could have found enough mediocrities in his own country without going across the Atlantic for others." [123]

With a faculty assembled, the Catholic University of America commenced instruction in 1889, with thirty-eight clerical students enrolled in the university's only school, the School of Theology. [124] Some students were, of course, seeking advanced degrees, either licentiates or doctorates in sacred theology; others were simply continuing their theological education without plans for a degree; and still others, although they had finished their theological studies in diocesan seminaries, did not even possess the bachelor's degree. For these latter students, the University conferred the bachelor's degree in theology. The curriculum of the school of theology was divided into four departments : dogmatic, moral, and scriptural theology and historical theological studies. Degree requirements were set out along the following lines. For the licentiate, a purely ecclesiastical degree almost totally unknown in the United States outside Catholic seminaries, two years of study were required along with a six-hour written examination on subjects from the four departments and a private and public oral defense of fifty theses. The doctorate in sacred theology demanded four years of study, a dissertation of at least one hundred printed pages, demonstrating "original power and personal research and it had to be approved by the faculty and published," and a satisfactory public defense of seventy-five theses, "along with the dissertation, for three hours on each of two consecutive days." [125]

Cardinal Manning turned out to be less than a prophet when he

[122] *Ibid.*

[123] Quoted in Maurice F. Egan, *Recollections of a Happy Life* (New York, George-H. Doran, 1924), p. 185.

[124] Patrick Henry Ahern, *The Catholic University of America, 1887–1896* (Washington, Catholic University of America Press, 1948), pp. 36–37.

[125] *Ibid.*, p. 38.

doubted the capabilities of the University's first faculty, for the theses and dissertations produced by the first students were impressive testimony to the high standards this faculty set. During its early decades the Catholic University had a narrow academic scope and it failed to fulfill the most rigorous definition of a true university, but its dissertations, after all the best evidence of its scholarship, are still available to prove that this school was much more than an advanced seminary. No apologies were needed for its scholarly quality even during its most infant years. Yet there were other aspects of genuine university life in which its accomplishments were low.

Catholic colleges had been preoccupied with student discipline for a century; seminaries were assiduous in the supervision of moral life among their students; and the Catholic University found it easier to comply with established conventions of college life than to blaze any new trails toward creating a university environment. Thus rules that might have been appropriate for children were imposed on students who were ordained priests. Many clerical students had come to the University anticipating the liberal academic climate befitting a university and were bitterly disappointed to find they were housed in a monastery instead. And Keane, sometimes so liberal on other issues, had a blind spot on discipline : he was unable to understand why students resented being treated like schoolboys; moreover, it surprised him to discover that well-qualified, promising students often refused to attend the university.[126] Nowhere in the record of his rectorship was Keane weaker than on this matter of discipline, and he was publicly critical of students who thought they should find an atmosphere at the university different from the one they knew at the seminary. His rigid policy included supervising all student activities and sometimes supervision meant only the limitation of personal liberty in the interest of what the Rector chose to call good order. It was when he took this hard line that he began to find support among prelates who had opposed him before. Bishops who had wondered whether or not the university could ever succeed, especially under Keane's direction, now advised him to stand by his guns and expel any priest-student who questioned the wisdom of the university's disciplinary code.

The adaptation of the regulations to the age and maturity of the students enrolled was never seriously considered; all students were required to live in common dormitories under the direction of Sulpician prefects. The rules governing conduct were plentiful and taboos were numerous, but two were especially juvenile : students could not leave the university grounds without permission and smoking in rooms was prohibited. Compliance with all rules was expected to be exact. A system of demerits was invented and a student's deportment was reported regularly to his bishop. So much was

126 *Ibid.*, pp. 30–40.

made of discipline that some bishops, now interested in what a real university could do, began to wonder whether or not there was some higher objective toward which the university might aim. Diocesan seminaries had trained priests for their spiritual and sacerdotal life; had the university been established to make them monks? Compared with what one might expect in an authentic university climate, the paternal atmosphere at the Catholic University, with its fetishes about student conduct, was both ridiculous and disappointing and unworthy of a great institution. For the most part, its students were mature, capable, dedicated priests assigned to the university because of their academic and intellectual promise, but the strident disciplinary code bespoke a narrow ecclesiastical mentality still too restrictive to embrace the idea of a university.[127]

Despite these inexcusable disciplinary preoccupations, the Rector and the board of directors soon discovered it was a mistake to keep their attention fixed on rules of good order, for the university was growing and its growth needed direction. Legally the university was authorized to confer degrees in theology, philosophy, natural science, mathematics, history, humanities, law, and medicine; papal rescript allowed it to conduct advanced studies in philosophy, theology, pontifical law, as well as other studies normally maintained by universities of the world. The old doubts about what the university should be—a complete institution of higher learning or only a high school of theology—were voiced with less regularity and with much less fury than before. It is probably correct to assume that toward the end of the first decade of its existence most American bishops were beginning to take for granted what had seemed so clear to Spalding : the Church in America needed a university more than it needed a big seminary. It was left, then, to the managers of the institution to make the Catholic University what most interested persons wanted it to be. In 1895, two schools, one of philosophy and the other of social sciences, were added to the already existing school of theology, and nine departments supplemented the four original ones. Both these new schools and the new departments organized within them were indicative of the departures the school was capable of making from a total commitment to ecclesiastical studies. The new departments were : philosophy, mathematics, physical science, biological science, letters, sociology, economics, political science, and law. And it was at about this time that friends of the Catholic University tried to wrestle away from Georgetown her schools of law and medicine. We have already seen the results of this academic tampering.[128] Undoubtedly, as the Catholic University prepared to enter the twentieth century her sights were set on becoming in reality the first Catholic *university* in the United States.

Adding schools and departments involved, of course, the recruitment of

[127] *Ibid.*, p. 41.
[128] See pp. 217–218; 227–228.

faculties to conduct them, and this was never easy; so the Rectors who followed Keane were introduced to some of the problems he had faced earlier. But they had some new ones too : the retention of outstanding professors, especially if they were Americans, was sometimes impossible, for the faculty of the Catholic University, far more in the public eye than professors of Catholic colleges, were inevitably considered for promotion in the hierarchy : a number of the University's most distinguished professors became bishops. This practice, when still in its beginnings, is known to have worried the university's first Rector. Archbishop John Ireland gave Keane some advice which he was powerless to follow : "You must educate your professors and then hold on to them—making bishops only of those who are not worth keeping as professors."[129]

Besides faculty recruitment and retention, the University was faced with the always explosive problem of maintaining good relations with the Catholic colleges of the country. In the first years, because there was uncertainty about what the university would prove to be, the Catholic University appeared to the colleges to be only a minor threat to their security. But the misguided attempt engineered by the Papal Legate to abstract Georgetown's schools of law and medicine and transfer them to the Catholic University became a clear sign of the ambitions some persons had for the University. The Catholic colleges, moreover, were trying their best to achieve university rank and the competition of the Catholic University was a deterrent. If the new University were to admit only clerics as students, then the colleges might see their road to success somewhat more clearly, because the lay Catholic population would be left for them to educate; or if the University were to remain true to its original intent of offering only graduate studies, then the colleges would have the whole field of undergraduate education for their domain. As it turned out, however, the original plans for the University were tentative rather than fixed : undergraduates were admitted to the Catholic University in 1904, although only male undergraduates were formally acknowledged to be students of the University; women students were educated through an arrangement with affiliated houses of studies. The decision to admit undergraduates appeared to the University's managers to be imperative, for without the income from undergraduate students the school could not remain solvent; and the decision to educate women, although only on an unofficial basis, was dictated by the needs of the Church to have communities of sisters qualified to conduct parish schools. As a matter of fact, the University's faculty was considerably more sensitive to this need than the University's board of directors, for the former had voted in 1894 to admit women, but the board of directors, all bishops, refused to countenance coeducation. This prohibition remained in force

[129] Quoted in Ahern, *op. cit.,* p. 50.

until 1928, when female graduate students were officially admitted to the University, but it was not until 1946 that laywomen undergraduates were officially recognized as students. What with these changes in admissions policies, attempts to broaden the curriculum and the tendency to welcome lay students, the relations between the Catholic colleges and the Catholic University seldom reached the level of academic cordiality. Yet by 1930 it became fully apparent that, even with the Catholic University conducting broad graduate and undergraduate programs which attracted men officially and women unofficially, there was still plenty of room left in the field of higher learning for American Catholic colleges. Even the colleges which had matured into university status found their academic lives and futures unthreatened by the presence of the University in Washington.

Promise and realization

On entering the twentieth century, and now more than a century old in America, Catholic higher learning presented a variety of faces : at the head of the list stood the Catholic University with its commission to be the major Catholic school in the United States, but not very far down were the promising Catholic colleges—Georgetown, Fordham, Notre Dame, and St. Louis—where university-type studies had been experimented with for a quarter of a century. Then came dozens of men's and women's colleges of all characters and qualities; some, unquestionably, were good under-graduate schools, others had yet to reach the lower levels of respectability; and a few should never have been established. But through all these schools ran a common thread of ambition to achieve a place in the American world of learning and in most of them these ambitions were expected to be served by adding programs of graduate studies. In a word, every Catholic college, irrespective of its resources, its location, or any reasonable evaluation of its success, wanted to be a university. And these ambitions were natural enough, although probably unrealistic, for such schools were living in the age of the university.

It shortly became obvious that neither the Catholic University nor the better-known Catholic colleges, where graduate departments and schools had been added, could monopolize Catholic higher learning beyond the bachelor's degree. Even if the Catholic University had been more centrally placed, genuine competition would still have been possible, for its initial charge committed it to the higher education of religious persons and this tended to diminish its attractiveness for lay students; so other Catholic schools could be assured of a clientele. Then Georgetown, Fordham, St. Louis, and Notre Dame—none of them had a commanding geographic location and even if they had had, it is unlikely that any one, or all together, would have been able to offer all the graduate education opportunities a more enlightened Catholic population now thought it wanted. There was room for all Catholic colleges to move toward their ambitious goal of associating graduate studies with existing undergraduate curricula.

Setting a legitimate goal was one thing; attaining it was quite another. In the early nineteen hundreds Catholic higher learning, including the Catholic University, was uncertain of its direction and unsure about its philosophy, and was, moreover, almost totally bereft of any university tradition from which to obtain guidance. Besides, among the teachers and administrators in early twentieth-century Catholic colleges, only a handful had any direct experience of university study and none had been involved in managing the complex academic arrangements of universities.[130] So without models of their own to follow, except those they could faintly recollect from what they had read about European universities and in Newman's *Idea of a University,* which they studied as literature but refused to regard as educational theory, they could depend for guidance only on what they saw going on around them. Their own experiments with postgraduate studies were there, of course, but they preferred to forget them, believing, no doubt, that they were short of the necessary standards; more up-to-date, but no more dependable, paradigms could be found for university management among the actions taken by such schools as Georgetown and Fordham; but the model that seemed most useful, and also most orthodox because of its creation under the direction of the hierarchy, was the Catholic University. So Catholic colleges began by imitating the school they really intended to compete with, and this always caused them some difficulty. Yet such imitation was entirely natural, possibly unavoidable. If the colleges were to become universities, at least some of their religious faculty members should have advanced university degrees, and where could such students go unless they attended the Catholic University? Thus, coming from the school in Washington, graduates of the Catholic University introduced policies of wider university academic management with which they were only partially familiar.[131] It is probably fair to say that prior to 1930 Catholic colleges working toward university standing were trial miniatures of the Catholic University of America.

Yet, even if the Catholic University proved to be the first and, for a while, the best model for Catholic colleges to follow, it proved in the long run to be only one among many available for imitation. Beginning timidly, and intent upon preserving their image of Catholicity, the Catholic colleges chose to ignore nonCatholic universities around them, and in so

---

130 Power, *op. cit.,* p. 235.

131 Henry J. Browne, "Pioneer Days at the Catholic University of America," *Catholic Educational Review,* 48 (January, 1950), 29–38.

doing they were continuing a policy of planned indifference to nonCatholic higher education which had been in force for more than a hundred years. But whether or not they would have continued voluntarily to follow this policy of paying small attention, if any, to their nonCatholic counterparts is a question that need not be asked, for, as it turned out, conditions in American higher learning effectively prevented them from doing so. There grew up college and university academic societies and regional accrediting associations to set standards of academic quality and acceptability; if Catholic higher schools were to take their places in the world of learning and, moreover, if they were to keep academic faith with their students, they would have to become members of such associations.[132] In becoming members they surrendered some of their freedom, it is true, but they were also introduced to theories and practices of higher education which, left entirely to themselves, they probably would have missed. Thus, the closer Catholic colleges came to becoming universities, in fact as well as in name, the more like their nonCatholic counterparts they became and this meant that some of their chronic problems became even more serious.

Many Catholic colleges, although by no means all, were just beginning to master the art of being undergraduate schools and were achieving reasonable standards at this level when the responsibilities of graduate education were thrust on them. As a result, the established undergraduate academic organization suffered some loss and injury in competition with new graduate departments, and the chronic problems of faculties, finances, and facilities became more critical. Catholic colleges which set up graduate departments, divisions, and schools often did so mistakenly, believing, or hoping, that advanced instructional facilities would cost nothing, and that a flood of graduate students would help fill their depleted treasuries. This was a myth current among college presidents and not recognized as such : and during the early years of the twentieth century, when classrooms and laboratories were often only half filled with students, graduate programs were inaugurated in the belief that they would fill them. Had they been less isolated from the academic world around them, presidents might easily have learned of the notoriously poor record graduate programs had as income producers.

But perhaps too much can be made both of Catholic college isolation and of the increased cost of graduate teaching; both are somewhat beside the point. The early Catholic graduate schools often ignored distinctions between undergraduate and graduate classes, allowing students from both divisions to mix in the same classes, so it was probably true, for a time at least, that income could be increased by adding graduate studies. The feeling was common, and plenty of documentation could be mustered on

[132] P. M. Limbert, *Denominational Policies in Support of Higher Education* (New York, Teachers College Press, 1929), pp. 91–106.

this point by simply leafing through the catalogues of a few colleges of the period, that programs of study for the master's and sometimes the doctor's degree could be added without altering or multiplying the courses offered, without making appointments to the faculty, and without enlarging college facilities. This was all a great myth too, but it went unrecognized and unchallenged for a long time.

The first graduate departments, as we have seen, and the first graduate schools, too, for that matter, lacked genuine graduate quality and university character. Naming the courses almost without reference to standard was something which had had its origin in these schools a half-century earlier and it was an obstacle to growth and improvement; for as long as the colleges sincerely believed their work to be praiseworthy, the prospects for higher standards or better quality were foreclosed. Undoubtedly Catholic colleges sincerely aspired to university standing—it is unthinkable that they either desired or planned for inferiority—yet they failed to perceive that high-quality institutions were not produced by wishful thinking. Almost overnight a school would move from solely undergraduate educational obligations to add programs for advanced instruction and sometimes for the highest degrees—all legal enough because state legislatures had been too generous in the charters they issued to foundling colleges—[133] with a faculty barely adequate to the demands of a modernized undergraduate course. And thereafter these professors would have to teach graduate classes too. Yet to fulfill the expectations set for these graduate programs was fairly easy, because nowhere in them was anything said about research and independent inquiry. These key phrases, to which Georgetown had paid lip service in the 1890s,[134] were never translated into action. Had they been, hardly any early twentieth-century Catholic college would have engaged in graduate instruction, for with faculties composed of men who had never spent a day doing scholarly work, and with curricula which were only continuations of undergraduate courses or duplications of them, the most obvious and necessary criteria were missing. Faculty appointments were too often internal promotions, with all the perpetuated disadvantages of inbreeding; standards were viewed with thinly veiled complacency or nonchalance, as witnessed by a Catholic college petition to the North Central Association of Colleges and Secondary Schools in 1933 asking the Association to recognize ordination to the priesthood as equivalent to the Ph. D. degree.[135] The schools themselves displayed a studied indifference to the quality of their instruction. But all this had a sufficient excuse : what-

133 John S. Brubacher and Willis Rudy, *Higher Education in Transition* (New York, Harper and Row, Publishers, 1958), pp. 339–340.

134 *Catalogue of Georgetown University, 1895–1896,* pp. 25–29.

135 "Proceedings of the Commission on Colleges and Universities," *North Central Association Quarterly,* 8 (July, 1933), 44.

ever deficiencies the course might have, it was none the less praiseworthy, because its content was protected both by Catholic orthodoxy and the truths already the common possession of all educated Catholics.[136] With truth in their grasp, what need had professors or students for research and what justification was there for continuing the quest for knowledge?

For purposes of advanced instruction, college facilities were no better than the faculties. These schools, especially the older ones, had been founded, and their buildings had been constructed, in the belief that they would always be what their founders said they should be—simple colleges. So such things as libraries, laboratories, faculty offices, and places for students to study were seldom adequate to the needs of basic undergraduate teaching and were totally inadequate for the requirements of graduate work. The Catholic University probably had the best library, but its holdings totalled only 17,000 volumes in 1889 and its books were selected with theological and philosophical studies in mind.[137] The usual college library, to which reference has already been made, was theologically and classically selected, and even within these limits the selections were hardly adequate for advanced scholarly study. For the most part, Catholic college libraries were useless for purposes of graduate research. But if libraries were bad, or nonexistent, so were laboratories, study rooms for students, and office and conference space for professors. In the last respect, which could hardly have been an oversight, one must assume that clerical architects had designed college buildings without ever taking into account a professor's need for a place to study, conduct his research, or confer with students. And some of these buildings were designed at a time when such professional responsibilities were readily apparent.

But if all these things militated against university quality and status, they were really of minor importance when compared to the official academic attitude toward knowledge prevalent among Catholic higher schools. Knowledge might be good for its own sake—at least Newman had said so, and it was difficult to controvert him—but knowledge worth having was already known and somehow readily available within the Catholic deposit of knowledge. Research to discover something new, effort to push back the boundaries of knowledge, was a profitless enterprise.[138] With this official attitude, graduate schools could not have been expected to prosper; but, without reference to the part specifically to be played by graduate schools, it proved also to be a serious impediment to the discovery of things yet unknown in God's world. In actual fact, for the first half-century of their

---

[136] George Bull, "The Function of the Catholic Graduate School," *Thought,* XIII (September, 1938), 364–380.

[137] Power, *op. cit.,* p. 236.

[138] George Bull, *op. cit.*

history, Catholic graduate schools left forfeit the authentic and genuine objectives of university education.

Yet, amid the run-of-the-mill academic practices allowed in Catholic colleges and the half-hearted efforts to upgrade the quality of instruction to meet university standards, there were some good omens for the future. A few prominent Catholic scholars demanded a better performance from Catholic schools; a few visionary presidents allocated resources for the development of genuine graduate programs; and a handful of dedicated, yet eccentric, professors proved that everything worth knowing was not already in the colleges' handbooks of knowledge.[139] There were enough of these undercurrents for reform and improvement, just enough prodding from accrediting associations, enough dissatisfaction from students who had been exposed to the courses, and enough illustrations of university worth and work from nonCatholic universities in the United States, to make the Catholic schools undertake some self-examination in the matter of their graduate programs. Rather than wait for outside agencies to condemn them and put them out of business, as was done in a few instances when regional accrediting associations withdrew accreditation from graduate departments or refused to accredit them in the first place, Catholic colleges took action on their own initiative. And here credit must be given to the Jesuit colleges, for they were the first to see that something should be done.

In 1936 the Jesuit Educational Association decided to propose a set of norms to be used for appraising graduate work in the Jesuit colleges of the United States. The intention of the Association was not to suppress graduate study at any Jesuit college, but quite clearly the Jesuits were sensitive to the differences in quality existing between their own schools, other Catholic colleges, and the better nonCatholic universities of the country. Samuel Knox Wilson, a product of the English universities and President of Loyola University in Chicago, was a ready spokesman for reform within the Catholic colleges which then called themselves universities, and he doubted the wisdom of Catholic higher education continuing to isolate itself from conventional university standards. "It well may be," he wrote, "that Catholics have imitated the worst features of secular education and have neglected the best features of their own. Devotion to scholarship, however, cannot be one of the worst features of secular education, since only here and there have Catholics imitated it. And the waste of trained talents in Catholic colleges—that is really a matter for tears and compunction."[140] Wilson was recounting almost a half-century of close association with Jesuit colleges of the Middlewest when he wrote this article. And his attitude,

139 Karl F. Hertzfeld, "Scientific Research and Religion," *Commonweal,* IX (March, 1929), pp. 560–562.

140 Samuel K. Wilson, "Catholic College Education, 1900–1950," *Catholic School Journal,* 51 (April, 1951), 122.

one which strongly counseled the improvement of standards, dominated and encouraged such statements of policy as the one produced by the Jesuit Educational Association. The standards recommended by the Jesuits touched upon five key points : faculty quality, effective academic organization, adequate libraries, sufficient research facilities, and degree requirements consistent with normal university practices.[141] The Jesuit document, it must be added, assumes a rather special significance when one recognizes it as the first of its kind to issue from a Catholic source.

First on the list of the Jesuits' proposed requirements was a faculty fully qualified to carry on its duties of advanced graduate instruction, and this meant that something more than a mere appointment to the faculty was necessary to determine who should teach graduate school courses. Affirming that it was probably neither necessary nor desirable for professors to commit themselves solely to graduate teaching, the statement went on to endorse an administration of teaching which would allow professors time for a thorough preparation of their lectures and seminars, for conferences with their students, and for their own research and publication. In the consideration of a professor's time, the document was even more specific : "It is recommended that, if sixteen hours per week of lower division instruction be considered a normal load, then twelve hours of upper division teaching and eight hours of graduate instruction be considered equivalent full loads; and that proportionate deductions from these be made for the direction of graduate students and especially for the supervision of research. The guidance of one candidate for the doctorate is at least equivalent to one hour a week for graduate teaching." [142]

Obviously, since these loads were being recommended as minimum standards to be met by the schools, existing practices must have departed from them. From other sources we know that this was so, for the colleges routinely assigned professors to graduate and undergraduate courses, assuming the demands for both to be the same, and frequently allotted professors twenty or more hours of instruction per week. These attitudes to faculty deployment, discussed in an earlier chapter,[143] were continuations of old policies which had been in force since the days when the colleges employed the class teacher. Class teachers, of course, had taught all day. In addition to the issue of teaching load, the standards proposed by the Jesuits required any professor assigned to graduate classes to have qualifications in "scholarship and research at least to the level of the doctorate in the subject for

141 Jesuit Education Association, "Norms Proposed by the Committee on Graduate Studies of the Jesuit Educational Association for Its Guidance in Appraising Graduate Work, 1936–1937," quoted in Power, *op. cit.*, pp. 354–358.

142 *Ibid.*

143 See pp. 90–111.

which he is chosen."[144] The Ph. D. degree itself was not demanded, perhaps because it could not have been required at this time; yet it is clear that the principle of faculty competence at this level was to be emphasized. Actual possession of the doctoral degree was, in any case, preferred : normally the requirements of scholarship, research involvement, maturity and experience should "presuppose the actual degree of Doctor of Philosophy and some years of teaching experience. Whether a professor has the equivalent of the doctorate for the purpose of graduate instruction is to be judged not only by scholarship in the field of which there is question but principally by published research. On the other hand the possession of the actual degree creates only a presumption of fitness, not a proof."[145]

While this statement of standards merits praise, it must also be admitted that it was somewhat premature in its demands for faculty competence : probably less than twenty-five percent of the graduate teachers in Catholic colleges actually possessed the Ph. D. degree and hardly five percent of the graduate professors in these schools were engaged in any serious research or publication. It was due partly to this statement of minimum faculty standards that Catholic colleges in the North Central Accrediting Association pressed their earlier appeal that the Association should recognize ordination to the priesthood as equivalent to the doctoral degree.[146]

Effective academic organization, in this Jesuit document, meant three things. First, it meant that curricula should be properly designated for lower, upper, and graduate classifications and that departments, divisions, and fields of specialization should be respected. Second, it meant the organization of a graduate school which would have jurisdiction over the courses taught, the students admitted, and the degrees conferred. Finally, it meant that the graduate school should be administered by a dean "who has the graduate outlook, who is not in charge of the administration of any undergraduate school or college, and who is responsible directly to the president of the university."[147]

The statement insisted upon adequate libraries for graduate study, and adequacy implied the provision of "all the ordinary tools of scholarship in the field of the course, such as bibliographies, abstract journals, finding lists, collection of documents, texts and monographs, and especially bound files of all important learned journals in that field."[148] Trained library personnel were also essential, the statement continued, and "a reference

---

[144] Power, *op. cit.*, p. 355.

[145] *Ibid.*

[146] "Proceedings of the Commission on Colleges and Universities," *North Central Association Quarterly*, 8 (July, 1933), 44.

[147] Power, *op. cit.*, p. 356.

[148] *Ibid.*

librarian and a dictionary catalogue are indispensable." Research facilities, cubicle space and study tables in the library stacks, "collections of source materials, extensive files of learned journals covering not only the entire field but its supporting fields and its backgrounds" were also essential. While admitting that no library could have everything, the statement nevertheless doubted whether anything other than "unusual journals may be borrowed with good grace from another institution," and went on to say that these unusual journals, especially the ones written in foreign languages, were "perhaps the most costly part of the equipment for graduate study." [149] This last statement is illuminating, for it clearly indicates both the level and the scope of graduate work under discussion : the Jesuit Association was preoccupied with graduate study in the humanities and had not paid real heed to the instructional demands, the cost of equipment, or the laboratory facilities for scientific study. Yet laboratory facilities were not entirely ignored. After admitting that the needs of research would differ from one field of specialization to another, the document asserted : "In the physical sciences the research equipment, in addition to learned journals, will embrace instruments, laboratory space, and shop facilities." [150]

Finally, the writers of the document undertook to wrestle with the issue of requirements for the master's and doctor's degrees, and when they did they recognized that their statement must not sound provincial or second-rate. Minimum standards must be capable of implementation in all Jesuit schools, for, they said, "We must rather visualize our degrees, not as given by this or that institution, but as conferred by a Jesuit university, so that rightly or wrongly, praise or blame will attach to the Jesuits. Therefore, the requirements laid down everywhere should be a little above the average of what is generally considered good practice." [151] And the good practice they were talking about meant that candidates for master's degrees should, first of all, come to the graduate school with solid undergraduate majors and minors. With such sound initial qualifications, they should then follow closely coordinated major and minor fields in their course work for the master's degree and in the end should have completed a balanced graduate program of study. Before master's degrees were conferred on students, the graduate dean should know that they had at least twenty-four hours of graduate credit in their curriculum, contact with the literature of the whole field, a respectable thesis which involved research methods, and the approval of a committee of experts from the department in which the study was undertaken. "A one-man Master's degree under ordinary con-

[149] *Ibid.*, p. 357.
[150] *Ibid.*
[151] *Ibid.*

ditions," concluded the section on master's degree requirements, "is not good practice."[152]

The degree of doctor of philosophy was approached with considerable care, but since so few Catholic colleges were involved in granting it, the statement about it in this set of norms had no need to be long. The writers began by saying that programs for doctoral degrees "cannot be justified," unless an adequate library and extensive research facilities could be provided, together with a graduate faculty in the department numerous enough to introduce the student to the many sides of scholarship in the field and "to evaluate his achievements and qualifications in the light of the whole field of scholarship to which his research belongs." Departments staffed by only one professor, the document averred, should never engage in doctoral-level study.[153]

The statement of standards for graduate work prepared by the Jesuits indicated an awareness among Catholic educators that the realities of university study would at last have to be faced; these realities could not be dismissed nor could Catholic colleges expect an indulgent smile while nonCatholic universities were held strictly to account. The issues of faculties, facilities, finances, and good students were all burning ones and Catholic universities, during the decades following 1930 were obligated to face them, for if they did not they would be left without students willing to pursue advanced study. As it was, because the Catholic universities were unable to keep pace with the developments in university teaching during the 1930s and 1940s, they had some trouble in attracting the better students to their graduate schools. Yet heroic efforts were made from time to time to improve the quality of the graduate schools, and from 1930 to 1945, it is probably safe to assume, most graduate master's degree programs in the best Catholic colleges were usually respectable. This was due in part to a general unwillingness of the Catholic universities to dilute their resources by engaging in graduate programs in science, where facilities and equipment were becoming inordinately expensive, or by adding doctoral studies to their graduate syllabi. In 1955, fifteen years after the period of development had closed, nine Catholic graduate schools were offering doctoral programs in some departments—Boston College, the Catholic University, Duquesne, Fordham, Georgetown, Loyola (Chicago), Notre Dame, St. John's (New York), and St. Louis University—but only four of these endeavored to conduct what amounted to comprehensive doctoral programs.[154] The requirements set out by the Jesuit Educational Association unquestionably benefited the Catholic universities by alerting them, in a way not done

[152] *Ibid.*, p. 358.
[153] *Ibid.*
[154] *Ibid.*, p. 237.

before, to the imperative need for good standards and high quality in all graduate teaching.

But even with this standard before them, it would be naïve to suppose that all Catholic colleges, even all Jesuit schools, observed it to the letter. If it had been taken as a statement of unalterable policy, dozens of Catholic colleges would have closed the doors of their graduate schools by 1940. Again, as they had done so often before, the colleges tried to find a way to observe the letter of the law while remaining indifferent to its spirit. This severe indictment is valid only for a limited period, however, for improvement did come to Catholic colleges; but it came slowly and painfully. The way to circumvent the 1936 requirements, which in any case never had the force of law, was to find a special feature in what the individual Catholic college was doing which could neutralize the scholarly demands the norms had endorsed. We know that faculties in Catholic colleges in 1936 had among their credentials a dangerously low proportion of doctorates;[155] we know too that there were few promising scholars among even the best professors; so somehow scholarship and research as a matter of policy had to be minimized in favor of something tangential about which the colleges could boast. They began by emphasizing the fact that they were teaching universities, where what the students wanted to learn came first, and where the scholarly productivity of faculties could be paid very secondary attention. It was even suggested that research and publication could be obstacles to good teaching and there was just enough truth to this assertion and enough confirmation of it in the experience of the major universities to make it believable. Some Catholic college presidents came close to making a career out of downgrading research and legitimate scholarly enterprise while emphasizing the pedagogic talents of the faculty.[156] And when they did so they were usually on safe ground, because few educators were certain of the limits of good teaching, and there were no ready means to measure the pedagogic quality of Catholic college faculties.

Despite some genuine and reasonable doubts which might have been raised on the issue of teaching vis-à-vis research and publication, the Catholic college line lauding teaching over research was seldom anything more than a defense mechanism : Catholic colleges could hardly boast about their scholars, because they had so few, but they could talk about their teachers. And talk they did. Sometimes this emphasis on teaching gave the colleges an antischolarly image in the academic community and this image, coupled with doubts which nonCatholics harbored about

155 John D. Donovan, *The Academic Man in the Catholic College* (New York, Sheed and Ward, 1964), pp. 80–84.

156 Celestine J. Steiner, "Some Current Trends in College-Industry Cooperation," *National Catholic Education Association Bulletin,* 50 (November, 1953), 7–14.

academic freedom for teachers in Catholic schools, did the stature of Catholic colleges and universities no good. Of all the questions debated on Catholic college issues, the literature is as ample on this matter of research versus teaching as on any other.[157] When it came to affirming or denying the place of scholarship in Catholic schools, authors would generate great enthusiasm and rush into print; unfortunately so many argued from the doubtful position of vested interest that research and publication were seldom preferred, or even given a fair hearing, in comparison with the art of teaching students what they did not know. It took Catholic colleges and universities a long time to realize that a nice balance should be maintained between research and teaching; and they are still trying to make this realization come true on their campuses.

Yet, quite apart from unreasonable caveats against research, publication, and scholarship, Catholic colleges had good excuse for failure to meet the scholarly requirements of the Jesuit pronouncement. Paramount among the reasons for this failure, and the only one that needs notice here, was the matter of resources : the colleges simply could not afford to allow a man to remain away from the classroom, for it was in the classroom that revenue was produced. It is probably incorrect to assume that if the Catholic colleges had had enough money, all other problems of quality education would have disappeared at once during the first fifty years of the twentieth century, but money could have solved some of the important ones. As we have said, the Catholic colleges had no wish to be inferior schools; they usually tried to do the best they could with the resources at their disposal. And these resources, almost without exception (although one important exception was the endowment of men from the religious communities) were limited to income from student tuition. Financially deprived, devoid of sizeable endowments, frequently in debt for the most basic instruments of college teaching and learning, Catholic colleges were too poor to be high quality universities. Their progress in future decades and any marks of quality they might achieve would depend almost entirely upon their ability to support their various programs more generously, and as we move into the period of awakening we shall see the extent to which this was true.

157 Donovan, *op. cit.*, pp. 103–105.

III
The period of awakening:
1940-1970

I I

The great debate

For several decades after their founding the first Catholic colleges in the United States were insensitive to any criticism, regardless of its source, and notoriously complacent about their stature as American schools for higher learning. Of course, competition (to the extent that they felt any) was, in any case, keen only from a few of the country's older colleges. Thus, Catholic colleges enjoyed a doubtful luxury of isolation and wore a public face of haughty self-assurance. Religious, moral, and intellectual objectives, inextricably entangled, made it especially difficult to tell whether the institution was a school, a monastery, or a church. In any case, the colleges prospered just enough during these early years to enable them to think seriously about more ambitious projects during a period of development, a period wherein they added to their academic structure, allowed their missionary and moral objectives to diminish in importance, fashioned multiple curricula, commissioned graduate departments and schools, introduced professional studies, experimented with coeducation, and created colleges for girls. On the surface these were all excellent developments, but at the same time they complicated the lives of the colleges and made it extremely difficult for them to continue to operate as appendages of the Church, on the one hand, and as schools with aspirations for academic identity, on the other. Perhaps the colleges could have survived any crises which might have arisen within the system itself and thus continued along their pleasant, unhurried, conventional ways untroubled by the outside academic world, if their public had been willing to accept its designation as a minority culture in the United States. But that public refused to accept such a role and it was incumbent then on the colleges to strip away some of their natural conservatism and to reclothe themselves in a fashion suitable to the demands of a modern world. This was a hard task and its fulfillment was accompanied by considerable unease and ferment.

This unease about purpose, quality, and status endowed Catholic colleges with historical distinction, for nowhere else in the history of higher education in the United States is there any evidence of public colleges or private universities in concert passing through similar periods of critical self-examination. What concerned the Catholic college community most was its image and the quality of the education it offered its students; as a corollary the colleges were interested to know what place their students occupied in American life and the extent of their intellectual influence.

Catholic college quality

In 1955, John Tracy Ellis, then Professor of Church History at the Catholic University of America, was asked by the Catholic Commission on Intellectual and Cultural Affairs to address its annual meeting, held that year at Maryville College in St. Louis, on the subject of American Catholic scholarship. Ellis delivered a paper entitled "American Catholics and the Intellectual Life," [1] wherein he cited several indictments of the failure of American Catholics "to produce national leaders and to exercise commanding influence in intellectual circles, and this at a time when the number of Catholics in the United States is exceeded only by those of Brazil and Italy, and their material resources are incomparably superior to those of any other branch of the universal Church." [2] While Ellis' thesis was by no means original—nor did he claim originality for it—and while he was not talking directly to the colleges or placing them in the center of the national intellectual stage, what he had to say, if ignored for long by the colleges, would surely put in jeopardy what respect the public then felt for them. Two options were open : first, the colleges could use their considerable talent for polemic to controvert or neutralize Ellis' case; or, second, they could take his analysis seriously, find their appropriate position in the intellectual arena and try to ensure and strengthen it. At one time or another most colleges tested both options. In the end, however, the use of polemic to discredit the cogent arguments of the most recent spokesman for the raising of the level of Catholic scholarship and intellectual life was empty and unconvincing; the evidence was too clear to be denied. The colleges therefore adopted the second option, now really the only one left open to them.[3]

[1] John Tracy Ellis, "American Catholics and the Intellectual Life," *Thought,* XXX (Autumn, 1955), 351–388.

[2] *Ibid.,* p. 351.

[3] Arthur A. North, "Why is the American Catholic Graduate School Failing to Develop Catholic Intellectualism?" National Catholic Education Association *Bulletin,* LIII (August, 1956), 181–189.

Unfortunately they had marked time for so long that the task confronting them—a task which amounted to making intellectual agencies out of places they had for so long called schools—was monumental and costly and the time lost and the talent wasted through many years of inactivity could never be regained.

Apologists for American Catholicism could find a variety of good reasons why Catholics had not been more active socially, politically, and intellectually,[4] and these reasons should not now be discounted, for they contained elements of truth. But the historical point is clear : Catholic colleges had been warned repeatedly years before Ellis delivered his famous address, an address which, for all its illumination and careful reasoning, had a fundamental message which had been articulated in various ways several decades earlier. Orestes Brownson, in trenchant *Review* articles, had warned Catholics against losing an intellectual grip on American life, and he had prescribed, too, a radical reappraisal of the colleges.[5] Yet Brownson's warnings were called diatribes [6] and were countered by the broadly phrased ecclesiastical rhetoric of pastoral letters in which—inexplicable advice—parents were told to keep their children's education consistent with their station in life.[7] Catholic schools and colleges were further counseled in these letters to maintain the course of action they were then following and the standards they already had because those standards were both good and true and far superior to anything in secular schools.[8] Yet bishops were not alone in praising virtue unnecessarily at the expense of learning; they were joined by well-intentioned writers, anxious to defend the Church's schools by misinterpreting the fundamentals of scholarship. Such a one—a layman, who as a student had studied in European universities—was Austin O'Malley. As late as 1898, he could write an eloquent apology for Catholic colleges, apparently innocent of the sort of scholarship he chose to defend :

The Catholic college is intended for the teaching of history that can talk for at least one page without lying, of literature that has the foulness cut out of it; . . . The Catholic college is also intended to teach the elements of metaphysics and ethics, to replace histories of erroneous systems of philosophy and sneers at scholasticism made by men who, through ignorance of technical terminology, could not understand Catholic philosophy if they honestly tried to study it. It also

[4] Thomas T. McAvoy, "The Catholic Liberal College and American Studies," *Catholic Educational Review,* 54 (May, 1956), 295–311.

[5] Edward J. Power, "Orestes Brownson on Catholic Higher Education," *Catholic Educator,* XXIII (February, 1953), 275–278.

[6] Father Edward Joos to Orestes A. Brownson, October 27, 1859. UNDA.

[7] See "The Pastoral Letter of 1866" in Peter Guilday, *The National Pastorals of the American Hierarchy, 1792–1919* (Washington, D. C., National Catholic Welfare Conference, 1923), pp. 215–216.

[8] *Ibid.,* pp. 280–284.

teaches Christian doctrine, but almost half its work should be devoted to that moral education that is effected by discipline. The end of education is not so much learning as living, and intellectual education alone does not conduce to good living.[9]

O'Malley's assumptions, concealed as they are by his rhetoric, are hard to discover and confront face to face, but clearly he rejects histories that are nonCatholic, philosophy that is not scholastic, and philosophers who are unfamiliar with or unschooled in the esoteric philosophical language of scholasticism—although one may fairly doubt their inability to learn it if they chose. He also makes the dogmatic assumption that higher learning should devote about half its time to the formation of good morals and character. This was already the creed of the colleges; O'Malley, so far from blazing a new trail, was simply re-marking one which had been used for a century.[10] This was conventional Catholic wisdom with respect to higher learning and anyone, prelate, priest, or layman, who questioned it did so at his own peril.

The voices of caution and convention could hardly quiet all doubts, and such doubts about the course of Catholic higher learning were sometimes spoken publicly, as in the case of what John Lancaster Spalding had to say about the meaning of a university in the Third Plenary Council.[11] There is a good deal of evidence, however, suggesting that, for the most part, Spalding's discourse fell on deaf ears.[12] Even earlier, the famous Jesuit, Augustus Thébaud, whom we have met before in these pages, had revealed his anxieties about the quality of Catholic colleges, not even exempting the schools of the Society from his critique.[13] And while the colleges were more open to public view than the seminaries, and therefore fairer game for public discussion, Talbot Smith could nevertheless raise some searching questions about the nature and the quality of seminary teaching.[14] But these doubts were always spoken with reserve, admitting more good than bad in Catholic higher learning, and finding more to recommend than to correct in connection with it. Whatever else might be

[9] Austin O'Malley, "Catholic Collegiate Education in the United States," *The Catholic World*, LXVII (June, 1898), 295.

[10] Sebastian A. Erbacher, *Catholic Higher Education for Men in the United States, 1850–1866* (Washington, D. C., Catholic University of America, 1931), pp. 64–68.

[11] In John Lancaster Spalding, *Means and Ends of Education* (Chicago, McClurg and Co., 1897), pp. 212–216.

[12] John Tracy Ellis, *The Formative Years of the Catholic University of America* (Washington, D. C., American Catholic Historical Association, 1946), pp. 101–111.

[13] Augustus J. Thébaud, *Forty Years in the United States of America* (New York, United States Catholic Historical Society, 1904), pp. 350–351.

[14] John Talbot Smith, *The Training of a Priest: An Essay on Clerical Education, with A Reply to Critics* (New York, Longmans, Green and Company, 1908).

said, even the most outspoken critics would agree, Catholic higher learning, when it was authentically Catholic, was concerned with eternal truth and with this ultimate concern its virtue was always assured.

The reservations and doubts referred to, discoverable in the rhetoric of responsible, often prominent persons close to the Church, belong to the nineteenth century; the twentieth century brought a different perspective; at least, the new voices then speaking in critical tones about Catholic colleges were no longer so willing to countenance (as their earlier counterparts had been) the tenets of the past simply because they were old and supposedly true. Moreover, these new voices were impatient for reform. Yet they could speak with urbane responsibleness, pointing to weaknesses, but always trying to find some strengths to compensate for them and balance the negative components in their appraisals. In 1922, Carlton J. H. Hayes, the noted historian and for several decades a professor of History at Columbia University, told the graduating class at the College of New Rochelle of the great need the Church in America had for intellectual leaders.

We boast of twenty million Catholics in this country, but how many of them are scholars and scientists, artists and critics? . . . It is true that our Catholic colleges are annually turning out thousands of young men and women with academic degrees. It is true also that the non-Catholic colleges and universities throughout the country are annually turning out other thousands of Catholic young people with academic degrees. Nevertheless, it must be confessed that altogether too large a proportion of these thousands have gotten little or no intellectual stimulus from their four years' training. Too many of our young people go to college for purely social reasons. Too many go for athletic reasons. Too many go for financial reasons. How to earn a few more dollars than one's father or how to move in a more exclusive social set than one's mother has been the predominant ambition. Truly intellectual interests are a by-product.[15]

What Hayes stressed here were the motives of the students, and he seemed to lay at their door the principal blame for a lack of Catholic intellectual leadership. At the same time his indictment of the nonCatholic college student was equally severe. Yet Hayes' address, later published in *The Catholic Mind*,[16] clearly implicated the Catholic colleges in academic ineptitude.

A few years later, James Burns, writing in *Commonweal*, took a new line in calling attention to a seldom noticed fact of Catholic college life : clerics had no monopoly over scholarship and teaching skill and if Catholic colleges were to be both broad and versatile in their opportunities, laymen should have a more prominent role in them.

[15] Carlton J. H. Hayes, "A Call for Intellectual Leaders," *The Catholic Mind*, XX (July, 1922), 267.

[16] *Ibid.*, pp. 264–267.

If our universities are to be as productive as they should be of the highest scholarship, we must provide the means for bringing more laymen into their faculties. The kind of talent which makes the true university teacher is comparatively rare. It is no respecter of place, or station, or vocation. It cannot be created through any system of training, however elaborate, and it is not always an accompaniment of university degrees. It is as likely to be found among the laity as among the clergy. Hence, to exclude laymen from a university faculty, or to keep their number down to an inconsiderable fraction of the whole, would be to condemn the institution, in advance, to a position of relative academic inferiority.[17]

Burns, writing in 1926, advanced as the obvious reason for the low proportion of laymen on Catholic college faculties a lack of endowment funds among such colleges for the support of lay teachers, and undoubtedly the financial issue was an important deterrent to faculty development. Yet we know from clerical attitudes about faculty standards (attitudes developed in the nineteenth century) that something more than money was involved. The problem was rooted in the nagging doubt among Catholic college managers whether any layman could be either as effective or as learned a teacher as a cleric, whether laymen on faculties could be counted on to follow unquestioningly the directions of superiors, or whether parents would patronize a Catholic school wherein any but a small minority of professors were lay. It is probably fair to assert that the addition of laymen to Catholic college faculties correlates with their growth in collegiate stature; as faculties became predominantly lay the colleges became more thoroughly academic. But proof that this relationship was causal as well as correlational is lacking. In any case, the place of laymen on Catholic college faculties attracted little attention in the great debate about the quality of Catholic higher learning. The important, but now incidental, lay-clerical issue was a tug of war contested behind college walls and out of public view.[18]

An issue with more profound implications now became the subject of fairly open discussion, an issue which could hardly avoid affecting the colleges. Were American Catholics capable of cultural involvement and leadership? In 1927 George N. Shuster, in *The Catholic Spirit in America,* expressed the view that "Catholics have not even done what might reasonably have been expected of them to foster letters, speculation, and the arts." [19] This charge had more sting to it than most of the earlier ones, for

17 James Burns, "Failures in Our Higher Schools," *Commonweal,* IV (November 3, 1926), 636.

18 James Maguire, "A Family Affair," *Commonweal,* LXXV (November 10, 1961), 171–173; and Oscar W. Perlmutter, "The Lay Professor," *Commonweal,* LXVIII (April 11, 1958), 31–33.

19 George N. Shuster, *The Catholic Spirit in America* (New York, The Dial Press, 1927), p. 115.

the older critics who had been prepared to admit the slightness of Catholic contributions to American culture were also quick to append an excuse. Because Catholics had so many cultural, political, and religious hardships to put up with, no one had a right, they argued, to expect much from them. And this comfortable and entirely believable excuse was now impaled by Shuster's doubt whether Catholics had done even as much as could reasonably have been expected. Such an indictment was both bewildering and disturbing and even the best excuses lacked the ring of conviction.

Sometimes the colleges became involved in the debate over Catholic cultural accomplishments to the extent that members of their faculties spoke and wrote about them. And when they did they were either defensive and apologetic about the colleges' cultural tradition or optimistic about what cultural centers they would soon become. Sandwiched between these two points were the comforting or terrifying excuses (depending on one's point of view) that Catholic culture in America suffered irreparable harm either because the clergy were celibate, and therefore the best minds in the Church were prevented from perpetuating their kind, or that the Church's mission was what it was—mainly nonintellectual—in America because of the strong Irish influence over the American Church.[20] In either case, no solution could be offered because the laws of celibacy for the Catholic clergy were fixed and the impress of Irish influence was too deep to be excised. What in effect was being suggested, by writers who found and used such arguments, was that the American Catholic inheritance was final and in its immutable state would always be outside the mainstream of American life.

Closer to the colleges, however, and beneath the usual apologetic statements, were some fairly perceptive analyses of the conventional American Catholic attitude to culture and science, an attitude which seemed to be contagious for generation after generation of Catholic college students. The Church's dogmatism, the confidence of its spokesmen with respect to what was and what was not true, the tendency to narrow rather than broaden the circle of knowledge, the determination to indoctrinate students in the excessive rights of authority, all lessened the chances of the development of attitudes of scholarship conducive to that cultural involvement and productivity so many people had been talking about. But these analyses were rare and for the most part were never very popular among garden-variety Catholics; more popular were the statements pointing to the vital contributions Catholic scholars had already made in a number of fields.[21] No doubt some accomplishments merited notice, but they counted for relatively little when compared with the monumental dimensions of the

[20] Ellsworth Huntington and Leo F. Whitney, "Religion and Who's Who," *The American Mercury*, XI (August, 1927), 438–441.

[21] Francis W. Power, "Research in Catholic Schools," *America*, XLI (May 18, 1929), 131–133.

cultural issue. Again, there was a haste to point out that some Catholic colleges sponsored scholarship publications; a few, in addition to their scholarly journals, had institutes or research stations.[22] And then there was the business of proving that Catholic colleges of the better variety were already spending more money on research than some of the best non-Catholic colleges of the United States.[23] But worst of all was the attitude, fortunately seldom widely broadcast, that cultural and scientific accomplishments to which Catholics did not contribute were of no consequence anyway, because only a Catholic scholar could be truly enlightened and thus give truth its proper interpretation. This view added up to the stark and, for Catholics, pleasant fact that the prize of the scientific and cultural race was theirs after all, for their nonCatholic confreres were incapable of understanding truth even if they fell over it. Such attitudes have a fairy tale quality and are hardly believable, but they were expressed even as late as the 1930s.

In 1938, John A. O'Brien edited *Catholics and Scholarship: A Symposium on the Development of Scholars* wherein it was clearly stated that Catholics were too little visible in proportion to their numbers and that the provision for producing scholars in Catholic higher schools were extremely limited.[24] Even though this view was called iconoclastic by persons who refused to admit of any inferiority in Catholic institutions, its acceptance was fairly general among the colleges themselves, and for a while the strange attitude was current that Catholic colleges were willing to take for granted, and accept as a fact of life, their academically subordinate status. It was almost as if the Holy Spirit had decreed their inferiority and they would accept it without murmuring. Despite the quality of O'Brien's book, hardly any perceptible action was taken by the colleges to open avenues for higher and better scholarship among their students. This was a time when bold steps were unlikely, for World War II was just over the horizon and colleges were wary of overcommitment. So for the next ten years, although some Catholic spokesmen still discussed and illuminated the issue of Catholic scholarship and the colleges' part in it, the clock of progress stood still. In 1947, with the war over, the issue was still waiting for resolution and again John A. O'Brien, in an address to the National Catholic Education Association, entitled "The Need for Catholic Scholars, with Suggestions for Their Development,"[25] decided to take the lead. O'Brien correctly identified the change that was coming over the world of higher

[22] *Ibid.*

[23] Julian Pleasants, "Catholics and Science," *Commonweal*, LVIII (August 28, 1953), 510.

[24] John A. O'Brien, ed., *Catholics and Scholarship: A Symposium on the Development of Scholars* (Huntington, Ind., Our Sunday Visitor, 1938), p. 16.

[25] National Catholic Education Association *Bulletin*, XLIV (August, 1947), 250–261.

learning, and he maintained that the Catholic colleges should devote the major share of their efforts for the next decade to correcting any deficiencies in their system. The deficiencies which militated against the production of scholars were, he said, the result of "the heavy teaching load with which our faculty members are generally burdened;" [26] the best way to produce scholars was to cultivate their development, first, among college teachers. This would mean that the colleges should offer various benefits to their faculties, especially sabbatical leaves. But, in addition, "Faculty members with the ability and eagerness for research should be encouraged to undertake it by administrators and religious superiors. . . . Research work requires suitable facilities in laboratory equipment and in library. . . . Adequate financial compensation is essential for the development of lay scholars." [27]

O'Brien chose to concentrate on the faculty of the colleges, and had perhaps too little to say about other features which also needed considerable improvement (such as the quality of the students); and in concentrating on the faculty and placing confidence in administrators and religious superiors who themselves were almost totally unfamiliar with research and sometimes uncertain of its promised rewards his case was at its weakest. For irrespective of the inner logic of Father O'Brien's discourse, the persons from whom initiative would have to come were generally unwilling to take it; or, equally seriously for their prospects, the colleges were simply incapable of bearing the cost of sabbatical leaves for faculty, of research facilities, or of lighter teaching loads for their professors. Following O'Brien, John Courtney Murray,[28] Leo R. Ward,[29] Edward A. Fitzpatrick,[30] and William F. Cunningham[31] all, during the next few years, exhorted the colleges to improve. But the time was not quite ripe. In 1955, now the right man at the right time, John Tracy Ellis delivered his famous address, and most of the fundamental improvements in Catholic higher learning, which have literally changed its face, date from that hour.

The principal weight of Ellis' charge was simply and directly laid, and, moreover, it was a charge that many times had been voiced by assistant professors in the faculty rooms of Catholic colleges. These men must have been surprised to learn that ideas they had so often exchanged in the privacy of coffee breaks were now being given so much attention in

[26] *Ibid.,* p. 253.

[27] *Ibid.,* p. 256.

[28] John Courtney Murray, "Reversing the Secularist Drift," *Thought,* XXIV (March, 1949), 37–43.

[29] Leo R. Ward, *Blueprint for a Catholic University* (St. Louis, B. Herder Book Co., 1949).

[30] Edward A. Fitzpatrick, *The Catholic University and the World Today* (Milwaukee, Bruce Publishing Co., 1954).

[31] William F. Cunningham, *General Education and the Liberal College* (St. Louis, B. Herder Book Co., 1953).

national periodicals. Ellis recognized that the colleges alone could not put Catholics in the mainstream of American cultural accomplishment, but, on the other hand saw too how little could be achieved without them. Whatever the colleges did would affect the cultural conditions on which a true intellectualism is based. And at this point, Ellis maintained, the colleges were actually betraying not only their long-standing traditional allegiance to Catholic higher learning but to their students as well : "they spent their energies in the mad pursuit of every passing fancy that crossed the American educational scene, and found relatively little time for distinguished contributions to scholastic philosophy." [32] Perhaps Ellis was giving scholastic philosophy more attention than it really deserved, for we have since learned of the willingness of philosophy departments in Catholic colleges to play down their attachment to scholasticism and to add other philosophical emphases to their syllabus. But the point, nevertheless, was clear : Catholic colleges should concentrate on those areas and fields of knowledge where the possibility of their contribution was greatest and should leave to the other colleges those subjects and fields of professional study wherein they had no special competence or aptitude.

Woefully lacking in the endowment, training, and equipment to make them successful competitors of the secular universities in fields like engineering, business administration, nursing education, and the like, the Catholic universities, nevertheless, went on multiplying these units and spreading their budgets so thin—in an attempt to include everything—that the subjects in which they could, and should, make a unique contribution were sorely neglected.[33]

Other defects to which Ellis alluded, ones we now easily understand, were caused by a lack of planning, indeed a duplication, in the founding of American Catholic colleges. The simple exercise of counting colleges in a geographic section of the country leads us to suspect that some were unnecessary and that all were starved for resources to achieve adequacy. This is an important point, and it bears on what Ellis considered to be a central theme; but it was related chiefly to undergraduate colleges, and Ellis, now concerned with the development of scholars, wanted to talk about graduate schools.

I mean the development within the last two decades of numerous and competing graduate schools, none of which is adequately endowed, and few of which have the trained personnel, the equipment in libraries and laboratories, and the professional wage scales to warrant their ambitious undertakings.[34]

[32] John Tracy Ellis, "American Catholics and the Intellectual Life," p. 374.
[33] *Ibid.*
[34] *Ibid.,* p. 375.

These conditions were usually openly admitted by the schools—for there was no point in trying to conceal poverty—and sometimes they were spoken of with faint hints of pride; but Ellis demanded an end to this false humility, which at best was educationally unsound and untrustworthy, pointing out that "the result is a perpetuation of mediocrity and the draining away from each other of the strength that is necessary if really superior achievements are to be attained." [35]

There was little hope, Ellis assumed, that marginal schools would decide voluntarily to abandon collegiate ambitions in favor of Catholic colleges better qualified to conduct the important business of higher learning. So the best chance, he thought, for Catholic higher learning lay in the fact that current fiscal conditions would inevitably lead many schools to bankruptcy.

I realize that this may sound extreme, but in my judgment the danger of insolvency, and that alone, will put an end to the senseless duplication of effort and the wasteful proliferation that have robbed Catholic graduate schools of the hope of superior achievement in the restricted area of those academic disciplines where their true strength and mission lie.[36]

Ellis emphasizes the faulty use of the resources available to Catholic colleges, attributable particularly to an urge to keep up with the academic Joneses, but there is yet another facet to the whole issue : he detects an absence of love for scholarship for its own sake among American Catholics, "and that even among too large a number of Catholics who are engaged in higher education." [37] Unwilling to place the responsibility for this defect on the American Catholic temperament, he nevertheless alleges it to be a major impediment to significant, disinterested scholarship. Yet we should hardly be surprised at this lack of commitment to scholarship in the Catholic college of the period of awakening, for its seeds were never planted in the earlier colleges conducted in affiliation with the Church. True, lip service had been paid to liberal learning, but when hard decisions had to be made, the studies that really counted in Catholic colleges were those which would produce rewards of another kind : the seminary, the capstone of the college system for so many decades, was not intended to be a landmark of liberal learning, yet it was praised as the highest and best of all educational institutions. The professional schools and departments were given pride of place on every Catholic college campus that could afford them, but the professional school never promised anyone anything in terms of scholarship or disinterested study. The Catholic college of the twentieth century

35 *Ibid.*
36 *Ibid.*, 376.
37 *Ibid.*

avoided any deep commitment to scholarship or to love of knowledge for its own sake, despite what Newman had said in his *Idea of a University*,[38] because in its long history in the United States the Catholic college had refused to recognize scholarship, or learning simply for the sake and joy of knowing, as having any special value.

Finally, Ellis charged the Catholic college, and almost all Catholic education, with having misunderstood the role of moral or character education. He called it "the overemphasis which some authorities of the Church's educational system in the United States have given to the school as an agency for moral development, with an insufficient stress on the role of the school as an instrument for fostering intellectual excellence." [39] While admitting, as any prudent person would, the importance of moral formation as a school objective, Ellis maintained that the philosophy of education embraced by Catholic educators regularly confused the objectives of education with those of schooling. The latter, he did not doubt, "must maintain a strong emphasis on the cultivation of intellectual excellence." [40]

Why, after 1955, the Catholic college community should have taken so seriously reasoned statements about its shortcomings, when it had refused to heed them before, is a mystery. In any case, the debate which had started so early and lasted so long was at last beginning to have some effect on the actions of the colleges. While it would be too much to suppose that they at once amputated the courses and departments which served only to weaken them, they began to give profound thought not only to their public image but to the academic quality of their work. And in an age where the business of higher education was becoming more competitive, it was important for the colleges to give serious consideration to their quality. In any case, the arguments so well developed by Ellis were reinforced by those of others who, taking the same theme, sought to give it broader application and fuller illumination. In 1957, Gustave Weigel wrote "American Catholic Intellectualism : A Theologian's Reflections," [41] and in 1958 Thomas F. O'Dea published his *American Catholic Dilemma: An Inquiry into the Intellectual Life*.[42]

Weigel essayed to clarify the meaning of scholarship and spent a good deal of time in his paper on this point, for, he said, "the general Catholic community in America does not know what scholarship is."[43] He pointed to some interesting misconceptions among Catholics :

38 John Henry Cardinal Newman, *The Idea of A University* (New York, Double-day & Company, Inc., 1959). There are various editions to this great book.

39 John Tracy Ellis, "American Catholics and the Intellectual Life," p. 378.

40 *Ibid.*

41 *Review of Politics*, XIX (July, 1957), 275–304.

42 (New York, Sheed and Ward, Inc., 1958).

43 Weigel, *op. cit.*, p. 299.

One common persuasion among us is that intellectual is the same as intelligent. . . . Others consider a studious temperament to be scholarship. . . . Another common persuasion among our people is that smart boys should go into the priesthood [but what is not recognized] is that priestly formation need not be scholarly nor is scholarship its true aim. . . . The seminary wants to train ministers of the Church. It hopes that some of them will become scholars but it does not consider it its function to make them so.[44]

Then, turning to the role of the colleges, his attention was directed, first, to the pre-eminent reputation of philosophy : "in Catholic institutions it is held up as a high point of scholarship, all other secular disciplines being inferior to it."[45] Traditionally the home of reason and the lodging of wisdom, philosophical study as practiced in Catholic colleges discouraged students from using their reason originally. Problems were proposed and answers were given; students were expected to memorize philosophical dicta.

His [the student's] problems and the precise problems of his time are not considered. Instead, . . . questions are treated mathematically; to each word in the question a definition is given *a priori*. The definitions are then analyzed and compared. Finally a synthetic residue of all the definitions is given as the answer to the question.[46]

An important obstacle to scholarship then, stood in the very powerhouse where it should have been generated, Weigel argued, but the greatest impediment to scholarship among Catholics was, he said, an

obsession with the apologetic defense of Catholic positions. . . . Orthodoxy is a constant preoccupation, producing an abiding compulsion to make this orthodoxy capable of overcoming unrecognized deviations within the group and critical attacks from without.[47]

Weigel's perceptive analysis was valuable; both the objectivity of his article and its carefully reasoned statements helped keep the debate on a high level. Possibly even more important, he kept open avenues for discussion at a time when they were in danger of being closed by persons who, on the strength of their protracted intimacy with Catholic colleges, were beginning to publish rejoinders, wherein they cleverly argued down the indictments made of Catholic culture and, specifically, of Catholic higher education. A service similar to that of Weigel's article was performed by O'Dea's book which, instead of multiplying the points of criticism (un-

44 *Ibid.*
45 *Ibid.*, p. 300.
46 *Ibid.*
47 *Ibid.*, p. 304.

necessary, anyway, because those on the agenda were already ample) undertook to interpret, explain, and illuminate the weaknesses evident in Catholic culture. The reputation of Ellis, Weigel, O'Dea and others as scholars did much to add weight to the indictment, for there were still plenty of pulpit orators who thought they could demolish the whole issue of Catholic scholarship with one breath of sermon rhetoric. Those who listened, for example, to Robert Gannon, a former president of Fordham University, must have been convinced that what Ellis had said about the colleges, and what others, both before and after him, had concurred in, were nothing more than ill tempered diatribes or petulant pettifogging.[48] A book with the quality of O'Dea's brought the issue into perspective : its basic themes did not disappear with the dramatic gesture of a hand or dissolve in a catchy oratorical phrase. The time had come to consider these allegations and it was too late to dismiss the charges as meaningless and unfounded.

So the great debate over college purpose and quality did what few debates had done before : it identified the principal issues facing American Catholic colleges and indicated a number of ways in which the colleges might seek to redress their weaknesses.

The nature of the Catholic college

After more than a century and a half of their existence in the United States, one may think it extraordinary that anyone associated with Catholic colleges should have been uncertain about their nature or their principal commitment. It may seem no less unenviably unique that after such a long time the colleges should have been equivocal in their expressions of stated purpose. We know how in their first tempestuous years those Catholic schools called colleges were actually misnamed : they were really elementary and secondary schools, but no one was offended when they flew the more ambitious colors of a college. We know they achieved the standing of higher schools only after expending inordinate effort that could not have been generated in the first place without the dogmatic assumption which monopolized higher learning to prepare young men for the priesthood. We heard talk in the years of development about liberal and professional courses, and later we saw the colleges add professional schools, to be followed shortly by graduate departments engaging in studies leading to the master's and sometimes the doctor's degree. John Henry Cardinal

---

[48] Robert I. Gannon, "Enough Breastbeating !" *The Catholic Mind,* XVI (July–August, 1958), 314–318.

Newman had written a great book on the subject of university functions,[49] and thousands of his careful readers enthusiastically accepted everything he had to say about the philosophy of higher learning. Nevertheless, even with so much evolutionary growth as institutions, the insights of experience in teaching and learning, and the wisdom codified in books like Newman's, the Catholic colleges of the period of awakening were obviously unsure of what they ought to be, or sometimes, what they were. Despite the lateness of the quest, they were still looking for a definitive elaboration of their nature.

They had dogmatic assurances from their spiritual leaders—the American episcopal hierarchy—of their distinctiveness from and their superiority over the secular colleges of the country,[50] yet Robert Hutchins criticized them for being too much like the colleges which on principle rejected philosophical and theological inspiration.[51] Despite Hutchins' high credentials as an educational leader in the United States, it is indeed surprising that the leaders of Catholic higher education in 1937 did not think it strange for him to address them on their legitimate means and objectives. For this to have happened at all, or for the educators involved to have, first, invited him and, then, stayed to listen to what he had to say, speaks well both for them and for the colleges they represented.

Hutchins said he had heard a number of things about Catholic colleges from diverse sources and, with this information for basis, he found it necessary to level a scandalous accusation at Catholic educators:

"In my opinion, . . . you have imitated the worst features of secular education and ignored most of the good ones. There are some good ones, relatively speaking —high academic standards, development of habits of work, and research."[52]

These good features of secular education, Hutchins continued, although subject to some qualification, were seldom duplicated by Catholic colleges, and

"experience does not make me think that the standards of Catholic institutions are nearly so high as ours, nor that Catholic students acquire the habits of work of students in other colleges. Neither is real research, as an ideal, cherished as much in Catholic universities as in others."[53]

The general tone of Hutchins' message was not unfair to the stature and quality of Catholic colleges, but his assertion that Catholic colleges

[49] The Idea of A University (New York, Doubleday & Company, Inc., 1959).

[50] See Guilday, op. cit., pp. 190–191.

[51] Robert M. Hutchins, "The Integrating Principle of Catholic Higher Education," College Newsletter, I (May, 1937), I.

[52] Ibid.

[53] Ibid.

were the weakest of all American institutions of higher learning was clearly too sweeping. If his criterion was the University of Chicago, he was entitled to judge the standards of Catholic colleges as not being "nearly so high as ours," but in comparing Catholic colleges with all other American colleges, his conclusion was simply inaccurate. The same reservation must be made in connection with his remark about research in Catholic vis-à-vis other colleges.

In quick succession Hutchins listed the principal bad features of secular education, which, for the most part, he thought, were being copied by Catholic colleges : athleticism, collegiatism (about which he is unclear), vocationalism, and anti-intellectualism. "All these things produce the disintegration of education." [54] And in all these things, Hutchins maintained, "Catholic education is as bad as, maybe worse than, secular education. My charge, then, is that Catholic education is not Catholic enough." [55] It had, he said, forgotten its great tradition of allegiance to things of the mind, along with its tradition of excelling in the liberal arts.

This central tradition might have been upheld by the hierarchy of studies which existed when all universities were Catholic but which has now disappeared. In these days philosophy, in most universities, is merely one department of fifty or sixty. Any attempt to secure its rightful position in the hierarchy would be long and arduous and in a secular university would be vain. In your universities, however, it should be a success. Unless this is done Catholic education will never be Catholic enough. The best service Catholic education can perform for the nation and all education is to show that the intellectual tradition can again be made the heart of higher education.[56]

Hutchins' partner and co-worker for the cause of liberal learning, Mortimer Adler, had some advice for Catholic higher education also. He admonished its leaders to listen to Hutchins. Writing in *Commonweal* in 1939, he admitted to understanding why Catholic educators might be impervious to any critic who attacked the ends of Catholic education,

because somehow these ends are implicated in the central truths of the Christian religion, and there is a dogmatic confirmation for the conviction of reason about them. *But certainly that is not the case with the means!* The truth of Catholicism in religion and philosophy, for example, is no warrant for the efficiency or intrinsic excellence of the way religion and philosophy are taught in Catholic schools. Only the liberal arts can provide the standard for judging excellence in teaching, for measuring the efficiency of educational means or inventing others; and the liberal arts are neither pagan nor Christian, but human.[57]

54 *Ibid.*, p. 2.
55 *Ibid.*, p. 3.
56 *Ibid.*, p. 4.
57 Mortimer Adler, "Can Catholic College Education Be Criticized?" *Commonweal*, XXIX (April 14, 1939), 682.

The point Adler wanted understood—one that was frequently misunderstood—was that Catholic education would be better and its self-scrutiny more thorough if such distinctions were clearly perceived. Keeping them in mind, Catholic educators "would be more cordial to an adverse discussion of their means, especially if it comes from friends." [58]

Hutchins and Adler were extraordinarily friendly toward Catholic higher learning, despite its alleged weakness, yet their advice to the colleges was seldom taken at face value. Its importance, however, was not entirely discounted, for the advice these men offered actually led Catholic college presidents and deans to consider previously dormant questions, and to look behind the broad rhetoric of their predecessors to more fundamental factors in the process of providing a decent education. Old pronouncements were no longer very convincing, so it was necessary for the new generation of Catholic college managers to rethink the whole business of appropriate objectives for their colleges. Their own mentors were less than sufficient, for even Newman's *Idea of a University* sometimes seemed to miss the mark of what the American Catholic college could or should be.

The American educational experience (principally nonCatholic, yet only infrequently blatantly secular) provided illustration in practice and theory in print amply sufficient to guide Catholic educators in charge of colleges into the mainstream of higher education's contemporary purpose, and this much Catholic educators themselves willingly admitted. But there was another dimension to the discussion. What was a Catholic college? This question had never been noticed, let alone answered, in documents so long circulated in the United States covering the fundamental issues of college purpose. There were monumental omissions in the commission given to the Catholic colleges right from the beginning, together with hazy implications that what had not been said forthrightly could not be articulated—it had to be absorbed intuitively. Aside from this mystery, it had long since become clear that the traditional ideas of higher learning fashioned during the medieval period, though containing permanent elements of worth, could not be transmitted without some translation. Once again the theories of higher learning had to be removed from the tomes on library shelves. A great part of the history of education is an exercise in recounting such transmogrifications, and the history of higher education in the United States is not an exception.

For long content to abide comfortable generalizations about the objectives of Catholic higher education, spokesmen for the colleges did not, until after the Second World War, begin to take seriously the business of determining precisely what Catholic colleges could and should be. It was now next to useless to talk about being principal citadels of learning in the

[58] *Ibid.*, p. 683.

United States, because such citadels were already erected in the great state universities and a few extraordinarily gifted private colleges. But in the many-sided world of American higher learning there had to be something the Catholic colleges could affirm as their special goal, and now the spokesmen began to stake out the claim. And, in doing so, they tacitly assumed that most of the statements about the questionable quality of Catholic higher learning were correct. Plenty of room was left, nevertheless, for a clarification of the purpose of the Catholic college, even if the issue of quality had to be left on one side.

The Report of the President's Commission on Higher Education, to which a minority view expressed by Catholic members was appended,[59] had, in 1947, spoken enthusiastically about the need to democratize American higher education and the prospects for so doing. The high school, for at least half a century, had been a school for all the children of all the people and now, the Report said, the same philosophy should guide the colleges. For some students a full four-year college program should be supplemented by years of graduate or professional study; for others the undergraduate college would be enough; and for still others the two-year college should suffice. And this two-year college should be located near students' places of residence, thus making additional costs for room, board, and travel unnecessary. Whether Catholic college educators saw a special danger in this further democratizing of higher learning or whether they felt the community-type college would create unwelcome competition for their own schools, is hard to determine. At any rate, as was so often the case before, Catholic educators began by opposing what on its face was a truly progressive step : they argued that higher educational opportunities, especially if given at public expense, should not be expanded. In the end, however, vested interest was forced to surrender and Catholic college spokesmen retreated from their position of opposition to wider opportunities for higher learning. Then, allowing a brief time for adjustment to the idea of a new liberalism in higher learning, we hear Catholic college leaders advocating not retrenchment but a renewed effort to broaden the opportunities available.

It is now a time of preparation in which we must prepare the great mass of our people through our educational system for a greater Christian civilization and thereby also prepare the leaders who will achieve the tasks confronting us. The one immediate obligation which is placed on us is one of high excellence at every level of our educational system and above all in a strong intellectual life whereby we shall be able and shall deserve to assume that intellectual leadership

---

[59] *Higher Education for Democracy:* A Report of the President's Commission on Higher Education. Vol. I. *Establishing the Goals* (New York, Harper and Row, Publishers, 1947), pp. 1–49.

and to carry out that creative intellectual effort that alone will bring success and answer the challenge of history.[60]

This objective, however, was sometimes lost to sight behind the attitudes surrounding Catholic higher education, and these attitudes were clues to the nature that education had been assigned by tradition and practice. "The first of these I shall call the defensive or apologetic attitude in educational work. . . . The second attitude is what I shall call the pseudo-pietistic attitude." [61] Preventing the cultivation of irreligious habits and tendencies and actively promoting the salvation of souls were, of course, goals to which Catholic colleges might pay allegiance, but in doing so they must be certain to keep the principal purpose of an educational institution intact.

The Catholic educator, when his institution falls below high standards in literature or science, in research or teaching, is not to be less concerned but more than a secular educator, for he has a less perfect work to offer to God. And he who is tempted to excuse failings on the ground that education is not his ultimate interest is being tempted to a sort of blasphemy against the nature of things as God made them and a sort of sacrilegious use of his own high motives.[62]

So the call now was not only to make Catholic higher education excellent but also to make it authentically Catholic, and the latter assignment was a huge one which inevitably caused a good deal of trouble.

It was good and necessary for the Catholic college to be a Catholic community internally but its Catholicism should also be externalized or, as John Courtney Murray put it, it should "be a point of departure for a missionary effort out into the thickening secularist intellectual and spiritual milieu. Their [the colleges'] function in the Church and in regard to the children of the Church requires to be completed by discharge of a function in the world and in regard to those who stand without. . . ." [63] Murray was asking Catholic colleges to be intent upon producing new kinds of apostles who should first be scholars. And scholarship, he said, is not an automatic result of piety, "as if one would love learning simply because one loves God."[64] The acquirement of it is somewhat more complicated and difficult: "Basically, one loves learning simply because one loves learning, and for this high love is willing to submit to the rigorous disciplines of the scholarly life. It is not possible therefore to "promote"

---

[60] Robert Henle, "The Future Challenge to Catholic Education," National Catholic Education Association *Bulletin,* XLV (August, 1948), 281.

[61] *Ibid.,* pp. 282–283.

[62] *Ibid.,* p. 285.

[63] Murray, *op. cit.,* p. 41.

[64] *Ibid.,* p. 43.

scholarship any more than it is possible to improvise it." [65] Still, it is possible both to create conditions wherein a natural impulse for learning can assert itself and to provide an environment friendly to the ideals of scholarship, and these should be the principal preoccupations of the Catholic college.

Among the exhortations to make the Catholic college a springboard for a profound Christian intellectualism were heard a few erudite exclamations which now appear somewhat obscure. Writing in a highly significant book about the nature of the Catholic college, Leo R. Ward confused his readers :

The Catholic higher learning, then, has as its end learning and higher learning and Catholic higher learning. Any other end, no matter how excellent, is secondary, remote, and ancillary. The Catholic higher learning ought to be itself. Other ends may be good; but if promoted to the rank of specific end, they are out of place and cause confusion and evil. Let Catholic higher learning learn to be itself; let it simply be Catholic higher learning.[66]

Fortunately, Father Ward is clearer later on when he writes that the main problem of Catholic higher education (he associates it with college purpose), is neither financial nor athletic, but one of persuading persons most intimately connected with the colleges to believe profoundly in intellectual values. How could Catholic college teachers influence their students to love standards to which they themselves were indifferent?

In this period of violent and active debate over college purpose two fairly distinct camps were formed : one affirmed the traditional and conventional nature of the Catholic school and college. Since it was a servant of the Church, argued this camp, the college should aim first at the salvation of souls. The other camp was determined to have schools and colleges which, while embracing the visible signs of the Catholic Church, were really duplicating the work of nonCatholic universities. Neither argumentative position seemed to promise what more serious thinkers believed to be the purpose of Catholic higher learning, and, moreover, nothing could be found in Newman's work to give comfort to either camp.

Yet there was an uneasiness which even the official language of college publications was unable to conceal and it was sometimes expressed in this way :

There is serious disagreement between those who are emphasizing the necessity of higher educational standards and those convinced that our schools are not Catholic enough. The latter feel, for example, that there are too many Catholic teachers of economics who would be flattered to be told that their courses—with

[65] *Ibid.*
[66] Ward, *op. cit.,* p. 103.

the exception of a prayer before and after class—are identical with those offered at the Harvard School of Business Administration. They are right in pointing out that the class in religion at present is often only an extra chore for students of a Catholic grammar school, or that a scientific course in theology is not at present the central discipline of any existing Catholic university; that Catholic schools have sometimes paid too high a price for quick accreditation.[67]

Accreditation, it must be said, could hardly be held responsible for lowering standards in Catholic colleges or in any way affecting their genuine Catholicity. In any case, the confusion of aim apparently indigenous to the Catholic college—sometimes a determination to be extremely and ardently Catholic even at the expense of secular scholarship, at other times officially Catholic but actually indifferent to the critical features of Catholic higher learning—was redressed in the 1950s, and Catholic colleges, while considering the question of their quality, began also to examine their fundamental purpose. This examination, the historical record suggests, was done with some unevenness and with glaring omissions, but eventually a majority of American Catholic colleges came to accept a commission expressed as follows by William F. Cunningham, the dean of American Catholic educational philosophers :

As an intellectual agency the specific, essential function of the Catholic college is to bring about the intellectual, emotional, and volitional development of its students as contributing citizens in a free society and apostolic members of the Church. In addition to this, however, the college as a community has supplementary functions to perform, through which it aids other community agencies achieve their specific functions.[68]

Although the Catholic college is neither a clinic nor hospital, it will be concerned about its students' health; while not a home, it will perform some of the functions of a home; and not being a vocational institute, a playground, a police station, or a monastery, it will, nevertheless, be concerned with the broad training of its students for their social well being (with good order and reasonable discipline as conditions for life in the college community), and with the students' religious life.

It will have a vital religious program which, in addition to the development of the intellectual virtues through the curriculum, will develop the moral virtues through a life of Christian self-denial on the campus, and the theological virtues through private devotion and public worship with active participation in the liturgy of the Church.[69]

[67] Joseph E. Cunneen, "Catholics and Education," *Commonweal,* LVIII (August 7 and 14, 1953), 438.
[68] Cunningham, *op. cit.,* p. 35.
[69] *Ibid.*

Avoiding obscurity, Cunningham set out an ideal organization of the various functions of the Catholic college and, though it went unrecognized at the time, he expressed what was to become later in the period of awakening the policy followed by a majority of Catholic colleges. The debate over purpose ended by being more productive than most observers would have been willing to predict : without really changing the nature of the Catholic college, its essential functions as an educational institution were clarified within the context of the denominational doctrines it embraced.

Theories of higher learning

Except for Thorstein Veblen's famous work, *The Higher Learning in America*,[70] American higher education has been almost entirely free from broad theoretical expositions and general critiques. Perhaps Veblen's book made up for dozens of milder books that might have been written, if anyone had thought theory essential. In 1930 Flexner was of the opinion that "no sound or consistent philosophy, thesis, or principle lies beneath the American university today." [71] In any case, it appears to be true that Catholic higher education, despite the broad commission given the colleges by the prelates, and reinforced from time to time by pastoral statements and conciliar documents, was left to itself to work out its own theories. But for a long time, as we have seen, no need was felt for theorizing, for speculating about the policies governing higher learning, because it was confidently assumed that everything worth saying about objectives and policies had already been said. The function of an educational leader was to ensure the teaching of established truth and it was expected that his efforts in this direction would be unstinting. There was really no need to discuss curricula; seeking proper correspondence between graduate and undergraduate levels was unnecessary; problems pertaining to the role of the faculty in the affairs of the school were left untouched.

Catholic college managers were unconcerned about such things, so in actual fact there never had been an explicit theory of Catholic higher learning. Perhaps a definitive theory is still lacking; yet during the period of awakening some events served to bring Catholic colleges to the threshold of theory building. Leo R. Ward's book, *Blueprint for a Catholic University*, is a good illustration of the thinking that was stimulated, although Ward was not himself a college administrator, with responsibilities for day-to-day

---

[70] Thorstein Veblen, *The Higher Learning in America: A Memorandum on the Conduct of Universities by Business Men* (New York, Viking Press, 1918).

[71] A. Flexner, *Universities, American, English, German* (New York, Oxford University Press, 1930), p. 213.

academic decisions, but a philosopher who preferred to take a long, careful look at the prospects for the Catholic college.

Remembering both the old days, when the colleges had been content to familiarize students with selections from the classics and set them to work writing their compositions as classical writers had written them, and also the changes introduced when the colleges began to depart from their classical preferences to add a variety of practical courses and religion, Catholic college leaders found it hard to realize that their academic communities no longer housed only undergraduates. They liked to call their schools universities and even small colleges without full graduate schools liked to have some departments offering studies leading to master's degrees, so it was important for them to act like universities. But how did universities act? Where were the good examples which could be imitated? The most obvious examples were seminaries or, if religious orders conducted colleges, their own houses of study. But in the end the basic pragmatism of these leaders saved them from trying to remake the school they called a university along strictly religious lines. Perhaps the experiences of various communities with the Catholic University of America, wherein monasticism prevailed for a long time,[72] gave them pause. But if they were to find an example anywhere, and if at the same time they were to project an image of serious Catholic efforts in the field of higher learning, this model could not well be any other than the Catholic University of America. For a long time, and surely up to the beginning of the period of awakening, Catholic college leaders looked for guidance to the school in Washington.

One of the hallmarks of the period of awakening was that Catholic educators became somewhat less restricted and provincial in their educational outlook : when they wanted illustrations of colleges in action they could take them from nonCatholic as well as Catholic schools. This was probably what Hutchins had warned them about a few years before,[73] but what Hutchins had said did not dissuade Catholic colleges from looking for *exempla* in their nonCatholic counterparts. In the end, it was probably beneficial that Hutchins' warning went unheeded. In any case, taking a lead from nonCatholic colleges became an official exercise. Still, simply finding out what other schools were doing, reading and following their policies, could not solve every Catholic college problem. And one problem which constantly plagued Catholic colleges was related to teaching—the communication function of the college—and research—the discovery of knowledge.

Of course, the Catholic college of the nineteenth century had been

[72] Patrick A. Ahern, *The Catholic University of America, 1887–1896* (Washington, D.C., Catholic University of America Press, 1948), pp. 30–40.

[73] Hutchins, *op. cit.,* pp. 1–3.

dispensed from considering these functions as dichotomous, for it never took seriously the assumption that treasuries of knowledge were still waiting to be mined. The college of the early twentieth century had been a college where teaching—communicating the truths which college faculties possessed —was supremely important. But where this minimal attention to research might have been acceptable in a college (that is, a school without a complex organization or high aspirations), it would never do in a respectable university. For as long as any man could remember, the university had been charged with the assiduous preservation and communication of knowledge, but it had been charged, too, with the development of novel ideas and the laying bare of fresh knowledge. How could Catholic colleges pretend to be universities if they were either unable or unwilling to engage in research? Yet if they decided to cultivate a legitimate research function, which professors were going to be responsible for it and where were they to be found? It could be taken for granted at the close of World War II that few professors on Catholic college faculties were either interested in or qualified for research.

A choice now lay before the colleges, one embodying three alternatives. Teaching could be elevated to the pinnacle of college purpose and nothing detracting from it would be countenanced; research could be introduced by adding special professors and equipment, often with a great expenditure of resources, and this innovation could be publicized as a distinctive and separate addition to the university; or the college could encourage its teaching professors to use their own time and the modest resources of their departments for ephemeral research and equally ephemeral publishing. If the last course were chosen, the college president could then praise his faculty for its sensible wedding of teaching and research; if special research units were organized, the college president could assure his public that research at his college was no infringement upon teaching; and if research was disregarded, then the president could proudly proclaim that his college was true to its purpose of educating students, and that it left to other agencies the business of uncovering new knowledge. For the most part (only a few of the larger and stronger Catholic colleges were exceptions) Catholic colleges decided to take the last of the three alternative courses : they could claim to be—and to a great extent could fulfill their claim—teaching institutions where student needs were of the first importance, where the students would be able to study with prominent professors *before* entering the graduate school. They would not have to spend their undergraduate career entirely in the classrooms of teaching fellows of subordinate rank and possibly inferior qualifications.

For colleges deciding to test the treacherous waters of university research, the natural sciences proved most attractive, although, it must be admitted, most such colleges entered the sciences lacking the essential resources for this concentration. If Catholic colleges had capitalized on their strengths, they would have embarked on philosophical, theological, and humanistic research, where their traditional tools were better and already somewhat more available. But this was not the right and contemporary bandwagon. What is more, research funds were seldom available in the humanities, so colleges took the direction promising the greatest rewards. And the research budgets for the schools which took this step were by no means inconsequential as Julian Pleasants commented in 1953 :

The larger Catholic universities, such as Notre Dame, Catholic University, Marquette, and St. Louis, are spending in the neighborhood of a half-million dollars a year apiece on research in the natural sciences, and the extent of their investment is increasing rapidly. This investment is more than many state universities reported to the New York *Times* last year, more than that of many old established colleges, like Amherst or Colgate, not a great deal less than Duke's $850,000 or Stanford's $1,000,000. Needless to say, it falls below Princeton's $2,200,000 or Minnesota's $5,250,000 or Illinois' $7,214,000, or Cornell's $14,850,000. Besides what the larger universities do, some of the smaller Catholic colleges, particularly girls' schools, are making modest but well-planned forays into research, and are qualifying for grants.[74]

These colleges—Notre Dame, Catholic University, Marquette, and St. Louis—were exceptions, and in assuming this exceptional stance did not always have the full support of their own faculties in the budgetary allocations for research. Besides, the smaller colleges, and the girls' colleges, did not account for much of the foundation and grant money distributed over the next quarter-century. To the credit of both the smaller men's and girls' schools, they ceased their forays into the field of scientific research. In any case, having pointed to the colleges making the substantial investments in research along with policy commitments to it, and the much larger number refusing to budge from their determination to be teaching colleges exclusively, we have illustrated the variations of theory among Catholic college leaders and policy makers. According again to Pleasants,

the basic difference between this modern world which values research so much, and the Catholic segment which values it so little, is that the Catholic part had given up the virtue of prudence, and the modern world, through the advance of science, rediscovered it. The temptation to give up prudence for formalism is an ever-present temptation for Catholics, since we have it on the highest authority that 'the children of this world are more prudent in their generation than the children of light.' [75]

[74] Pleasants, *op. cit.,* p. 510.
[75] *Ibid.,* p. 513.

No doubt the issue arises in a number of Catholic colleges in the 1970s, for there is still some bewilderment about how to manage research in a college or whether it should be put up with at all. But a great deal of the confusion abated during the period of awakening with wide agreement on the following generalizations : products of research in any university should be used to inform teaching; with research opportunities professors on the faculty would provide themselves with scholarly stimulation; and with a producing, vital faculty the university would achieve an academic momentum sufficient for keeping its programs excellent.

Yet, while debates raged over the relative merits of teaching and research, other matters of basic curricular concern were being dealt with too. We remember the traditional, although sometimes misunderstood, commitment of nineteenth-century Catholic colleges to liberal learning, but we saw also how the colleges fondly embraced professional curricula. Now, and as a matter of policy, how were liberal and professional studies to be evaluated? Whatever theory might have said about the nature of a Catholic college, Catholic colleges during the period of awakening were not prepared to scrap any of their professional schools of law, medicine, engineering, education, or journalism. Amid the tensions, college communities could still assert the primacy of liberal learning and thus remain true to what seemed to be the legacy of Catholic education. In this area, as in so many others, it took theory a long time to reach the level of day-to-day application, but whether or not theory was followed, we need to know what it was.

Liberal learning, we have said repeatedly, had had lip service paid to it during the formative and developmental years; but in addition to the verbal allegiance regularly accorded the liberal arts, the colleges, it must be admitted, had a genuine affection for them. Yet, for all this, they allowed the arts to be displaced because students and the public generally put a higher value on practical studies. So it was in this context of divided loyalty that a theory of liberal learning was proclaimed. And in its assessment of liberal learning, the Catholic college was not alone, as it had not been alone in running after all those kinds of education that tended to wear away the liberal image of the old college, but was moving along pace for pace with most colleges of the United States. Evidence of the interest of nonCatholic colleges in liberal education is plentiful, but is attested most fully in the Report of the Harvard Committee, *General Education in a Free Society*,[76] where a determined effort was made to state a theory of liberal or general education with which the colleges could be comfortable and which would improve the quality of education. Nothing so elaborate as the Report of the Harvard Committee proceeded from the conclaves of Catholic college leaders, although a number of perceptive

[76] (Cambridge, Mass., Harvard University Press, 1945).

analyses and suggestions were made for reestablishing commitments to liberal learning.

It should be said, first, that had the Report of the Harvard Committee used the term *liberal* instead of *general* to describe the kind of education it believed ought to have pride of place, then Catholic colleges would have taken greater notice of it, and perhaps would even have adopted it as a guide for the formation of curricula they saw over the horizon. Yet the reason for the Harvard group's substitution of the word *general* for *liberal* was reasonable in the light of the considerable hostility generated toward liberal education ever since John Dewey's elaborations had declared liberal learning anathema in democratic schools. No other statement about liberal learning and the mission of the American college was quite so complete or so thoughtful as the Harvard Report, a judgment which takes into account Robert Hutchins' *Higher Learning in America*,[77] Harry Gideonse's *The Higher Learning in a Democracy*,[78] Mortimer Adler's *Art and Prudence*,[79] and Henry Wriston's *The Nature of the Liberal College*.[80]

Room remained, amid all the discussions about liberal education, for the elaboration of a Catholic interpretation of liberal learning. Two such interpretations, both made by Catholic scholars, one by a philosopher and the other by an educational philosopher, were those of Leo R. Ward and William F. Cunningham, and both showed qualities of scholarly insight and precision. In his *Blueprint for a Catholic University* Ward affirmed the end of the university to be "intellect and its values for the personal life and social body;" and in the university this end must be maintained by the persons who comprise the academic community, although this maintenance should not be aimed for "altogether independently of cosmic order." [81] The problem, he wrote, may be stated as follows : "The best thing in the university is learning, culture, and strong, appreciative, and sympathetic minds." If these are absent from the university, if they do not figure large in its objectives, then "nothing else is of any use in the university." [82] If this is the bedrock principle for Catholic college policies on liberal learning, if this is the foundation of their educational building, then which studies are most effective in securing the objectives of this intellectual culture?"The studies which tell us most about man, and in which man is best affirmed, are the most important for man." [83] By this

---

[77] (New Haven, Conn., Yale University Press, 1936).
[78] (New York, Farrar & Rinehart, 1937).
[79] (New York, Longmans, Green and Company, 1937).
[80] (Appleton, Wis., Lawrence College Press, 1937).
[81] Ward, *op. cit.*, pp. 174–176.
[82] *Ibid.*, p. 181.
[83] *Ibid.*

principle history would be first on the list, because it makes us most aware of those matters relevant to ourselves, "but man cannot be really known in his roots and growth unless known in relation to nature and God." So, following Ward's interpretation, "sciences and philosophy go ahead of history as telling us about nature, and philosophy and theology go ahead as telling us about God, and we may say that psychology as telling us about man goes along with history and undoubtedly in front of mathematics and sciences that tell us for the most part about nature." [84] But there are still other studies to be reckoned with, for example, literature and the arts, which have "a liberating and emancipating effect; their specific good is to be enjoyed, but they also afford refinement to the feelings and a power of discrimination and appreciation." [85] Which studies are best, and which should have pride of place in the Catholic college? "Commonly those that are most human and most personalistic in content and in their effect are the most proper and valuable to a man as a person and as a member of society." [86] There are other studies which may make some claim on the university, and they may be prosecuted because they have a practical value for mankind, but, according to Ward's interpretation of Catholic liberal learning, they should have a subordinate position on any hierarchy of studies in Catholic colleges.

In the fourth decade of the twentieth century, with so much to study and so many studies having an apparent worth for men, it was admittedly hard to find any unchallenged principle of order. Yet, a few years after Ward wrote his perceptive book, William F. Cunningham essayed to state the problem and offer tentative solutions in the language of an educational philosopher. Cunningham's record as an open-minded thinker, always sympathetic to ideas other than his own, and remarkably free from dogmatism, made his ideas more interesting and attractive to his nonCatholic colleagues, among whom his views were studied with care, than to his Catholic confreres. Still, what he had to say was a fully contemporary interpretation of Catholic liberal learning: he published his theory in a book entitled *General Education and the Liberal College.*

Cunningham departed from the dogmatic assumption, so long affirmed in Catholic attitudes toward liberal learning, that the only route leading to a decent education (always called liberal) was the classical curriculum. And what he called the appropriate outcome of liberal education was not merely skill in language or traditional erudition, but, rather, the shaping of people "with a philosophy of life that is characterized by a deep sense of social responsibility which they will carry with them and make operative in whatever cultural situation they may find themselves after gradu-

---

[84] *Ibid.,* pp. 181–182.
[85] *Ibid.,* p. 182.
[86] *Ibid.,* p. 183.

ation from college." [87] Such a purpose, according to Cunningham, allowed for freedom in the curriculum and admitted, as fully- enfranchised subjects in the liberal syllabus, language, theology, philosophy, history, literature, fine arts, visual arts, music, mathematics, natural science, and social science.[88] This theory refused to restrict the options for liberal learning to the traditional curriculum of a college of liberal arts. It welcomed liberal studies in the curricula of schools where a principal focus was preparation for life. Knowledge was not belittled, yet it counted for less than the discipline which could, and should, be the outcome of liberal learning. In elaborating his theory of liberal education, Cunningham clearly committed every part of higher education to its creation and commissioned all studies to aim at disciplining the mind rather than just informing it. The discipline he wrote about was not the discredited nineteenth-century doctrine, but the growth of mental attitudes, aptitudes, and habits, and he quotes Henry Wriston's definition of discipline with approval :

Discipline . . . is the essential mode of thought in a field of study, the inherently characteristic mental method of attacking that kind of problem. The discipline is a type of intellectual experience involved in a successful approach to a problem of knowledge . . . it refers not to the form only, but to fundamentals, to essential qualities without which the subject may not be successfully mastered.[89]

Any study worthy of a place in the college curriculum is capable of generating a degree of mental discipline, although some subjects may be more generative than others. What are these disciplines, the sought-after products of liberal education? Cunningham listed them as : disciplines of thought—perspective, unification, precision, objectivity; disciplines of feeling and emotion—appreciation; disciplines of action—responsible citizenship, Christian life ideals, freedom, intensification; and the universal discipline—expression.[90] The student, Cunningham concluded, who achieves the fruits of study—the disciplines—will have a liberal education, and the title of the course he has taken will not matter much.[91]

Free from the ominous language and the compelling rationalism of philosophers who could prove to their own satisfaction which studies could be allowed in the curriculum of a liberal college, Cunningham's theory was one that permitted Catholic colleges of the period of awakening to maintain an up-to-date curricular image, to retain their professional and vocational curricula, and to develop their studies as knowledge exploded around them, while still affirming their allegiance to the efficacy of liberal learning.

[87] Cunningham, *op. cit.*, p. 129.
[88] *Ibid.*, pp. 101–114.
[89] Wriston, *op. cit.*, pp. 146–147.
[90] Cunningham, *op. cit.*, pp. 137–152.
[91] *Ibid.*, p. 153.

With the nature of the liberal college redescribed, and absolved from uncertainties about what could and could not be judged respectable as the core of higher studies, Catholic colleges were free to examine their presuppositions concerning, first, the upward extension of college study—what should graduate education be?—and, second, the downward extension of the undergraduate curriculum—what was the function of the general college? [92] In common with all colleges of the country which had introduced graduate programs on a permanent basis, Catholic colleges were troubled not only by the cost of such advanced study programs but by the lack of a code setting out the way in which graduate and undergraduate schools could live together on the same campus, sharing the same faculty, the same facilities, and the same commitment to Catholic doctrine, but all the while acknowledging disparate educational objectives. If both could be maintained, could an appropriate balance be struck where one would not seek to dominate, and then succeed in dominating, the other? Few Catholic college presidents were willing to preside over a college community where one or the other school was about to be strangled. But how to avoid academic strangulation of either the undergraduate or the graduate program in a college seeking excellence in both research and teaching turned out to be a true conundrum, and, so far as anyone can tell, one that is no nearer resolution in the 1970s than it was in the 1940s when it first began to appear as a critical issue.

On the other side of the college, that is, on the side where efforts were to be made to increase the opportunities for students to gain some college experience without enrolling in a bachelor's degree program, a few Catholic colleges, prompted by pressures from the public, created two-year units (avoiding the designation of *junior college*) expecting them to approximate closely to the pattern of the conventional junior college for the last half-century. These units were named variously, but they liked to think of themselves as general colleges. At best, the general college could expose its students to the first stages of liberal learning and could thus claim to be performing a service to a vast number of students who, either because of lack of ability, interest, or resources, could not aspire to the full four-year course. Always an experiment, the general college betrayed its theoretical justification—increased educational opportunity for young persons—by disappearing from most Catholic college campuses when the facilities of the college began to be fully used by students pursuing the four-year college course. Despite its demise, the plan was sound and plenty of educational justification could have been found for offering

---

[92] Urban H. Fleege, "The Graduate School and the Program of General Education," National Catholic Education Association *Bulletin,* 45 (August, 1948), 287–302; and John A. Kemp, "The College in Preparation for Graduate School," National Catholic Education Association *Bulletin,* 51 (August, 1954), 228–233.

Catholic college students a two-year course, which, whether preparatory or terminal, could have contributed greatly to general culture. In the 1970s, however, the general college in Catholic institutions appears to be a dead issue.

But if Catholic colleges of the twentieth century in some respects failed to capitalize on opportunities which seemed to have educational merit, they profited from their maturity as academic institutions in relegating their athletic programs to subordinate positions in an institutional complex. Some, seeing the error of their earlier ways, abandoned intercollegiate athletics altogether. But this was an extreme action not fully consistent with the *mores* of American college life. If we assume that colleges intending athletic de-emphasis were on the right track, they faced predictable hazards in implementing such policies. Their alumni, who remembered most of all the athletic glories of their own college days, reacted unfavorably to any policy which seemed to tarnish the image of their *alma mater*. It took a brave college president to withstand the petitions of alumni who could see no justification for taking their athletic teams out of public view, and it was a fortunate one who could find his way through the financial maze without their generous help. To their credit, however, most Catholic college presidents found a reserve of fortitude equal to the resolve of disgruntled alumni. And in this respect, aid came from an unexpected source : the federal government.

Until the mid-1950s, Catholic colleges stood opposed to any form of federal aid to education as a matter of policy, and this included aid to the lower as well as the higher schools. But economic realities finally caught up with them. Guided by a simple pragmatism, the higher schools, seeing federal money for research grants, operational development, buildings and facilities available, simply chose to apply for it. In that moment they forgot what for decades they had heard about the ugly apparition of federal control that might follow federal aid. While it may be true that no Catholic college, or any other college for that matter, liked its independence eroded by having to depend on federal subsistence, the survival of the schools often did depend on their abandoning their old fears about federal control. Perhaps the colleges traded a dependence on alumni for a dependence on government, but in this exchange the Catholic colleges obtained one bonus at least : they could dictate their academic course without making obeisance to athletics. To detail the record of federal involvement in Catholic higher education is impossible here and, in any case, this is a story which at present has no imperative need of the telling. During the period of awakening the colleges discovered the federal government's capacity for being a generous friend without smothering the individuality or curtailing the independence of the colleges it helped.

Throughout most of their history, the Catholic colleges in the United

States came into public view mainly through their administrative officers; first, the president, and then, when subordinate administrators appeared, vice-presidents and deans. Except in the past two decades, these officers were always in clerical orders, which added immensely to their stature among American Catholics, who for a long time took the trustworthiness of education for granted if it was managed by religious persons. In the twentieth century, however, mainly because of developments in curricula and the introduction of specialized subject matter, it became necessary for the colleges to add laymen to their faculties, and the more prominent lay and clerical professors began to receive notice as ornaments of *academia*. In the 1960s, the forgotten man in Catholic higher education—the student —began to assert himself. First he assaulted and then demolished the doctrine of *in loco parentis;* next he challenged the right of college officers to conduct the college's business without the benefit of his counsel. At first this latter challenge fell on deaf ears, and then, when it became apparent how serious students were about their rights in an academic society, spokesmen for Catholic colleges began to declare that, if students wanted to manage colleges, they should go elsewhere, for student meddling with administrative and faculty prerogatives would not be tolerated in a Catholic institution. Yet this edict, for all its obvious elements of common sense, was hasty and discounted the fundamental sympathy college faculties and administrators had for a principle of college government allowing for student participation in institutional management. In the end, because of the soundness of student recommendations for their involvement and the zeal with which they advanced them, the custodians of college control compromised. In the 1970s only the rare Catholic college refuses to invite students to share in the determination of college policies, and during the short history of this striking innovation it is hard to find instances where students have failed to demonstrate their maturity and responsibility. To the credit of students in Catholic colleges, as well as to that of the administrators, this long step in the reform of college government toward a fuller democratization has been taken with few major interruptions in the day-to-day operations of the colleges and only rare denials to any student of his right to obtain the education he came to college to get. Even high praise understates the good sense and responsible action of Catholic college students in the 1960s.

If the period of awakening was generally a time for the resolution of conundrums, it was a time also for the re-appearance of one old one in a new guise : how is the Catholic college of the United States in the 1970s different from any other college? In what sense can it be called *Catholic?* We know, of course, that such a question would not have been put in this way to the nineteenth-century college, nor, for that matter, to colleges of the first half of the twentieth century. They were distinctively Catholic because their curricula were heavily loaded with courses in theology and philosophy; their emphasis on moral and religious formation was unrelenting; and their public policies were generally embellished with religious rather than academic language. Now, however, most of this had changed. Could it be true that in its quest for respectability the Catholic college had lost its faith? This question remains troublesome to many Catholic academicians and the answer still eludes them. Yet to others the answer is simple and can be given easily: a *Catholic college,* they aver, is at best a misnomer, at worst a contradiction. It remains for Catholic scholars to establish the nature and scale of the colleges' relationship to the Church whose endorsement it bears and whose intellectual traditions it essays to maintain. The best justification for the continuation of Catholic colleges as such, and at the same time a balanced statement of their distinctiveness, was made by Charles F. Donovan, whose interpretation may yet become a principal code for guiding Catholic colleges in the twentieth century. The Catholic college, Donovan maintained, should "provide the same education one would get in any good college, while making possible formal courses in theology and Church history and out-of-class worship ceremonies." It should "keep alive the quest for and discussion of personal and social values, which in the increasingly secular and scientific world tends to get dropped out of college education." It should, moreover, "continue intellectual inquiry in those realms of reality that modern scholarship, which wears blinders and cuts off investigations not objectively verifiable, tends to ignore, especially the metaphysical." Finally, the Catholic college must "keep vital the pluralism of American culture and help resist the homogenization of contemporary mass society. . . ." It must "do the thinking of the Church," and provide a place "where the sociology, theology, and movement of the Church get thrashed out openly, fully, rationally, and sympathetically." [93] It remains to be seen what Catholic colleges will do with such a reasonable and perceptive elaboration of their character and purpose.

[93] Quoted in "The Changing World of Catholic Education," *Columbia College Today* (Fall, 1966), p. 24.

12

The changing world
of Catholic higher learning

Curriculum

From 1900 to 1945 Catholic college catalogues describing programs and curricula reminded one more of nineteenth-century schools than of contemporary colleges. After World War II, however, colleges which for so long had looked fondly to their past began to think seriously about enlisting in the present. After 1945 new courses and departments began to appear, and some respite was offered students from a fully prescribed course of studies. Requirements in courses in religion or theology were often modified because students needed more time to study sociology, psychology, science, and a variety of vocationally oriented subjects. Philosophy, long justified for its disciplinary value—a claim evidencing a good deal of truth—as well as its power of putting students in intellectual contact with life's ultimate purposes, was subject to reorganization. At long last the curricular face of the college began to change substantially.

In 1945 almost every Catholic college required its student to take sixteen semester hours of credit in religion or theology courses, and a few demanded as many as twenty-four semester hours.[1] Philosophy, similarly privileged in the curriculum, followed religion in staking out its claim, for relatively few students could graduate without courses in the history of philosophy, logic, cosmology, ethics (two in this subject), epistemology, and metaphysics, obtaining thereby a minimum of twenty-one semester credits

---

[1] J. Evans, "Theology at American Universities," *Tablet,* 220 (December 24, 1966), 1453–1454; D. Degnan, "Secularizing Catholic Colleges," *America,* 118 (May 25, 1968), 696–697; R. Grismer, "Christian Formation in the University," *Catholic Educational Review,* 66 (November, 1968), 523–532; and A. App, "Religion: A Unifying Principle for Universities," *Social Justice,* 58 (March, 1966), 440.

on their transcripts.[2] At this time, departments of psychology were under-developed or unknown, as were departments of sociology and political science. Courses in rational psychology sometimes appeared in philosophy depart-ment syllabi, and educational departments added educational psychology, but psychology as a subject worth studying in its own right, subordinated neither to philosophy nor education, earned little attention. Sociology, as a rational rather than an empirical study, was traditionally wedded to ethics; political science, when not paying allegiance to philosophy, was superin-tended by history. Variety in curricula was discouraged by an attitude which discounted any product of empiricism, so additions to fields of knowledge were extremely limited, and these limitations were not imposed by a dearth of financial resources.

The bounds to curricular development, it should be noted, were broken in the period of awakening, and it is unnecessary to list here all the amendments to the syllabus of learning the new age assembled.

The most fundamental changes of the new era occurred in the discip-lines which for more than a half-century had been regarded as the curricular *sine qua non* of Catholic higher education—theology and philosophy. First, historically, because theology was assumed to be untouchable and unsus-ceptible of any compromise, departments of philosophy were remade and courses, such as psychology, which could now claim scientific respectability, were stripped from them. Cosmology was jettisoned too, because in the light of sophisticated scientific knowledge it was plainly impossible for philos-ophers to sustain pretensions of scientific competence when they were ill-equipped to speak the language or handle the data of modern natural science. Second, the inflexible grip scholastic philosophy had maintained over the curriculum for so long began to relax, partly because of the keen sense of self-criticism of which philosophy faculties were capable, and partly because other philosophical systems, formerly mentioned only in the history of philosophy, and then only to be ridiculed and rejected as intellectual nonsense, were given a fairer hearing and were subjected on increasingly frequent occasions to serious study.[3] At long last contemporary philosophic

---

[2] Paul E. Campbell, "What Makes a Catholic School Catholic?" National Catholic Educational Association *Bulletin,* 179 (September, 1954), 426–430; F. Lonsway, "The Liberal Arts and the Changing Curriculum," *Catholic School Journal,* 67 (April, 1967), 75–76; and J. P. Whalen, "The Problem of College Theology," *Catholic Educational Review,* 57 (December, 1959), 583–590.

[3] J. Donceel, "Philosophy in the Catholic University," *America,* 115 (September 24, 1966), 330–331; Gerald F. Kreyche, "The Philosophical Horizons Program at De Paul University," *New Scholasticism,* 39 (October, 1965), 517–524; R. McInerny, "Thomism in an Age of Renewal," *America,* 113 (September 11, 1965), 358–360; and J. Dieska, "Philosophy in Catholic Higher Education," *Social Justice,* 60 (October, 1967), 184–189. The most illuminating, as well as the most up-to-date,

thought was countenanced, for now Catholic philosophers began to take seriously what the man in the street was well aware of—that anyone who refuses to be part of contemporary life can hardly expect to influence it. Despite the undoubted significance of these shifts in philosophic perspective, it must be admitted that philosophy now began to assert its credentials as a liberal study worthy of men's best efforts. The college largely succeeded in stripping its courses of the professional orientation which had been inherent in the seminary philosophy course. As we have noted before, seminary philosophy curricula had for a long time been the models which the colleges felt compelled to imitate.

Theology courses sought to justify their ambitious nomenclatures : both their titles and their descriptions promised a determined academic assault on the treasure possessed only by the "queen of the sciences." Yet, in actual fact, few professors of theology were equipped by training or temperament to open avenues in theology to fundamental scholarly inquiry; they had long understood their commission, an understanding befitting persons who were the products of a professional seminary education, to be considerably narrower and far more practical than anything a serious academic pursuit of theology might entail.[4] Theology department faculties were not totally at fault, however, nor were their perceptions completely incorrect, for in reflecting the policies deeply inbedded in Catholic higher education, they were simply teaching their courses in the way they believed the higher administrative echelons in the college and the Church wanted them taught : they were there to convince students of the truths of dogma and apprise them further of the discipline of the Church.[5] Had their approach been missionary, to convert, rather than homiletic, to instruct a doctrine and in the end to improve both the character and the religious virtue of the students, then good excuses might have been found to justify their practices; but as it was they essayed to recommend their procedures as being consistent with the intellectual goals of Catholic higher learning.[6] What they succeeded

---

of the studies on philosophy is Ernan McMullin's "Philosophy in the U. S. Catholic Colleges : A Survey." His conclusions were reached on the basis of a questionnaire sent to 277 Catholic colleges. 180 colleges responded. McMullin's work is apparently available only in typescript.

[4] Campbell, *op. cit.*; and Fergal McGrath, *The Consecration of Learning: Lectures on Newman's Idea of a University* (New York, Fordham University Press, 1962).

[5] The Hierarchy of the United States, "Religion in Action," *The Christian in Action,* November 21, 1948; J. Leary, "The Bishops and the Catholic College," *Ave Maria,* 10 (February 10, 1968), 6–9.

[6] Francis M. Crowley, *Why A Catholic College Education?* (Washington, D. C., National Catholic Welfare Conference, 1926); Francis C. Wade, *Teaching and Morality* (Chicago, Loyola University Press, 1963); and E. Kevane, "A Note on Catholic University Objectives," *Catholic Educational Review,* 66 (March, 1968), 196–200.

in achieving had been achieved repeatedly in the catechism classes most Catholic college students had completed years before; and hardly anything in the curriculum qualified for a place in higher learning.

With a curriculum lacking intellectual challenge, with a faculty often unable to generate enthusiasm for its function, and with no clear sign that any other functions would be recognized, theology succeeded only in getting a bad name among a majority of Catholic college students. Quick to label theology classes a waste of time, they were prone also to condemn the department's teachers. While Catholic colleges had no previous record of taking notice of student complaint, it must be remembered that now the colleges were living in a new world and the voices of student dissent and their demands for reform were not easily ignored.[7] Students thus forced colleges to reexamine their century-long commitment to a formal teaching of Catholic doctrine in a dogmatic, nonacademic manner. Again, because they were obviously uneasy with the heavy theology requirements, college officers undertook to moderate them. The schools which had been in the habit of demanding one three-hour course in theology for each of eight semesters reduced this requirement by half, to twelve hours; others which had started with lower demands dropped the requirement to eight hours of theology for the bachelor's degree.[8] For a brief time this satisfied the students, not so much in that they had a sense of having fulfilled their responsibility to reform in a field where they felt reform was needed, but in that they had relieved themselves in part of a duty to study subjects which previously had been imposed on them. Huge reservoirs of resentment to academic authoritarianism had been loosed on institutions whose culpability was somewhat in doubt. The broader question of theology as a study with legitimate college and university credentials was as yet untouched, and in the end it was a question which the students were unready to answer. Still, ferment continued and college officers were moved to accelerate their quest for reform in theology curricula. And at this point we meet the more liberal attitudes and pronouncements of the Second Vatican Council, without

---

[7] J. Simmons and P. Grande, "The Student-Administration War of 1966: The Strategy of Escalation," *Catholic Educational Review,* 64 (December, 1966), 582–592; Robert Hassenger, "Student Freedom on the Catholic College Campus," *Ave Maria,* 109 (February 8, 1969), 7–12; and P. H. Ratterman, *The Emerging Catholic University* (New York, Fordham University Press, 1968).

[8] P. McKeever, "Seventy-Five Years of Moral Theology in America," *American Ecclesiastical Review,* 152 (January, 1965), 17–32; Sister A. Carr, "Evolution of a Program in College Theology," *Living Light,* 5 (September, 1968), 76–86; D. Dugan, "Sell-Out in College Theology," *America,* 117 (November 18, 1967), 605; J. L. McKenzie, "Theology in Jesuit Education," *Thought,* 34 (Fall, 1959), 347–357; R. W. Rousseau, "Theology and Culture in Catholic Colleges," *Perspectives,* 5 (October, 1960), 25–29; and Whalen, *op. cit.*

which, one may suppose, the progressive action of more recent years would have been impossible.[9]

The better Catholic colleges in the 1960s undertook revisions in curricula which could hardly have been imagined in 1945; they reduced their theology requirements as low as nine or six hours, removed from their syllabus all required courses, added Biblical studies, minimized the emphasis of the doctrinal and dogmatic approach, and, finally, added professors who were Protestant and Jewish to teach courses in nonCatholic branches of theology.[10] Courses in Catholic theology remained, and some such courses continued to embody the doctrinal approach, but students were free to register for them or not as they chose. Theology in these schools was considered to be an important part of a university curriculum, but its claim upon student time was judged to be neither superior nor inferior to the claim of any other department. In the end, theology courses were subjected to the vagaries of academic competition, where quality could attract students to register or where popularity, relevance, or the ease of a professor's marking system could be factors as important as scholarly standing in the formulation of student choice. Such courses, freed from institutional support, would now sink or swim on the basis of their academic credentials, scholarly appeal, or popularity in what was judged, for good or ill, to be an awakened academic community.

Along with the catharsis sweeping away old assumptions about the superior status of theology and philosophy, and the multiplication of new fields of study in the curriculum, Catholic colleges ventured into new areas, or perhaps only revisited old ones, when they introduced interdisciplinary studies.[11] The nineteenth-century curriculum with its humanities, poetry, and rhetoric years, for example, was probably interdisciplinary; but these curricular patterns had been forsaken in favor of a departmental organization of studies, because in the twentieth century departments were the fashion. Yet, the departmentalization of curricula had become subject to criticism for abandoning the integration of knowledge,[12] and Catholic

[9] Vatican Council Declaration on Christian Education (English translation), *Catholic Educational Review,* 64 (March, 1966), 145–158.

[10] Lewis Mayhew, "The Desirability of Catholic Higher Education," *American Benedictine Review,* 19 (December, 1968), 427–436; G. Sloyan, "The New Role of the Study of Religion in Higher Education: What Does It Mean?" *Journal of Ecumenical Studies,* 6 (Winter, 1969), 1–17; and T. Ambrogi, "The Catholic University in an Ecumenical Age," National Catholic Education Association *Bulletin,* 64 (November, 1967), 21–26.

[11] Eugene Grollmes, "Catholic Colleges: The Pearl Called Uniqueness," *Catholic Educational Review,* 65 (September, 1967), 361–375; and Lonsway, *op. cit.*

[12] Bernard T. Rattigan, *A Critical Study of the General Education Movement* (Washington, D. C., Catholic University of America Press, 1952); and John J. Ryan, *The Idea of a Catholic College* (New York, Sheed and Ward, 1945).

colleges, seeing their American counterparts experimenting with inter-disciplinary curricula, decided to follow suit.

Professors

Unquestionably fundamental in their effect, curricular changes in Catholic colleges were nevertheless, in the period of awakening, overshadowed by the larger perspective faculties began to bring to their work as members of an academic community. For a while early in this period, the presidents of Catholic colleges discovered the word *family,* and on almost every occasion when such talk was at all appropriate they spoke of *the university family,* by which they meant the relationships existing, or those that could be made to exist, between faculty members and administrators.[13] But all this talk about a collegiate family (really a revival of paternalism dressed in captivating rhetoric) was inconsistent with the role faculties now per-ceived for themselves. They scorned the pronouncements presidents were prone to make, and the presidents, shortly seeing the error of their ways, abandoned domestic terminology. No doubt elements of truth lingered in the familial analogy, especially as it applied to religious confreres assigned to a college faculty, but laymen were not to be so convinced about a relationship in which they were asked to relinquish their hopes of playing an effective and professional role in university life to the president, the father of the family. The era of unlimited presidential authority was past, a new age was dawning, and even when faculties could not interpret the omens for that possibly still-distant time when they would become full partners, they were confident that eventually their voices would have to be heard. Fulfillment of their hopes came sooner than they expected.

The presidents of Catholic colleges, it should be admitted, were neither forced to relinquish their authority, in which charters and statutes sustained them, nor were they tricked out of it by the cunning of professors : it was gratuitous action on the presidents' part that delegated some academic authority to the faculty. And this was a sign, we should think, that the caricature of the Catholic college president as a man jealous of his authority and unwilling or unable to surrender or delegate any of it is unjust. For the most part, college presidents had conserved their authority for what they believed to be the schools' good during the whole of the nineteenth and the first decades of the twentieth century, and their rejection of

[13] R. R. Macgregor, "The Catholic Lay Professor," *America,* 33 (September 12, 1925), 513–514; and Charles Rice, "The Plight of the Professor," *America,* 85 (September 8, 1951), 543–544, 548.

petitions from faculties asking for shared responsibility in academic organization was justified by one good excuse at least : faculties were unready to cope with issues of college management. But by this time, say around 1955, many Catholic college faculties were equipped to take a hand in college government, and what is more, they could demonstrate their qualifications for assuming this responsibility.

Faculty participation in college control was evidenced in a number of ways, such as the implementation of policies on academic freedom, appointments to the faculty, tenure arrangements and tenure decisions, salaries, curricular renovation and innovation, admissions practices and policies, and the determination and supervision of academic standards.[14]

Catholic college spokesmen had for long proudly proclaimed the existence of full academic freedom in their institutions; sometimes they boldly asserted that only in a Catholic college was academic freedom possible.[15] What they should have said was that Catholic college faculties had been carefully selected on the basis of religious orthodoxy and it was impossible to imagine them ever thinking about or actually teaching anything in conflict with the official policies of the college or the established doctrines of the Church. Catholic colleges enjoyed their image as safe schools to which parents could send their sons and daughters never doubting the colleges' ability to protect their morals and insulate their faith. The old-fashioned Catholic college sincerely and convincingly affirmed orthodoxy, but confused orthodoxy and academic freedom, and at the same time failed to understand that nothing of consequence pertaining to academic freedom could ever have been tested in its environment. Yet, when colleges matured to university standing and some professors began to enter fields of social science research, when questions of population control, Communism, the rights of free enterprise, the rights of labor, and the sociology of the family became both relevant to their publications and their classrooms, the comfortable pronouncements of Catholic colleges were put to the test. Was academic freedom authentic? Could professors conduct their research without interference? And could they report their findings without jeopardizing their positions on the faculty? Were there conditioned inhibitions which really made most of the talk about academic freedom fanciful?

---

14 J. K. Durick, "The Lay Faculty: A Reply," *Commonweal,* 21 (April 19, 1935), 699–701; and William H. Conley, "The Lay Teacher in Catholic Education," National Catholic Education Association *Bulletin,* 59 (August, 1962), 25–30.

15 Ronald W. Roloff, "Are Our Colleges So Bad?" *The Catholic World,* 185 (June, 1957), 267; Francis P. Donnelly, *The Progressive Conservatism of Catholic Education* (New York, Fordham University Press, 1936); Virgil C. Blum, *Freedom of Choice in Education* (New York, Macmillan Company, 1958); and J. Lawler, "In Defense of the Catholic University," *Catholic Mind,* 65 (January, 1967), 21–27.

Faculty handbooks reaffirmed the colleges' allegiance to what was called the "proper interpretation" of academic freedom : professors were free to teach truth, to pursue it wherever it might lead, as long as they did so responsibly and as long as they refrained from teaching or writing anything either remotely or explicitly contrary to the doctrines of the Catholic Church.[16] But who was to determine truth? Who would define responsible teaching? And who was to decide at what precise point a teacher strayed into heterodoxy?

Besides, the question of the rights of a professor as a citizen sometimes arose : could he, for example, denounce the anti-Communist tactics employed by Senator Joseph R. McCarthy of Wisconsin? Could he lend his name to the political campaigns of various candidates, some of whom might be unpopular with persons from whom the college expected benefactions?[17] Could he stray from the philosophic traditions of scholasticism? And could he deal in a strictly scientific way with such psychological questions as free will and determinism? Even in the 1970s it would probably be wrong to interpret the climate of Catholic colleges to be so liberal as to be indifferent to a professor's public declarations on many, if not most, of these issues. Conservatism is almost indigenous to Catholic college faculties, and it may be some time before the fundamental issues in academic freedom are put to the ultimate test. Yet, even if we assume that this is a fair appraisal of conditions in Catholic colleges, it must be admitted that a procedure for managing disputes over academic freedom has been established, and that perhaps a majority of Catholic colleges in the United States have either formally adopted or informally endorsed the 1940 *Statement of Principles on Academic Freedom and Tenure* defined by the American Association of University Professors.[18]

We know how faculties in the old colleges were assembled. The term recruitment would be used incorrectly in connection with them. Positions on the faculty were first filled by members of the religious community; if, after the resources of the religious community were exhausted, vacancies remained, then laymen would be sought, sometimes as temporary employees

[16] J. Kennedy, A. McNally, and A. Hennessy, "Academic Freedom on the Catholic College Campus," *Sign,* 47 (September, 1967), 29–31; Philip Gleason, "Freedom and the Catholic University," National Catholic Education Association *Bulletin,* 65 (November, 1968), 21–29; C. Donahoe, "Heresy and Conspiracy," *Thought,* 28 (Winter, 1953), 528–546; and M. Sheridan, "Theology and Academic Freedom," *America,* 116 (May 6, 1967), 681–682.

[17] Rice, *op. cit.*

[18] This statement received the official endorsement of the AAUP in 1941 and the Association of American Colleges in the same year. The only Catholic scholarly association to endorse it officially was the American Catholic Philosophical Association in 1966. See Edward Manier and John W. Houk, *Academic Freedom and the Catholic University* (Notre Dame, Ind., Fides Publishers, Inc., 1967), pp. 207–225.

and sometimes as more or less permanent additions to the faculty. Availability rather than qualification was important, and only infrequently were judgments made, once a religious or lay teacher had joined the faculty, about the quality of his work. When decisions about such appointments were made presidents or deans made them, sometimes with and sometimes without consultation with the faculty. It was hard to tell what qualifications were sought. But this practice halted abruptly in the better Caholic colleges when faculty members were asked to recommend persons of scholarly quality who might be invited to join the faculty.[19]

This procedure, indeed new in the experience of Catholic college professors, was not handled with alacrity or with great success. There was always the human tendency amongst the "old guard" not to recommend for faculty appointment a person who might prove to be an academic threat, and an attitude of this sort made faculty upgrading a slow and tedious process. In the end, however, it came to work reasonably well—at least, better than the old method—and while there could never be any guarantee that recommendations would be totally free from an incumbent's vested interest, department faculties usually recognized the obvious : the quality of their department and its reputation in the world of scholasrhip affected them directly. By adding mediocre colleagues, they were only depressing their own academic prospects. So, in order to ensure the recruitment and appointment of the best teachers they could afford to pay for, Catholic colleges, rather than wait for applicants to seek them out, actively engaged in faculty talent hunts.

In order, however, to attract well-qualified persons to their faculties, Catholic colleges were required, whether the administrators liked it or not, to offer competitive salaries, fringe benefits, and tenure. It would be hard to determine with historical exactitude either when tenure was formally instituted at Catholic colleges or which college was the pioneer in establishing it. It is clear, of course, that long before tenure became a legal precept in Catholic college statutes, it was, or could be, an unwritten law of faculty life.[20] Thus, certain lay professors (because tenure was not usually offered to members of religious communities) were assured of permanence in their positions by the traditions of the college, and this guarantee of permanence was usually as good and as certain, although not a matter of written policy, as the legal tenure assured by statute.

---

[19] Ward Stames, "The Lay Faculty," *Commonweal,* 21 (April 12, 1935), 667–668.

[20] Macgregor, *op. cit.;* Conley, *op. cit.;* Robert Hassenger (editor), *The Shape of Catholic Higher Education* (Chicago, University of Chicago Press, 1967), pp. 193–201; "Catholic Scholars Urge University Autonomy," *National Catholic Reporter,* 3 (August 2, 1967) 3; J. Leary, "The Layman in Catholic Higher Education," *America,* 116 (March 25, 1967), 414–417; and Paul C. Reinert, *Faculty Tenure in Colleges and Universities from 1900 to 1940* (St. Louis, St. Louis University Press, 1946), *passim.*

Tenure, however, before the objective of legality became explicit, was destined to play a significant role in upgrading Catholic college faculties. Before tenure policies were adopted, Catholic college administrators assumed their freedom to correct mistakes in faculty appointments anytime such mistakes became obtrusive, by simply dismissing the unwanted faculty member. They were similarly absolved from the careful planning of future faculty requirements, for, if it became clear that a certain professor was no longer needed, he too, could be dismissed. No doubt, because it did not need to live with its past mistakes, if it chose not to, Catholic college administration was freer to modify its curricula than was the college where the lists of professors tended to prescribe the courses to be taught. But if this freedom was a luxury few colleges capitalized it; in any event, the essential adjustments in curricula were not on the side of retrenchment but on the side of expansion and enrichment. If tenure was to be taken seriously, and there is no indication that Catholic colleges were not serious, prudent judgments would have to be made, first, about the need for additions to the faculty and, then, when appointments were made, whether or not the professors involved should be advanced to tenure status. Once tenure was granted, the college had a clear legal obligation to the professors.[21]

Who should make these important decisions about the quality and competence of recently-appointed faculty members? In their early experiences with tenure, Catholic colleges assumed, perhaps naturally enough in view of their traditional adherence to administrative control, that the proper officer to make such decisions was either the president or the dean. In larger colleges, the dean made his recommendations to the president, who then acted on them; in a small college, where the president still took a fairly active part in day-to-day administration, and where he tried to learn his faculty's strengths and weaknesses at first hand, the president reserved tenure decisions to himself.[22] But this was an administrative technique manageable only in a small, uncomplicated school.

In the university, where administration could not be close to the classroom or the laboratory, such procedures vested in the administration, and susceptible to all kinds of unreliable evidence, proved to be hard to manage and, in the end, unacceptable to the faculty. The faculty, then, was called upon to participate in a matter critical to the quality and standards of the school. Department and college faculty committees were either appointed by the administration or elected by the faculty itself to make tenure recommendations to the president. In the end, of course, he

[21] John D. Donovan, *The Academic Man in the Catholic College* (New York, Sheed and Ward, 1964), pp. 174–175.

[22] Darrell F. X. Finnegan, *The Function of the Academic Dean in American Catholic Higher Education* (Washington, D. C., Catholic University of America Press, 1951), pp. 17–24.

was responsible for making the final decision, but now his judgment was informed by evidence from good witnesses. The principles governing tenure procedures in Catholic colleges, while based generally on the *Statement of Principles on Academic Freedom and Tenure* made in 1940 by the American Association of University Professors,[23] are, as yet, so diverse that to deduce from them any common code is plainly impossible. It should be clearly stated, however, that this diversity exists in the method of arriving at tenure decisions, and not, at least as far as a majority of Catholic colleges are concerned, in the adoption of tenure policies.[24]

Catholic college faculties, while relying heavily on support from the standards for faculties stated by the American Association of University Professors, and regularly using the ammunition supplied by the Association to accelerate the adoption of tenure and salary policies, have been surprisingly remiss in active participation in this Association.[25]

At one time, before the advent of the period of awakening, this lack of involvement in the one professional group which could have helped them most could have been excused. Administrators declaimed against the work of the Association and threatened to dismiss any faculty member who either joined the AAUP or tried to organize a chapter on the campus.[26] Their antipathy toward the AAUP was matched only by their dislike for and fear of faculty unionization, which they regularly anathematized.[27] So taking this intransigent attitude at face value, as it was meant to be taken, and coupling with it the native reluctance of Catholic college professors to enter the world, either for academic conferences or for professional improvement, we find therein the principal reasons for their noninvolvement, a noninvolvement with some permanent features.[28] Besides, in the trust a Catholic layman, who happened to belong to a college faculty, bestowed on a priest, and the fundamental paternalism infecting both administrators and professors, we find another reason why Catholic college teachers refused to look outside the gates of their own college for any

[23] For a reprint of the Statement see AAUP *Bulletin,* 51 (September, 1965), 388–389.

[24] G. Dalcourt, "Lay Control of Catholic Colleges," *America,* 117 (October 14, 1967), 412–414; Hassenger, *op. cit.,* pp. 193–201.

[25] Henry J. Browne, "Catholics and the AAUP," *Commonweal,* 65 (October 5, 1956), 7–14.

[26] Rice, *op. cit.,* and Macgregor, *op. cit.*

[27] C. Cogen, "The Professional in Labor," *Labor Leader,* 22 (August, 1959), 3; and Brother G. Paul, "Report of Discussion Meeting of College Presidents on the Rights of the Lay Faculty in Our Colleges and Universities," National Catholic Education Association *Proceedings,* 48 (1951), 161–162.

[28] Jerome G. Dalmation, "Confessions of a Catholic Professor," *America,* 86 (October 6, 1951), 9–10.

steppingstones to professional advancement.[29]. Such action, they thought, smacked of a disloyalty unacceptable to professors and condemned by administrators. In trying to be true to models of Catholic higher learning, for which they had little or no responsibility, faculties too often turned out to be untrue both to themselves and to the fields of knowledge they represented. But this was a state of affairs subject to change, and change it did.

And now for the best of reasons the colleges were contributing to the dethronement of administrative supremacy: in their quest for higher faculty standards they were appointing persons whose credentials were equal to those of professors in nonCatholic institutions. If conditions of employment and the standards in use in academic matters proved unsatisfactory, these persons would leave the college, and how would the college replace them? By appointing more fully qualified persons to their faculties Catholic colleges increased the chances of unrest and ultimately of a further diminution of administrative control. In general, too, the greater mobility of all persons in society argued indirectly for a stronger voice for faculties in the management of Catholic colleges.

Still, the AAUP was seldom sought as a remedy for the ills Catholic college professors felt; and even in 1969 an almost insignificant number of Catholic college faculty members had joined its ranks.[30] But, while this is true, the old antipathies for local AAUP chapters have tended to disappear, and when chapters are organized their membership, though small, is not generally, as it once was, augmented by religious members of the faculty sent by the administration to spy on the proceedings. A lack of enthusiasm for active membership in the ranks of AAUP has not, as we have already suggested, deterred these same faculties from using such things as AAUP salary classifications as gauges for judging their own salary schedules.[31] Among colleges in the United States, the first objective was the raising of the average in the salaries of various academic ranks to the norms published by the AAUP. For a long time Catholic colleges, while generally sharing this aspiration, were content with the gentleman's "C" on the AAUP salary scale. In the period of awakening, with higher aspirations, most seek, and a number have obtained, "A" standing on the AAUP scale for at least some of their professorial ranks.[32]

[29] Willis D. Nutting, "Mark Hopkins, the Log and the Dollar," *Commonweal,* 52 (April 14, 1950), 8–10; Arpad Steiner, "Creative Scholarship," *Commonweal,* 25 (January 22, 1937), 347–349; and Donnelly, *op. cit.*

[30] B. H. Davis, "Report of the General Secretary," AAUP *Bulletin,* 55 (June, 1969), 159–161.

[31] W. J. Baumol and P. Heim, "On the Financial Prospects for Higher Education: Annual Report on the Economic Status of the Profession," AAUP *Bulletin,* 54 (June, 1968), 182–241.

[32] W. R. Bokelman and L. A. D'Amico, "Comparison of Salaries and Student Costs at Catholic Institutions with Salaries and Costs at Other Private Institutions," National Catholic Education Association *Bulletin,* 58 (November, 1961), 27–32.

During the period of awakening, Catholic colleges discovered committees and quickly adopted the committee system, a practice in vogue among other American colleges for decades.[33] Committees were elected or appointed to make recommendations on various policies pertaining to collegiate functions, and probably more significant than any other committees were those concerned with curricular renovation and innovation.

About 1945, deans, having by then discovered the complexities of curricular management, decided to seek the help of department heads or, as they were called in some Catholic colleges, department directors.[34] So, to begin with, the committee system was largely a way of employing the prudence of department heads, who now considered common problems in concert. But, it should be observed, the department head was at least partly a representative of administration, and seemed to many members of the faculty to have too little in common with them to be a fully accredited colleague. As long as colleges took seriously the definition their handbooks gave of department directors and heads, the resources of faculty talent for rebuilding curricula were hard to mobilize.

At the beginning of the period of awakening (as we have stated, about 1945), department directors and heads were appointed either by deans or presidents and they were charged with the conduct of their departments. Among their responsibilities were such items as selecting textbooks for various courses (with the approval in some colleges of the province prefect of studies), assigning professors to teach the courses, prescribing or approving syllabi for all courses in the department, recommending promotions and salary increments for department members, and from time to time, usually once monthly (if handbook prescriptions were followed rigorously), convening the department's teachers to make announcements of policy and to give routine directions.[35] Thus authority formerly lodged with the president in the old college, and later delegated to the dean, was now delegated further to the "leader" of a department. Perhaps this was a sincere effort to bring the government of departments closer to the operational level; it may, on the other hand, have been a clever ploy to make the faculty believe it was being enfranchised to manage academic affairs.

Whatever the motivation for this transfer of authority, it turned out to be a mistake. Department growth, the attraction of talent to faculties, and the utilization of the scholarship and academic insights of the rank and file were all limited by the appearance of authority now residing in the

---

[33] John S. Brubacher and Willis Rudy, *Higher Education in Transition* (New York, Harper and Row, Publishers, 1958), pp. 354–355.

[34] *The Faculty Handbook,* The University of Detroit, 1949. At this school, departmental director was an academic rank one step above the rank of professor.

[35] Edward J. Power, *A History of Catholic Higher Education in the United States* (Milwaukee, Wis., Bruce Publishing Co., 1958), pp. 157–158.

hands of a department chief. So, sensing the hostility generated against this innovation, the colleges decided to modify the terminology they normally used and thus make the whole system less offensive. They deleted all reference to directors and heads and began to use the term *chairman* as a title for identifying department leaders. Yet in most colleges the change was purely nominal, for during this interlude department chairmen were not, in fact, chairmen : they were not elected by their colleagues; only infrequently were department members consulted before a chairman was appointed; their tenure as chairmen was decided outside the department; and they were not in any sense accountable to the department for their decisions.[36].

With all the evidences of democracy, whether in student government, student participation on university committees, deans' councils, or even in the college and university academic senates, so recently organized in a few Catholic colleges,[37] the earlier citadel of authority, the power of the department leader, is intact. And curricular reform and innovation, because, as the colleges are now organized, it must really begin on the department level, is made to depend on the goodwill, the vision, or the wisdom of a department chairman.

Despite the difficulties arising from an inability on the colleges' part to become more fully democratic, curricular reform and innovation have been realities of the past decade. Largely by chance, but occasionally by design, department chairmen have been appointed who recognize innovation as essential and inevitable, and instead of being hustled by events in the direction of innovation, have determined to shape the innovations themselves. Usually men with enough foresight for this have a natural prudence which helps them also to use the resources of talent in their departmental colleagues in the business of shaping department objectives and curricula.

While department organization has tended to isolate fields of study and to make their management the special responsibility of the department, the broader faculty voice is seeking a hearing, and in the colleges college-wide curriculum committees are now appearing. On the university level, moreover, the more prestigious and progressive schools—Boston College, Fordham, St. Louis, and Notre Dame are examples—are experimenting with academic senates through which the entire faculty is capable of influencing academic policy.[38] For the complex (university) institution,

[36] P. Collins, "The Department Chairman : Move Over Rover," *Catholic Educator,* 36 (December, 1965), 30–32.

[37] J. Leary, "The Layman in Catholic Higher Education," *America,* 116 (February 18, 1967), 251–253.

[38] Theodore Hesburgh, "The Changing Face of Catholic Higher Education," National Catholic Education Association *Bulletin,* 65 (August, 1969), 54–60; Gerald

these policies usually recommend a basic liberal or general education for all students during the first two years of college study. Yet, it should be admitted, this experimentation with liberal learning and its deployment in the college's curriculum is only beginning.[39]

Because of their recently improved status, the faculties have come to think that they alone can speak with authority on curricular matters. Contemporary student power, however, has caused them to revise some of these newly formed opinions about faculty autonomy.[40] Students seeing their vital interests affected by what they are required to study, have asked for, and in may instances have obtained, the right to make their opinions felt on curricular organization and reorganization.[41] While usually respecting faculty prerogatives in the determination of curricular policies (and for so doing Catholic college students must be given credit for an unusual amount of common sense), they have demanded formal means for representing their own attitudes and opinions. In the 1970s students are being listened to, more in some colleges than in others, but everywhere with a tardy realization that students have a right to express their concern about a subject so important to them as the content of their college course of study.

In recognizing a contemporary fashion to captain one's own fate, especially in college studies, as having elements of validity, the historian's memory is too good to allow him to forget the chaos inflicted on universities of the past when they mistakenly surrendered control over learning to persons whose qualifications to pursue knowledge were sound enough but who had no experience whatever in arranging for its preservation, transmission, and expansion in the university. If student appetites for college control become insatiable, and if college faculties and administrators continue to feed them, the integrity of man's one great intellectual agency will be put in dire jeopardy and the universities of the United States will become intellectual wastelands. To avoid such a catastrophe Catholic and nonCatholic colleges alike must learn to balance the tensions generated

Kreyche, "American Catholic Higher Learning and Academic Freedom," National Catholic Education Association Bulletin, 62 (August, 1965), 211–222; and D. O'Brien, "A Job for the Laity: Catholic Higher Education in North America," Tablet, 221 (February 18, 1967), 175–176.

[39] J. Sherer, "Ferment on the Campus," Month, 226 (December, 1968), 325–331; E. Shuster, "Why a Catholic Liberal Arts College?" Social Justice, 61 (May, 1968), 40–49; and M. Sheridan, "A Rationale for Changes in Catholic Colleges," National Catholic Education Association Bulletin, 64 (November, 1967), 11–14.

[40] "Control of Catholic Universities," Ave Maria, 105 (January 28, 1967), 4–5; M. Marty, "Catholic Colleges in a Time of Change," National Catholic Reporter, 3 (February 1, 1967), 8; and Simons and Grande, op. cit.

[41] J. Walsh, "Law and Order on the Catholic Campus," Commonweal, 90 (September 19, 1969), 562–563; Robert Hassenger, "Student Freedom on the Catholic College Campus," Ave Maria, 109 (February 8, 1969), 7–12; and Ratterman, op. cit.

by student activists with their own profound convictions about the fundamental purpose of any school : they must continue teaching what needs
to be taught. Taking into account legitimate student recommendations
(although they are frequently demands) and remaining alert to fairly stated
student needs are attitudes which belong to the order of common prudence,
but the university, although it exists for students, must never acknowledge
them to be its master.

Professorial standards in Catholic colleges, long a matter of compromise
and ambiguity, took a decided turn for the better in the early years of
the period of awakening. An old portrait is easily recognized : in it clerical
members of the faculty took precedence over laymen, and laymen were
seldom heeded when questions of policy were opened for faculty discussion.
In the old college, the rare faculty meeting was convened for the purpose of giving out information, but if other issues were to be discussed, the
laymen on the faculty were excused from the room.[42] Such practices must
have been demeaning, but, given the conventional opinions current in
Catholic higher education, it was entirely natural to reserve the discussion
to those vitally involved, and laymen, by definition, were not intrinsic to
the college.[43] No one seriously entertained the possibility of allowing laymen
to know plans for the college, or in any way to share the secrets of college
management.

This portrait may be continued for a moment longer. In it we see,
besides the clear dominance of the clerical professor, whose credentials
were good or bad, it made no matter, a figure who comes from outside the
college to influence and sometimes to dictate the day-to-day operations of
the college. This is the prefect of studies or, perhaps under some other
title, the representative of the religious order's superior.[44] When he arrives
at the school for a periodic visit, he wants to know how things are going,
so he calls on the president, and the president, a subordinate officer to and
an appointee of the religious superior, makes his academic report. The next
stop for the prefect of studies is the dean's office, where again he obtains
a report of the college's operations; then he proceeds to the offices of
selected department heads, who until the period of awakening were always
clerics, and sometimes to the classrooms of the teachers.

This tour of inspection enabled the prefect to prepare his report
to the religious superior (although some prefects were commissioned to
change academic practices and institute new ones on the spot), who always

---

[42] Power, *op. cit.*, p. 104.

[43] Sebastian A. Erbacher, *Catholic Higher Education for Men in the United
States: 1850–1866* (Washington, D. C., Catholic University of America, 1931),
pp. 79–82.

[44] William J. McGucken, *The Jesuits and Education* (Milwaukee, Wis., Bruce
Publishing Co., 1932), pp. 221–222.

wanted to know how exactly the school was fulfilling the educational directions he had given and, of course, how orthodox its teaching was. As for orthodoxy in particular, the prefect of studies hoped to ensure it by insisting that the textbooks used be approved by him.

The appearance of a prefect of studies was most common in Jesuit colleges, where the prefect, whose office was prescribed in the *Ratio Studiorum,* had extensive influence over operational and instructional policies, standards, and practices.[45] More recently, although the office of prefect still exists, the prefect himself seldom appears at a college, and never in the classroom to get a first-hand view of teaching. In the past decade or so the prefect of studies has surrendered his control over the materials of instruction, including textbooks, to the professors.

Both external and internal controls over teaching became less necessary —an adjective applicable only if we assume they were once essential— when religious and lay faculties became more fully qualified. Plans for the academic training of lay professors, however, were seldom the business of the college managers. They first met the lay professor when he applied for a position and could then judge whether or not he had appropriate credentials. With members of the religious community, however, more control could be exercised.

Here the prefect of studies participated in the organization and faculty improvement of colleges manned by teaching orders by superintending the academic preparation of young priests. Once a priest was ordained (with Jesuits, before he was ordained), he was asked to select a field of study and enroll in a graduate school to complete his work toward an advanced academic degree. The prefect of studies, acting as the educational spokesman for the provincial, or some other religious superior, guided these prospective scholars to a graduate school, supervised their progress through their studies, and recommended teaching assignments for them when their degrees were obtained. In unusual instances, sometimes depending on the force of a prefect's personality, a young cleric's field of studies would be selected for him. He would seek a doctorate in a field of study where the college needed a teacher. But knowing that intrinsic motivation, or personal attraction to a field of study, was better than an edict, religious superiors preferred to allow candidates to make their own choices.

The record of colleges for men, especially since the advent of the period of awakening, in sending their personnel on to graduate study, often at state and nonCatholic private universities, helped to lessen the atmosphere of inbreeding for which all Catholic colleges were criticized in earlier years.[46]

---

[45] *Ibid.*

[46] Samuel K. Wilson, "The Genesis of American College Government," *Thought,* I (December, 1926), 415–433.

We have already said that Catholic colleges were seldom able to involve themselves in the business of a prospective lay professor's academic preparation. Neither their attitudes toward faculty development nor their resources qualified them to encourage post-magisterial or post-doctoral studies for their faculties, and sabbatical leaves were no more than promising possibilities that faculties now and then dreamed about. While these generalizations are undoubtedly valid, they may, nevertheless, be susceptible to minor amendment. A college here and there did on occasion invest in the preparation of lay faculties by supporting some of its most promising graduates through doctoral studies. The support varied from loans to outright grants, with the understanding that the person so supported would, after completing his graduate studies, return to the college for an agreed period of time, usually three or five years. This practice, however, was not fully exploited by the colleges, and Catholic colleges always understood such arrangements to be *ad hoc* expedients outside the realm of institutional policy.

Colleges for men took the lead among Catholic schools in developing and improving the qualifications of their faculties, and for this they deserve some credit.[47] Somewhat less praiseworthy, however, was the tendency of Catholic women's colleges to prepare their faculties of religious women in their own classrooms, ignoring for the time the need for advanced academic degrees.[48] They feared the influence of the secular university and even that of the larger Catholic universities where graduate study had obtained, even by 1935, a fairly solid beginning. By 1955 these intransigent attitudes in Catholic women's colleges had changed for the better. From that time these institutions became more sensitive to the critical need for faculty development if their schools were to obtain and retain accreditation, so communities of religious women, pooling their resources in artful ways, created the Sister Formation Movement, commissioning it to find means for the better preparation of teachers.[49]

While Sister Formation, it must be said, aimed more at the lower schools than the colleges, its impact was felt in many Catholic women's colleges and helped college faculties to meet the standards required for

[47] Allan P. Farrell, "Catholic Men's Colleges," *America,* 76 (January 18, 1947), 436; and "Report of Section on the Improvement of College Teaching," National Catholic Education Association *Bulletin,* 51 (August, 1954), 244–245.

[48] William F. Kelley, "Observations on Some Catholic Colleges for Women," *Catholic Educational Review,* 48 (May, 1950), 311–315; and M. Regina, "Can the Mother General Afford to Send Sisters on to Graduate Study?" National Catholic Education Association *Bulletin,* 58 (August, 1961), 141.

[49] John O. Riedl, "Scholarship and the Sisterhoods," *Sister Formation Bulletin* II, (October, 1955), 4; and W. J. Dunne, "Personnel Policies for Sister College Teachers," National Catholic Education Association *Bulletin,* 56 (August, 1959), 131–141.

accreditation. More importantly, improved faculty quality tended to ensure a decent education for the women students enrolled.

Despite the determined action of colleges for men and colleges for women in this age of awakening, acceptable academic standards (acceptability being understood here to mean accreditation) were hard to attain and then to maintain. In 1970 approximately twenty percent of the Catholic colleges in the United States lacked accreditation with their regional accrediting association and, according to a recent Danforth Foundation study, another twenty percent were considered to be of marginal quality.[50] A general opinion, although, it must be admitted, the firm evidence to support it is lacking, prevails that not a single Catholic university can be considered as belonging to the front rank of American higher learning despite the extraordinary effort of the past to achieve academic excellence in such schools as Fordham, St. Louis, Notre Dame, Marquette, Georgetown, and Boston College (among the larger, predominantly men's schools;) Manhattan, St. John's in Minnesota, and Providence (among the smaller, mainly men's colleges;) and Manhattanville, Immaculate Heart, Trinity, and Mundelein among women's colleges.[51]

Without trying to determine college rank, or even to assert that no other Catholic college belongs on this short list, we may aver that these schools are unquestionably good, though even among them the existence of one library capable of serving the dual functions of teaching and research is doubted by some commentators.[52] The largest library collection in a Catholic university, at St. Louis, numbered 691,000 volumes in 1966.[53] Only Georgetown, Boston College and Fordham have Phi Beta Kappa chapters.[54] Judgments on the adequacy of libraries to support graduate programs in the academic fields surveyed by the Cartter study[55] are inevitably colored by arbitrary or subjective evaluation. Yet, if we use the criteria of total volumes, volumes added annually over the period in question (1953–1962), and periodical resources, find the average of these criteria for all universities and assign an index of 1.00 to the average, each library can be assigned an index number below or above the average and thus provide some basis for making a qualified objective judgment on merit. Harvard's cumulative index (volumes in library, annual acquisitions,

[50] M. Pattillo, "The Danforth Report and Catholic Higher Education," *Catholic Mind*, 64 (June, 1966), 36–46.

[51] "The Changing World of Catholic Education," *Columbia College Today* (Fall, 1966), p. 20.

[52] *Ibid.*

[53] *Ibid.*

[54] Neil G. McCluskey, "Phi Beta Kappa and Catholic Colleges," *America*, 98 (February 22, 1958), 597–599.

[55] Allan M. Cartter, *An Assessment of Quality in Graduate Education* (Washington, D. C., American Council on Education, 1966), pp. 114–115.

and periodical holdings), the highest of all, was 5.29; Johns Hopkins' cumulative index, which assigned it to group two, was reported as being between 1.50 and 1.99; Michigan State, in category three, had a cumulative index of 1.00 to 1.49; Notre Dame, in category four, had a cumulative index of .75 to .99; Catholic University, Fordham, Georgetown, and St. Louis were given a cumulative index of .50 to .74, and were assigned to the fifth category (out of six) of universities considered in the survey.[56] Boston College, excluded from the study because it did not confer an annual average of ten doctorates for the 1953–1962 period, computed its cumulative index by applying these criteria to the years 1963–1964 at 1.17.

Students

In its infant years American higher education took the position that its quality depended first on the efficiency of its administration and then on the competence of its faculty. If some assurance could be had about the praiseworthiness of presidents and professors, then, without doubt, the standards of the college were good. The quality of students was ignored, for in the old college it was hard to see what relationship they had to institutional excellence. But this was academic myopia at its worst; to the good fortune of American higher learning it did not last. The old time colleges, it is true, talked about entrance requirements long before they set any standards for admissions.[57] And setting standards took time, but eventually the best colleges set them. It soon became evident that the level of college studies advertised and the reputation of a school depended not only on its administrators and teachers but on the ability, motivation, and curiosity of the students as well. Long neglected, students suddenly became important to the colleges who wanted their superiority noted.

While this was going on in the better nonCatholic colleges of the United States, Catholic colleges were content to remain unconcerned about entrance requirements and standards.[58] A recapitulation here of the history of admissions during the formative and developmental years is unnecessary for we either know or can guess that this was an aspect of college life in which there was no clear policy. Students who applied were admitted, and it hardly ever made any difference whether or not they were prepared to follow a *college* course of studies.[59] Without any solid American Catholic

---

[56] *Ibid.*, p. 115.

[57] Erbacher, *op. cit.*, pp. 83–84.

[58] Power, *op. cit.*, pp. 115–116.

[59] Augustus J. Thébaud, *Forty Years in the United States of America* (New York, United States Catholic Historical Society, 1904), pp. 331–332.

tradition for higher learning, and without the criteria to judge the standards necessary for the college course, college managers contrived to achieve
a great variety in content and instructional quality. Bachelor's degrees
were awarded promiscuously, but only the brave commentator would
attempt a generalization about their worth. And worth, interestingly enough,
was seldom tested by any agency outside the college itself. Eventually,
of course, accrediting agencies appeared, but their influence on Catholic
colleges was restricted largely to the twentieth century, probably more
exactly to the years of awakening.[60]

Before accrediting agencies appeared to apply a standard, if often
arbitrary, definition of acceptability to the college course, few external
controls guarded academic quality. Catholic college graduates, secure in
their own cultural assumptions, were disinclined to seek graduate degrees,
so it was hard for graduate schools to make general assessments of the
extent to which students were prepared at entry and thus inform the
colleges about their standards. Professional schools attracted the bulk of
Catholic college graduates who aspired to study beyond the four-year
college,[61] but since professional curricula were seldom based on or integrated
with elements of liberal learning, it was again almost impossible to make
any dependable judgments about undergraduate education.

The cultural and educational disadvantages suffered by Catholic
college students began to disappear in the period of awakening and this
was a good indication of the improving quality of the colleges, for now they
began to enroll students who could base their educational expectations on
home-instilled appreciation of learning. In 1966, forty-five percent of the
students enrolled in Catholic colleges had fathers whose educational accomplishments included graduation from high school, and this should be
compared with fifty-two percent of students enrolled in all four-year
colleges of the United States whose fathers had proceeded so far up the
educational ladder.[62] In terms of a college education the statistics for
fathers were more favorable : nineteen percent of the students in Catholic
colleges had fathers who had earned a college degree, compared with
seventeen percent of the students in all four-year American colleges whose
fathers had similar educational credentials.[63] Like advantages obtained on
the maternal side : eighteen percent of the students in Catholic colleges

[60] "Reducing Abuses in Accreditation," *Catholic Educational Review,* 51 (November, 1953), 628–629.

[61] B. W. Kunkel, "The Representation of Colleges in Graduate and Professional
Schools in the United States," *Bulletin of the Association of American Colleges,*
XXVI (October, 1941), 449.

[62] A. W. Astin, R. J. Panos and J. A. Creager, *National Norms for Entering
Freshmen—Fall, 1966* (Washington, D. C., American Council on Education,
1966), p. 22.

[63] *Ibid.*

had mothers who had earned college degrees, compared with sixteen percent of the students in all four-year colleges.[64]

While it would probably be claiming too much for these statistics to say that cultural and educational advantages were now on the side of Catholic college students, for the percentages would be markedly different if data from elite nonCatholic colleges only were compared with those from Catholic colleges, it is no longer necessary to assume that the short-comings of Catholic institutions can be charged principally to the student and the lack of motivation and of educational and cultural values that he brings to college with him. "This condition," Greeley wrote, "was probably at the root of most of the other problems and . . when and if American Catholics left their immigrant mentality behind, there would be the beginnings of an intellectual development."[65] The period of awakening, it appears, ushered in an era for Catholic higher learning where cultural and educational hobbles were largely discarded.

No secret is betrayed when we say that during the years before the awakening Catholic colleges produced few graduates with scholarly and scientific ambitions : only a small number were granted their doctorates and generally they fared poorly in winning graduate fellowships.[66] But this was not a permanent condition and the next decade, as we shall see, showed considerable improvement. Improvement can be noted, too, in connection with the commitment Catholic college students were capable of making to advanced study, if commitment can rightly be inferred from the number of doctoral degrees obtained by graduates of a sample of the better Catholic institutions : more of their graduates earned doctorates during the seven-year period, 1960–1966, than had been earned by the graduates of the same colleges during the preceding forty years.[67] The conferral of doctoral degrees upon graduates of Catholic colleges has, in the past decade, progressed at a rate above the national average.[68] This is important, because of the normal assumption that the number of a college's graduates capable of earning a doctorate provides a rough measure

[64] *Ibid.*, p. 23.

[65] Andrew M. Greeley, *Religion and Career: A Study of College Graduates* (New York, Sheed and Ward, 1963), p. 11.

[66] R. J. Knapp and J. J. Greenbaum, *The Younger American Scholar* (Chicago, University of Chicago Press, 1953), pp. 58–59.

[67] National Academy of Sciences (National Research Council), *Doctorate Production in United States Universities, 1920–1962,* Publication 1142 (Washington, D. C., National Research Council, 1963), pp. 89–112.

[68] James P. McIntyre, *A Study of the College Choices of the Children of Alumni and Alumnae of Selected Catholic Colleges,* unpublished doctoral dissertation, Boston College, Chestnut Hill, Mass., 1967, p. 40. See McIntyre's summary article "Catholic College Graduates," National Catholic Education Association *Bulletin,* 65 (November, 1969), 37–50.

of the college's ability to graduate students who can compete successfully on a national basis.[69]

Similar judgments can be made about colleges when the number of their graduates who win national fellowships is taken into account. According to a recently published college guide,[70] Woodrow Wilson fellowships and National Science Foundation fellowships provide a reasonable basis for making balanced judgments. If we accept this statement at face value, and judge from the number of such fellowships awarded to graduates of Catholic colleges, it is possible to conclude, McIntyre maintained, that on Woodrow Wilson fellowships Catholic colleges rank slightly above the national average and that on National Science Foundation fellowships their performance is about average.[71] While admitting that a general appraisal of Catholic colleges must take more into account than the performance of students either in graduate schools or as competitors for nationwide fellowship programs—admitting too, with Kunkel, that "We must look at the product of the college with greater care than ever before to arrive at a more definite knowledge of what the colleges are accomplishing,"[72]—we are nevertheless able to discern some grounds for optimism among Catholic colleges in the United States. Students in Catholic colleges of the 1960s were obviously better prepared than their counterparts of a half-century earlier, and what is more,. they appeared to have been more talented as well.[73]

The colleges anxiously capitalized this talent by establishing various curricular and extracurricular opportunities for its further development. Thus honors programs were instituted in many Catholic colleges, although because of their endless variety a generalization about their nature or quality would be hazardous.[74] In addition, independent study has finally achieved respectable standing among Catholic colleges and, again, variety rather than uniformity characterizes the plans for this.[75] Experiments with the college year, of which trimesters and inter-sessions are examples, although they are sometimes aimed only at greater productivity from the college plant, have a serious innovative side : they are intended to create an environment more favorable to high quality learning.[76]

[69] McIntyre, *A Study of the College Choices . . .* , p. 40.

[70] James Cass and Max Birnbaum, *Comparative Guide of American Colleges* (New York, Harper and Row, Publishers, 1966).

[71] McIntyre, *A Study of the College Choices . . .* , p. 44.

[72] Kunkel, *op. cit.*

[73] James A. Davis, "Intellectual Climates in 135 American Colleges and Universities," *Sociology of Education,* XXXVII, No. 2 (Winter, 1963), pp. 128–135.

[74] Eugene Grollmes, "Programs for Superior Students in American Colleges," *Catholic Educational Review,* 42 (January, 1964), 34–38.

[75] *Ibid.*

[76] Andrew M. Greeley, *The Changing Catholic College* (Chicago, Aldine Publishing Co., 1967).

More important than amendments to the college curriculum, which may or may not have encouraged scholarship, was the determination of the colleges to seek the best students available rather than just wait for them to come to school. In pursuance of this policy, Catholic colleges became exceptionally attentive to their scholarship programs and tried regularly to augment the funds which were budgeted for recruiting talented students.[77] Talent searches of all kinds were instituted, some, of course, prosecuted with more vigor than others.

In one aspect of talent search Catholic colleges, until the late 1960s, were strikingly remiss : black talent. Although there was no formal adoption of segregationist policies, the history of Catholic colleges in the United States leads the historian to conclude that black students were unwelcome in their classrooms. Perhaps the Catholic college record was no worse than that of the majority of colleges in the country; it was common practice to take for granted the lower aspirations of the black student and, in the consideration of the educational opportunities at college level, to leave him out of account. Most Catholic colleges, whether north, south, east, or west, were white schools and so they remained perhaps even as the result of covert policy, until late in the sixth decade of the twentieth century.[78] If any justification existed for this indifference to black students, it must be found in the conventional attitude that Catholic colleges were schools for Catholic students, and since few black Americans were Catholics,[79] it would be natural to find few black students on the rosters of Catholic colleges. The Catholic Church in the United States was a white man's church and Catholic colleges, in recruiting both professors and students, found it easy and comfortable to follow the Church's example.

Apart from such sociological insensitivities, Catholic colleges in the United States during the period of awakening not only educated their students better but also had better students to educate. McIntyre's careful study of selected Catholic colleges warrants the conclusion that Catholic college students "today are no weaker academically, nor are they products of families which are less educated or less affluent than the students in other types of colleges."[80] The student graduating from a Catholic college in the 1960s was more likely to continue his advanced education in a graduate school than in a professional school, and this indicated an

[77] J. O. McAuliffe, "Are We Doing Enough to Qualify Our Students for Scholarships?" *Catholic Educator,* 29 (June, 1959), 710–712.

[78] Augustine Dominic, "The Catholic College Man and the Negro," *American Catholic Sociological Review,* 8 (October, 1947), 204–208; and Lafe F. Allen, "College Education and the Negro," *Commonweal,* 49 (January 21, 1949), 370–374.

[79] J. McLinden and J. Doyle, "Negro Students and Faculty on Catholic College Campuses," National Catholic Education Association *Bulletin,* 62 (February, 1966), 1–49.

[80] McIntyre, *A Study of the College Choices . . . ,* p. 181.

acceleration of cultural maturity among American Catholics. McIntyre, assessing the attitudes of Catholic college graduates of a generation ago, concluded that alumni have a high regard for the quality of the education they received in the Catholic colleges they attended, and most of them either have sent, or intend to send, their sons and daughters either to their *alma mater* or to another Catholic college.[81] Whether the loyalty of alumni by itself is a mark of the quality of the education provided by Catholic colleges may be debated; it does, however, stress an important point —graduates' perception of the worth of their own education—an item which any college ignores at its peril.

In sending children to college, Catholic parents who attended Catholic colleges themselves were usually more anxious for their sons than their daughters to have opportunities for higher learning.[82] Interestingly enough, Catholic college graduates who were not parents expressed a high degree of loyalty to the Catholic colleges from which they themselves graduated. Parents represented in the study were willing to make considerable financial sacrifices in order to send their children to Catholic colleges, even though, in many instances, a more economical kind of higher education was available. Of course, many Catholic parents, themselves graduates of Catholic colleges, found it impossible to send their sons or daughters to a Catholic college. And the principal deterrent was financial. Yet in connection with family size and college attendance an interesting statistic emerges: "Although the percentage of children of Catholic college graduates who attend all types of colleges decreases as the number of children in the family increases, the opposite is true for Catholic college attendance. As the number of children in the Catholic college graduate's family increases, so does the number of children who attended a Catholic college."[83] McIntyre found, in addition, that Catholic college graduates were convinced of the need for maintaining Catholic colleges and, moreover, that Catholic higher education was judged to be as important for boys as for girls. Whatever shortcomings Catholic higher education may have, and alumni of an earlier generation were able to identify many, Catholic college graduates are extremely loyal to the Catholic college from which they themselves graduated. All of which led McIntyre to argue that "Since these graduates represent a very influential segment of American Catholicism, this loyalty augurs well for the future of American Catholic higher education."[84]

Despite their protestations of loyalty as alumni, few Catholic college graduates, it must be admitted, would recognize their *alma maters* if they were to return as students in the 1970s, and the feature which would strike

81 *Ibid.*
82 *Ibid.*
83 *Ibid.*, p. 182.
84 *Ibid.*

them as most novel would be the enfranchisement of students in the college community. Catholic colleges have changed more in the management of student life than in any other way. The doctrine of *in loco parentis,* we know, was discarded; and students, less regimented in their scholastic approach, were able to choose freely from a variety of electives, and, moreover, were allowed to decide whether they would or would not attend classes regularly. Up to 1960 almost every Catholic college required regular class attendance, and this was true of graduate as well as undergraduate classes. A student's absence was noted by the professor and after a certain magic number was reached the student could be failed for excessive absences. While some Catholic college professors (in company with colleagues in nonCatholic universities) continued to insist on regular class attendance, and penalized students who stayed away from class too often, official policies countenanced voluntary class attendance.[85]

To the graduate of an earlier generation this was a novel feature of college life, and he questioned whether or not students were ready to cope with their new-found freedom. Other more significant features were evident too : student government, campus councils, and student senates became part of college government and began to have a role in the determination of academic policies. In most Catholic colleges a share in policy-making was conferred on students without the outbreak of violence or the threat of it, but in others the principle that students should have an effective voice was not accepted easily. At first, some college presidents who doubted (mistakenly as it turned out) the seriousness of students' intentions and the depth of their convictions counted on a positive statement defining the students' role as a subordinate one in the college—to be led but not to lead— to defuse the student movement for participatory college democracy. Thus, we find from President Theodore Hesburgh of the University of Notre Dame an almost classic declaration along these lines.[86] In effect, Hesburgh told students that the control of Notre Dame was not their business and that if they were determined to involve themselves in college government they should find some other school to attend.[87] This hard line won the acclaim of many prominent persons the country over, leaving some college presidents wishing they had taken such a stand. In the end, however, it was a policy not even Notre Dame could sustain.

Without following the development of student power from college to college, we can generalize about the outcome of the students' determina-

[85] J. Simmons, "The Catholic Student: His War Against Protection," *Ave Maria,* 104 (October 15, 1966), 6–9.

[86] "Hesburgh's Law; Notre Dame University," *Commonweal,* 89 (March 14, 1969),

[87] Theodore Hesburgh, "Action in the Face of Student Violence," *Catholic Mind,* 67 (April, 1969), 13–19; "Hesburgh Labels Protest Tyranny," *National Catholic Reporter,* 5 (December 4, 1968), 5.

tion to have a voice in matters affecting them. A majority of Catholic colleges appear to believe that a recognition of student power is very nearly a condition for survival. So either by turning over to students the control of student life or by allowing them to play a vital role in policies governing academic issues, Catholic colleges escaped what in the beginning had all the signs of a disastrous struggle for power. Such a struggle could have had no winners. Thus the management of student publications, cocurricular activities, food services, housing, and general student discipline was granted (some say surrendered) to students. Freedom to leave the campus at will, to return without having to meet any curfew, to have visitors in college residence halls, with or without restrictions, changed the face of Catholic college student life and made it practically unrecognizable to a graduate from any earlier era.[88]

It remains to be seen, of course, whether these liberalizations of traditional Catholic college codes of student conduct will contribute to the kind of academic excellence the colleges want and which students, too, say they are seeking. In any case, these changes are evidence of the Catholic college's willingness to allow students to become full partners in twentieth-century American higher education.

Administration and organization

Striking changes in student life in Catholic colleges should not blind us to other metamorphoses, which although less dramatic, are nevertheless highly significant. If we are intrigued by what Catholic college graduates of a generation ago would find unfamiliar in their *alma maters,* we should not be satisfied to stop at student life. College administration expanded at a furious pace, and administrators multiplied so fast over a decade or so that it was difficult for the colleges to invent new titles for them. In the old college a student was fully aware of the president and generally familiar with the dean; save for the prefect of discipline, other administrators, if the college had any, seldom came into contact with students. But in the colleges of the period of awakening, the best-known officer of administration (best-known at least, to the students) was the dean of student affairs, and nothing about him or his office reminded anyone of the old-fashioned prefect of discipline.[89] The dean of students' commission was to cooperate with students in managing student life and to coordinate their activities. He was not an enforcer of college law. Perhaps no other

[88] Ratterman, *op. cit.;* and "Catholic College Students and Parietal Hours," *America,* 115 (December 10, 1966), 767–768.

[89] Power, *op. cit.,* pp. 158–159.

administrator was more important to the college's educational efficiency, its academic image, or its future than this dean. And instead of being a jumped-up ranker, or an under-used clerical professor, he was usually a well-educated, highly skillful professional person capable of finding his way through the myriad issues arising in a day's work.[90]

Even to attempt to list the titles of the various administrative officers to be found at present in Catholic colleges is a risky procedure, for there are so many and they vary greatly from school to school. We shall not try to make such a list here.

The proliferation of administrative offices, while undoubtedly a fact of contemporary college life, is not by reason of that fact necessarily praise-worthy. Too frequently, we must suppose, Catholic colleges, impressed by the organization of business, industry, and nonCatholic universities, simply imitated administrative constructs without ever pausing to consider whether or not such prototypes suited them. If any one office was handled by Catholic colleges with the freshness of discovery, despite its nominal standing in the old days, it was the office of vice-president. Larger Catholic colleges had as many as from four to a dozen, and smaller colleges from three to half a dozen vice-presidents. Why several were needed, and just what so many vice-presidents could do, remains to this day a mystery to the rank-and-file Catholic college professor.

Yet if the delegation of authority appears to be one aspect of Catholic college administrative policy, another, the centralization of basic control in boards of trustees, suggests a movement in the opposite direction. The traditional role of a Catholic college president had been to govern his college, and he remained in office as long as his actions satisfied his religious superior. For legal purposes (officially the college was a corporation) every college had had a board of trustees, but boards of trustees, as we have seen, were neither visible nor effective elaborators of college policy.[91] Their stature was nominal and at best they were sounding boards for the college president or convenient scapegoats for his mistakes. In his personal public relations he could blame the board for decisions for which they had no responsibility. The president alone was the man who counted.

In the period of awakening, however, two considerations arose which argued for a vitalization of boards of trustees. First, the identification of the college as the creation of a religious order or a diocese threatened its public image, and Catholic college administrators, capitulating to super-ficial public opinion, began to believe what they had so often heard, that, at bottom, educational policy and religious commitment are unavoidably hostile. Catholic colleges would be better schools, ran the gratuitous assump-

[90] Robert Hassenger, "Competence, the "Pro," and the Catholic Student," *National Catholic Guidance Counseling Journal,* 10 (September, 1966), 233–234.

[91] Power, *op. cit.,* pp. 148–149.

tion, if the basic control legally granted to boards of trustees were actually exercised by them. If this were the case, and if such boards were composed of persons not necessarily connected with the religious order originally responsible for the school, wider experience and an almost cosmic perspective might be utilized in shaping institutional and academic policies.[92] Second—and this was probably the genuine reason why the colleges took their step toward corporate control—by establishing the ultimate power in boards of trustees, colleges could assume the legal standing of corporations freed from religious and denominational ties. A college would then simply be private; its old identity as a denominational school was legally discarded. This device could have the effect of making a college eligible for public money which might be available to private, but not church-related colleges. Schools which for so long had feared the encroachments of public support and control were now doing everything within their power to qualify for public largess.[93]

In the 1970s, this transfer of control from a religious superior and a president to a board of trustees, only some of whose members may belong to the religious order which founded the college, is in the early processes of experimentation.[94] A relatively small number of Catholic colleges have reorganized along these lines : St. Louis University, the University of Notre Dame, and Boston College are the most prominent schools now testing a new corporate model.[95] Whether or not this model will work is debatable. And whether or not these schools are sincere and serious about their plan to relinquish basic control to boards of trustees, which might have a majority of laymen, is not yet clear. Still, we should be reminded, a board of trustees with fundamental policy as its prerogative is hardly a novelty in American higher education. Hundreds of American colleges were managed in this way for decades and some have had an academic success far above the average by following the policies outlined by such boards of control.

[92] "Catholic Scholars Urge University Autonomy," *National Catholic Reporter,* 3 (August 2, 1967), 3; "Control of Catholic Universities," *Ave Maria,* 105 (January 28, 1967), 4–5; and D. Degnan, "Secularizing Catholic Colleges," *America,* 118 (May 25, 1968), 696–697.

[93] William Conley, "New Directions for Financial Support," *Catholic School Journal,* 67 (September, 1967), 35–39.

[94] T. Blackburn, "Orders Turning Over Colleges to Lay Trustees," *National Catholic Reporter,* 3 (January 25, 1967), 1.

[95] "Lay Majority on New Board Control Turnover at St. Louis University," *National Catholic Reporter,* 3 (February 1, 1967), 3; "New Board of Trustees at St. Louis University," *Catholic Mind,* 65 (March, 1967), 1–4; M. Papa, "Notre Dame, Portland Give Laity Control," *National Catholic Reporter,* 3 (February 1, 1967), 1; and J. Reedy and J. Andrews, "Control of Catholic Universities; Holy Cross Rethinks Its Relationship to Notre Dame and Portland Universities," *Ave Maria,* 105 (January 28, 1967), 16–19.

Experimentation

The history of American Catholic higher learning is notoriously short of daring educational innovations, but during the period of awakening Catholic colleges became uneasy with their almost total inertia in matters of curriculum, academic organization, and administrative practice and tried to redress their conservative image. They adopted a more tolerant attitude toward change without in any sense endorsing revolution, and thus earned some slight revision in their reputations as custodians of the *status quo*. There had, after all, been reasons for their academic conservativism, reasons based on the scholastic dogmas Catholic educators had allowed to evolve along with their educational practice. There was a myth, lodged somewhere in the Church's missionary commission, that *dicta* elaborating the right course of instruction for all formal education were to be found in canonical promulgations. If Catholic colleges either already possessed, or might have these *dicta* for the asking, how could innovation and experimentation be countenanced? Some Catholic college leaders showed every sign of believing this myth.[96]

But the days of the educational old guard were over by the time the Second World War ended, and what remained of their determination to preserve a formalized past was further undermined by the attitude toward education of young men (mostly war veterans) who now came to populate the classrooms. Old academic and disciplinary codes were unsuitable for these men, although mere boys might have put up with them. So innovation had the support of serious, mature students as well as of significant numbers of administrators and faculty.

There has, for some time, been an informal assumption that faculties actively campaign for change and administrators automatically strive to block it. This view may contain more truth than fiction, if one is thinking only of nineteenth-century colleges; but even then it turns out to be no more than an interesting half-truth. Whatever inertia the president and dean may have demonstrated in order to keep higher learning safe and inviolate, only pure fiction could maintain that faculties were always in the vanguard for innovation and found change universally praiseworthy. They were comfortable with things they knew and understood. If we

---

[96] John J. Kane, *Catholic-Protestant Conflicts in America* (Chicago, Henry Regnery Company, 1955), pp. 62–68; Ronald W. Roloff, "Are Our Colleges So Bad?" *The Catholic World*, 185 (June, 1957), 267–270; W. Gurian and Leo Ward, "Catholic Universities in a Secular Society," *American Benedictine Review*, 19 (March, 1968), 91–102; and E. Kevane, "A Note on Catholic University Objectives," *Catholic Educational Review*, 66 (March, 1968), 196–200.

move away from the nineteenth century and into the twentieth, we begin to find Catholic college faculties slightly more liberal than their administrators, in articulating the urgency of the need to modernize educational organization.[97] Whether or not faculties were really progressive, or were simply indulging either in a verbal freedom which an administrator, because of his responsibility to the whole academic enterprise, could ill afford, or in creating contretemps for an administration toward which they had developed sharp antipathies, can only be matter for speculation. It is probably fair to assert, although only tentatively, that faculties wore a veneer of progressivism and were quick to preach retrenchment when a significant and far-reaching innovation, or one touching their vested interest, seemed imminent.

Still, as we have seen, curricula were brought up-to-date in the Catholic colleges of the period of awakening; and this sometimes cost the colleges more money than they could afford to spare. The problem often took this form : a curricular change, say the elimination of an old required course, left the college with professors apparently qualified for the course dropped but lacking the versatility, skill, or background to handle new courses in the curriculum. What could the college do with these professors? Usually the colleges decided that the best policy was to live with their past, keeping unneeded and unused professors on the faculty, and simply absorbing their salaries as an operational expense. College financial officers, of course, declaimed against such waste, and it was the fiscal balance sheet more than any cadre of intransigent administrators or professors which blocked the avenues of progress and halted projected innovations. In the last analysis, it was probably neither academic myopia nor lack of goodwill which immobilized Catholic colleges, but insufficient resources to afford the changes which even then must have appeared inevitable.[98]

Eliminating certain required courses from the curriculum, expanding the curriculum, introducing new courses and programs, and reducing faculty teaching loads to allow time for study, research, and writing brought many a Catholic college to the verge of financial disaster. And this is to take into account only the undergraduate curriculum. On the graduate level, believing no doubt that the public would notice and esteem only those schools which acted like universities, Catholic colleges adopted policies of expansion and improved quality as essential. None of these policies was inexpensive.

[97] Robert Henle, "The Future Challenge to Catholic Education," National Catholic Education Association *Bulletin,* 45 (August, 1948), 281–285; J. Pleasants and R. Bauer, "Resources for Research," *America,* 76 (November 2, 1946), 123–124; and Edward F. Clark, "Undergraduate Preparation for Graduate Study and Intellectual Leadership," National Catholic Association *Bulletin,* 55 (August, 1958), 141–143.

[98] A. B. Corrigan, "Financial Problems in Catholic Colleges," *America,* 89 (April 11, 1953), 38–41; and Willis D. Nutting, "Mark Hopkins, The Log and the Dollar," *Commonweal,* 52 (April 14, 1950), 8–10.

Poverty was the universal and undebatable element in Catholic college history. Here all colleges met on common ground and all at one time or another shared similar experiences of imminent bankruptcy. Undoubtedly the Catholic Church could have helped the system of higher education establish and maintain fiscal equilibrium. But the Church chose not to do so.

Recognizing the multiple difficulties under which they had to work, Catholic colleges, nevertheless, engaged in reform, revision, and experimentation with their educational programs. While their experiments with the college course were conducted in a climate of excessive caution and, in addition, usually imitated a similar experiment in a nonCatholic college, they occurred often enough to prove that Catholic colleges were still alive. The great issue facing the colleges was seldom where or with what to experiment, but whether or not experimentation was justified in the first place. When this issue was finally resolved in the affirmative, the colleges tried something new, mainly with curricula, as we are aware, but also with academic and faculty organization, as we have also seen. Outstanding among these new developments were research professorships, sabbatical leaves for professors, reductions in curricular requirements for students, the introduction of electives, the offer of scholarships to superior students, the tailoring of programs of study for disadvantaged black and white students, the creation of honors programs, and the institution of programs of study abroad.[99]

Experimentation, which tended to imply a rejection of some dogmatic attitudes about education, was never intended to be limited to curriculum, and one of its most interesting sides was evidenced in a testing of the conventional policy of separating the sexes in Catholic higher learning. It is as unnecessary here to review nineteenth century experiments with coeducation as to recapitulate the dire predictions of disaster directed at the colleges involved in them,[100] in order to perceive what colleges in the period of awakening were capable of doing. In the absence of any clear educational edict unequivocally proscribing an integration of men and women in higher education, it was left to the colleges to decide their own policies. This much, at least, was new.

Implementing a freedom that two decades earlier would have been inconceivable, the collegiate citadels of male education were assaulted with the prospects and promises of coeduation. Colleges which added graduate

---

[99] Neil McCluskey, "The New Catholic College," *America,* 116 (March 25, 1967), 414–417; and M. Sigler, "Summer Study Abroad," *Catholic School Journal,* 66 (April, 1966), 48–49.

[100] Santa Clara University, "The Impact of a Value-Oriented University on Student Attitudes and Thinking," Cooperative Research Program Project No. 729, Office of Education, Santa Clara, Calif., 1961; and George N. Shuster, *Education and Moral Wisdom* (New York, Harper and Row, Publishers, 1960).

schools at the turn of the century had, of course, admitted women to graduate classes; in addition, some Catholic colleges, by now complex institutions, had professional schools of education and nursing wherein women students were welcome. But even in the larger, more complex institutions of its kind, the college of arts and sciences, the custodian of liberal education and the guardian of a revered educational past, remained closed to women until the third or fourth decade of the twentieth century. Catholic colleges for men, if their historical record is at all authentic, simply refused to countenance coeducation and this inflexible attitude was not seriously eroded until the sixth decade of the twentieth century. Notre Dame, entering into an arrangement with St. Mary's College (a Catholic college for women across the highway from the Notre Dame campus), began to exchange students and professors, without becoming formally coeducational, in 1969.[101] By 1971, however, St. Mary's College had achieved the full status of a coordinate college in its now consummated relationship with Notre Dame. Holy Cross College, respected for its adherence to the honored traditions of Jesuit education, adopted a policy of coeducation in 1969, with the intention of implementing it as soon as possible.[102] And Boston College, an ornament of Catholic higher education in the period of awakening, announced in 1969 that in the fall of 1970 all its colleges, including its prestigious College of Arts and Sciences, would become coeducational.[103]

While it is plainly impossible to argue that coeducation in the 1960s was in any sense a novelty to American higher education, or even that it was new to Catholic higher education,[104] in rejecting the archaic traditions opposed to coeducation elite Catholic colleges like Georgetown, Notre Dame, Holy Cross, and Boston College demonstrated in a convincing way their willingness to compromise their past and suppress their anxieties about modern educational practices in order to meet the future face to face.

The adoption of coeducation without, or with only slight, reservation was a sign of still other metamorphoses in educational policy : gone was the assumption (which had been out of style for decades) that women were incapable of mastering curricula shaped for men; gone, too, was the determination to keep higher education firmly within the boundaries of that conventional moral code which dogmatically affirmed the existence of dangerous temptations when men and women were educated in the same classrooms and billeted on the same campus. Because coeducation always raised the question of housing, the colleges which adopted new policies

[101] *Notre Dame Alumnus,* Spring, 1969; and see Sister Anita Marie, "Catholic Colleges: Merger: Answer or Obstacle," *Jubilee,* 16 (May, 1968), 43–46.

[102] *Boston Globe,* May 12, 1969.

[103] *Boston Globe,* April 25, 1969.

[104] Power, *op. cit.,* pp. 141–143.

on the admission of female students were required to face the housing issue forthrightly. Could they continue to assume responsibility for the morals of their students, a responsibility which many educators acknowledged would be increased greatly if men and women lived together in the same college? Would they even try to accept this responsibility? Would it not be better, as many spokesmen put it, to admit the college's inability to alter or police the morals of youth and thus allow students to live according to the moral code they had when they came to college? On the level of theory many Catholic college leaders found this latter admission distasteful, yet on a practical level they recognized how powerless they and their colleges had become on the issue of character education. Further and more liberal experimentation with coeducation sometimes meant assigning men and women to residence halls located side by side, or, in a few extraordinary instances, assigning them to different floors of the same residence hall.

Behind the greater willingness to adopt new policies in higher learning was the Church's more tolerant attitude toward the modern world evidenced in the documents and *dicta* of the Second Vatican Council. The Council's statements on higher education were neither particularly innovative nor profound, but they were made in a spirit of cordiality and progress; so colleges in the United States seeking justifications for new departures in educational policies and practices could usually find them in the balanced views of compromise characteristic of Vatican II. The Council's goal, we must remember, was to rebuild the Church along contemporary lines and not to reform higher learning.

The spirit of tolerance so evident in the pronouncements of the Council was a good omen, too, for a change in the policy governing a college's financial support, the policy which for so long had made Catholic colleges hesitant about seeking such support outside the circle of their immediate friends and alumni. The ugly apparition of a state waiting to destroy religion was forgotten, and the colleges, being totally realistic about their chance of survival in an age wherein higher learning was becoming inordinantly expensive, and wherein it was hardly possible for the student, by means of tuition money, to continue to carry the entire financial burden of the college, began to make representations to state and federal governments for various kinds of financial assistance. We have seen how they began to modify their church-related corporate structures in order to make a better legal case for their petitions. In addition to learning new ways to obtain public money, Catholic colleges acquired the use of the techniques of professional fund raisers to finance expansions of curricula and plant, and to improve the financial status of their faculties. Besides all this, they turned to private foundations and began to develop programs which might prove attractive to them and thus generate some financial support; they freed members of their faculties to engage in the kind of research which might warrant help from outside. Colleges, with praiseworthy foresight, began to budget their own funds for research and program development, allowing the early stages of a project to be paid for from their own funds before seeking assistance from outside agencies. They learned quickly that to get government, industry, and private foundations to subsidize them, they would first have to demonstrate a confidence in their ventures by supporting them with their own resources. The success of this technique was effectively demonstrated in a huge money grant made available by the Ford Foundation to colleges in the United States (including Catholic colleges) as an endowment for faculty salaries.[105] The criterion the foundation used for making its awards was always the amount of effort colleges had made on their own to better faculty salaries.

Any account of the financial support available for Catholic higher education must make reference to the scant (or in most cases nonexistent) endowment of the colleges. The solution to endowment problems was so obvious, yet so difficult or impossible to implement, that elaboration here is unnecessary. Another aspect of endowment, however, is either neglected or simply taken for granted : the endowment of men.[106] Catholic colleges, managed, administered, and staffed by religious orders and communities were beneficiaries to the equivalent of hundreds of millions of dollars from the contributed services of thousands of dedicated persons. Without this extraordinary endowment of men (unmatched by that of any other colleges of the United States), Catholic colleges could not have survived and any discussion of their future would now be pointless.

Yet, aside from endowment of either money or men, the colleges learned another way of adding to their income without harming the image of academic excellence they were determined to achieve : evening and summer schools were organized. The former, in particular, were intended to perform a useful community educational service, and to a great extent they succeeded; and while educational good was being done, the colleges found such evening schools quite profitable. Summer sessions, too, could help balance the colleges' books.

Long years of fiscal impoverishment, along with some improvidence in using their resources, made it imperative for Catholic colleges to seek profitable educational sidelines, without jeopardizing their hard won academic reputations, to assist them in the battle for solvency.

---

[105] J. Franklin Ewing and Margaret Donnelly, "Private Foundations: A Catholic View," National Catholic Education Association *Bulletin,* 53 (November, 1956), 7–14; and Lloyd Davis, "Catholics and Eight Foundations," *America,* 100 (January 17, 1959), 460–461.

[106] "End of Living Endowment?" *America,* 116 (February 25, 1967), 269.

13

The quest for excellence

Throughout the greater part of its history Catholic education in the
United States presented a single face to the public, so it is usually
possible to make generalizations about Catholic colleges with reasonable
assurance of their equal applicability to all institutions. Yet, as Catholic
higher education matured, selective processes (which were often nothing
more than fortuitous circumstances) interposed and destined some colleges
for the sidelines of educational notice and projected others to the center
of the academic stage. But good luck, while sometimes a valid, if super-
ficial, explanation for success, must not be taken with complete seriousness
where Catholic colleges were involved. No doubt good luck was a factor,
but in the end more than good luck was necessary. If colleges were to distinguish themselves they would have to make their own luck. The persons
perforce nominated to pull the many strings needed to make Catholic
higher education work were the presidents : the future of the colleges was
in their hands.

Vision, leadership, and risk

A considerable amount of space was given in earlier chapters to showing,
first, how much Catholic colleges depended on their principal educational
officer, the president,[1] and then, more recently, to reciting the erosions of
presidential authority to the point where he was but one man, though an
important one, among many in shaping the policies which affected life in
the Catholic college and in recommending them to boards of directors for
ratification.[2] Yet, despite these erosions of authority, he was, throughout

[1] See pp. 70–86.
[2] See pp. 440–442.

most of the period of awakening, the responsible officer on whom the destiny of the college most depended and enough authority still resided in his office to make the college community respond to his will. Many Catholic college presidents may have known what needed to be done to make their institutions competitive in a keenly competitive educational society, but along with this knowledge of the appropriate academic direction went another kind of knowledge, equally essential, which in the long history of Catholic schools had never earned much attention : it was necessary to master administrative technique.[3]

The more complex the college, the greater the difficulty in conditioning it to accept common purposes, to establish priorities for concerted action, and then to make the necessary effort to achieve these goals. At best, these purposes were never accomplished easily or without friction, but the successful college president was able to communicate his hopes for the college without creating too much opposition (an opposition often fed by the fear of change), and then to set in motion the machinery to realize these hopes without antagonizing either faculty, students, or the college's loyal public. What was needed were men of clear vision, with patience to mobilize the forces within the college, and then with enough courage to strive vigorously to reach the desired goals. Some Catholic college presidents were exceptionally clear thinkers; others had an abundance of courage and enthusiasm; still others were masters of executive technique. The mere administrator too often lacked, on the one hand, vision and, on the other, an ability to elicit zeal and devotion for his plans. Presidents who succeeded had qualities of leadership in the optimum proportion, but since such men appeared seldom (if it is fair to judge from the few Catholic colleges which made definite progress toward their objective excellence), only a handful need details about them recited here.

Some subjectivity is unavoidable in expressing an historical opinion on the relative quality of Catholic colleges and universities, for the evidence seldom admits of one conclusion only. Yet Catholic higher education had pace-setting institutions throughout its history, and in various historical periods different schools demonstrated that they were clearly in the vanguard of educational innovation (witness, for example, St. Louis University's promotion of the four-year curriculum) or were setting new standards for educational quality among their counterparts. By these criteria, the names of Georgetown, Fordham, Notre Dame, Boston College, St. Louis, and Catholic University may be singled out for particular mention.

Apart from what may be a subjective judgment, there is fairly good evidence that Catholic colleges, when rated on the capacity of their graduate faculties and on the adequacy of their graduate programs in selected fields of study, were not acknowledged by their co-workers in

3 Erbacher, *op. cit.,* pp. 69–78.

American higher education to be superior in many fields of advanced instruction. Still, an emphasis on graduate education may distort the picture of quality somewhat, concealing almost as much as it reveals, for it may fairly be doubted whether the absence from a college of a doctoral program of high standing is any proof that undergraduate instruction there is necessarily deficient. As a matter of fact, the caution exercised by a Catholic college in refusing to expend its resources on graduate education may well have been a blessing in disguise, for in refusing to dilute its energies the college may actually have been asserting its right to be considered as an undergraduate institution of quality.

In returning to the issue of graduate education, however, we are faced with the sobering evidence presented by Allan M. Cartter, in *An Assessment of Quality in Graduate Education* (Washington, D. C., American Council on Education, 1966). In this American Council on Education rating made in 1964, only those universities were assessed which had conferred an average of ten or more doctorates during the years from 1953 to 1962, a criterion which left out of account one or two fields of study for which advanced graduate instruction was offered in several Catholic universities.

Only the Catholic University of America was rated among the top twenty universities, and that rating was achieved in the category of those universities offering doctoral work in the classics.[4] In other fields of study the names of Catholic universities appeared only infrequently : in classics, in addition to Catholic University, Fordham was rated 'adequate plus' on its faculty and 'acceptable plus' on its graduate program.[5] In English, Notre Dame was rated 'adequate plus' on its faculty.[6] In French, Catholic University and Fordham were rated 'adequate plus' and 'acceptable plus' on faculty and program.[7] In philosophy, Notre Dame was judged 'adequate plus' on faculty.[8] In Spanish, Catholic University was rated 'good' on faculty and 'acceptable plus' on program.[9] In history, Notre Dame's faculty was rated 'adequate plus.' [10] In pharmacology, Georgetown's faculty and program were rated 'adequate plus' and 'acceptable plus' respectively.[11] In chemistry, Notre Dame's faculty was rated 'good' and the graduate program was scored 'acceptable plus.' [12] In mathematics and physics, it was

[4] Cartter, *op. cit.*, p. 21.
[5] *Ibid.*, pp. 20–21.
[6] *Ibid.*, p. 22.
[7] *Ibid.*, pp. 24–25.
[8] *Ibid.*, p. 28.
[9] *Ibid.*, pp. 30–31.
[10] *Ibid.*, p. 38.
[11] *Ibid.*, pp. 52–53.
[12] *Ibid.*, pp. 62–63.

Notre Dame again, rated 'adequate plus' on faculty and 'acceptable plus' on program.[13]

These ratings, together with a reasonably objective estimate of progress made in the last couple of decades, suggest that something further should be said about five Catholic colleges—Boston College, Notre Dame, St. Louis, Fordham, and Georgetown. Their success in the period of awakening must be credited to the men who led them through these years of striking adjustment to new academic horizons.

These schools, perhaps, had advantages not fully shared by a majority of Catholic colleges the country over. All east of the Mississippi River, four out of the five were located in large metropolitan areas with a significantly large Catholic population to provide a solid base for student enrollment, and all had distinguished themselves even earlier as schools capable of offering a decent education. Without exception, late in the period of development, they tried the route to success and notoriety by fielding memorable football teams, but in the post-war period, except at Boston College and Notre Dame, football was played down almost to the point of extinction.[14] But even at Boston College and Notre Dame, where football continued to be important and where athletic schedules still reminded the alumni of past days of glory, the policy was clear : academic reputations are built and sustained in the classrooms, the libraries, the scholar's study, and the laboratories, not on the gridiron.[15] Excellence, it was plainly understood, if a goal worthy of institutional commitment, was the outcome of a dedication to academic ideals in which the quality of the faculty and students counted for much more than national sport ratings or the reputation of football coaches.

So easily stated, these ideals were never easy to attain. And this is where we must forget some of the advantages of fortune with which these colleges appear to have been blessed, because other Catholic colleges of similar size and public prominence, also located in metropolitan centers, were unable to match the achievements of these five schools. We can recognize and acknowledge the wish of the run-of-the-mill Catholic college to be a school of reputation and a fair haven for scholarship, but wishful thinking alone never fulfilled ambitions. At this point the human dimension of leadership became critical : it was necessary for the presidents of ambitious colleges to take calculated risks. They had to invest whatever resources their colleges had, and sometimes to jeopardize their own reputations and careers, in order to advance toward that worthwhile goal whose attainment was by no means certain—excellence in scholarship.

[13] *Ibid.,* pp. 66–69.

[14] J. Leary, "More Than Their Share; Basketball at Catholic Colleges," *Columbia,* 45 (March, 1965), 8–9; and Waldemar Gurian, "Football Capital or Intellectual Community," *Commonweal,* 51 (October 14, 1949), 17–18.

[15] *Ibid.*

Never just public relations men, the presidents of the best schools recognized, nonetheless, the importance of communicating their high ideals to the collegiate community. Their first task was to convince a critical and skeptical lay and religious faculty that the goal of scholarly excellence was worth reaching and, then, that they were profoundly serious about the journey toward it. With the faculty on the president's side, if occasionally disagreeing with his choice of administrative techniques, it was then necessary for top administrators to demonstrate by act rather than just by precept their pledge to compete in the front line of academic endeavor. This meant an investment in faculty talent and qualification which in years past few presidents would have thought worth the trouble; it meant pruning the faculty of unsatisfactory professors or, if pruning could not be done with fairness, then bearing bravely the cost of retaining mediocrities in positions where they would not impede progress and waiting for attrition to produce the final solution. It meant something more than telling current faculties (or new appointees) that their work was important and that by it the college would be judged; it meant creating an environment wherein scholarship and scholarly instruction could flourish. It meant, moreover, an investment of college resources in research, because in the interests of scholarship time and facilities for research were paramount.[16] But most of all it meant strong leadership along with clearly defined institutional objectives, and this the best presidents, and the most successful ones, were able to furnish. We have said before that the successes and failures of Catholic higher education in the United States depended principally on the presidents, and the recent history of these five schools goes a long way toward confirming that assumption.

In the vanguard of Catholic college leadership in the period from 1950 to 1970 stand three presidents whose accomplishments were of such a high order that they literally rescued Catholic higher education from academic oblivion. Thus not only their own colleges stand in their debt : all Catholic higher learning does so too. If, in fact, Catholic higher learning reached an historic turning point in the two decades from 1950 to 1970, Michael P. Walsh (Boston College, 1958–1968),[17] Paul Reinert (St. Louis University, 1949–   ), and Theodore Hesburgh (University of Notre Dame, 1950–   ) were the men most responsible for setting the new compass course.

Although these leaders displayed marked differences in manner, temperament, and academic background, as well as in their style of administration and their appearances in public, they met on common ground in a

16 Sister Mary Ellen O'Hanlon, "Research and the Professor," *Commonweal*, 16 (June 29, 1932), 238–239; and Arpad Steiner, "Creative Scholarship," *Commonweal*, 25 (January 22, 1937), 347–349.

17 After his resignation as president of Boston College in 1968, Father Walsh became president of Fordham University.

determination to improve the quality of their schools and in a commitment to the goal of academic excellence. At another point, too, their aspirations coincided : the future of Catholic higher education, they were agreed, depended on its ability to prove its worth to the public, in marketing terms to produce what was wanted and valued by customers. The age of the college, they perceived, belonged to American history; the age of the university was the present and the future.[18] Whatever Boston College, Notre Dame, Fordham, Georgetown, and St. Louis had been, and however meritorious their histories had always and honestly projected a college image, and true to that image had been preoccupied with communicating tested cultural and literary inheritances to their students. This commitment (never regarded as unimportant) was by no means ignored, for these colleges, and the presidents who called the academic tune, were never representatives of eclectic educational theories : admitting a common core to basic culture, they assumed that one of the important obligations of a college or university was to perpetuate this core as a vital, living tradition. They were true to their past, but being true to old traditions was not the same as being paralyzed by them. Leaders with foresight were able to broaden the objectives, and to explore new horizons for Catholic higher learning. The presidents rightly concluded that if their schools were to be truly significant institutions on the American educational scene they would have to create a new image and, moreover, that this new image would have to be a true one, not one gilded for observation from a distance.

This meant becoming universities in fact as well as (with the exception of Boston College)[19] in name. To achieve this undoubtedly herculean task it was first of all necessary to state clearly what the aspirations of the university were, and no less necessary to continue and even improve the quality of the undergraduate education then being offered. Besides, means had to be found to make the goal of university a realistic aspiration. This was the work undertaken by the courageous presidents we have named, and no one would have been much surprised if they had failed. That they succeeded must have been a cause, not of self-satisfaction, but of considerable pride.

Tensions in university life appear to be more acute in developing institutions than in those already over the threshold of maturity; so it should not be thought that academic development at Boston College, Notre Dame, Fordham, St. Louis, and Georgetown in the past ten to twenty years was

[18] Theodore Hesburgh, "The Vision of a Great Catholic University," *Catholic Mind,* 66 (February, 1968), 42–54.

[19] Early in Father Walsh's tenure as President of Boston College, he appointed a committee to recommend a new name for the school. The committee's commission was too great however for it had too many people to please. Besides to change the name of an institution almost a century old seemed presumptuous. In the end, nothing was done.

accompanied by serenity and composure. Faculties sometimes doubted the wisdom of making a university commitment, and resented what seemed to be a lack of attention to the objectives of undergraduate instruction. On frequent occasions, when it was necessary to find replacements for persons in key academic positions because they were no longer suitable by temperament or qualifications for their new role, attempts at minor revolutions had to be put down and intrepid confrontations faced out. But the mere fact that there could have been such reactions to the direction the colleges were taking meant that the colleges really were beginning to live in another world, for what occurred could not have happened in the colleges of the developmental period and did not happen in some colleges of the period of awakening which, for whatever reason, chose easier routes to educational survival.

What it meant to be a university was seldom entirely clear, and the scholarly attitudes of tradition-minded faculties ensured that many would assume the answer could be found by going to authorities. Somewhere a model must have been secreted away waiting for just such a moment for its revelation.[20]

This new breed of presidents, however, was understandably impatient with old-fashioned formulas, even when they could be unearthed, or with definitions of university education meant for Europe, for ecclesiastics, for gentlemen, or only for scholarly reading and satisfaction, but, in any case, not for the modern university in twentieth-century America. They were forced to follow a largely unblazed trail, and when they did they were bound to make directional errors; they were almost certain from time to time to make academic investments that paid no dividends. But here again courage and forthrightness served them well : mistakes could be acknowledged and corrected; bad academic investments could be reclaimed and what was left could be reinvested. There was no point, and this the presidents knew, in pretending always to be right; what was more important was always to be seen to be working toward the ultimate objective of full standing among respectable and responsible academic institutions, in which it would be axiomatic to meet modern life more than half way.

If they could reject the ponderous formulas from the arcana of the past with impunity, it was not always so easy to relocate the priorities of institutional purpose. The heart of the Catholic college was always assumed to be the college of arts and sciences, and though science was more often given lip service than actual attention, this assumption was nevertheless evident. Nothing should be done, the old guard never tired of saying, to sacrifice the commitment Catholic colleges made to liberal learning.[21]

20 Francis P. Donnelly *The Progressive Conservatism of Catholic Education* (New York, Fordham University Press, 1936), pp. 1–15.

21 Ronald W. Roloff, "Are Our Colleges So Bad?" *The Catholic World*, 185 (June, 1957), 265–270.

Allow secular schools to be universities, but let Catholic colleges be true to their honorable tradition of humane learning. What, then, the presidents of the new age had to prove first was that they, too, felt a commitment to liberal learning and would do their best to preserve it, and afterwards that they would not be bound to a role of simple preservation. Instead they would use the foundations of the college as the bedrock for academic progress and build upon them. Nothing was to be sacrificed : all segments of the college were to benefit from the upgrading they envisaged.

Academic lieutenants were important to the presidents, for the colleges were far too complex to be managed single-handed. Here, of course, the tactics of the most prominent college presidents varied considerably. Where the President of Boston College, Michael P. Walsh, jealously guarded his prerogative of determining basic educational policy and managing its exe-cution on a day-to-day basis (although always allowing deans and depart-ment chairmen considerable initiative), both Presidents Hesburgh and Reinert were more generous in delegating policy-making functions to trusted lieutenants.[22] For the most part, neither at Boston College, Notre Dame, nor St. Louis, was the faculty brought into policy making, for the Presidents were uncertain about their faculties and were not confident that their spirit had been sufficiently infected by presidential idealism. Later, when it became clear that faculty sentiment was on the side of progress and quality, policy determinations could be delegated to professors. At that stage we find these schools organizing senates and other types of faculty bodies concerned with academic policy.[23] But this kind of liberalism was forced to mark time while faculties were being led toward and ap-prised of the new frontiers of higher learning.

Leaders must sometimes act with dispatch and such action can be mistaken for ruthlessness. But if these colleges were to become universities worthy of the name, the removal of incapable or incompetent persons from important positions was imperative. In other instances the college had simply outgrown an incumbent officer. Such issues had to be faced more often than the presidents liked, but house-cleaning was never a preoccupa-tion with them. They organized new teams for the administration of

[22] The literature on the administrative style of Presidents Walsh and Hesburgh is scant. William B. Faherty, *Better the Dream: St. Louis University and Community, 1818–1968* (St. Louis, St. Louis University, 1968), pp. 363–393, gives a fairly full account of President Reinert's methods.

[23] Edward Manier and John W. Houck (editors), *American Freedom and the Catholic University* (Notre Dame, Ind., Fides Publishers, Inc., 1967); "Control of Catholic Universities," *Ave Maria,* 105 (January 28, 1967), 4–5; J. Leary, "The Layman in Catholic Higher Education," *America,* 116 (February 18, 1967), 251–253; Neil G. McCluskey, "The New Catholic College," *America,* 116 (March 25, 1967), 414–417; and M. Marty, "Catholic Colleges in a Time of Change," *National Catholic Reporter,* 3 (February 1, 1967), 8.

college affairs, yet this never meant lopping off hundreds of heads. More evident than any imagined ruthlessness was the pragmatism the presidents adopted and applied to every aspect of university life. There was no handbook of the details of university management; they were without tested formulas for the change from college to university. If there were no edicts why act as if there were? What was left, and they were always perceptive enough to see it, was the test of pragmatic common sense. Policies and practices that *worked*, that produced the upgrading desired, were accepted. When policies needed revision they were revised, but results counted more than rhetoric. And policies confirmed in practice to be wrong or useless were discarded. It may be said, without in any sense impugning their orthodoxy, that the distinctive administrative style of the new presidents was their pragmatism. And they could be fully pragmatic in managing their schools without ever endorsing one line written by pragmatic philosophers.

The style of presidential action was abetted and made evident by spokesmen who, interested in the future of Catholic higher education, turned to their typewriters. This was not simply a matter of rushing into print with apparently novel but immature ideas, for some factions among faculties and some administrators in various Catholic colleges had been pondering at length the status of their institutions and had some definite views about academic improvement. But Catholic timidity vis-à-vis authority left few spokesmen with the temerity to test their ideas in public before they had some sign that what they had to say would either be welcomed or given a fair hearing. Here, again, the presidents cultivated the ground for innovation in Catholic college life, for in their pronouncements and by their action they gave the signal for responsible debate on the changes in the operation of colleges that were thought desirable. Such discussion, in their view, was both welcome and desperately needed.

John Tracy Ellis was unquestionably candid in appraising American Catholicism and the degree of intellectual life among educated Catholics,[24] but his candor was stimulated by the determination for reform already evident in the work of the five élite colleges. So the elements of openness in their leadership had a cumulative effect: slowly but surely others appeared who were willing to make recommendations about the reshaping of the colleges. But before reconstruction could begin, and especially if it was to have intelligent direction, the schools must first know their weaknesses. This principle led them to make self studies.[25]

Cunningham's prescription for liberal education in the general college

[24] John Tracy Ellis, "American Catholics and the Intellectual Life," *Thought,* 30 (Autumn, 1955), 351–388.

[25] See L. J. Lins (editor), "Basis for Decision," *Journal of Experimental Education,* 31 (December, 1962), 89–228.

retained professional and paraprofessional curricula in which the colleges had already made considerable investment. Moreover, these were courses many college students wanted.[26] But what Cunningham had said about liberal education was basic to any movement to return the human sciences to a more significant place in college curricula. In various articles, too, John J. Kane introduced the sociological dimension, and his perceptions were sufficiently striking to make persons associated with the colleges (who previously had expected little from sociology and knew less about it) see higher education as an integral part of American Catholic culture.[27] The educational literature of the period was filled all at once with the articles of writers taking a stand on Catholic higher learning. Some of these set out informed opinions about what the colleges should or should not do; others supplied important and interesting data comparing Catholic and non-Catholic higher education. McCluskey's article on Rhodes Scholars[28] was far more convincing to the progressive Catholic professor, and more revealing too, than any of the defenses hastily thrown up around the Catholic colleges by persons who not only disliked the thought of change but were convinced of the superiority of those colleges.[29]

Lawler,[30] Meng,[31] Smith,[32] Weigel,[33] Svaglic,[34] Cavanaugh,[35] Ong,[36] Donovan,[37] and O'Dea[38] all belong to the same category of enlightened

[26] William F. Cunningham, *General Education and the Liberal College* (B. Herder Book Company, St. Louis, 1953), pp. 120–129.

[27] John J. Kane, "The Social Structure of American Catholics," *American Catholic Sociological Review,* 6 (March, 1955), 25–30.

[28] Neil G. McCluskey, "Too Few Rhodes Scholars," *America,* 95 (April 7, 1956), 26–30.

[29] Robert I. Gannon, "Enough Breastbeating!" *Catholic Mind,* 56 (July–August, 1958), 314–318.

[30] Justus G. Lawler, "The Mission of Catholic Scholarship," *The Catholic World,* 183 (July, 1956), 262–269.

[31] John J. Meng, "American Thought: Contributions of Catholic Thought and Thinkers," National Catholic Education Association *Bulletin,* 53 (August, 1956), 113–120.

[32] Fidelis Smith, "Mediocrity: Flight from the Challenge of Self," *Homiletic and Pastoral Review,* 57 (April, 1957), 595–600.

[33] Gustave Weigel, "American Catholic Intellectualism: A Theologian's Reflections," Review of Politics, 19 (July, 1957), 275–304.

[34] Martin J. Svaglic, "Catholics and Learning," *Commonweal,* 67 (October 4, 1957), 9–10.

[35] John J. Cavanaugh, "American Catholics and Leadership," an address delivered December 15, 1957.

[36] Walter J. Ong, in *Frontiers of American Catholicism* (New York, Macmillan Company, 1957), pp. 9–10.

[37] John D. Donovan, "The American Catholic Hierarchy: A Social Profile," *American Catholic Sociological Review,* 19 (June, 1958), 98–112.

[38] Thomas F. O'Dea, *American Catholic Dilemma: An Inquiry into the Intellectual Life* (New York, Sheed and Ward, 1958).

Catholic scholars who essayed to introduce precision and scholarly respectability to the debate over the need for change and the nature of the changes recommended. But these men could hardly have spoken at all had it not been for the new climate in Catholic higher learning which, for the most part, was an achievement of this new breed of presidents.

Ironing out old issues

Prior to 1945 it was the unusual college president or professor who took very seriously the role of research in the Catholic college or university.[39] Without articulating the principle, although actually accepting it, most of the teachers associated with these colleges were confident they already possessed all really worthwhile knowledge. If now and then professors like Julius A. Nieuwland, of the University of Notre Dame, should conduct clandestine experiments in chemistry, Edward A. Doissy and John Auer of St. Louis University should work on insulin and pharmacology, and James B. Macelwane and Francis A. Tondorf on seismology,[40] they could be labeled eccentrics unable to use their time more profitably, or followers of interesting but unpopular hobbies. The historian or the litterateur, interested in finding new or deeper interpretations in his speciality and writing about them, was pictured as a recluse who, somewhat antisocial, preferred the dusty shelves of the library to the company of persons in the club and common rooms. What these curious professors were doing was taken with little seriousness until they were successful in uncovering something new, and then they could be praised for their perseverance and their accomplishments and the luster they added to the college. But they were seldom positively encouraged to continue their research, and what is more, their good example led to the conversion of few disciples. Academic environment and intellectual assumption allowed scholarship to wither; the general run of professors who met their college classes belonged to that long list of invisible and unremembered scholars who were supremely confident that truth was in their grasp. And fortunately for them they had learned this truth early in their careers, so that even study, to say nothing at all of research, was superfluous.[41]

39 Edward F. Kenrick, "Scholarly Publication," *America,* 101 (May 9, 1959), 304–305; J. Pleasants and B. Bauer, "Resources for Research," *America,* 76 (November 2, 1946), 123–124; and Sister Mary Ellen O'Hanlon, "Research and the Professor," *Commonweal,* 16 (June 29, 1932), 238–239.

40 Francis W. Power, "Research in Catholic Schools," *America,* 41 (May 18, 1929), 132–133.

41 Weigel, *op. cit.*

Attitudes toward scholarship needed radical revision, for who could be motivated to pursue truth if the prize had already been won? Both insight and leadership were essential, then, if scholarship was to be rescued from the swamp of inattention and indifference and, for the first time in Catholic higher education in the United States, given a fair hearing. Again, the presidents were the key figures, for without their encouragement those who would have to become producing scholars would be reluctant to take the first step. Demanding the product of research was tried—and this tactic produced some good results—but more than persuasion and presidential edicts were necessary for the very great majority. Example counted most and here the presidents, although they themselves (if we consider Walsh, Hesburgh, and Reinert) were men with a scholar's credentials and capable of leading their faculties part of the way, could not do everything. The burdens of administrative duty were too heavy to allow these Presidents the enviable luxury of the productive scholarship they had engaged in prior to taking up their presidency, so they had either to import scholars who would supply the necessary example or find men among their own faculties who would react to their encouragement. Neither alternative was easy and neither produced immediate results. To import seasoned scholars sounded straightforward enough, and these Presidents were willing to assume the financial burdens of recruiting professors from other universities; but the qualified scholar with a reputation to protect was understandably uneasy about associating himself with even the most reputable Catholic college. He might come for a year or so as a visiting or distinguished professor, but he was disinclined to abandon for very long the more receptive and friendly climate of a state or private university.[42] Recruiting ambitious young scholars to strengthen faculties could be tried, but here, of course, Catholic colleges were competing with all other colleges and it was never easy to corral talent of the sort needed. The young scholar, fresh from his own doctoral studies, was not anxious to become a pioneer in the scholarly wilderness of Catholic higher education. So, in the end, the universities had to depend mainly on home-grown talent. That is, they had to encourage their own professors to qualify themselves as scholars and to lead the way on the road to better scholarship.[43]

To accomplish this some teeth had to be put into salary and promotion procedures. These, however, were new rather than old issues, at least in their management, so we shall defer them until later.[44]

[42] Sister Charlesetta, "Why Not Exchange Teachers in Catholic Colleges?" *Catholic School Journal,* 60 (December, 1960), 22.

[43] John A. O'Brien, "The Need for Catholic Scholars, with Suggestions for Their Development," National Catholic Education Association *Bulletin,* 44 (August, 1947), 249–261.

[44] These issues were nevertheless receiving official attention early in the period of awakening. See, for example, Brother G. Paul, "Report of Discussion Meeting

The attitude toward scholarship had to be changed and it could be changed successfully only when the faculties recognized, as Socrates said, "that men begin to learn only when they realize they are ignorant." With scholarly motivation approved as official policy, the Presidents were then faced with the need to correct the dogmatic attitude shared by so many professors that, if they had mastered their fields of knowledge to a level sufficient for classroom competence, nothing more should be expected. They were content to enlist in that vast, unrecognized army of invisible scholars which, the propaganda of the college had said, was world-wide.[45] These Presidents, however, were unimpressed with slogans, catchwords, and proclamations of satisfaction. They knew, as the more astute professors also knew, that the Catholic colleges, while lacking neither human talent nor men with something to say, had no great desire to share their academic and scholarly conversations with their colleagues in other institutions or with the general scholarly world. For one thing, they were unused to the rarified air of productive scholarship and for another they had, beneath their self-assurance, a fundamental inferiority complex. If they were ready to engage in research, the rank and file were genuinely apprehensive about publication.[46]

In the face of the old issue of indifference to scholarship and the deep-seated aversion to publication, the Presidents inaugurated new policies whose consequences we shall relate in the next part of this chapter.

Apropos of publication, it must be admitted that these Presidents failed to make good use of one instrument which, although not very active, was fully at their disposal: the college press.[47] A few colleges, and all the good ones, had college or university presses, but they were reserved mostly for religious tracts, for institutional histories, or for intramural publications and, for the most part, were not available to those well-qualified scholars on the campuses who might have used them. No doubt, the revival of the college press would have been expensive, but its presence as an outlet for good scholarship would have accomplished two things : it would have given faculties a means of publishing books that were unattractive to commercial publishers; and it would have added a scholarly luster to the institution. This opportunity the Presidents missed. But recognizing the need for publication, they missed few chances to encourage and sometimes to subsidize the scholarly journals that now began to make a regular appearance from the good Catholic institutions : the *Review of Politics*

of College Presidents on the Rights of the Lay Faculty in Our Colleges and Universities," *Proceedings* of the National Catholic Education Association, 48 (1951), 161–162.

45 Erbacher, *op. cit.,* pp. 79–82.

46 Kenrick, *op. cit.;* O'Hanlon, *op. cit.*

47 J. B. Amberg, "Why University Presses?" *America,* 101 (June 20, 1959), 451–452.

from Notre Dame and *Thought* from Fordham exemplify the best of this type of publication.[48]

Productive scholarship grows with encouragement, does not materialize overnight, and is never the outcome of mere wishful thinking. So much was obvious to the new Presidents. They hastened to accelerate the maturity of scholarship on their faculties by improving the quality of their graduate school departments. Starting slowly and working with one department at a time, they added enough academic depth to make their master's degree program respectable and then moved on selectively to the doctoral level. By this time it was entirely clear that the reputation of a university was based in part on the quality of its doctoral programs, and that it would be difficult or impossible for these colleges to take their places among the good universities of the United States without respectable graduate schools.[49]

For reasons still obscure, however, the concentration of effort at the graduate level was directed at those fields of knowledge for which the colleges were least equipped and which were also the most expensive, namely, the various fields of science. Reading the sentiments of the times, the presidents must have thought that this was the area in which the colleges, once committed, would attract the greatest degree of public attention. But there was another aspect of the matter, too, and it should be noted: although upgrading scientific instruction and scientific research cost tremendous sums of money, these were fields where outside funding was possible. If the colleges invested their own resources in science, they might hope to obtain grants which, in the long run, would more than balance anything the college itself had spent. This rationale undoubtedly had a good deal to recommend it, for when such grants were obtained the college's expenditures were returned many times over. But at the same time the colleges were left with an investment and with a commitment which was often more than they could afford. Riding the waves of popularity, the presidents allowed themselves the luxury of betting on science to get them started and then, later, returning to the social sciences and the humanities to attempt the same procedure in more favorable conditions.

When the period of awakening began the elite Catholic colleges had already organized a variety of undergraduate programs and curricula, sometimes as divisions of the basic liberal arts college and sometimes as separate schools. Some of these programs unquestionably needed revision and some of the separate schools had outlived the needs that had produced

[48] Neither of these journals was the product of direct presidential action, although they may be taken as being representative of the kind of support the presidents could give to scholarship and its outlets.

[49] Arthur A. North, "Why is the American Catholic Graduate School Failing to Develop Catholic Intellectualism?" National Catholic Education Association *Bulletin,* 53 (August, 1956), 180–189.

them in the first place.[50] This reorganization, however, although perhaps necessary to future growth, was not urgent, so the Presidents tended to allow the old programs to continue. Their colleges, they felt, lacked the academic strength to break new ground in undergraduate education. They were, moreover, generally satisfied with the main outline of their undergraduate colleges of arts and sciences. Reorganization was less important to them than a renewed dedication to liberal learning. And even the wisest heads found it impossible to agree on the direction of this renewal.

The presidential tasks for this new era were both multiple and monumental and they included, in addition to the items we have noticed so far, an entirely new dimension of presidential leadership, that of convincing students, professors, alumni, and the colleges' loyal friends that the renaissance in Catholic higher learning was essentially the effect of an idea whose time had come.[51] It would be hard to deny that the caliber of leadership in the half-dozen or so best Catholic colleges was extraordinary and unexpected; but, while giving these Presidents their just and historic due, we must also recognize that they were the right men at the right time in Catholic college history. The idea of respectable and responsible Catholic higher learning had matured to the point where, even with leadership of lesser quality and vision, the colleges would have changed markedly from what they had been at the advent of the period of awakening. Change was in the wind, and fortunately for the best Catholic colleges they were led by men capable of using it to the full in the quest for excellence.

The next concern to the Presidents was the matter of public relations. They had to expunge the memory of presidential appearances and pronouncements in the day of the old colleges, when complacent advertisement of supposedly high academic standards had simply created a public attitude of cynicism and disbelief. At the beginning of the period of awakening, few American educational leaders believed Catholic colleges counted for much. While as a matter of courtesy and good politics they invited Catholic college leaders and spokesmen to various academic conferences, they never listened seriously to what they had to say and were unimpressed by what they had to contribute. In the beginning, then, the new breed of Presidents, recognizing that they had to listen and watch, looked for ways to convince their nonCatholic confreres of the seriousness of their purpose and, moreover, of their willingness to learn the lessons history had taught other

---

50 Cunningham, op. cit., pp. 24–27.

51 Theodore Hesburgh, "The Changing Face of Catholic Higher Education," National Catholic Education Association Bulletin, 65 (August, 1969), 54–60; Theodore Hesburgh, "The University in the World of Change," Catholic Business Education, 17 (Summer, 1966), 36–45; and Theodore Hesburgh, "The Vision of a Great Catholic University," Catholic Mind, 66 (February, 1968), 42–54.

colleges. This was one important part of public relations; but there was another. It must be made clear, they concluded, just what the objectives of Catholic higher learning were, and they were determined to stress the essentials of education more than the elements of orthodoxy. In pursuance of this aim, they had to expurgate the old intramural notion that whatever was called Catholic was necessarily trustworthy and praiseworthy, and they sought to enlist the aid of all the colleges' friends in the gigantic task of projecting a new image for their schools. This image should be that of an excellent school which was also Catholic, rather than, as before, that of a Catholic institution to which a school was subordinated.[52]

In speaking to the public the colleges now used all the techniques of communication available and the Presidents never missed an opportunity to express their ideals in public. Realizing that, if they alone were interested in remaking the colleges, failure was almost certain, for leadership could do only so much, they became, in the best sense, academic missionaries who could preach the gospel of academic quality and be entirely sincere and convincing about it. It was unnecessary for them to be pulpit preachers and, for the most part, they tried not to capitalize on their religious vocation or to be anything more or less than responsible agents for their colleges. Their appeals were directed at men's minds rather than at their emotions or their religious sentiments.

In addition to bringing new ideas and new methods to the business of Catholic higher learning, the new era of leadership also brought the notion of selective rejection of old policies and practices. First, authoritarianism as a way of college life was rejected : next to go was the abiding principle, almost an article of faith, that truth was hidden away in the treasuries of Catholic doctrine and religious idealism :[53] finally, there was the dispatch of the ancient shibboleth that secular learning was worthless.[54] Without surrendering to secularism, the new leaders accepted the apparatus of secular scholarship along with much of its idealism, but rejected the philosophy of life on which it was based. In the end, these Presidents spoke a language of compromise whereby their colleges entered the mainstream of American higher learning without embracing the values of secular life. Compromise along these lines was imperative, but it was never easy to maintain and administer, as the colleges have since learned.

[52] Allan P. Farrell, "Catholic Colleges and Public Relations," *Catholic Mind,* 46 (January, 1948), 56–61.

[53] D. Bonnette, "The Doctrinal Crisis in Catholic Colleges and Universities and Its Effect upon Education," *Social Justice,* 60 (November, 1967), 220–236.

[54] Austin O'Malley, "Catholic College Education in the United States," *Catholic World,* 67 (June, 1896), 289–304.

New issues

The idea whose time had come brought with it an agenda of problems proving that Catholic colleges had really entered contemporary life. And, as before, the Presidents were the central figures. The way in which they motivated their faculties to scholarship and then rewarded them for their efforts has already been described. As a matter of policy the better colleges instituted salary, tenure, and promotion statutes and devised practices for their superintendence.

In the old college, the president paid professors whatever he thought they were worth, and always as little as possible. The professor, perforce representing himself, and thus somewhat disadvantaged, could seldom do anything more than trust the goodwill, the justice, or the charity of the president to keep him and his family financially solvent. Faculties never spoke with a single voice and showed themselves remarkably indifferent to any action which would guarantee improvement in their status. Eventually, no doubt, they would have generated enough fortitude to challenge the age-old paternalism of the colleges if conditions had remained unchanged, but, happily, they were absolved from such action because new policies were introduced by enlightened administrators. Paternalism was discarded; salaries were negotiated according to fairly definite and reasonably well-known schedules; individual bargaining, while always possible, was out-of-date. Tenure, adopted somewhat equivocally, nevertheless ensured a freedom of action and an openness for debate and discussion heretofore unknown in Catholic schools. Promotion, now intended and administered as a reward for accomplishment, replaced archaic codes wherein professors' promotions were based on years of service.[55]

The administration of these college policies (final decisions being reserved to the president) was delegated to committees composed of professors and administrators. Promotion to the various academic ranks (now generally recognized) was guided by policies which required evidence of scholarly maturity and reputation. And a faculty member unable to meet the minimum requirements of scholarship within a specified period of time was separated from the faculty. Elements of institutional self-protection were obvious in up-or-out policies where men had to be promoted to the rank of associate professor within, say, six years after joining the faculty or leave. Despite the obvious need for such protection, if the institution was to achieve its announced goal of faculty quality, there were signs of uneasiness and sometimes of revolt among persons on the faculty directly affected by

55 Oscar W. Perlmutter, "The Lay Professor," *Commonweal,* 68 (April 11, 1958), 31–35.

such policies. It became necessary on occasion for presidents to guard their policies against faculty assaults on them, and when the presidents took this stand they appeared in an unenviable role, as defending procedures that were temporarily unpopular. Yet they correctly perceived that if promotion and tenure were to have any significant meaning, and if both were to be used as instruments for upgrading the colleges, they would have to defend their policies and adamantly maintain them even when to do so made them extremely unpopular.

Contests between the presidents and the professors sometimes left scars, but they were really signs of collegiate robustness; they demonstrated the existence of a Catholic college climate wherein academic freedom was tolerated. They led, moreover, to the development of clearly articulated policies for academic government, replacing the rule of personality with the rule of policy.

Every perceptive president realized the practical limits to presidential authority. The day of the academic autocrat was gone. Policies had to be stated clearly and implemented effectively and fairly, but policies were only a beginning on the long road to academic success. The faculty, too, had vital interests and they needed forums in which to express them. It was necessary, in all probability, for dynamic and perceptive presidents to drive the bandwagon of college management over the early stages, but they could hardly expect, later on, to administer complex institutions alone. While this was undoubtedly clear to Presidents Walsh, Hesburgh, and Reinert, it was not so clear to the run-of-the-mill Catholic college president. Misunderstanding the legitimate part a faculty might play in shaping policies which affected them profoundly, the administration of St. John's University in New York created in 1965 a historic confrontation between themselves and several members of the faculty.[56] While the tendency still persists to evaluate this confrontation solely as a debacle or a catastrophe (as it may well have been for the college involved), it nevertheless demonstrated the power of a faculty to modify or to halt the operation of a huge college.[57]

This incident at St. John's was so clouded by charge and counter-charge that its authentic history may always be obscure. It all began with a dispute over salary increments which, it was alleged, were promised to the faculty with the beginning of the academic year 1965-1966. When these promised increments were forgotten and when negotiations between faculty organizations and administration proved fruitless, some of the faculty decided to strike and thus force the college to close. Student support was solicited by the faculty, a fairly easy maneuver because the administration,

[56] F. Canavan, "St. John's University; The Issues," *America,* 114 (January 22, 1966), 122-124.

[57] J. Leo, "Strike at St. John's," *Commonweal,* 83 (January 28, 1966), 500.

partly due to its own ineptitude, was made to appear sinister, and for several days instruction at St. John's was seriously interfered with, although never completely brought to a halt. The administration made a fatal mistake in dismissing several professors whom it considered to be ringleaders in insurrection. Intransigent, unbending in its refusal to allow the usual processes of academic consultation, and insensitive to what it was said to have promised in the first place, the administration had taken up a position that was almost untenable. And to add to these exercises in bad judgment— evidence of which an institution can ill afford to have on the public record—the college officers decided to conduct the school without the members of the dismissed or striking faculty by importing student members of the religious community from seminaries and houses of study. Thus revealing their lack of loyalty to academic standards by using persons to conduct university classes who had none of the credentials of the academic guild, St. John's officials put both the institution's reputation and its academic accreditation in jeopardy.[58]

Drastic shifts of administrative personnel brought cooler heads and firmer leadership; communication was restored between faculty and administration and eventually agreements were reached which allowed the school to resume normal operations. The St. John's incident, an object lesson in the futility of depending too heavily on authority to impose order on an academic community, was also a warning to Catholic colleges throughout the United States that faculties had a frightening reserve of power which could be mustered for responsible or irresponsible use. How college leaders acted could dictate the extent of the responsibility the faculties might choose to demonstrate. If a full recognition of the faculty's role in the life of Catholic colleges and the faculty's right to be involved in all institutional policies was the outcome of the St. John's incident, then the lesson so difficult to learn was probably worth all the unrest and acrimony. St. John's, then, rather than appearing the culprit of the period of awakening, may, by harking back to threadbare authoritarianism, have offered itself as a martyr on the road to Catholic college progress.[59]

Realizing for the first time the tremendous power of the faculty, the *ex-officio* leaders of Catholic colleges during the first years of awakening were faced, as never before, with the monumental task of channeling and directing this power. With good leadership it could help the colleges; leaderless it could destroy them.

While faculties were finding and testing their strength, students were disposed to make their voices heard too. The old-fashioned docility of the Catholic college student, although still welcomed and somewhat evident,

58 "Academic Freedom at St. John's," *America*, 115 (December 17, 1966), 795.
59 J. Hitchcock, "Reflections on the St. John's Case," *Catholic World*, 203 (April, 1966), 24–28; and "Victory for St. John's," *Commonweal*, 84 (June 24, 1966), 382.

was reserved for the classroom and the chapel. The admissions policies of the leading presidents had emphasized the need for talented students and when talented students came to the campus they brought with them not only their capacity to perform well in the classroom and the laboratory but an almost insatiable determination to have a responsible role in shaping their academic destinies. But apart from academic questions, in which they had an abiding interest, they wanted to be able wholly to manage their own domestic affairs. They wanted to share in the formulation of academic policies and for this they were willing to bargain, but they demanded the right to make their own regulations concerning discipline, housing, and, generally, the quality of campus life. Neither timid about assuming power nor reluctant to express their convictions about how to obtain it, students posed problems for college administrators which no writer of textbooks had ever illuminated. There were no beaten paths to follow and the presidents, along with their lieutenants, were severely tested to maintain that environment of reasonable equanimity in which the important business of teaching and learning could be continued.

Yet, as we saw before, the fundamental values of Catholic college students never stood out more clearly than in the common sense they displayed and the mature judgment they evidenced in eschewing violence and the threat of violence in their encounters with college administrators. Only once, when students manned picket lines in support of the faculty at St. John's University, did reason come close to being sacrificed to expediency.[60] Catholic college campuses were free from assault by students; presidents' and deans' offices usually were spared invasion; and violence, either as a means or as an end in itself, was rejected. Either Catholic college students entered college with a basic sense of responsibility or they were taught how to be responsible after they got there. Irrespective of where they learned that responsibility, they deserved praise for it; with students acting responsibly it was easier both for administrators and faculties to emulate their good example. The freedom of Catholic colleges from student-bred strife, we should say, was no accident, nor was it due merely to the respect college students had for religious leadership of the colleges. Leadership was responsible and responsive, to some extent, no doubt, because students allowed the rule of reason to work.

Students and faculty, with their new involvement, raised many fresh and unexpected issues for the leaders of the colleges of this period of awakening to handle. But fresh issues did not stop within the structure of college life. Knowledge was exploding in and around the colleges. It was hard to believe that the college curriculum could do justice to everything that should be known any more than that the colleges could satisfy the

[60] J. Leo, *op. cit.*

appetites of persons who, while desirous of adult education, were unable to matriculate in college classes.[61]

Visualizing the colleges in the modern world as more than places where classes were held for persons working toward academic degrees, the leaders of the new college era organized special sections in the college to be of service to those who would use them. Thus, institutes for research and teaching were organized outside the regular college curriculum; centers for continuing education grew up on campuses where two decades earlier the mere suggestion of such things would have been scoffed at. Under the new leadership and in the new age, Catholic higher learning assumed new dimensions by recognizing that it could be of service to its community, however large or small, and by departing from the traditional notion that everything taught in the college must somehow be applicable to degree requirements.

The vision of college presidents, of faculties, and of students, when converted into campus realities, cost a great deal of money, and money was always a critical issue for the colleges. The presidents were determined to find ways to deal with this persistent issue which, they knew, would never disappear of its own volition. College development funds were established and drives were organized; both were conducted in a highly professional, efficient way. Sometimes they were coupled with promises from foundations whereby the foundations would match dollar for dollar whatever the colleges raised in their development drives. These fund-raising drives, the invention of the presidents of the colleges of this period, while never as successful as the presidents would have liked, were always productive enough to allow the colleges to do things they otherwise could never have done. Money was unable, however, to solve all the questions and issues facing the Catholic colleges of the 1950s and 1960s, but it helped to answer many of them.

Marking out the goal

During the period of awakening, Catholic higher education was faced with the titanic task of setting and marking out its goal, and Catholic colleges were likewise sensitive to the urgent need for aligning complementary institutional goals. The possible alternatives were limited, but this did not make decision easy. First, moral formation could be restored to the primacy it had in the old college; second, intellectual development could

---

[61] Leo V. Ryan, "The Role of the Catholic College in the Field of Adult Education," National Catholic Education Association *Bulletin*, 60 (August, 1963), 171–178.

be accorded pride of place; third, moral and intellectual development could be set in balance, with the expectation in the long term of forming a decently educated person fully possessed of both intellectual and moral autonomy.

When the period of awakening began, the tendency of many Catholic college spokesmen was to accentuate the intellectual side of higher learning while leaving moral formation to take its chances. This emphasis, perhaps, was natural and predictable, for it was obvious to perceptive leaders— especially the three Presidents we have named—how much scholarly up- grading the colleges needed. And several Catholic colleges nailed intellectual excellence to their educational masts. By improving faculties and recruiting talented students they hoped to compete with the best colleges of the land. But while this goal was always possible, if difficult to reach quickly, it soon became evident that academic excellence was hardly the shibboleth to distinguish Catholic from nonCatholic colleges : nor could it justify the existence of Catholic colleges in the first place. Catholic colleges should be good schools, so much was agreed upon, but they should be something more. Their distinctive quality was hard to find on the intellectual level or in the allegiance they paid to scholarship. But it could be found, they remembered, in the fundamental Christian message that Catholic colleges and universities were capable of translating into the language of educational purpose and process.

In the old college system the Christian message had been stated in negative language and a long litany of prohibitions was recited and applied both to scholarship and to life. But in following the progressive advice of Pope John XXIII, the colleges found a way to state their code better. "It is very widely, and we fear, very generally believed, that true Catholic duty requires us to take our stand for a past civilization, a past order of ideas, and to resist with all our might the undeniable tendencies and in- stincts of the human race in our day," Pope John wrote in the encyclical *Pacem in Terris*.[62] The Catholic college should therefore be the first Catholic institution to reject the ancient and mistaken notion that educa- tion's only purpose is to reclaim the past. The commission from Pope John was clear : the Catholic college should guarantee "the right to freedom in searching for truth, and in expressing and communicating . . . opinion, and in pursuit of art—within the limits laid down by the moral order and the common good." It should be serious about its "duty of seeking and possess- ing [truth] ever more completely and profoundly." It must recognize the "right to share in the benefits of culture . . . to a basic education . . . to technical and professional training . . . [and] to go on to higher studies;" and finally it should endeavor to prepare its students "to occupy posts and

[62] Quoted in P. J. Hallinan, "The Responsibility of Catholic Higher Education," National Catholic Education Association *Bulletin,* 60 (August, 1963), 145–152.

take responsibilities in human society in accordance with their natural gifts and the skills they have acquired." [63]

Recognizing its inability to replace the home, or the church, or to blunt the inchoate influences of society, the Catholic college should constantly seek to reinterpret the doctrinal values that gave it life in the first place by ensuring a human and Christian climate wherein precept is translated into action. But it should do more. It should be a repository for responsibility in scholarship, a responsibility bred on the moral convictions of the Christian inheritance, and a scholarship equipped with all the skills, appurtenances, and insights available to men in the contemporary world.

Correctly seen, the goal of the Catholic college in the 1960s, without any implication of a wishful superiority over other colleges of the country (for such an implication would obviously be arrogant and presumptuous), was to employ the best techniques of scholarship and instruction and to add —and this was distinctive—a two-thousand-year legacy of Christian wisdom to intellectual and moral ideas.[64]

The future

What the remaining three decades of the twentieth century hold for Catholic higher learning is largely a matter of speculation and conjecture; yet we know enough about Catholic and nonCatholic higher education and the passion for higher learning that has inflamed the United States to make some cautious projections. Two dimensions to the future are worth noting : what Catholic colleges must do as they move along, and what they must avoid doing. What they must avoid may, in the long run, be more significant than what they must do. A perceptive and articulate spokesman for Catholic higher learning, Charles F. Donovan, has stated with admirable precision some of the imperatives for the future. "The one thing we must avoid," he writes, "is altering our purposes or softening our ideals in the hope of creating a more acceptable image. This would be senseless surrender. And our secular critics would be quick to ridicule supposedly religious institutions that tried to turn themselves into pale copies of secular colleges." [65] Then he proceeds to recommend that Catholic colleges should capitalize on the opportunities the years ahead will produce; while forthrightly rejecting gloom because there will be inevitable crises, which only

[63] *Ibid.*

[64] *Ibid.*

[65] Charles F. Donovan, "Implications for the Future of Catholic Higher Education," National Catholic Education Association *Bulletin,* 60 (August, 1963), 144.

the myopic optimist would refuse to acknowledge, he recites the reasons why he thinks the years ahead will be "years of vigor and progress for Catholic colleges and universities." With increased enrollments "the next few decades are bound to be boom years for Catholic higher education." With so great a need for colleges, many of which will have to be new foundations, the "relative age and sophistication [of Catholic colleges] in collegiate affairs will give us a certain prestige among American colleges and universities." The United States is a land of great wealth, which American Catholics share : "American Catholics have the resources and the will to back us in our educational enterprises." The atmosphere, Charles Donovan maintains, is growing more receptive to the real academic contributions of American Catholic colleges; "the chances for a fair and intelligent appreciation by secular educators and by the general public of the operation and efforts of Catholic higher education will be at their brightest in the remaining years of the century." [66]

Signs, moreover, are evident that opposition to public support for private education is weakening and there seem "to be genuine efforts by influential people not connected with the Church to find a way of ensuring the survival—not the vestigial survival but the lusty continuance—of private colleges and universities." Finally, he asserts, the colleges have the challenge of their "own vocation, the challenge to survive not as colleges but as Catholic colleges. . . . As Catholics and as Americans it is our duty and our bracing opportunity to continue, to strengthen, and improve the work we are doing in higher education so that our colleges and universities will stand as vital examples of the possibility and the reality of higher education that is genuinely religious." [67]

Perhaps there will be a pooling of resources by the association of Catholic colleges that are geographically close to each other (a long overdue experiment) or perhaps a moratorium will be declared on the founding of additional Catholic colleges in order to support more adequately those presently in existence. Other issues, impossible now to foresee, may arise, but the future of Catholic higher learning depends mainly, the lessons of history teach, on the colleges' determination to be true to their past, that is, genuinely to cultivate the religious and cultural perspectives they are heir to.

[66] *Ibid.*, p. 145.
[67] *Ibid.*

Bibliographical essay

Although the footnotes throughout the book are intended to provide the principal documentation, I am persuaded that some comments on bibliography are clearly in order and should prove useful to a reader who wants to go beyond what has been done in this book by consulting some of the primary and secondary sources himself.

I. Catholic Church history, biography, and religious community history

Various Church histories have appeared over the years, some general, some special, but all have been cognizant of the unique role education has occupied in religious history. Higher education, it is true, has not been a preoccupation of Church histories, yet both Theodore Roemer, *The Catholic Church of the United States* (St. Louis, B. Herder and Co., 1950), and John Gilmary Shea, *History of the Catholic Church in the United States* (New York, John G. Shea, 1888), provide a broad historical context both for the Church in America and for higher education as one of the ancillary endeavors of the Church. A special function of Catholic education, shared always by the colleges, was to help the Church sustain religious faith. And in a country which was often hostile to Catholicism, it is important to know such studies as Gerald Shaughnessy's *Has the Immigrant Kept the Faith?* (New York, Macmillan Company, 1925). A background for anti-pathetic sentiments toward Catholicism in certain historical periods of American social evolution is evidentially supported in Sister Mary Augustina Ray's *American Opinion of Roman Catholics in the Eighteenth Century* (New York, Columbia University Press, 1936); and a threat to all religion from an education without theological perspective is evidenced in Burton Confrey's *Secularism in American Education: Its History* (Washington, D. C., The Catholic University of America, 1931).

One side of Church history is the book or monograph on religious development in the United States. Another is biography, wherein an individual ecclesiastic's impact on religion, education, and life in the United States is significant enough to warrant a life story. Many Catholic bishops have their biographies, and among these books the reader finds considerable unevenness; but the best frequently throw some light on the evolution of higher education during an historical period, or during one person's lifetime. One of the best of these biographies (especially

473

worthwhile for the historian of Catholic higher education in the United States) is Peter Guilday's, *The Life and Times of John Carroll* (New York, Encyclopedia Press, 1922), for Carroll was the founder of Georgetown College and Georgetown, in turn, became the principal institutional paradigm for Catholic college development in the United States.

Still another side of Church history vis-á-vis the growth of institutions for Catholic higher learning is represented in the accounts of the fortunes of religious communities in the United States. Among such communities the Society of Jesus takes a place of undoubted prominence, so Gilbert Garraghan's three-volume *The Jesuits of the Middle United States* (New York, America Press, 1938), Thomas Hughes' four-volume *History of the Society of Jesus in North America* (New York, Longmans, Green and Company, 1907–1917), and William J. Mc-Gucken's *The Jesuits and Education* (Milwaukee, Bruce Publishing Company, 1931) must be mentioned. To these may be added Charles G. Herbermann's *The Sulpicians in the United States* (New York, Encyclopedia Press, 1916), and Brother Angelus Gabriel's *The Christian Brothers in the United States, 1848–1948* (New York, Declan X. McMullen, 1948).

II. General college history, Catholic college history, and seminary history

In a country where higher learning has always received attention and where thousands of colleges and universities have been established, it would be surprising indeed if the literature were barren of books and articles wherein historical report and interpretation were made of colonial and national higher education. All such studies cannot be cited here, but those which contain a special background for this book bear notice.

Richard Hofstadter and C. DeWitt Hardy, in their *The Development and Scope of Higher Education in the United States* (New York, Columbia University Press, 1952), have exercised the greatest economy of space in presenting, with insight, an historical picture of higher education as it passed through, first, the age of the college and, then, the age of the university. Richard Hofstadter's and Wilson Smith's two-volume *American Higher Education: A Documentary History* (Chicago, University of Chicago Press, 1961) makes available the principal documentary foundations wherefrom colleges and universities in the United States gained their inspiration and generated their forward thrust. John S. Brubacher and Willis Rudy, *Higher Education in Transition* (New York, Harper and Row, Publishers, 1958); and Frederick Rudolph, *The American College and University* (New York, Alfred A. Knopf, Inc, 1962) are responsible for the most recent general histories.

Somewhat more special studies, mentioned here because of their exceptionally keen insights into the fundamentals of American higher learning, are those of Beverly McAnear, "College Founding in the American Colonies, 1745–1775," *Mississippi Valley Historical Review*, XLII (June, 1955), 24–44, and George Paul Schmidt, "Intellectual Crosscurrents in American Colleges," *American Historical Review*, 42 (October, 1936), 46–67, and "Colleges in Ferment," *American Historical Review*, 59 (October, 1953), 19–42. What has stood for nearly forty years as the definitive work on college founding is Donald Tewksbury's, *The Founding of American Colleges and Universities Before the Civil War* (New York, Teachers College Press, 1932). Amid all the ferment of college founding and development, one figure, the college president, dominated the college scene, and he more than anyone else translated collegiate ideals into educational reality. Although the president's importance is always sensed in the historical literature, it has yet to be fully documented in accredited history. When this will be done is hard to say, but George Paul Schmidt's, *The Old Time College President* (New York, Teachers College Press, 1930) was a brave and significant beginning.

Written along the same lines as general histories of higher education in the United States, but centering on Catholic colleges, a number of scholarly books have essayed to establish the evolutionary boundaries of Catholic higher learning. And following, too, the example of general college history they have tended to separate higher education for men from that of women. Thus Sr. Mariella Bowler's *A History of Catholic Colleges for Women in the United States of America* (Washington, D. C., Catholic University of America Press, 1933) undertook to do for colleges for women what Francis P. Cassidy, *Catholic College Foundations and Development in the United States, 1677–1850* (Washington, D. C., Catholic University of America, 1924), and Sebastian A. Erbacher, *Catholic Higher Education for Men in the United States, 1850–1866* (Washington, D. C., Catholic University of America, 1931), did in their studies for colleges for men. In 1958, I wrote *A History of Catholic Higher Education in the United States* (Milwaukee, Bruce Publishing Company), a first effort at putting this vast subject between the covers of one book.

The only general history of Catholic education in the United States—J. A. Burns and Bernard J. Kohlbrenner, *A History of Catholic Education in the United States* (New York, Benziger Brothers, 1937)—has no more than one chapter on higher education, yet this valuable old book allows one to see how Catholic colleges and universities grew up in a climate of Catholic determination to provide adequate and safe instruction on all levels of learning. This same determination, although now seen only in the perspective of the colleges, is evidenced in a principal primary source for Catholic college history, the *Catalogues of the Colleges of the Society of Jesus in the United States, 1857 to 1896.* Some enterprising, although unidentified, person was responsible for collecting and binding the Jesuit college prospectuses for a forty-year period. These highly valuable volumes are deposited in the University of Detroit Archives.

Important, too, and often for primary sources, are Edmund J. Goebel, *A Study of Catholic Education During the Colonial Period up to the First Plenary Council of Baltimore, 1852* (New York, Benziger Brothers, 1937); Augustus J. Thébaud, *Forty Years in the United States of America* (New York, United States Catholic Historical Society, 1904); and Agatho Zimmer, *Changing Concepts of Higher Education in America Since 1700* (Washington, D. C., Catholic University of America Press, 1938).

David R. Dunigan's delightful master's dissertation at St. Louis University in 1938, *Student Days at Holy Cross College in 1848,* is filled with information on the lighter sides of college life. Unfortunately it is the only study restricted to this theme.

Catholic colleges for women have not attracted as much scholarly interest as colleges for men, yet such studies as Sr. Leo Joseph Devine's unpublished doctoral dissertation at Boston College, *A Study of the Historical Development of Co-education in American Higher Education* (1965), Sr. Margaret Marie Doyle's *The Curriculum of the Catholic Woman's College* (Notre Dame, Ind., University of Notre Dame, 1932), and Mary Syron's unpublished master's dissertation at the University of Detroit in 1956, *A History of Four Catholic Women's Colleges,* have not only given Catholic women's colleges good historical representation but have contributed considerably to the chapter in this book on Catholic higher education for women.

In a country where so much attention was paid to religious education, various histories of seminaries should be expected, although usually to fulfill local needs or merely to satisfy institutional pride. With few exceptions such studies are of little help to a work centering on collegiate education. Yet Catholic colleges were almost naturally motivated to follow seminary models in building their own educational programs, and for the most part the philosophy of Catholic higher education had its home in the seminary. Thus, such books as John Talbot Smith's two studies, *Our Seminaries: An Essay on Clerical Training* (New York, Longmans, Green and Company, 1896), and *The Training of a Priest: An Essay on Clerical Education with a Reply to Critics* (New York, Longmans, Green and Company, 1908), and Lloyd McDonald's *The Seminary Movement in the United States, 1784–1833* (Washington, D. C., Catholic University of America, 1927) are unquestionably useful to the college historian.

III. Institutional histories

A useful, and more often than not dependable, source upon which the generalizations of college history may be based is the institutional history. It is possible to make the point even more strongly: institutional histories are essential sources which no college historian can ignore. Perhaps both public and private colleges in the United States have had their natural leaders—that is, institutions which have set the pace in their perceptions of what college education should be and in the implementation of these perceptions. Harvard and Yale are regularly mentioned as institutions which have been in the vanguard of private higher education in the United States; schools like the University of Michigan have created models for public higher learning to follow; and among Catholic colleges, if one takes the long historical look, Georgetown must be accorded a position of leadership.

Georgetown's position of prominence in Catholic college history seems to be demonstrated, too, in the attention given her by historical studies, for more books have been written about Georgetown's history than about that of any other Catholic college. Chief among these, because of its undoubted excellence, is John M. Daley's *Georgetown University: Origin and Early Years* (Washington, D. C., Georgetown University Press, 1957), wherein Daley begins his study before Georgetown's founding and continues it down to the 1830s. Joseph T. Durkin, *Georgetown University: The Middle Years, 1840–1900* (Washington, D. C., Georgetown University Press, 1963) traces Georgetown through her highly significant developmental years. Added to these fairly recent histories are three old, but still highly valuable books: James S. Easby-Smith's two-volume *Georgetown University in the District of Columbia* (Chicago, Lewis Publishing Company, 1907); J. Fairfax McLaughlin's *College Days at Georgetown and Other Papers* (New York, J. B. Lippincott, 1899); and John Gilmary Shea's *A History of Georgetown College: Memorial of the First Century* (New York, P. F. Collier, 1891).

The Catholic University of America, similar in many respects to Georgetown in playing a leading role in Catholic higher education (although obviously for a much later period), has been studied carefully in its various stages of development. John Tracy Ellis, *Formative Years of the Catholic University of America* (Washington, D. C., American Catholic Historical Society, 1946) inaugurated a series of highly respectable monographs: Patrick Henry Ahern, *The Catholic University of America, 1887–1896* (Washington, D. C., Catholic University of America, Press, 1948); Colman J. Barry, *The Catholic University of America, 1903–1909* (Washington, D. C., Catholic University of America Press, 1953); and Peter E. Hogan, *The Catholic University of America, 1896–1903* (Washington, D. C., Catholic University of America Press, 1949).

From this point on, with only a few exceptions, Catholic colleges had their historical story told each by a single book, and it is necessary to observe that, while every such book contains a good deal of valuable information on formation and development, these studies were not always intended to fulfill the careful canons of objective historical writing. Frequently they were instruments of public relations and sometimes they were written as commemorative volumes. All this means that among such institutional histories one finds a great deal of unevenness. Still, although in varying degrees, all are valuable.

Mark V. Angelo, *The History of St. Bonaventure University* (St. Bonaventure, N. Y., Franciscan Institute, 1961), and Irenaeus Herscher, "The History of St. Bonaventure University," *Franciscan Studies,* 11 (September, December, 1951), 365–424, recount the principal Franciscan involvement in higher education in the United States. Colman J. Barry's *Work and Worship: A History of St. John's Abbey and University* (Collegeville, Minn., American Benedictine Academy, Historical Studies Number II, 1956) is an excellent history of the Benedictines' work in religion and higher education in Minnesota. Sr. Mary David Cameron, *The College of Notre Dame of Maryland* (New York, Macmillan Company, 1947), introduces the Catholic women's college to serious historical scholarship. And Thomas J. Donaghy's *Conceived in Crisis: A History of LaSalle College, 1863–1965* (Philadelphia, LaSalle College, 1966) is the only book-length historical treatment of the work of the Christian Brothers in higher education.

M. P. Dowling's *Reminiscences of the First Twenty-Five Years at Creighton* (Omaha, Neb., Burkley Printing Co., 1903) is a somewhat rambling account of the first years of Creighton University. More authentic history of college development is represented in David R. Dunigan's *A History of Boston College* (Milwaukee, Bruce Publishing Company, 1947). The extremes of the old and the new history can be seen in two books on St. Louis University: Walter H. Hill's *Historical Sketches of St. Louis University* (St. Louis, Patrick Fox, 1879), and William B. Faherty's *Better the Dream; Saint Louis University: University and Community*

(St. Louis, St. Louis University Press, 1968). Despite the intrusion into Faherty's book of religious community life and activities, he has wrtten an unquestionably competent history of the university. In connection with St. Louis University, it is important to mention again the three-volume work of Gilbert J. Garraghan, *The Jesuits of the Middle United States* (New York, America Press, 1938), for Garraghan looks closely at the Jesuits' work in higher education, both at St. Louis and elsewhere in the Middlewest. In addition to this book, Garraghan was the author of the following illuminating articles: "The Beginnings of St. Louis University," *St. Louis Catholic Historical Review*, I (January, 1919), 85–102; "Fordham's Jesuit Beginnings," *Thought*, 16 (March, 1941), 17–39; "Marquette University in the Making," *St. Louis Catholic Historical Review*, II (April, 1920); 417–446; "Origin of Boston College," *Thought*, 17 (December, 1942), 617–656; and "Some Early Chapters in the History of St. Louis University," *St. Louis Catholic Historical Review*, V (April, 1923), 99–128.

Raphael N. Hamilton's *The Story of Marquette* (Milwaukee, Marquette University Press, 1953), and Arthur J. Hope's *Notre Dame, One Hundred Years* (Notre Dame, Ind., University of Notre Dame Press, 1943) are both detailed and careful academic histories; somewhat less so, because of the abundance of ecclesiastical detail, is Mathias M. Hoffmann's *Story of Loras College, 1839–1939* (Dubuque, Ia., Loras College Press, 1939). Yet the latter is interesting principally for its attempt to prove that Loras College is the oldest Catholic college in that section of the United States, a proof which at best is left at loose ends.

Edward F. Kennelly's unpublished doctoral dissertation, *A Historical Study of Seton Hall College* (New York University, 1944), is the only serious study of the history of Seton Hall University. Despite what some think is an ambiguous title, Michael J. Kenny's *Catholic Culture in Alabama* (New York, America Press, 1931) is the only authentic history of Spring Hill College. Walter J. Meagher wrote a doctoral dissertation at Fordham University in 1944 on *The History of the College of the Holy Cross*, and later, along with William J. Grattan, wrote *The Spires of Fenwick: The History of the College of the Holy Cross, 1843–1963* (New York, Vantage Press, 1966).

With one exception, Wilfred Schoenberg's *Gonzaga University: Seventy-Five Years* (Spokane, Washington, 1963), the institutional histories yet to be mentioned are quite old: the two-volume history by Mary M. Meline and Edward F. X. McSweeny, *The Story of the Mountain: Mt. St. Mary's College and Seminary* (Emmitsburg, Md., The Weekly Chronicle, 1911); Thomas C. Middleton, *Historical Sketch of St. Thomas of Villanova* (Villanova, Pa., Villanova College, 1893); Oswald Moosmüller, *Bonifaz Wimmer: Erzabt von St. Vincent in Pennsylvanien* (New York, Benziger Brothers, 1891); Thomas T. Taaffe, *A History of St. John's College* (New York, Catholic Publication Society, 1891)—St. John's name was subsequently changed to Fordham; and Francis X. Talbot, *Jesuit Education in Philadelphia: St. Joseph's College, 1851–1926* (Philadelphia, St. Joseph's College, 1927).

IV. Criticism and general evaluations

For the first half-century of its experience in the United States, Catholic higher education enjoyed the luxury of freedom from criticism and evaluation. On the one hand Catholics who might have had something to say about the educational process were strangely silent about the issues of college quality and purpose; on the other, nonCatholic spokesmen were generally indifferent to what Catholic colleges were doing. Thus, in the years of first founding Catholic college issues were never found amongst the burning questions of the day. This complacency was challenged, first, by Orestes Brownson, and from Brownson's time (about 1840) on, although there was by no means a flood of opinion, or anything like a controversy about Catholic higher education, the subject was thought about and discussed fairly regularly in print. The articles and books that have centered on Catholic higher education are sometimes characterized best as exercises in educational polemic, for there is always some note of charge, countercharge, and apologetics; yet there are also a few carefully reasoned and researched studies which add a tone of objectivity and responsibility to what may be described as a debate over the significance and place of Catholic higher education in the United States. But the point should probably be made that history is not compounded of reason and good judgment only; imprudence, acerbity, discord, distrust, and misconceived perceptions have their impact also. Thus in this section of bibliographical comment the reasoned and judicious book and article appear alongside what must clearly be labeled as academic polemic, for both, it seems to me, have their legitimate place in educational history.

As often as not, I think, Catholic college spokesmen were motivated to take to print to state a point of view regarding Catholic higher education because someone outside the circle of Catholic confidence had somehow stepped on Catholic academic toes. Timothy Brosnahan's "President Eliot and the Jesuit Colleges," *Sacred Heart Review,* 23 (January 13, 1900), 1–30, and *The Courses Leading to the Baccalaureate in Harvard College and Boston College* (nd.; np), are excellent examples of a Catholic reaction to outside criticism. At the same time, Brosnahan's strong response is about the only clear statement of the attitude among Catholic college educators on the question Eliot was then raising: the place of electivism in higher learning.

Long before Brosnahan assumed the role of principal apologist for the Catholic way in higher education, Orestes A. Brownson had penetrated the indifference to educational issues and had written deeply disturbing articles about the nature and the purpose of Catholic college education. What Brownson had to say was usually regarded as, at least, mischievous, if not dangerously bordering on the heretical, so it is hard to believe that he commanded a very large following. Yet, even when an attempt was made to dismiss him as a troublesome eccentric, it was hard to forget the principal issues he raised. The following articles which bear on higher education may be consulted in his collected *Works:* "The School Question," *Works,* XIII, 243; "Catholic Schools and Education," *Works,* XII, 496; "Liberal Studies," *Works,* XIX, 433; "Necessity of Liberal Education," *Works,* XIX, 97; "The Scholar's Mission," *Works,* XIX, 77; and "Our Colleges," *Brownson's Quarterly Review,* 15 (April, 1858), 209–244.

J. A. Burns, *Catholic Education: A Study of Conditions* (New York, Longmans, Green and Company, 1917), while not a study of higher education, is a thorough examination of Catholic education and thus illuminates the basic problems faced by the colleges and other Catholic schools. Much more recent, and directed at colleges in the United States, is Allan M. Cartter's, *An Assessment of Quality in Graduate Education* (Washington, D. C., American Council on Education, 1966). This study is capable of telling Catholic universities something about themselves.

Debates over the meaning of liberal learning have gone on at every Catholic college campus for the past fifty years, so against this background of uncertainty William F. Cunningham's *General Education and the Liberal College* (St. Louis, B. Herder Book Company, 1953) takes on added significance, not as history, but as a determined effort to bring some unity of liberal purpose to the thinking of educators in Catholic colleges. On the same level of significance are Charles F. Donovan's "Implications for the Future of Catholic Higher Education," National Catholic Education Association *Bulletin,* 60 (August, 1963), 137–145, and John D. Donovan's *The Academic Man in the Catholic College* (New York, Sheed and Ward, 1964).

Once Catholics began to think seriously about educational quality, it was only natural for them to publish their thoughts. And the names and publications that follow, although they cover a broad historical range, must be understood as reasoned opinions about the quality and purpose of Catholic higher education:

John Tracy Ellis, "American Catholics and the Intellectual Life," *Thought,* XXX (Autumn, 1955), 351–388; James P. McIntyre, "Catholic College Graduates," National Catholic Education Association *Bulletin,* 65 (November, 1969), 37–50; and his Boston College doctoral dissertation in 1967, *A Study of the College Choices of the Children of Alumni and Alumnae of Selected Catholic Colleges;* John A. O'Brien, *Catholics and Scholarship: A Symposium on the Development of Scholars* (Huntington, Ind., Our Sunday Visitor, 1938); Thomas F. O'Dea, *American Catholic Dilemma: An Inquiry Into the Intellectual Life* (New York, Sheed and Ward, 1958); Austin O'Malley, "Catholic Collegiate Education in the United States," *The Catholic World,* LXVII (June, 1898), 289–304; George N. Shuster, *The Catholic Spirit in America* (New York, The Dial Press, 1927); Augustus J. Thébaud, "Superior Instruction in Our Colleges," *The American Catholic Quarterly Review,* VII (October, 1882), 81–109; Leo R. Ward, *Blueprint for a Catholic University* (St. Louis, B. Herder Book Co., 1949); Gustave Weigel, "American Catholic Intellectualism: A Theologian's Reflections," *The Review of Politics,* 19 (July, 1957), 275–306; and Samuel Knox Wilson, "Catholic College Education: 1900–1950," *Catholic School Journal,* 51 (April, 1951), 121–123.

Index